The Bone War of McCurtain County

A True Story of Two Ordinary Men's Quest for Treasure and
Their Epic Battle Against Extraordinary Odds

Expanded Edition

Russell Ferrell

Rabelais Publishing
Waxahachie, Texas

Copyright 2013 by Russell Ferrell

The Bone War of McCurtain County

All rights reserved,

Including the right of reproduction

In whole or in part in any form

The rights of Russell Ferrell to be identified as the author of this work
has been asserted by him in accordance with sections 77 and 78 of the Copyright,
Designs and Patents Act, 1988

1-560086051

Rabelais Publishing
148 Brushy Creek Rd.
Red Oak, Texas 75154
rabelaispublishing@hotmail.com

ISBN 978-0-9833551-0-6

This Book Is Dedicated to all Amateur Paleontologists and Naturalists

Especially to the Memory of Sid Love
September 19, 1923 – November 21, 1997
One of the Greatest Amateur Paleontologists in History

For Halee, Christian, Maison, and Aiden

About the Author

Russell Ferrell is a Southerner and native Texan who lives in Red Oak, Texas with his wife Waynetta and their four dogs and three cats. He has worked as a journalist, educator, and cattle rancher. He was working on several book projects in the historical area when he put them aside to tell Hall and Love's story.

Contents

Acknowledgements i
Preface ii
Prologue vii

1 From the Ouachitas to the Great Lakes 1
2 It Happened In McCurtain County 4
3 In Search of the Pit with the Golden Wood 21
4 An Enclave of Secret Treasure 32
5 A Glimpse Back In Prehistoric Time 40
6 The Quest for the Bones 48
7 Fading Memories – Cephis Hall In Redneck Heaven 65
8 Locked In A Time Capsule 78
9 The Backwoods Country – The Lure and Lore of Timber, Marijuana,
   and Fossils 82
10 Sid Love Joins the Expedition 88
11 Mysteries Along the Mountain Fork 92
12 What Species of Dinosaur Is This? 104
13 McCurtain County – 100 Million Years Ago 109
14 Indiana Jones – Southern Style 117
15 The Bone Diggers Reach a Quandary 119
16 In the Pathway of Travail 123
17 Cephis Lays It on the Line 126
18 Despairing Minds 131
19 The Identity of the Creature is Revealed 134
20 The Boss Lays Down the Law 141
21 Overshadowing the Dig 148
22 On the River's Edge 154
23 The Gilded Ages of Dinosaur Discoveries 163
24 Lightning Strikes the Diggers 172
25 A Mysterious Visitor Comes Calling 176
26 The Bone Tally 184
27 The Strange Encounter at the Gem and Mineral Show 188
28 In the Clasp of Academia 192
29 A Clash of Cultures – Trickle-Down Fossil Manna 195
30 The Visit to Langston's Bone Lair 204
31 In Search of the Skull 208
32 A Skull Worth A Million Dollars 212
33 The Dig Comes to an End – the Valuable Cargo is Transported to the Lab 215

34	Haggling With the Professor	218
35	The Low Down Filthy Capitalist	222
36	The Bone Heist	225
37	Dark Conspiracies Forming	230
38	The Free Market in Bones	234
39	Bones of Contention	238

Photo Album 243

40	The Box of Bones	251
41	"Only Dead Fish Go With The Flow"	254
42	House Bill 2014	261
43	The Enforcer	268
44	Legal Recourse	271
45	In the Shadow of Perdition	275
46	A Dream Turns Into A Nightmare	279
47	The Gestapo Knocks on the Door	283
48	The Fog of Legalities	287
49	Legal Action	290
50	The Bone War	293
51	The Lamb and the Beast	297
52	Official Inquiry – An Inside View	304
53	The Legal Showdown	312
54	Full Pockets – Time for A Spending Spree?	315
55	Cephis Stretches for the American Dream	318
56	Empty Pockets – Cephis Feels the Pain	321
57	Southern Comfort	325
58	Legal Pleading	329
59	The Hard Sell	331
60	Legal Intercession	338
61	To the Core of the Bones	345
62	Dark Forces Converge	347
63	The Dinosaur Tempest – The Feds Move In	350
64	A Buyer Steps Forward	352
65	Acrocanthosaurus Versus T-Rex	355
66	The Jewel of the Ouachitas	362
67	The Crystal Lode – Cephis Strikes Again	365
68	OU Scientists Probe the Bone Site	368
69	A New Order is Imposed on the Forests	372
70	The White Knight	375
71	Fran is Unveiled at Black Hills	378
72	The Raid	381

73	After Shocks	386
74	The Dreamer	391
75	The Cast	393
76	Fundraising – Making the Dream Come True	396
77	The Monster is Showcased – The Celebration at the Museum	399
78	The Last Controversy	401
79	Creationists Hound Cephis	405
80	The Tail of the Tale	409

Notes-Sources 413
Index 421

Acknowledgements

Other than the author, there were two other people who made a significant contribution in making this book into a finished product. First and foremost was Cephis Hall, who spent countless hours in personal interviews relating his story to the author. His colorful narrations aided the author in composing the script and making his story come to life. The other was Jessica Love, no relation to Sid Love, who did the art work and designed the front and back cover. Jessica is a very talented young artist whose services were very valuable and indispensible.

Special thanks also to Susan Uttendorfsky at Adirondack Editing who did an excellent job editing the raw manuscript. Susan is a dedicated and first rate editor.

In addition, a number of other people played varying roles and made small contributions to the total effort. Thanks also to Jean Akin, Marissa Alanis, Dr. Rich Cifelli, Dr. Kyle Davies, Waynetta Dennis, Wayne Edgar, Jeanie Garris, Eric Gray, Joyce Hall, Steve Due, Thomas Ferrell, Jim Griffin, Walter Hamilton, Marcia Hodgeson, Morris "Coach" Hodgeson, Jim Honeywell, Harold James, Kenny Joiner, Christopher Jones, Jeff Jones, Levi Jones, Susan Kennedy, Carl LeForce, Neal Larson, Peter Larson, Kimberly Martin at Jera Publishing, Henry Moya at the Museum of the Red River, Charles Nation, Lemuel Richards, Dr. Lewis Stiles, Royce Tidwell, Bob West at McCurtain Daily Gazette, Carolyn Williamson, and Ron Wolfe at the Arkansas Democrat Gazette.

Preface

This book venture started when my son Thomas and his wife Kasie were on vacation at Beavers Bend State Park and just happened to stop off at Cephis Hall's rock shop on Highway 259 near Hochatown, Oklahoma to examine his rocks and collectibles. My two grandchildren, Halee and Christian, love rocks and no doubt were instrumental in prodding their parents to stop for a visit, thus bringing the family in contact with the rock shop and Cephis Hall. My son and daughter-in-law engaged Cephis in conversation about his dinosaur adventure and got a glimmer of the nature of the story, which apparently captured their imagination and interest.

Within days of their return home to the Dallas area, Thomas called and informed me about what he had learned about Cephis Hall and the dinosaur. At the time, I was working on a book about barbarians and while not seeking another writing opportunity, found myself intrigued with the tale. Thomas explained that the story sounded amazing, although he had only scratched the surface. He explained that he wanted to investigate the subject further and considered it a prime prospect for a book.

He convinced me to go with him to interview Cephis. We left that following weekend and spent two days interviewing the homespun rock hound at his home and reading over local newspaper stories. We both deemed the story worth telling, and since nobody else wanted to tell it at the time, we had inherited the job. We decided to take on the project as a father-son team. But unfortunately, Thomas, working as a software engineer at the time, was too constrained by the requirements of his job and had little spare time to devote to the project. Consequently, the endeavor fell totally on my shoulders. I thence became the caretaker of Cephis Hall and Sid Love's story – an intriguing story that deserved to be told.

Over the past three years, I traveled back and forth to southeastern Oklahoma on weekends to investigate and research the story. Although my forte is history, I had a modest background in science, particularly biology. The undertaking required me to buttress and polish up my mediocre knowledge of dinosaurs and paleontology. In research for this book, I read a number of books and publications about dinosaurs and the great fossil discoverers of the past. I learned that most major dinosaur excavations have been undertaken by professional paleontologists. In the case of Cephis Hall and Sid Love, here was an instance where two amateurs had taken on the entire excavation task with no financial or back-up support from Ph.D's or a university staff. This was a rare phenomenon in the scientific world – perhaps the only time in history in which such an undertaking by amateurs proved successful. Amazingly, their excavation turned up a rare and valuable find that soon became a center of controversy and conflict. It was in the aftermath of the recovery that their real troubles began.

I interviewed many people with firsthand and secondary knowledge of the story. I spent a considerable amount of time reading old stories from the local newspapers and concluded that Cephis Hall probably had his name in the local papers more than any single individual over a span of several years during the early to late 1980s when he was active not only in local fossil discoveries and nature tour guiding, but also mineral prospecting and geologic exploration. He is McCurtain County's foremost naturalist and the discreet holder of many deep secrets about McCurtain County's hidden geologic treasures.

I tried to approach the story from many different angles and intricacies. The best source, of course, was Cephis Hall himself. I found him not only an interesting narrator, but honest and straightforward as well. This is his story and it is told from his point of view. And I believe his story, although it may in some ways reflect his bias and personal feelings, is generally accurate and truthful as best as can be garnered from weighing the evidence and consulting the sources. His narrations were largely confirmed by local newspaper stories or through interviews with parties or persons possessing firsthand knowledge of the subject.

The book was written piecemeal as the story was gradually uncovered over a three-year period of investigation. I was busy weighing new facts and details until the very end. I had to learn the story as I progressed with the investigation and research. It is an amazing story and one I really did not begin to fully appreciate until I became deeply engrossed. I began to realize its amazing quality sometime after I had written Chapter 22. It was about that time that I truly realized I had gotten hold of a real jewel in the rough. Professional authors had totally overlooked this story and allowed a untested writer to step into the void and garner the meat.

A couple other writers had tried to write this book, but for untold reasons had fallen by the wayside. One journalist I encountered who himself had considered taking up the challenge bluntly told me that the story needed to be fictionalized if I wanted to sell any books. In essence, he implied that the real story was simply too boring for a fickle, dumbed-down American readership with a short attention span and disdain for complexity. I guess only time will tell whether or not he was right, but it was my humble opinion that the real story could rest on its own laurels and needed no fabrication or exaggeration. What I offer to the reader is a true story principally told from the main character's point of view. Frankly, I could not have fictionalized or romanticized a better story. In this case, truth is better than fiction. In my biased opinion, this is not just an adventure story, but a true epic. Real flesh and blood stories like this are as rare as a newly-discovered, fully-articulated dinosaur specimen. It is my privilege to have been entrusted with this story. I have done the best I could with it. I eventually found the real story to be much more astonishing and meritorious than I had initially imagined.

Shortly after I commenced my research and writing endeavor, a few of Cephis' close confidantes tried to convince him to go with a more established author. They recommended he bring in Bob Burke from Tulsa – the man that had written more books than any native Oklahoman. Cephis refused and continued to stake his hopes on my effort. A man of intuition, he was willing to give an unknown writer a shot, and he stuck with me even when the initial first few chapters did not turn out so well. If this book becomes a success, it is as much a testament to his presentiment and openness as it is to any writing talent that might be assigned to the author.

Sadly, it must be said that the other hero of the story, Sid Love, passed on before I was able to get his point of view. Would the book have been different had he been alive to narrate his own experience? Perhaps there would be some changes or additions. Certainly more light would have been cast on a few gray areas. However, I am thankful to have had the honor of putting into print the ordeals and struggles of Cephis Hall and his partner Sid Love, and I hope that my work reflects well on Sid and would have met his approval if he were alive today to read it.

Finally, the bias and point of view of the author must be addressed. If the main character has his particular insight and frame of reference, so too does the author. I had the opportunity to read a few parts of some chapters of this book at local writer's workshops in the Dallas-Fort Worth area. In one instance, I was accused of having a bias against academia. To such a charge, I respond to the negative and aver that I have the utmost respect for academia. I will acknowledge, however, that the arch protagonist of the book, Cephis Hall, seems to have such a bias and that his bias is colored by his own personal experience, and rightly so. Since this is his story and reflects his point of view to a considerable extinct, that bias cannot be negated.

Some readers or reviewers might claim the author has an inherent bias against large corporations, or at least against multi-national corporations, and that assessment would generally be correct. The author believes corporations have too much power and too much influence over government, the electoral process, the legal system, public opinion molding, the media, the government's purse strings, the private lives of individuals, and the direction of society. As a result of this imbalance of power, the society and economy have become destabilized and the democratic process undermined. The repeal of Glass-Steagall and the deregulation of commercial and investment banking led to the financial meltdown in 2008 and a near collapse of the entire economic system which was only averted through massive bailouts of too-big-to-fail institutions. The author is not alone in this assessment. Many social scientists and left-leaning political pundits agree. As widely noted in the press and media, main street America extensively distrusts big banks and Wall Street.

The author asserts that he has no particular negative sentiment against Weyerhaeuser per se, but it must be admitted that the principal character of the story, Cephis Hall, likely harbors such an unaffirmative predilection as well as a sizeable portion of the local population of McCurtain County, perhaps the majority. Despite some of the contents of the book not exactly projecting a benign corporate image of Weyerhaeuser, the author actually believes Weyerhaeuser is a good corporate citizen, at least in a relative sense – far more flexible and citizen-environmentally friendly than many, if not most, giant corporations that impinge directly on the environment, community, and labor relations.

The author, who has some legal training, has another inherent bias that may also seep through parts of this book dealing with the legal subjects. That bias is against the legal system and reflects an amorphous disdain for lawyers, the State Bar Association, and Texas courts based on firsthand personal experience as a plaintiff against wealthy defendants. The author believes most Americans share his bias and distrust of the legal system. The life experience and sentiment of the author does indeed color some of the pages of this book as it relates to the legal system. But from the point of view of a social scientist, this sentiment is more grounded in objective reality than capricious prejudice.

The author interviewed many people in the research of this book. Some potential interviewees were simply unavailable or unwilling to consent. In most cases, the names of Weyerhaeuser officials and employees were changed out of respect for their privacy. I was unable to locate some of the principal Weyerhaeuser officials, namely the character identified by the pseudonym herein referred to as "Joe Bueno." Regardless, it was felt that there was not much that could be added or detracted by the real "Mr. Bueno" that would fundamentally change the story in any way. I was able to largely confirm the veracity of Hall as it related to his dealings with "Mr. Bueno" through other sources and a review of the legal case file contained within the records of the National Archives.

Neither Dr. Wann Langston nor Dr. Jeffrey Pittman responded to my email requests for an interview. I took that as an obvious sign of a lack of interest and did not press the issue. Still, despite their conflict with the story's heroes, I tried to paint them in a most favorable light. In regard to Dr. Langston, I referenced his long-standing distinguished career and accomplishments. In the case of Dr. Pittman, I noted his accomplishments made after completing his university studies and obtaining his Ph.D.

I found Dr. Rich Cifelli and Pete Larson to be most cordial and receptive during our personal contact. The two men were quite affable, and it was a pleasure to have had the opportunity to interview them. True gentlemen they were. Unfortunately, Allan Graffham was in very bad health at the time I started my research and had passed away before I had a chance to interview him. Other than the two main characters, Cephis Hall and Sid Love, Allan Graffham played a principal third-person role. As a result of his ensuing conflict with the two protagonists, he is seen in both a positive light and a negative dark side, as both a hero and villain.

It is hoped that this book will be both entertaining and informative. Like the story and its heroes, this is a bold book with a broad reach of interjected topics. Scholarship combines with epic adventure.

The book is basically about nature, treasure hunting, a dinosaur discovery and excavation, and the struggles of the two men in the aftermath of that recovery. The author has thrown in some science, history, political commentary, and controversy to supplement and enliven the story line. Hopefully, this added material complements rather than detracts from the story. The first 34 chapters of the book deal largely with the discovery and excavation phase of the story. After Chapter 34, the story takes on a new dimension and changes tone as the nature of the story transforms. Chapters one and two largely cover biographical and historical material and strive to establish the tone and setting of the story. Chapters seven, thirteen, twenty-three, and fifty-one infuse historical and sociological topics that indirectly relate to the story. Readers only interested in the story aspect might choose to browse and skim through those chapters. You have chosen an amazing story and should find it quite compelling. For any communication to the author about this book, the author can be contacted at the following email address: acrocantho2010@yahoo.com.

Prologue

In the spring of 1983, Cephis Hall, an Arkansas hillbilly, and Sid Love, a Choctaw Indian, discovered a valuable cache of buried treasure along a mysterious bend of the Mountain Fork River in southeastern Oklahoma. They dug the prize from the catacombs of a long-deceased creature from the early Cretaceous Period. The discovery set in motion a chain of events that would alter their lives forever. The two men could not foresee the obstacles, the turmoil, and the controversies they would ultimately face as they embarked upon an epic journey and conflict against mighty foes in a David versus Goliath scenario.

Discoveries of rare antiquities and exotic treasure do not always bring fame and riches. Sometimes they bring trouble, conflict, and heartbreak. A perennial kernel of truth was inherent in their conflict, one which exists in all battles: the underdog is expected to lose, and usually does. Only in rare instances in history is this forlorn fixture of normalcy repealed and the tables turned. Throughout humanity's story, wars have been fought over riches and territory. It is still so today, albeit disguised in a bureaucratic and ideological cloak. In ancient times as well as modern, the antagonist with the greatest arsenal and resources usually wins.

The two Okies became embroiled in a titanic struggle for ownership rights to the treasure they uncovered – a cache of cryptic bones encapsulated in mystery. To protect their vested interest, they were propelled into a "bone war" over the rights to the paleontological stash buried in the sediments and crust of an ancient mud slab laid down in the Age of Dinosaurs. Their war would become "The Bone War of McCurtain County" – a war fought over the spoils of their dig and for the title to the valuable collection of fossils discovered.

The Bone War of McCurtain County reverberates back to an earlier bone war – the bitter conflict between two eccentric and aristocratic scientists of Gilded Age America (1880 – 1910) a century earlier. The Gilded fossil plunderers Othniel Marsh and Edward D. Cope, two of America's earliest paleontologists, battled each other for the rights to the spoils of Mother Earth and every dinosaur fossil which they could lay their hands on. Two antagonistic factions from the fledgling science of paleontology coalesced around these two central figures of dinosaurian iconography.

The rival scientific camps traded countless barbs while venturing out into the badlands of western America in an invidious attempt to outdo the opposition and bring heraldry to their cadre. America's first fossil war interjected a torrent of egos and eccentrics into a brew of controversy and animosity. This was a competitive war of numbers in a contest to outdo the rival in the tally of discoveries made and credited.

Cope and Marsh were in a contest to find, identify, and count their specimens and tally their scores. Comparatively, Hall and Love became ensnared in an odious struggle to retain ownership rights to the fruits of their toils. The obsession of Cope and Marsh to uncover fossilized riches in the West mirrored Hall and Love's quest to unlock mysteries along the Mountain Fork some 100 years later. A latent lust to gather the spoils of nature propelled both sets of antagonists forward into divisive confrontations. The Bone War of McCurtain County, however, had a different twist. This was a war over ownership rights to one of the single greatest dinosaur specimens in the history of paleontology, and the opposing factions were not equally matched. Hall and Love's war over fossils occurred during a time that might also be aptly called a Gilded Age.

The close parallel between the first Gilded Age antagonists of Cope and Marsh and the second Gilded Age antagonists of Hall and Love against their institutional enemies cannot be easily ascertained. This is due in large part to the fact that the circumstances surrounding the two wars are quite different – even though the social, economic, and political settings of the two ages are somewhat similar. The Cope-Marsh war was waged across the vast national and panoramic venue of the Great American West, whereas Hall and Love's battle was parochial, with an obscure view. But a bone war is still a war, and the constitutional makeup of the antagonists always colors the story.

The two Okies of McCurtain County did not battle peer competitors or rival camps of scientific explorers, but an intact system – an institutional and bureaucratic milieu at the apex of the American Empire. Their venue of battle was in the rural South rather than the great American West and in the wetlands of southeastern Oklahoma rather than the dry lands of the western outback. Unlike aristocrats Marsh and Cope, who were locked in peer combat, these men were of modest means and under-financed, and they faced off against people and institutions with much greater resources in wealth and power. They did not stand a chance, but they were sufficiently naïve and infused with ample visceral and moral conviction to attempt the impossible.

The social, economic, and political setting of their struggle (1980-2010) was much like that earlier Gilded Age (1880-1910) of the robber barons and, in both eras, a dinosaurian craze of sorts – a Jurassic and Cretaceous fixation – had pervaded the media realm. Sensationalism and dinosaurian hype became ensconced in the minds of the masses while people and great institutions made money from dinosaurs.

The dinosaurian mania of the two Gilded Ages entertained and inspired great wonder and awe in the consciousness of Americans. Pictures and stories about the alluring monsters of a more primitive, pristine, and beastly age were etched as indelible images in the beguiled minds of the modern mammalian rulers.

During these two prolific eras of dinosaurian discovery – of bounteous Jurassic and Cretaceous treasure – new names in science and paleontology emerged, both professionals and amateurs. In the modern Gilded era, among the amateur ranks, two bucolic naturalists from the rural hinterland of the southern US, Cephis Hall and Sid Love, would ascend and make their mark in the arcane world of paleontology. The fireworks from the Bone War of McCurtain County brought their names into the limelight as the world learned snippets about their struggles and accomplishments. This is their real story — a tale of two men's meteoric rise from obscurity to the pinnacle of amateur acclaim.

Hall and Love, as small-time entrepreneurs, battled both oligarchy and oligopoly. Their struggle provoked the ire of the modern timber barons and helped bring about a reactive policy of corporate retrenchment in southeastern Oklahoma. Corporate openness toward public egress and liberal use of their pervasive timber estates soon hardened into a rigid, distrustful, and intolerant attitude toward recreationists. The outcome of the Bone War accelerated a revision of corporate land-use policies and eliminated easy public access to the vast corporate timberlands. Rockhounds and naturalists like Hall and Love were locked outside the gates and put under surveillance.

Where once open roads had been freely traversed without hindrance, gates were erected to seal off the corporate forests from citizen intrusion. The open timberlands became fully privatized and closed. Fishing, cattle grazing, rockhounding, hiking, crystal digging, bird watching, fossil collecting, etc., were denied to the general public. Frontier customs and practices passed down from an earlier era were thus altered forever.

Sparse, clandestine patches of cannabis weed that had been cultivated in forest clearings as late as 2006 became a distant memory as methamphetamine and other addictive drugs supplanted pot; and virtually all the timber roads through Weyerhaeuser lands had, by then, been gated. Treasure hunting and harvesting had been banned for perpetuity. The open frontier ended. Easy access to the forests was denied.

Cephis and Sid are real-life American heroes whose story played out in the land of Okies and Arkies on both sides of the Mountain Fork River. A landscape riffled with backwoods banality, archaic frontier mentality, religious zealotry, Ouachita foothills melodrama, and "corporate bestiality" set the tone and tenor for the tale that unfolded. This book is a poignant and mordantly vivid account of two men's quest for treasure and self-respect while in pursuit of their own unconventional and unauthorized piece of the American Dream.

CHAPTER ONE
From the Ouachitas to the Great Lakes

Cephis Hall was born May 10, 1941, near Mena, Arkansas, and grew up on a small farm amid the lingering shadows of the Ouachita Mountains in the aftermath of the Great Depression. There were few jobs to be found in the city, and many family farms across the nation were ravaged and their owners bankrupt. Cephis and his family were dirt poor. Prosperous people in the city sometimes made fun of Cephis and his family because they did not dress perfectly and talked funny. He and his family were sometimes called "hillbillies" by those city folks who dressed well and had plenty of money to spend.

In the aftermath of that great economic catastrophe, agricultural prices were still too low for the Halls' small, 160-acre farmstead to earn enough income from their crops and livestock to support a family. During the period of 1930 through the 1950s, waves of seasonal migrations moved itinerant families across the nation in search of fieldwork. Agricultural labor was still in demand in rural America as late as the 1950s, and native-born, white workers performed much of that labor at a time when there was only a trickle of migrant laborers crossing the border from Mexico. Cephis Hall's family was among those migrant farm families seeking agricultural work.

In the pall of the Great Depression, people in search of work were not particular about the labors they performed to earn economic sustenance. People were still humble enough to work in the fields picking cotton, watermelons, or tomatoes, and were not afraid of hard, back-breaking labor, sweat, dirt, or danger. These conditions were accepted by the laborers of the time as part of the natural order of work. Cephis Hall's father was one of these people.

The Hall family did not buy into the California Dream that propelled so many of their rural brethren ever westward in a desperate search for agricultural fieldwork during the darkest days of the 1930s calamity. Cephis' family were Arkies, rather than Okies—more mountain folk than prairie folk—and less inclined to move west in search of a blissful fantasy in sunny California.

The family's home base was a small farm in the foothills of the Ouachita Mountains in rural southwest Arkansas. Unlike their poor brethren, the Halls chose a path which led them to the cooler climate of the Great Lakes region.

The Halls found what they were looking for in Indiana near the glaciated lakes close to Elkhart, a vicinity south of Lake Michigan. The large commercial growers in the area were contracted by the Campbell Soup Company to grow and supply tomatoes, so seasonal field hands like the Halls worked the fields and picked the tomatoes for these contract growers.

Cephis' father, Robert, was a diligent laborer, and Cephis would grow to become much the same kind of man. Robert was not too proud to pick vegetables in the field, but was ambitious enough to work hard and gain recognition as a reliable employee with proven organizational and leadership skills. Soon Robert Hall earned the title and responsibility of supervisor, and ultimately rose to be superintendent over the fields and field hands, who were both white and Mexican migrants.

Robert worked out an arrangement with the contract growers so that every summer in late June, he and his family could arrive in time to work and supervise the fields, then return to southwestern Arkansas in early September to tend their own crops.

Americans and Mexicans came from all directions to pick tomatoes. The family of renowned Mexican-American singer Freddie Fender picked tomatoes in the fields of Indiana with the Halls. The Hall family earned extra cash, and because Cephis' father was a field superintendent, he earned considerably more than the typical tomato picker.

While working as a young boy in the fields of Indiana near the remnants of the glaciated lakes – Cephis picked up his first fossils—the small remains of ancient marine animals. Such natural oddities are common on the lands southwest of the Great Lakes area. They were corrals, brachiopods, and crinoids, although he did not know what they were at the time. The idea of these ancient, once-living things transforming into rocks captivated his imagination. He trained his eyes to scan for such natural relics on the ground and in the earth, and began to also find them at home on the lands of rural Arkansas. Picking up fossils, rocks, relics, and Indian arrowheads became a hobby. As he grew older, his interest in fossils and rocks continued and he became what some people call a rock hound, or naturalist.

He took the best of his small fossilized pieces to school in his pockets to show them to classmates and to ask his instructors what they were. His teachers did not know, and the students did not care. His classmates, perhaps even his teachers, thought he was rather odd and different.

Some of the older children made fun of him and called him names. Out of meanness or spite, some of the boys even stole his pocket treasures.

Cephis grew into a rather tall, skinny, and gawky teenager—perhaps an early forerunner of the nerd before the term was invented. As a youngster, Cephis was more interested in natural things rather than technological gadgets, and more curious about geological science than physical science; in other words, he gravitated to biology rather than physics, and nature rather than technology.

As a teenager, Cephis did not fit in well with the more popular students—the celebrities and the jocks. He was sometimes bullied in school by the more dominant students who were generally from the more affluent families. Cephis didn't play sports in high school; instead, he was studious and preferred to spend his time in the library reading *National Geographic* or other nature publications.

He was conscious about being poor and developed sensitivity to an array of social and economic factors and the innate privileges that class and money seemed to convey and the social distinctions they engendered. These early experiences from school made an indelible impression on his psyche.

Although entrepreneurial in outlook, Cephis had no illusions or fantasies about becoming rich. He sided with the "little guy" and was well versed in the plight of the underdog. He would, in later life, become entangled with powerful persons and forces in which he performed the role of the underdog to the hilt, quite literally and admirably. As a small business owner, he soon discerned the reality of economic power and learned about the multi-scale and monopolistic enterprises that overshadowed small businesses.

Hard work was his hallmark. After years of strenuous and dangerous labor as a lumberjack and miner, Cephis toughened and transitioned himself into a physical dynamo that would not be intimidated by the size, stature, or status of any man. Sweat, dirt, and danger were his constant companions.

For years he searched the woods and hills of southwestern Arkansas and southeastern Oklahoma for treasure—rare and valuable minerals and fossils—and gradually he learned where the jewels in the rough were hidden. Along the edges of bluffs, ravines, and creeks, he ferreted out rare gems and crystals formed and shaped by geological forces deep within Mother Earth.

It was his love of geological treasures that spurred him onward in pursuit of an impractical dream. And this pursuit eventually brought him face-to-face with unforeseen and deleterious forces. His passion for quartz crystals and fossils propelled him into direct conflict with scores of foes and belligerents who stood in the way of his dream.

His quest for hidden treasure would take him on a great adventure as the underdog in a titanic struggle against enormous odds. The struggle would be over the rightful ownership of a rare and valuable dinosaur. After wresting one of the greatest dinosaur specimens in paleontological history from a viscous and hardened earthen embankment, a bitter struggle against the forces of man ensued, with the victor to garner the acclaim and spoils, while the loser would get nothing. It was an all-or-nothing, winner-take-all contest and brawl to the bitter end.

CHAPTER TWO
It Happened In McCurtain County

It is a well-known contemporary fact of life that the rich and powerful rule and the poor must simply obey. This reality can be evidenced in the daily workings of the courts, legal system, government, business, and virtually every arena of life. The little guy is at a disadvantage, and the powerful always win. At least that is the conventional belief, and the evidence to support that thesis is ever so compelling. The rich and powerful may sometimes dispute it, but that is just an exercise in public relations, if not outright propaganda.

Once in a blue moon, however, the above modus operandi of life is repealed and the little guy holds his own or even triumphs against those dominant forces that perpetually want to regulate his behavior and fix the outcome in their favor. The saga of Cephis Hall and Sid Love is about one of those rare exceptions to the rule and demolishes the universal belief that the powerful always win, regardless of circumstances, truth, and justice.

Even though the Great Depression had passed, these were still hardscrabble times for dirt-poor rural Arkansans and their neighboring Okies to the west. The typical family was much like the Halls, scratching out a bare subsistence on a small family farm. The rural people of the Ouachita foothills were castigated with the emblematic label of "hillbilly"—the same stigma relegated to their kindred mountainfolk of the Ozarks and Appalachians.

There were no unionized factories in southwestern Arkansas during these lean times that offered good pay, fringe benefits, and the standard forty hour workweek. Franklin Roosevelt's New Deal had already ended the social and public works programs that employed thousands of rural Arkansas folk during the darkest days of the Great Depression. On the other hand, families were generally closer, and society was more closely-knit. Extended social relations and friendships seamed together a more cohesive society across a broad front.

In sharp contrast, there was the small class of the patrician rich, who moved largely in their own circles, and then there was most everybody else, who were all poor to some degree, some dirt poor. As might be expected, the "wealthy snobs" and the "working slobs" lived on opposite sides of the tracks. Although they may have interacted with each other more than do the rich and poor of today, their social worlds were far apart and in sharp contrast.

Perhaps the time, place, and style of life that captured Hall and his family during these early years qualified them as not mere stereotypes, but as genuine "Arkansas hillbillies." This is often used as a regional pejorative term, like the epithet "Okie" that labels and sometimes stereotypes the neighboring Oklahomans. The term was loosely used to describe the condition and behavior of a large cross-section of people who were tied to the land in an abject state of deprived material and cultural existence. During the early and mid-twentieth century in rural Arkansas and Oklahoma, one could find an abundance of destitute people on the land who were conspicuous in their appearance and behavior. The whole lot of these people, with their grimy, tattered clothes and all, were broadly cast with that label and stigma of "Okie."

The stereotype of the Okie conjures up archaic images of destitute farm families from the Great Depression era packing up their lifetime-belongings in a worn out, clanking old truck, and fleeing from a panoply of misfortunes and disasters in a desperate quest for the ever-elusive Promised Land in California, or elsewhere in the American West.

"California Dreaming" had beckoned them westward to a distant Mecca – a sunny, warm, coastal oasis on the western edge of Pax Americana. It was a land of "milk and honey" and boundless opportunity—or so they imagined in their naïve and idyllic fantasies.

The Depression, drought, howling winds, dust storms, infertile soils, hunger, and the banker's bulldozer had pushed them off their lands and onto the roads like nomadic gypsies. Desperate, but full of hope that God would provide and protect, their naïve intuitions and aspirations drove them onward.

Across the Heartland they poured—over muddy, bumpy, and pot-holed roads—down Route 66, the highway of promise and hope—through the golden arches and into the "fields of dreams." Many fell by the wayside; but many others ultimately reached their destination. A throng of prairie Sooners and hillbillies cascaded into the Golden State by the tens of thousands. John Steinbeck's *Grapes of Wrath* describes the images precisely.

The Okies were God fearing creatures of the soil, fleeing both the wrath of God and man. Although moral and righteous, the images they cast as they trekked westward across the heartland of America were hideous and despicable to those people whose space they'd suddenly invaded, and who viewed them with suspicion and scorn. The greetings they received from the communities they entered were never warm or friendly. The Promised Land they initially encountered was more like purgatory than paradise.

After encountering ignominious exploitation and heart-wrenching disappointment, the Okies and Arkies eventually settled and found economic subsistence in the military factories and farm fields from Barstow to Bakersfield, which became a hillbilly enclave.

The country singing legend, Merle Haggard, whose parents had traveled that same path, was born in 1936 while his family was living in an abandoned railroad car in Bakersfield.

The Haggards left their small farm near Checotah in eastern Oklahoma in 1934 and traveled west down Route 66 to seek refuge in a sunny, idyllic agri-paradise. Reality was less sanguine. The Haggards and Okies, hungry and praying for work in the fields, were boarded up in old cardboard boxes in "Hoover camps."

The term "Okie" was coined in the 1930s to identify those distressed migrants as a people, in whole or in part. Today the term usually just means somebody from Oklahoma. A different array of stereotypical images has been foisted for the "Arkansas hillbilly."

The hillbilly was a product of the backwoods and mountains, as opposed to the open prairie and soil for the Okie. More rural and isolated than the typical Okie, the hillbilly was inclined to conceal his sins and indiscretions behind the hollows, hills, and pine forests in which he dwelled. These were not always puritanical, god-fearing, Bible thumpers like the Okies on the expansive prairies. Sometimes, these were vicious and feuding peoples driven by prurient instincts and desires. They seldom resorted to migration to escape their problems, staying in place and enduring their hardships with whatever palliatives they had within easy grasp.

They were often suspicious of strangers who wandered off the beaten path. A small and crudely constructed whiskey still might rest in a concealed corner behind the house. Moonshine was plentiful and indulgently used to assuage the lingering misery of poverty and isolation. A bottle of white lighting was often in easy reach to wash away the incessant bleakness, at least for the moment.

The "Okie" and "Arkansas hillbilly," like obverse sides of the same coin, represent images that endure and endear to this very day. These two socially descriptive terms represent distinctive peoples. They are unforgettable relics from an earlier era. Both still persist as regional and historical icons and remind us of a tougher but simpler time when an agrarian economic and social order prevailed throughout the American heartland. Although America had gradually emerged from the untamed frontier by the late nineteenth century, people were still brutally oppressed by awesome forces unleashed by man and nature. Even in a modern, mass, transient society, there are still people in rural Oklahoma and Arkansas who identify themselves by such terms, whether they know their true connotation or not.

This was a world in stark contrast to the urban, high-tech, globally integrated economic order of the twenty-first century—a world dominated by high technology and multi-national corporations. The great majority of the people were still tied to the land. Production of food was the mainstay, not production and consumption of consumer goods. These wind-swept, ordinary people had similar experiences— experiences marred and shaped by poverty and isolation, which sometimes turned into despair and desperation.

The above Okie description stems from that imagery depicted by John Steinbeck in his popular novel *The Grapes of Wrath* and pertains to the destitute Oklahomans fleeing the Dust Bowl experience that afflicted large portions of the state, particularly the northern and western prairie areas, during the Great Depression era. The experience did not reach McCurtain County or the contiguous counties of Pushmataha and LeFlore in southeastern Oklahoma. It was a phenomenon of the prairies, not the forested or mountainous areas.

The people of southeastern Oklahoma and southwestern Arkansas were very similar in character and lifestyle—living in the foothills of the Ouachita Mountains in a similar economic environment. The Arkansas people have sometimes been referred to as "Arkies," perhaps an imitation of the term "Okie,"

The term "hillbilly" is more obscure than the term "Okie." Apparently it was derived from the Ulster-Scottish (or Scots-Irish) settlers who had migrated from Northern Ireland to America and then promptly moved out west to settle the frontier Appalachians. The origin of the term goes even further back. Its antecedents were coined by the Catholic supporters of King James II, who was defeated by William, Prince of Orange—a Protestant aspirant to the English throne—at the Battle of Boyne in 1690. The supporters of William, mostly lowland Scots, were called "Orangemen" and "Billy Boys" by the opposing Catholic troops loyal to King James. The names endured. The Lowlanders brought their songs and ballads pertaining to the battle and their support of Prince William with them to America.

The names they earned at the Boyne would eventually be corrupted into one—"hillbilly." These descendents of the lowland Scots were the great frontiersmen who settled and tamed the American West. This nickname would stick and ultimately tag them when they moved further west from Appalachia into the Arkansas Ozarks—thus nicknamed "Arkansas Hillbillies."

The imagery for the "Arkansas hillbilly" was simply transferred from the existing Appalachian version, just given a slightly regional twist. Apparently, the images of the feuding Hatfields and McCoys of Appalachia have also been mixed into the cultural iconic brew.

Cephis Hall, quite aware of what the connotation meant in an earlier era, openly referred to himself as an Arkansas hillbilly and a country bumpkin. Most people would not dispute this claim. He toned a peculiar rural accent in his speech, such as the conversational phrase "like that there" that he frequently interjected in the middle of a spoken phrase or sentence. Cephis sedulously flaunted this hillbilly aspect of his persona as if to make a statement. He was proud of his Ouachita roots.

He possessed a conspicuous "Arkansas hillbilly persona" in mannerisms and outlook—a set of folkways likely derived from the cultural epicenter of the Appalachian highlands, which, in turn, harkened back to the Ulster Plantation in Northern Ireland, and ultimately to the border areas of lowland Scotland. His ancestral folks were the same people who had stood with William Wallace, "Brave Heart," who, with his ragtag army of Scottish peasants, soundly trumped the professional army of King Edward I of England at the Battle of Sterling Bridge in 1297 and sent Edward's troops reeling and limping back across the border into England.

A close-knit family structure and a disciplined, sod-busting, Ouachita-hills rearing had molded both the interior and exterior of Hall. Perhaps the hardships he endured in his early years conditioned him to deal with the future hard knocks he would one day receive as an adult. Such a condition of poverty can cut two ways, both strengthening and weakening a person at the same time.

Hall was the son of two states. Both Oklahoma and particularly Arkansas lay claim to the distinction of being home to both the rebellious Southern redneck and the reclusive uplands hillbilly. Both of these iconic symbols, although in sharp contrast, stem from a wider cultural heritage of the rural South oft described as "Cracker Culture." This broad, inclusive ethnic-cultural milieu encompassed a whole repertoire of rustic distinctions: hill-folks, po-folks, good old boys, white trash, etc., of which hillbilly and redneck are merely peculiar brands linked within that more comprehensive context of rural southern whites. Cracker cultural hegemony extended from that expansive set of bucolic lands from Appalachia to the southern flatlands—a broad stretch of Southern majesty that included the mountains of West Virginia, Kentucky, and Tennessee; the hills of Arkansas; the cotton fields of Alabama, Georgia, and South Carolina; the Mississippi delta; the panhandle of Florida; the swamps and bayous of Louisiana; and the pine forests of southeastern Oklahoma and east Texas.

During the colonial era in America, the Crackers were described as a rambunctious frontier people with a general defiance of authority. They were seen negatively as a hooligan population with no allegiance to the British Crown who often changed their abodes and squatted on unoccupied lands. The Cracker gave rise to all the Southern stereotypes and caricatures, such as hillbilly, that we know today. Over time, the term "Cracker" eroded into a racial slur for bigoted, backwoods Southern whites (Ste.Claire*)*.

Most assuredly, the early descriptions of migrating "crackers" were biased and distorted. More than just a residue of stereotypes, the cultural contributions of these people to the social moorings of the nation have been profound. "Cracker culture" has radiated across the entire nation, and its impact is seen in many areas such as religion, politics, taxes, music, race relations, gun laws, recreation, and distrust of government. Dixie is rising and the entire nation is being "Southernized." "The South is no longer geography—it's an attitude and a philosophy about government." (George Wallace) In the midst of this transition, Southern rednecks and good old boys came to vastly outnumber the Appalachian-cloned hillbillies, who are a dying breed.

In the decades before World War II, hillbillies, particularly those of the bucolic, Arcadian Ozarks, elicited big fanfare that drove a considerable national curiosity and fascination with the caricature. "The imagery, often a form of buffoonery, was used to entertain and parody. But with the rise of the Cold War, internationalism, and a cultural and economic homogeneity instilled by advertising and mass marketing after WWII, the nation was looking outward and there was little interest and curiosity in 'things hillbilly'." (Blevins)

The stereotypical caricature of the perennial Arkansas hillbilly is seen as that of the shiftless squatter forever mired in rude and base instincts—a drunken (on moonshine, of course), slovenly, violent, illiterate, fiddling, backwards "clodhopper" confined amidst the dismal isolation of the hills, hollows, and pine forests of northwestern Arkansas (Blevens).

Cephis Hall, "the jewel of the Appalachian juggernaut," negates that pejorative imagery. Far from being lazy or shiftless, Hall may have been the hardest working pine dweller who ever lived. He was also upright and moral and had a sense of fairness and equity in all things measurable. The same could be said for his partner, Sid Love, although Sid failed to qualify for the brandished hillbilly stigmata. Cephis hardly ever kept hound dogs, not even coon dogs, though it had been rumored that he harbored stills in the nearby woods.

Rather than moonshine, hogs, and hills, Sid was linked to Choctaw aristocracy, agricultural mercantilism, and a panorama of river-valley flatlands imposing a fading legacy of cotton fields and antebellum mansions once occupied by his great-grandfather, Robert M. Jones, one of the wealthiest traders of the Old South.

Both Arkansas and Oklahoma are mired in contradiction. The old symbols of the past are in a constant tug of war with the forces of modernity—the planter versus the industrialist; the redneck contrasting the urbane professional; the cultivated plantations of the South set against the rugged isolation of the Ozarks and Ouachitas; opulent shopping malls contrasting vast corporate grain fields; open grazing versus barbed wire fences; zealous evangelicalism versus secular scientific empiricism.

Cephis was reared an "Arkie"—sometimes referred to as an "Arkansas razorback"—a distinction in which he reveled. The attitudes and mannerisms garnered from the hills and fields of Arkansas carried over to his adult life amidst the pine forests of southeastern Oklahoma. From farms to forests, crops to logs, he gradually transitioned into a bona fide Okie after having moved to southeastern Oklahoma. With a leathered, parochial finish, Appalachia and Dixie were etched on his stark, sinewy persona like the coarseness of coal and bolls of cotton.

A religious-oriented upbringing, an instilled time-honored set of morals, values, and convictions, and a uniquely rural life experience had honed Cephis Hall into a person with a rare combination of qualities not often seen in the modern world—a plain-spoken, straightforward, down-to-earth, rough-hewn rustic with an unwavering penchant for honesty, equity, and truth. Also, Cephis was an oddity of mixed contradictions. He was like a rare coin—on one side a backwoods hillbilly who seemed to have never cracked a book, on the other side a studious, book-worn nerd with a rural, homey accent who in some plush quarters might be perceived as having a loutish, unpolished appearance. In one instance, he was an avid Bible thumper and quoter, while on another, an adherent and strong defender of science and evolution. He was seemingly anti-intellectual on the surface, but intellectual to the core underneath. Poverty had coalesced with perseverance and perspiration to shape his life chances and color his demeanor.

Hall completed high school and managed to develop eclectic interests in the scientific areas of geology and biology and learned from a more practical application of skills applied in the field. It would be easy to underestimate this man's knowledge base, until he begins to converse and elaborate about geological principles he largely learned out in the real world. Despite his unpretentious demeanor, he conveyed an uncanny expertise of the naturalist world.

In 1963, Cephis married Joyce, a resident of his rural Arkansas community, and moved to DeQueen, Arkansas, just east of the Oklahoma state line. Hall then became a contract trucker for a poultry company before relocating across the state line to Eagletown, a small community in McCurtain County, Oklahoma.

In Oklahoma, he became employed as a carpenter for the giant construction firm Brown & Root before finally taking a job as a contract logger. During this period from 1966 to 1978, Cephis and Joyce's three children, Angie, April, and Alan were born.

Eagletown is located on Highway 70 about fourteen miles east from Broken Bow, Oklahoma. Now largely an abandoned town, it was livelier in the early part of the twentieth century while serving as one of the camps (or perhaps more accurately, company towns), established by the original Dierks Brothers timber company—then known as the Choctaw Lumber Company. These camps had narrow-gauge rail spurs leading into the hills and valleys where virgin timber was cut, then skidded with mules, and loaded onto railcars to be hauled to the mills. Broken Bow, to the west, was developed in 1912 as one of the largest mill sites of the Choctaw Lumber Company. The camps were abandoned in the late 1930s once the virgin hardwood timber had been cut. The company's workforce packed up and left and Eagletown went into a precipitous decline.

In the early nineteenth century, Eagletown was a thriving center for the newly arrived Choctaw Indian Nation. In 1830, the Choctaws signed a treaty with the federal government that dictated the trade of their lands in Mississippi for remote lands in Oklahoma between the Canadian and Red Rivers. The following year, through forced removal, they began moving from Mississippi to Oklahoma and finally scattered over about ten counties of Oklahoma. About 6,000 Choctaws would be moved per year for three consecutive years. Eagletown was founded by that first wave of Indians.

Eagletown became an annuity town. Each year, Choctaws from the surrounding area came to town to get an annual payment. The leaders of the Choctaw Nation had to ride on horseback to a disbursement center in Little Rock to get their funds.

Eagletown was also an early cultural center for the emergent Choctaw Nation. One of the first schools to educate Choctaw children was established at Eagletown by a missionary brought in from Mississippi for that very purpose.

During this period, the federal government built one of the first major roads in the state for the purpose of moving supplies and Choctaws from Little Rock, Arkansas to Fort Towson, Oklahoma with Eagletown as a major stopover. That same military road was traveled through Horatio to Eagletown and eventually linked a community called Hoorah, which became known as DeQueen, Arkansas. This early primitive road eventually became Highway 70, a major transportation artery in southeastern Oklahoma and Arkansas.

Highway 70 now links the county's two predominant cities, Idabel and Broken Bow. Idabel, with a population of about 7,000, serves as the county seat and the hub for agriculture, shopping, and county government operations. Its sister city, Broken Bow, has a population of about 5,000 and is a hub for timber and tourism. Big-rig logging trucks are frequently seen rolling through the thoroughfares of Broken Bow. Idabel straddles the Red River valley, and its surrounding landscape was once dominated by King Cotton. Cotton was still king as late as the 1950s, but corn and cattle are now the principal agricultural products.

McCurtain County, located in the southeastern corner of Oklahoma, is a tiny enclave of Dixieland and strategically located where Arkansas, Oklahoma, and Texas intersect. Ethnically, the bulk of the population is composed of two types of people: Choctaw Indians and descendants of Scots-Irish frontiersmen, or a mixture of both. The flag, God, football, alcohol, country music, hunting, fishing, barbecuing, and apple pie, not necessarily in that order, are some of the most cherished pastimes for the locals. The place offers a pinch of frontier culture derived from a motley blend of Choctaw, Old Dixie, and Appalachia, and a contradictory jumble of progress and stagnation.

Only the southeastern corner of Oklahoma is noted as part of the traditional South. The remainder of the state is generally considered southwestern. McCurtain County is pegged loosely in what may be considered the "Confederate South" or "Dixie." In earlier times, it was actually known as "Little Dixie", a distinct region that took its name and identity from the Cotton South and represented a western fringe of the classical and purist of the Southern states: Alabama, Mississippi, Georgia, Louisiana, and South Carolina. Little Dixie was settled largely by Choctaw Indians, displaced citizens of the Old Confederacy moving west, and land hungry frontiersman from Appalachia moving southwestwardly. Migrating white Southerners brought their unique Dixie cultural characteristics, while the white folks of the Appalachians and Cumberlands carried a peculiar mountain culture that originated ultimately in Scotland.

The landscape of McCurtain County in the late twentieth century was more like the "Old South" than the "New South." Still a rural-based economy, it was a far cry from the new suburban South with its expanses of glitzy malls, mirror-glass office parks, sprawling subdivisions, and prolific corporate iconography like one might find in affluent Dallas County or in Newt Gingrich's Cobb County, Georgia.

Lumber, tourism, cattle, and poultry are now the major industries and employment underpins of the local economy. The giant poultry king, Tyson Foods, is probably the largest employer, at least since the beginning of the twenty-first century. Within the forest products industry, Weyerhaeuser and International Paper are the other two major employers in the county. Like most rural areas of America since the 1980s, McCurtain County has seen a decline in population as the younger generation continues to seek career opportunities elsewhere.

The two sister cities are unmistakably blue collar, as evidenced by economic demographics, occupational patterns, and dress and appearance. Stylish designer clothes or three-piece suits are not conspicuous in the open forums and streets. Dress is modest and casual, if not drab.

Choctaws are evident in the stores, communities, schools, and streets. Choctaw prominence also registers in tourist landmarks and recreational icons. The Choctaw Casino and tourist center in Broken Bow bring in gaming enthusiasts and cash to the local economy.

This area of southeastern Oklahoma, in and around the principal cities of Broken Bow and Idabel, is now dominated by monoculture plantations of Loblolly Pine. These new stands of pines have replaced the virgin hardwoods. The piney woods are interspersed with numerous streams and creeks that flow generally southward and meander through the low-lying valley as they drain the surrounding foothills of the Ouachita Mountains.

While living in Eagletown, Cephis became acquainted with the local crystal trade in and around Hochatown, Oklahoma, a small community north of Broken Bow. Years earlier, he had been active in the crystal trade in Arkansas. In the Hochatown locality, he found a productive area and began searching the backwoods of this new crystal zone.

The zone has veins running generally across the Ouachita uplift. A unique geologic structure, it is literally a rock hound's paradise. Although not big enough for commercial ventures, it attracts serious collectors from all over the world.

Quartz crystals are found in "vugs" or "pockets" at various places along a vein of hydrothermal quartz and must be mined by hand, or by mechanical digging. Successful digging of quartz requires meticulous care and good technique. Such skills cannot be learned overnight, and require extensive practice, largely by trial and error.

Hochatown is a small, picturesque village on the southern edge of the Ouachita National Forest and at the base of the Kiamichi Mountains. This is a scenic and quaint tourist area, less than a five-minute drive to a major tourist attraction.

Nearby, beautiful Broken Bow Lake and popular Beavers Bend State Park are nestled in the foothills at the base of the Kiamichi Mountains. The cold and clear flowing Mountain Fork River, teeming with trout, flows through the heart of this popular state park. The park was built during the Great Depression by President Franklin Roosevelt's Civilian Conservation Corps (CCC) after citizens of Broken Bow and Idabel raised $1,800 and purchased 1,200 acres of cutover land known as Beavers Bend from the Choctaw Lumber Company.

In August 1935, 208 enlisted CCC men began building barracks, water works, telephone lines, and sewer systems. In addition, the CCC constructed park cabins, a concession building, a swimming area, fencing, and a major access road. Many of these original buildings are still in use today. The Rooseveltian public works projects were designed to put a restless rural population back to work. In those days, disenfranchised hellions and hooligans threatened the social order. Roosevelt's "tree army" restored forests, fought forest fires, planted trees, and constructed fire towers, roads, dams, trails, and telephone lines.

The Mountain Fork is a major focal point within the county—a scenic, natural marvel that entices tourists. Hunters, fisherman, canoeists, and other recreationists flock to the area. The area also attracts naturalists and collectors of artifacts and minerals. Log cabins dot the landscape in and near Beavers Bend.

Hochatown has been a center of interest for more than just recreation and crystals. For decades, it was known as the moonshine capital for the state of Oklahoma. This distinction refers not to just Prohibition or the Great Depression era, but a period as late as the early 1970s when major moonshine operations shipped cases of bootleg whiskey across the entire length and breadth of the nation. Shipments of moonshine reached major cities like Chicago and Los Angeles.

The American South was the moonshine capital of the nation, and Hochatown was a rural hamlet within that region. By the end of Prohibition over 280,000 stills existed in the US, most of them in the South. Southern stills supplied the moonshine for the nation during Prohibition. Moonshine was not just tradition for the people of Appalachia and Dixie, but a true folk custom brought all the way from their ancient Celtic homelands.

While collecting crystals in the Hochatown area, Cephis became acquainted with local still operators, and landed a part time job driving shipments of sugar to several local stills. In McCurtain County, a local resident often had to work two or three jobs at the same time to earn enough to support a family, and Cephis was no exception. Some locals even claimed Cephis was a moonshiner in his younger days. He knew all about the moonshine craft with an intimacy that could only come from firsthand participation in the tricks of the trade, but there is no evidence of him ever having operated stills.

The larger moonshine stills were lucrative businesses in those days. People who believed that major stills were operated by "squalid rednecks" from the backwoods were patently mistaken. Prominent local families owned these larger stills and hired people with business savvy and political connections to manage the operations.

The smaller stills were generally only a local, single-family enterprise designed to supply the immediate family, local kin, and neighbors, rather than a distant market. It was one of the few ways of making money without stealing in those days.

The only thing illegal about brewing custom made whiskey was not paying taxes on it, and ever since Alexander Hamilton's day, most Southerners believed that alcohol should not be taxed. This sentiment was widely held among the small, yeoman farmers of the western hinterland. When Hamilton, a staunch federalist who wanted to increase the size and power of the federal government through taxation, needed to raise revenue to erase the war debt, he cast his ravenous eyes on the small whiskey trade of the frontier farmer class. He chose to tax the distilled spirits produced by small farmers, rather than shakeout revenue from the wealthy industrialist and merchant classes on the East Coast. In 1791, he persuaded Congress to pass a law that imposed a burdensome whiskey tax on western settlers. This tax was highly resented by pioneer farmers who depended on whiskey for comfort and income (whiskey was actually used as a medium of exchange). A full-scale whiskey rebellion erupted.

In 1794, the rebellion was put down by a militia force of some 13,000 men, led personally by Alexander Hamilton, President George Washington, and General Henry "Light Horse Harry" Lee, the father of Confederate General Robert E. Lee. This was probably the first rumbling of a regional conflict within the new nation—the industrial and commercial eastern seaboard set against the western, mountainous frontier.

In southeastern Oklahoma, whiskey production remained viable long after Prohibition ended. Secluded amidst the bluffs of the pine forests, small-time still owners who were less soundly financed could build a small still operation into a larger one. Much would depend on one's skill and guile, and perhaps even more importantly—political connections. It was always necessary to have the protection of the local sheriff, who always got his cut. The federal Revenuers could bust a still only if they had an undercover agent working on it, or if it was turned in for a bounty by some poor snitch that would probably get killed if he were ever discovered. Otherwise, it was usually an accident when a large operating still was found. As for the small stills operating since the 1930s, reviews of old newspaper clippings tell of numerous busts of small still operations throughout the county. The busts were usually made by local law enforcement.

A local sheriff, Gene Thorpe, was reputed to have operated at least one of the major stills in McCurtain County. This was probably an ideal business arrangement. The nature of the business dictates that one must pay off the local authorities. If true, this sheriff-operator probably got to pocket what ordinarily would have been a nondeductible business expense.

Moonshine was generally, at least for the big operators, a stable and well-managed business in those days. Occasionally, some moralist do-gooder might cast a scornful eye and make a little noise, but as long as law enforcement could be paid to look the other way, the operator remained in business. The major operations were well financed and the organizational model was sound—often resembling a hierarchical corporate organizational chart.

The organization was replete with a division of labor into specialties and an extensive infrastructure for the production, storage, marketing, finance, sale, transport, warehousing, distribution, and delivery of the product. Major buyers were the bars and nightclubs of major cities across America. The largest bulk-buyers were wealthy and prominent people in the community, including important politicians, who kept bottles handy for friends at social gatherings.

Moonshine was not mass-produced, but custom made. Liquor made from corn rather than sugar was mellow and preferable to store-bought or industrial whiskey. Although stronger proof, it was smooth and went down well. Good quality moonshine did not irritate the senses and was more addictive, or at least more pleasing, than bonded whiskey. The quality of the taste insured a continuous market.

The Hochatown area was an ideal setting for moonshine operations because of the many clean, cold, spring-fed streams that ran through the isolated backwoods, which were indispensable for the condensation and distillation processes. Also, the seclusion of the forests provided a backdrop for isolation and concealment.

Old timers remembered one still operation that had people working in eight-hour shifts and had a whistle that blew when each shift was over—just like a manufacturing plant. After Prohibition ended, Oklahoma was still a dry state and did not vote to legalize whiskey until 1959.

But the moonshine business was still hanging on in McCurtain County as late as the 1960s until a new landowner arrived on the scene. In 1969, Weyerhaeuser, a giant timber corporation from out of state, moved to the county. It bought out the existing holdings of an old mainstay timber company, Dierks, and subsequently purchased additional timberlands throughout the county. Weyerhaeuser soon acquired nearly 900,000 acres in Southeastern Oklahoma, almost 700,000 acres in McCurtain County alone. Nearly overnight, it had become the largest landowner in the county, owning more than 50 percent of the land base. Nationwide, Weyerhaeuser owned six million acres of timberland with nearly two million acres of holdings in Arkansas and Oklahoma combined.

The paternal Dierks' family empire was more akin to the dynastic capitalism of the nineteenth century, whereas Weyerhaeuser, the new monolithic timber concern, was the archetypical modern corporation—a mixture of old and new industrialism, the old and new economy, publicly owned rather than family owned, multi-nationalistic, oligopolistic, scientific management, information age technology, and Wall Street finances.

When arriving on the scene in southeastern Oklahoma, Weyerhaeuser was more akin to an old-line, industrial corporation—more a production machine than a high tech, informational company. The very nature of its business, timber and building materials, militates against it becoming a truly enlightened "knowledge corporation" encapsulating modern organizational democracy in consonance with "knowledge workers" and computer technology. The mechanized assembly line of Taylor or Ford is a closer fit than the computerized, white collar-staffed, informational platform. It requires a hierarchical management and staffing arrangement—a command and control approach, unlike that of twenty-first century high tech companies like Yahoo, Apple or Google with more liberated workplaces. In these companies, the organizational chart is centered more on the computer chip and a decentralized information flow.

Weyerhaeuser's 2007 Investor's Guide reveals that the company owned or leased 6.4 million acres of land in the United States (including 663,000 acres in Arkansas and 549,000 acres in Oklahoma/Texas) and 15.1 million acres of land in Canada for a total controlling interest in North American lands of approximately 21.5 million acres. Weyerhaeuser also owned or managed some 514,000 acres in four foreign countries: Uruguay, Brazil, New Zealand, and Australia. Its operations are divided into five divisions: Timberlands, Wood Products, Cellulose Fibers, Real Estate, and Containerboard, Packaging and Recycling. Most of its manufacturing plants are located in the United States and Canada. In addition, it has several manufacturing plants in Mexico that make linerboard and corrugated boxes.

In no short order, Weyerhaeuser began to make its presence known in McCurtain County after its arrival in 1969. The intrusive company began to build private roads throughout its extensive landholdings on top of pre-existing public roads and began casting suspicious eyes on strangers and intruders. Almost a decade later, in 1980, Weyerhaeuser would claim that the 80,000 miles of timberland roads built over old public roads were then "Private Roads" even though public access had not been denied during the previous thirty years. Apparently, at least many believed, they had started calling them private roads in a legal attempt to avoid liability for accidents.

Weyerhaeuser's new private roads began to cut through previously isolated backwoods that few people, except maybe moonshiners, cared to visit. The stills were no longer guaranteed concealment, and Weyerhaeuser officials could not be trusted for a wink and a nod.

Additionally, Weyerhaeuser did not operate like Dierks. The Dierks family corporation had always maintained a liberal policy in regard to public use of its timberlands. But this policy did not originate from a generous heart; it was due to a binding Trust Agreement between the State of Oklahoma and the Dierks Lumber Company in exchange for taxing their forestlands as "wasteland.

Finally, Weyerhaeuser managed its timber farming operations differently. It utilized a monoculture plantation system, and the company's practice of clear-cutting and heavy reliance on fertilizers, herbicides, pesticides, and defoliants resulted in these chemicals being washed into the previously pristine streams, which denigrated their purity and quality. Also, the extensive grading and construction of new roads throughout the timberlands and the radical clear-cutting of the pine plantations created erosion problems that further jeopardized the quality and integrity of the streams.

A clean moonshine product could no longer be obtained. The quality of the product was seriously compromised with reduced water quality. The future was indeed bleak for the moonshine industry in McCurtain County. A large portion of the county's underground workforce needed to find a new occupation—perhaps with Weyerhaeuser, now the county's major employer. Cephis himself landed a new job as a logging contract-employee for a prime Weyerhaeuser contract logger.

The paper business is very competitive and cyclical, especially lumber and building materials, which are tied directly to the housing market. The housing market, in turn, is very sensitive to interest rates and the normal cyclical gyrations of the national economy. There is enormous overhead, and the margin between costs and sales is low.

Management is under constant pressure to control expenses and must continuously assess these high, fixed costs in light of the low margins and onerous encroachment of the business cycle. There is enormous pressure to realize savings, but there are limits as to how far management can go in cutting costs.

Weyerhaeuser and the other U.S. timber companies cannot easily respond to these pressures in the same manner as most other American industries. It is simply not feasible to relocate existing paper and lumber operations to other countries like Mexico, China, or India, where labor and other input costs are extremely low. Lumber and paper mills serving the national market must be located near the supply source of raw timber to realize maximum economic efficiency. Otherwise, transportation costs would spiral out of control. Rather than move all production facilities overseas and import finished products back into the U.S. market, Weyerhaeuser streamlined operations by cutting its workforce and contracting out much of its production and service operations.

While working for a contract logger, Cephis for years plied his trade within the logging craft and stoically endured the constant pains, wear, and tear that are a veritable hallmark for the occupation. The experience toughened him both physically and mentally. Not just physical pain had to be endured, but unrelenting mental anguish and the inexorable trepidation that accompanied the inherent occupational insecurity of contract-logging. The employee turnover rate in the industry was extremely high, and Cephis had already outlasted most.

During his tenure within the trade, Cephis continued to drive from Eagletown to Hochatown in search of recreation and diversion from his harsh occupational reality. In those days, gas was cheap and the frequent drives were not a financial burden. His primary pursuit was crystal collecting and he proved to have an uncanny ability to find them. Some people believed he had a kind of ESP or sixth sense—an innate ability to project mind over matter.

Cephis was a local country boy who had risen in the undistinguished ranks of that loose collective of local naturalists: rockhounds, fossil collectors, botanical fanciers, bird watchers, wildlife conservationists, and environmentalists of all stripes and persuasions. He became an expert on quartz crystals, and before long, his name became synonymous with crystals. He also became a crystal dealer and had small-scale commercial dealings in minerals. His fine minerals were sold to museums and his exquisite quartz crystals to private collectors, even to dealers in Switzerland and Germany. Mineral enthusiasts began flocking to him for guidance on finding crystals. Before long, he began offering and instructing tours for people looking for crystals.

Nature and treasure hunting was encoded onto his DNA. His treasure hunts were not limited solely to natural and geological wonders, but riches buried by the hands of man and enshrouded in mystery and lore. Hall searched for buried Confederate gold at the Pine Knot Crossing where the Old Military Trail crosses the Little River. Although he didn't find gold coins, he did, with electronic equipment, detect naturally occurring gold in a nearby sandstone formation. Although it was never proven that the gold bearing strata was feasible to mine, the discovery fed into the myriad of legends already circulating around southeastern Oklahoma, including Big Foot (*Mother Lode Waiting to be Found, The Oklahoman*, Page 23A, October 16, 2005).

Hall knew the back roads and back lands of McCurtain County. When people were looking for natural phenomena of an earthly genre, they turned to Cephis Hall for guidance and direction. The most popular nature guide of McCurtain County, he operated Ouachita Mountain Tours, a local tourist service for naturalist sightseers and mineral prospectors. The tours were more recreational and educational than commercial.

Cephis, nicknamed "the Crystal of the Ouachitas," was an anachronism as a nature guide. He is a classic, old-timey nature guide, who entertains school children and adults with the stories, legend and lore, and magic of the natural world. He and Sid were vestiges of a vanishing class of American naturalist explorers, dinosaurs like the ones they sought buried in the earth.

Hall's naturalist style is a throwback to an earlier dawning before the turn of the twentieth century when naturalist adventurers had the sway of the land. But now he and his ilk have been eclipsed by the academic specialist. Antiquated, but still active, Hall's naturalist explorations were becoming pressured on many fronts.

When the highly regarded Neal Suneson from the Oklahoma Geological Survey at the University of Oklahoma visited McCurtain County in June of 1990 to explore and sample the geological treasures of the county, he chose Cephis Hall as his nature guide. Hall took him to the places he needed to see in order to locate prominent rock and geological formations as well as to assess the overall natural and geographical features of the area. While on stay in the county he was asked, "How good is Cephis Hall?" Suneson responded, "He's good. He keeps his eyes to the ground. After you know what you're looking for, and he does, then you need good eyes just like hunting squirrels in trees…he will certainly be valuable to anybody who wants to go directly to some of the marvelous locations in the county. He already knows where they are." (*McCurtain Daily Gazette*, June 1, 1990)

Cephis says he learned to excavate fossils from the techniques he learned digging crystals—a similar procedure. He also learned patience, where to look, and where not to look. His interest in fossils grew from a natural curiosity about rocks—about how they changed and evolved. "To be a good fossil hunter," he says, "you must have good eyes that can spot textural and color differences." "Finding fossils and crystals," he further adds, "involves a physical and spiritual connection—pure mental concentration."

His life experience had uniquely prepared him to endure hardship and adversity with a spiritual tenacity. He learned perseverance as part of his normal, daily routine. His childhood experience with poverty and his hazardous occupation as a logger toughened him both physically and mentally. He learned to deal with stress on a daily basis and generally took negative incursions in stride. His unpolished mien was that of a raw, razor-thin, dirt-splattered Okie with calloused hands, denim jeans, and "fields of dreams." As the world around him changed literally by the minute, his down-to-earth simplicity remained intact and incorrigible. Cephis, like all his kindred, was bound to the people and the land from whence they came.

His humble origins and modest background transcribed and outwardly projected a kind of delusive personality and demeanor that easily caused an opponent to underestimate him. This, conceivably, gave him an edge in tight situations. His extraordinary character and inner strength was not readily apparent on a first, or transitory, encounter. The impression he initially conveyed was that of simple, country folk. And this is the impression he still conveys.

While a young boy growing up at the base of the Ouachitas, Cephis inculcated a dream. Even as he navigated through adulthood and eclipsed the fourth decade mark, the childhood dream never left him. Conceived in the hollows and hills, it was more about natural treasures than monetary riches—more down to earth and devoid of opulence. Cephis was never obsessed with becoming rich, but had no reservations about lining his pockets.

Of course, there are different versions of the American Dream: a chicken in every pot, a car in every garage, the Horatio Alger rags to riches exemplar, celebrity status, nirvana in suburbia, etc. And yes, there is the underside of the American Dream: mass unemployment, poverty, criminality, victimhood, drugs, incarceration, Wall Street malfeasance, political corruption, etc.

But Hall's dream was unique. Envisioned and inspired from his prodigious nature experiences as he encountered both living and non-living things from a boy to a grown man, his dream was to discover and extricate a rare and valuable dinosaurian fossil and make his mark on the scientific and naturalist world. He was not a credentialed scientist, but rather an intrepid explorer of nature. To some, he was a quintessential treasure hunter who had found his share of interesting relics, even if the grand prize had long eluded him. The problem was that his American Dream was unauthorized and did not fit neatly into the status quo. His dream meandered across a murky stream of diverse venues: buried treasure, dinosaurs, greed, corruption, moonshine, pot fields, quartz crystal, amateurism, elitism, corporatism, legalism, academic snobbery, religion, politics—and these were all irreconcilable. Nevertheless, his dream (and his story) represents a small piece of bucolic, backwoods Americana, as well as fulfillment.

Cephis had bought into a tenuous version of the American Dream that was poised to "reap the whirlwind." His dream, despite his sincere intentions, was subject to the caprice of others who were wealthier and more powerful than he. His ambition would bring him to the brim of abyss and cataclysm. On the edge of an artificial waste-laden pit despoiled by industrial pollution, Cephis hoped to find remnants of giant mystifying saurians with fierce roars, horrid claws, and razor-sharp teeth that lived more than a hundred million years into the deep primal past.

Cephis Hall and Sid Love were part of that loose network of naturalist explorers and collectors who scoured the American Outback for sparkling jewels and crystals. Cephis, a man of humble origin, and Sid, a man of more luster but modest still, hunted treasure in out-of-the-way places. They had uncovered rare and valuable natural bounties and man-made booty within secretive enclaves without molestation or hindrance. But it was in 1983 when things started to change and their troubles began.

A dream, and a will to pursue it, can result in war.

CHAPTER THREE
In Search of the Pit with the Golden Wood

In McCurtain County, the winter of 1983 had elapsed and faded into the recent past. Spring had arrived and ushered in a new natural order. Wondrous sounds and scents filled the air. Flowers flaunted their bright new blooms, and birds competed for the best nesting sites. A rich tapestry of fresh colors adorned the trees and shrubs, and the forest came alive with the reawakening of animals and insects. An occasional light gust of wind circulated through the open forest and ruffled the leaves and cooled the surroundings. The peaceful and harmonious vibrations of spring could be felt all around.

A veil of verdant green now painted and pervaded the previous pale and dormant landscape. Wonderful and welcomed rains filled the creeks and streams to overflow, bringing life-sustenance to the grassy lands and renewing the promise of a bright beginning. The animals of the forests and meadows awakened from their winter somnolence as revival and energy permeated their senses.

With the warmth of the sun and greening of the plants, the ground-dwelling animals of the prairies had taken their cue and bustled with renewed vigor. As darting shadows bounced across the meadows and forests, the stirrings of life embellished the landscape with intensity. The abounding arrival of spring inspired new drives and ambitions. Dormancy had ended. Life was in transition.

Cephis Hall also stirred and emerged from his winter torpor. A cold and harrowing winter had confined his family to the warm, indoor shelter and fireplace for many days of the long winter season. The cold, rainy, and icy days kept him away from his work of felling trees on Weyerhaeuser lands and interrupted his hobby of collecting crystals and fossils. But as the sun brightened, the clouds cleared, and the foliage greened, he was anxious to resume his perennial life activities of cutting pine trees, planting gardens, and digging crystals.

In addition to prospecting, Cephis, in a garden clearing amidst the pines, grew organic vegetables that tasted nothing like supermarket produce or the poor-quality, impostor vegetables bought at Southern roadside stands. Those vegetables were erroneously presumed to be locally grown, but are actually brought in from California, Florida, or Mexico, where they were commercially grown by agri-business with loads of pesticides, petroleum-based phosphate fertilizers and cheap, semi-indentured labor. It was a bait and switch ploy designed to foist off low-grade produce to naïve green-purity seekers. In contrast, whatever came out of Cephis' garden was a vine-ripened delight.

Not long after the blooms of spring arrived, Cephis made his way back into Weyerhaeuser's forests to earn a living. As the daily temperatures rose, the grounds of the pine stands thawed and dried, and the timber roads became passable. The roar of machines pierced the solitude of the forests.

Activity within the forests intensified and dollars began to flow swiftly through the local economy. The life force of springtime and the lure of money stimulated the social and recreational life of the community. McCurtain County was not just a timber economy; it was also a tourist economy. For Hall, the desire for recreation and social involvement with friends now came to the forefront. The two needs were combined into one activity—crystal hunting.

That early part of spring in 1983, a friend stopped by for a social visit. Louis Pruitt, a local coon hunter, told Cephis about what he had seen during a recent hunt near the Mountain Fork River. He stated that he had shined his flashlight on a gully and had spotted not a raccoon, but something that looked like fool's gold on wood. The distinctive sheen on the petrified wood was a natural manifestation he thought might interest Cephis. Cephis listened intently to his description and directions to the location of the sighting.

Pruitt's details did pique his curiosity. Based on the description, Cephis suspected the shining fool's gold on the wood was actually iron pyrite on carbonized wood – an indication of something ancient—perhaps of the Cretaceous Period.

The Cretaceous Period stretched back more than one hundred million years and was the time of the dinosaurs. Whatever it was that Pruitt had seen might be worth collecting. Besides, this was an indication that the Cretaceous strata was accessible, and offered hope that the remnants of some other life form might be attainable. Perhaps an animated organism of real flesh and blood reminiscent of the Cretaceous had once been active in the immediate area and its remains near at hand. Perhaps something else from that ancient era might just show up, possibly bones, maybe even dinosaur bones.

Cephis had always dreamed of making a major dinosaur discovery. It's a dream that mystifies not just amateur naturalists, but credentialed scientists as well. The thrill of the discovery, the challenge of the excavation, and the notoriety and recognition that follows is an enticing proposition. Great discoveries are made by amateurs and professionals alike. Quite often, the mere discovery is rewarding enough for the amateur. The daunting task of excavation is nearly always performed by the professionals who are subsequently called to the site.

Academicians and field scientists might search a lifetime and never make a noteworthy discovery. Many "three-piece" scientists prefer the computer and air-conditioned lab to the harsh elements often encountered in the field. A spade and a pick are not the instruments of choice for many white-collared scholars. The most sedentary of the "armchair professors" prefer their "collegiate ivory towers" as inveterate havens from the cutthroat competition of free market capitalism and the daily grind of the workingman's world with its accustomed grime, toil, sweat, low pay, and long hours. Manually demanding work and scholarship are sometimes incompatible.

Unfortunately, finding and excavating dinosaurs is hard work and not well suited for the pampered and leisured. It tarnishes the digger with dirt under the nails, sweat on the brows, and soiled and tattered clothes—not an elegant prospect for a cloistered scholar. Most dinosaur discoveries are made by either amateurs or commercial collectors accustomed to the difficult trench-work in the field. More than eight out of ten of all significant fossil finds are made by amateur fossil enthusiasts.

A noteworthy example of some world-class, highly successful commercial collectors is the Larson Brothers, Pete and Neal, of the Black Hills Institute of Geological Research in Hill City, South Dakota. These scientists hunt fossils for a living and have unearthed several of the greatest Tyrannosaurus Rex specimens in the world. The Institute has been the leader in paleontological excavations and preparation since 1994 and supplies museums and collectors with the finest in professionally prepared fossils and cast replicas. It is involved in all phases of dinosaur preservation—excavation, preparation, mounting, molding, and casting. Black Hills sells dinosaurs and mounted cast replicas to private collectors and international museums.

Pete Larson, who grew up on a ranch in South Dakota, is known as the Indiana Jones of South Dakota. To some of his peers in academia, his methods of excavation are a bit unorthodox. Larson has been known to utilize a bobcat mini-bulldozer at the fossil site to move the large outcroppings of material encasing the bones before moving in close for the dig with a bayonet from an M-16 rifle. Larson has become the world's most successful dealer in the bones of T.rex and other prehistoric specimens retrieved from the great western plains of Montana, Wyoming, and South Dakota.

The Larson Brothers and their scientific staff are indisputably field scientists and apply their stock and trade knowledge to the actual physical world with the manual use of hand tools to scratch, pick, dent, dig (or whatever it takes) to get to the specimens in their natural geologic context. Although sometimes criticized for collecting specimens for a profit, these scientists have made an enormous contribution to the world of science. Their efforts have greatly increased public accessibility to view and enjoy these rare discoveries as mounted fossils and cast replicas at museums across the nation. This is a case of the private interest working for the benefit of the public interest.

Pete and Neal Larson were naturalist explorers and collectors long before they became commercial fossil preparers and dealers. They parlayed their credentials and skills into a highly successful enterprise, the Black Hills Institute. Like Cephis Hall, they possessed an innate curiosity about natural objects and a passion to collect and study them. They were uncredentialed field explorers before they became scientists and lab technicians. The two brothers had actually visited McCurtain County on a few occasions in the 1970s in search of precious minerals and fossilized treasures.

By the 1970s, McCurtain County had become world famous for its local deposits of quartz crystal. Cephis Hall, the jewel persona of rockhounding, would become, in the eyes of both locals and outsiders, the man most closely linked with this popular crystal trade.

Although the Larsons did not meet Hall during their 1970s visits, their paths eventually crossed in the late 1980s as the McCurtain dinosaur discovery became a collection of world renown. The Larsons would become intimately linked with the Cephis Hall dinosaur story that unfolded over the course of an entire decade, from the mid 1980s to the late 1990s.

As a collector like the Larsons, Cephis had for years been a connoisseur of natural geological museums and displayed and donated rare minerals to regional museums. He gained considerable recognition from the avid rock and mineral collectors who admired his collections. Now he contemplated the prospect of his life-long dream—finding a major dinosaur specimen.

Finding a rare mineral was one thing; finding a rare dinosaur specimen a whole new experience. A feeling of euphoria engrossed his mind. What if there really was something rare and valuable lying in the pit next to the ancient carbonized wood that Pruitt had described? He had a hunch, a preconception that something big and important was lying buried just beneath the mud and he was determined to find it.

A few days later, Cephis got into his late 70-model Chevrolet truck and drove out of Eagletown on Highway 70 to find the gully with golden-colored wood. It was about 8 a.m. on a Saturday morning in late March. He had arranged to meet his friend Sid Love at the site. Sid was driving from Idabel.

Smitten by a passion for rocks and fossils, Hall set out to claim his earthly prize and consecrate his dream as reality. He headed west over the bridge across the Mountain Fork River and traveled approximately one mile past the river to the marker where he saw the old Tiner School building on the left side of the highway. He made a left turn and entered a remote, low-lying, timbered area. The road did not deteriorate into potholes and washed out places as he anticipated. Surprisingly the road was better than expected. Weyerhaeuser owned and operated a fiberboard plant located on the left side of the road just two miles south of the Highway 70 turnoff. The plant was still active and operating three shifts of fifty to one hundred employees. Most likely, the county kept the road maintained to accommodate the needs of Weyerhaeuser and its employees.

After traveling the first three miles south and passing the fiber board factory on the left, Cephis arrived at a four-way stop. The routes heading straight (south) and right (west) took travelers past secluded ranches and isolated homesteads, while the course to the left (east) led into a remote river bottom. Going east toward the river, the landscape quickly transformed into a flat, brushy, dense vegetation zone. As he made his last left turn, the river came into view within the tree line to the right. The directions given by Pruitt were precise.

The gravel road going east from the four-way stop was not well traveled. It was probably built and maintained to provide access to an old gravel pit near the river. Perhaps it was a continuance of an old frontier trail leading to a river crossing used by pioneers in the 1800s before the bridge was built further to the north. The road accorded access to the west bank of the Mountain Fork.

The swampy terrain near the water's edge was snake and mosquito infested and likely harbored alligators. This was clearly off the beaten path and offered no attractive tourist destination. Few people cared to venture into this bottomland near the untamed river area.

The river was only about ninety feet from the gravel road and visible beneath the tree line. Cephis needed to follow the gravel pathway north along the riverbank for about a quarter mile until it ended at the edge of the gully. Traveling onward, he watched for a historical landmark known as the Tonihka Crossing.

As he looked out across the river, he was sure he had found it. This was an old pioneer river crossing steeped in history and lore. Though he had heard about it since his early years, he had never seen it. This riverine monument was located about 300 yards past the last left turn. After stopping his car for a few minutes to look and contemplate, the scenic beauty of the river cast its reflection and created a visual sense of awe.

The Mountain Fork River, a tributary of the Little River, is one of the major water arteries of southeastern Oklahoma and among the most scenic and popular rivers in the state. The ninety-five mile long river begins its course in the Ouachita Mountains near the Oklahoma/Arkansas state line. It flows southward through the Ouachita National Forest and joins the Little River in McCurtain County about ten miles southeast of the city of Broken Bow. In McCurtain County it has been dammed to create the beautiful Broken Bow Lake. It is one of the officially designated scenic river areas included in the Oklahoma Scenic Rivers Act.

The river is a cool-flowing stream that passes generally over beds of rock and sandstone. The gravel and rock-embedded bottom give the river its clear and pristine appearance. The river stretches about thirty to fifty yards across, but can swell into a much wider stream after heavy rains. It is about two feet deep in its most shallow parts and typically fifteen-feet deep in its deeper parts.

The Tonihka Crossing was an old wagon and stagecoach-fording pathway across the river. Native Americans and early white settlers had used it since the early 1800s as a crossing. A natural shoal had formed where a rock outcropping extended across the river channel. This location of the river had originally been used as a game trail for herds of buffalo and deer. It was subsequently altered and improved by the hands of man to make it even more passable. It stopped being used as a passage after a bridge was finally built around 1926 near the location of the existing bridge on Highway 70.

The shallow crossway had been named for John Tonihka, a member of a prominent Choctaw family. He had initiated the construction of the crossing to make it useable for wagons and stagecoaches. Tonihka and his party of workers have been given credit for cutting the high embankment on the west side of the river to facilitate easier travel up the steep side of the embankment. A crew organized by Tonihka used shovels and picks to carve out a gradual slope and trail through the high embankment. After the work performed by Tonihka, more than just herds of bison or riders on horseback could ford the river—the river ford could also be navigated by four-wheeled vehicles.

In pioneer times, the river sometimes became impassable due to high waters and swift currents after heavy rains. The swollen river could delay or strand a party for days. Delayed travelers were often forced to camp near the river bank and wait till the river's raging currents subsided. These vulnerable people might fall victim to robbers and bandits who made the rounds in search of stranded stagecoaches with valuables or hapless, encamped families. Marooned travelers were quick and easy targets for armed desperados on the prowl.

If a party were stranded at the river's edge for a considerable time, they might deplete their rations and become hungry. In that predicament, they might be forced to resort to the bounty of nature for sustenance. During the first half of the 1800s, fishing and hunting was good, but sometimes people were not skilled or lucky at finding food. There is a tale of a family that became exceedingly hungry while encamped and waiting for the swollen river to subside. The family became desperate enough to try eating an old black crow that the father had shot near the riverbank. It just didn't work. It was too tough. The taste was terrible. Crows are inedible.

The Tonihka Crossing was a historical marker that most of the locals cared little about. As Cephis looked out across the river channel at the still visible outline of the historical crossing, he pondered some old pioneer tales. Unusual things had happened here. He was staring into the face of history—a place where people had encountered innumerable dangers and hardships along the river's edge. People had been drowned, assaulted, shot, stabbed, robbed at gunpoint, or even killed while waiting to cross the river. It must have been a harrowing experience to be trapped on one side of the cascading river and at the mercy of the treacherous currents. These unpleasant thoughts passed as he started his truck and drove on.

Sure enough, as he continued along the west side of the riverbank, he soon reached the end of the gravel road where he parked in a grassy area about fifty feet beyond its terminus. He was thirty minutes early, and Sid had not yet arrived. He figured he might have a short while to wait for his friend, so he used the spare time to examine and assess the surrounding area. The landscape seemed similar to a flat and dusky scrub forest.

On a closer examination, however, the surroundings showed more distinction and color. In the background to the north, he spotted lush green vistas, and in the foreground, a marshy area interspersed with cypress, willows, and other aquatic-thriving plants. To the west and south, the drier bottomland was laced with tangles of bushes, low, thorny shrubs, and intermittent elms and pines. To the east was a labyrinth of tree trunks and vines that formed the border of the west bank of the Mountain Fork. This rich stand of vegetation provided cover for many living things that sought moisture, nutrients, and sunlight from the brim of the river. Some of the trees were matted together with distended, creeping vines hugging their bark. The trees leaned over the river from both banks.

As he cast his eyes on the terrain in front of him, he immediately spotted the gully partially hidden by brush and weeds about thirty feet in front of him.

While looking down inside the gully, a concrete abutment (or weir) immediately caught his attention. It sealed off the end of the gully and looked odd and out of place. A closer inspection revealed a gate built into the abutment. The gate apparently served as an outlet for entrapped water.

The weir had been constructed at the east end of the gully and designed to release water when the gate was opened. The metal gate stood about two feet high and eighteen inches wide. It had to be manually opened and closed.

The design was dismally inadequate. Erosion had carved out a small fissure underneath the gate, and the water flowing through the gully had washed out the edges where the abutment adjoined the walls of the gully. Rising water poured through the eroded gaps, rendering the gully ineffective as a containment reservoir. Whatever the intent of the builder, the work of nature had been the decisive factor.

Ahead and to his right, he saw a stream bed that carried water in a northerly direction toward the marshy area. This stream bed ran on the east side of the abutment, but curved to the left (north) and connected to a nearby slough. The water from the gully entered the streambed after it had flowed through the gate outlet or past the eroded sides of the concrete abutment. It then flowed toward the slough, which simultaneously conveyed murky water southward from the opposite direction during heavy rains. At the point of their confluence, the dark, nutrient-rich water of the slough mixed with the water in the streambed and turned eastward into a creek that discharged into the river about 200 yards downstream to the south.

The gully looked entirely artificial—a disparagement of a perfectly natural process. It was also blatantly ugly—an atrocious example of human tampering and despoilment of a creative work of nature. Whereas Mother Nature had gradually and modestly sculpted a natural drainage pathway over many decades or centuries, this eyesore had been suddenly and violently imposed on the natural order. It had been dug to intersect the original course of the small stream that drained generally west to east. In effect, whoever had dug the gully had rechanneled the preexisting stream.

The water retained within the slough and surrounding marshy area to the north was stagnant and colored by the dissolved putrefied matter of dead aquatic plants. The slough and marshy land served as a natural settling pond—an ecological filtering system. The aquatic flora of the marshy settling area absorbed the effluent from upstream, including inorganic and toxic residue. The thick water in the slough was retained in a natural confinement area during dry periods, but swift water flow caused by heavy rains pushed the stagnant water down its natural course.

The preexisting stream that now fed directly into the gully was a natural flow that meandered, twisted, and turned along its course. Before the gully had been constructed, the stream had entered the slough further to the west. The gully impeded the original dispersal into the slough, thereby militating against ecological cleansing. The new course bypassed the original drainage pattern. This intrusive alteration was an ecological abomination and blemish on the landscape.

Both the stream channel flowing into the gully and the stream channel at the rear of the weir were shallow, only about two feet deep. The gully was about eight feet deep, twelve feet wide, and 50-75 yards long. Cephis estimated the original depth to have been about seven feet. But erosion had carved the bottom deeper. It ran west-east, and stopped about eighty yards (as the crow flies) short of the curving river. The small stream fed into the west end of the gully and a small stream led out from the east end of it. After the imposition of the gully and the concrete weir, the stream water was impounded until the gate was opened.

As Cephis studied the drainage system, he wondered about the source of the stream. Why had it been diverted from its original course? The end result was that the drainage pattern that previously allowed the stream water to disperse and settle within the slough and marshy area had been permanently altered. The ecological benefit of natural settling and filtering had been lost.

This realization raised several other questions. For what reason had it been dug, and who had dug it? Who owned this land? Cephis immediately suspected that Weyerhaeuser was the culprit. Weyerhaeuser must own this land. Perhaps it was part of the property connected to the fiberboard plant he had passed on his drive to the site, he thought.

After his visual survey of the surrounding terrain, Cephis cast his eyes into the pit and peered along the sides of the gully. It looked to have been dug by a backhoe. The existence of the gully as a containment reservoir seemed rather bizarre. But despite the distraction, Cephis could not lose sight of his purpose for being there.

He walked along the edge of the gully while glimpsing downward. As he scanned along the bottom in search of any conspicuous woody material, Sid drove up. Cephis was relieved to have company after investigating the site for over thirty minutes. Cephis turned around and walked through the high grass to greet him.

Sid showed up in his typical field garb: loose clothing consisting of a jumpsuit (or coveralls) and sturdy work boots. Cephis wore his usual work clothes suited for lumberjacking: denim jeans, casual shirts, construction boots, and a ball cap.

Sid arrived in his late 70s model GMC pickup and parked beside his partner's truck. The two men were good friends. They had known each other for years. Sid was almost full-blooded Choctaw. He was short and stocky in physical proportion with distinctive Indian features. He was generally reticent and reserved—not likely to engage strangers in spontaneous conversation. Indians have been enduringly repressed and consequently preferred low-key isolationism.

Sid was a commercial refrigeration repairman who operated his own successful business. He was also an avid hunter, fisherman, and outdoorsman, keeping in the best tradition of his Indian-Celtic heritage. Although not an aggressive or outspoken person, Sid was active in the community and held leadership positions in several organizations. He served as both president and board member of the McCurtain County Genealogical Society and the McCurtain Gem and Mineral Club.

He stood above the crowd in the genealogical society. His pedigree was remarkable. His line of descent was just a few generations distant from one of the wealthiest and most distinguished Americans of the nineteenth century, Robert M. Jones, who was also his great-grandfather.

Robert M. Jones was the first millionaire in the Choctaw Nation and one of the wealthiest men in the American West. Jones had many leadership roles, which included being president of the United Nations of the Indian Territory and being a delegate to the Confederate Congress at Richmond. His assets included 500 slaves, 289 mercantile businesses, and at least two steamships that operated between the Southern plantations and New Orleans.

Sid may have inherited his business acumen from his famous great-grandfather. He managed money and resources wisely and was organized, detailed, and efficient in handling records and financial matters. Sid was not rich, but he was financially comfortable. He had assets, but not instant liquidity.

Cephis, unlike Sid, seldom fished or hunted for meat, but for sport, he occasionally took practice with the bow and arrow. Although having a sprinkling of Indian blood, Cephis was almost the opposite of Sid in outward appearance and demeanor. He was a gangly, six-foot, ball cap-wearing, hawk-nosed amateur whose body was scarred by numerous chainsaw injuries. He was gregarious, out-spoken, and sometimes blunt to the point of being offensive. In addition, he was reliable, stubborn, determined, and combative—features he perhaps inherited from his Scots-Irish ancestors. These traits had served to catapult both the Ulster Irish and their descendants, the Appalachian frontiersmen, into new lands and destinies—first from northern Ireland across the oceans to America, then westward over the mountains and into the wilderness where they struggled against long odds, treacherous enemies, and grim and foreboding landscapes on their way from Virginia and Pennsylvania through the Ohio Valley and into "Kantuckee," Tennessee, Missouri, and the deep South.

Cephis's strong sense of individualism and resolve stemmed from family generations inured to a hard life on the isolated frontier. This life was encapsulated on the edge of civilization and urbanity and had little deference for government or judicial authority. His ancestors, largely Scots-Irish settlers, were at the forefront of westward expansionism from the mid 1700s until the early 1900s. They were nearly always poor, sometimes lawless, but always courageous.

This Scotch-Irish heritage and rural way of life gave Cephis a sense of southern identity that had always defined and helped him weather the storm of uncompromising change as it swept over the entire society. His roots were in the soil of "Little Dixie," even as rampant technological and social change uprooted the moorings of his insular world view. This incorrigible identity had accorded him continuity in an onslaught of transformation that threatened to remake his known world into something unfamiliar and transient.

Cephis Hall was a living embodiment of the Scots-Irish legacy: he was white, Southern, rural, individualistic, religious, patriotic, pugnacious, and rebellious. In the eyes of some silver spoon-fed, eastern establishment, Ivy League preppie like the pseudo-Texan and cowboy-poser George W. Bush, he might have looked like some "oak grove shadowed," countrified hick, but by heaven's grace, he was not some damned "redneck." Or was he?

Cephis and Sid were indeed rural Southerners, but one could not easily pigeon-hole them in any particular category to meet a predetermined cultural label. The personalities and values of the two men were complicated, but blended well together in both their sedentary and ambulatory activities. Both were home grown, country boys who had risen in the sundry ranks of local naturalists. They were passionate promulgators of nature's marvelous treasures—collectors of a unique stripe that blended naturalism with industrialism and idealism with pragmatism. Both had been active members of the McCurtain Gem and Mineral Club for decades, and had served in leadership roles.

The two men were deeply inspired and prodded by nature – or at least by the attractive products of nature. Their personalities were in some ways complementary and in other ways diversionary. As both naturalist collectors and industrial practitioners, the two men had made an unsentimental compromise with the modern world. These were folksy, down-home boys who were rapidly being overtaken by the forces of change and modernism.

Like former President Theodore Roosevelt, one of America's foremost amateur naturalists, the two men were more interested in field work than lab work. They would rather explore and search the outback, than sit in front of a microscope as a section-cutter or lab experimenter. They preferred the pick or shovel to the book or research manual, but did not shy away from books and research when it came down to a pinch. They felt more at home in the midst of nature than the confines of a classroom or laboratory.

Cephis was a treasure hunter—pure and simple. He sought the beauty and gleam of quartz crystals dug out of Vugs along cliffs and bluffs. Such "gems of nature" radiated from hidden crevices to excite and warm his heart. Nature was his sanctuary, the backwoods, his haven.

Sid's family background was more urbane and citified, although his Choctaw roots brought him closer to nature. His grandparents had been quite prosperous in decades prior and were part of that old Choctaw aristocracy warped and diluted in the great stretch of chronology and space as the workings of Father Time altered and obliterated the landscape and the people upon it. Now it was only tradition and memory that kept him clinging to what vestiges remained of his Choctaw roots. Nature was part of that Indian heritage and Sid, like Cephis, combined nature as hobby with commerce as livelihood.

The two had been together on many occasions searching the rough-hewn backwoods for precious geological products. But this time, Cephis felt in his heart that they had gotten a good lead that might yield something exceptionally unique or exotic.

Cephis made his way down the banks of the gully and began to trudge along the bottom. There were several inches of standing water inside, and the ground was muddy. Sid chose to walk along the top and survey the upper portion of the wall.

As Cephis tread along the bottom of the pit, his boots occasionally bogged down in the mud. He walked the entire length of the channel several times and located a conspicuous thirty-foot span. In this vicinity, he spotted numerous pieces of pyrite-covered wood. The iron pyrite had given the wood a fool's gold color just as Pruitt had described. Cephis believed this to be ancient wood, perhaps as old as the Cretaceous Period. They knew they had come to the right place.

Cephis suspected he might be standing in the midst of a prehistoric bed that once contained ancient life, including dinosaurs. He concentrated his search in this specific area, and began examining the sides of the embankment, especially along that thirty-foot span where the carbonized wood was seen. Within minutes, he was abruptly distracted from his concentration. Sid was complaining that there was nothing there, and he was ready to leave. His discomfort was intensified by the hordes of mosquitoes feasting on his blood. This was not like the usual Sid, who was tough and seasoned. Perhaps, for some reason, his mind was elsewhere on this particular day.

The two men had been at the site for more than an hour. Cephis, somewhat irritated with the impatience of his partner, decided it was time to go. He grabbed a couple of pieces of carbonized wood and emerged from the pit. Before the two men left, he tried to share his enthusiasm with Sid, but Sid dismissed him. The two men said goodbye and departed in their separate vehicles. Cephis knew he would be back; but next time he would be alone.

CHAPTER FOUR
An Enclave of Secret Treasure

Cephis was eager to return to the river, but he first had to survive another week of treacherous and dangerous work as a contract logging employee cutting hardwood timber in the forests with a chainsaw.

The backwoodsman was inured to the strenuous demands of slashing timber in Weyerhaeuser's pine forests and digging crystals in the pine bluffs. Tall and lanky and perhaps weighing 150 pounds dripping wet in his prime, he was as tough as any hulking Pacific lumberjack who had ever severed a Sequoia.

Like the indomitable dinosaurs of lore, he was durable, resilient, and did not give up easily. His toughness and backwoods aura sometimes caused others to accuse him of being a redneck.

But what kind of redneck might Cephis be? Why, he didn't even chew "tobacker" and seldom cursed or boasted out loud. Cephis, of Scotch-Irish and Indian descent, had the outward persona of a redneck, but did not really fit the mold in a psychological sense. A true redneck tends to reject reason and abstract intellectualism, while embracing passion. Cephis, on the other hand, was more complicated than the average redneck. He did not don the mantle of willful ignorance and thoughtless action. He was, in many ways, a careful man, a man of thought, integrity, and industry. But still, the question lingered. Perhaps an innate "redneckedness" exists in all Southerners, no matter how much culture they acquire.

Maybe Cephis was more roughneck than redneck. It was all rather nebulous, but relative. Owing to all that physically demanding work, Cephis lacked the conventional Southern beer paunch. The Southern obesity epidemic never touched the lumberjacking, crystal-digging Hall.

The redneck image is in the eyes of the beholder, and a person who claims to be (or not be) one must take into account the image he projects and the definition of the audience. Although the origin of the redneck moniker has been traced to the Scots-Irish, it no longer specifically applies to a particular ethnic group. Besides, most Americans would not recognize a person of Scots-Irish descent. Their outward appearance is indistinguishable from the masses, and virtually anybody who exhibits any of the associated traits can be labeled a redneck. It is true, however, that rural Southern whites are broadly cast with the redneck stigma.

In its origin, the moniker was not necessarily a pejorative term, but the modern stereotype sometimes represents a viciously subjective label. Over the decades, it became an invidious caricature for the presumed uncouth and racist white Southerner and has now taken on more of a cultural resonance, rather than an ethnic marker. Redneck culture enveloped southeast Oklahoma in much the same way it shrouded the Deep South and rural America. "Redneckery" is as American as apple pie.

The redneck is maligned by both plush, conservative elites and comfortable, liberal intellectuals. Although the stereotypical redneck has sometimes been virulently condemned for being racist, sexist, and violent, the stigmatized caricature often does not hold water. The redneck hologram is often exaggerated and steeped in misperception. In the nineteenth century, both the tidewater aristocrats of Old Virginia and the carpetbaggers and Yankees from the industrial north had impugned and slandered the redneck brand. In modern times, sophisticated urbanites, whether lavish conservatives or enlightened liberals, castigate rural rednecks for their parochial backwardness and unrefined behavior.

The term redneck means different things to different people. A real redneck is perceived as one capable of kicking down any door or the ass of any malevolent intruder. Cephis was quite capable of defending himself, but did not look for reasons to fight. Another thing largely ruled him out as a redneck: the incompatibility between the redneck mindset and scientific mindset in much the same way that the religious fundamentalist differs from the secular, empirical scientist. Cephis had a scientific mind; therefore, it would be a bit of a stretch to classify him as a true redneck. He possessed an investigative, pragmatic, and objective world view.

Redneck or not, powerful and prominent people in McCurtain County would soon have to deal with this oak-hardened man who cut trees and dug crystals for a living. Cephis would rip through the *prima donna* egos of those supercilious elites like a chainsaw slicing through the trunk of a tree—first measuring them up and then cutting them down to size. His vocation as a logger had taught him how to surmount a tall obstacle—be it person or object—by truncating the ego from the mind, or the limbs from the trunk.

Logging is one of the hardest and most dangerous occupations in the world. A logger has to be in exceptional physical condition to endure for more than a short time in the trade. It has one of the highest accident and casualty rates of any occupation; at least it did during the time when chainsaws were still being widely used. Cephis operated a commercial 26-pound Stihl chainsaw—the best chainsaw on the market— but it was heavy when toted onto mountainsides.

Insurance coverage for chainsaw-wielding employees had become unattainable. The occupation was so hazardous that large commercial timber companies virtually eliminated chainsaws. In the early 1990s, Weyerhaeuser and their logging contractors began phasing out chainsaw crews and replacing them with crews operating heavy machinery, which was still dangerous, but less so than chainsaws. Purchasing such heavy machinery required a massive capital investment of tens of thousands, even millions, of dollars, thus putting the contractor in stringent debt. Chainsaw operators were still used, but only on the sides of mountains where heavy machinery could not operate.

On Cephis's next visit to the river, he planned to go alone so he wouldn't be distracted. The first visit to the site with Sid had yielded nothing. Other than the pyrite-coated, carbonized wood, there were no significant leads. But he had barely taken a glimpse and not even scratched the surface. Finding the location of a hidden dinosaur cannot be accomplished in a few minutes or even a few hours unless pure luck intervenes, which rarely happens in the real world. A degree of faith is needed to continue the effort after initially encountering failure, and then repeated failure.

Much knowledge and skill is needed to find a dinosaur skeleton hidden from obvious view. A successful searcher must be well endowed with the needed abilities to visually survey and assess the topographic features of the site. The search requires close scrutiny of the fine details of the surface area and recognition of the immediate geologic features worked over time by Mother Nature. Places where the surfaces have eroded, fissured, or layered are points upon which to focus. Personal attributes such as good eyesight, patience, concentration, and the ability to pay close attention to detail are needed to decipher the contextual and textural characteristics of a specific location.

Some say it takes a kind of natural, innate ability, like a sixth sense or ESP, to be really successful at tracking down dinosaur remains. Others argue unequivocally that only scholastic education and skills learned through academic training and professional field experience are of any account, while everything else is of trivial merit. Those who have such an inherent bias might also argue that only credentialed scientists can be successful in finding dinosaur bones overlaid in their natural context.

But whatever school of thought others might hold, Cephis was eager to put his ESP to good use in an attempt to ferret out fossilized treasure from an artificial reservoir. After surviving another week of hard timber cutting without injury, he was eager to return to the Mountain Fork in pursuit of his agenda.

A bright, crisp, blue-sky morning illuminated his buoyant optimism. The stratified layer along the wall of the gully looked compelling. There was a reasonable prospect that something intriguing lay concealed beneath. The search started as mere intuition—a driving force catapulted by his mind, which accorded a solid feeling that he was on the right track.

An ability to project mind over matter had brought him within reach of a treasure trove from the prehistoric past. A self-taught ability to discern geologic formations had enabled him to hone in on a specific location.

Although his prior visits had failed to turn up anything tangible, he retained a feeling of elan as he drove toward his destiny along the river. The clearheaded lumberjack had an insatiable ambition to unearth bones and was filled with vigor and perspective. The beauty and captivation of the riverfront enhanced his concentration and focus. Cephis felt better prepared this visit and ready to expend all daylight hours, if necessary.

He parked his truck at the edge of the pit and prepared for work. Before breaking ground, he paused for a moment to take in the scene.

His resolute eyes focused on the horizon where hope merged with reality and where the vastness of the forest and sky met in a seamless projection that reinforced his belief in God and reverence for nature. The sights and sounds of the forest reinvigorated his senses and uplifted his spirits. Two contrasting panoramas accented the serene river setting. In the early dawn, the bright glare of the sun radiated the misty overhang of the breezy forest; conversely, just after dusk, the dark haze of the sultry summer night was punctuated by the sounds of chirping frogs and chattering insects.

After a few minutes of delightful nature worship, the more utilitarian aspects of his search came to the forefront. Although tempered by thick humility, he oozed with confidence. Even if he never discovered anything of scientific value, his visits to the Mountain Fork were reaping spiritual benefits. He found solace and peace along the tree-shrouded riverbank—a kinship with nature he always enjoyed. There was no buzz of the chainsaw; only the sounds of nature penetrated his ears and consciousness. The vegetation clusters hugging the river were moderately lush, vividly green, and relatively pristine. The fragrances of flowers filled the still air. The expedition merged ambition with spiritual harmony in a naturalist's Shangri-La.

As he scoured along the pit for traces of ancient life, the animation of real life enchanted him as never before. The river scene combined leafy opulence with the exuberant scents and sounds of wildlife. The leaves and branches of trees rustled and swayed in the wind as they simultaneously nestled the stirrings of tiny animals.

The river frontage he had staked out for inspection radiated a rich diversity of life contained within several distinct mini-ecosystems: a tree-rimmed riverfront; a sparse, scrubby forest; a marshy slough; a brushy bottomland; and even some dispersed patches of grasses and weeds. The terrain was flat bottomland and teemed with life, much of it camouflaged and hidden from view. It manifested a fascinating tableau of timeless nature—tranquil and relatively unscathed by the forces of man.

Occasionally, Cephis spotted deer, squirrel, or rabbits in the brush, but they quickly scampered out of sight. Birds perched in the trees serenaded their neighbors for hours at a time before taking flight in response to instinct or some biological drive. The dense bushes and trees along the river held mysteries of their own and stirred his imagination.

But despite the beauty and serenity, something seemed rather odd; something wasn't right. During wind gusts, Cephis detected noxious, chemically tainted smells, and he noticed occasional bare spots of brown turf amidst stands of verdant green. The purity of green and the taint of chemicals seemed to coexist. This was the way toxic pollutants worked—slowly, but lethally. The effects on the environment and the living organisms were stealthy and insidious—eventually overwhelming the organism in cell toxicity, which manifested as cancer.

Cephis snapped out of his enchantment with nature to buckle down to business. Nature watching was superseded by dinosaur searching. He was about to enter the artificial realm—the manmade gully that contained wastewater conveyed from the upstream factory.

On his prior search of the pit, he concentrated on the most propitious geo-strata pattern. He found an intriguing location along the north wall of the pit—a few feet west of the concrete abutment and about four feet up from the bottom of the gully. Now, as he arrived for his third visit to the site, he planned to break the surface and peer inside.

He climbed down into the pit and waded through shallow water. It had rained earlier that week, and surface water had entered the stream channel from the west and flowed eastward along its normal course. A torrent of water had cascaded through the gully and cut a path until it found an outlet through the weir gate or the washed-out, peripheral edges of the abutment. The force of water abraded rock and clay strata, and in this instance, may have worn down various portions of the gully wall.

Erosion is an important factor in both the preservation and discovery of dinosaurs. After an animal dies, sediments cover the stripped carcass before transient predators scavenge and scatter the bones. The eroded sediments that wash atop the skeleton settle in place, encase the bones, and continue to compact and harden over time. Minerals contained within the compacted mass thence enter the bones, harden them, and aid preservation.

The entombed skeleton must be sealed off from oxygen and aerobic bacteria for millions of years. Given the right internal conditions, fossilization occurs. The process of erosion eventually works in reverse to expose the skeleton. Running water and wind gradually wears away the hardened embedment and exposes bones leaching from their bed that thence become accessible to the hands of man.

While sloshing in the mud, Cephis scanned the gully and spotted several small, distinct pieces lying in front of him. He did not remember seeing these on his last visit. They were the same color as the pyritized wood, but smaller and more rounded. Were these rocks or something else?

If they were not carbonized wood, what were they and where had they come from? Had they entered the gully from upstream, or had they washed out from some hidden stronghold? He paused for a few minutes to ponder these questions and make a comparison.

He moved closer and picked up some of the fragments. None seemed to fit the external pattern of wood and were all identical in structure and fit together like pieces of a puzzle, or, like fragments of a larger bone.

The distinctive, rounded pieces had to be fragments of either wood or bone. Each piece was about two inches long and two inches wide. He confirmed that their external pattern was different from the carbonized wood. His curiosity was piqued; he knew that wherever there were bone fragments, there were likely intact bones.

In front of him was that portion of the north wall where he had previously noted a thin layer of sand amidst the gray clay. This layer was about three inches thick and four feet up from the bottom of the pit. He believed this unique layer of sand represented the Antlers Sand Formation—a sand layer found almost exclusively in southeastern Oklahoma which was deposited during the Cretaceous Period more than 100 million years ago. He fixed his attention there, and checked to see if these bone fragments corresponded to anything embedded in the composition of sand and grayish clay. He tried to match the fragments with any material concentrated in that portion of the wall and looked for indications of the same color, shape, texture, and structure. If they had come from the layer of blue-gray clay directly astride the thin layer of sand, the bones might be ancient.

No large mammals existed during the age of dinosaurs. The only living mammals of that period were tiny rodent-like, nocturnal creatures. Mammals did not emerge from their dark concealed places, diversify into different ecological niches, and evolve to become larger species until well after the extinction of the dinosaurs some 65 million years ago.

While studying the dark clay directly above the sand layer, Cephis noticed that the fragments were a color match to the indented clay, an indication that both the fragments and carbonized wood had broken loose from this same level.

As he scraped along the clay layer, beads of sweat formed above his eyebrows. The clay fell in chunks. Suddenly he saw part of an embedded fossil. His heart pounded, his pulse surged, and his head swirled.

He also noticed pieces of carbonized wood loosely commingled in the clay layer above the bone. To get a better glimpse, he needed to separate the hard clay from the fossil. Having initially used a pick and shovel to break the overburden, he now changed to a smaller, specialized tool—a metal probe that looked like a modified screwdriver.

He chipped at the clay in a meticulous manner until he penetrated about one foot into the interior of the wall. He was on the first leg of what would become a long journey of excavation.

After several hours, the outline of a giant appendage took form, and he could discern the distal ends of the bone. He loosened the remaining clay surroundings to nudge the bone loose from the substrate. It lay sideways atop the sand.

He stood back to take in the sight. His eyes sparkled as the significance of the discovery weighed in on him. He was the first human to see this monstrous bone, or so he imagined. A joyous fog temporarily clouded his normally pragmatic mind. He surmised it to be a large leg bone (femur)—part of the skeletal remains of a large animal, most likely a dinosaur. The revelation had tapped a wellspring of hope and elicited both elation and perplexity.

Within seconds, the tenacious bone hunter collected his rational coolness and began pondering relevant questions raised by the discovery. What was concealed deeper within the clay? Were other bones hidden inside the wall? Could this stratum contain an entire skeleton? He knew it would take considerably more work to obtain answers and was ready to make the sacrifice. This kind of arduous work was proximate to digging crystals, and that was his hobby. At this point, there was no stopping Cephis Hall; he had been smitten with "bone fever" and aroused by "dinosaur fervor."

As he continued to dig around the femur, he detected the vague outlines of other fossils. He thought he might be seeing part of the other femur. Was this a bone bed? Was this a bone bed of a dinosaur skeleton? The bones appeared coal-black, likely colored by carbon. Dinosaur fossils are usually a brownish color. Unique processes of nature had worked to color these bones distinctly.

After digging for seven hours, Cephis was tired and hungry and dusk was approaching. In the distance, packs of coyotes howled and yapped down on the river. He could return another day to remove the femur and the other bones tucked beneath it.

The thought of being on the cusp of a major discovery excited him. But he faced daunting work just to determine what he had uncovered, let alone free it from its crusted enclave. The removal of the visible fossil might reveal what lay hidden in the cavity behind it. If the femur or other pieces could be recovered, perhaps an identification of the animal would follow. That was the most interesting part of the whole experience—learning what kind of creature had bequeathed its bones.

Perhaps only a few bones were left. Many had likely eroded out of the wall or had been destroyed when the gully was originally dug with a backhoe. He had to learn the truth and let the cards fall into place. If this were indeed a complete dinosaur skeleton, he needed to obtain permission from the owners of the land. But they might not grant it. Or, they might call scientific experts to the scene. The bones would then elude the grasp of their true finder and he would be ushered to the back of the stage.

One favorable fact persisted. This was an isolated area where few people cared to explore. It seemed unlikely that anybody would stumble upon this site, or if they did, it was even more unlikely such a wanderer would notice the bones. Even so, they probably wouldn't bother to dig or call for a scientific team to investigate. The majority of the local population was not scientifically minded. A few might come to fish or hunt, but not to prospect for fossils.

Waiting for the owner to act or for scientific experts to show up would cause an unneeded delay. Cephis was determined not to let that happen. Nature had taken millions of years to solidify and preserve these bones. Now she threatened to undo this wondrous state of preservation in short duration. Erosion had already taken its toll. This was a race against time—a race to save these valuable fossils from the encroaching ravages of nature. If they were not extracted soon, the remaining bones might erode from the embankment and be lost forever.

Cephis would continue until he determined what kind and how many bones remained. If this was something big, a contact with the landowner was inevitable. This river location might be public land, but more likely it was private and owned by Weyerhaeuser. Certain laws might apply, depending on who actually owned this riverfront property and whether it was public or private land. He had broken ground on an excavation that would eventually bear bitter fruit.

The hawk-nosed amateur had barely tapped the surface in his initial quest to wrest a world-class dinosaur specimen from the water-laden backlands of McCurtain County. His initial thrust into the Cretaceous crust was the beginning of a journey of dinosaurian scale that would unleash a host of personal ordeals and distortions. The daring dig would bring Cephis Hall into direct conflict with scores of adverse foes and belligerents. It would strain and warp the relations between a giant timber corporation and the local community; bring the issue of private land use to the fore; and shake the world of paleontology to its core.

CHAPTER FIVE
A Glimpse Back In Prehistoric Time

B efore his next jaunt to the pit, Cephis took time to reflect on his situation. Was he on the brink of uncovering something with significant implications for science? An intriguing mystery weighed on him as he realized he might be resurrecting an ancient creature that had lain undisturbed for millions of years. As he pondered the prospect of a major discovery, he felt certain that the key to the present could be found in the past. A picture of dinosaurs emblazed within their natural context began to haunt him.

Cephis thought hard about the lives and deaths of the dinosaurs, and drew on his extensive knowledge of them as he considered the questions which lay before him. He'd always had a colorful imagination and excitement took hold of him now as he traveled back in time to when dinosaurs walked the earth. The images of dinosaurs he had seen in books suddenly became real in his dream.

The outline of another world came into focus—a primeval world much older and more natural than today's. Giant flora and fauna—trees standing up to two hundred feet tall—towered over the landscape, and stupendous plant-eating animals over twenty feet tall and eighty feet long roamed the planet. Inland seas, lakes, rivers, and lush foliage dotted the natural setting and provided sustenance for the gigantic life forms. Archaic species of gymnosperms, conifers, cycads, ginkgos, and ferns dominated the botanical scene. Oxygen levels were as high as thirty-five percent (in the late Jurassic Period) compared with about twenty-one percent today. This warm climate, abundant rainfall, and high atmospheric oxygen level made life more prolific for dinosaurs, the dominant life form on earth. Fueled by an abundance of water, sunshine, and oxygen, this lush environment bestowed a banquet of food for the herbivorous dinosaurs which, in turn, became a feast for the carnivorous dinosaurs.

Cephis conjured up vague images of strange and awesome creatures stirring in the mists. A medley of fierce and majestic beasts in all sizes, shapes, and colors haunted the landscape. The creatures proudly displayed an assortment of evolutionary characteristics that Mother Nature had shaped over scores of millennia in response to a precarious world. Each change in the environment had led to a corresponding change in the vegetation and consequential adaptation of the plant eaters. The bodies of the carnivores then evolved to adjust to the physiological change in the herbivores. These bizarre and miraculous bodily adjustments had enabled them to survive. With survival hanging in the balance at every turn, these revolutionary external features were uniquely designed not just for feeding and hunting, but also for defense or attack.

As the activity heightened in the background, Cephis caught transient glimpses of a whole panoply of dinosaur belligerents parading their defiant weapons in full view before a hungry world: armored dinosaurs, plated dinosaurs, horned dinosaurs, spike-finned dinosaurs, bone-headed dinosaurs, duck-billed dinosaurs, and even flying reptiles—the Pterosaurs, perhaps the most mysterious creatures to ever glide through the earthly skies. As Cephis closed his eyes and fixed his concentration, the images became vivid and real.

He saw great predators like Tyrannosaurus Rex stalking the ancient forests and valleys in search of prey. As these beasts pounded the earth with their massive weight, they let loose a crescendo of fierce and strange bellowing sounds, transforming the landscape into a zone of terror. The primeval killers were on the prowl. Suddenly, a monstrous T.rex and horned Triceratops were locked in mortal combat—the outcome was a draw with both animals limping away seriously injured.

Great herds of herbivorous dinosaurs were on the move. They were looking not just for green and succulent leaves, but to escape from these horrifying carnivorous behemoths lurking at the edge of the forest. In some quarters the herds had panicked, and a stampede of sorts had taken place. Their natural instinct was to seek safety through flight or sheer numbers—precisely the strategy used by today's great mammalian herds on the African Serengeti whenever lions commenced their hunt.

Along the lakes and streams were gentle grazing giants: eighty feet in length and fifty tons in weight. These giants extended their necks to reach a height of forty feet, enabling them to graze on lofty trees. These peaceful plant eaters did not break and run in response to a deep-seated instinctual fear. They stood their ground when carnivores approached and routinely carried on their normal activity of gorging themselves with tons of green vegetative matter. Too slow to run away and their brains too small to form defensive strategies, their defense was their sheer size. They were simply too big, even for T.rex.

Cephis envisioned migratory highways congested with droves of herbivores moving together in search of sustenance. Lurking in the background behind trees or giant rocks were flocks of raptors scouting for an easy meal. They waited for a lone straggler too weak or sick to resist. But if an easy target did not appear, these fearsome ambush predators were capable of taking down any healthy, low-grazing migrant that wandered off the beaten path.

Suddenly, the raptors launched their surprise attack against an adult duck-billed dinosaur. Four of them sprang upon the innocent *Hadrasaur*. They leaped on its back and slashed deeply into the unfortunate creature's hide and flesh, causing gaping mortal wounds with their deadly claws. The contest was over quickly, and the victors devoured their victim before T.rex arrived on the scene.

Pound for pound, the raptor, especially the Utah Raptor, was the most terrifying dinosaur on earth. About six feet tall and weighing 1,500 pounds, he was fast, strong, agile, and loaded with fearsome weapons—including twelve-inch killing claws on both hands and feet. With extremely sharp teeth and specialized lungs to fuel him with plenty of oxygen and energy, he was the ultimate killer.

Raptors were small, bird-like dinosaurs that hunted in packs. Although they had hollow bones like modern birds, their appendages were very strong. Their skeletal design was similar to a modern turkey.

Other bird-like creatures swarmed the skies. Giant Pterosaurs soared overhead looking for carrion meals much like a vulture or condor. One such Pterosaur, the giant Quetzalcoatius, had a wingspan of up to forty-nine feet and weighed as much as 300 pounds.

Still, there were visions of tiny, humble, and obscure creatures—furry, warm-blooded, rodent-like animals scurrying to reach the safety of their underground burrows. The rumbling and shattering noise from the killing grounds evoked their survival instinct. A keen sense of sight, sound, and smell, and a highly adaptive fear-response enabled them to react and quickly find sanctuary. These were the early ancestors of modern mammals that branched off from reptiles before the evolution of the dinos.

Their place of refuge was the darkness of the subterranean world. They ventured into the other world—the world of daylight and ghastly reality—only when absolutely necessary. These visits to the otherworld were sporadic, short, and horrific. These smaller creatures knew, or sensed, that giant beasts strode and lurked about. Their greatest risk was not merely in being eaten, but in falling beneath a giant footstep to be trounced into oblivion. They occupied an insular world of their own: secretive, hidden, and shadowy. It was an innocent, small world couched within a larger, monstrous world.

As these beastly images faded into the recesses of his mind, Cephis caught glimpse of a closer, more tangible beastly reality—the bones of his own Mountain Fork specimen. Now here lay another beast and one of close proximity—a beast that had once stalked and haunted these very lands. This mysterious creature was about to reemerge in a less animated form as a pile of bones bearing value as an object of science. As this fleeting impression passed, Cephis pondered other questions to be raised once his beast was gingerly introduced to an awaiting world.

What would he do with the fossils? How could he identify the creature that had imparted them? What would the bones say about the creature and its ancient world? What might they disclose about how the dinosaur lived, and could they elicit insight on the elusive question of how it had died? What could the remains of this lone dinosaur tell the world about dinosaur biogenesis, dinosaur evolution, dinosaur ancestry, and dinosaur extinction?

Cephis had no doubt he was facing a daunting task, but one that offered an enlightening experience. He held a life-long interest in dinosaurs and fossils and had dug up a few bones in his time, but nothing significant like this prospect portended to be. He was thinking in terms of something extraordinary. He was imagining a bone bed. His mind was running wild. He needed to get back closer to reality—to the more mundane and sensible.

He needed to draw on his knowledge base and devise an empirical perspective. For now, he would reflect on the perplexities at hand by distilling his knowledge from books and science. He needed to address as well as sort through some fundamental questions about dinosaurs in general. Geological, biological, and paleontological science would establish the framework. After constructing his foundation of dinosaur knowledge, he would have a more accurate view of dinosaurs in general and could apply that knowledge to the understanding of his own dino prospect.

He had already confirmed the presence of a few fossils and partially uncovered a large appendage he assumed was a femur. He had dug out around the sides of the femur and hoped to remove it on his next visit. Upon removing the femur, he might be able to determine if there was an intact skeleton, or just a few scattered bones.

Cephis was aware that giant carnivorous dinosaurs captivated the minds of the public. The awesome Tyrannosaurus Rex was the largest and most fearsome carnivore of the continent. The species has held the public in awe for decades and become a ubiquitous icon representing the top of the line, apex predator. T.rex is the quintessential symbol for beastly preeminence and the undisputed King of the Dinosaurs. T.rex reigned supreme in North America during the late Cretaceous Period. It stood about sixteen feet tall, was over forty feet long, and weighed about six tons.

Cephis knew that most paleontologists considered a T.rex specimen of at least ten percent complete to be significant. Since a T.rex has approximately 300 bones, a find of thirty bones was significant. Had he encountered the bones of a T.rex?

Cephis speculated that his dinosaur might be from an earlier era, most likely the early Cretaceous. If so, he might have something rare and unique. Whatever it was, he hoped it turned out to be a carnivore. Carnivores have a certain mystique that dazzles the imagination. To find a creature equivalent to the ferocious T.rex killer, but much older, would indeed be significant.

The Age of Dinosaurs began during the Mesozoic Era about 225 million years ago (mya). The Mesozoic Era covered three periods: the Triassic Period (251 to 200 million years ago); the Jurassic (200 to 146 mya); the Cretaceous (146 to 65 mya). It was a world dominated by monstrous beasts that held a tight grip on the animal kingdoms during their Golden Age. If the dinosaurs had not become extinct some sixty-five million years ago, mammals would never have arisen—hence human beings would never have succeeded in taking over the planet.

The dinosaurs suffered three or four major catastrophes, and each episode thinned the ranks of scores of previously perched dynasties that were, in turn, replaced by new clans better suited to a changed environment. After each fall, the dinosaur kingdoms recouped their evolutionary fortunes and rose again to complete terrestrial dominance. Old species evolved and new species arose to replace those which had become antiquated in a transient world.

Primitive dinosaurs first appeared in the Triassic Period 250 mya. These earliest dinosaurs shared the terrestrial realm with a diverse host of four legged beasts—principally mammal-like reptiles. The dinosaurs seized power and subordinated the lesser creatures under their sovereign rule. They assumed important roles in the macro-niche of the planet—of mega-predator and mega-herbivore. The older clans were forced to adapt and live in the shadows of the ruling beasts by changing their body forms or occupying a concealed micro-niche outside the purview of dinos.

The dinosaurs grew to enormous size and spread to inhabit the entire planet. The environmental conditions that caused this gargantuan growth spurt were established in the Triassic Period. The late Triassic was a high carbon dioxide period, which facilitated plant abundance. Since the plants of that era were not very nutritious, early plant-eating dinosaurs were forced to ingest more plant matter for basic sustenance. Digesting plant material is difficult, so it was necessary to evolve a bigger and bigger gut. Consequently, the body enveloping the digestive tract had to enlarge. Over time, both the gut and the body evolved, and the animals as well as their guts, increased in size.

At the end of the Triassic (200 mya) and the beginning of the Jurassic, the oxygen level in the atmosphere increased. The dinosaurs, with their large lungs and air sacs, were able to take in more oxygen. This higher intake of oxygen increased the oxygen level in their tissues and magnified their energy and growth. More oxygen intake transformed dinosaurs into larger herbivores. Carnivores subsequently adapted by evolving into larger-sized predators. During the early Jurassic, there was a move toward gigantism among dinosaurs, which allowed them to dominate the planet. This was the true Age of the Dinosaurs. But gigantism turned out to be a double-edged sword by making them more vulnerable and susceptible to changes in the climate or ecosystem.

About 65 mya, a great asteroid struck the earth off the Yucatan Peninsula of Mexico. The giant impact sent up enormous clouds of soot, ash, and dust into the atmosphere that blanketed the planet—creating what scientists have called a "nuclear winter" when referencing the probable outcome of a nuclear war. Sunlight could not penetrate the worldwide conflagration to reach the surface. Consequently, earth's climate cooled and photosynthesis halted.

Plants began a massive die-off across the planet, and large herbivores succumbed to starvation and disease. The large carnivores had a feast for a while, but their food supply was soon gone. The bigger the animal, the more certain was its extinction. The only strictly land-born animals that survived were the smallest of creatures—the tiny nocturnal mammals. The largest air-breathing survivors were the crocodilians, which were semi-aquatic detritus feeders. The only reptiles to survive the mass extinction at the end of the Cretaceous were all members of the groups that exist today: turtles and tortoises, lizards, snakes, crocodiles, and alligators.

Until new discoveries shed light on the nature of dinosaurs, they were believed to have been cold-blooded like all other reptiles. Reptiles are lethargic, slow, and, like the crocodile, rely on ambush of prey. Over time, evidence mounted that the theropod* dinosaurs were active, swift, agile, and wide-ranging predators. There is now a consensus among scientists that they were warm blooded, and their nearest living relatives are the birds. Although dinosaurs like T.rex were not reptiles, it is generally accepted that they shared a common ancestor with the crocodile and ultimately stemmed from a reptilian line. (*Theropod dinosaurs were flesh-eating, saurischian dinos that walked on two hind legs, rather than four.)

Carnivorous theropods shared many features with the birds. They had hollow bones like birds. The bone histology of theropods, with numerous vascular holes throughout, confirms they had high metabolisms and grew rapidly—more like birds than reptiles. Cold-blooded reptiles have few vascular canals throughout their bones, while warm-blooded birds have many. Some scientists believe that feathers evolved on the scaly skin of theropod dinosaurs before the actual appearance of birds. Birds are supposedly descended from raptors—a class of theropod dinosaurs.

The heyday for the dinosaurs was the late Jurassic and early Cretaceous. This was a time when gigantism became the norm and allowed dinosaurs to assume complete dominance of the planet for 160 million years—an incredible accomplishment. The dinosaurs were distinctly set apart from their more primitive reptilian ancestors. Their legs were directly underneath their bodies. They were walkers rather than crawlers. This distinction set the stage for the emergence of an enduring and unprecedented earthly rule.

The dinosaurs represent indisputable proof that the strongest and most dominant animals on the planet, even with an unprecedented record of success, can succumb to powerful forces of nature. Extinction is a normal outcome of evolution. Over ninety percent of all organisms that ever lived are extinct. Mass extinction events are seen in the fossil record. The occurrence of mass dinosaur extinctions has been pinpointed at the end of the Triassic, the end of the Jurassic, and the end of the Cretaceous periods. At the end of each extinction event, a door was opened for new kinds of dinosaurs or other creatures to emerge. However, the extinction of the dinosaurs at the end of the Cretaceous was total and ended the long earthly reign of these amazing creatures.

Climate change is a frequent culprit in extinctions. A shift in climate affects vegetation, and those plant feeders making a successful adaptive response to the new flora will gradually surpass the herbivores that are unable to adapt to the new plants. A change in herbivorous body structure or feeding habit necessitates an adaptive change in the carnivores. Temperature or moisture variations impact some species more than others. When the environment changes, animals must adapt, migrate, or die.

Volcanic eruptions accelerate climatic change. Massive volcanic ejections of carbon dioxide and sulfur dioxide into the atmosphere have played a part in warming the earth. Sporadic episodes of high carbon dioxide throughout Earth's long history created global warming and a consequential unbalancing of the ecological status quo.

"The asteroid that struck the Earth 65 mya is estimated to have been about six miles in diameter and traveling at around fifty thousand miles per hour. It struck the Earth with the unimaginable force of 100 million megatons of TNT. The crash blasted out a crater 180 miles across and impacted the earth along the northern portion of the Yucatan Peninsula and the Gulf of Mexico." (Jacobs, *Lone Star Dinosaurs*)

The asteroid impact hypothesis is the prevailing scientific explanation for the dinosaur extinction of the late Cretaceous Period. But there are other plausible theories.

A more earthly scenario posits that the extinction resulted from a massive pulse of volcanic activity that occurred at about the same time as the asteroid impact. This was a more gradual extinction scenario based on the effects of volcanism over an extended timeframe, whereas the sudden wipe out attributed to the asteroid may have taken less than a century to produce the same results.

At the end of the Cretaceous, the atmosphere was thick from ash and the toxic gases spewed from active volcanoes in various areas of the globe, particularly India. Horrendous flows of lava blanketed the earth. Trillions of tons of toxics such as carbon dioxide, sulfur, and chlorine were injected into the atmosphere. The flora and fauna were subjected to recurring exposures of corrosive acid rain over tens or hundreds of thousands of years. Consequently, global environmental conditions deteriorated, even before the asteroid hit.

The evidence for both theories is seen in the rock and fossil record. The two events overlapped and the killing mechanisms were essentially the same. Both scenarios disrupted photosynthesis and the food chains, leading to starvation and disease. The evidence that both events happened is seen in a layer of soot conflagration found in the earth stratum. Millions of microscopic carbon spheres are found in this layer representing the end of the Cretaceous. In the so called K-T boundary, the strata of rock laid down at the end of the Cretaceous, are significant traces of iridium and shock quartz, which are indicative of an asteroid impact.

A combination of several causes doomed the dinosaurs. Volcanic eruptions and climate change initiated their demise; an asteroid impact was the final straw. The two events combined in a sort of one-two punch that sealed the fate of the dinosaurs and brought their earthly reign to a tragic end. In his marvelous book, *Hell Creek Montana*, Lowell Dingus argues that the volcanic eruptions could have caused the iridium at the K-T boundary. The iridium may have been brought up from deep inside the earth by massive volcanic activity. It is also noteworthy that in many samples of the Cretaceous-Tertiary clay, arsenic and antimony were found along with the iridium in quantities more indicative of a volcanic source than a meteorite (Wilford, *The Riddle of the Dinosaur*).

Below this K-T boundary, rich quarries of dinosaur fossils are found; above it none are found. Atop this layer, the preponderance of mammalian fossils gets larger as one ascends into the Tertiary strata. At higher levels, larger sized mammalian fossils are found, giving clear evidence that mammals proliferated and evolved larger over time. The Tertiary Period represented the rise of mammals; the late Cretaceous represented the demise of the dinosaurs.

The biological record shows that the dinosaurs were the most resilient animals to ever occupy the planet. Yet, they ultimately lost in the struggle for survival as they perished in an environmental catastrophe. They could evolve and adapt to gradual environmental change but not to sudden, catastrophic change. All animals, including man, are sensitive to environmental change and there is an ultimate threshold, a point of no return, for all species. Once the limits of environmental tolerance are exceeded, extinction is inevitable. That is the principal lesson to be derived from the legacy of the dinosaurs.

Suddenly, the lightning struck and the thunder roared. Refreshing rain poured down from the heavens to renew the earth. Cephis was jolted from a deep sleep. His mind reawakened to reality. Where were the dinosaurs? A reality check informed him: this was the twentieth century and humans now controlled the planet. The dinosaur images receded into his unconscious realm, but the dinosaur questions acutely penetrated his consciousness. He wanted to learn more about them and how their fossil remains and legacy might be wrestled from the bowels of the earth. The dinosaur prospect lying in wait near the banks of the Mountain Fork now weighed on his senses. His mind refocused from living dinosaurs to earthen-bound fossils.

CHAPTER SIX
The Quest for the Bones

As Cephis contemplated his situation, images of fossilized bones in their geologic context replaced live dinosaurs from the prehistoric past. A yearning to return to the river's edge eclipsed his mundane thoughts. Although elated about his dinosaur prospect, flurries of negative thoughts invaded his consciousness. Optimism was tempered by bone-hard reality. The odds of uncovering something truly unique were stacked against him.

His normal, innocent world was about to be transformed. He would soon learn that a major dinosaur discovery can be hazardous to one's health and state of mind – that it can unleash a plethora of worries and problems. His life was about to become more hectic and stressful as he commenced his struggle to wrest the quarry of a one hundred million year old creature from its ancient bed. He was not sure what lay ahead, but an uncertainty connected with the dinosaur encroached upon his mind.

Cephis was aware that every year millions of fossils "weather out" on North America's rolling escarpments. Wind, water, and geologic up-thrust magically transform the landscape to reveal traces of embedded treasure that had lain dormant for millennia. Most of these bits wash out of their clandestine havens and are lost to posterity. Once becoming palpable after millions of years of concealment, there is seldom anybody at the site to collect them. Thus, they become exposed to the natural elements and disintegrate.

The quest for fossils is a race against time – a race against the proclivities of a capricious Mother of Nature. If people had timely access to the land and fossils, whether on public or private lands, more fossils would be found and preserved before being lost forever. Unfortunately, there are innumerable obstacles that prevent human access and timely intervention. Most fossils are lost. A few are found.

The fossilization process is a marvelous work of nature. The process unfolds over an enormous time span. The right conditions must exist at a given moment to initiate the process. Only a fraction of the creatures that ever lived become fossilized. Still yet, only a tiny percentage of those fossils are ever found. Their sheer rarity makes them precious. Their very uniqueness makes them attractive. The riddles and mysteries locked within them tell much about ancient life in a mystifying prehistoric world while adding awe and curiosity to their dimension. The archive recorders know scientific detail only about what is found and nothing about what is not found.

The majority of fossils reveal themselves where geological history reaches the surface in rock outcrops. Fragments are usually the first traces of ancient life to appear. The paleontologist recovers the fragments and hopes to locate more. He then uses them to piece together a scheme or pattern that gives clues on where to focus his immediate attention. Deciphering fragments, whole bones, and skeletons – he pieces together his version of history. These amalgams of ancient life help describe the ancient environment as it may have appeared at the time, whether deep or shallow marine, inshore or continental slope, lacustrine or alluvial. Every geological period hosted distinctive kinds of animals and plants. The recognition of these distinctive species gives evidence of when the analogous rocks were formed.

For many creatures, we have only bits and pieces (fragments of bone), which must be screened through an onerous melange of scientific analysis to tease out the most minute details that impart a tentative identification. This practical fact of scientific realism makes finding an articulated dinosaur skeleton all the more exciting. An articulated specimen eliminates a lot of investigative work and virtually all guesswork. Unfortunately, many dinosaurs are known only from tantalizing fragments.

It all begins when an animal dies and is covered with sediments before its bones decay. A flood can deposit a meter or more of sand and mud in a single event – thus entombing carcasses lying on the flood plain. A flow of sediments must occur within a propitious timeframe immediately after the creature expires.

Just as the forces of nature must work to cover, embed, and ossify bones, so too they must work to uncover or weather them out. Rivers cut through plains. Mountains weather or erode away through the work of wind or water. Glaciers move and scrape rock while dispersing sediments, minerals, and even fossils. Seas erode cliffs. Lakes and rivers dry up and their exposed sediments erode away. It has been said that erosion is the paleontologist's best friend. As the hidden treasures leach out from their dormant resting place, they must quickly be recovered or be lost forever.

If skeletons are submerged in water, sediments such as mud or sand must quickly cover them if they are to be preserved. Layer must be deposited upon layer – sand, silt, and mud. The sedimentation and preservation process is a long and delicate one. The initial sediments are covered with additional sediments that compress the original impoundment – thus cementing them into rock and entrapping the skeletal remains. Mud is turned to clay, sand into sandstone, lime into limestone or chalk. During this sedimentation phase, water seeps into the bones and dissolved mineral salts in the water gradually change the bones into rock. The bone has become mineralized or petrified. Now harder and heavier, stone instead of bone, it is a mirror image of the original bone. Fossils are usually harder than the matrix containing them.

There are thousands of amateur collectors in North America, a few hundred university paleontologists, and about a hundred commercial collectors. Amateurs find most of the loose fossils on the surface. If uniquely perceptive or lucky, they might find the beds from which they came. The majority of articulated skeletons still embedded in the earth are excavated by either university paleontologists or commercial fossil collectors. Indeed, few amateurs have the means or skills to perform excavation. Their principal contribution in the field is finding the locations of the specimens.

Finding dinosaurs is not easy, but the onerous task of excavating them is an even greater challenge. It has taken as long as twenty years to excavate articulated specimens embedded in hard rock. The great cost of such a project, often pushes expenditures beyond the reach not only of amateurs, but also institutional or commercial collectors. Indeed, it has often been necessary to have a wealthy benefactor such as an Andrew Carnegie as a sponsor. Depending upon the nature of the impoundment in which the articulated skeleton is encased, the project is best undertaken by a scientific team from a major university or a commercial enterprise with deep pockets.

As a rule, the great bone hunters of early paleontology (the mid 1800s to the beginning of the twentieth century) have been independently wealthy or had the financial backing of wealthy scions or great academic institutions. In those early days, most field excavators were born and bred, full-fledged members of the aristocracy. The aristocrats were the only people who had discretionary time for independent study or exploration. Only men of privilege entered the field of science. The common people spent virtually all their wakeful moments struggling to make a living. Most could not read or write, or were overshadowed by superstition and religious dogma.

During the second half of the nineteenth century, science in America was young and struggling for a firm footing in a changing world. It was a raw science in a raw land. American men of science had no particular training or distinguishable credentials. Many were medical doctors. America was far behind Europe and much of the world in science. In the mid-nineteenth century, America had no great universities, no royal societies, and no esteemed academies. Americans saw science as impractical at best, irreligious and blasphemous at worst. Indeed, many biblical fundamentalists and creationists still, to this day, regard science – or at least its major underpinning, evolution – as outright heresy.

This anti-science stance may seem a contradiction, perhaps an atrocious display of hypocrisy, to secularist-minded people perceptive enough to observe these same science bashers basking in the delight of modern technology, which is incontrovertibly derived from scientific knowledge. Some writers have warned of organized collusion between evangelicals and Republicans to wage concerted war against science in the name of Christianity. The war already rages at both the local and national levels: fundamentalist political lobbying for compulsory prayers in public schools; the inclusion of creationist teaching (sometimes referred to as intelligent design) in the science curriculums of public schools; attempts to post copies of The Ten Commandments in public buildings; anti-evolutionary preaching from the pulpit; political endorsements and campaign contributions to culturally conservative politicians; and local censorship and banishment of politically incorrect textbooks.

Secularists file lawsuits against local school boards dominated by religious fundamentalists. The issue of contention is usurpation of the scientific curriculum. Secularists oppose inclusion of creationism and exclusion of evolutionism. They contend that only evidence obtained from scientific observation and experimentation rationally explains natural phenomena, and that faith-based explanations have no place in science.

The literal interpreters of Genesis aver that a divine being (the Abrahamic God of Judaism) created the heavens and earth in six days. They not only reject evolution, which undergirds modern biology, but also Einstein's theory of relativity; Steven Hawking's quantum physics; and the Big Bang Theory for the origin of the universe, a major prop of physics. Many Biblical literalists also dispute the principles accounting for the formation of rock strata and mountains over millions of years, which are the fountainhead of geology.

This war between science and secularists on one side, and religious fundamentalists on the other, has been politicized. It will continue to be waged in the courts, the schools, the media, and the halls of legislatures.

Creationists, through their political connections with the Republican Party, are tapping into the enormous financial resources of multi-national corporations and super-wealthy individuals. Mega-corporations like Wal-mart, Monsanto, or Koch Industries own or control more monetary assets than most independent nation-states. Forget the petty $50.00 or $100.00 contributions from small-time, true believers. For the multi-nationals, millions of dollars is mere pocket change. If these corporate money machines don't squander their profits on extravagant bonuses and profligate golden parachutes for their high-dollar CEOs, there will be plenty of loose change for charities, and the creationists should expect to get their share. If creationists are successful in enlisting the political and economic clout of the multi-nationals, a lucrative portion of an enormous "empire of wealth" might be lavished upon them and used to buttress their "intelligent design" and "creationist" agendas. Tax exemption is one thing; corporate subsidization another.

As they become endowed with the largess of the greatest corporations in the world, creationists will inevitably win the war against science. Well-connected, fundamentalist leaders might collude with high profile public relations firms, lobbyists, culturally conservative media pundits, and high dollar politicians to dismantle the cultural status quo that maintains a barrier between religion and science, and church and state. Science will not only be politicized, but empirical research and the scientific method might be overshadowed by religious faith. There is a great irony contained therein. It is the corporations that are the greatest beneficiaries of scientific research.

A recent turn of events suggests that creationists may be winning the war on science. The 70,000 square foot Creation Museum costing more than twenty-seven million dollars opened May 28, 2007, in Petersburg, Kentucky, with much fanfare and a blue-ribbon celebration involving celebrity-status, conservative politicians from neighboring states. The cause snared more than seven million dollars from corporate donors and more than twenty-one million in private donations. On the other hand, the American Museum of Natural History, one of the greatest museums in America, couldn't find a single corporate sponsor for its Darwin Exhibition recently built to celebrate the life of Charles Darwin.

Unwavering fundamentalists with strict interpretations of the Hebrew Bible (the Old Testament) claim that the earth is 6,000 to 10,000 years old and dinosaur pairs were boarded on Noah's Ark during the Great Flood. They denigrate scientific research and forecasts about global warning in favor of an End Times apocalyptic prophesy they claim is inevitable despite what man may do, or not do, about his destructive technology and harmful environmental practices. Man now has the technology and means to destroy the planet – a power previously reserved only for God. Biblical prophecy is one thing; self-fulfilling prophecy another.

The new Creation Museum in northern Kentucky takes the Genesis account of creation as fact, when in reality it can neither be proven or disproven. The museum replaces the scientific method with biblical literalism in exhibitions portraying dinosaurs as meek creatures living harmoniously within the Garden of Eden. Tyrannosaurus Rex is presented as a docile, plant-eating animal that could be petted or ridden by children. Only after Adam & Eve sinned and were cast out of the Garden, did dinosaurs begin to eat flesh. This creationist museum is more like a Disneyland theme park than the typical science museum. It seems intended to enchant children with its high-tech, state-of-the-art, animated dinosaurs and Fred Flinstone-like human robots moving freely about in friendly cohabitation.

There are 160 separate exhibitions in all that utilize animatronics and high-tech, special effects to dazzle the audience, particularly children. The exhibits tear apart the very tenets of geological science – depicting the miraculous Grand Canyon as having been created in a mere span of weeks, rather than carved out by erosion over millions of years. The great canyon formed when water collected after Noah's flood breached an earthen dam and rushed in quickly to carve out the canyon. The prodigious numbers of fossils strewn about the earth's surface are a result of the massive flood detailed in Genesis. The museum also goes against the scientific grain on global warming, which has become almost universally accepted as fact (not theory) by climatologists.

In late nineteenth-century, Gilded Age America, science was a rather novel and motley patchwork of knowledge. Geology and paleontology were the youngest of the branches. Science, especially the new disciplines, needed standards, rigor, integrity, but most of all, discoveries. It needed tangible results from practical exploration of the real world. The knowledge base needed to be bolstered through evidence derived from the lab and field. Geologists had only recently learned from observed rates of erosion and sedimentation that it took millions of years to build rock strata. New fossil discoveries in the American West during the mid 1800s were beginning to advance the field of paleontology. These new fossil discoveries would in turn be used to match and fix the ages of rock.

The remains of the first dinosaur in the United States were found on an expedition to Montana in 1856. Joseph Leidy, a professor of anatomy at the University of Pennsylvania's medical school, identified those first bones. Two years later in 1858, this pioneer in paleontology also found the first partially articulated dinosaur skeleton in America, the Hadrosaurus. Another early paleontologist of Leidy's day, the famed Edward Drinker Cope, discovered the second significant American dino skeleton in 1866. In 1877, the first complete dinosaur was found in Como Bluff, Wyoming.

These early discoveries in the remote American West ignited a Jurassic treasure quest for bedrocks of bones hidden in rugged western terrain. These fossils attracted public interest and galvanized well-financed bone hunting expeditions to wrest them from the rough outback.

From the beginning, the new American nation sent its surplus population continuously westward into new frontiers. First, there was a land rush. Wave after wave of settlers followed the trails westward in search of a new agricultural beginning. Farmland was the commodity that propelled people onward.

A number of decades later, another rush sent people packing and moving westward, ever westward, in search of another precious commodity – gold. Amidst this frenzied rush for gold during the nineteenth century, a new precious commodity was discovered – fossils. As there was a gold rush in the American West, there was also a fossil rush, just on a smaller scale. A lust for gold was soon followed by a lust for fossils. Land, gold, and bones have driven Americans westward throughout the late nineteenth century.

During this westward expansion, bones were pervasive across the landscape – bison bones and human corpses littered the Great Plains, not to mention the plenteous remains of strange, gigantic creatures not yet distinguished or understood. In southeastern Oklahoma, both then and now, the fossilized remains of such monstrous beasts were rare or non-existent.

The Plains Indians thought both the gold and bone prospectors to be insane. The bone hunters were a special curiosity for them. They were viewed as bad medicine – irreverent toward nature and spirits. Indians believed that the petrified bones lying atop the soil were the remains of an extinct race of giants. Sitting Bull was aware that strange, haunted men like Leidy and Cope were prowling around Indian Territory looking for these oddities. The Indians never quite understood exactly what kind of bones they sought and what their significance meant for a growing body of knowledge known as science.

These were the romantic days of fossil hunting in wide-open expanses of western plains. Traveling by horseback and wagon, these early geologic explorers saw wild Indians and old mountain men plying their fur trade. This western dinosaur rush was as exciting and dramatic as the famous gold rushes of the same era. Just like the western gold rush of the nineteenth century, the dinosaur rush was filled with enormous dreams, ambitions, and egos. Although the bone hunters were fewer in number, there was no less fervor.

In Medieval Europe, whenever dino bones were exposed, people assumed them to be the bones of giant mythical dragons. Due to strong religious feelings, the peasants never imagined that these mysterious giants had stalked their very lands for tens of millions of years before Noah and the Great Flood. In ancient China, they were also thought to be the remains of dragons and were ground to powder for prized magical and medicinal potions. These skeletons represented the real dragons of antiquity. The dinosaurs found in Europe and Asia were seen in both a mythical and mystical light. For many people of Asia, there was deep religious significance attached to the bones.

No doubt, the great explorers Meriwether Lewis and William Clark, commissioned by President Thomas Jefferson to explore and chart the unknown American West during the early 1800s, encountered countless numbers of prehistoric fossils lying loose on the ground. In those times, American science had little conception of what these mysterious bones represented. Lewis and Clark were baffled and had no clue as to their identity. Decades later, creationists attributed the giant, three-toed tracks discovered in the limestone beds south of Hudley, Massachusetts, to the raven Noah sent out from the Ark to find land. Evolutionists later classified these fossilized tracks as belonging to bi-pedal animals with the feet of birds – theropod dinosaurs. Evidence of feathers was eventually discerned on the bodies of some of these mysterious creatures. Evolutionary scientists eventually linked birds to both reptiles and dinosaurs.

Evolutionists and creationists continue to squabble over the meaning and significance of dinosaur fossils, not to mention the ongoing controversy over their age and methods of dating. As more newly-discovered fossils sift through scientific scrutiny, a clearer picture of the tapestry of life emerges, but the argument between empiricists and faith-based literalists magnifies with time. Until the emergence of an intense, but peculiar, fossil collecting rivalry in the expansionist American West, fossil recoveries came in at a trickle and their decipherment was equally dismal.

In the later nineteenth century, two wealthy scientists, Edward Drinker Cope and Othniel C. Marsh, took fossil collecting to a whole new level. A quest for discovery was enhanced by a contest of egos. The two men launched a life-long rivalry to outdo each other in finding the most dino bones in America. While conducting expeditions in the West, they contended with warring Indians; hordes of buffalo and other wild beasts; primitive transportation (foot, pack mules, horseback, wagons, rowboats, and barges) and living conditions; perilous terrain and almost unbearable climate; and numerous other obstacles and dangers, both natural and man made. Although friendly with each other at the outset, relations between the two men unraveled. Their disparate personalities collided; their enormous egos antagonized.

The rivalry between the two men was sparked after Marsh insensitively pointed out a technical lab error made by Cope. Cope had mistakenly put the skull of a specimen on the tail and the articulations of the vertebrae were reversed. This effusive denigration was done rather arrogantly in the presence of an esteemed colleague, Joseph Leidy. The two men bickered and dallied for a while, but soon there was no doubt that Cope had botched it.

Marsh had flair for defrocking the pseudo-exalted – flesh and blood humans or statuesque giants. He was ever given to opportunistic and flamboyant debunking of myths and fallacies, and was the man credited for exposing the Cardiff Giant as a hoax.

This rebuff of Cope's scientific abilities was a mortal blow to his ego and would not be forgotten or forgiven. It didn't help that Marsh seemed to take personal satisfaction in derogating his fellow scientist before the entire American scientific community. Up to that point, the two men had been cooperative peers, if not friends. Unlike Marsh, who had lettered credentials and hallowed Ivy League degrees, Cope was a self-made scientist whose laurels rested solely on the results of his visible works. It was too bitter a pill for Cope to swallow. The brash, acerbic, and supercilious Marsh was not a man inclined to freely offer up apologetic gestures, not even to his fellow scientist. Marsh was always looking to gain the edge.

An insult had catapulted a rivalry. A rivalry had instigated a war – a bone war over who could recover, identify, document, name, and classify the most specimens of the dinosaurian orders. These fossil-seeking titans struck out on countless excursions in all directions across the mountains, plateaus, and plains of the wild American west to seek glory and distinction and— most importantly—triumphal recognition over the despised foe. The war hosted two gallant antagonists: Cope, the precocious field naturalist, versus Marsh, the degreed academician turned field scientist.

Cope used horses and wagons to transport fossils from the badlands to the banks of the Missouri to await a river streamer to journey them downstream to a point that linked the railroad line. These expensive expeditions ultimately pushed him to the brink of his financial rope. Cope ran out of money before Marsh and thereby ended up on the short end of the stick in terms of numbers of specimens counted and attributed. Both Marsh and Cope obtained the first of their collections from the upper Jurassic beds of Colorado and Wyoming.

Marsh, with all his financial and institutional backing, got special consideration from the U.S. government. The hero of the Civil War, General Phil Sheridan, ordered his best military scout, William "Buffalo Bill" Cody, to escort Marsh's expeditions into western Indian Territory. On the open plains, his expeditionary crew hunted large herds of elk and buffalo. In the more mountainous areas, they fought off grizzly bears and nests of swarming rattlesnakes. Professor Marsh, owing to his wide range of territorial expeditions and political connections, had the opportunity to encounter and meet some of the most famous celebrities of the Wild West: Cody, Sheridan, General George A. Custer, Chief Red Cloud, and Wild Bill Hickok, to name only a few. Marsh was nicknamed "Bone Medicine Man" by the Pawnee Indians.

The quest for bones by these peerless pioneers of paleontology captivated the public interest and set off a Jurassic Gold Rush in the form of dinosaur bones. Tons of fossils emanated from the American West and were shipped in great trainloads to the elite educational centers and museums of the American East.

These bone barons and rustlers filled up whole museums and initiated a public rave for magazine articles and encyclopedias with photos and data about these megathons. They also filled people's minds with wonder and bemusement. A plethora of wondrous creatures from the ancient past captivated the public imagination.

Cope discovered and described fifty-six new dinosaur species, while Marsh claimed and documented eighty new species in total. Cope and Marsh introduced not only new species, but also new methods of exploration and excavation. Their techniques for preserving and shipping bones are still used today. As the American West yielded an enormous bonanza of fossils, these true pioneers were building up the new science of paleontology.

Marsh, with greater financial resources than Cope, won the competition in the quest to recover and document the most fossils from the great western frontier. But Cope won the larger war – the war for respect and admiration within the scientific community. Cope was a more amiable person and had not projected the same egregious coarseness and cutthroat competitiveness exhibited by Marsh. Consequently, he won the war on the personality and public relations fronts and is a more respected icon of science than Marsh, even to this day. The flaming eccentricities of these two titans of science were unleashed not just on the rustic backlands, but also on the pages of newspapers and scientific journals and in the minds of a public in awe.

A reasonable person might surmise that with science so young, the world so large, and the American West so vast, the colossal egos of these two indomitable bone competitors could easily be subsumed, indeed, sublimated and diluted, in the great stretch of space, change, and time of the American West during the late nineteenth century. But such was not the case. Their drives and ambitions could not be contained. Their egos radiated out to propel the greatest competition in the history of science and the greatest spree of fossil discoveries in all of history.

While Germany had the great universities and France the most recognized academies, America had the immense, peerless laboratory that was the West and it was there that the great rivalry and melodrama of the Cope-Marsh bone war played out. It provided a mysterious, picturesque backdrop that fueled the public imagination. Their caches of bones are still on display in museums for the enjoyment of the masses and continue to be studied by scientists even today.

Thanks to Cope and Marsh, the fledgling field of paleontology made a giant leap forward, as many new specimens were brought forth for close scientific scrutiny. These specimens proved invaluable to a new science trying to establish credibility among its peers. These marvelous fossils yielded clues to the ancient past – a world of gigantic creatures and unparalleled splendor in mega-flora and foliage. The American West provided a living laboratory for the likes of Marsh and Cope and in time, living museums would be erected where great bone quarries had been prospected by the founding fathers of paleontology. The Dinosaur National Monument was erected at the very site where one of the greatest dinosaur quarries had been worked. This prolific quarry located just east of Vernal, Utah, was developed into an exhibit-in-place and became a major tourist attraction.

Great tangible evidence from the Jurassic and Cretaceous eras now decorated the halls of academia and the labs of science departments in the midst of the greatest centers of learning. New standards, techniques, measurements, principles, etc. were established. The knowledge base of the nascent science of paleontology expanded prodigiously. The needs of science were being met. American science was catching up with Europe.

Cope and Marsh were different and alike in several ways. Both were independently wealthy and supported in their scientific exploits by wealthy family members. Both roamed and explored the remote and rugged back lands of the American West in search of petrified booty that could be ravished from Mother Earth. Cope was a self-made scientist; Marsh, a degreed academician. Marsh was funded by a major university and sometimes by the government. Cope was an independent contractor who bankrolled his own operations, and was more like a commercial collector – perhaps a forerunner of the modern fossil dealer.

Another element of their enduring conflict stemmed from competing beliefs. Marsh was a Darwinian and much of his work was focused on proving the thesis of Darwin's Origin of the Species. Cope was raised as a devout Quaker and could not accept the absence of divine design in nature.

It did not hurt that the two men had enormous egos that blended with their own peculiar quirks of eccentricity. The bigger the ego, the more likely one thrived in the wild and wide-open West. Paleontology was, and still is, a profession for individualists. The contemporary paleontologist still retains a dab of the adventuresome spirit, even in the midst of a modern morass of mass conformity. He makes a career out of wandering off the beaten track into barren deserts or desolate mountains. He is an explorer of the past – the recorder of a period of time before history began.

The two competitors were of kindred spirit – engaged in a romantic adventure to uncover iconic treasures from a remote and unrecorded past. These pioneer explorers, working within the province of a new field of science, were charged with the task of describing the immensity of the story of life from a hint here, a fragment there. The inveterate clues to a distant shred of life were often discovered by chance – by the lucky blow of a geological hammer in the right place on the right day of the year – by a spontaneous improvisation of the intricacies involved in the quest for fossil discovery. Through the competitive labors of Marsh and Cope, new vistas of dinosaur life were revealed and the antiquated vision contained in the past was profoundly changed. They found whole skeletons in the West, rather than just bits and pieces.

Both Marsh and Cope became consummate field scientists able to withstand the extreme rigors and demands of exploration in the wild and barren American West.

Exploration and excavation were their principal hallmarks and stocks-in-trade. They excelled in the techniques of discovery and excavation. It was principally their goal to get the specimens out of the earth and into the lab where they could be analyzed and studied by others with inscrutable scientific credentials. This was an extremely onerous task given the drastic environmental conditions often encountered in the wilderness of the American West. It was an undertaking that only the most experienced, resourceful, gifted, and soundly financed could achieve on a level they attained. Getting all these precious relics into the university labs and museums for public amusement was, indeed, a daunting task.

Despite the unglamorous and grueling field work, the two men maintained a flair of eccentricity throughout the whole ordeal. Cope wanted his brain preserved and measured against Marsh to continue the rivalry after death. His brain still sets in a jar in the museum at the Wistar Institute. The self-made scientist still holds the record for scientific publication with more than 1,200 papers.

Other pioneering scientists prospected the Great American West and hit major bone quarries. Earl Douglas, another great name in paleontology, found the single greatest concentration of skeletons anywhere in the world – a true western bonanza in dinosaur bones. Over a fifteen-year period, he shipped 350 tons of fossils back to the Carnegie Institute from Vernal, Utah. He discovered and excavated the single largest dinosaur bone bed in the West. From the discoveries of Marsh, Cope, Douglas, and a few others, came enough bones to fill all of America's major science museums.

The Carnegie Museum of Pittsburgh financed the excavation at Vernal, Utah that was then known as the Carnegie Quarry and now known as Dinosaur National Monument. Earl Douglas developed the quarry. The dig grew to an inordinate and unprecedented size. Over a few years, the excavation produced a mass quantity of dino bones unequaled in the history of dinosaur collection. A trench some 600 feet in length and 80 feet deep was cut through the sedimentary layers. Many articulated skeletons were exposed and removed. Bones of giant swamp-dwelling sauropods along with other Jurassic era species such as Stegosaurus and Allosaurus were recovered. It was the largest concentration of Jurassic dinos ever discovered (twenty or more articulated skeletons and parts of other skeletons representing about 300 additional individuals).

Douglas believed this massive dino graveyard was once a sandbar in a river – a shallow place where the carcasses of dead animals floated downstream, lodged at the sandbar, and subsequently covered with sediments. Over time, the river dried up and the massive mound began slowly eroding away.

Andrew Carnegie, the great steel baron, was a major player in the western dinosaur rush. It was his money that financed the museum and quarry excavations. Another great industrial plutocrat, the financier, J.P. Morgan, was heavily involved. He financed the freight cars and rail spurs that transported the bones from staging and loading points in the West to the major cultural centers of the large eastern cities. As a result of

Carnegie's money and the tenacity and expertise of Douglas, the Carnegie Museum has the greatest assemblage of Jurassic dinosaurs in the world.

Carnegie made sure that a little of the glory rubbed off on his good name. A major specimen, *Diplodocus carnegiei* was named in his honor. Carnegie had an ego of his own and made sure that this exceptional dino bearing his name was made available to a wider audience than just the Carnegie Museum. He supplied the funds to make an entire cast of the skeleton, bone by bone, which was an inordinate task in those days. He wanted a series of duplicates. Thousands of casts were made. These casts of the skeleton were donated to other museums. He paid for everything. His name still lives as Dinosauria memorabilia.

Another great bone hunter of the age was Barnum Brown of the American Museum of Natural History in New York City. On the Howe Ranch in Wyoming during the 1930s, Brown located one of the most concentrated deposits of Jurassic skeletons ever found. It was believed this mass of dinosaurs had been trapped in a water hole and succumbed in their tracks. Brown also developed another great quarry known as Bone Cabin, a few miles north of Como Bluff, Wyoming.

Brown was also famous for his flat boat trips down the Red Deer River in Alberta, Canada. While floating down the rock-encrusted river, he did some prospecting within the dinosaur-bearing sediments along the banks. He was later joined by two other noteworthy prospectors, the Sternbergs (a father and son team), and the trio explored and dug along the cliffs of the river with phenomenal success.

The collections were freighted back to the museum where they were carefully unpacked and entered into the permanent archive. The scientific description of the fossils starts at this juncture. A complicated dino specimen with many pieces can take years to piece together and study.

In the laboratory, the encasings of burlap and plaster are removed and the fossils cleaned. Any new pieces noted during the process are inserted into their proper places in the numbered sequence.

Excavation, transportation, and delivery of the specimens to the lab are not the end-all objective of the exploratory undertaking. A discoverer of a prime specimen never rests until the skeleton makes its way into the arena of public exhibition. Only then can the public become captivated by the mystery and uniqueness underlying the magnificent beastly display cast before their eyes. The marvelous exhibit bestows credit and recognition to the discoverer's name and accomplishment.

Not just the task of excavation makes the exploration daunting; the cost of preserving and assembling a quality display framework is time consuming and expensive. The end product is not just a well-preserved specimen that makes a collector proud, the ultimate goal is a visibly-displayed, enthralling exhibit that holds the public in wonder.

The excavation and recovery process is tedious and delicate; so too is the process of casting and molding the specimen into a museum showpiece. Tons of fossils sit in museums or university storage rooms for years, or sometimes indefinitely, because of a shortage of funds to prepare them or the space to display them. It takes about twenty days of lab preparation for every day spent in the field excavating. Only the most unique and valuable specimens ever find their way onto display booths at museums or science exhibits.

Fossilized vertebrates are generally found through meticulous surface prospecting. An effort is made to locate the producing horizon in order to determine whether additional parts of the animal or unrelated pieces from another species are present. In many cases, the specimen has completely weathered out of the rock and the horizon of origination cannot be located or determined.

Most dinosaur discoveries are made in the western United States. Such states as Montana, Wyoming, Utah, Colorado, and South Dakota have yielded copious quantities of bones in their rough, outcrop areas known as The Badlands. The immortal Badlands play host to a lot of geologic activity where the earth's surface is endlessly shaped, altered, formed, and reformed. The best fossil sites are usually in the remote, rocky regions. In the Badlands, the terrestrial landscape is rugged and the climatic conditions harsh. In the "baddest lands" one can encounter a roasting sun by day and freezing winds at night. Because of the difficult terrain and harsh weather, an excavation endeavor is usually a long, tiring process that requires great perseverance and physical endurance. It is a difficult task in its own right to reach or access these remote, isolated places by vehicle or foot.

Despite the extreme difficulties encountered in prospecting dinos in the American West, most articulated remains are found in the Badlands. In less remote lands, such as eastern Oklahoma, articulated skeletons are extremely rare. The West is truly a unique fossil fabrication domain. Its diverse patchwork of geological formations offers revealing insight into many epochs of life's primitive history.

In the American South, a few sorted dino bones are found each year, but seldom a noteworthy articulated skeleton. There is less geologic activity in the American South and East compared to the American West. The more active geologic processes of the mountainous West magically work to uncover and expose rock-embedded fossils. Fragments of bone are usually found first. Then sometimes, whole, intact bones are found. Finally, if one is extremely lucky, a prolific bone bed containing intact skeletons found barely beneath the surface.

In the moist environments of the American South, skeletal remains erode and wash out quickly. The moist environment facilitates rapid disintegration of bones left lying on the open ground.

Fossilized bones partake of the characteristics of the rock or strata in which they are entombed. Although fossils embedded in rock are more difficult to excavate, they are also more likely to remain intact as articulated skeletons. Extensive rock formations in the western Badlands harbor articulated dinosaur skeletons. The drier climate of the West preserves exposed fossils longer than the moisture-laden South. The West has less vegetation, thereby making it more prone to erode and expose the latent fossils. Vegetation retains moisture and impedes erosion.

Fossils embedded in rock do not erode out of their quarries as swiftly as those in softer matrix like clay or sandstone. Eroded gullies and hillsides are good places to prospect. Rocky streambeds are excellent place to scope. Prospectors find loose fossils or slabs of fossiliferous rocks on the slopes or in place. For fossil hunting, the West is the best and the East is the least.

The very best places to look for fossils are areas with fresh exposures of rock – where rocks are crumbling or wearing away. The weathering of sides of mountains causes skeletal pieces to break loose. In the deserts of western America, wind erosion brings a new crop of bones to the surface every year. Howling desert winds erode away rocks that contain fossils. Most often, only one piece at a time comes to the surface. Once dinosaur bones have been discovered in a particular area, it can be assumed that there are more to be found.

Volcanic ash and dune sands often cover deposits laid down on dry lands. In numerous locations within the Badlands such as the area around Medicine Bow, Wyoming, bone beds are abundant. At times, the ground has been littered for miles with bones of gigantic dinosaurs weathered out of their beds. Dinosaur bones are distinguished by their gigantic size and peculiarities not seen in reptiles or mammals.

Dinosaur fossils, like all skeletal remains, are found only in rocks formed from the sediments in which their remains were buried – sediments like mud and sand. Those sediments are changed into sedimentary rock, including clay and sandstone. Rocks formed directly from the molten interior of the earth are called igneous rocks. These rocks, often made of granite and basalt, never contain fossils of any organic sort.

The matrix embedding fossils must be chipped and scraped away – often a slow, tedious process. The overburden (the soil, rock, and miscellaneous debris covering the fossil-bearing rock) is often removed with explosives or large mechanical excavators. After the overburden is blasted or mechanically scooped away, large pick-axes, shovels, hammers, and chisels are used to remove the smaller aggregations of rock still encrusting the bones. Once the embedded fossil becomes visible, smaller hand tools such as awls and trowels are used to carefully crack or scratch around the specimen to loosen it from the immediate concretement. Once fossils are within grasp, smaller hand tools like ice picks, dental picks, and brushes are used for the finer and delicate debridement.

By traversing the layers of rock, one embarks on an odyssey back though time. Each layer represents a page in the book of history for a particular region and is filled with geological and evolutionary scenes that remain locked in the landscape. By applying the geological principle of superposition (rocks on the bottom are older than rocks on the top), one can analyze the geological and evolutionary changes that occurred over the course of the earth's geologic history. The story is told in the strata of the rock, including the soil or rock composition, minerals and fossils that are present, the extraneous debris that can be sifted out, and evidence of ancient vegetation that once thrived in the region.

As one moves from the higher, younger layers into lower, older layers, there is tangible evidence of climatic and geologic influence, localized natural resources, and the types of ancient life once present. The content of the plant and animal fossils tell the story as they identify the cast of living organisms that once inhabited the area.

The sediments, plants, and animals vary from environment to environment, location to location, and these can be discerned inside the layers. Each fossiliferous layer contains distinct events in the saga of life for the local area. Each rock layer represents a different verse or moment in the geologic and evolutionary history of the area. As a person descends into lower zones of the earth's strata, he or she experiences geologic time travel. Over time, as these different geological layers are worked by natural erosional processes, they expose and reveal their precious contents. As they bear forth their unique antiquities, science benefits if there are enthusiastic collectors like Cephis Hall nearby to locate and retrieve them from the last clutching grip of Mother Nature.

Hall had read about the legendary paleontologists – the almost super-human exploits of Cope, Marsh, Douglas, and Brown, who scoured the great American West and uncovered tons of fossils that enchanted a curious public for decades. These paragons of bone prospecting held a certain charm, a certain mystique, and a certain curiosity for him. Their stories helped cultivate his life-long interest and inspired him toward an ambitious quest for the most unique natural rarities of McCurtain County.

The famed Edward Drinker Cope was a man to whom he most related, despite the vast differences in their social and economic backgrounds. Cope was born into the American aristocracy. Hall was born of humble origin in the cultural backwater of the Ouchaita foothills. But the small man often emulates the great man in his own small way, within his own small sphere.

Hall perhaps captured a tiny glimmer – a mere trace – of the kind of magic and wonderment that must have enshrouded the life of Edward Drinker Cope in his earliest prospecting days before fame and public notoriety made its enduring mark. Hall had experienced the thrill and splendor of finding truly wondrous relics of man and nature – objects of rarity, purity, sheen, and luminescence. His marvelous collections — whether antique or contemporary – had attracted followers and admirers.

Like Cope, Hall was a self-made naturalist who had obtained the greatest portion of his stock of knowledge directly from his first-hand interaction with nature. He boasted a journeyman's resume of countless hours of practical work experience in the field. The intrepid Hall, in a small measure, mirrored the impetuous Cope.

Cope and Hall were alike in other ways. Both men were not just naturalists, but miners and businessmen. Cope searched for ore veins and invested copious sums of money in silver and gold mines in the Great American West and Mexico, much of it lost or swindled. Cope, like Hall, collected not only fossils but minerals while searching for bone beds and ore mines. Cephis, too, searched for ore lodes and as an accompaniment to his dinosaur dream, he sought to find and establish commercially viable mineral quarries in his own backyard of McCurtain County.

Like Cope, Hall had a penchant for viewing the geological past in its actual or imaginary form. He was able to fill in fine details of hypothetical vistas by detecting the workings of transformative geologic forces and discerning the continuity between the present and past.

Hall was a man of modest means forever tied to the continuous role of grinding out a living and supporting a family through hard, excruciating work within the timber economy of McCurtain County. The demands of his trade required that his naturalist prospecting be local and of short duration. He did not have the time or financial means for a rendezvous to the Great American West to mount a prospecting campaign, not even a mini-expedition on the slimmest of shoestring budgets. Despite his life-long interest in minerals, fossils, and antiquities, he would never get the chance to prospect in the Great American West. His lack of financial resources and discretionary time sealed his fate.

Unfortunately, there were few fossils to be found in and around southeastern Oklahoma, but for a man of modest means and confined to a local hunt, McCurtain County was not a bad place to be. There were extensive mineral rarities throughout the county – including a rich source of quartz crystal – that offered a means to quell a latent lust for the enthralling products of Mother Earth. Hall had begun his life-long quest for the best geological items that McCurtain County had to offer.

His drive for these natural rarities could hardly be satiated, especially given that his prospecting options were largely confined to minerals. But he was not complaining. He loved prospecting minerals and the local area offered a reasonable prospect for assuaging his lingering obsession. Still, it would be nice if there were a few more fossils around. Nevertheless, he would accept his fate and let the chips fall where they may. He would have to be happy with what he could find locally, although that spark of optimism had never completely subsided. Someday he hoped to find a world-class fossil specimen, despite his dismal prospecting hopes largely confined to southeastern Oklahoma.

There was always a need for recognition – a need to be noticed and respected among his peers. As his expertise in crystal collecting increased, he became a figure of prominence within his own peer community. First, he attained notoriety among local quartz collectors and naturalists. Later, he gained national recognition among this larger network of rare mineral enthusiasts, otherwise known as rockhounds. Cephis had found specimens of interest for not just the locals, but a national audience as well. Museums knew his name. Rockhounds from near and far had heard of him, and many had seen and admired his collections.

Hall, at times, was somewhat of a dreamer and had an innate longing to catapult his name into the annals of the great naturalists of history. Instead of just another Arkansas hillbilly who grew up and lived a quiet life in the shadows of the Ouachitas and was soon forgotten, he wanted recognition and a place in paleo-dino history. It was an impractical dream – illusionary at best, psychotic at worst. He, more than anyone, knew that the reality of his situation did not pan out for such a scenario. To capture a large following, he needed a major fossil discovery. Rare rocks would not suffice, although they might garner some recognition from the rockhounds. The reality of the situation was clear. The prospect of making a significant fossil discovery in McCurtain County was extremely remote. Still, the dream never left him.

As he pondered the legacies of the great paleontologists – Cope, Marsh, Douglas, and Brown – he knew he could never come close to their accomplishments, certainly not in quantity and likely not in quality. But perhaps with one great strike, he might launch his own notoriety as a great discoverer within the realm of science. One great finding and successful excavation of a truly rare specimen might get his name inserted as a footnote in the historical annals of paleontology. It would certainly help if the specimen was found in an unlikely place – a place that had never offered up its hidden treasure to a receptive world. Finding a rare fossil in a rare location would be a true distinction and achievement. At last, he would garner some respect from an indifferent public. With that notch under his belt, he could truly claim to be an amateur paleontologist without encountering irksome scorn and skeptical stares. At least he now had a prospect. Tomorrow was Saturday and he was set to resume his work at the pit. He had located a gigantic femur that needed to be recovered. Tomorrow offered the hope of a new beginning.

CHAPTER SEVEN
Fading Memories – Cephis Hall In Redneck Heaven

While the sun crept up from the shadows of the early morning blackness, a rooster stationed outside strutted, flapped, and pierced the solitude with his boisterous "cock-a-doodle-do." With the rooster's announcement of the crack of dawn, sunlight penetrated through the window shades and lit up the previously dark bedroom. The rustlings of God's creatures punctuated the early stillness as they paid homage to the rising sun. The promise of a new day had begun.

On a normal workday, Cephis would already be on the road headed for the timber stands and a long, grueling day of toil for a workingman's wages. But today he had different plans. Tempted to sleep late on a Saturday morning, he began to stir and think about the day's activities that lay ahead. He tossed in the bed and looked outside the window. One glance informed him that a beautiful Saturday morning was in the cards. He felt lucky.

He had waited impatiently all week for this day to arrive and could scarcely contain his excitement as he hopped out of bed and got dressed. Soon he was outside loading his truck with the tools and supplies he needed. While loading, thoughts of the gigantic leg bone entered his mind as he glimpsed its visual image. On his last visit to the pit, he had left it partially uncovered inside a crevice. Today, at last, he was going to recover it and learn what secrets were buried along with it.

By the time Cephis finished loading his truck and returned back inside, Joyce had breakfast prepared. He felt lucky again, but in a more profound way. He and Joyce had enjoyed an idyllic, traditional marriage for twenty years. They had known each other since their school days. Their life together was straight out of a storybook—like a romantic dream. Their life was simple but full of the truly important things. Joyce had been a wonderful companion, and they had three precious children together.

Life might be hard, but it had many bright spots, and Joyce was the brightest. She had stood by his side during every ordeal and was the only family member who staunchly supported his daring dig at the dinosaur pit.

Cephis sat down to a full-course breakfast tailor-made for a man with a hard day's work in front of him. This was an old-style, down-home, Southern breakfast – one to accommodate a hungry man with the most energy output per caloric input: fried eggs, bacon, biscuits and gravy, hominy grits, butter, and home-canned raspberry preserves. Cephis helped himself to generous portions. He needed them. Digging up dinosaurs was hard work.

The breakfast was much like the hearty, country-style breakfast Cephis had often enjoyed as a boy growing up on a small farm in southwestern Arkansas. His family was poor, but they usually ate well at breakfast. As he relished its fine taste, he began thinking about the past — about his own family heritage and culture. This frontier-style breakfast was inherited from his forefathers — the Scotch-Irish pioneers of nineteenth century America. These were the very people who had settled and tamed the western frontier.

Cephis knew his family roots were Celtic and Indian. He also knew something else; he was born an Arkansas razorback but had been blessed to later become an Okie. His family tree included both mountain folk of Appalachia and rebels of Ole Dixie – a motley blend of many types: yeomen farmers and cattle herders; coon hunters and cock fighters; deer hunters and catfish noodlers; isolated moonshiners and God-fearing city folk. He was tied to both the hard, rocky soil of the Ouachitas and the soft, loose sod of the Mountain Fork Valley.

His background was rural; he was both Arkie and Okie. He was shaped by the land and the people who worked it. He had picked a little cotton in his time.

American history books portray nineteenth and early twentieth century rural America as an egalitarian nation of small, family-owned farmsteads, but this was not so in rural southeastern Oklahoma, where dour folks on a somber land paid rent or shared crops with the landlord. The rural experience in southeastern Oklahoma was fairly uniform – most people were either tenant farmers or sharecroppers – and the one-horse plow was more common than the John Deere tractor.

Those unhappy renters of the most eroded and poorest quality soils were often in debt bondage and subject to the caprice of an exploitive landlord, banker, or merchant. Folks not sharing their harvests with landlords worked in company towns, lumber mills, timber camps, or cotton mills.

"Little Dixie's large landowners were not in the business of farming the land. Instead, they farmed the farmer." The region was an isolated premarket society where prices were set not by economic laws but by coercion. Local landlords and businessmen gradually dismissed cotton and came to rely on land speculation, usury, and not infrequently, criminality to support themselves. "The wealthy and the criminal had a nearly insurmountable advantage over the poor and the ethical." Consequently, Little Dixie's key economic enterprises resembled piracy more than they did marketplace exchanges (Thompson 24, 25).

Although a remote fringe of the agrarian South, in Little Dixie one would fine little, if any, of the archaic iconography depicting magnolias, white-columned, antebellum mansions, mint juleps, mirthful darkies, cavaliers, and tapestries of beam-draped moonlight illuminating quaint cottages amidst idyllic, serene landscapes. Not a trace of Southern gentility or *nobles oblige* was to be found.

Southeastern Oklahoma or Little Dixie as it was called during the Gilded Age, was one of the poorest regions of the nation and became a hotbed for radical populism. The land sowed not just crops, but a seething unrest and discontent that eventually erupted into redneck revolts, as alienated rural folk joined the agrarian revolts (then known as the Populist Movement) that were sweeping the nation. Sharecropping and tenant farms were America's form of serfdom – at least until cotton fields were converted into wheat or grazing land and serfs evicted off the land in a process similar to the enclosures of England.

As cotton fields were turned over to wheat or cattle, there was less need for sharecroppers and field hands; expensive machinery was used for harvest. As people became useless on the land, they also became restless. Tiny shacks amidst rustic landscapes became hovels of misery and despair. By the early 1900s, dispossessed tenant farmers began a decades-long exodus from their impoverished, overpopulated, and underdeveloped lands. The landlords burned their shacks to discourage squatters.

Before 1880, the western frontier was still open and farm families who fell on hard times could move on to homestead newly opened territory. But by the end of the nineteenth century, all the arable land of the continent was owned — much of it by big operators — and millions were landless. Therein lay the sprouts of the Green Corn Rebellion, the Wobblies, and agrarian revolts.

People had hopes, desires, and innate longings that could not be assuaged; destitution was the reality that continued without ease amidst unrelenting dreams. Both Celts and Indians endured these hardships. Oklahoma was a land of mixed lineage, a strain of Celtic and Indian genes. Man-made disasters like bank failures and the Great Depression were horrid enough, but God unleashed environmental calamities that compounded the suffering.

Cephis' family roots in America went way back. His ancestors had experienced much and seen plenty. He nostalgically looked back into the remote past and got a glimpse of the distant forces — both God-ordained and man-made — that shaped the landscape and gave Oklahoma its regional flavor. Before Oklahoma became a recognized territory, there was the open frontier and the people who settled it. These people had moved ever westward and extended the frontier into Oklahoma.

The frontier no longer exists, but the story of these people endures. Their story is Oklahoma's. It is also Cephis Hall's.

Scots-Irish settlers flowed down the Great Philadelphia Wagon Road between the 1730s and 1770s into Virginia, Appalachia, and the Southern states. Pennsylvania was a staging ground for the Scots-Irish. As Pennsylvania grew more crowded and less welcoming, the Scotch-Irish headed south across the Susquehanna River, along the Alleghenies, and down the Shenandoah Valley, or traveled other routes into the South and Appalachia.

These Celtic peoples would come to dominate the Appalachian region. It was from this pivotal cultural hub that these people radiated out and disseminated their folkways, social customs, and ethnic traditions to a wider geographical area, including Arkansas and Oklahoma. From that cultural focal point in the Appalachian region, migrating Celtic settlers brought this frontier way of life ever westward into the Ouachita regions of Arkansas and Oklahoma.

The Celtic "mountain culture" was isolated, clannish, self-reliant, fiercely independent, and distrustful of strangers and outside authority, much as it had been in the highlands of Scotland centuries before. The Celtic "cotton culture" of the Deep South had many of the same cultural traits and traditions, but was more market oriented, less isolated, and less independent.

The white people who settled Oklahoma were largely Scots-Irish or ethnic-Irish. These were Celtic peoples with roots going all the way back to the Celtic enclaves on the Isles of Britannia. Forget the Anglo-Saxons, the Pilgrims, the Puritans, the Quakers, and the Yankees. Those were the English and Dutch settlers. Few of them made the journey to the American South during the eighteenth and early nineteenth centuries.

Grady McWhiney, in his book *Cracker Culture*, claims Southerners and Northerners were two different peoples. Southerners, he claimed, came mostly from the Celtic fringe of the British Isles – the northern uplands of England, Wales, the Scottish Highlands, and Ireland – while northerners came mostly from the lowlands of the southeastern half of Britain.

While the English formed the backbone of the American aristocracy, the Irish and Scots-Irish shaped the character of the American working class. The Catholic Irish helped socialize later European workers and transmitted elements of their own culture to European immigrants. The Scots-Irish, an older American ethno-culture, were instrumental in Americanizing immigrants as they moved westward. The values of Jacksonian democracy and individualism and the Scots-Irish code of honor, self reliance, equality, and courage were adopted by migrants on the frontier (Walter Jackson Mead, *The Jacksonian Tradition,* National Interest, Winter 1999-2000, 11-12). New immigrant groups have traditionally gravitated toward this culture in a quest to assimilate and call themselves American (James Webb, *Born Fighting*).

The true western frontiersmen were the Scots-Irish Presbyterians (sometimes called the Ulster Irish or Borderers). The Scots-Irish Protestants had an entirely different immigration experience than their Irish-Catholic cousins. Their American experience was uniquely rural and deeply rooted in the land.

Soon after arriving on the eastern America seaboard in the early 1700s, the Scotch-Irish faced derision and discrimination from local English populations. Fiercely independent, they promptly set out for the western hinterland and, over time, many arrived in the heart of Dixie and established successful farms and cattle operations, and gradually fashioned a regional identity that became the Confederacy.

Blending their imported Celtic culture with the frontier setting, some became slaveholders and plantation owners. A considerable number became impoverished "white trash;" the majority, however, became the sturdy, independent yeoman farmers, including cattle herders. The plantation aristocrats of the Deep South, many of whom were self-made men from the ranks of the yeoman class, were more rustic, earthy, and crude than their counterparts, the aristocratic English planters of Tidewater Virginia.

"The Old South was a thinly populated area of untouched forests and vast grazing lands and ideally suited for the clannish, herding, leisure-loving Celts who relished whiskey, gambling, and combat, and who despised hard work, anything English, most government, fences and other restraints upon them or their free-ranging livestock." (McWhiney, *Cracker Culture, Celtic Ways in the Old South*, 8)

The American South is largely a world existing apart from the mainstream – alienated from other regions and people by its own unique habits, traditions, and imbedded cultures. In the modern era, as the Southern male became urbanized and industrialized, and with the flow of jobs from the farm to city, an internal struggle ensued to cling to elements of rural manhood – more specifically, ruggedness, toughness, and a connection to the land (McGhee 139).

No longer geographically and culturally isolated, the South is now part of a national commercial culture that has adopted the same values and beliefs that were once uniquely Southern (Applebome 15). In a sultry process of "Southernization," America is becoming a redneck nation. Southern redneck culture – messianic religiosity; a preference for small government and the states' rights of Calhoun; the rejection of reason and intellectualism; country-western music; rustic, outdoor recreation; simple answers to complex questions, etc. – has gained national hegemony and evolved into mainstream. Celtic popular culture has trumped Anglo-Saxon culture.

The Southern states that became the Confederacy were a nascent Celtic nation, in fact, if not in name. The predominant ethnic composition of the American South was Protestant Scotch-Irish. There were also scads of ethnic Irishmen, Scotsmen, and Englishmen. Celtic culture played a predominant role in shaping the social character of southeastern Oklahoma and southwestern Arkansas.

The ancient Celts were a mysterious, war-like people that remained fragmented as separate tribes. Although never united as a single nation, these people once controlled most of pre-Roman continental Europe, and have been called the fathers of Europe by some historians. From their ancient homelands on the grassy steppes of Eurasia to the dark forests of central and Western Europe, the Celts remained dominant over vast territories until Julius Caesar invaded Gaul and conquered.

Their most formidable foes were the Romans of ancient times and the English of the modern era. They were constantly on the frontier edge and in the pathway of empires on the move. Having ancient roots as one of the great Indo-European peoples of the Eurasian steppes, they had an equestrian-based herding economy and were famous for having invented trousers (breeches).

The ancient Celts were dreaded foes in combat and feared by all enemies, even the Romans, who suffered the disgrace of having their shining city on the Tiber sacked by the Celts in 390 BC. The ancient Celts practiced psychological warfare and so terrified and intimidated their opponents that many foes dropped their weapons and ran before the battle was joined. These were the same tattooed people who painted their bodies blue before going into battle naked against the heavily armored Romans. They collected the heads of their slain foes, soaked them in cedar oil, and kept them in chests as souvenirs to show important guests, much as their modern-day redneck descendants decorate their walls with the trophy heads of deer, moose, elk, and other majestic herbivores.

The Celts worshipped nature and swift and cunning animals like the elk or boar. The hog has always been an icon for the Celts, and is the favorite meat of modern-day Southerners. One can see the remnants of this boar cult at University of Arkansas Razorback football games with their mascots and chants. The craze of barbecue in the South stems from a Celtic heritage.

Over time, mega-trends in the wider society have changed the cultural patterns of modern-era Celts. Continuous evolutionary adaptations to changing technologies have altered and shaped the cultural milieu of the Scots-Irish in America, who are most emblematic of white Southerners. From chariots to pickup trucks; from druids to evangelical preachers; from tribal affiliation to Confederate nationalism; from moonshine runs to the Indy 500; from farms to armament factories…the Celts have made their compromise with the modern world.

The exertion of rampant technological and social change has gradually transformed the Celtic Southerner into the modern iconic redneck. Today, such things as truck stops, rodeos, coon dogs, Copenhagen snuff, Confederate flags, and a demeanor sometimes characterized by swagger and bravado symbolize (or stereotype) redneck culture, which stems largely from the Scots-Irish. Celts worked in stout occupations as policemen, lumberjacks, miners, longshoremen, soldiers, construction workers, and cattlemen—to name only a few.

But throughout it all, some things remained constant: a sentimental attachment to the land; a war-like mentality; a penchant to wander and migrate; a belief in a divinely awarded after-life; a tribal outlook and a distrust of centralized authority; an attachment to a herding economy as embodied in the American cowboy; a predilection for alcohol in the most expedient form; and meat as a staple of the diet.

For the true rustic Southerner there is only one meat—pig, the meat traditionally favored by the Celts. "As the Southern cook rotates the slabs of meat over flames, the juices crack and sizzle, and the redneck becomes once again the hunter and provider, recounting his glory days. Hunting has long been part of the redneck mystique; a gun is the essential symbol of redneck power as they wield guns to fulfill their traditional role as hunters." (Bultman 248)

The Celts have often been equated with the Indians of North America and have actually been called the Indians of Europe. Over centuries, the Celts and North American Indians had interacted and intermarried. Perhaps a constant life on the edge of nature experienced by both these peoples had given each insight into the heart and soul of the other. The fusion of Celtic frontier passions and Choctaw Indian pastimes laid the foundation for the emergence of an anomalous regional culture in southeastern Oklahoma.

This unique cultural flavor added a distinctive twist to rural-based recreational expressions as rednecks, hillbillies, cowboys, and Indians melded their outdoor passions into nature-based recreational activities. Verdant hills and pine forests provided the natural backdrop for Indian-Celts like Cephis Hall as they maneuvered their way through this hazy maze in the shadows of the Ouachitas.

In the early nineteenth century, the Native American populations of the southeast were forcibly relocated to the newly formed Indian Territories of the southwest in what would become the state of Oklahoma. They would make their mark on the history of the region that comprised their new tribal lands and play a pivotal role in the formation and character of the future state of Oklahoma. Their culture and agrarian-based economies were more akin to the agricultural South than the mercantile North. Celts and Indians have had a long association and affinity throughout American history. This is demonstrated in similar cultural patterns as much as it is in the commingling of genes. In sympathy with their native-American counterpart, the Celts preferred not to live under the yoke of civilized society and resisted civil control.

Those Celts and Indians who eventually settled in McCurtain County had a major impact on the cultural and economic heritage of the community. Frontier traditions endured, and the fine imprint of Celtic folkways was indelibly etched on the local psyche. A preference for country living was rooted in a frontier heritage that endowed these people with strong ties to family kinship and an attachment to the land and community. Such Celtic or Native American pastimes as hunting, cattle herding, gambling, Blue Grass (or country-western) music, dancing, recreational alcohol consumption, and old-style Southern hospitality have made their mark on the local character and social disposition of the people.

These culture-based activities became a focal point for the local community and fostered a rural-based economy centered on recreation, tourism, cattle, moonshine, and timber. Recreation was enjoyed in the natural outdoor setting and was family oriented and church centered. From the earliest times, family, church, or fraternally organized picnics were often held outdoors as a favorite recreational activity in McCurtain County. The allure and mystique of forests and timber held a strong grip on the imagination of the locals. A popular fraternal and social organization was *The Woodmen of the World,* which promoted close links with nature and scenic woodlands. Before there was radio or television, hillbilly bands entertained the locals with music delivered by blue grass singers and the strings of guitars, fiddles, and banjos.

Rural Okies and Arkies preferred their sports intermixed with competitions amidst nature, at least until football took root. Nature was incorporated into recreation and was later commercialized as a major component of the local economy. Fishing and hunting were always at the forefront of recreational activities for the locals as pastimes, or even a way of life.

For southeastern Oklahoma, like the rest of the South, recreation congealed with a rural-based culture practiced within a shrinking nature domain outside the confines of the metropolis. The frontier culture of the Celts lives on in such redneck folk customs as moonshine, raccoon hunting, cockfighting, catfish noodling, and other backwoods sporting arcana. As the sport of angling grew alongside the commercialism of tournament fishing, the locals distinguished their fishing style by reviving the old, lost art of hand fishing. This reawakened style of fishing, now known as grabbling or noodling, originated as a backwoods sporting activity enjoyed by frontier Celts and Indians. The art involved the finesse and technique of catching large catfish with the bare hands.

Giant flathead catfish, some weighing as much as a hundred pounds, were literally probed and felt out from under rocks, crevices, and holes along riverbanks. After being bitten by the fish, the "noodler" grabs and grapples the fish with his bare hands until it is subdued. The noodler eventually emerges triumphantly with his trophy in hands, or lives to tell another story about the great fish that got away and about his eagerness to return another day for another fray.

The sport gets in one's blood and has been passed down from generation to generation. Noodling is an authentic sporting activity in Oklahoma. It is folk tradition.

Okie noodling is becoming mainstream. The Okie Noodling Tournament is in its thirteenth year and is a living testimonial to the enduring legacy of the western frontier and the Celtic and Indian inhabitants who practiced the art. The Celtic frontiersmen and Native Americans colored the territory and state with a unique blend of art, recreation, and folklore.

Other great frontier pastimes transmitted from generation to generation in McCurtain County, even into modern times, were the recreational pursuits of hunting and trapping. In rural communities, these arts have been passed down from father to son over many generations during the span of more than a century. As with fishing, hunting often provided a considerable part of the subsistence and basic protein needs of rural Oklahomans during the nineteenth and early twentieth century. Trapping provided extra income to cash-starved, backwoods families through the sale of furs to national fur distribution syndicates.

Until the Great Depression, one could make good money from the sale of hides of fur-bearing animals, including beaver, otter, mink, fox, and raccoon. An extensive fur trading network existed in North America until the early 1920s, perhaps vestiges of the old Astor fur-trading empire. Furs harvested on the frontier were sold to regional fur dealers, who shipped them to large consolidation hubs in major cities like St. Louis or New Orleans, where they were further prepared for an ultimate destination to New

York or Europe. Jewish merchant families controlled the fur export business from an international distribution center in New York City.

By the early 1920s, the fur trade had diminished greatly due to over-trapping and excess hunting of fur-bearing animals. The wild stock of beavers, otters, fox, and mink had been greatly depleted and were on the verge of extinction. The double whammy of the Great Depression coupled with a scarcity of supply had virtually dried up the fur trading markets. Even if a fur could be had, few people could afford one. Paper money was scarcer than furs. With the death of the fur industry, the endangered fur-bearing animals made a comeback and are again plentiful in southeastern Oklahoma.

In frontier times, raccoon hunting was as much a sport as a means to income and sustenance. Frontier families often had packs of coon dogs that treed coons by the light of the moon. Prior to the 1930s, the hides of raccoons typically brought five dollars apiece, which was good money in those days. Sharecroppers and subsistence farmers often worked the fields during the day and coon hunted at night – combining sport and subsistence in one activity.

Although coon hunting is still a local sporting activity, it has lost much of the popularity, allure, and mystique it once enjoyed in the backwoods of Oklahoma, Arkansas, and east Texas. Although the sport is not unique to Oklahoma, it was the backdrop of the hills of eastern Oklahoma that provided the inspiration and setting for several books about this quintessential, backwoods American tradition, including *Where the Red Fern Grows*, which was made into a popular movie in the early 1980s.

Coon hunting has had its share of famous adherents. George Washington came to be called the Father of Coon Hunting, as well as the Father of the Country, after receiving seven coon hunting dogs known as Grand Bleu de Gascogne hounds as a gift from a squire friend in France.

Some rural Oklahomans liked their entertainment on the raw and earthy side. One form of recreation combined gambling, nature, spectator sport, bravado, and bloodletting all in one contest. The sport of cockfighting thrived within the backwoods, mountain glens, hollows, and hills of the American South for scores of decades until the animal rights movement shut it down.

"In a more distant past, cockfighting was a sport for kings. Henry VIII had a sumptuous cockpit, encircled by coops belonging to the lords and princes of the realm. Even Clergymen joined in the sport, holding cockfights at church and awarding prayer books to the winners." (Bilger 32)

Some of the most famous American presidents have been associated with cockfighting. "George Washington loved a cockfight for the spirit of anarchy it embodied. By 1830, Andrew Jackson was fighting cocks on the White House carpet, and cockfighting was a national pastime." Abraham Lincoln, a former cockfighting referee, had a philosophical flare in regard to the sport and chickens. He was once reputed to have commented in response to complaints about the cruelty of the sport: "As long as the Almighty permits intelligent men, created in His image and likeness, to fight in public and kill each other while the world looks on approvingly, it is not for me to deprive the chicken of the same privilege." The legality of cockfighting boiled down to a fight between the morality of the animal rights activists and the individual freedom of the cock fighters. (Bilger 56)

The sport likely originated in the Celtic homelands of Europe, Ireland, and Scotland and was transplanted to the American South, including Oklahoma. It started out as a gentleman's sport, but became a poor man's game after the fall of King Cotton. The allure of the sport still registers as an iconic symbol within certain Southern venues, such as the football games of the University of South Carolina where the mascot is the gamecock.

Two trained gamecocks – dinosaur descendants with attached spurs and supercharged with vitamins, hormones, proteins, and steroids – are thrown into a pit and slash it out in mortal combat. The owner of the chicken still standing or breathing walks away with the purse. The sport still endures underground in remote places out in the sticks, much as dog fighting does in the inner cities.

In another passion, Southerners, like their Celtic ancestors, have always been riffled with the goad of gambling, which lay at the heart of game cockfighting. In modern times, this passion has taken on an institutional flare as Las Vegas-style casinos have proliferated along the marine coasts and river fronts of Biloxi and Shreveport, as well as small Oklahoma cites like Durant and Broken Bow—from floating casinos along the Mississippi coast to glaring Choctaw recreational complexes in the Red Man's State.

The great state of Oklahoma is a converging ground for Celtic Americans and Native Americans. Indeed, a sort of mixing pot between these two peoples has been stewed. While the Celtic frontiersmen migrated ever westward toward Arkansas and Oklahoma, the five civilized tribes of Cherokee, Choctaw, Chickasaw, Seminole, and Creek – already infused with Celtic blood – were being forcibly removed from their native lands in the American South. They were relocated westward onto federally designated Indian Territory in what is now Oklahoma.

The Indian Removal Act of 1830 authorized President Andrew Jackson to initiate the removal of Native Americans from their native lands in the southeast to newly designated lands in the Indian Territory of what became Oklahoma. The Act had exchanged Indian lands in the southeast for unoccupied lands west of the Mississippi River. The discovery of gold and valuable minerals on Indian lands had been the prime impetus for the forced relocation.

The Choctaws were the first tribe to begin relocation in 1831 and were soon followed by the Seminole in 1832, the Creek in 1834, the Chickasaw in 1837, and the Cherokee in 1838. All these relocations imposed enormous hardships and dangers on the migrants. The most horrid and notable of these forced relocations was the Cherokee removal of 1838. This desultory migration experience was known as the Trail of Tears and resulted in considerable loss of Cherokee life from the harsh wintry elements, famine, and disease encountered along the trail.

The Indians, for the most part, arrived in the Oklahoma Territory first, but white Celtic settlers were close behind. These Southern Celts competed with the Indians for open cattle grazing lands. The pastoral way of life had existed for millennia in Ireland, Scotland, and Wales until English colonialists dispossessed the Celtic people from their own native lands. Celtic frontier people managed to revive this pastoral way of life in the American South and West. Southern Celts, like the Indians, were rural at heart and deeply rooted in the land. But market and technological forces would push them off and huddle them into urban centers.

The Okies have left the soil for the city. Oklahoma underwent enormous social, economic, and political change over the balance of the twentieth century. Despite rampant urbanization and change, the descendants of frontier Celts and North American Indians still prefer life in a rural setting and there is a yearning to return to the land. Native Americans continue a tenuous hold on what remains of their tribal territories.

The Southern Celts and Native Americans coalesced and consolidated the Oklahoma Territory, bringing it to statehood on November 16, 1907. Oklahoma is an Indian name meaning "home of the red man," which comes from the Choctaw language.

Although there are 39 tribal governments throughout Oklahoma, most of Oklahoma's Native Americans do not live on reservations. Instead, they have become assimilated into the cities and small towns across urban and rural Oklahoma. Within the larger society, they have struggled to maintain their unique cultural identity.

Although Native American tribes still occupy and control their own tribal lands and reservations within the state, the predominant ethnic identity of Oklahoma is a mixture of Irish and Native American. Virtually all white Oklahomans who can trace their families' roots back several generations on Oklahoma soil have Native American genes. One of the most famous sons of Oklahoma who claimed mixed ancestry was the great Olympic champion and professional sportsman Jim Thorpe, who was half Irish and half Native American.

Oklahoma is at a cultural crossroads between the Old South, the Old West, and the American Southwest. The state represents a cultural admixture of the old Confederacy, the frontier Celts, the cowboy, and the Indian.

The pastoral legacy of the Celts was transplanted in Oklahoma. Great cattle trails and open range ultimately gave rise to dynastic, barbed wire-enclosed cattle ranches. These great cattle barons consolidated huge rangelands in the western portion of the state. By the early twentieth century, the cattle industry flourished across the entire state. Western ranchers, Native Americans, southern settlers, and eastern oil barons all played major roles in the new Oklahoma and had a great impact on the history, culture, and economy of the state.

In 1907, Oklahoma became the 46th state to join the Union. It currently has about 3.5 million residents and is ranked 28th in population. The "Red Man State" has the second largest Native American population of all the states – over 398,000.

The state has somewhat of an identity crisis. Is it the South, the West, or the Southwest? Although it is overwhelmingly Republican, evangelical, and conservative – one of the reddest of the red states that gave George W. Bush and John McCain their greatest electoral margins – it has a diverse and colorful list of famous Americans: the homespun humorist Will Rogers; the singer-songwriter Woody Guthrie, who lived and worked in migrant worker camps in California and told about the experience in folk tales and folk songs; and the eccentric and oil-financed U.S. Senator James Inhofe, who believes the abounding warnings emanating from scientists about global warming are a gigantic hoax.

As Cephis finished breakfast, his thoughts about Oklahoma heritage and family roots faded in the background. It was time to get on the road. He was hoping to gain a historical lesson of his own from the day's experience by learning something about an ancient creature that had once been a local Oklahoma inhabitant during a time when the lands were wilder than the frontier, even wilder than the Wild West, and more pristinely violent than the Civil War. If he could learn something about the creature, he might learn something new about Oklahoma – about its primeval, prehistoric past. He hoped that knowledge gained about the creature might yield insight into the natural ecological setting of the ancient Mountain Fork Valley during the time of the Cretaceous Period. His new passion was digging dinosaurs and he had no spare time to engage in popular redneck pastimes. Everything was subordinate to his mission, even recreation.

Cephis had a knee-jerk response to all those who disliked rednecks: "Wait till you get stranded on a lonely rural road somewhere south of the Mason-Dixon Line. You will appreciate a redneck then. They are the most helpful to strangers in dire straits."

The dinosaur digger said goodbye to Joyce and informed her that he expected to be home before dark. He hopped into his pickup and headed westward on Highway 70, away from Arkansas and deeper into the great state of Oklahoma. Shortly, he passed the main strip of what remained of the old frontier settlement of Eagle Town. After crossing over the bridge and looking down at the clear-flowing Mountain Fork, he would be at the dig site in minutes. The drive was short – only a fifteen-minute trip. He had found a fossil bed literally within his own rural neighborhood. His dream was close at hand.

Cephis was not born wealthy and privileged like Professors Cope and Marsh. Although he would never be able to conduct large-scale fossil expeditions out in the vast American West, he now had a promising fossil prospect at hand and within easy commute. Maybe his fossil prospecting luck was about to change.

As he spotted the landmark Tiner School Building and turned off State Highway 70 onto Craig Road, he began thinking about the bone site and assessing the prospective situation. Several advantages were obvious. He had easy access to the site by automobile. Quite literally, he could drive to the edge of the pit. There was no need for an airplane or transcontinental automobile drive to reach a prime prospecting site. There was no need for wagons, boats, mules, or horses to transport supplies in and fossils out, much the way Cope and Marsh had done in the badlands of the Great American West over a century prior. There was no need for tents, outback cabins, bedrolls, or other crude living accessories. There was not even a need for a motel. This was an amateur fossil hunter's dream come true.

The specimen was not embedded in hard rock, but enmeshed in a softer matrix that disaggregated readily in water. The skeleton was concreted in non-indurate, fine-grained sedimentary rock like siltstone, mudstone, or clay stone. Seemingly it would be relatively easy to clear the overburden, break the soft rock into chunks, and access the fossiliferous horizon.

All the right ingredients were in the recipe to make this a quarry that could be tackled by a local, amateur paleontologist with limited resources. In other words, this specimen was tailor- made for Cephis Hall. If it turned out to be an articulated skeleton, as he suspected, there would be considerable sacrifice in time and labor to recover it, but no primitive discomfort or horrendous expenses. Seldom does such a confluence of favorable factors coalesce at a single dig site for an individual paleontological project. Still, there would be challenging limitations and obstacles to overcome, many of which were unforeseen.

The working conditions would still be hard and demanding, but nothing like a western excavation project portended. At times the heat, humidity, mosquitoes, and water moccasins might be intolerable, but those distractions were nothing compared to walking on an isolated, rocky outcrop within a scorching, barren desert, which presented its own unique hazards, including beds of rattlesnakes and prowling mountain lions and wolves.

Within minutes, he had driven up to the edge of the gully. His heart fluttered as he got out of his vehicle and walked over to peer inside the pit. Everything appeared undisturbed. He was still in business. It was time to remove the giant femur from its embedded resting place. He hoped to learn some new facts by the end of the day, particularly about what kind of ordeal awaited him. It was time to get back to work.

CHAPTER EIGHT
Locked In A Time Capsule

A beautiful Saturday morning energized Cephis with an added impetus to resume the dig. He stood inside the pit with his feet planted squarely on the floor and his eyes fixed on a monstrous femur lodged in the wall—an alluring appendage locked in a time capsule sealed for millennia.

Water more than a foot deep covered his boots and sloshed around with every step. Standing water filled the gully after a fast-moving thunderstorm had moved through two days prior and saturated the God-blessed, fertile soil of southeastern Oklahoma. The storm had pierced the solitude of the night and snapped him out of a vivid dream about dinosaurs.

On his last visit to the site he dug along the sides and top of the femur. Unable to recover it at that time, he left it about seventy-five percent exposed as it lay atop a bed of sand-stone. A torrential downpour could have ruined his prize had the femur eroded out of the wall. With foresight, he left the fossil embedded in a thin concretement of clay as an extra precaution, and because of that, the femur was undamaged.

As he assessed the immediate area around him, he still wondered who had imposed this artificial abomination—the gully—on the landscape. Despite the artificial defilement, the place exuded a haunting and intriguing connection to the ancient past. He was standing amid the confines of an ancient grave, a hallowed ground that entombed many secrets.

As Cephis readied his tools, an atrocious creature appeared overhead. Amidst the clear morning sky glided a large carrion seeker—an ugly and despicable vulture hovering now above him. The creature, a swooping scavenger with a wide-span, appeared from out of nowhere after detecting the faint scent of putrid flesh. It glided downward rhythmically, and then flew upward in synchronized motion. Whole swarms of these invidious creatures would soon arrive on the scene.

These opportunistic trackers of death had their purpose in the ecological niche and projected a hideous presence when invading the quiet, open space. Their survival and ubiquity purveyed a lesson about life and evolution—for they, like all living birds, were the lone descendants of dinosaurs. Their way of life as scavengers had existed since time immemorial. Despite their contemptible appearance and loathsome lifestyle, they served as nature's clean-up crew—recyclers, restorers, and sanitizers of the terrestrial landscape. Without them, the smell of rotting carcasses would taint the surroundings and spoil the air.

Also soaring in the majestic sky was an indistinct waterfowl. Cephis looked more closely and realized it was the indomitable Great Blue Heron, one of the most enduring icons of North America's wetlands. Its amazing sweep was strikingly agile, effortless, balanced, and rhythmical—a true aeronautical marvel. Wherever there was water, there were also fish, and these birds had skillfully adapted to preying on them within their own specialized riparian niche.

With its long, pointed yellow bill, white head, blue-grey plumage, long neck, and skinny legs, the Great Blue Heron wades in water and spears fish with its sharp beak. This is a grand and picturesque bird—a fitting subject for the artist's brush. It is four feet tall, six to eight pounds in weight, and has a seven-foot wingspan. It is a solitary feeder but establishes its nests and raises its young in colonies.

In the case of the Great Blue Heron, Mother Nature has endowed a dinosaurian descendant with proven resilience against the ecological depredations of man. It has surmounted the bleak prospect of extinction and evaded the endangered list in spite of its habitat being plundered. The Great Blue Heron is abundant in southeastern Oklahoma, thanks largely to the extensive wildlife sanctuaries established and maintained by farsighted conservationists. Such scenic wildlife preserves as the McCurtain County Wilderness Area, the Ouachita National Forest, the Little River National Wildlife Refuge, and most importantly of all, the Red Slough Wetlands Management Area are magnificent conservation preserves that attract birdwatchers and wildlife enthusiasts from all over the nation.

Although the Great Blue Heron continues to thrive, such is not the case for many other waterfowl species. Indeed, many have already disappeared, and their existence is known only through some distant photograph, painting, or the lamentable nature stories of elderly environmentalists and bird watchers who care about such things as magnificent birds. Until recent decades, the great family of waterfowls had represented a living testimonial to the success of a water-borne life with fish on the daily menu—a course of existence lasting for millions of years, but now under intense pressure.

Before man went on an industrial binge and overloaded the ecosystems with pesticides, herbicides, and other industrial toxins, the great waterfowls of North America had a pervasive presence on the water-borne landscapes. Human over-development of the wetlands and aquaculture operations are rapidly desecrating and destroying their habitats.

While Cephis stood in the midst of an ancient dinosaur graveyard, the progeny of dinosaurs swooped in; a stark reminder of the enduring adaptability of those awesome creatures from a distant age.

The living descendants of the dinosaurs, the birds, have almost matched the diversity and tenacity of their dinosaur forebears. They come in all shapes and sizes, inhabit all types of environments, disperse and migrate across the entire globe, occupy many different levels of the ecological niches and food chains, and get their sustenance and make their livings in many different ways. Since the demise of the dinosaurs and the rise of mammals, they have been among the most successful inhabitants of the planet.

Cephis was captivated by the magnificence of these awesome birds as they plied their vocational trade of making a living through scavenging and fishing. He watched from a distance while they performed their routine rituals. The distraction of the bird show was amusing, but he had to get back to his immediate task—severing the remains of a deceased bird ancestor from the gripping debris of its ancient habitat.

On his last visit to the bone site, Cephis had breached the exposed overburden and broken into the softer clay matrix. He pinpointed his effort above that conspicuous thin layer of sand along the wall of the gully. Using the pick, shovel, and rock hammer, he commenced his thrust near the top of the gully and worked downward and laterally. After detecting the dim contour of a lengthy bone, he used modified chisels to meticulously efface the concreted barrier that housed the fossil.

Upon reaching the margins of the giant femur, he switched to a more intricate method of exhumation using a type of large screwdriver with a curved tip. This novel screwdriver had been designed by Cephis and then custom-made at a local machine shop where the tips of different screwdrivers were heated at varying temperatures so each bent at different angles. Thereby, each screwdriver had a different curved tip. An assortment of such instruments provided flexibility and matched the different angles and contours of the concretions.

Cephis methodically used these specialized screwdrivers to scratch and abrade the aggregate – a tedious process allowing penetration to where a clay-laden pedestal of matrix still clung to the bone, which held the femur secure.

Now, as he resumed his work to free the femur from the last grip of matrix, Cephis used delicate instruments such as brushes, awls, or ice picks. To avoid slipshod methods, he reviewed some notes and ground rules before plunging in too deep.

A common mistake in specimen quarrying is not allowing sufficient space and room around the skeleton (or bone). As Cephis chipped the matrix, he tried to maintain ample distance from the outer margin of the bone. From his own field experience, he knew that an excavator should work down to a level below the horizon, and then gradually work inward. Wherever bone is encountered, one should work laterally until it is possible to safely work inward again.

Cephis knew that when prospecting large specimens, such as articulated skeletons, one must expose bone surface, and when necessary, separate them into small enough units to handle expeditiously with the equipment at hand. Any exposed bones should be cleaned and treated with consolidant. When fragments cannot be reattached immediately, their associations should be carefully marked prior to wrapping and labeling, especially where there are a number of fragments or individual items to be removed. A map showing the location of each bone needed to be sketched.

He could protect the small fragments by wrapping them in paper toweling, and cover the large pieces with protective jackets, while leaving some matrix affixed to protect them. As he began scraping to loosen the substrate beneath the femur, he feared the bone might shatter.

After two hours of delicate work, a close inspection revealed that the bone was fractured in three places. Each section would have to be removed separately. Other than the fractures, the shaft looked stable. At this point, it was necessary to abrade underneath and carefully pry the femur loose from the pedestal. The femur sections seemed solid enough that plastering them was unnecessary.

Cephis retrieved a unique tool made of bamboo and shaped like a chisel specifically designed for prying. Each piece, when freed from obstruction, was carefully placed on a piece of ¾" plywood about four feet long and two feet wide. Success!!!

He sprinkled loose sand and clay to form a nest of gummy clay material around the three separate pieces as they lay atop the plywood. This kept them intact and immobilized in transport. He covered them with burlap stapled to the plywood, making them ready for portage.

Before leaving the site, Cephis examined the void space from where the femur was removed and sighted the vague outline of another large appendage—perhaps the matching femur. It lay sideways in the same spatial arrangement as the femur.

The bone bed had scarcely been tapped and he had struck pay dirt. Perhaps his intuition was accurate. Maybe he had found a bone bed that sheltered at least one articulated skeleton. He had uncovered a superannuated vestige of raw nature, and now expected nature to deliver up more secrets.

The length of the femur was roughly four feet and in three pieces, each about eighteen inches long. The diameter of the bone shaft was about eight inches. He estimated that the complete bone shaft weighed in excess of one hundred pounds.

The pallet would not be easy to carry up the embankment, but Cephis was strong and fit. Years of hard labor in the timber stands had conditioned him. He could tote it.

He struggled as he carried the specimen up the embankment and over to his pickup parked at the edge of the pit. There was no need for teams of mules or heavy equipment to move this precious commodity. He gleefully loaded the valuable cargo into the back of his truck and carefully drove off. He would return soon and often. The pit would become a second home. His life would soon be changed forever.

CHAPTER NINE

The Backwoods Country – The Lure and Lore of Timber, Marijuana, and Fossils

Cephis Hall triumphantly made it home with his prized specimen and stored it in his workshop.

As he curiously analyzed this rarity, cautious thoughts juxtaposed with his gleeful sentiment. At some point he would need to consult a paleontologist. He was not sufficiently versed in dinosaur anatomy to make his own composite identification. The appendage reminded him of a giant turkey bone. Aha! Was it a theropod or sauropod? A carnivore or herbivore? Was it hollow or solid?

Cephis knew that if the femur was hollow, it was probably from a large, bi-pedal predator like T. rex. Hollow bones are a hallmark for carnivorous, theropod dinosaurs—the line that gave rise to the raptors and, ultimately, birds. This very creature had once roamed the coastal plains of what is now southeastern Oklahoma via the locomotion provided by this very leg bone.

As Cephis looked closely at the appendage, he saw that it was an unusual, coal-black color and manifested a tainted veneer of gold-colored iron pyrite. Moisture associated with pyrite poses a destructive scenario. The bone would eventually decay unless properly treated. With that realization, despair swept over him. He knew he had to keep the femur dry and adequately ventilated, and eliminate the pyrite, or at least control it.

If the fossil could be kept dry, the pyrite might flake off or simply be brushed away. To preserve the bone over a relatively long period, a technique for eliminating the moisture was needed. But southeastern Oklahoma is a moist place, the very reason why few fossils are found in the region. In a moisture-laden environment, the biological nemesis, mold, forms in the cracks and threatens viability.

Cephis was aware of a few homegrown tips on fossil preparation. The fractured pieces could be temporarily glued together with the old, tried-and-true Elmer's Glue. When it came time to disassemble and reattach them, the glue could be dissolved with water. After a thorough cleaning, the bone might be further protected with a clear brushing of shellac. Any obstreperous matrix still clinging to the appendage could be soaked away in acetic acid. If silicified or pyritized, it might be soaked overnight in hydrochloric acid to inhibit further contamination. Pyrite was a natural substance made from a combination of iron and sulfur and occurred naturally in moist environments.

A person might think that hollow bones are weak, but this isn't necessarily the case. Fossilization not only preserves, but hardens and strengthens. Hollow bones were an evolutionary adaptation for speed – reducing the weight of the animal and thereby aiding in mobility. They represented a unique adaptive response to a predatory lifestyle enjoyed by giant, bipedal, terrestrial dinosaurs.

As Cephis further examined the femur, he noticed a two-inch hollow space in the center. His heart raced as adrenaline surged – hollow bones are a diagnostic evolutionary feature of meat-eating dinosaurs. The femur was likely from a giant, theropod dinosaur – a carnivore that once stalked the swamplands of the ancient locality now known as Oklahoma. This was what he had hoped for. Several nights prior, he had experienced a mystical vision of a giant, terrifying, flesh-eating dinosaur in his sleep, and it wasn't T. rex. He had always dreamed of finding the fossilized remains of such a monster. This was not a small raptor, but a giant predator.

Cephis was certain he had a dinosaur with distinct physiological and behavior traits: large, bipedal, carnivorous, theropodic, hot-blooded, and energized by great quantities of food (high metabolism). Only a paltry number of dinosaurs bearing such traits are known from the scientific record. He wondered if his specimen was already known, or was he dealing with something unidentified and uncatalogued? The femur was much too large to be from a raptor. Could it be from an *Allosaurus*? He did not think the stratum was old enough to house a Jurassic bone bed.

Spontaneously, his thoughts about the uniqueness of the bone were replaced by questions about his unusual predicament. How would he proceed in identifying the creature, excavating the remains, storing and preserving them, and contacting the owners of the land?

To a large extent, he would have to make up the plans as he went along in the course of the game and improvise at every quarter – assuming the game didn't get cancelled. He would do all he could to keep himself eligible and active in the contest – one against the forces of nature and man that might obstruct the excavation, damage the goods, and stifle his life-long ambition.

He was certain he had seen another large appendage only a few inches behind where the femur had lain, and the indistinct protrusions of others. In all probability, he had located a genuine bone bed in which rested the remains of an articulated skeleton, laid down during the ancient Cretaceous. Perhaps there were multiple skeletons.

The pick and shovel, or even a bulldozer, might resolve the conundrum. The undertaking would be arduous, with innumerable obstacles and risks. But whatever the burden, Cephis knew he had to stay within the law. He had to straddle the fence, cover his bases, and most importantly, his behind. Surely, the lords of the land kept post over this great corporate dominion.

Digging and moving dirt might catch somebody's attention. A casual onlooker might think he was digging graves and burying bodies instead of practicing science. The situation required him to keep a vigilant watch for the timber magnate's baronial knights and servants patrolling the sovereign realm in search of wayward peasants and sinners who were up to all sorts of sordid, heretical mischief, such as Wiccan ceremonies.

Cephis couldn't delude himself into thinking he could single-handedly excavate an ancient quarry containing multiple skeletons without somebody finding out about it. The undertaking could last years and might require the use of heavy equipment to strip away the hard earth. Still, he thought he had some leverage over the situation. Leverage provided by a long-established precedent hewn out of the woodland commons through a customary practice that allowed public use of the commercial timberlands. He wouldn't be thrown in jail merely for trespassing unless he had done something illegal or immoral, or, of course, managed to arouse the ire of the managerial barons.

Ambling around the river's edge or recreational activities such as fishing, swimming, or picnicking might not invite much attention. But digging? That would surely incite curiosity and raise some eyebrows. Cephis needed to be subtle and submissive, if cornered, and avoid any suspicious behavior. Soon he must go to the baron or one of his underlings and ask permission. He mulled over how he could frame the issue to the corporate officialdom without inviting officious and meddlesome prying. He did not have an answer off the cuff and would have to figure it out later.

If Cephis was cornered and confessed to digging up dinosaurs, he might invite a whole sortie of probing questions. "Why is a plantation serf playing field scientist on the timber lord's estate—even if it is an isolated wasteland along a lonely river?"

The interrogation would flow like a Spanish Inquisition. *"Oh yeah, what kind of dinosaur?" "Is it worth anything?" "What do you know about dinosaurs?" "What else you been up to?" "What's in this for me?" "Show me the dinosaur." "Nope, we cannot approve your project. If you bring a shovel out here again, we'll escort you off in chains to the vault at the high lord's castle, or, at the very least, have you arrested for trespassing."*

Fortunately, the first great timber empire of McCurtain County, Dierks, had always allowed easy public access to their vast private lands. Innocent loitering or recreation on their domain had generally been tolerated as long as it was lawful. It was like a tradition—a symbiotic and paternalistic relationship that went back several generations and obliged the great, capitalist enterprise and its local subjects into a mutual understanding and customary practice. Easy public access to the timberlands had become a precedent. The Dierks empire had been permissive. This lingering, liberal attitude just might accommodate the spading of dinosaurs.

But now there was a new kid on the block. And he was not just a local entity. He was a powerful, multi-national corporation that seemed to have little reverence or deference for local tradition or custom. Weyerhaeuser was the new owner and overseer of the plantation. The company's huge "feudalistic" styled estate was international but had a firm grip on the local forest. The organization's tentacles of influence reached out across the county and the state and into the halls of Congress, the highest courts, the federal bureaucracy, the ivory towers of academia, the greatest boardrooms, and the loftiest perches of Wall Street.

In this case, Cephis was like a simple peasant perilously treading on the premises of a great, manorial estate—an expansive, corporate domain of conspicuous wealth, power, and privilege. This giant timber company was the economic lifeblood of the county—an omnipotent economic institution that exercised real control over the region. It could stop commoners dead in their tracks and make them quiver in their boots.

For all practical purposes, it did not just make the law by pulling strings behind the scenes—it was the law. The Weyerhaeuser corporatocracy cast an imperious shadow over the entire county and conveyed an implacable message to all commoners: *Heed your ground and tread lightly*. It would be both a feudal, and futile, mistake to become embroiled with this omnipresent corporate being. The timber sovereign was the rule behind the throne in McCurtain County, and kings have a long tradition of routinely executing their subjects and arbitrarily throwing peasants in the dungeon.

Such awesome political power, both public and private in scope, comes with the territory for any mega-corporation operating in a small community—particularly the company town. It's as natural as the practice of "divine rule" during the age of medieval monarchs and theocrats. The outreach of this corporate leviathan serves both good and bad purposes and is emblematic of any great economic and political institution that generally exercises free will at the local level.

Through an organized system for local control: regulation of the local workforce, political influence peddling via the spread of great stashes of cash, granting favors to important people, doing good public deeds through charities and private spending on much neglected public needs, massive lobbying, control of the local media, political campaign swaying, control over local political appointments and regulatory agencies, etc., the sovereign would impose its will.

The situation required Cephis to walk a fine line in dealing with this corporate megathon. He needed to be very circumspect, show proper deference and humility, and use acceptable diplomatic protocol.

Hall knew he would always have an alibi for being near the river—fishing and recreation. But that would not suffice when the evidence of excavation—piles of dirt and rock, a big hole in the earth, and giant bones protruding in plain view—was blatantly visible to any curious visitor at the site. He could only go a little farther in clandestine mode. If the bone bed was extensive, he might need to utilize heavy earth moving equipment such as a backhoe, which certainly could not be concealed.

His best strategy was to continue his surreptitious work until he determined the size of the bone bed and the approximate number of bones. Thus far, he had dug about two feet into the wall. Fortunately, the femur had lain sideways across the horizontal plane of the sand layer, rather than lodged vertically or inwardly. Retrieving the femur had been relatively easy; the other bones would be more difficult. To fully excavate a large dinosaur, he might have to dig a tunnel tens of feet deep or wide and use heavy equipment to strip the overburden. Once he had a firmer grasp of the challenge, he could then make a more rational decision about how to proceed in dealing with the landowner.

It was clear by now that he was going to need an extra set of hands in order to proceed to the next level of excavation, and he was getting weary doing all the work alone.

One of his greatest fears was the inherent risk of vandalism. There were no security guards posted to watch over the site. He tried to conceal all evidence of digging, but that was no guarantee against somebody finding the site and maliciously pillaging it. And there was another concern.

A shadowy, itinerate farmer growing marijuana about 200 yards from the dig site worried Cephis. The farmer had planted his crop in a concealed clearing near the river. The sheriff might become suspicious and put them both on the radar. Thieves, marijuana peddlers, and pot pillagers might presume Cephis to be the man with the "golden crop of weed" and demand information about its whereabouts.

Cephis was quite aware that secretive, private patches of marijuana were interspersed throughout the county. Small farmers grew them in secluded clearings on their own lands or on the company's lands. Criticism and complaints were constantly leveled against the police, who frequently busted the small hobbyists and backyard growers but never seemed to get around to finding the larger, commercial crops nestled within the pine stands of Weyerhaeuser's immense land holdings. The expansive, corporate timberlands seemed to offer refuge from police intrusion.

As in medieval times, there were outlaws in the forest. Scores of unsavory, backwoods characters haunted the deepest fringes of the shadowy woodlands. But these were not malevolent vagabonds in hiding or benevolent Robin Hoods in waiting. They were black market entrepreneurs who cultivated plants, cooked up concoctions, or used the seclusion of the forest to conceal illicit activities. In times gone by in European countries, the medieval forest was a place of contention between commoners and nobles. Commoners were not allowed to harvest game in the royal forests. The forests and the game belonged to the king and nobles. The royal forest was a legal jurisdiction patrolled by the sheriff, the most hated royal official, who used false arrests, abuse, and violence to keep commoners at bay.

The extent of unmolested wildlife roaming the area amazed Cephis. The lack of hunters surprised him. Cephis wondered, "Where are the hog hunters? And where are the coon hunters?" Their absence was obviously not a result of a lingering medieval attitude toward game conservation. He was unaware of any corporate wildlife harvesting guidelines on company lands other than existing state laws enforced by game wardens. Did Weyerhaeuser, the likely owner of this land, have its own private security to supplement public law enforcement, or were hunters choosing more accessible lands elsewhere?

Medieval Europe had an effective wildlife conservation program—all venison was reserved for royalty and aristocracy, less than five percent of the population. As a result of this restrictive resource management program, peasants became ever more dependent on their lords to allow them to work their vast manorial landholdings for a meager, hand-to-mouth existence. Hunting was a luxury accorded only to the king and barons. The common man, peasant or serf, had only one purpose in feudal society: labor for the lord. Peasants were brutalized and oppressed by knights raiding the countryside and taking their animals and valuables. Serfs were the personal property of nobles and treated accordingly.

Fortunately, modern McCurtain County was not a true medieval-styled society and landholding patterns had changed since the Middle Ages. Life was now more complicated. The woodlands were no longer owned solely by the king and a small coterie of nobles. Since the end of feudalism, mixed categories of ownership had evolved: private, corporate, and public; small, medium, and large landholdings; local, out-of-area, out-of-state, and even trans-national ownership. Whether this dinosaur-laden riverfront was owned by a public, private, or corporate entity, the risks were many; the potential reward, enticing.

In addition to dangers from human intervention, there were also environmental risks. Cephis faced personal dangers, and there were countless risks related to safety and health.

A field paleontologist, amateur or professional, needed accurate records and adequate field data. The pieces needed to be labeled and documented. Maps needed to be drawn and photos taken. Cephis sought a personal assistant, somebody he could trust. Only one person came to mind—Sid Love.

Tomorrow he would return to the site with hopes of learning what remained hidden within the bone impoundment. He needed to know what kind of task awaited him, how many bones could be recovered, and what it would take to uncover them. Planning would be necessary, but he could not devise a viable plan without ample knowledge of the work order. Would Sid Love be willing to help and, together, could they figure out how to deal with Weyerhaeuser?

CHAPTER TEN
Sid Love Joins the Expedition

Cephis was a proud dinosaur discoverer and on his way to becoming a genuine bone connoisseur. He would get intimate with the bones—even pamper and baby them with tender loving care. They needed his most conscientious attention. He was determined to do his best to preserve and protect them. They were too rare and valuable to neglect. More than that, they offered potential for an enhancement to his rank and status within the naturalist world.

The massive femur and its associated bones could shed new light on the local paleo-history and elicit considerable interest from researchers. Sedentary, arm-chair scientists would have a field day studying his specimen. This was his showpiece—his master stroke. He wanted to paint an alluring picture for scientists and laymen alike as he shared his product with the world.

The magnificent femur was a raw testament to his recent success as a navigator of the Cretaceous rock strata. Single-handedly, he had struck a mother lode in a wretched, abandoned mud layer of an ancient swamp pit.

Cephis was willing to share the spoils with a partner. He couldn't do this job alone. He called Sid Love that evening and invited him over to inspect the prize.

Before Cephis broke the news of his discovery, the two men exchanged their usual convivial small talk. As Cephis narrated the news, Sid dismissed it as a joke. But Cephis reiterated the story and finally got his attention.

In their phone conversation, Cephis painted a rosy picture of an enormous black bone tainted with gold. Cephis wasn't exaggerating. Quite literally, the bone was splotched with a gold-tinted luster caused by the pyrite contamination. Sid was a little skeptical, but receptive to taking a look. He always enjoyed visiting with Cephis and Joyce, and especially savored Joyce's delightful, home-cooked meals.

Before Sid arrived, Cephis cleaned his prized specimen—brushing off the remaining clay still adhering to the bone's rigid surface. Using Elmer's Glue, he cemented its three sections into an intact composition. The bone sections could later be disassembled and reattached permanently with quality glue. The bone needed professional treatment using the best methods known to modern science.

An astonished Sid laid eyes on the huge femur. This wasn't a cow or mammal bone. He was seeing it up front and personal. The aura of the bone was vivid and jolting—

unlike the impersonal and detached experience one gets from viewing such a monstrous appendage in a museum display.

Sid related to the fossil. Like Cephis, he was an enthusiastic naturalist with considerable field experience. In token with his Indian forebears, he mixed art with nature in a spiritual concoction. He prospected for crystals, petrified wood, rare minerals, and fossils, and was an accomplished lapidary who transformed his collection pieces into art. He made fine jewelry out of rocks, dinosaur fragments, and even dinosaur "poop" (coprolite).

Sid embellished his collections by prospecting in the immense outdoors of the American West, especially the rugged, mountainous regions of Wyoming, Colorado, and New Mexico. Within those vast, panoramic landscapes, the products of nature were plentiful and easily retrieved by amateur collectors. He had never struck a fossil quarry, but had found numerous dinosaur fragments which he artistically transformed into necklaces, beads, bracelets, and earrings—some so alluring that his Indian ancestors would be proud. He brought back stashes of petrified wood and agate, which he polished and converted into showpiece specimens.

In areas of southeastern Oklahoma and east Texas, the two friends had collected impressive stocks of marine fossils, including shark teeth and bones of a massive *Mosasaur*—a giant reptilian species that thrived in the ancient inland seas of North America. One of the most prolific prospecting sites they visited was along the gravel bars of the north fork of the Sulphur River, a few miles west of Paris, Texas. They came home with huge tote sacks and baskets of ancient marine relics and found multiple uses for these unique pieces as souvenirs, jewelry, or gifts. These items were sold, traded, and donated to museums.

Sid had an appreciation for dinosaur bones. But despite his spontaneous interest and curiosity, he lacked the degree of commitment that usually marked Cephis. The two men needed to keep their eyes on the prize and the benefits that would accrue from a successful excavation. A tangible benefit or product was dangled like a carrot and Sid demonstrated his serious motivation as an indispensable assistant.

Sid had great confidence in Cephis, and Cephis had great respect for Sid. The two men forged an enduring partnership. This undertaking would prove to be their longest and greatest quest for discovery. It was a project that would consume their time, energy, minds, and money for years. It became an obsession. The obsession would reap its rewards and benefits. But a fact often overlooked is that great accomplishment can also have a dark side. There would be a negative side to the ledger.

Sid was ready to come on board for the big dig. What else could he do? His interest and curiosity were aroused. How could he turn down an opportunity like this? Besides, he was more than willing to assist his friend for the mere sake of friendship. He was now a believer, and he too wanted confirmation of the identity of the creature. The mystery had quickly ensnared him, making him eager to tour the pit and see what else Cephis had uncovered.

That following morning, the two men set out for the dinosaur pit. As they drove toward the Mountain Fork that early Sunday morning, neither could fathom the ultimate outcome that their long and strenuous endeavor would bring. They could not imagine that their specimen would end up making dinosaur history —even shake up some of the core and inviolate beliefs about theropod predators in North America. That was still more than four years away. They still had a long road to navigate. Both Cephis and Sid accepted the challenge with eagerness—perhaps a bit naïve about what the excavation would ultimately entail. They liked working on the edge with elusive prospects shrouded in suspense and mystery. They never knew what might turn up with each swivel of the spade or thrust of the pick.

These two men would spend hundreds of hours working together on the lonely edge of the river. Every weekend, any free time after work, every holiday and vacation, any spare time they could garner was expended digging bones. Their friendship became stronger, their social bond tighter. The two men shared the experience of the big dig—a dig that lasted years and eventually unearthed one of the most extraordinary dinosaur specimens in history. They would share the gold, the glory, and, ultimately, the grief that accrued.

They represented a contrasting set of backgrounds and personalities. One was a half-baked, cool-temp Choctaw Indian, who was reticent and shy. The other was a sun-blistered, sawdust-splattered Celtic hillbilly, who was an inveterate babbler and grappler. One was a commercial refrigeration repairman; the other, a fast-cutting lumberjack. One was more focused on the small, beautiful ornaments of nature that could be enhanced into artwork or jewelry, the other more interested in the big picture—geological forces and features that gave rise to unique earthly creations. Sid saw value in the smallest of things, while Cephis saw value in the larger objects—the bigger the better. Both men were consummate shufflers of the stratigraphic layers.

The two men brought their unique abilities, personalities, and skills to the project in a consummate and complementary fashion. Neither man would waver; both would stand the test of time. Only two such uniquely endowed men possessing a strong sense of friendship, trust, compatibility, determination, and cooperation could weather the storm and survive the ordeal that awaited them. At the time they began their fantastic journey, Cephis was a strapping 42-year-old, Sid, a vigorous 57. Both men were entrepreneurs and seasoned naturalists, but they were not accomplished dinosaur excavators.

It was simply inconceivable in the early 1980s that McCurtain County could deliver up such a magnificent treasure and that two raw naturalists from the local area might rise to the occasion and stun the paleontological realm by successfully excavating and saving the dinosaur from certain destruction. Until that opportunity arose, Hall and Love appeared to be dismally bound to indulge their naturalist hobbies and museum passions exclusively in the mineral sphere and fade into desolate mediocrity.

The duo would gain notoriety as two green-horned amateurs who managed to accomplish what few of the greatest academic minds of science had been able to do—locate and extricate a world-class dinosaur specimen from a wet location in a region where no articulated dinosaur skeletons had ever been found.

As they passed along the west bank of the Mountain Fork and drove up to the edge of the pit, they could not conceive what destiny would bring. The future was illusory; the present was real. They could not see beyond the next bone and that's the way it would largely go—one bone at a time until the entire mystery was solved. Each obstacle, each intricacy, each adversity, each dilemma would be met and surmounted with innovation, flexibility, and practicality. The project was conducted in a piecemeal fashion. One step at a time and one piece at a time, the two men would ultimately put the puzzle together. Given enough time, the bones would fit and the riddle of the dinosaur would be solved.

CHAPTER ELEVEN
Mysteries Along the Mountain Fork

On his last endeavor at the bone site, Cephis discerned another large bone lying directly behind where the femur was lodged. He surmised it to be another leg bone – perhaps a tibia or the matching femur. Also, he could see the outlines of several other indistinguishable pieces partially visible within the clay embedment. The work order was simple – extend and widen the existing embrasure and expose the fossils for a clearer assessment.

While in transit to the Mountain Fork, Cephis and Sid discussed plans for the day's dig. As their vehicle rolled up to the edge of the pit, their objective was threefold: enlarge the stratum incision, assess the contents of the embedment, and liberate the accessible bones. Once those objectives were met, they needed to determine if there was a discernible layer or formation that fit a pattern that could be deciphered and tackled in an orderly and methodical manner.

The femur had been extracted from a cavity dug barely one foot into the wall of the gully, about four feet wide. They needed to enlarge the pocket size by extending its width and depth. The hole had to be hollowed out to enable elbow room and easier access.

If an articulated skeleton was embedded, their small hole would have to be expanded into a massive tunnel. Unless they secured heavy earth-moving equipment to strip the overburden, they needed to become tunnel rats. Tunneling deep within the gully posed a risk of collapse and live burial. Cephis and Sid did not wish to be entombed with the dinosaur. Since this was a secret mission, nobody would know the location of their final resting place. They would become enshrouded in mystery, like the dinosaur.

They arrived at the site shortly before sunrise and unloaded their tools and supplies. This day was going to be different. Cephis now had a partner and felt relieved to have company. An extra set of hands lightened the workload.

Immediately upon arrival, the two men commenced digging. They shared the workload to accommodate the abilities of each man and promote maximum efficiency. The tunnel was only big enough for one man at a time. Since Cephis was younger and more adept at excavation, he bore the brunt of the digging. Sid assumed most of the documentation and legwork.

In deference to Sid's Choctaw heritage, Cephis christened a new name for the dig site – the Tonihka Crossing – the name for the old frontier stagecoach crossing located about two hundred yards down the river. Sid agreed. It was a fitting name.

The Tonihkas were a prominent Choctaw family with deep roots in McCurtain County. In the 1840s, one of the leading members of the clan, John Tonihka, constructed the crossing with the aid of local manpower, using picks, shovels, and axes to cut a pathway along the west bank of the river. The human-engineered features of the crossing were now barely visible; nature had largely reclaimed what man had once altered.

Sid could relate to Choctaw prominence. He was the great-grandson of Robert M. Jones, a high ranking member of the Choctaw Tribe and an influential leader when the tribe still occupied its ancestral homelands in the state of Alabama. He was aristocracy – Indian style – and a large trader-merchant on the Tennessee River near Florence, Alabama, with political connections within the state of Alabama – connections that reached all the way to Washington. Although too involved in commerce to serve as chief, he was probably a member of the tribal council.

Robert Jones was of mixed blood—about ¾ Choctaw and the remainder Celtic. He started life as a cotton and tobacco farmer, but soon parlayed his talents to become a large commodity trader. He owned a fleet of boats and shipped salted meats, wild game, furs, fish, grains and other commodities down the Tennessee River to major ports in the South.

As a large commodity trader, he had a reputation for honesty and paid his debts in a timely manner. He took good care of his Negro servants. It is believed he had a loyalty bond with his slaves.

Prior to the forced resettlement of the Choctaws beginning in the early 1830s from their tribal lands in the South to the western lands of Oklahoma, the federal government made friendly overtures to Jones in an attempt to entice him to leave early. The federal government feared he had become too close to Southern leadership.

Through the offer of a large land grant in the designated Indian Territory of Oklahoma, Jones was persuaded to relocate months ahead of the tribe. He was awarded several thousand acres of prime farmland along the Red River that extended northward to the settlement of Hugo, Oklahoma.

Jones reestablished his shipping business along the Red River with farms and trading posts located at strategic points. He built a large mansion approximately two miles from the northern banks of the river, and managed six large plantations from Foreman, Arkansas to Durant, Oklahoma, as well as sugar plantation in Louisiana. After his first wife died, he married into another prominent Choctaw-European family – the Loves – whose sons served as officers in the Confederacy. After the Civil War, he freed his 200 slaves, who thence elected to stay on the land as sharecroppers.

The large landholdings established by the Jones' family patriarch were passed down for several generations to heirs, and divided into smaller and smaller plots. Sid inherited a parcel of this once-great holding – some of it still in his family's hands. Sid was not born poor, but his inheritance from what was left of the great family fortune was small. He lived in a rather modest house in the city of Idabel.

The dig resumed where Cephis left off. Initially, he used a pick and spade to abrade the outer rim of the hole and enlarge the opening to about four feet in diameter. This would give him more room to maneuver inside the crevice and allow easier access to the fossils.

After clearing more space, he redirected his efforts toward freeing the large leg bone, which was now more distinguishable. Digging around the bone in a concerted effort to separate it from the surrounding matrix was tedious. Progress was slow as the hours elapsed. Whenever Cephis tired, Sid assumed the digging so the action could be sustained and maximization of time realized.

After clearing space along the sides and rear, Cephis chipped at the matrix atop the bone until establishing a hollow void around it. A thin layer of soft clay, left purposefully for protection, still coated the bone as it rested on a bed of sandstone.

A close examination of the appendage revealed that it had several fractures along the span of its shaft. Recent water seepage had likely caused deterioration, requiring it to be plaster-casted along its entire shaft. Rubber bands were affixed to further secure it. Fastidious care was needed to remove the bone intact.

The fossil was covered with plastic wrap before burlap strips soaked with plaster were applied around it. This application stabilized the bone and kept it from shattering while being dispatched from its bed. They would have to wait a few hours for the plaster to dry.

Soon the sun would set and darkness would cast its sleepy pall over the Mountain Fork. Both men were hot, tired, sweaty, and dirty. But that didn't matter. They needed to finish the job and take the relic home to safety.

While taking a break, they discussed their situation. Unless they botched the effort, they would have another trophy to add to their collection. Despite their fatigue, they were teeming with excitement.

They had made considerable progress in widening and deepening the hole, and in separating the leg bone from its enclosure. Within a few hours, the appendage would be freed from the stifling impoundment. They would not be leaving empty-handed.

The two men took out their food and drinks, and as they ate their last sandwiches, extraneous thoughts entered their minds. Cephis, always a curious surveyor of the geologic landscape, began to think about the surrounding topography and was momentarily puzzled. Only having dug a few feet beneath the top level of the gully, they had hit the Cretaceous layer. How could that be? What ancient geologic forces had sculpted and fissured this local landscape over the ages? A massive buildup of natural sediment had been corrosively worn down. Had man intervened to reshape the terrain?

Telltale signs of ancient life were all around. Pieces of shining, petrified wood tainted with pyrite and as old as the Cretaceous were strewn about. Prehistoric leaves and vines had been dug out of the wall of the gully. Small, water-worn cobbles, shaped by the force of moving water over millions of years, were copious. Signs of water immersion, both ancient and recent, could be detected by any astute observer of geologic and hydrologic forces.

Other things were obvious. Man had indeed altered the topography. First, the two men were working in the midst of an old gravel pit. Motorized digging equipment with large buckets had shaved the surface. Although difficult to detect the contours, the ground level had been lowered by several feet. Also, the gully's use as a waste-holding reservoir was an obvious human innovation, having been dug by a backhoe several years prior.

Besides the man-made alterations of the terrain, industrial effluents and toxic wastes were carried to the immediate vicinity by the stream flowing eastward from the Craig fiberboard plant, about a mile to the west, and had likely contaminated the localized ecosystem of this once-pristine river. Cephis had heard about massive fish kills in this vicinity of the river and was aware of the aspersions cast on the fiberboard plant.

During their excavation, they were annoyed by the intermittent encroachment of the inauspicious smell of rotten eggs. The abhorrent smell tainted the fragrant scents blown in from flowers near the river bank. The pleasant aromas of nature faded away, being overpowered by the imposing stench seeping from below. The smell was most noticeable whenever they were resting or taking a break.

Quite obviously, sulfuric acid or some other strong chemical was leaching out of the soil, and the fumes occasionally irritated their eyes. Sid wondered if he and Cephis were working in the midst of a polluted wasteland. Had industrial chemicals saturated the grounds and permeated the watershed? Were toxic carcinogens percolating to the surface and inflicting insidious harm to their bodily organs? The two men were forced to either bear it or ignore it. Sometimes they alleviated their discomfort by practicing self delusion – changing their thoughts or conversations, reorienting their work, or walking away until recouping.

Not just abominable smells and worries about toxic chemicals distracted them. Swarming insects plagued their dig. On the terrestrial front, they were sometimes tormented by ants, spiders, chiggers, and ticks; while flying pests were the scourge of the dusky air currents.

Rest breaks were a time to retreat from their many adversaries. They usually sought shelter under a shade tree or where thick, matted grasses accorded a soft place to sit or lie. Such retreats allowed time to reflect.

Cephis was certain this area was an ancient floodplain shaped by timeless geologic forces. Great flows of water once cascaded through this low-lying valley. Sediments were deposited, and in time, worn away. Over eons, a fast-flowing stream captured the run-off from the local watershed and gradually carved out a channel – ultimately to become the Mountain Fork River.

Until the river became deep enough to capture the surrounding drainage and convey it southward, the entire area was likely a gigantic swampland or lagoon with abundant diversity in vegetation and animal forms – including the monstrous theropod dinosaur whose grave they were now molesting.

They were caretakers of the creature's legacy. It was an enchanting proposition. The duo walked in the monster's tracks whenever they strolled about the streambed. As a large theropod, the creature was likely the apex predator of the region and roused fear and panic from the local herbivores whenever it prowled nearby.

More than one hundred million years ago, the creature stalked this low-lying plain in search of sustenance. It likely hunted around water sources where there was a rich assortment of plants and prey. The lush vegetation of these wetlands attracted a bounty of plant eaters, which provided the predator an ample meat market.

But something unusual happened. The creature did not die of old age or natural causes. It met a sudden and violent death. Its carcass was quickly covered by an enveloping barrier before scavengers could scatter its bones to the four corners. Perhaps it died in or near water and was quickly buried by water-born sediments. The answer to the mystery was likely locked in the strata of the bone bed. With the recovery of a few more bones, perhaps they, or some professional bone seer, could shed light on the cause of the creature's demise.

As the two men rested and pondered the intricacies of the surrounding landscape, little did they know that they were not the first to scratch the surface of the dinosaur's tomb. Apparently, this was a trampled path, and they were not the only intruders to violate the sanctity of the dinosaur's grave. Several years earlier, there were other diggers at the site. The river is full of many surprises and conceals many secrets. The river's edge plays host to a whole array of mysteries.

As early as 1981, a Broken Bow High School student, Jeff Jones, was the first to retrieve bones from the site – almost two years before Cephis began his excavation. Jeff and two fellow classmates, Jason Norrid and Kelly Mundell, were visiting Jeff's grandfather, Louis Jones, at his riverfront home located about a mile downstream from the dinosaur site.

While exploring the backwoods along the river in search of petrified wood, the three boys climbed down into a gully and spotted something very peculiar. An unusually large bone was embedded in the eroded wall about four feet up from the floor, lying flat on a carved-out ledge. The bone was anchored only by the clay substrate beneath it, and held the three teenagers in awe for several minutes.

The giant bone was enticing and a "cool thing" for a trio of teenagers to come across during a frivolous frolic in the forest. Curiously, the boys began to peer and probe at the strange object. They wanted to retrieve and take it home as a souvenir.

After all, one didn't find something like this every day. Perhaps somebody could tell them what kind of bone it was.

Mother Nature made the job of retrieval easy for them. Erosion had carved out the embedment that once concealed and protected it. All they had to do was dig underneath it. Using only their bare hands, they loosened the substrate beneath and gently dislodged it.

A grayish color, perhaps sun bleached and washed by rain, it was so heavy that surface water could not wash it away. Being exposed to the elements, it was amazing that it was still intact – or so they thought until they attempted to handle it. The shaft splintered into three separate pieces, each about eighteen inches long.

The bone was brittle and reminded Jeff of petrified wood. Erosion had exposed other bones inside the gully. Jeff wanted to get this collector's piece home safely and come back another day to see what else could be retrieved.

Soon thereafter, he and his father, Levi, visited the site with picks and shovels and spearheaded a primitive excavation. The father-son team dug up several odd-looking pieces – including four vertebrae from the creature's spine – each the approximate size of a basketball and weighing about fifteen pounds.

Levi and Jeff returned back to the site four more times and came home with additional pieces. Soon, there were no more visible bones and the excavation came to a halt.

The Jones family remained curious about the fossils, but could not find anybody to give them a credible identification. Most believed they were scorched cow bones. The people they consulted were not very inquisitive or imaginative, and spouted knee-jerk, banal answers.

Jeff took a piece of the large femur bone to his high school science teacher, Darrell Williams, who had no clue as to what it was. The best guess he could garner was a bone from a Wooly Mammoth. Jeff donated the piece to the science lab in hopes that somebody might take an interest and identify it. Levi had the best hunch; he suspected they were actually dinosaur bones.

Three generations of the Jones family had a personal connection to the bones. To their chagrin, nobody could identify them. The grandfather, Louis, soon grew tired of them and began giving pieces away to friends. He gave a piece of the femur and one of the vertebrae to a local veterinarian, Dr. Lewis Stiles. These fossils had circulated around McCurtain County long before Cephis initiated his dig.

Jeff finally donated a few pieces to the Forest Heritage Center at Beaver's Bend State Park, where they came under the scrutiny of the park naturalist, Christi Silvey, who took an active interest. She finally took them to the University of Oklahoma at Norman in hopes that a paleontologist could put a name and face on the creature. She was disappointed by the university's apparent lack of interest. The scientists did not identify the remains; the identity search ended after the university claimed they lacked sufficient funds to delve further into the matter. However, some of the locals actually believed that a university team had finally driven down in a van and made an investigation of the site, but returned empty-handed.

Christi Silvey donated the bones to the university and that was the last known about that particular set of bones that originated with the Joneses. Supposedly, they were being held in storage somewhere on the campus, most likely within the science museum.

The femur piece that Jeff donated to the high school disappeared without a trace. The only pieces from the original Jones collection still known to be on display in McCurtain County are those pieces that were given to the local veterinarian, Lewis Stiles, who owns and operates the Gardner Mansion & Museum on Highway 70 near the Oklahoma-Arkansas state line.

A local brick mason named Royce Tidwell recovered another set of bones about a year after the Jones' discovery, and months before Cephis commenced his dig. Tidwell did not happen upon the site by accident – Levi Jones gave him directions to the pit.

After arriving and inspecting the site, Tidwell noticed the edge of a vertebrae protruding out of the gully embankment. He took a knife and trowel and worked the vertebrae loose. In the aftermath of a little dirt shuffling, he recovered a second vertebra. After more exertion, he finally grew restive and departed the scene. However, he left with a hunch that more bones still lay concealed beneath the surface.

A few months later, Tidwell revisited the scene and found orange engineering stakes marking the location. This was rather perplexing, but he saw no evidence of fossils or excavation. At that point, he simply lost interest, went home, and never returned. To this day, he still retains the two vertebrae as souvenirs.

Tidwell was more insightful than the typical county resident. He suspected from the beginning that his vertebra were from a deceased dinosaur. He consulted scientific authorities about his fossils but obtained no answers as to their identity. Like the Jones family and Silvey, he finally just gave up. They had all concluded that a university staff could be detached and indifferent.

The first person to ever set eyes on the bones was an employee of the Craig fiberboard plant named Jay Westbrook. Westbrook was a backhoe operator given the assignment of excavating the gully in the late 1960s or early 1970s, soon after Weyerhaeuser bought out Dirks and took over the fiberboard plant.

Westbrook cut a deep furrow into the earth and widened, deepened, and lengthened it into a gully twelve feet wide, eight to ten feet deep, and about seventy yards long. The infamous gully was born, but in the process, several large bones were torn loose from the subsurface.

Westbrook was curious about their unusual size and appearance. He informed the plant managers of what he had uncovered. As usual, they were too obsessed and stressed with managerial duties and had no time for or interest in such things. Massive, strange-looking bones were not a priority. They brusquely informed him that they were nothing but cow bones and instructed him to get back on his backhoe and complete the project.

The first real opportunity to uncover a world-class dinosaur specimen was lost due to neglect and indifference. Bones continued to erode out of the embankment for over a decade, and as a result, a one-hundred percent articulated skeleton was whittled down to sixty-five percent.

The bones proved quite elusive and resilient in their resting place. Thanks to the obtuseness of man, they remained anonymous in their quiet and reclusive enclosure until Cephis Hall arrived.

The potentially greatest dinosaur discovery of all history was debased to "one of the greatest dinosaur discoveries of the twentieth century." From the period of Westbrook's exposure to the commencement of Hall's excavation, thirty-five percent of the bones weathered out of the bed and disintegrated into dust. A once-in-a-millennium opportunity had completely eluded Weyerhaeuser, the Oklahoma scientific community, and a sundry cast of local citizens.

Had a professional scientific field team been brought to the site and put to work immediately after Westbrook's revelation, a one hundred percent solution might have been realized. The discovery of a one hundred percent articulated theropod dinosaur has never been accomplished in the history of paleontology. A twenty percent recovery is considered a sheer stroke of luck.

The haunted abode did not easily relinquish its treasure – a few pieces here and there, a few small discoveries, but a number of lost opportunities. The Jones family, Christi Silvey, and Royce Tidwell tried to get the scientific world to take notice, but all experienced an icy reception. The last hope for the world was in the hands of Cephis Hall and Sid Love.

The Jones clan had the greatest intimacy with the bones until Hall made his debut. That was easily understood, for Louis Jones and his sons were the eyes and ears of the river. Not much happened along the river without the knowledge of Louis Jones. Jones, the "Old Man of The River," retained many secrets about river shenanigans, some his own doings.

Louis Jones was an old timer in the county. Born of mixed Irish and Indian stock, he still held true to his frontier heritage. He was a living exhibition for the pure and unadulterated "Old Oklahoman," an atavistic reminder of an earlier era. His life was colorful and full of many experiences. The Great Depression made its mark on the man during his early years. The traumatic events and profound changes that impacted McCurtain County in the early twentieth century etched an enduring imprint on his outlook on life. (Louis Jones and Robert Jones are unrelated, or if so, distantly.)

Louis Jones was born in 1913 and experienced hard times in his early years. His uncle Henry, a lawman for the Choctaw Nation, brought the family from northwestern Arkansas to McCurtain County in the 1890s. Uncle Henry worked as a deputy for "Hanging Judge" Isaac C. Parker (1838 – 1896), who presided over the Western

District of Arkansas in Fort Smith, which included the Indian Territory. During the late 1800s, the region comprising western Arkansas and eastern Oklahoma was a wild, untamed frontier inhabited by legions of outlaws and bandits. Judge Parker and his deputies were charged with the task of restoring law and order to these wide open badlands.

Eastern Oklahoma during that period was known as the outlaw capital of the world. The reclusive mountains, hills, forests, caves, and clean water sources throughout the territory provided ideal hideouts for gangs of bank, train, and stagecoach robbers, cattle and horse thieves, counterfeiters, solitary ruffians and bandits of every stripe, and prowling desperados looking for an easy buck.

The wild and lawless frontier of eastern Oklahoma was infested with many notorious and infamous outlaws including the Dalton Gang, John Wesley Harden, Frank and Jesse James, and Belle Starr – the "Bandit Queen."

The Robbers Cave State Park near Wilburton, Oklahoma, displays one of the most popular and widely used outlaw hideouts of the late nineteenth century. A large cave camouflaged within the rugged landscape provided perfect cover and shelter for long-term habitation and concealment from the law. Outlaw legends grew around Robbers' Cave beginning in the Civil War years when deserters from both the Union and Confederacy hung out in the area. After the war, guerilla bands and gangs of robbers made it a rendezvous site between raids.

Eventually, the law penetrated these isolated sanctuaries and caught up with the outlaws. The bandits were rousted out and forced to find new abodes elsewhere. Some lawmen like Louis Jones' uncle Henry were successful in apprehending some of these fugitives and bringing them to justice before Judge Parker.

The outlaws of the Wild West were a dying breed as times changed. As society became more urbanized and industrialized, horse and cattle thievery became less attractive and trains and stagecoaches were no longer viable targets for would-be robbers. The era of Prohibition (1920s) and the Great Depression of the 1930s opened up new opportunities for criminal enterprise and ushered in a new kind of outlaw – the bootlegger and gangster, in particular. The nature of outlawry changed with the changing times, and the Great Depression fostered a new era in crime and lawlessness.

As a young man during the Great Depression, Louis Jones rode freight trains across the country going from town to town looking for work. He was among the vast numbers of so-called hobos who made their way around the country hitching rides on freight trains and managed to see the egregious and perverse sights of a wretched and devastated nation. Those hobos witnessed and experienced firsthand the desperation of millions of hungry, jobless, rootless, and restless people trying to survive the cataclysm of a devastated financial system that afflicted the entire nation.

He had ridden a train out to California looking for work picking vegetables and fruit in migrant labor camps and ended up working on a large ranch, where he took up the sport of bare-knuckles boxing. The ranch hosted boxing contests between the ranch hands and locals. Louis proved to be a very good fist brawler. The famed boxer Max Baer also lived and fought at that same ranch, but moved on to bigger and better things as the professional heavyweight champion of the world. Louis and Max had made contact – Louis served as his sparring partner on the ranch.

During the Great Depression, boxing was the favored sport of the poor – and that meant most of the people. Fighting, whether in the ring or watching from a distance, was a cathartic way for the downtrodden to relieve anger and pent up frustration. The Charles Bronson movie of the 1970s, *Hard Times*, dealt with the subject rather vividly. Louis made the circuit and eventually plied his boxing skills in McCurtain County and at one time was considered the bare knuckles champ of the Broken Bow area.

He, like most people of that era, took whatever kind of work he could find in order to survive. He worked on road gangs using mules to grade roads and dig ditches, labored as a sharecropper and row farmer, and hoed cotton from dawn to dusk for fifty cents a day. He even spent time in the CC Camps, organized by the Civilian Conservation Corps, a Depression-era, New Deal make-work program for distressed rural areas that put unemployed people to work building roads, bridges, and other public works projects.

In better times, Jones became an entrepreneur and owned and operated his own service station, liquor store, and tavern. In his spare time, he engaged in an old, traditional, frontier enterprise that had been a way of life for the pioneer people of Appalachia and the sand hills of the rural South since the 1700s – bootlegging whiskey.

Louis knew many people in the county. Because of his vast life experience, kindheartedness, extensive social connections, and keen listening ear, people often came to him for counsel concerning pressing issues, or sometimes merely sought a referral to the right person who could address their particular concern. He became something of a backwoods celebrity for the country folks of McCurtain County.

The Depression had been a harrowing experience for Jones, but it had taught him much about life; how to survive and cope with adversity and hardship. It had both exhausted and strengthened him. Burdened with constant stress and worry that had to be surmounted, the taunting experience toughened and inured him to the travails and trauma of a devastated economic and social landscape. Following the Depression, Jones returned back to McCurtain County, where he lived out the balance of his life under the shadow of that unforgettable and tumultuous life experience. Over time, as the indelible experience became a more distant memory, he began to season and mellow, like an aged barrel of vintage Scotch whiskey.

In his later years, Louis lived in an isolated cabin on the edge of the river – a far cry from a modern, sleek, two-story brick house in a shiny new suburb. Although a little on the raw and earthy side, he was also charismatic, friendly, and outspoken. He had many wise, homespun tales with which to entertain and spoke from experience. A popular man in the county, he threw shindigs on weekends, and people were considered lucky if invited. He always livened up the festivities with fresh moonshine served directly from his home-brewed still.

It is no surprise that Louis Jones was among the first to know about the bones; he also had insight into the environmental atrocities committed along the river. He knew about the degradation of the water quality by the industrial and timber operations of Dierks and Weyerhaeuser.

He had seen repeated occurrences of sizable fish kills in the early 1960s. Large numbers of dead fish were seen floating in the river alongside his house. Some washed up on the bank and became an aromatic abomination. During extreme episodes of fish extermination, the water turned a dark, rancid color and emitted a foul, noxious odor.

He knew that Dierks discharged raw industrial waste from the Craig fiberboard plant and that Weyerhaeuser had tried to mitigate the problem by building a containment reservoir (the gully) near the river in an apparent attempt to monitor water quality and control-and-time discharge events.

The problems with the fish kills always occurred in the summer when the temperature of the river was high and the oxygen and water levels low. During the rainy season, water was released from the upstream dam, creating a heavier flow of cold water downstream.

During the wet period, the wastewater released into the river was easily diluted in the heavy flow – a kind of "dilution is the solution to pollution" remedy. Unfortunately, during summer, the dam released less water and any large discharge of industrial chemicals during that period spelled danger for the local fish population.

Thus, the gully was excavated and a concrete weir and aperture installed to contain the wastewater until the water level in the river rose and the discharged wastewater could be diluted in the fast-flowing stream. It was simple – discharge on high water level, contain on low water level.

But the containment reservoir no longer worked. The concrete abutment had eroded out and there were no timed discharges of wastewater. The Craig plant was still operating.

In a way, for Cephis and Sid, it was kind of like making a deal with the devil. Sacrifice the fish but save the dinosaur. If the containment reservoir had still worked, it would be impossible to excavate inside the gully. The dinosaur would have to be forgotten and sacrificed on the altar of environmental quality.

With the containment reservoir out of order, what risks were now posed to the river and a couple of dino excavators who toiled for scientific truth inside the bottom of a waste-holding pit? To the river's detriment, if not their own, Cephis and Sid were willing to take their chances and felt lucky for the opportunity to strike a bonanza in bones. It was a pragmatic trade off; they were not idealists, anyway.

As they continued their long break from the arduous toil, the smell of rotten eggs again invaded the air and jolted their senses. Since it was easier to bear the odorous distraction while working, the duo resumed their digging. Cephis took up a position inside the manhole and chipped away at the matrix; Sid got the supplies ready for the extraction of the big bone. With ample time left before sunset, they attempted the bone removal.

The appendage came out precisely the same way as the femur. Cephis gently pried underneath the bone until he could release the hold of the matrix and liberate it from the dark underworld of the dinosaur mausoleum.

After carefully prying and nudging, the bone popped loose. Snug in the plaster jacket, it would soon be ready to be reintroduced to the living world. Success! The bone was placed on a plywood pallet and made ready for transport.

The two men had moved a great deal of dirt that day. Cephis was eager to get the bone home, unwrap it, study and admire it. This raw product of nature held great fascination for both Sid and him.

The two men were proud of the day's accomplishment. They had successfully removed another gigantic bone from the pit and uncovered several others that could be accessed on their next venture. They had hollowed out a five-foot wide by five-foot tall opening in the gully embankment. The hole was tunneled four feet into the wall and there was now ample room to maneuver inside. But the hole was going to have to get much bigger.

CHAPTER TWELVE
What Species of Dinosaur Is This?

Things were looking up for Cephis and Sid. They had successfully brought home another large appendage and exposed a few other fossils. A cache of visible bones awaited their return. Even if the only pieces left to recover were those clearly visible inside the earthen cavity, they had the greatest inventory of dino bones ever uncovered in McCurtain County. There was no longer any doubt; they had hit a genuine bone bed.

After removing the appendage, they saw the outlines of ribs, but most astonishing were the extensions of spines attached to vertebrae. The bizarre-looking spines were protruding from the wall with their jagged ends outward.

They had never heard of a North American theropod with spines on its back. The spines reminded them of sail fins, a feature common on mammal-like reptiles during the early Triassic Period, millions of years before dinosaurs arose. But the two men were aware that all those early, fin-backed creatures of the Triassic (250 – 200 million years ago) had gone extinct or evolved into smaller mammals. Besides, those unique Triassic creatures were quadrupeds that walked on all fours.

Was their beast a high-spined carnivore that walked upright? Had they encountered a new phenomenon in theropod anatomy?

They were anxious to return to the Tonikha Crossing, but the first order of business was to get their fragile specimen unloaded and placed in a safe place to be unwrapped and analyzed. The two men lifted the large piece of plywood out of the pickup bed and hand-carried the cargo into Cephis' workshop as if it were a block of gold. They placed the plywood bearing their new trophy on the concrete floor next to the femur. The burlap strips were carefully unwrapped, the plastic covering removed, and the bare bone exposed. Curiously, the two men stared at the naked appendage and compared it to the sister fossil.

The new piece was shorter and thinner in diameter and a little lighter in weight. Although the first bone weighed one hundred pounds, this bone weighed only about eighty pounds. They looked at the distal ends of the new relic and confirmed its hollow interior. Around the outer edge of the hollow portion was the same pyrite contamination. The piece was likely from the same animal. The new appendage confirmed their original supposition concerning the first—if the first bone was the femur, the new one had to be the tibia.

Despite the tibia's fissures and poor condition, it remained intact. Their preparation wrapping of coated burlap and careful handling reaped a huge dividend. The emaciated bone could be coated with shellac as a preservative, and hardener and glue applied as needed. With care, this could still be a showpiece item. Pyrite contamination was a perfidious and enduring problem and constantly wracked their minds with trepidation.

As the two men admired the pieces, they pondered the intricacies of their discovery. Although the identity of the creature still eluded them, some visible clues started to emerge. Step by step, piece by piece, a picture of the creature and its local habitat was being painted. The brush strokes were still blurred, but gradually, an image of the beast and its local Cretaceous environment were coming into clearer focus.

The true enigma of the dinosaur could not be solved until more bones were recovered, particularly the all-important skull, and evaluated by scientific experts. But certain evidence elicited further questions and pointed toward tentative answers. They had a large and ferocious apex predator with peculiar back spines—a theropod from the early or middle Cretaceous Period. Apparently, the creature once terrorized the swamps and lagoons in a floodplain near the Atlantic shore.

During the early Cretaceous, what is now known as the Gulf of Mexico extended further inland and may have reached within a hundred yards of the dig site, making the southeastern edge of what is now McCurtain County ocean-front property.

Cephis Hall's mind kicked into overdrive and abounded with imagination and speculation. A key to unlocking the identity of the creature was to analyze and relate the peculiar anatomy of the animal with its local environmental context.

Visible geologic and biologic signs present at the site offered clues to the remote past and buttressed their preconceptions about the regional landscape and its flora and fauna during the early Cretaceous. The dig site parameter contained an abundance of carbonized vegetative material—layers of compacted wood and preserved leaves, still fibrous after millions of years—indicating an ancient floodplain.

What species of giant carnivorous theropods with high spines hunted near water sources during the early Cretaceous? Had any such creatures lived in the southern lowlands of North America? What kind of prey did they feast on—armored, herbivorous low-browsers, sauropod high-grazers, fish, or all of the above? These were beguiling questions and accorded a realization that the key to solving the identity conundrum was to consult the biological record to learn which peculiar theropods habituated southern coastal plains.

Cephis envisioned a large lagoon with a bowl-shaped bottom. The dinosaur may have attempted to retrieve a meal and became trapped in a quicksand-like bog and subsequently was buried alive. The creature could have been submerged under mud and silt and sealed off from oxygen and the living world for over 100 million years. This theory was pure speculation, but plausible.

Based on what they knew about the creature's anatomy, it was a biped with surrealistic dorsal spines—a sail-backed dinosaur that walked upright. Almost an oxymoron—no such theropod was known to have lived in North America during the Cretaceous. Their curiosity burgeoned.

Cephis was aware that a giant, predatory theropod known as *Saurophaganax maximus was* found in the Morrison Formation in western Oklahoma in the late 1930s by a WPA* work crew under the supervision of renowned University of Oklahoma paleontologist J. Willis Stovall. (*The Works Progress Administration was a New Deal jobs program initiated under the administration of Franklin D. Roosevelt during the Great Depression.)

Could their bones be from a *Saurophaganax maximus? (Saurophaganax maximus* remains have been found only in the state of Oklahoma. Senate Bill 1185, Section 98.6 – state – fossil, April 14, 2000, declared *Saurophaganax* the state fossil of Oklahoma. A restoration of the animal is on display at the Sam Noble Museum of Natural History in Norman, Oklahoma.)

The *Saurophaganax* invokes a polemical controversy among paleontologists. Some have designated it as a separate genus, others consider it a close relative of *Allosaurus,* while a third camp considers it a full-fledged member of the *Allosaurus* clan, just an exceptionally large specimen. Perhaps for that reason, it is often confused with *Allosaurus* and is not widely known by the general public.

Saurophaganax maximus was an interesting Jurassic specimen that rivaled, or maybe surpassed, T. rex in size and ferocity. The giant may have been in excess of 45 feet long, 16-17 feet high, and 5-9 tons in weight. This ancient Oklahoma native was known to have horizontal laminae at the base of the dorsal spines, rather than high spines or a sail back. Besides, *Saurophaganax* was a creature of the late Jurassic (155-145 mya.), like *Allosaurus,* and probably tens of millions of years older than their high-spined specimen. In addition, the *Saurophaganax* bones were dug out of the Morrison Formation, which is a lower (older) stratum than the Antlers Formation, the strata that contained their mystery bones. These facts basically ruled this creature out.

The duo was aware of a whole class of dinosaurs known as spinosaurs, or by the more formal family name, *Spinosauridae,* which were so named and classified because of the tall neural spines growing on the back of their vertebrae. This family of theropods includes: *Spinosaurus, Baryonyx, Suchomimus,* and the *Irritator.*

The most interesting of the lot was the *Spinosaurus.* The *Spinosaurus* (spiny lizard) is thought to be the largest terrestrial predator ever to walk the face of the earth—larger than even T.rex and *Giganotosaurus.* The bizarre creature lived during the middle Cretaceous (112 to 85 mya) and was estimated to be as long as 56 feet and weighing 7-9 tons. It had distinctive spines as long extensions of the vertebrae. The skull was almost six feet long. This huge predator-scavenger was more reptilian than avian.

A sail back formed from skin connected and enshrouded the tall neural spines (in excess of six feet) growing on the back of the vertebrae. The skin sail may have been brightly colored and used for display purposes, possibly to impress a potential mate or scare off a competitor, if it could be changed to a warning color by "blushing" it red with blood. The sail covered a large surface area and might have absorbed heat to warm the body, or, if turned away from the sun, to dissipate heat and cool the animal. Because of this unique adaptive structure, some paleontologists questioned whether or not *Spinosaurus* was warm-blooded.

This unusual creature lived on the edge of the inland water bodies and frequently entered them in search of prey. Like other members of the *Spinosauridae* family, it had anatomical similarities with the crocodile and was more crocodilian than typical terrestrial theropods. The *Spinosaurus* embodied a monstrous chimera—a creature with a long, narrow snout, conical teeth without serrations, elongated jaws, raised nostrils and interlocking teeth—features common to the crocodile. Most likely it had adapted to eating fish, but occasionally it cornered small dinosaurs for dessert.

The *Spinosaurus* is believed to have been bipedal, but occasionally resorted to a quadruped position. Like something out of a horror film, it looked much like a giant crocodile that walked upright, but more fierce and deadly. Although it was longer and taller than T.rex and had more robust arms, it was lighter built. Also, its jaws and teeth did not have the killing power of a T.rex.

In the 2001 film, *Jurassic Park III*, the *Spinosaurus* was portrayed as a larger and more powerful creature than T.rex. When the two monsters locked in a horrendous battle, the *Spinosaurus* ended up victorious by snapping off the head of the T.rex. Such a performance garnered the *Spinosaurus* alluring fanfare among young dinosaur enthusiasts, who subsequently bought T-shirts and other memorabilia that displayed the conquering monster's bold and fearsome image.

Also within this specialized class of theropod dinosaurs was another giant predator-scavenger known as *Suchomimus*, a crocodile mimic (due to the shape of its head). Like the *Spinosaurus*, it too adapted to eating fish and had the long, low snout, narrow jaws, and other crocodilian features. It was about 40 feet long—almost the size of a T.rex. A smaller version of *Spinosaurus,* it also lived during the Cretaceous (125 to 112 mya).

The *Spinosauridae* family of theropods had several things in common with Cephis and Sid's specimen. They had spiny fins on their backs and lived during the Cretaceous Period. They made their living in and around swamps and waterlogged landscapes. Despite the common features, this group was ruled out of consideration—none of the *Spinosauridae* family members were known to have lived in North America. The remains of *Spinosaurus* and *Suchomimus* have been found only in North Africa. The mystery remained intact.

Unable to locate a category of dinosaur to match their specimen, they cast their thoughts upon the natural history of the local area. What kind of salient features of the local environment had attracted and nurtured such a monstrous beast? Why had it chosen to haunt the ancient landscape of McCurtain County? What kinds of flora and fauna had lured this mysterious creature to the local scene and coaxed it into an evolutionary adaptation suitable for the local neighborhood? Why had these biological adaptations become antiquated and the creature extinct? Or, if the creature did not become extinct, into what did it evolve? It was time to take a closer examination of the ancient landscape and natural history of southeastern Oklahoma, particularly prehistoric McCurtain County.

CHAPTER THIRTEEN
McCurtain County – 100 Million Years Ago

When studying the human animal, behavioral scientists place great emphasis on context— the great debate over nature versus nurture comes into play. Which is more important in determining behavior and life potential—the environment or the genes? Although genes play a major part in setting the parameters, animals, especially humans, do not live in a vacuum or bubble. They are shaped by the environment and their responses and adjustments to their surroundings. How they cope and adapt determines the level of their success. The environment determines the lifestyle and the lifestyle influences the cultural milieu, which shapes behavior. Animals must adjust and change within their changing environment or face extinction. Evolution—both biological and social—is a continuing process.

The issue of context was important for Cephis and Sid. In order to better understand their dinosaur and possibly identify it, they needed to better understand its context—the natural environment that molded its behavior and determined its way of life. The environment could shed clues to its behavior and way of life and possibly cast light on its cause of death. If the species had gone extinct at some point during the Cretaceous era, the environment would have been the decisive factor in the cause of that extinction.

In the time of the Cretaceous, McCurtain County had its own unique geographical and biological backdrop—a local ecosystem that encompassed a unique blend of climate, terrestrial landforms, resources, flora, and fauna. The local ecological setting was defined by this peerless comportment of biotic and abiotic factors, and these essential components determined the types of local inhabitants, the degree of speciation, the growth of populations, the diversity of niches, the structures of the food chains and webs, and all elements of animal behavior and interaction. Understanding the environment and the role it played in shaping animal behavior was essential in comprehending the nature of the beast itself.

Southeastern Oklahoma has transformed over the ages. Whole dynasties of creatures arose, evolved, expanded, morphed, and died out within that environmental context. Animals had to adapt to environmental change or suffer a reversal in fortunes, even extinction. Throughout the ages, there have been instances of sudden cataclysmic changes or single extinction events, including the asteroid impact 65 million years ago (mya) that is believed to have extinguished the dinos. In those rare episodic events, animals could not evolve or adapt quickly enough to avoid annihilation. If they managed to survive such a cataclysm, they were either preordained with a special adaptive potential or simply lucky. If unlucky, they became extinct.

By studying the ancient environment of McCurtain County, Cephis and Sid hoped to get a better understanding of the natural forces that shaped and modified that living world by gradually transforming the organisms that thrived and died within that archaic context. Just as the current environment determines the quality of life for modern citizens, the environment of the archaic past determined the quality of life for the prehistoric denizens.

The two men's objective was to trace the events that played out in McCurtain County over the eons since the early Cretaceous. With that deeper understanding, they hoped to tease out from that broad context of place, space, and time just where in the overall scheme of things their dinosaur actually fit.

Southeastern Oklahoma has always been a wet zone, and in the 21st century, it is still the wettest part of the state. During the Cretaceous, water was pervasive; it soaked and saturated a broad stretch of the green terrestrial landscape. This was a riparian world richly endowed with the basic biological necessities: water, carbon dioxide, oxygen, nitrogen, mixed nutrients, and loads of detritus and organic matter. This plentiful mixture of necessary biotic and abiotic factors helped nourish and sustain a green world that harbored a rich diversity of life.

Southeastern Oklahoma averages fifty-six inches of rainfall per year, the highest in the state. The area encompassing McCurtain County is within this wet zone, averaging about fifty inches of rain per year. In the area of Oklahoma City, the state capital, the average is only thirty-two inches. Due in part to this abundance in moisture and nutrients, southeastern Oklahoma has richly endowed soils and extensive canopies of native hardwoods and pines that house an abundance of wildlife, including 110 species of birds recorded in the wilderness area boundaries.

The southeast corner of the state near the Red River is only 325 feet above sea level. The state drains generally from the northwest to the southeast and has carried rich deposits of sediments and nutrients in that direction for eons. The most eastern Oklahoma soils outside the limestone belts are made from a base of clay and shale mixes.

The Antlers Formation was on the north shore of the ancient Atlantic sea. The geographical area of the Antlers Formation consisted of a large flood plain that drained into a shallow inland sea to the southwest. A few million years later, this sea expanded to the north and merged into the western interior seaway by the later Cretaceous. The sediments of the Formation were laid down in coastal swamps in the midst of this large flood plain.

The Antlers stratum consists of sandstone and clay laid down in the early Cretaceous about 110 mya. It is a band of strata that extends across north-central Texas, southeastern Oklahoma, and southwestern Arkansas in a pattern marking the edge of what was then the Gulf Coast. The formation covers about 150 miles of silty to sandy mudstones—fine to coarse-grained sandstones that are poorly to moderately sorted and cemented with clay or calcium carbonate. Most of the dinosaur remains found in the Antlers Formation have been teeth, not articulated skeletons.

The paleo-environment comprising the terrestrial land that formed the Antlers Formation was probably similar to that of modern-day Louisiana—with extensive forests, deltas, bayous, and lagoons. Along this ancient coast lived a wide assortment of dinosaurs, including *Deinonychus*, a small, raptor-like theropod; *Tenontosaurus*, the large herbivorous, ornithopod dinosaur; and the unknown apex predator that Cephis and Sid were working to uncover and identify. The *Tenontosaurus* is the most common dinosaur found within the Antlers stratum.

This same Antlers Formation runs through the lower southern part of McCurtain County. The site of the Cephis Hall dig site was just north of the ancient shore of the expanded Gulf of Mexico. Nobody knows exactly how far the actual shoreline was from the site, but is assumed to have been within 200 yards. The shoreline along southeastern Oklahoma gradually retreated southward during the Tertiary until it reached its present level. The state's general pattern of east- flowing drainage had its beginning in the Tertiary Period.

As the Gulf to the south and the inland sea to the west transgressed, habitats were destroyed and populations condensed into smaller space. As the seas regressed, new habitats were formed and more living space was accorded, thereby speeding the rate of evolution. The more prolific areas for fossil prospecting are found near areas that were once coastal zones because this was where life prevailed and where sediments formed.

The Rocky Mountains in the West formed in the late Cretaceous and early Tertiary eras. This up-thrust was accompanied by a broad uplift of all of Oklahoma, which imparted an eastward tilt to the entire state and caused a final withdrawal of the sea.

At various intervals in the remote past, forces within the earth caused portions of the Oklahoma land mass to alternately sink below and rise above sea level. Shallow seas and thick layers of marine shale covered large portions of the state at different times. Limestone and sandstone were deposited in adjacent areas, while sandstone and shale were laid down as alluvial and deltaic deposits near the ancient seas.

When these areas were later elevated above the seas, earlier deposited rocks and sediments were eroded and exposed, much as happens in modern terrestrial areas. Uplift was accomplished by gentle arching of broad areas or by the formation of mountains in areas where rocks had been intensely folded, faulted, or thrust upwards.

Three major mountain belts are found in the southern portion of the state: the Ouachitas, the Arbuckles, and the Wichitas. They represent areas of folding, faulting, and uplifting during the Pennsylvanian Period of geologic time and have exposed a variety of structures as these fold belts were brought to the surface: igneous rocks and thick sequences of Paleozoic sedimentary rocks. These uplifts are good locations where one can search and collect fossils.

Mountains form as they rise out of the surface of the earth due to the forces of plate tectonics, and are subsequently deformed over millions of years by the abrasive forces of wind, ice, and water. Such was the case with the Wichita and Arbuckle Mountains, which were once connected to the Rockies. Ever since that summit of greatness, Oklahoma's mountains have been eroding.

The Ouachita Mountains are part of a mountain belt that extends from Alabama to Mexico. In the US, the only sections of this great belt not buried by younger rocks are the Ouachitas in Oklahoma and Arkansas, and the Marathon Mountains in west Texas.

According to the *McCurtain Daily Gazette* (June 28, 1990, Volume 85, Number 15), in the early 1990s, Neil H. Sunneson and his crew from the Oklahoma Geological Survey were mapping the Arkoma basin of the Ouachita Mountains while conducting geological surveys of southeastern Oklahoma. Sunneson was interested in a particular rock found near Broken Bow. It was greenish in color and according to Smithsonian Institute expert Richard Fiske, this particular slab of rock which extends north to Watson is volcanic matter blown from a tremendous underwater explosion about 400 million years ago. Cephis Hall led the crew to the site. It comprised a large layer of material that had blown out of a volcano somewhere in the Gulf of Mexico. This material had scattered in the direction of Oklahoma and Arkansas, both of which were underwater at the time.

The greenish volcanic layer called the Hatton-Tuff came from the Gulf of Mexico after a big eruption. McCurtain County was under deepwater sea at the time of the massive underwater volcanic eruption, pouring igneous rock into the county.

So many layers of old rock had been laid on top of the surface by upheaval that the hard rock that should be on the bottom is on the top. Evidence of this is seen in some of the oldest rock in North America being layered on top of the hills just north of Broken Bow. Things are confusing when looking below the earth in McCurtain County. The formations are tricky in depths as far down as 30,000 feet. Many upheavals have thrust rock that would normally be found on the bottom up to the top, and vice versa. This is perhaps one reason why dinosaur remains have been so hard to find in the county. (*McCurtain Daily Gazette*)

During his tour of McCurtain County, Sunneson was amazed at the potential treasures in the county. Titanium was found in small pieces and picked up off the ground—indicating the possibility of mineable quantities. The Herkimer diamonds that are found in the northern part of the county are actually quartz crystals with pyramids at both ends. Oil and gas formations were likely in sufficient size for drilling. In Suneson's own words, "a clash between oil people and mineral folks is coming."

There are several major sedimentary basins in the southern half of Oklahoma, including the Ouachita basin. The basin was at the southern base of the present Ouachita Mountains. Sediments eroded from the Ouachitas and were deposited within the basin over eons of geologic time. Above the alluvial flood plains, the valleys picked up sediments carried from the higher Ouachita lands to the north and conveyed them southward to the lowlands. The flood plain near the ocean was the recipient of sediment deposits, but subsequently lost them as a result of horrendous floods and swift-flowing torrents cascading across the flood plain.

The ancient Cretaceous environment comprising the Mountain Fork dig site reminded Cephis of the Louisiana bayous. Tall conifers and cordaites grew upward from little patches of land surrounded by water. In ancient times, the swamplands were more extensive and pronounced. At the time of the Cretaceous, the Mountain Fork, if it even existed, was nothing more than a narrow, shallow ditch. Vegetative growth in the area was heavier than today.

The proof of the extensive vegetative growth was in the pit. Cephis and Sid scooped out hardened, compacted masses of fossilized plants—even low-growing species that may have represented some of the earliest progenitors of flower-bearing plants. A hodgepodge of plant debris—vines, leaves, pieces of trees, seed pods, and the branches, twigs, and limbs of trees and other woody, fibrous material—was found lying atop the bone bed. These flattened trees had been compressed and hardened within the strata. As Cephis and Sid penetrated into the overburden atop the bone bed, they were forced to use jackhammers, picks, and chisels to break the hardened fossilized material.

At one level below the bone bed, a layer of leaves that looked like straw and cypress needles was uncovered. Embedded between the leaves and the bone bed were globs of pyrite and marcasite (often used to decorate ladies' jewelry) about one inch by four inches in size. Scattered amidst the fossilized plant debris were also bits and nuggets of dinosaur dung, scientifically known as coprolite.

The Ouachitas formed during the Pennsylvanian era (340 mya). This mountain range, along with the Appalachia chain, was among the highest and most prominent mountains in what today is known as the United States. During the period that the Mountain Fork beast stalked in the shadow of the Ouachitas, these mountains were breaking down rapidly and the sediments washed into what was becoming a permanent drainage system, generally flowing north to south but veering to the east. By the late Tertiary time, the Ouachitas had worn down to foothills.

At the time of the Cretaceous, a wide expanse of lowland swamps extended from approximately the current location of Eagletown in the east all the way to the current site of Broken Bow to the west, and beyond. Throughout the Cretaceous, there was evidence of periodic super floods that conveyed massive amounts of surface water and sediment southeastwardly within this large swath.

Sediment deposition enriches the soil, which in turn nourishes a wider diversity of plants and animals. A rich vegetation cover attracts herbivorous grazers, which in turn, attracts carnivorous feeders, and an apex predator moves in and sits atop the food chain. The swampy area of the ancient Mountain Fork flood plain was full of life and attracted many animals seeking sustenance. This coastal wet zone contained an immense cornucopia of living things and was a good place to find a meal.

The weather was warm and seasonal with ample rainfall. The first flowering plants were beginning to evolve, and over time magnitudes of plant eaters were fine-tuning their feeding apparatuses to take advantage of the new style of plant growth. The changing environment was setting the tone and tune for evolution. A flowering of plants radiated across the valley floor and provided lush vegetation and fodder for low-grazing herbivores. Amidst this dense vegetation, mega-predators scoured the landscape for fresh meat.

Within the swamplands, dense and lush vegetation covered the small islands and all surface lands not submerged in water. Teeming herds of herbivores feasted on the rich foliage within the lush valley, but were weary of treading too deeply into the swamps, for in the swamps, mobility was limited and this presented a risk of being cornered by the monstrous apex predator—the "Terror of the South."

Deep within the thickets and brush, loud and heinous noises could be heard—screeching, rumbling, thrashing, and bellowing—the sounds of life; the sounds of death; the sounds of mundane, day-to-day activities—of movement, communication, seduction, mating, reproduction, competition, predation, and feeding. All these sounds were stilled with the arrival of the apex predator—the ruler of the ancient McCurtain County flood plain. Normal activities came to a screeching halt whenever its presence was felt or sensed.

The monster was conspicuous; its size and fierceness was intimidating. Its presence on the scene fomented terror and panic. Adrenaline surged and flight ensued. It was difficult for the monster to stalk its prey without being noticed. Life was difficult—even for the apex predator. But kill it did; and its species had successfully reproduced and inhabited a large part of the southern range of the North American continent.

The king of the McCurtain County flood plain was a missing link in the evolution of theropod dinosaurs. Few of its remains had been found. The creature was a mystery not only for Sid and Cephis, but also for the scientific community.

This dinosaur stood atop the food chain for southeastern Oklahoma during the early to middle Cretaceous; perhaps it was dominant across the entire breadth of the North American continent. *Allosaurus* was extinct by the late Jurassic. T.rex did not arrive on the scene until some fifty million years later.

Because of a dearth of fossil evidence, it would be difficult to construct a theoretical food chain for the local environment or identify the cast of creatures listed on the menu. It would be safe to say that the monster fed on smaller herbivorous dinosaurs. Perhaps it worked in family pairs to bring down giant sauropods.

The giant stalker of the ancient wetlands was likely a solitary hunter. The wicked-looking spines protruding from its back imparted a menacing, almost armored look to this awesome predator. Like most giant predators, it was probably an opportunistic feeder—taking a meal any way it could—preying, ambushing, or scavenging.

Although the specimen being uncovered may have been a swamp dweller, the species was probably adaptable to a wider range of terrestrial habitats. Cephis and Sid believed their specimen, unlike the water-borne *Spinosaurus,* was a more versatile predator whose diet consisted of more than fish. Their "swamp monster" occasionally lived around water, but not in it. Being truly opportunistic, it likely ventured into the swamps and made its kills on the edge of the water. Very likely, at opportune times, it confiscated carcasses from smaller predators. During its heyday, it ruled the valleys and swamps. Nothing could compete with it.

Because of its enormous size, the solitary carnivore required an expansive hunting range. It devoured an enormous amount of flesh, and a sizeable territory was needed to supply that meat. In a rich, bio-diverse swampland or river valley where the vegetation was thick, the plant feeders were plentiful and concentrated. This was an ideal hunting environment that sustained more top-line predators than other kinds of ecosystems. This concentration of meat in a single, generalized area likely shrank the required territorial size needed to sustain the apex predator.

Within the swamplands, it resorted to ambushing and scavenging, as its mobility may have been impaired. In the more open lands within the valley, it likely was an active hunter, perhaps chasing down the young, the sick, the lame, and the old. Like many theropods, it had limited cranial capacity for hunting strategy, yet it may have been the most successful predator that ever lived.

The fossil record denotes two species that were common in southeastern Oklahoma during the Cretaceous: *Deinonychus* and *Tenontosaurus. Deinonychus* was a small raptor that hunted in packs and was a nasty little predator—fast and cunning, possessing fearsome claws and killing accessories.

The apex predator could easily subdue *Deinonychus* if it managed to corner it, but not without risking serious bodily injury. *Deinonychus* could inflict some ghastly wounds with its fearsome claws. Very likely *Deinonychus* was not a choice meal from the normal menu. It might have been scavenged, but was not actively hunted by the "Terror of the South." Fish may have been a staple, but most likely the prime cut was the *Tenontosaurus.*

Tenontosaurus (tendon lizard) was a medium-sized ornithopod—a descendent of *Iguanodon*. It was about eight feet tall, twenty-three feet long, and as much as two tons in weight. It lived contemporaneously with *Deinonychus* and the "Terror of the South." With a long tail and neck, it walked mostly on two legs, but probably walked quadrupedally (on all four limbs) when browsing on low vegetation. A horny beak was used for shearing off low vegetation. *Tenontosaurus* had no body armor, and, except for its relatively large size, was somewhat defenseless.

Perhaps the only defense it had against a large theropod predator was the protection of the herd. Other than that, it could either run, or if cornered, could swat with its long tail or deliver a solid kick with its hind legs. The *Tenontosaurs* probably laid their colonies of eggs in the higher and drier plains to the north of the coastal area, but did most of its feeding in the lowland areas.

The low-grazing ornithopod was definitely hunted by hungry flocks of *Deinonychus*. Evidence of the predation is seen in the fossil record. The broken teeth of Deinonychus have been found with the skeletons of *Tenontosaurus*.

Tenontosaurus would have been an easy meal for the "apex terror." With its wicked claws and sharp, serrated teeth, the high-spined monster would have quickly overpowered and dispatched the defenseless herbivore, easily making mincemeat out of its flesh.

It must have been a merciless spectacle—the humble meek against the fierce, omnipotent giant. The struggle would have been over very quickly. The *Tenontosaurus* performed a specialized role within this primeval environment—a sacrificial offering of food for the sustenance of the king of the beasts.

The giant bipedal, high-spined theropod once stalked these ancient swamplands in search of an easy meal. Its bones had been uncovered, but its exact identity remained to be solved. As a diverse selection of food was on the menu, its diet was varied. It might have been a specialized fish eater like *Spinosaurus*, but the verdict was still out. Now, at least, Cephis and Sid had a better understanding of the ancient environment that sustained the creature—until that one fateful day during the early or middle Cretaceous when it met its sudden and tragic end.

CHAPTER FOURTEEN
Indiana Jones – Southern Style

The two rogue dinosaur hunters returned to the bone bed the following day. They had hollowed out a small manhole in the gully wall—picking and hacking their way through the rock and clay embedment. They resumed work where they had left off from their last visit. Inside the hole, spines attached to vertebrae were visible and extended outward. The diggers also detected several ribs dispersed in the clay matrix.

Diligence and caution were critical—a single thrust of a blade, pick, or chisel at the wrong place with too much blunt force could damage a precious bone. However, a bludgeoning from a blunt instrument was not the only risk to a prized commodity. The specter of water was a perilous threat to the entire treasure trove. Flood waters backing into the gully could submerge the manhole and dislodge the fossils from their concretement or cause fungi rot to infect the bone crop.

After heavy rains, water stood three feet deep inside the gully, making working conditions difficult and miserable. Often times, work was delayed for days until the water subsided or evaporated. Standing water posed its own unique set of concerns—swarming mosquitoes and swimming cottonmouths (poisonous water serpents) invaded the pit. Also, there was an ongoing concern about toxic chemicals washing into the gully from the Craig Plant upstream.

For the diggers, water was both a blessing and a curse—cool, refreshing, and life sustaining, but a hindrance to digging "dinos in the rough." Both the world of the dinosaur and the world of the diggers were intricately linked to water. On this day, they wouldn't be removing any bones but they would make a considerable dent in the matrix that enveloped them. With days of slow, steady work, several ribs and vertebrae might be ready for extraction.

This day would not end in glorious triumph. No wondrous, giant bone of antiquity would come out of the pit. There was nothing on the agenda but hard, tiring work in the hot, sweltering sun. Summertime was creeping up on them. It was only late spring in southeastern Oklahoma but it felt like the middle of July—hot, humid, and uncomfortable.

Normally unwavering, the two men became tired and bored early in the day. Rest breaks were often taken. As usual, the wonderful fragrances of spring were intermittently debased by the impetuous intrusion of the horrid smell of rotten eggs. Only when the odorous abomination subsided did the diggers get a little breathing reprieve.

Curiously, they wondered if the smell was caused by sulphur dioxide or hydrogen sulfide. Or was it from a more sinister source imposed by man's deadly concoction of chemicals? Amidst many concerns and questions, the diggers were poised to move forward.

The search was panning out. Where would it lead? What obstacles lay ahead? Would the landowner be agreeable to further exploration? What would they do with the fossils? A showdown was coming. They faced a confrontation with corporate bureaucracy and academia.

A long road filled with potholes lay in front of them, and they were determined to navigate it. Their sally was bold to the verge of recklessness and vigorous to the edge of pithy audacity. They were doing it Indiana Jones style.

Timbered questions would come out of the mud to perplex them. As soon as their work became public, more questions would bombard them from all sides.

Today's dig was unfruitful. They were approaching a roadblock, and their drive and energy was sapped. Maybe it was time to assess the future of their project. At this juncture, clearheaded thinking was more important than digging. They needed to map out a strategy. The bones had to be saved, and they had been requisitioned to perform that duty. If not them, then who?

CHAPTER FIFTEEN
The Bone Diggers Reach a Quandary

Collecting minerals and crystals can be both a hobby and obsession that can drive a person to out-of-the-way places. The glitz and sparkle of a rare gem has a dynamic of its own that lures one ever closer in the direction of that scintillation.

In the fall of 1983, a naturalist-collector named Allan Graffham and fellow collector Wayne Edgar were carousing around McCurtain County in search of quartz crystal and other rare minerals. Graffham, a non-university affiliated paleontologist, had visited the county in prior years with fellow geologist Pete Larson of South Dakota. The two men had scouted the backwoods of McCurtain County and found small caches of mineralized treasure. On this trip, however, Graffham and Edgar were not finding what they were looking for.

Graffham lived in Ardmore, a neighboring city to the west in Carter County. Larson sometimes flew in from South Dakota. When the two men got together, they usually went prospecting. They enjoyed sampling the sundry selections of quartz crystal to be found or bought in the local area. In the 1970s and 80s, the two men were young and possessed an adventurous spirit.

Larson would go on to become one of the most respected paleontologists in America. Both Larson and Graffham were destined to play pivotal roles in the story of Cephis Hall and the dinosaur, but those events were years away.

Only several years after the commencement of the dig did Cephis and Sid become acquainted with the two paleontologists. By that time, Graffham and Larson were prominent commercial dealers in fossils. Wayne Edgar, the director of the Goddard Youth Camp and museum, would also play a major part in the dinosaur story.

While in the city of Broken Bow, Graffham and Edgar stopped off at a local service station to fill up. Herman Snow, a personal friend of Cephis, owned the convenience store. Snow kept a shelf selection of Hall's finest quartz crystals. Graffham spotted the crystals and was impressed with their quality and luminescence.

"Where did you get these?" he asked Snow.

Snow answered, "I got them from Cephis Hall, the man who knows where all the local treasures are hidden."

"Well, we need to meet that guy," Edgar retorted.

Both men purchased a few of the exquisite crystals, and after a short, friendly chat with Snow, convinced him to give directions to Cephis's house, which was located about fourteen miles east of town near the Oklahoma-Arkansas state line.

The two treasure seekers set out to find Hall. Within minutes, they crossed over the Mountain Fork River heading east toward Arkansas. It was about an hour before sundown. They hoped to catch the treasure expert at home and purchase more of his quality quartz. But more importantly, they hoped to learn something worthwhile about the local geology.

Their arrival was timely; the treasure man had just finished his supper and took the two men into his rock shop. Graffham and Edgar found what they were looking for: an exquisite selection of fine quartz crystal. The best specimens were not for sale, but even the least attractive pieces were better than the typical crystals they found elsewhere. The two men thinned out their wallets, and Cephis freed up shelf space for new, freshly-mined McCurtain gems.

As the three men walked out of the treasure shed, Graffham spotted something rather odd lying on a shelf near the door. They were fossils. A closer look revealed them to be from a dinosaur. Cephis quickly noticed Graffham's interest.

"Those are a couple of loose fossils I found in the forest and I don't know what they are," Cephis said.

"What you may have here is the high-spined lizard," Graffham responded.

Cephis paid scant attention to the comment, thinking it was said in jest. He had never heard of such a thing as the "high-spined lizard."

As Graffham walked out the door, he handed Cephis his business card.

"Call me if you ever need anything," Graffham said.

Cephis stuck the card in his wallet without looking at it. Graffham and Edgar got in their car and drove away.

The two men had entered Cephis' world for the first time, and it would not be the last. Little did Cephis know that Graffham was a renowned commercial fossil dealer and Edgar had influential ties to the state capitol.

Cephis retired to bed early; grueling work awaited him and Sid the next day.

Before sunrise that following morning, Sid showed up at his best friend's front door in time for breakfast. After stuffing themselves on pancakes, eggs, biscuits, bacon and gravy, the two men drove off in search of a fresh ensemble of bones.

Shortly after arriving and unloading their tools, they began the ritual of chipping away at the matrix. A tunnel about five feet wide, three to four feet high, and about twelve feet deep had been dug into the interior. Their dogged determination had propelled them within reach of a treasure trove of ossified antiquities. As soon as a single fossil – or a few – could be distinguished inside the cavity, the vague silhouettes of other mystifying bones were detected. On the periphery, new bones were continuously cropping into view.

The two anonymous diggers had struck a Comstock Lode in the midst of an obscure paleontological site. Nobody had ever made a significant dinosaur find in McCurtain County. The area was too wet to house a fossil fabrication preserve. Dinosaur remains are rarely found in the forest.

Inside the mine, the men uncovered several bones flattened and fused by pyrite. The ribs were not curved, but shattered by the overburden and proved particularly onerous to dislodge. They had to be taken out in blocks, and would take more than a month to retrieve. The recovery of the vertebrae and attached dorsal spines followed in logical sequence.

The two men innovated as necessary. They used sturdy, custom made wooden boxes hand-crafted by Sid and cushioned with sheets of foam rubber to protect the valuables and keep them secure. Plastic milk crates were used to store and transport small pieces of plant material and other small rarities.

Open-air containers ensured adequate ventilation. They screened the dirt to sort out small pieces of vegetative matter, tiny mammal fossils, stomach stones (gastroliths), bits of dinosaur feces (coprolites) and assorted small relics. That task was accomplished via the use of small boxes with 1/4" to 1/16" screens. Every inch of sub-surface compaction was combed and sifted. Nothing was taken for granted. Scientists could pick and choose what was valuable and worthy of scrutiny. Posterity would know the full truth of what was overlain and recovered from this ancient grave.

Each fossil ready to be removed from the impoundment received an application of sealer to harden and preserve it. Elmer's Glue was used to fill in the cracks. A jacket enclosure of burlap strips was placed around weak pieces before handling. Despite great caution and care, some bones still shattered. They cleaned, reconfigured and restored the fossils the best they could.

Sid took photos of the fossils in their natural geologic context and again after having been recovered as distinct pieces. He also made homemade videos and hand sketches of the bone bed showing each piece in relation to others. For amateurs, the duo was uniquely organized and approached the complicated task with a spirit of professionalism that approached – or in some cases exceeded – experienced field scientists.

Safely removing the vertebrae and dorsal spines from the crusty matrix was of utmost importance and required a cautious and methodical pace. The vertebrae with attached spines were the unique core attributes of the specimen – perhaps the defining characteristic of the mysterious species.

Some of the dorsal spines were separated from the vertebrae, while others were still attached. They dislodged each vertebra separately and paired the loose spines with their matching vertebrae. In some instances, vertebra were fused together with pyrite and had to be taken out as an intact clump.

The spines extending from the vertebrae spanned two feet and represented a primal and mysterious dinosaurian accessory. They were the key to unlocking the riddle of this mysterious beast. The specimen was not a T.rex. Much older and rarer, it was as big and ferocious as T.rex.

While removing the ribs, they detected a skeletal pattern with a semblance of articulation. To delineate this structure, they paired the liberated pieces with those still imbedded. Chevron spines, vertebrae, neural spines, arms, hands, and shoulder blades were all discerned as an outline of an articulated skeleton.

They had photographs and real bones to show the world, but at this point, all they wanted was positive identification. But for the time being, they wanted to remain anonymous and keep their quarry a secret. The world would simply have to wait until they sorted things out. Their secret would be revealed at the right moment and place and they didn't yet know when and where that would be.

This was a forensic case. The crime scene was one hundred million years old. There had been a death, and the bones were all that were left to tell the story. They needed to consult a professional to identify the post-mortem remains, but didn't know whom to consult, or whom to trust.

They settled on contacting Dr. Bob Slaughter, a paleontologist at Southern Methodist University in Dallas, because SMU was the nearest university with a trained paleontologist on staff.

Clear photos with quality images were presented for Slaughter's examination. To their amazement, Slaughter was unable to identify the dinosaur. He believed it was a large plant-eating dinosaur from the Antlers Formation of the lower Cretaceous. Beyond that, he offered no suggestions, referrals or assistance. The two fossil extractors were baffled and disappointed. Had they uncovered something so rare that not even an expert forensic paleontologist could unlock its riddle?

They had presented compelling evidence that their specimen was a meat-eating theropod with spines extending from its vertebrae. The photographs depicted hollow bones, and they had mentioned that to Dr. Slaughter. The photos of the vertebrae with protruding back-spines should have been a clear cue for speculation; few North American dinosaurs, herbivorous or carnivorous, manifested such a trait. The two men were unsure where to turn or what to do next. Hopefully, there was an expert somewhere who might be able to pin a name and identity on their rusticated denizen.

The situation had Cephis worried. He stayed awake at night thinking about how to sidestep the pitfalls and surmount the obstacles. His obsession strained his relationships. Some people thought he was crazy and didn't understand what he was doing. All his family, except Joyce, was losing faith. Despite being demoralized by this lack of support, he was determined to stay the course. There was no turning back; they had crossed the Rubicon. There was no quitting, they were in too deep. Somehow, they had to get approval from the owner. Somehow, they had to complete the dig.

CHAPTER SIXTEEN
In the Pathway of Travail

Two ornery bone prospectors were in a whammy of a dilemma. They had uncovered the remains of a rare and valuable dinosaur, but on private property that wasn't their own. This fact raised a number of troubling questions. Their lives were about to get more complicated as they became imbued in an imbroglio of intrigue, conflict, and controversy.

They were a relentless duo immersed in an urgent mission to save the remains of a unique dinosaurian specimen—a specimen clouded in mystery and perplexity. The fossil recovery team had invested too much time and money to merely walk away or turn the project over to the landowner or an outside interventionist. Besides, they had a vested interest in the ultimate outcome—they had attained an intimate attachment to the memory of the creature—deep to the core of its bones.

The duo harbored an ingrained fear that the owner would have no interest in completing the dig. He was unlikely to share their passion or their appreciation for the fossils. That owner was likely Weyerhaeuser, a gigantic, multi-national corporation and one of the largest landowners in the world. But could the corporation's inherent indifference, obtuseness, and lack of appreciation for nature and the tenets of science work to their advantage? Could a couple of homespun backwoodsmen put the mighty corporation at ease with their mission?

There was a slight chance that they might be able to sort of squeeze through the cracks and go unnoticed in the larger scheme of things. A pile of antiquated bones probably had no relevance to a stressed cadre of corporate officials bent on achieving the corporation's short term goals of making the numbers to impress Wall Street and appease higher management at corporate headquarters.

The giant timber empire was not owned or controlled by one man or family; it was like a monster octopus with many tentacles or layers of management stretching out in all directions at many heights and levels. This realization dawned on the two tunnel trenchers like a pristine silver bullet striking them squarely in their foreheads. Their strategy was obvious—they had to access the appropriate level of management.

Going to the very top of the corporate pyramid was out of the question—it was just not feasible. Corporate headquarters was too distant, too aloof, and too impersonal. The "bigwigs" in Tacoma probably wouldn't even talk to a pair of "local yokels" from the backwoods of southeastern Oklahoma.

Going to the lowest rung of the managerial ladder might promptly invite suspicion or intrusion. They might have better luck approaching the corporate hierarchy at the regional level. That level was far-enough removed from the daily workings at the local office to have an interest in "localized dinosaur poop" and too distant from national headquarters to be held directly accountable. It was perhaps their best forum for manipulating "the corporate system" to their advantage.

They had no definite proof that Weyerhaeuser actually owned the riverfront property that had for so long harbored a secluded bed of arcane fossils. People had told them Weyerhaeuser owned the land, but what did they know? Obviously, the Craig Fiber Board Plant located about a mile to the west was part of the vast Weyerhaeuser domain. Accordingly, it was plausible to assume that the eastbound, riverine front was part of that same tract—after all, it was a repository for waste and toxic chemicals washed downhill from that facility.

They couldn't take the obvious for granted by prying directly into the local affairs of the Craig Plant and inviting suspicion. Confronting rank and file employees at the plant might alert management. It would be time-consuming and cumbersome to go to the county tax office and research the elusive ownership veil of an austere piece of riverfront property. They needed confirmation of ownership from an inside source that wouldn't elicit suspicion. Cephis actually had a connection through his boss, a private contract-logger who was on Weyerhaeuser's payroll, and he was also acquainted with a member of Weyerhaeuser's management team.

John Piezyck, a Weyerhaeuser supervisor over the contract loggers, was a kind of green horn from the Pacific Northwest and relatively new to the logging trade. He was still learning the ropes from a kind of bottoms-up approach.

Piezyck, rather good natured and well liked by logging employees, was a link between the contractors and corporation. The logging employees worked for the contractor and were not under Weyerhaeuser's managerial umbrella. Piezyck was more like an inspector than a supervisor.

Cephis had met Piezyck on the job site and would never forget their first encounter, and neither would Piezyck. Piezyck was young and naively interacted with the rough-hewn lumberjacks, who sometimes took advantage of him.

On one instance, Piezyck sat down for a free-spirited conversation with the stump-edged loggers and in a feeling of camaraderie began inadvertently chewing tobacco and dipping Copenhagen snuff. Instead of impressing the rednecks, he made a spectacle of himself. He doubled up and spilled out the contents of his gut on the open ground in full view of a watchful audience. He was too raw, his stomach too sensitive. The backwoodsmen got a chuckle out of it, but Piezyck's troubles for the day were not over. Later that afternoon, he suffered another misfortune when a tree fell on top of him. It was just not his day.

While conducting his routine inspections, Piezyck unknowingly walked into the pathway of a falling tree cut by Cephis and was knocked to the ground. Fortunately, only the branches, and not the trunk, nailed him. Although visibly shaken, Piezyck came out from under the limbs with only a few bruises. Cephis was relieved.

Despite this singular setback, Piezyck was on his way up in the organization. He was a fast learner who got along well with people.

Piezyck would certainly know if Weyerhaeuser owned the riverfront property to the east of the Craig Plant, and Cephis was eager to ask him. Cephis and Sid needed a sense of direction in order to successfully navigate through the labyrinth of Weyerhaeuser's multi-tiered, managerial structure. Cephis hoped Piezyck could give them a referral and set them in the right direction.

Piezyck confirmed that Weyerhaeuser did, in fact, own the riverfront land and that it was part of the Craig tract. Piezyck, without suspicion, referred him to a man named Joe Bueno at the regional office in Wright City, about thirty miles northwest of Broken Bow.

Cephis hoped Bueno was a man detached from the mundane activities of the Craig Plant, and also a man lacking interest in such things as dinosaurs and fossils. Maybe Bueno had more to worry about than a dingy dig along the river's edge?

His span of managerial oversight was much broader than the Craig Fiberboard Plant. He had responsibility over almost two million acres of land in southeastern Oklahoma and southwestern Arkansas. Why would he care about a little bone digging along a secluded bend of the river? And what would a coterie of stressed-out, corporatized, middle managers know about dinosaurs? Probably not much! The less they knew the better. The further away they stayed the better still.

If Cephis obtained approval from Bueno, the local managers of the Craig Plant would likely consent and stay out of the way. This was the best the two fossil proprietors could hope for—an unmolested continuance of their dig and ultimately the completion of their mission. Cephis started making plans to visit Wright City and talk to Bueno.

CHAPTER SEVENTEEN
Cephis Lays It on the Line

Over a span of weeks, Cephis repeatedly attempted to schedule an appointment and engineer a public relations coup with the regional manager of the giant timber corporation, but failed. The duo continued the dig, even as outside temperatures soared to a brutal 103 degrees. Despite working in a dark cave that offered shelter from the blistering sun, there was no escaping the heat and misery.

The electric lamp, powered by an outside generator, gave off light, but also considerable heat. The conditions inside the manhole were cramped and confining, with barely enough room for one man to maneuver. The monotonous chipping of the matrix sent dust and debris whirling about. The two men's backs ached, their knees buckled, their arms and wrists throbbed, and sweat poured.

Cephis, normally a toiler in red dirt, was plastered with a grayish haze from the swirling dust unloosed by the chops of his pick. A bit haggard and stooped, he emerged from the hole "bone tired" to get a breath of fresh air. And rest? Why rest was for people who did not dig dinosaurs or decapitate pine trees.

This was not glamorous work. Few comprehended, least of all appreciated, the physical sacrifice of such an undertaking. People might wonder and marvel at the amazing treasures displayed at fabulous museums – the gigantic bones of extinct prehistoric beasts – but had no concept of the sacrifices made to recover such a prize from the bowels of a begrudging earth.

The two bone liberators extended their reach inside the wall cavity to almost fourteen feet. More bones came into view – reminding them of how much further they had to dig. The endeavor was reaching a limit; they had dug about as far as they could in a tunneling mode. Even with the installation of support beams and braces inside the tunnel, it was still dangerous. They were at a point where they could either count their bones and walk away, or secure permission to use a backhoe to clear the overburden.

Although they had chosen the most difficult path to excavation by hand-tunneling straight into the wall stratum, they had also taken the most conservative route in an earnest effort to save the skeleton. Had they initially scooped into the surface level with heavy equipment, they would have run the risk of digging too deeply and scouring fossils. The weight of a backhoe bucket could easily crush a whole layer of precious bones.

Thus far, the two diggers were on a roll – a slow, torturous movement that by any stretch of the imagination was progress. They might be progressing at a snail's pace, but at least they had saved the bones – thus far. The two men had much to be proud of. Few amateurs had managed to get this far in recovering an articulated skeleton without calling the professionals to finish the job.

There was nothing intricate or fancy about their project. Keeping it simple – that was the southern way. Complexity was to be avoided at all costs, and the two men could afford little monetary losses. Anybody trying to cut corners would surely have garnered a different result. This was really no job for unfinanced amateurs, yet they met each challenge with vigor and enthusiasm. They had achieved success on a level equivalent, or perhaps exceeding, that of highly-experienced field paleontologists. They were out to prove something to themselves and the world.

They had recovered a femur, a tibia, and a number of ribs, vertebrae, and spines, and were moving in closer to a whole new crop of bones. Amazingly, they were doing everything right and had a reasonable chance of uncovering the entire skeleton, or at least what was left of it. No matter how many fossils had been lost to the elements, the two had a significant discovery.

Over the past week, Cephis had repeatedly called Bueno's office to set up a meeting. His secretary always gave some excuse—Bueno was out of the office, in a meeting, or just not available. Cephis knew he was getting the run-around, but he persisted. Maybe the secretary would eventually get tired of putting him off and finally let him talk to the elusive Bueno.

At last his timing was right. The secretary answered the phone and stated that Mr. Bueno was in the office, and then inquired about the nature of his business. Cephis explained that he was seeking permission to dig up some fossils down on the Mountain Fork and wanted an appointment with Bueno. The secretary put him on hold and came back with an answer—Mr. Bueno could meet with him that Thursday afternoon. Cephis quickly consented.

Two days later, Cephis showed up at Bueno's office in Wright City, hoping that Bueno was a reliable manager who kept his appointments and his word. The secretary led Cephis into a private conference room where he was met by the boss.

Bueno had a certain machismo and swagger that sometimes comes with a title such as manager. His appearance and demeanor cast him as a man of "timbered" importance. The walls sported sundry plaques and awards attesting Bueno's devoted service to the company.

Bueno, like Napoleon, was a rather short, stocky man who stood about five feet eight inches tall and weighed 180 pounds. To Cephis's dismay, he was from New Jersey or somewhere on the East Coast judging from his distinct accent— "a damn Yankee." Initially, the boss seemed more like a city slicker or paper shuffler than a log cutter – perhaps a little incongruous in a leafy province where hicks habituated the sticks and pine trees shaded the landscape.

The pompous Bueno made an interesting quick study. Although a little pudgy in the middle, he was tanned and seemingly fit. With a no-nonsense look, he was a bit like cardboard—somewhat smooth, but rough on the edges. He had a sharp, raspy voice that left little room for compromise. As they sat down, Cephis studied the man more closely, a clearer image formed.

Bueno was a little too rude to be a true gentleman, too rough and tumble to be urbane, too crude to be genteel, and too boorish to be a sophisticate. Although schooled and citified, he seemed more like a blue collar knave who had risen in the dismal ranks of hard hats and now puffed on cigars as a show of bravado to remind the under-caste of his meteoric rise.

Despite almost complete dominance over its realm, the giant timber corp tried to maintain a flexible public relations front with the local community. At this moment in time, Boss Bueno held the fate of both the diggers and the bones at his discretion. The life-long dream of Cephis Hall, and his elusive horizon of paleontological aspirations, hung in the balance.

In medieval times, the great manorial lords, less than half of one percent of the population of Europe, owned all the forest lands and only they could hunt, cut trees, or for that matter, dig, on those sacrosanct lands. In the twentieth century, there were still great landlords and such, but their dominion over the forests had diminished.

The medieval serf had to display the proper gesture of submission when imploring the lord of the manor. A peasant might be required to prostate himself before his lord. Thanks to the liberal reforms of the Enlightenment Age, such servile social conventions were no longer appropriate.

As they began to talk, it became apparent that several things were working in Cephis' favor: the audacious Bueno knew little or nothing about dinosaurs and for that matter didn't care; he was burdened with many company concerns and didn't want to spend time hassling with worthless fossils.

Perhaps Bueno was a reasonable man who wanted nothing more than to be left alone to handle company business and fulfill his obligations to the organization. Maybe he would make the first move. As for Cephis, he was willing to pay his dues. If Bueno were going to ask a favor, he would do his best to fulfill it. Hopefully, the meeting would engender a stamp of approval for completion of the mission with no onerous strings attached.

Cephis could not offer him a bribe—as efficient as such a transaction might seem on the surface. But given the gravity of what was at stake, even that deplorable option couldn't be taken completely off the table. Desperate men can do desperate things. Above all, Cephis was a practical man and well aware of the stakes. The bones had priority here, not some chivalrous code or conventional play on morality.

Cephis was sure Bueno had no idea what was at stake or how important his decision would become for the future of the bone diggers, the dinosaur, and the science of paleontology. For Bueno, the issue was mundane and of small account; for Cephis

Hall, it was a crucial and pivotal moment of his life. For science, it would prove to be a momentous decision.

A cigar-chewing, corporate officiate sat across the table from a good old country boy. Bueno brusquely scoured the modest woodcutter with an aloof, skeptical stare. Perhaps it was his method of intimidation. Anyway, there was no doubt about who was in control. The meeting was being held on Bueno's watch and the corporation, through the personage of Bueno, would dictate the terms.

Cephis, normally vociferous, was very reserved. Although Bueno somewhat talked down to him, like a lord to his serf, Cephis desperately wanted to work things out. He was a submissive petitioner who didn't want to annoy the man in any way. His whole paleontological future rested on the decision of this one man.

As Cephis and Bueno engaged the issues, an undertone feeling of "If you don't cause me any trouble, I won't cause you any" seemed to surface. Both men had responsibilities that were, frankly, a little tiring, and both wanted to move on as quickly as possible.

Apparently feeling detached and indifferent, Bueno tried to contain his impatience with the irrelevant spiel emanating straight from the mouth of an authentic southern backwoodsman. He acted as if he had little time to waste in a conversation with a rustic commoner about an obscure pile of bones.

Looking at Cephis with flinty eyes, Bueno shifted in his chair and glanced deliberately at his watch. "Mr. Hall," he said in a chilly tone, "I'm a busy man. What can I do for you?"

"Well," began Cephis, "I found some bones near the Mountain Fork. I think they might be dinosaur bones. I've done some hand digging and recovered a few pieces. I like to dig up fossils like that there feller over in Choctaw County. I might need a backhoe to recover those that are left. I do rock and fossil collecting for a hobby."

Bueno listened politely, but skeptically. He knew Cephis worked for a Weyerhaeuser logging contractor and his trustworthiness could be verified from his employer; that basic fact alone warranted a paltry consideration. If the request were legitimate and harmless, it might be seriously entertained. What could be so bad about an eccentric hillbilly digging up a few bones near the river? Besides, Weyerhaeuser, as a legacy from the Dierks' era, still allowed people to hunt, fish, and graze cattle on company land.

But Bueno framed his principal concern with a question: "Can we depend on you to maintain a low profile and not go to the media about this?"

"Yesseh, I will mind my own business, and not tell anybody, least of all the newspaper folks," said Cephis.

"Can we also count on you not to take your friends out on company land to snoop around or cause problems?"

"Yesseh, of course."

A dinosaur skeleton in McCurtain County was rarer than the elusive footprints of Big Foot. Dinosaurs are rarely ever found in forests. Bueno must have prefigured that whatever this insouciant hillbilly was digging up on company land, it was likely of no consequence.

Bueno, rather prosaic in his own right, was simply incapable of conceiving anything significant coming from the labors of what he erroneously perceived as a babbling, pining "buffoon." The request to dig seemed harmless enough—at least he was not poaching, growing marijuana, or cooking methamphetamines.

Bueno was not aware of any specific laws that prohibited dinosaur digging on the company's timberlands. Neither was he aware of any specific company policy that addressed or governed the digging of animal bones on company land.

Bueno responded to Cephis in typical bureaucratic fashion. He stated he needed to talk to his superiors in Tacoma, Washington, and would try to have an answer for him in a few weeks. This was not exactly what Cephis wanted to hear, but it did leave room for hope. By mutual understanding, Cephis agreed to stop digging until permission was granted. The two men quietly exchanged courtesies and Cephis walked out of the conference room and headed home.

Cephis now had to wait on an arbitrary, bureaucratic response from out of state. Permission to continue the dig hinged on one of the most important landowner decisions of modern paleontological history. The fate of the bones rested on that decision.

CHAPTER EIGHTEEN
Despairing Minds

The bone excavators were stymied in a limbo of uncertainty—held in suspense by the arcane proclivities and caprice of a multi-national corporation based in far-away Tacoma, Washington. Their life-long goals and aspirations were held in check by a toplofty decision to be handed down from the epicenter of a nebulous corporate hierarchy centered in the luxurious suites at the national headquarters. The diggers were held captive by the arbitrary mind of the Corporation.

While the bone question sifted through the lofty halls of corporate headquarters, the mind of Cephis Hall fluctuated across a wide spectrum of emotions—some rational, others irrational. Although he agreed to stop digging until permission was granted, he wondered what he would do if approval was denied or put on indefinite hold. What if the decision was never made or simply shuffled to a "suspense file" and held in limbo indefinitely? Possibly, the decision might be lost in the vastness of the corporation with no single person or office having been delegated responsibility to decide the issue. Perhaps nobody within the immense organization wanted to assume responsibility or accountability for the problem, and it had been pocket-vetoed and derogated to die a slow, corporate death due to lack of interest.

In that scenario, what would Cephis Hall—a man built and primed for action—do? Could he simply let his dream sit idly by while the bones disintegrated into dust? Could he fathom the loss of one of the greatest dinosaurian specimens of history? He knew he already had too much time, money, and emotional energy invested to sit passively while the ultimate dinosaur specimen of the twentieth century eroded away.

Neglect, indifference, and bureaucratic inertia could seal the fate of the bones. But what could he do? His hands were tied. If he were caught shoveling dirt before the question was decided, his hope for approval might be jeopardized. If discovered digging after a denial had been issued, he could be charged with trespassing and thrown in the dungeon.

The diggers had not fully anticipated the psychological turmoil that accompanied a feeling of powerlessness. The Corporation was pulling the strings, and they were the puppets. The bone collectors found themselves in an indeterminate waiting mode that fostered a delirious dilemma and wariness.

The ambitious duo was impatient. They were galvanized for action and success, not inaction and failure. To be restrained by an elusive and capricious corporate regime was almost unbearable. To sit patiently and wait on a distant and dubious decision from an aloof corporate boardroom was simply untenable.

The two diggers were engulfed in a "quagmire of bones" that captivated them, but also smothered them in a state of bewilderment. They had to find a distraction to absorb their energies and attention while the issue worked its way through the grist mill of the corporate decision-making process. While they waited on their answer, they needed to find a way to move forward with their endeavor without violating the terms of their agreement not to dig.

They decided that this psychological stand-down presented a timely opportunity to resume their attempt to learn the identity of their partially unearthed specimen. If they could learn its identity, at least they might know what the world would lose if their request was denied. As a last resort, if the specimen was as rare and unique as they suspected, they might be able to convince Weyerhaeuser of the scientific worthiness of the project and the need for professionals to finish the job. Maybe they might even be allowed to continue their participation alongside the professionals. If they couldn't get full access, it was better to have limited participation and recognition. Most of all, it was imperative that the skeleton be saved.

The duo had struck out on their previous attempt to get the creature identified. Maybe this time they needed to consult with a different kind of scientist or institution. On this new attempt, Cephis decided to reach out to a modest university—a small town college rather than a rich, hallowed institution in a metropolis. Dr. Slaughter, at the prestigious Southern Methodist University, had been a flop, and it had not been particularly pleasant dealing with him. They wanted to find a competent scientist who was more casual and down-to-earth—a man more like themselves.

The two men did researching and telephoning in an attempt to locate scientists able to lend assistance in identifying the specimen. With few paleontologists in Oklahoma, they extended their search into nearby states. They were not having much luck until a tip came in from a friend in Oklahoma City, Chet Hazelwood, who had a personal contact with an acclaimed professor at Midwestern State University in Wichita Falls, Texas. Hazelwood personally knew Dr. Walter Dalquest, and provided his phone number.

What they learned about Dalquest was intriguing, and several things were particularly appealing. He was not a paleontologist, but a biologist—more specifically a vertebrate zoologist—and considered top-notch in his specialty. He was very versatile and adept in the field—a true naturalist and field scientist.

Working as a biology professor at MSU since 1952, he had published seven books and 173 research articles in mammalogy, ornithology, ichthyology, and vertebrate paleontology. He was self-educated in the field of paleontology—a credential that particularly appealed to Cephis. Interestingly, he had the distinction of having had a new genus and species of primate, *Diablomomys dalquesti*, named in his honor. Finally,

Dalquest was noted for his distinguished study of the mammals of Veracruz, and had been dubbed one of the last truly great hands-on American mammalogists.

Amateur naturalists like Hall and Love could identify with this man. He was an inspiration. Dalquest was the closest thing Cephis had found to his hero and mentor— Edward Drinker Cope—a man who, like himself, had learned the science of paleontology and the art of fossil digging by trial and error and hands-on endeavor.

Although Dalquest did not hold a degree in paleontology, he had extensive field experience and knowledge of dinosaurs. What they wanted was a hands-on guy with intimate knowledge of fossils—a man who had not just studied them, but dug and handled them in the routine course of business. Paleontologist or biologist, it didn't matter—intimacy with the bones was the crucial credential. To them, Dr. Slaughter seemed more like an arm-chaired elitist than a true field scientist.

MSU had a different institutional flavor than SMU. It was a small but highly respected public institution located in a modest city amidst the tumbling prairie flats of northwest Texas. Dalquest had chosen to tenure at this small university of about 6,000 students—a fact that revealed something about his character that was particularly appealing to the two country boys. Cephis wasted no time in contacting the prospect; no interview was needed, only a willingness to examine the fossils and venture an opinion.

The telephone conversation with Dr. Dalquest went well. Dalquest agreed to inspect the fossils and do his best to identify them. Cephis mailed him some very clear photos, the most important ones being of the vertebrae and spines.

Within a few days, Dalquest responded by phone with an answer. The two men had indeed uncovered a marvelously rare and unique specimen. Their minds were temporarily put at ease— a reprieve from the corporate intrigue that had suspended their digging and held the project at bay. Finally, they knew what they had been digging, and what they hoped to rescue from the stranglehold of Mother Earth. All they needed was a reasonable and compliant corporation. Science would be the repository and beneficiary of an ensuing data flow about one of the planet's greatest predators. The specimen might even prove to be a missing link in the theropodian line of descent. If they could finish the project, it would prove to be a win-win situation, for both themselves and paleontology.

CHAPTER NINETEEN
The Identity of the Creature is Revealed

The creature had finally been identified. The mystery that palled over the enigmatic pile of bones was lifted. The river's edge had delivered up a long-dormant secret that would befuddle and mystify the world of science and laity alike. Ancient McCurtain County had once hosted one of the greatest predators of all time, and its legacy would soon be unveiled and introduced to the world. The riddle wrapped in an enigma and enshrouded in a confounding conundrum had yielded to tangible reality. The pile of elusive bones could now be penned with an identity and connection to the ancient past.

Infused with passion and impatience to resume the dig, the indomitable Hall was confined and held at the tender mercies of an arbitrary corporate hierarchy. This was an almost unbearable predicament and had captured the ardent prospector in its woeful throes. The corporation had cramped his style of action and stifled his ambition.

Desperate for any positive word, Cephis continued to call Mr. Bueno's office about their pending request. Each time he was brusquely informed that Bueno had not received a response from his superiors. The corporate chain of command was slow and cumbersome. Perhaps the answer had to trickle down through several layers of management until it reached Bueno personally.

The anxious bone liberators were kept on edge in a state of inanimate uncertainty. The bones had been encapsulated – frozen in time – in a period now known as the Cretaceous, but were ready to be liberated. The two bonesmen were also suspended in time pending Weyerhaeuser's approval. But how long would it be?

Every day the suspended bones were left untended meant a potential loss for science and their ambitions. A half-exposed dinosaurian quarry was vulnerable to the harsh elements and the wanton depredations of uncaring humans. How long could they sit and wait for an arbitrary, hierarchical decision to filter through a far-flung corporate informational loop comprising several layers of management?

They wondered how the world would greet their new specimen, if they were allowed to save it. Surely it would prove quite intriguing. It was big. It was ferocious. And it was mysterious. The high spines on its back added a new dimension—making it alluring and compelling as a rare and unique predatory specimen. Perhaps the scientific data to ultimately accrue might elucidate a new chapter in dinosaurian genealogy or a new era of "theropodian enlightenment."

Dinosaurs have long provided a fascination for modern humans. They harken back to an enchantment with giant, reptilian-like dragons that are couched in mythology, fantasy, heroics, and medieval lore. In both classical and medieval times, bones retrieved loose from earthen works were considered to be dragon bones, and the folklore that accompanied these bones romanticized the aura of the medieval dragon slayer. The dragon that was slain by the chivalrous knight was, in reality, a dinosaur.

The Chinese continue to hold a resounding degree of reverence for the bones of dragons and dinosaurs. The bones of such creatures are both precious icons and utilitarian products at the same time. China now has stringent government programs in place to protect dinosaur fossils on their lands. Once considered simply irreverent, it is now also criminal for a Chinese peasant to deface or discard these sacrosanct relics of nature and folklore. Even to this very day, the Chinese consider the mythical bones a sacrament and grind them into medicines and aphrodisiac potions.

Children are especially enamored of dinosaurs, and the mystifying creatures have a captivating hold on their imaginations. The fantastic size and ferocity of these monstrous beasts are conspicuously evident, yet they are safe as a child fantasy because they no longer exist as living animals.

Dinosaurs are a unique blend of fantasy and reality, and allow children, and even adults, to be scared – but at a safe distance. Dinosaurs leave plenty for the human imagination and satisfy a need for adventurous curiosity. In all their mystique and intrigue, they shed light on man's place in nature and the universe. Beginning in the late seventeenth century with the dawning of the Scientific Age, as reason replaced mysticism, there has been a movement away from using the supernatural as explanation for all things mysterious and unapparent. Gradually, the concept of the dinosaur became rooted in empirical science rather than mythology, religion, or folklore.

Dinosaurs also allow children and adults alike to engage in mental time travel, while at the same time providing a transcendent reality by dispelling the pervasive anthropocentric bias that places humans as the measure of all things. Cultures that worship an anthropomorphic god as their deity of preference may wish to isolate the bones as irrelevant relics of an archaic mythology that is far removed from modern orthodox theology. The dinosaurs ruled the earth for tens of millions of years before humans arrived to establish their celestially sanctified rule.

For Cephis Hall, the dinosaur represented a more practical proposition rather than a "divinely enthralled memento" to be worshipped or a magical potion to be internalized. Worshiping dinosaurs was one thing; extracting them from the earth, another. Scientific empiricism and faith-based mysticism were irreconcilable to Hall, an ardent champion of fossil-based scientism. The grinding of bones into medicines or aphrodisiacs had no relevance for him; the right to dig up the remains was the overriding concern. Science was his forte, not mysticism or religion. In Hall's mind, the bones were so rare and enthralling that they deserved a place of permanence in nature – of hardened solidity to be possessed by the generations throughout the ages. It was all about tangible intactness, preservation, and display.

Finding the fossils is difficult enough; excavating them, a more daunting challenge; but getting them into a prepared collection presents another set of obstacles. These almost insurmountable difficulties are compounded beyond the pain of description if there is an ownership or property rights dispute – especially when the contester is an all-powerful economic institution with almost limitless resources.

The telephone call from Dr. Dalquest came like a bright array of sunshine and cast fresh air over a cloudy and convoluted spectrum. Light was shone on darkness, hope sprinkled amidst pessimism, and clarity supplanted confusion. "You have found the mysterious, high-spined lizard," stated Dalquest, "and you were right about some of your assumptions." Cephis's ears perked and his heart skipped a beat.

The high-spined lizard was known from only a few bits and pieces found here and there, mostly in Oklahoma and Texas. No articulated skeleton of the species had ever been found. The creature was named *Acrocanthosaurus atokensis* by two legendary scientists, J.Willis Stovall and Wann Langston of the University of Oklahoma. In 1950, the two men had found a few fossils of the creature in neighboring Atoka County, to the northwest of Broken Bow. The name "Acrocanthosaurus" was coined in recognition of the high spines on the animal's back, while "atokensis" was so chosen after the county in which the first bones were found. It was definitely a native of Oklahoma and considered a "Lone Star dinosaur" in neighboring Texas. The word "akros" in Greek means high, the word "akantha" means thorn or spine, and "sauros," of course, means lizard.

Before Cephis and Sid's discovery, only limb bones, vertebrae, a few spines, and assorted teeth from the monster had been found and recorded. This giant carnivore lived in the early Cretaceous, roughly 115-100 mya, mostly in semi-tropical areas near the sea. It was a saurischian (lizard hipped) dinosaur, and believed to be the apex predator in North America during that period. In fact, it was the largest bipedal theropod to have ever lived on the continent, with the sole exception of T. rex, who arrived some 45 million years later. Most likely, it stepped in to fill the void as apex predator of North America that was left open after *Allosaurus* went extinct in the late Jurassic. Since a few remains of the animal had also been found in Utah and Maryland, it was believed to have inhabited the entire continent, but definitely thrived in the South.

Its two outstanding characteristics were the protruding spines on its neck, back, and tail, and the three claws reaching out from each forelimb. The wicked, curved claws of the *Acrocanthosaurus* measured about six inches in length and were a unique killing accessory endowed by a Mother Nature bent on bestowing maximum efficiency in capturing and holding prey, as well as tearing flesh apart from bones.

Its thin, sharp, serrated teeth were lethal to the bite. These teeth, like steak knives, were designed for tearing flesh apart, just as the claws; whereas, the larger, more conical-shaped teeth of the T. rex, like railroad spikes, were designed for crushing bones. The Acro was better designed for killing than scavenging and ate flesh, not bones.

Dalquest informed Cephis that the fossils examined from the photographs matched existing Acro findings. If that was not enough to peg the creature, the unique vertebrae and attached spines were a dead giveaway — no other North American animal of the Cretaceous era was known to have such features. The Acro was a one-of-a-kind.

Although the mysterious spines may have been the conspicuous anatomical apparatus that allowed Dalquest to identify the specimen, the high spines remained the most baffling physiological component of the animal's skeleton and posed daunting evolutionary questions. Science had not arrived at a reasonable consensus on what purpose the high spines served. Speculation had preceded and would abound in the future as scientists scrutinized the newly catalogued bones.

The typical, generic postulations assumed the spines served as a fearsome display to competitors or a sexual attractant to a potential mate, or might have been involved in such mundane things as communication, fat storage, or temperature regulation. However, the most compelling thesis to emanate out of the scientific community was that the spines supported a ridge of muscle over the animal's neck, back, and hips. Rather than supporting a skin sail like *Spinosaurus*, the spines had attachments for powerful muscles like those of a modern bison, probably forming a tall, thick ridge down its back. This anatomical arrangement allowed more surface area for the attachment of large muscle and ligament sheets, which awarded the Acro a suspension bridge-like stability in grappling large prey or yanking carcasses to a safe feeding spot. This was a truly powerful predator with uniquely adapted tools for catching, holding, killing, and eating its prey.

This monster was blessed with the most advanced killing instruments ever possessed by a dinosaurian apex predator, including some of the most efficient tools for capturing prey. Nothing matched the efficiency of this specialized killing machine until the arrival of the raptors. Even still, it would likely take four or five of the typical small raptors to match the killing power of one Acro. This ultimate predator was larger than *Allosaurus* and may have been larger than T. rex.

An exceptional raptor that could likely lower the odds against Acro was the giant Utah Raptor. Like the Acro, this fearsome predator, a native of Mongolia, arrived on the North American continent in the late Jurassic after *Allosaurus* had departed the scene. These terrible flesh slashers played a leading role in the movie *Jurassic Park*. They were kick boxers whose wicked hind feet were transformed into large curved knives that could disembowel with a single thrust. They were more than twice the size of the average raptor and weighed a thousand pounds or more.

These creatures, like most birds, were monogamous and formed bonds of male-female pairs that hunted together and shared the parental duties of caring for their own nest of chicks. A single pair of these vicious killers may have been a close match for a single adult Acro. In Robert T. Bakker's extraordinary book, *Raptor Red,* the leading character, a female Utah Raptor, and her mate meet up with an adult ridge-backed Acro and the battle scene is true carnage.

The family structures of both the raptors and acros were likely built around a large female – a pattern which is rare in meat-eating reptiles and mammals, but is the norm for one category of predators – carnivorous birds like owls, hawks, and eagles. For many paleontologists, raptors, tyrannosaurs, and other flesh-eating theropods are seen as giant, ground-running birds. Fossil trackways of ridge-backed acrocanthosaurs found in Texas show them hunting in pairs like Utah Raptors as they stalk herds of herbivores (Bakker, *Raptor Red*).

Both the raptors and acrocanthosaurs emerged on the North American continent sometime between the end of the Jurassic and the beginning of the Cretaceous and were in fierce competition to corner the meat market. Many paleontologists believe the raptors and acros were both related to *Allosaurus,* but their lines of descent have not been determined. Both the acros and raptors inherited significant features of the allosauroid body plan.

The claw design of the raptors departed somewhat from that of the allosauroid family by transforming a talon fit for grabbing and holding prey into a weapon for slashing (Bakker*).* The unique evolutionary design of their wrist bones gave the entire allosaur hand the capacity to swivel quickly from side to side; the raptors had managed to retain that swivel feature of the allosauroid hand design. The raptors were masters of the quick dash and slash – they ran up to their victims and slashed with Ginsu knife-like claws (Bakker).

The ridge-backed acros retained, virtually intact, the complete allosauroid hand claws with the thick tips designed more for holding prey than slashing. The raptors discarded the archaic allosauroid model forepaws by evolving long, slender fingers that wielded narrow, knife-like claws (Bakker). Having retained the allosauroid foreclaw features, the acros are generally considered a closer relative to the *Allosaurus* than are raptors.

The Acro foreclaws were shaped more like grappling hooks than steak knives. Notably, the Acro was blessed with substantially larger and stronger forearms than T. rex. The forearms of T. rex were very short and small, and not evolved for the purpose of grappling with giant sauropods.

Although the acros were at the top of the food chain in the early Cretaceous, the Utah Raptors were one notch below them. Very likely, they both attacked sauropods. The acros usually attacked them in pairs; the Utah Raptors likely hunted smaller herbivores in pairs and sauropods in large packs. The two species of predators used different techniques of predation – the acros were grapplers with enormous body strength and balance for wrestling giant sauropods, while the Utah Raptors were kickers and slashers, pure and simple. Most likely, these two top predators occasionally stole kills from one another. The Acro's *coup de grace* was the bite rather than the slash.

The acros probably arrived on the North American scene first and prevailed at the top of the food chain for millions of years until their numbers crashed. Their extinction opened the door for a short-term ascension of the Utah Raptor, which colonized the low-lying floodplains and river-edge forests that had previously been dominated by the acrocanthosaur clans. After the acros left the stage, the Utah Raptor reigned as top predator for approximately two million years and was likely superseded by more diverse flocks of smaller raptors (Bakker*)*.

The back spines of the *Acrocanthosaurus* were likely unique appendants evolved to aid in the technique of killing, and were not a sail-fin for display or temperature regulation. Endowed with the latest evolutionary tricks of the trade in the avocation of predation, the *Acrocanthosaurus* may have been the ultimate killing machine. This was no mere fish eater. The monster preyed heavily on sauropods and ornithopods, and was more than a mere swamp dweller like *Spinosaurus*. A subsequent analysis of the creature's feet revealed that it had small, four-digit feet (each footprint had three toes pointing forward and one pointing back – the typical avian pattern) and flat, instead of curved, claws, making it more mobile on rocky and hard surfaces. The creature may have ranged across the entire North American landscape (Neal Larson, *Dinosaurs Illustrated*, Winter Edition, 1996).

This uniquely equipped predator may have been ordained with an evolutionary calling to balance the population of sauropods during the late Jurassic. By preying on the over-populated sauropods, it provided stability and homeostasis to an unbalanced ecosystem. Apparently, the *Allosaurus* had not been up to the task. During its reign as apex predator, sauropod populations soared. The Acro – or something – must have checked their population as sauropod numbers had plummeted by the early Cretaceous Period.

This was the same dinosaur whose fossilized footprints had been discovered along the rocky banks of the Paluxy River at Dinosaur Valley State Park near Glen Rose, Texas, by the legendary Roland T. Bird. The tracks, later identified as belonging to an Acro, were discovered in 1938 when R.T., as he was called, was in Texas tracking dinosaurs for Barnum Brown and The American Museum of Natural History. Bird was an eccentric field collector for Brown and traveled across the great American West and Mexico on a Harley-Davison motorcycle looking for fossils.

The tracks were astounding and captured a fleeting moment in time when a large, lunging carnivore chased a thirty-ton sauropod (*Brontosaurus*) along a central Texas stream now known as the Paluxy River, a tributary of the Brazos. The footprints of the two beasts were indelibly etched in the sediments which, over time, became rock. The fearless and determined theropod was in hot pursuit of the giant, and its footprints paralleled those of the sauropod—indicating it may have gotten close enough to take a brutal bite or thrash a deep laceration. Unfortunately, the outcome of the chase could not be determined; the tracks abruptly terminated before the contest was decided. Near where the tracks overlap, one of the theropod tracks is missing, as if contact was made and the carnivore was lifted off the ground and carried along by the larger, wounded animal (Jacobs 8).

Although not enough pieces of the animal were found to postulate a family history for the Acro, the swamp-borne spinosauridae family was definitely ruled out. Despite the common back spines phenomenon shared by the two races, *Spinosaurus* and its brethren were unequivocally from North Africa and apparently descended along a different evolutionary pathway. Because of the paucity of recorded acrocanthosaur fossils, not much else was known about it. The fossil record was skimpy and fragmentary; consequently, the species remained elusive for over thirty years.

Trying to enlighten his fellow field explorers, Dr. Dalquest did his best to relate his analysis and conclusion to the two inquisitors; however, there just wasn't much information out there. Although the lack of scientific knowledge about the species failed to quench Hall's thirst for detail, the sparseness of data about the species was actually a positive; it made the merit of the excavation and the product of the dig ever more worthy.

Dalquest ended the conversation by supplying a last tidbit of information – a referral. One of the scientists who had first encountered and named the species was still alive and practicing paleontology in Texas. Dr. Wann Langston had been a student of the famed J. Willis Stovall and was with him when the first Acro bones were found. These two men had recorded the bones in the archive and published research papers on the elusive predator. Dr. Stovall had passed on, but Langston was now the head paleontologist at the University of Texas in Austin and was considered the foremost living authority on the *Acrocanthosaurus*.

Before ending the conversation, Dr. Dalquest asked permission to forward copies of the photographs to Dr. Langston at UT for a final confirmation. Cephis consented. Langston received the photos and later affirmed Dalquest's identification. There would be no doubt; their specimen was a true member of the *Acrocanthosaurus* family.

Cephis was elated. His creature was unique – a rare comportment of the most advanced killing equipment of its time, and perhaps prior and thereafter. His dream of discovery had come true. This was exactly what he had hoped for. T. rex was common and redundant and, compared to this specimen, was rather a bore. This was unique, rare, intriguing, and exciting! His discovery criteria were satisfied and he couldn't ask for anything better.

But as quickly as his euphoria spiked, hard reality set in and tempered his elation and enchantment. The duo had sunk their shaft into one of the single greatest dinosaur quarries of history, but a mighty corporation stood in their way and threatened to turn a rich and active lode into an abandoned mine. It would be virtually impossible to complete their dig without the acquiescence of the most powerful economic institution in southeastern Oklahoma. Cephis eagerly got on the phone to relate Dr. Dalquest's news to Sid. Tomorrow he would call the office of Mr. Bueno and again inquire about their pending request to continue their dig.

CHAPTER TWENTY
The Boss Lays Down the Law

Cephis Hall had always desired to have his name recognized within that growing class of explorers and discoverers oft described as amateur paleontologists. These are the lonesome scouts and fossil hunters, who work behind the scenes, find most of the fossils, volunteer their labor, but get little of the credit and remain largely anonymous outside the circles of paleontological networks.

For the amateur, in order to obtain true recognition in the eyes of the public, it was necessary not only to make the discovery, but to extricate the specimen from the natural impoundment and be in the forefront of its introduction to an awaiting world. Once the excavation is turned over to a scientific team, the professionals end up with the glory and recognition for a successful recovery.

For Hall and Love, the onerous demands of excavation were almost insurmountable and more than an amateur could expect to overcome. There were pitfalls and road blocks at every turn, and always something to obstruct the course and remind the navigators of the challenges that lay ahead.

But Cephis had thrust his spade into the solid core of the quarry, digging deep into the stratum with abounding energy and determination. The project had potential to become a prototype for a successful amateur excavation of a major quarry by a two-man team operating on piddling resources. If they were successful in their recovery, they would become noteworthy in the world of science. If they failed, they would remain anonymous, and science would also lose. Their paleontological net worth was intrinsically linked to the inherent value of the bones.

Cephis and Sid had before them a specimen that met all the criteria for being a truly great discovery. If T.rex was already famous, this theropod dinosaur had equal or even greater potential. It was approximately the same size as T.rex,[*] lived about forty million years earlier, and served essentially the same role in the ecological order of North America – that of top line, apex predator. T.rex was king during the late Cretaceous; the Acrocanthosaurus was king during the early Cretaceous. But the Hall-Love specimen was different from T.rex in several respects. It was more rare and mysterious, and uniquely adapted for a specialized predatory function as a skillful grappler of giant sauropods. (*The size of dinos is constantly being reevaluated, and the trend in many cases is toward larger sizes than had previously been evaluated.)

Like the dinosaur, the two bone liberators had a thick crust of overburden hanging over them. Had they gotten in too deep? Were they already embedded in a quagmire? Even if they managed to get approval from Weyerhaeuser, they still faced a long road of recovery. They were encumbered by an obsession and could not turn it loose. Where would it all end? The ordeal was taking on a dimension and dynamic of its own that was starting to spiral out of control.

An obsession with a dinosaur can be a costly proposition. One case in point was the excavation and cleaning of the giant Seismosaurus (later renamed *Diplodocus hallorum*) discovered in New Mexico by David Gillette, the state paleontologist for Utah, in 1983. This gigantic sauropod, one of the largest ever recorded, was estimated to be as long as 150 feet and over 100 tons in weight. Gillette estimated that the excavation project would last his entire life, cost more than a million dollars to complete, and take five additional man-years, at $25,000 a year, to merely clean the bones. Still, even with that daunting task in front of him, he could not thwart his obsession. Without hesitation, he plunged head-long into the arduous project and could not call a halt, despite the odds. (Lessem, *Kings of Creation*)

The obsession can spur an impractical undertaking – costly beyond one's means in labor, time and money. Obsession can catapult one over the brink of a realistic paleontological endeavor, even to the point of financial ruin. It is necessary to get financing to cover the costs of excavation, transportation, storage and preparation. If not associated with an institution with deep pockets, one must by necessity undergo debt obligations or personal expenditures to satisfy the dictates of the lingering obsession.

Most excavators get scientific grants. In the case of Hall and Love, two amateurs were investing their own time and money and operating on a shoe-string budget. No salary, no grant, no financing, no back-up logistical support from a scientific institution, and no institutional sponsorship of any kind had been bestowed. But for now, that was the way they wanted it. Perhaps it was an obsessive case of grandiose naivete, but they wanted to do it their way. These were rash and bold proprietors building bone equity through muscle, sweat, and sheer dogged determination.

They were confident in their abilities to extricate the skeleton, but were not sure of the intricacies involved in the preservation and display of the specimen. Cephis was brash and daring while unafraid of publicity or self promotion; but he knew he was sinking into uncharted waters, and mud was already bogging him down. Getting the bones out of the earth was just the first stage of their project – the ultimate goal was a display mount in a major science museum. Many bones – some stupendous and mystifying beyond the norm – have never been named or catalogued and continue to gather dust as they sit idly for decades in university storage rooms.

Scientific protocol demands that a new discovery be announced by a formal description enumerated by scientific detail and a research thesis. The enormous cost, labor, and public interest in the Seismosaurus led Gillette to go public with his record-setting find long before he was able to complete the dig or analyze what he had dug up. That was the part of the project Hall and Love could not handle—they couldn't tell anybody about their discovery until they had dug and carted off the very last bone. Publicity is fine, but sooner or later, one needs to get the fossils into a prepared collection, and that is the real challenge. Even if Weyerhaeuser approved the dig, their difficulties and challenges were far from over. In fact, they were just beginning.

They were seeking to recover fossilized treasure buried on private land and not just any private land—this was land owned by one of the most powerful landowners in the world. If they didn't secure permission from Weyerhaeuser to dig and were caught in the act, they could be prosecuted for trespassing or theft. Still, even if they managed to recover the bones with permission, Weyerhaeuser might come back and contest ownership.

The precedents of law specify that on private lands the fossils belong to the landowner or revert to the landowner if they have not been deeded to or purchased by the fossil finder. If a landowner gives a fossil prospector oral permission to search on his land, is that tantamount to conveying ownership of any fossilized material recovered thereon? In their case, they were not seeking permission to prospect; they had already done that. They were seeking to recover what they had already found, and the landowner appeared to have no interest whatsoever in their fossils.

On public lands, title is retained by the public, which means the rights of ownership are usually transferred to a pre-designated public educational institution that is notified by the governmental land supervisor and accorded all rights of excavation in the public interest. Hence all paleontological riches become the possession of the public institution – usually a local university with a museum.

But in the case of Weyerhaeuser, things were a little convoluted and blurred – It was often difficult to determine where private enterprise ended and where public government started. It was a mixed economy, with Weyerhaeuser participating at all levels of economic activity and governmental involvement. The base of Weyerhaeuser influence extended out from the roots of the forest to all locales and levels of government from city hall to the federal bureaucracy. There existed a nebulous and reciprocal relationship between the private realm and public helm where money flowed back and forth between Weyerhaeuser and all levels of government – between private government and public government. One could not readily determine whether Weyerhaeuser roads or infrastructure was built by public or private finance. It was all a complicated maze.

Money flowed from several sources and in all directions to grease the machinery and keep the econo-politico system running smoothly. Tax revenues flowed in and funds were subsequently dispersed in accordance with the influence of lobbyists and special interest pressure groups. Politicians were bought and corporate-friendly tax policies, de-regulations, and subsidies doled out. Weyerhaeuser, like virtually all mega-corporations, had its hands in the public trough and subsidized the public till at the same time. Through revolving doors, the private and public interest had converged in what investment guru Jim Cramer has called a government of, for, and by the corporations.

Even though Weyerhaeuser was assumed to be a private entity, the two bone impresarios were fearful that some intrusive arm of public government, even the police, might come sniffing around and peering into their business. The situation seemed forever hazy, perilous, and uncertain.

To their advantage, the private landowner, Weyerhaeuser, was indifferent and had no conception of the true value of the fossils. The company assumed they were either worthless or of miniscule value. The landowner, as represented by regional land manager, Joe Bueno, just didn't want to be involved. He had a rather cavalier attitude – just don't bother me or take up any of my time. There was no time allotted for hillbillies or bones.

Weyerhaeuser was in the paper and building materials business – obscure and dormant fossils lying around on their vast timberlands were the least of their concerns. It was simply inconceivable for these production-minded, profits-driven, cost-conscious, efficiency-obsessed timber magnates to associate a world class fossil specimen with some diminutive, backwoods hillbilly. In their minds, Hall was not a legitimate scientific-minded explorer and excavator of the natural world, but a mere simpleton and charlatan.

For them, a credible scientific field project could only be conducted by men with esteemed credentials from renowned institutions who were full-fledged members of the scientific meritocracy. Amateurs like Hall were mere hobbyists and pretenders who did not know what they were doing, and since they were small scale, their project was bound to be down scale. Alas, they just wanted to get the hillbilly out of their hair and let him dig in the dirt on his own time.

After a long wait and many failed attempts, Cephis finally had Bueno on the phone. At last, Bueno was ready to give him an answer. Bueno stated he had talked to higher management and they had merely kicked the decision back down to the lower level and left it all in his hands.

In the spirit of maintaining harmonious relations with the local community, Bueno had decided to let the hillbilly dig but needed to have another face to face meeting to iron out the details. Also, Bueno wanted to see a few of the fossils as literal proof that it was really animal bones they were digging up and not something else. Cephis agreed to bring a few pieces and suggested they meet at the museum. Bueno concurred.

Bueno iterated that he was going to be in Idabel that Thursday evening and it would be convenient to meet on that day. Cephis obliged, and the meeting was set for Thursday at 7:00 P.M. at the Museum of the Red River.

Cephis and Sid knew that Weyerhaeuser was going to set the terms and lay down the law. They hoped the strings to be attached wouldn't bind them in merciless knots.

Their best hope was that Weyerhaeuser would just forget about them and stay away from the dig.

Although the meeting was supposed to confer the right to dig, the two amateurs hoped the meeting would emanate an unequivocal clarification regarding ownership of the bones. Bueno had asked them to bring a few pieces to the meeting for inspection, but would he set some kind of unwieldy terms requiring them to present their freshly recovered bones to the company for periodic inspection and possible confiscation? It was a dicey situation and left them in a state of dazed suspense.

Cephis did not want the meeting to become bogged down with legalistic questions and concerns – the more informal the meeting and terms of the agreement, the better. He knew the more the law was brought into the transaction, the more Weyerhaeuser was empowered. The laws, courts, and governments all favored the corporation. Two ordinary citizens, a hillbilly and an Indian, didn't stand a chance against such a monstrosity of money and power. It was kind of like begging the system for crumbs.

Cephis did not know exactly what to expect from the corporation. Would it engage in Machiavellian tactics to elevate the princely timber lords and decimate the lowly timber boors? The Corporation had the heavy hand and could slam it down on their worn fingers at any moment. It was used to getting its way in McCurtain County and had at its disposal an entire arsenal of stratagems and resources (financial, legal, and political) that could knock the two trifling prospectors dead out of the water with a double barrel blast like Dick Cheney on the hunting range with a sally of buckshot.

The legal system favored the participant with the deepest pockets and the most political clout, and that meant Weyerhaeuser. The police and local media knew who was prominent in the community and who was impertinent. Would the Corporation require paper work, contracts, and written agreements? Did they need lawyers? Would this affair turn into a legal fiasco?

Nothing legalistic had been mentioned by Bueno. Cephis would not beg the issue. He would come as the usual, down-home Cephis Hall—folksy, gregarious, informal, unpretentious, and straight forward. He would be as honest and direct as possible. Since the bones were unimportant to the Corporation, perhaps the meeting would be short and informal and not ensnare them in any odious or onerous bone-manifested stipulations.

Cephis was a man who always tried to be organized and prepared. He was not looking for an explicit written agreement, but needed a witness to what actually transpired at the meeting.

Cephis had a casual relationship with Greg Perino, the director of the Museum of the Red River. The two men had similar interests and collaborated on cultural antiquities prospects. Hall, the foremost naturalist of McCurtain County, was constantly prospecting the backlands and wetlands of McCurtain County in search of nature's bounty and sometimes came across archaeological prospects that interested Perino.

Greg Perino, like many of the citizens of McCurtain County, was of mixed Irish and Indian ancestry. He had come to the Museum of the Red River from the vaunted Gilchrest Museum of Tulsa. Antiquities and museums were his life calling. He was particularly interested in Indian artifacts, but also liked rocks. Perino was an expert on American Indian culture and had written several books on the subject.

Over the years of their association, Cephis had discovered several Indian burial sites throughout McCurtain County of Caddo or early Choctaw origin and introduced Greg to their locations. On a few occasions, Hall and Perino inspected the sites together. The two men shared mutual respect and trust.

Cephis had wisely suggested the museum as the meeting place. Bueno had taken the bait, never suspecting that the scraggy hillbilly had professional connections to the museum curator. Perino was working late that evening to make sure he was on hand for the fireworks.

As he walked into the museum, Joe Bueno, the quintessential corporate henchman, exuded confidence like a man who was in control. Cephis and Sid were less confident; they knew the Corporation was packing the ordnance and calling the shots. Upon arrival, the participants, Cephis, Sid, and Bueno, were taken to the conference room and the meeting got underway.

The parley had brought together an odd collectivity of personalities: a tall, lean and mean, loquacious hillbilly, a taciturn, short and rotund Choctow, an officious and imperious corporate timber magnate, and a scientifically-minded connoisseur of Native-American culture. Cephis Hall and Sid Love, the galvanized proponents of amateur paleontology, contrasted sharply with the formalized officiate of corporate self interest, regional executive Joe Bueno. The die was cast. The result of this meeting would determine the fate of the dinosaur and the paleontological future of the two backwater naturalists.

The four participants were seated at a large conference table. Cephis and Sid sat across from Mr. Bueno. At the end of the table sat the mediator of the contest, Greg Perino, the inscrutable museum curator who peered across the table through his rimmed spectacles at the imposing cast of motley and contrasting images. The conference had brought a strange consort of protagonists and imperatives face-to-face – the organizational man against entrepreneurs; formality contrasting informality; polished business attire differentiating casual dress; rigid legalism set against flexible opportunism; dogmatic corporate rationalism opposed to free-spirited naturalism; hierarchical symbolism and elitism astride from backwoods eccentricity and individuality; oligopolistic franchise versus free-enterprise; monopolistic dominance overshadowing free market initiative; and globalism versus provincialism.

Rather than Bueno playing the role of arch dictator, Perino would serve as facilitator to help foster a meeting of the minds. Perino's presence undoubtedly moderated the tone. He was a representative of an important institution within the community and served as a watchdog on Bueno. The issue of community relations became more relevant in this social context, and Bueno was compelled to spin a friendly face and project a positive corporate image.

The first order of business was the inspection of a sample of bones. Cephis brought in a box of assorted pieces consisting of a vertebra without the spine, an ankle bone, and a rib bone. Bueno dismissively looked at the bones without making any comments. He had no idea what they were. They might have been nothing but ubiquitous cow bones. Whatever they were, they failed to make an impression on him. He asked no questions and showed no curiosity. Presumably, he assumed they were worthless and was hence satisfied that the two-man bone consortium was really doing what they claimed.

The meeting lasted about thirty minutes. Sid was quiet throughout the discussion but paid close attention. Perino spoke few words. Bueno and Cephis did most of the talking. A sort of terse, sketchy agreement was ironed out, and the terms were specified orally. Since Weyerhaeuser had no official policy concerning fossil excavation on company land, Bueno refused to give any kind of written agreement.

Bueno stated in uncertain terms that Weyerhaeuser was not interested in the fossils and did not want to be involved in the project. The company would not provide any financial backing or support. No money, manpower, or equipment would be provided. Cephis retorted that he did not expect any.

Bueno mentioned no objection to the use of a backhoe to clear the overburden and didn't specify any details about how the land should be refurbished or restored. He did, however, request that the diggers maintain a low profile and avoid any publicity. No company inspection or visit was implied. He basically said: "Go dig; we won't bother you as long as you don't cause any problems."

The parties came to terms on this referendum on bones. Although Cephis and Sid had not secured written permission to dig, they obtained oral consent and had a witness to that fact. A burden was lifted from their chests. As they walked out of the museum that late summer of 1983, they felt that Weyerhaeuser was a good corporate citizen, and Bueno an honest and honorable man. Although not aware of it at the time, the two men had made a Faustian bargain.

They also felt elated because no onerous strings were attached to their excavation project. They were given the opportunity to put their minds back to work on the mine – a mine of enchanted bones lying in seclusion near the river bank. The moment called for some celebration and planning. A few cold beers would taste good. Back to the drawing board, they would resume the dig Saturday morning. The stage was set for a resumption of a long term, two-man, organized dig of dinosaurian proportion.

CHAPTER TWENTY-ONE
Overshadowing the Dig

Cephis and Sid left the museum that Thursday evening in a mood to celebrate. They were tempted to stop at the local tavern for a couple of cold beers but had second thoughts. Both men had given up alcohol years prior. They decided to map out their plans for the resumption of the dig in complete sobriety. Instead of the tavern, they stopped at a local family restaurant in Broken Bow, the Pier 49 on Highway 70, for an old fashioned, southern-styled meal of chicken fried steak, mashed potatoes with gravy, cornbread muffins, and green beans.

Over the conviviality of iced tea, they mapped their strategy for their ultimate conquest. They could not believe their luck. Weyerhaeuser had agreed to let them dig with virtually no strings attached. They were determined to make the most of their situation and win.

Still, these two ardent champions of nature—of rocks, dinosaurs, and fossils—were a bit uneasy with their long-term prospect. They knew the odds were long and the deck stacked against them. But having accepted that kernel of truth, their dream of a successful excavation was still a perceptible prospect, although perhaps a bit quixotic.

Regardless of the odds, they would give it their best shot. If they failed, they would not be blaming themselves. Most importantly, they wouldn't be filled with regrets about not trying hard enough and abandoning their dreams too early. Casting their treacherous obstacles aside, the two bone-driven exploiters of the Antlers Formation made ready to delve ever more deeply into the fossil-rimmed stratum of the early Cretaceous.

The obsession had propelled them onward and gotten them this far—perhaps it could take them all the way. Despite their lingering concerns about Weyerhaeuser's potential contest of ownership, the dig was on—although a bit of the previous zeal and naivete had faded. With a more rational and cautious stance, they forged ahead.

They were aware they might be investing thousands of dollars and man-hours on the project only to see it pilfered away by Weyerhaeuser's grasping hands. Despite the goodwill gesture by Bueno, they didn't trust the giant corporation. But like Gillette, they could not quit. The obsession had taken over their lives, and their lives would never be the same.

In a few days, the month of November would be upon them, and they could expect rainier and cooler weather. Winter would arrive to transform the landscape and impede their bone investiture. Still, wintry weather or not, they would be in the dinosaur catacombs gathering bones on every weekend and days off that Mother Nature could accommodate them. Weather permitting, the big dig would resume that Saturday morning.

The ruthless climatic elements were a normal part of any paleontological project and could not be factored out of the equation. During winter, they endured freezing temperatures and the chill of cold, northerly winds. In the summer, they contended with heat, humidity, and mosquitoes. The spring brought torrential rains and flash floods. They were working on Oklahoma's good earth, a place where weather swiftly fluctuated to extremes. Although the vexatious climate posed a disconcerting challenge, they were more concerned about other issues.

The obstinate entrepreneurs were engaged in a Herculean mining venture that would push them to their limits in time, resources, and capital. The dig looked as if it had no end. They felt more like battle-hardened warriors than bone-vested miners. The two peerless fossil collectors braved the elements and fought a protracted war against Father Time and Mother Nature. And there was always that ominous overhang—the looming prospect of Weyerhaeuser stepping in at any moment and clouding their bone horizon. The risks were numerous; the rewards, enticing. The dig continued on in sunny or cloudy weather.

The duo proved to be consummate dino diggers. They carved out a mine some fourteen- feet deep into the wall of the gully. From that vantage point, they determined that a bounty of bones lay in waiting and they were determined to get their hands on them.

The dinosaur skeleton was housed within a 30 x 40 foot quarry, but they wouldn't figure that out until almost three years into the future when the last remaining pieces were freed from their hallowed resting place. The bone bed was about six feet below the ground surface with easy access from the gully basin. The duo had excavated a hazardous tunnel complex braced by 4"x 4" posts with plywood sheets on top to prevent the roof from collapsing. However, inside the makeshift innovation, the duo never felt secure.

For the two nimble navigators of the Cretaceous strata, their research on dinosaurs was paying off. They now knew enough about dino anatomy to make a preliminary identification of the recovered fossils. They measured and sized the ends of the bones against adjacent appendages to decipher the skeletal arrangement, piece by piece. They made diagrams and temporary reconfigurations of the bones, while leaving the rest for the professionals to figure out.

The duo had expertise with more than fossils; they also knew the basics of geology and botany. They were aware that a sand layer with greenish tint was indicative of a marine layer, and had determined that their sand layer was not green. Although they worked in the midst of an ancient wet layer, it was not of oceanic origin. The two men were realistic; they knew that education could take them only so far in the field—the rest is instinct, and that is where they excelled.

The two men were cognizant of diverse strains of botanical life decorating the river-worn landscape and reveled in that diversity. They observed sparse patches of wildflowers growing in shadowed areas amidst the scattered willows. The riverfront area was still relatively pristine. Although the area had not been logged, some of the top sand had been commercially dug and hauled off decades prior. These lovely wildflowers had attained a foothold. Some were wild iris cloaked in every color of the rainbow.

Sid was a botanical enthusiast of the first order—native wildflowers were one of his passions. In keeping with his Indian heritage, he knew the names of virtually every local plant and flower, as well as which species were edible or not. Cephis learned from Sid that greenbrier twigs made a delightful salad. Like a true botanical hobbyist, Sid photographed the flowers and placed the images in collection albums. Throughout history, North American Indian cultures have had close association with natural herbs—appreciating their raw beauty and reaping their utilitarian gifts to man.

Cephis dug up a few of the flowers and tried planting them in his yard, but, as Sid had advised him, they did not live. They are picky about their habitat and are found only in a few rare places. By the late twentieth century, many species were isolated within the confines of large commercial estates, and Indians and hillbillies no longer had easy access to their enjoyment. Native flowers remain part of the eroding legacy of the Great American Wilderness.

Within the dig parameters, the craftsmen uncovered a rich bounty of petrified plant material with scientific merit in their own right, but it proved difficult enough to entice the scientific community to give a diligent assessment of the bones, let alone the plants. These two wild crafters of Cretaceous-laden flora were unable to interest botanists in their herbivorous fossils. Only the zest and zeal of a genuine *Acrocanthosaurus* interested science professionals.

When Cephis and Sid pictured the Acro's world, they didn't see a lush tropical rainforest, but an Albian world of dull green and brown—of conifers, cycads, ferns, horsetails, and ginkgoes—plants that are flowerless. The undergrowth was composed mainly of short ferns, ground pines, low-growing horsetails, and conifer seedlings, while taller conifers and palm-leafed cycads hovered over them.

Flowering plants were just beginning to emerge during the early Cretaceous and barely had a foothold within the landscape. The ruling clans of acrocanthosaurs were being shaped by Darwinian forces unleashed within these archaic botanical settings. The flora of the Cretaceous era was still devoid of reproductive color—bright colors and fruit bearing plants were still millions of years into the future. Very likely, the changing vegetation pattern over time, particularly the rapid spread of flowering plants, had a considerable impact on the transient environment and helped foster the ultimate demise of the Acro species. As the flora evolved and changed, everything else either changed or became obsolete in the struggle for survival. Changing climate and vegetation have been the principal omens of extinction over the ages.

As Cephis knew well, education and experience are the harbingers of success. He had learned how to protect fossils during excavation by steadfastly watching removals of Indian artifacts from excavation sites. He watched the plastering method utilized on Indian artifacts collected locally, and observed museum staff removing burlap strips from artifacts. Plaster jackets wrapped around antiquities kept them intact—like a cast on a broken arm.

He knew that earthen-bound dinos are laid out in the classic death pose where the body is curled up in the fetal position with the skull and neck bending inward, while the tail, also bending inward, pointed toward the extended neck and skull. As in theory, that is the way it seemed to be panning out as the bones were discerned one by one and removed from the pit, bit by bit. About 90 percent of the pieces had to be plastered before being moved.

By identifying certain body parts of the dinosaur, they anticipated which pieces might be encountered next. Sid drew maps showing the placement of each fossil in relation to the others. On the map of the bone bed, they plotted the probable location of the next bone waiting to be unearthed.

The two modest bone proponents were beginning to feel like paragons of dinosaur reclamation, epitomizing a rise to full-fledged amateur paleontological status. Their elusive claim to distinction was earned through diligent field exertion and practical bone compilation. Once their skeleton was acknowledged by a scientific world in waiting, their names would radiate from the provincial backwaters of McCurtain County to the exclusive enclaves of paleontological society. In the eyes of the locals, the two men were a precursor for nature exploration, but in the wider world, they would become the prodigy of amateur paleontology.

Their honorary amateur distinction was garnered through gritty field work, rather than sedentary lab work. The two men were making their paleontological mark as true, blue-collar, working-class heroes. Through the machinations and exertions of their paleontological endeavor, they basked in an aura of brazen machismo and unrepentant bravado.

The project pitted two local and ornery rockhounds against a cold, indifferent world and enormous odds, but they would surmount each obstacle with tenacity, creativity, and flexibility. These rugged, self-taught naturalists tenaciously explored the backwoods and dug deep into nature's bounty the hard way. They were not the privileged, spoiled, or pampered offspring of the leisure class. Practicality and hard reality, not comfort and academic serenity, served as their modus operandi. Hard work, perseverance, and extensive field experience made up for their lack of formal education in the classroom.

For the two daring diggers, the project was like a cathartic experience—a means to sublimate all frustrations and pent-up anger onto the bone impoundment. The bones had consumed their excess energies; there was no time left for extraneous mischief. But ultimately, they would pay a heavy price for their bone indulgence.

Their bone affair extracted a costly toll on their families and social relations. Tensions and resentments developed as the duo spent too much time in the pit and neglected other people and matters. However, their affection for the bones bonded the two men ever closer, especially during the darkest period of their ensuing trials and tribulations. Solidarity was sealed in their solitary struggle, and their friendship thus strengthened.

The diggers were intrepid, hard-hat journeymen engaged in a trek back through time—an arcane traversal through the dense layers of crust leading all the way down to the Cretaceous shelf and a reclusive bed of bones. It was now time to free them from their enduring confinement by stripping the overburden to allow easier access. The hardened outcrop needed to be peeled back to facilitate retrieval of the more estranged bones.

Cephis and Sid discussed the matter thoroughly over southern steaks and iced tea. At the conference, they had informed Bueno of their wish to utilize a backhoe to scoop off the overburden. Bueno had not objected. In fact, he didn't even respond. He did not take them seriously.

The two men did not bother to mention that they had already gouged out a fourteen-foot cavity in the side of the gully and it was no longer safe to work inside the cave. It was unlikely that Bueno could fathom anything that significant or complex coming from the works of a pair of simple country bumpkins shoveling dirt on the river front.

The working conditions had become unbearable and the fossils almost inaccessible. They didn't figure it was necessary to tell the corporation every bit of their "bone bizness." Some things were better left untold. The corporation didn't give a damn about the bones. Bueno had made that adamantly clear. It may have been the corporation's land, but those were damned sure their bones.

They were a bit wary of official intrusion from the Craig factory managers. The Weyerhaeuser fiber-board plant was located approximately one mile west of the dig site and in close enough range to allow easy snooping by plant operators. Cephis had mentioned virtually nothing about the factory at the two meetings; he had merely cited it as a reference point to help Bueno pinpoint the approximate location. They weren't even sure if Bueno would notify Craig officials of the digging taking place on their eastern periphery. The two excavators had the impression that Bueno cared little about the fiber-board operation because it was not under his direct purview. The timberlands were his principal responsibility.

The two explorers knew they would sooner or later meet up with Craig management. Although the gully was inoperable as a containment reservoir, the plant managers needed to monitor the chemical effluents being discharged into the river from time to time. Surely they had not forgotten about environmental quality.

That Saturday, Cephis and Sid returned to their quarry, inspected the site, and performed limited excavation inside the hazardous tunnel. They made arrangements for a backhoe operator to come out to the site. The backhoe work would cost $350, about $35 an hour, with no charge for road travel—a bargain even in those days.

They needed to get the overburden lifted as soon as possible—time was always of the essence in the bone digging business, and the tunnel might cave in at any moment. Once the overburden was removed, the two resolute diggers could get to the marrow of the bone bed and make real progress.

They were back in business and felt elated that Weyerhaeuser had approved the dig. They also felt lucky that the dig site remained undisturbed during their extended, corporate-imposed moratorium on digging. The dig was being readied to take on a new scale and dimension. Sid and Cephis, in a southern expression, were going "whole hog."

CHAPTER TWENTY-TWO
On the River's Edge

Near the yellow tips of the maple trees, some 100 feet to the left side of the road, as many as 100 marijuana plants brazenly grew – standing idle, tall, and budding with majestic defiance and haughty contempt. Cephis and Sid knew they were there. They had traveled the road many times while going to and fro to reach their quarry—before daylight and well after dark—for over a year.

Whether Cephis and Sid approved of their cultivation or not was irrelevant; it would not be wise to alert the authorities, for that might bring attention to themselves and their own cultivation of treasure in the shadows of the tree-laden Mountain Fork. They ignored the marijuana plants and hoped their audacious owner-cultivators would, in turn, ignore them and their cache of cryptic bones. While the marijuana magnates harvested pot by the light of the moon, the fossil entrepreneurs harvested bones by the blaze of the sun.

Marijuana is a beguiling and lucrative crop—a major market component of an extensive underground economy. From its market springs cash and all the concomitant trappings of an illicit revenue stream. In the 1980s, marijuana was the new black market gold of McCurtain County. Since bootleg whiskey was bottle-necked and discarded in the early seventies, cannabis weed became the prime crop on the block—a cash-cow par excellence. While Weyerhaeuser grew timber on an industrial scale, clandestine, backwoods businessmen produced weed on a cottage scale right in Weyerhaeuser's backyard.

But the cannabis plant had a down side. It was a high-risk economic proposition—a blending of high dollars and high rollers. Like the roll of a dice, a sudden spree of bad luck might put the enterprising grower out of business, or in jail. To see a pot crop growing unmolested in a serene and secretive forest clearing with hired hands tenderly nurturing its growth was a bewitching experience that did not leave one's memory very rapidly. It broadcast a blatant warning and subliminal message—stay clear and mind your own.

Along the torn path of the Tonihka Crossing where covered wagons once rolled and roving bandits once trolled, splendid rows of well-tended and well-nourished marijuana plants grew. It was a small agricultural enterprise sandwiched inside a huge agricultural empire.

The diggers conjectured, "Was this a sweetheart-sanctioned business arrangement modeled after the old whiskey stills that once dotted the backwoods throughout the county? Was somebody being paid to look the other way?" They wanted no part of the crop. It was best just to ignore the weeds and stay out of the way—lest retribution be inflicted harshly against them from some unknown source. Their business was bones, not pot.

Marijuana haze or not, they needed to get back to work. The venture had been spurred with a new imperative – a sanctioned approval to get to the heart of the bones and rescue them as quickly as possible without needless corporate intrusion.

The reinvigorated bone emancipators hoped to tread a course free from the outstretched, imperial hands of Weyerhaeuser. Corporate intervention was neither wanted nor needed. The venture was basically theirs to construct or deconstruct as they saw fit and tempered with an enlightened spirit of harmony with the fossils.

In order to get to the core of the bones, the top of the tunnel needed to be shaved off by a backhoe. The operator, a local named Wesley Cassidy, arrived and started the task of lifting the burden off the bones. He scooped into the top of the overburden and removed the over layer to within two feet of the bone bed. After this masterful piece of earth sculpting, the whole nature of the quarry was transformed. Instead of a cave embedded in a wall of a gully, there was now a deep, wide trench intersecting an artificially constructed levee.

After removing the top of the tunnel, the mechanized excavator cut an extended furrow about twelve additional feet so that the total length of the trench was about twenty-six feet long and its width of equal distance. The 26'x26' trench was lopped to within two feet of the underlying bone bed. The balance of the two-foot overburden was dug by hand. The dig team now had an open pit mine with visible and easy access to a distinguished bone horizon. They no longer had to stoop or crawl inside a tunnel.

Now the excavation was streamlined and bones by the dozens were found and lifted out of the pit—forever freed from the gripping clutches of an intransigent Mother Earth. They could soon add shoulder blades, neck vertebrae, pelvis bones, the clavicle, tail pieces, etc., to the list. The backhoe had worked a miracle.

In the days of Marsh and Cope, there was no heavy earth moving equipment. The overburden was either hacked through with picks and shovels or blasted away with dynamite. But near the banks of the Mountain Fork, dynamite was too risky and would make too much noise.

But now with the overburden cleared, they had an eight-foot deep trench intruding into the heart of the Antlers Formation and were geared to spade their way to a new ensemble of captivating bones. An unprecedented bone conquest was in the making – a conquest spearheaded by two unknowns ready to unearth one of the greatest single dinosaur specimens in history.

The two Okies from McCurtain were undeterred by hard toil and gritty dirt work. In fact, they seemed to relish it. Nothing seemed to hold them back. Ordinary and unremarkable on the exterior, these men were endowed with a remarkable gullet of internal strengths and convictions. Cephis and Sid possessed extraordinary true grit and were set apart from the sedentary and leisured. They were the salt of the earth—sons of soil and toil.

The dig would go on for weeks, months, and years. Each alluring piece dug out of the pit was added to their growing inventory and accorded more detail to the unfolding mystery, while moving them closer, inch by inch, to their ultimate conquest. The score was tallied one bone at a time. Each day at the pit brought new challenges and new experiences. Many questions were raised along the way, and new people entered their bone horizon and dabbled in their "bone bidness."

They did not encounter many people at the pit during the chill of the winter. But during the heat of the summer, they played host to scores of curious strollers who plodded upon the scene, probed into their bone proceedings, and questioned their legitimacy. Over the course of several years, they were bound to run into a few strangers who just happened to be passing by. These random visitors were always a mystery because there was no way of knowing their true identity or purpose. Precaution with strangers was always the prudent course.

For the most part, the few people they encountered seemed to have a reason for being out on the lonely riverfront—hunting, fishing, or collecting were the most common motives. On one occasion, they met a transient ambler who seemed lost and disoriented—a drunken Indian who had wandered off the beaten path.

In their entire bone digging adventure, this single encounter with the intoxicated Indian was the most mysterious. He was just moseying around for no apparent reason, and they were unable to tie him to anything or anybody. He seemed to have come out of nowhere, like a misty forest shadow, and faded into the stillness like a ghost of the meadow.

Upon his encroachment, the befuddled rambler asked rather inquisitively, "What are you guys doing?"

Cephis answered. "Oh, we're just digging for old bones."

After wobbling a little, the inebriated red man retorted rather diffidently, "Well, there ought to be a bunch around here; ain't this a graveyard?"

Cephis tersely responded "No." He actually lied; this really was a graveyard—of a long-forsaken dino denizen of a hundred million year vintage.

They visited with him for awhile, and he went on his way. It was a casual encounter that raised several questions, but never amounted to anything. Was it just a chance meeting? Or was the lone Indian pulling an investigation on them? Was the loose Indian somebody important who was prying into their grave robbing? Was he some deranged psychotic prowling the woods? Or was he simply working for somebody important and monitoring their every move? The drunken Indian remained a mystery.

This was a curious, and possibly precarious, situation. Two men were vigorously digging in a concealed location along the river with marijuana plants all around. To add more suspense to a dubious situation, on occasion a helicopter whirled above them as if it were doing surveillance duty—either policing the backwoods for marijuana patches or scouting for intruders who might plunder or steal the precious weed. There was no way of knowing if the choppers were official or private. One thing was obvious: the marijuana grove was closely watched and guarded— nobody ever messed with the fertile fields of pot.

Constant anxiety taunted the diggers. There was always the haunting prospect of the site being molested by some mindless, bone-headed predator or pilfered by spontaneous bone rustlers. During the spring, heavy rains caused the river channel to rise and floodwaters spilled over the embankment and threatened to inundate the bone bed and turn the precious relics into a mushy, fungi-infested powder.

The harried bone conquerors were on the edge of a water-rimmed abyss and threatened by a counterattack from the forces of nature. The bone bed was endangered on two fronts— stream water flowing from the west could engulf the gully, while from the east, rising flood waters from the river could deluge the entire river valley. A hundred-year flood was overdue, and such a centennial event would put the two bone-capitalists out of business.

It was mandatory to get the bones freed from the outdoor elements as soon as possible, but that could not be accomplished in the mere span of weeks, even with the most advanced technology, the most competent and expeditious field crews, and the greatest paleontological minds of the century. The hard-boned, expeditor crew of two would not rest until all the bones were gathered up and warehoused under lock and key.

During the course of their protracted dig, they continued to be distracted, and sometimes baffled, by uninvited interlopers who happened upon the site and caught them in the act. Shoveling dirt and prying up bones along the river can bring unwanted scrutiny from suspicious intruders. The "bone maestros" spun fictional yarns and fantastic lies to keep the meddlers at bay. They used creative genius and made up anything to detract from the true nature of their affair – the extraction of deceased dinosaur parts from private land. Mammal bones might not be intriguing—but dinosaur bones were an entirely different proposition.

Dinosaur bones conjure up passionate feelings and stir up evolutionary dissension and latent, mystical sentiment. The ensuing bone tempest can arouse curiosities and elicit discomforting inquisitions. When caught with shovel in hand, they lied about what they were scooping up: petrified wood, tin cans, lead, Indian graves, arrowheads, water pipes, elephant bones, etc. For each person they encountered, they had a different explanation for their dubious activity. Some people must have thought them peculiar or eccentric, if not insane. The whole objective of the ruse was to hide their bones and the true nature of what they were doing from the rest of the world.

People came by car, foot, horseback, and on rare occasions, by motorcycle. Most of their business was down on the river—fishing, camping, or swimming. Since the bone site was not far from the river's edge, any inquisitive stroller might wander into the weeds and beat a path to the bone bed. With each novel intrusion, the bone diggers had to strategize a plan to deflect attention away from themselves and their ongoing project. Through cunning and guile, they managed to disperse each uninvited visitor on his merry way—hopefully in a state of delusion and with their curiosity satiated. The duo wanted to remain unseen, unbothered, and unremembered, but that was virtually impossible.

On one hot day in the middle of May, 1985, a couple on horseback rode up to the bone trench and found the duo digging away. The horse riders were immediately suspicious. They could not fathom a couple of eerie sod busters working inside a massive trench in the middle of nowhere. It was a disturbing and haunting encounter for them. As they rode off, Sid could hear the woman tell her male companion, "Don't ever come back down here again."

The woman was appalled at the sight of loose bones lying around. Bones and graves represent a ghastly and ghostly experience for many people. No matter what kinds of bones are being exhumed, the mere sight of them is unsettling – perhaps reminding people of a crime scene or their own mortality.

Not every visitor was a stranger. On one instance in the springtime, the duo was accosted by a pair of acquaintances. Charles Nation, the local mortician, and his friend, Jack Vaughn, were out in the boondocks hunting arrowheads and Indian artifacts when they stumbled upon the bone abyss. They already knew about the old gravel pit near the river, but didn't know about the dinosaur grave. They were surprised to find Cephis and Sid shoveling dirt in the bottom of a deep trench.

They saw a huge open pit, but no bones. A large amount of fool's gold (pyrite) was lying around. The ground appeared to be a blue clay color and texture. The four men conversed casually and Cephis and Sid confessed to what they were doing. They personally knew the two men and felt they were trustworthy. They asked them to keep it quiet and not tell anybody what they had seen. Nation and Vaughn agreed and kept their word.

The trench was getting wider and deeper. The uncanny expeditors used shovels to scoop up the loose clay and a jackhammer to burst through the seams of the stone-hard matrix. When close to the margins, they scrapped the substrate meticulously with curve-tipped screwdrivers and an assortment of delicate instruments. Each day before leaving, they covered up the holes and bones with a few inches of smooth dirt to conceal any evidence of recent digging.

They used ramps to move the larger clumps of matrix-encased bones from the trench and engineered a wooden bridge across the concrete abutment to move fossils mounted on plywood panels. The bridge was made of sixteen foot, 2"x6" boards laid flat across the gully and supported underneath by vertically placed 2"x6" braces.

Whenever an employee from the fiberboard plant drove up to the pit, Cephis and Sid nonchalantly tried to stay cool and keep their distance. The Craig employees didn't care about their excavation and posed no challenge or questions.

One frequent visitor to the site was an employee from the Craig plant named Harold James, a water quality tester who took water samples from inside the gully. He was friendly and amiable. Cephis and Sid liked him and did not mind his occasional visits.

There was always enough water in the gully to take a water sample. The fiberboard plant had given up on its efforts to impound water inside the gully. Erosion had worn around the containment weir, and the gate was continuously open. Water inside the gully was rarely deeper than three feet. Mr. James was charged with the responsibility of filling BOD bottles for Biological Oxygen Demand testing—a simple test for oxygen and chemicals in water. The EPA and state water board were responsible for evaluating the results of water samples taken by Mr. James.

The two rogue treasure hunters had reverence for the local environment despite blatant evidence all around them that many people did not. This riverfront haunt had become a second home for them. The ebbing flow of the river, the solace of the tree-lined riverside, and the majestic rising and setting of the sun against the panoramic silhouette of the forest had soothed their inner souls. In their view, this riverfront property was a sanctuary from the complexities and troubles of the modern world, but it was clear that some people did not see it their way.

They were deeply offended by the invasive sight of multiple piles of trash dumped beside the entrance road as it wove its way along the river. Weyerhaeuser's majestic riverfront property was egregiously despoiled by these sorted lumps of mini-landfills. These despicable heaps of rubbish were an abominable sin against the pristine innocence of the local river zone.

In the midst of their spiritual haven, these wanton mounds of trash were a defilement of the aesthetic values of the two riverine conservationists. But, like the illegal marijuana growing less than a hundred feet from the nearest trash heap, there was nothing they could do. Weyerhaeuser certainly had not given this sordid disposal practice their rubber stamp of approval, but neither did they diligently send out company cleanup crews from time to time to police this once-pristine area. Weyerhaeuser largely ignored this bend of the river, and that worked to the advantage of the two-man bone-salvaging crew.

They thought they understood Weyerhaeuser's environmental dilemma, but couldn't understand these blatant transgressions of laws and nature. They feared they would soon see even worse things dumped along the river—large agglomerations of tires, batteries, asphalt roofing shingles, and computer monitors. They wanted to see nature in the raw, not piles of manmade garbage.

Their die-hard reverence for raw nature was apparently not appreciated by a segment of the local populace. The two embattled diggers were goaded and gored from all sides, like a pair of hapless Sooners being trampled by rampaging Lone Star steers.

They would be attacked on the right by scornful comments made by hard-core anti-evolutionists, evangelicals, and anti-environmentalists; and on the left by enlightened, public-spirited scientists bent on ridding the badlands and backlands from the encroachments of commercial and amateur bone poachers.

The two men knew the score—for their concerns about "environmental incorrectness", they would be mislabeled all sorts of disparaging names: ecology freaks, tree huggers, greenies, nature worshipers, communists, prosperity haters, organic nuts, etc. For their attachment to the bones and their success in retrieving them, they would be called such things as grave robbers, bone hustlers, bone idolaters, and bone thieves.

The two "pristine naturalists" were sometimes unfairly stigmatized as environmental extremists by wrong-headed locals. Were they out of touch with the prevailing local sentiment or was a portion of the community out of touch with their bone-intoned reality?

Although these were not a pair of starry-eyed reformers bent on changing the conservative social order of southeastern Oklahoma, sometimes they were mistakenly stereotyped as impractical idealists or visionary mystics. In reality, they were bone-hardened realists. Cephis Hall, the Indian-Celt, and Sid Love, the Celtic-Indian, were two of McCurtain County's finest—true-blue, dyed-in-the-wool proponents of "scientific rationalism" and "pragmatic naturalism" who just happened to be fascinated by dinosaur bones. Despite the scurrilous epithets, they refused to be detracted and thrust forward with their spades.

Sid and Cephis learned to live with the myriad episodes of distraction that frequently accosted them along the riverfront. They had heavy bones to tend and a burdensome workload. The large clumps of matrix-coated bones were a bit heavy for just two men of average size. They moved heavy bone clusters up the steep sides of the trench or over the boardwalk across the gully and used winches to slowly crank the heavy chunks of matrix-encased bones into their pickup. They worked from daylight to dark in both scorching heat and shivering cold.

On a few occasions, they were assisted by Harold James—the Weyerhaeuser employee who visited the site frequently to take water samples. Sid, the meticulous documenter, took photographs of all major events involving bone extraction and bone transport. The image of Mr. James was captured in some of those photographs—incontrovertible documentation of Weyerhaeuser complicity in their dinosaur extraction. A Weyerhaeuser employee, who they thought was a supervisor, was aiding and abetting their bone quest.

The pit teemed with movement and excitement. The pick was thrust, the hammer pinged, the saw buzzed, the chisel scraped, the shovel spaded, the jackhammer vibrated—the tools of the trade were in competent hands as the two craftsmen plied their trade amidst numerous distractions, unforeseen threats, and looming disasters.

Cephis and Sid dug in two-foot increments. If they failed to find anything in a two-foot perimeter, they dug in a different direction until they hit pay dirt. Each piece was accorded the respect and deference it deserved. Reverence for nature was expounded to encompass reverence for bones.

The hands and the finger digits of the dinosaur came out in a clump—the whole lump was plastered. Hundred-pound chunks of matrix and bone were liberated in an ordeal of ingenious extraction—two hands, two arms, and two shoulder blades. The shoulder blades were an intriguing marvel, marred by scars—teeth marks that had almost ripped the arm apart. One ankle bone had pyrite inside the hollow space and was beautifully colored with a yellow glaze—a gorgeous bone that was coal black on the outside and pyrite gold on the inside.

The wrist, arm, hand, and shoulder bones were all in relatively good condition and found lying close to each other. The leg, foot, and pelvis bones were likewise in good condition and found in close proximity. The gastro ribs were found scattered and loose amidst the bone rubble. Interspersed within the bone bed were fragmentary bits and pieces of coprolite— fossilized dinosaur feces. These "poop pieces" were about 1.5 inches in diameter. Each distinct piece was individually wrapped and put in a dedicated box.

As the bone venture inched forward bit by bit, the two bone-aroused exploiters of earth's hidden booty became ever more confident and competent. As the duo delved ever more deeply into the dinosaur grave and the encrusted mysteries of the Cretaceous layer, new bits of treasure were uncovered. In the location where the gastro ribs were uncovered, a neat little pile of rock pebbles was found. These were gastroliths—small, water-borne pebbles that were consumed by the dinosaur and utilized to grind up food in the gizzard. The pile contained about a dozen pieces. They were smoothly polished and beautiful in color and texture; about the size of the coprolite—approximately 1.5 inches in diameter—and dug up in a clump and kept separate from all other items.

Gastroliths were instrumental in an earlier dinosaurian adaptation for digestion. Over time, the stones were of less importance as jaw and tooth structures evolved and enabled more efficient chewing techniques. Special muscles developed that allowed the jaw to be rotated from side to side as the animal chewed. This allowed the teeth to grind food more effectively. The innovation lessened the need for the grinding work of gastro-stones inside the stomach.

The gastroliths found in the pit had an interesting twist. They had been transported inside the dino's stomach from afar. The gastro-stones, some scientists would later say, came from Utah and provided direct evidence that the acrocanthosaur species inhabited an extensive range across North America.

As the fossils accumulated over the months and years, the storage shed at Cephis' house in Eagletown no longer provided enough space to house the valuables. Sid had a larger building in Idabel that at one time had been an appliance store. The fossils were moved to Sid's abandoned storefront warehouse.

With the fossil inventory taking up more space, questions about preservation became crucial. The collectors spread out the bones inside the warehouse to enable a clearer watch for any changes in their condition. They continued to clean, prepare, and glue the fossils in an attempt to prevent additional cracks, and were on constant readiness to correct problems as they developed. A vigilant watch for any surface deterioration was maintained. With tender loving care, their bone-capital might compound by interest earned.

In their new role as warehousemen, Cephis and Sid dealt with a host of immediate and potential problems. The ordinary physical processes that acutely threaten fossils are mineralization, hydration, crystallization, and oxidation. Getting the bones safely out of the pit and keeping them free of moisture and temperature variation had mitigated these harmful processes. The biological processes were an immediate concern, and the bones needed to be assessed constantly for mold and mildew forming in the extensive cracks. Their specimen suffered from pyrite contamination. The effect of iron sulfide and exposure to air caused surface degeneration.

The dig had endured for three years and consumed their spare time. The rescued bones were now protected in Sid's warehouse. Although their dig was not yet complete, they now had breathing room. Their minds could now contemplate other issues outside the confines of the pit and warehouse.

The two bone-savvy progenitors of *Acrocanthosaurus* eminence were building a stash of fossils they hoped could one day be converted to cash. The ascendant rescuers had secured enough fossils to become enablers of *Acrocanthosaurus* rejuvenation with the means to promote the bones and themselves. The experience had become a platform for self-actualization. The unfolding story was no longer just about the dinosaur, but also about them. This ambitious pursuit also became a drive for self-respect and self-esteem. With their prodigious quantity of freshly-mined fossils tallied and credited, the world of science might someday pay a tidbit of homage to a pair of obscure amateurs from the "outback" of southeastern Oklahoma. Consequently, they would not disappear into the landscape—into nothingness like the dinosaur before its resurrection.

Despite their steadfastness in recovering the treasure, the two friends were changing. McCurtain County was changing. The whole American society was transforming. America during the 1980s was ruled by Reagan's cronies and entering a new Gilded Age that resembled the earlier gilded period one century earlier when robber barons ruled the land.

CHAPTER TWENTY-THREE
The Gilded Ages of Dinosaur Discoveries

The greatest era of dinosaur discovery occurred during the great American industrial boom of the late nineteenth and early twentieth centuries. That period of American history became known as the Gilded Age—named after an 1873 social satire by Mark Twain.

This was a period of massive capital spending on industrial infrastructure, heavy equipment, raw materials, and manufacturing facilities for an emerging consumer society. Also, the era gave rise to the age of fossil fuels—crude oil was harnessed and refined for electricity generation and motorized propulsion.

This First Gilded Age (ca.1880-1910) saw the creation of the modern industrial economy and the rise of monopolies, trusts, and great concentrations of wealth in the hands of a few industrial plutocrats such as John D. Rockefeller, J. P. Morgan, and Andrew Mellon. Factories and manufacturing capacity expanded, especially in the industrial East and Midwest. New inventions and production technologies spurred a manufacturing revolution leading to economies of scale, scientific management, vertical integration, segmented production roles by workers (division of labor), and the assembly line. A national transportation and communication network was also created. The corporation, then mostly known as trusts or monopolies, became the dominant form of business. The divine right of capital had replaced the divine right of kings.

The 1880s period hosted the bone war between Marsh and Cope, fought amidst the great panoramic theatre of the vast American West. Other great paleontologists like Earl Douglas and Barnum Brown were also prowling the great western outback seeking prolific beds of fossils.

The great industrial scions of the age, such as Andrew Carnegie and J. P. Morgan, took a personal interest in fossils and financed their excavation and transportation with grants of cash from their overflowing coffers. At the same time, they lavished endowments to elite, eastern-establishment universities like Yale (Peabody Museum of Natural History), The Smithsonian Institute, and the Philadelphia Academy of Natural Sciences.

In the late nineteenth century, valuable commodities in the West – cattle, grains, minerals, and fossils – were loaded onto railroad cars and transported overland to great industrial and educational centers in the Northeast. At the same time, the spirit of industrial expansion and the forces of modernism were propelled westward along with the migrations of people in search of land and what was still left of the American frontier. Gold and fossils were the most valuable of all commodities, and there was a lustful rush to secure these precious resources.

The second greatest period of dinosaur discovery (ca.1980-2000) happened during what might aptly be called a Second Gilded Age. This period also witnessed a great economic expansion and a relative increase in prosperity. In addition, this era ushered in a technological and market revolution that profoundly altered society, indeed, the world.

While the 1880s had been the most prolific period for dinosaurian recovery, one century later the 1980s would become the next greatest decade of dinosaur fossil consolidation as a new breed of paleontologists and new field technologies were unleashed to track down ever more obscure and difficult-to- access fossil deposits.

The 1990s continued the trend as renewed public interest and awareness of the giant behemoths, especially the carnivores, incited an incipient dinosaurian craze. The *Jurassic Park* movies of the 1990s animated the masses, much as the melodrama of the bone wars between Marsh and Cope had in the 1890s. A booming economy undergirded by frothy speculation and inflated bubbles of "irrational exuberance" enticed more funding for research and exploration. Both decades were a time of industrial transformation, technological modernization, and rampant social change.

The more extreme the social and economic conditions in Gilded Age America, the more it seemed to goad dinosaur discoveries. It was as if the great bone barons had fled into the wilds and barrens as a diversion from the insipid proclivities of the masses or the excesses of Mammon. Fossil mania may have been partly propelled in response to the underlying discordant tunes and malevolent tones of a disharmonious society.

Although these scientific explorers and fossil hunters were ambitious and acquisitive in their own right, they were not driven by a latent lust for monetary riches. While the aristocratic fossil hunters of the late nineteenth-century already had wealth, the scientific professionals of the late twentieth-century were motivated by a scientific imperative that did not allow time for an obsessive hankering after money. Both the aristocratic scientists of the nineteenth century and the professional scientists of the twentieth century had ventured out into the barren badlands in search of treasure that would line the walls of scientific museums, rather than their pockets.

The 1990s upsurge will likely prove to be the pinnacle for dinosaurian research and recovery for the foreseeable future as funds become scarce, budgets are cut, and resources trimmed. The travail and discord in the overall economy since the 2008 financial collapse may set the tone and parameters for future paleontological projects and discoveries. As goes the economy, so goes the dinosaur mania and the scientific research and infrastructure needed to sustain it. Fascination with dinos can only be sustained in a society free from the privations of an economy riddled with economic malaise and precipitous crashes.

During both the First and Second Gilded Ages there were great contradictions and extremes in social and economic factors. New business tycoons emerged on the scene – multi-millionaire industrialists arose during the first gilded period, while multi-billionaire technologists ascended during the second. There were great disparities in income and wealth during both eras – conspicuous squalor subsisted alongside audacious splendor.

Major national corporations became larger during the First Gilded Age, while multi-national corporations grew larger still during the Second Gilded Age. Productivity expanded during both periods, but the gains were inequitably distributed; the average worker's share of national income began to decline in the Second Gilded Age. From the 1980s onward, wages remained stagnant even while productivity increased and top corporate CEOs were lavished with riches beyond imagination. Jack Welch of General Electric was "paid some 1,400 times the average wage of his blue collar workers in the U.S. and 9,571 times the average wage earned by Mexican industrial workers who made up an increasing percentage of the GE workforce after production was moved across the border." (Thomas Frank, *One Market Under God*, 7)

Even though the standard of living and family income for the majority of American workers was slowly declining, there was an overall increase in productivity and GDP (Gross Domestic Product). Consequently, a generally ample supply of funds continued to flow to prominent educational institutions, which were, in turn, able to furnish funding for field exploration and fossil excavation. Partly due to the continuing bestowal of surplus funds, a new Gilded Age in dinosaur fossil recovery proliferated during the great stock market, real estate, and financial bubbles of the 1980s, 1990s, and early 2000s.

The Second Gilded Age saw the maturity of a profligate consumer society with mass marketing utilized by America's corporations to manufacture artificial needs and desires for their products. A great expansion in technological innovation, especially in electronics, led to the computer chip, the personal computer, and the Internet. In conjunction with this electronics revolution, a post-industrial, service economy evolved as American corporations relocated factories overseas. As this transitional service economy merged with a nascent information economy, electronics and computer chip technology made the Internet universal. This was the age of technocracy and a new breed of technological entrepreneurs like Bill Gates, Steve Jobs, Larry Ellison, and Michael Dell arrived on the scene to garner Wall Street financing in order to organize the new technologies into viable high-tech companies.

The new economic order of the Second Gilded Age developed an information revolution as profound as the industrial revolution – computers, software, and the Net instead of machines, assembly lines, and the division of labor; white collar more than blue collar; service workers instead of industrial workers. New advances in science and technology moved the science of paleontology to new levels. The new field scientists were now using state-of-the-art technology for exploration, communication, excavation, transportation, and preservation. By the 1990s, paleontology had become high-tech with the aid of GPRs, remote sensing devices, diffraction tomography.

Fossil discoveries, except those dug by FDR's government work crews, were paltry during the 1930-1950s. Fossil hunting was not a priority during those decades, and funding for science, other than for weaponry, was meager. But beginning in the 1980s, there was a great thrust forward in dinosaur recoveries. Thrilling new discoveries of T.rex, Utah Raptor, and Seismosaurus revived public interest, and the *Jurassic Park* movies added more enthusiasm for research. By the 1990s, a new breed of paleontologist had entered the field and initiated a renaissance in ways of thinking about dinosaurs. As in the 1880s, dinosaurs had again captivated the minds of the public, and this interest initiated an upswing in grants and funding for paleontological research and exploration. Dinosaur fervor was at its greatest in the 1880s and the 1990s.

Despite horrendous federal budget deficits, money has continued to filter down to educational and scientific institutions from both private and public sources. The availability of monetary grants has been the principal factor in the equipping, organizing, and success of fossil hunting expeditions, whether conducted in the first or second gilded ages. But the dinosaurian renaissance of the 1990s may have recently gone over the cliff. The resurgence in knowledge, research, and exploration for fossils may soon be transformed into a palling Dark Age as public funds allotted for science come up against the hard reality of unprecedented budget deficits.

In the early years of fossil hunting, the science of paleontology was an exclusive province of the elite; bones and aristocrats were inexorably linked in the minds of the public. In the 1880s, these wealthy scientists and fossil prospectors were able to bankroll their own expeditions or were supported by the largess of prestigious institutions of learning or wealthy Eastern industrialist benefactors. The growing concentrations of wealth at the top allowed the great accumulators of wealth to "trickle down" their blessings to the ambitious field scientists who were aptly scouring the Western badlands for prehistoric bone treasures.

In the time of Sir Richard Owen, Leidy, Cope, and Marsh, aristocrats had a monopoly on the bones. They had the fossil market cornered in the same fashion as their industrialist peers had the steel, oil, or financial markets cornered. They were the robber barons of bones, pillaging loose-lying fossils on both private and public lands with no resistance from owners.

Fortunate son Othniel Marsh was the nephew of millionaire banker George Peabody. Uncle George subsidized Yale with an endowment for a new museum with the stipulation that his nephew be made professor of paleontology. Whereas, E.D. Cope preferred to work independently with no university affiliation and funded his paleontological pursuits through his father's estate.

Fossils were precious commodities just as surely as were oil, gold, or copper. The graduated (or progressive) income tax was not enacted until the close of the First Gilded Age; government budgets were scanty compared to modern times. Thus, most financing for fossil expeditions ultimately stemmed from the private sphere, rather than a public source.

During the Second Gilded Age, although amateurs have been more active in discoveries, the actual excavation was left for the large paleontological houses with the needed resources, technology, and expertise to delve more deeply into the natural geologic context. The amateurs never strike out on their own to mine the large fossil beds. In excavation and recovery, the well-funded university staffs have a paramount edge. This was probably truer during the days of Marsh and Cope when there was no such thing as amateur paleontologists, only laborers and aides to the aristocratic field scientists.

In modern times, fossil collecting has become more equalitarian – not exactly a bedrock of pure democracy where every man is equal (or as Huey Long used to say: "every man a king") in the eyes of science and the law, but more open nonetheless. Unlike the 1880s, today's amateurs have more discretionary time to pursue their hobbies in the field. As they became more active in the later part of the twentieth century, a moniker or vocational namesake evolved for the pure field collectors who were non-degreed – "amateur paleontologists." These men were not titled, credentialed, or pedigreed, but made significant contributions to science and the expanding fossil inventories, nonetheless.

Amateurs without degrees have remained active in the field from the 1960s-2000s and made most of the discoveries, but the most skilled among this class of amateurs were supported by large educational institutions or worked directly under the supervision of university paleontologists. Despite the status quo favoring the lead paleontologist with the glory for the discovery and excavation, the field had become open enough by the 1980s that two unconnected moonlighters from obscurity – a backwoods Arkansas hillbilly and a small town Choctaw Indian – had slipped through the cracks and arrived on the scene to claim their own prized specimen, and a magnificent prize it was.

Field collectors had become more diverse – from bearded non-conformists with crumpled straw hats to three-piece suits; from weekend hobbyists to well-financed fossil entrepreneurs; from PhDs to high school grads; from urban sophisticates to rustic hillbillies, i.e. Cephis Hall. In the 1990s, one would never find a true aristocrat in the field digging bones.

Probably the most well known of the non-three-piece-suit types was Robert Bakker, PhD – "a fossil-junkie genius, the Galileo of paleontology," as Peter Larson described him in his book, *Rex Appeal*. Bakker, with beard, pony tail, and a crumpled straw hat, more than any other scientist, is credited for initiating the Dinosaurian Renaissance of the 1970s –1990s; and largely through his zeal and foresight, the dinosaurian mystique once again registered in the minds of the public, much as it had in the First Gilded Age.

Bakker explained the great paleontological leap forward as having more to do with a new surge of scientific funding made possible by the Cold War competition with the Soviet Union. Following the Russian Sputnik launch in 1957, the space race was on and American science needed funding for the ensuing contest in rival technologies with the ideological competitor. As Bakker put it, the craving for scientific funding was so magnified that a new era dawned – the Three-Piece-Suitification of Paleontologists. (Larson and Donnan, *Rex Appeal*, 17)

Up until then, funding for science was on a much smaller scale, and paleontology was not a fashionable branch. Much of the funding for science had been provided by wealthy private donors. World Wars I and II and The Great Depression reduced public funding for science, except in those areas pursued by the military.

Public funding for paleontology and biological specialties had not been lavish in the pre-Sputnik era, but now a paradigm shift was taking place. Largess was bestowed on all specialties, and a fraction of that public bequest trickled down to the coffers of elite paleontology departments.

This new source of funds set off a scramble by educational and research institutions, but the benefaction came with strings attached. Paleontologists now had to look and act the part of the white-robed lab researcher, rather than the field excavator in jeans and overalls, at least when under the scrutiny of the fund disperser.

"In the old days, there was a fraternity, a brotherhood, and instant camaraderie built from shared passions about ancient life." The common thread was the ensemble of bones that stitched together the enthralling story about life. You could spot a fossil enthusiast by that glee of enthusiasm on his face. (Larson 32)

"But within the profession, as Three-Piece-Suitification evolved, someone started noticing that maverick collectors tended to resemble Indiana Jones more than Prince Charming. And that the prince usually resided in museums and universities while Jones was out in the field or selling at a fossil fair. Even though museums had been built with purchases made from Indiana Jones's predecessors, an unexpected mutation began to divide paleontologists into groups based generally on whether or not they were independents, and especially on whether or not they sold the fossils they were finding." (Larson 32)

The Bone Wars epoch of fossil hunting (1870-1910) and the pinnacle of the Sputnik-Renaissance era (1970-2000) were the apogee for fossil discovery, but there had been a pivotal shift in the sources of funding for field exploration and excavation – from that of wealthy individuals and museums to corporations and individual taxpayers. In both eras, money generated from outside the halls of paleontology paid for digging equipment, wages, lodging, supplies, and landowner fees.

"The Renaissance was a bull market for whoever got there first. It also began to look more and more like the Bone Wars. In the updated version, however, Three-Piece-Suitification adopted a new, politically correct attitude that frowned upon treating fossils as commodities. Such behavior was called unseemly, even poisonous, and the act of selling bones to museums gradually became anathema. In some circles, commercial paleontologists themselves became anathema. After nearly 150 years of buying and selling fossils, commercialism in paleontology had become immoral." (Larson, 32, 33)

The three-piece Prince Charming wanted a monopoly on the bones and unfettered access to the lands that bore them. He wanted the great bone corridors free from trespass by rogue amateurs and commercial collectors. The Prince Charming also believed that only he should have access to public funding. "He blames paleontology's slide into immorality on Indiana Jones, and has suggested banning him from public lands." (Larson 33)

Indiana Jones has indeed made most of the modern fossil discoveries, and when that Indiana Jones has ample expertise and finances to excavate, he has proven extremely adept and successful in the field. And now, a neophyte style of Indiana Jones had entered the paleontological realm and was making his mark. It was as if a befuddling and humbling hoax had been foisted off on Prince Charming who was now flushed with public funds. What a contrast it was—money versus penury; the urbane sophisticate versus backwater coarseness; the credentialed versus the non-credentialed; the amply-equipped versus improvised makeshift; a large field team versus two lone diggers; high-tech versus crude, industrial-era implements; upscale versus down-home.

In the midst of the 1980s dinosaur upsurge, an obscure and miniscule hillbilly and his Indian compadre had been turned loose on a great private-commercial estate to ravish secluded treasure concealed within the perimeter-confines of a swift flowing river, a murky and marshy slough, a mysterious crop of clandestine cannabis weed, and a waste-laden pit.

This recovery team was outside the established province of institutional paleontology –beyond the pale of custom, tradition, norms, financing, and territory. "Establishment paleontologists" did not dig in McCurtain County, and wherever they did happen to dig, mostly in the Great American West, they were nearly always adequately equipped, supplied, and financed.

Now here in McCurtain County—the land of Little Dixie, of Choctaw prominence, the one-horse plow, a land once dotted with cotton fields, sharecroppers, and tenant farmers—were stationed two modest amateurs who had none of these paleontological luxuries, only pocket change, home-furbished supplies and tools, common sense, sheer determination, guts, and perspiration—yet they were winning and winning in a big way. They were short on cash, but long on sweat. They were men of the past, of the old school—not the sleek, crowning, high-tech future. They were not of the aristocracy, the meritocracy, the technocracy, or the corporatocracy. These were a pair of commoners from McCurtain County, the kind of men Andrew Jackson had championed when the frontier was young.

Where in the modern world of television, video games, shopping malls, mass entertainment, runaway urban sprawl, congested freeways, instantaneous gratification, self indulgence, mass persuasion through advertising, YouTube, and short attention spans would you find two such men who were willing to spend virtually all their spare time without pay, wresting a crypt of disintegrating bones from an ancient sepulcher embedded in a crusty layer of sediments laid down in the Age of Dinosaurs?

In the midst of a pall of elitism, mass spectacle and illusion, and hubris of power, Cephis Hall and Sid Love were sober and rational; they spoke with humility and in simplistic terms. They confronted a world torn by change, one step at a time, one thrust forward, and sometimes backward, while never bowing to authority or surrendering their resolve and convictions. They were not just champions of bones, but of individualism, of the common man against entrenched power, of individual liberty against the imposing corporate state. With the national attention span of Americans distracted and unable to keep focused, deep within a backwater enclave of McCurtain County resided two peerless men who could not be distracted or dissuaded from completing their mission. They were able to keep their eyes focused on the prize, even as dark clouds gathered on the horizon.

Cephis Hall had no delusions or pretensions. He knew his roots and walked in his own boots. He was an authentic person – a hillbilly from the sticks, and he made no attempt to conceal that. If he was not satisfied with his lot in life, with his true identity, he at least accepted its limitations and fate. He made no attempt to conceal his identity, or be something he was not.

Within a mass culture contrived and manipulated from above – of hidden persuaders, mass media, mass marketers, and mass illusions, there stood Cephis Hall, a man of simplicity and unpretentious authenticity who possessed a reality-based consciousness. Hall's down-to-earth sentience was rooted in the stability of a more constant world view, a world less influenced by rampant technological, economical, and organizational change. The rural backwoods of southeastern Oklahoma was slow to change and more likely to retain and nourish parochial and traditional values.

While the society at large was being transformed beyond recognition by the forces of technology, market dynamics, institutional restructuring, and corporate reorganization, Cephis Hall and Sid Love remained transfixed in their outlook and consciousness—immutable in their attitudes and values about life and how to live life. In this new American society defined more and more by illusion and fantasy—a culture of narcissism and celebrity worship—Cephis Hall and Sid Love were real persons who knew who they were and who they were not. They were grounded in reality and realistic ambitions. A reality check had told them that their flaming sense of accomplishment could quickly be brought low. Still, their confidence in the prospect for complete success was mounting day by day.

The bone quest was no endeavor for immortal fame, only mere recognition for their contributions and respect among their peers. They knew they would never become mass celebrities—household names in the public's mind. They were not trying to win via overt and invidious competition with others. The results of their success would likely bring only a feeling of success, of self respect, and of recognition within a narrow scientific community and a warm realization that they had contributed to the stock of scientific knowledge. Hall and Love were on the verge of becoming avatars for amateur paleontology.

Their accomplishment would represent more than just self-aggrandizement; it was advancement for science, for knowledge, and for public bemusement. The two men never lost sight of their goals and humble origins. They were almost finished. Just a few more bones, including the all-important skull, were yet to be recovered. They were closing in on the twilight of their rendezvous to resurrect the majestic aura of Acrocanthosaurus—"The Terror of the South."

CHAPTER TWENTY-FOUR
Lightning Strikes the Diggers

The two Okies from McCurtain headed west from Eagletown on Highway 70 in the direction of the clear-flowing Mountain Fork. They had a rendezvous with nature – an odyssey back through time with a mission to recover the remnants of the high-spined lizard and present them to the scientific world for examination and revelation.

The struggle had been with and about nature, but nature had its own moods, tempos, and inclinations. Nature, or a product of nature (the dinosaur), was not just the story; it was also the key – the driving force, the divining force, and the decisive force in unlocking the mystery and according access to the treasure that had been sealed off for eons from a paleontological endeavor.

The dinosaur had once lived and then died, and its remains ossified. Nature had a guiding hand in the creation, expiration, and fossilization of the creature. Nature also guided its primal forces in the process that allowed eventual access to the fossilized treasure. Once access was granted through geological or hydrological intercession, the recovery of the unlocked discovery needed the continuing cooperation of a beguiling Mother of Nature.

Through the workings of geological transformative forces, the untold mysteries locked up in the earth's strata are uncovered, compiled into data, and reported in scientific sources. But nature, after granting that access, can still intercede and close the door. At its whim or discretion, it can deny recovery of that creation. Nature, not man, has the final say in all things natural, even resources and treasure. Science would record the stats, a paleontological stash of unknown measure.

Time was moving quickly. It was already 1986; they were nearing the end of their quest. The two Okies were headed into their third year of shoveling gray sandstone and clay. They toiled inside an austere pit in the heat of the day. The dinosaur remains had been disturbed, and the fossils dug out of the mud; the grave earnestly molested, and the creature's identity wrested. Soon, the bones would be offered up to science as a world-class collection – an intriguing earthly manifestation.

The two bone maestros were on the last leg of their dig and confident of victory. Even if they never recovered the skull or another single bone, they had still won, at least in the excavation zone. Like a pair of bantam roosters, they had suddenly become cocksure and feisty, their minds filled with reckless anticipation. They oozed with confidence, perhaps a bit complacent.

At the beginning of the day, the skies were clear and blue. It was a warm Saturday in early May. The two Okies were aware that rain was in the forecast, but a rain scenario looked far away. As a storm appeared a more distant arising and time was abiding, the sun crept up amidst the pale blue horizon. The azure was tranquil, and the winds docile. Nature had coaxed its subjects into a smug disposition.

Perhaps they could get in a full day and avoid a calamitous melee. Rain looked distant; the bone bed still imminent. The brightness and glare of the sun belied any prospect of heavenly tumult. But in Oklahoma there is a constant caveat. When it comes to weather on a given day, it can swiftly change in a profound way.

In their sublime euphoria over their recent success, the two Okies let their guards down in jest. They left themselves vulnerable to a capricious wizard of nature. A godly alchemist was brewing up vaporous concoctions that soon discharged volatile strikes of lightning. Jolts of electrically-charged bolts came out of the blue.

A glitch of hubris penetrated their cognition and engendered a false premonition; they foolishly trusted their instincts rather than scientific prognostication. Their dig would become stanched, their plans wrenched, their bodies drenched, and their bones at risk inside the trench. Their minds seized with obfuscation, their excavation threatened with devastation.

The two amateurs made their way back for another stint in the trench, and began to scratch and chip away at the imprinted dents. Soon they would be strutting and crowing a tune of paleo-amateur grandiosity. It was a meteoric rise from total obscurity. They would ascend to the summit of amateur exaltation – the essence of amateur renaissance magnification.

The amateur exploits of Hall and Love would become important not so much for their quantity of products as their unique quality of specimen. They would join the ranks of the greatest amateur paleontologists in history and be on the same par with a Stan Sacrison or "Dinosaur Jim" Jensen. But that was still in the distant future. They had immediate problems with which to contend, and bones still to mend.

Jim Jensen was probably the greatest amateur paleontologist that ever lived. Although falling short of achieving a high school education, he worked for Harvard with great aspiration. Mammal paleontologist Alfred Romer was his inspiration, before taking a non-teaching position at another institution. He took a new job in the geology department of Brigham Young University with some hesitation. He had dreamed of finding dinosaurs since the age of ten. His dream came true in a discovery binge.

Under the tutelage of Romer, he looked for dinosaurs in Antarctica and Argentina. While employed at Brigham Young, he collected fossils across Utah and western Colorado. On a shoestring budget he dug up twenty-six quarries in twenty-three years. "Dinosaur Jim" collected thousands of bones, including the bones of two of the largest sauropods ever known. Supersaurus and Ultrasaurus came out of the earth, and awed observers with their magnificent girth.

Like Cephis Hall, he was not a trained scientist or temperamentally fit for bookish endeavor or scholarly script. His difficulties in scientific format, documentation, and writ, caused him considerable discomfort and discouragement.

Stan Sacrison discovered two of the greatest T.rex specimens of paleontological fame, with one of them named "Stan" after his own name. He was active in working with the Black Hills Institute in recovering their remains. Both Sacrison and Jensen made their discoveries in the American West, a fertile ground for great dinosaur claims. Jensen had close collaboration with a university, while Sacrison had close ties to a commercial entity.

Hall and Love had zilch for a budget and worked independently of a university. They had discovered and excavated probably the rarest carnivorous theropod in history. McCurtain County was not a propitious place for dinosaur recovery. It was a paleontological bleak zone. There were no major discoveries. Hall and Love were on their own.

As the two embattled diggers hacked away at the crust, it seemed like just another day from dawn to dusk. But nature had a nasty surprise in store. While the two besotted diggers progressed inside the trench, the firmament was ready to unleash a calamitous drench. A few fresh bones had been uncovered inside the ditch. They lay vulnerable and exposed in the dust of the pit, strewn atop the surface and ready to pick.

The diggers were unprepared for the storm sweeping in. It crept out of the stillness and cast a sinister spin. It overshadowed the verdant hills and valley below, and splattered the meadows and forest floor. The skies turned ominously dark; thick, foreboding clouds hung over the Mountain Fork. It was raw nature as brute force; it gave the stunned diggers little recourse. The immediate outlook became rather stark; the tides of the storm were precipitous and harsh.

Roaring gusts blew in from the west. The storm crept out of the stillness and suddenly became violent; it threw their orderly world into darkness and chaos. Strong winds crumpled and distorted the green stalks of weed growing near the river, while snatching leaves and branches from oak-wood timber.

McCurtain County was under siege. A deluge of rain beat down on God's humble creatures. It blew off Cephis's cap and smattered Sid with debris and mud. Their boots bogged down in thick, crusty crud.

Their clothes became wet, rumpled, and wrinkled; they were caught right in the middle of a heavenly sprinkle. The sprinkle became a torrential rain; it caused them considerable pain. As the rain battered the leaves of the old oak trees, it gave the diggers little reprieve.

A tumultuous onslaught overtook their elation; it splattered their faces with precipitation. Their consciousness was transformed into desperation; their minds worried and their egos deflated. Saving the bones was their objective and answer, but they were overwhelmed by the forces of nature.

The storm blew in quickly and changed the score. Within the mere blink of an eye, the atmosphere changed. The winds soared, the lightning flashed, and the thunder roared.

The harried bone diggers were caught in an odious trap, as the bones lay half-buried in a water-soaked, earthen vat. While desperate to save their magnificent treasure, they were overtaken by rising water besieging their artificial embrasure.

Thunder, lightning, wind, hail, and rain beat down on McCurtain County terrain. They were desperate to cover their fossilized treasure and retreat quickly to a safe haven. With torrential rain pounding them into submission, the two men worked frantically to stabilize their precarious situation.

CHAPTER TWENTY-FIVE
A Mysterious Visitor Comes Calling

While lightning struck in the background and thunder roared in the foreground, torrential rain battered Cephis's and Sid's soaked, shivering frames as they scrambled to cover the exposed bones. So far, they were fighting a losing battle. Standing water inside the trench posed a serious risk. The bones had to be saved. Nature was trying to reclaim the treasure.

Their strategy was simple: cover up the bones as quickly as possible and level the surface inside the trench to enable water to drain out into the holding pit. The piled-up tailings had to be knocked down or scooped out to prevent a dam from forming. This was no easy task.

Howling winds and cascading rain obstructed the diggers and the terrain, making the work difficult, if not in vain. Scattered piles of dirt had to be shoveled and leveled. Unfortunately, the loose dirt had turned to mud. Shoveling compacted crud was almost impossible.

The working conditions were atrocious. A lightning strike could fry them in their tracks. Nevertheless, they stood their ground. The bones were precious. The situation was dire and dark. The storm was one adversary the wily Cephis Hall could not outsmart. The diggers were in a world of hurt. They were desperate.

As usual, Cephis and Sid were forced to improvise. A shovel was of no value in this ordeal. Cephis grabbed a 2x4 board and tried to dislodge the hardened mounds of muck, but had limited success. Sid battered the compacted aggregations with a pick and gradually the obstructed clusters began to break. Cephis finally grabbed a rake and scraped along the bottom, working northward from where the trench intersected the waste-holding pit. Slowly, the standing water began to drain. The disheveled Okies were winning again. They might lose a few bones, but the quarry could be saved.

The mud mounds were leveled off and the floor of the trench receded toward the gully. At last, a reprieve allowed them to catch their breath and sigh a feeling of relief. While the rain poured, they stood in the trench and watched the water drain off their beloved bones.

As the waters retreated, the mud plodders covered any protruding bones. They scoured along the bottom looking for traces of fossils near the surface. They shoveled scoops of mud over any exposed protuberance and leveled it off. Although drenched, they had stood firm against a wrathful nature.

With mixed feelings, they were ready to retire. They were angry with themselves for having allowed this calamity to happen, but felt fortunate to have survived relatively unscathed. Most of their day was spent under the drenching spout of heaven and in shackles of mud. Wet, exhausted, and soiled with sludge, the two men parted company and headed home.

Sid and Cephis were thunderstruck; their outlook clouded and somber. They needed rest before returning. Although the gloom of the day's events unsettled them, their spirits were still resolute. Eager to assess the carnage, they wouldn't be away for long.

Cephis drove into his driveway, got out of his truck, and limped to his front porch. He removed his mud-encrusted boots and had Joyce bring his robe. Supper would be ready by the time he finished cleaning up. He was tired and ready for bed, but still hungry.

Harried and wearied, the shivering hillbilly sat down for supper. After only two bites and one gulp, the phone rang. Cephis reluctantly answered. From out of nowhere, a solicitous intruder invaded the solitude of Cephis Hall. While barely dry and calm, the mysterious voice on the other end piqued his curiosity.

"Cephis, my name is Jeff Pittman," the caller said. "I'm a graduate student at the University of Texas at Austin."

Cephis continued listening.

"I've heard through the grapevine about a dinosaur you discovered, and I wanted to offer my services," Pittman said. "I have a proposal to make and I'd like to talk to you in person."

Cephis was exhausted and ready for bed, and in no mood to meet this stranger. He was, however, quite interested in learning his motive and who had put him up to this solicitation. This young man was traveling through the area in route to UT, and had driven out of his way in hopes of meeting Cephis in person.

"Okay, I'll meet with you," Cephis said reluctantly.

What else could he do? He had to find out what force was brewing behind the scenes that might come out of the blue and strike him like a bolt of lightning.

The unexpected call raised some beguiling questions. He wondered how some third party from out of state had inside information about the dinosaur. To Hall's knowledge, the dig was a secret agreement between Bueno, Sid, and himself, and nobody had a clear conception as to what was really going on in the pit or what was at stake.

Bueno certainly was not telling anybody. He didn't care about the dig and had no idea a classic dinosaur specimen was in the works. The boss wanted the whole thing to remain discreet, thinking it was of no consequence and would fade away. Nobody from out of state should be privy to the veiled secret hidden amidst the clay rubble near the banks of the Mountain Fork. Who had tipped off this stranger?

Cephis was not interested in making a deal. What could be gained by collaboration with an out of state university? "Nothing," he thought.

Cephis and family lived about seven miles northeast of the quaint village of Eagletown in a rough neck of the woods just short of the state line, and about only a quarter mile from a strip of taverns and beer joints. The neon lights glowed in the dark and country music could be heard from Cephis' front porch on weekends. These were fighting and dancing clubs that captured the spirit of gun-slinging outlaws from the Old West.

Dives and dance halls straddled both sides of the highway. This was vintage Oklahoma, at least for the rural folks who liked their entertainment under the neon lights into the wee hours of the night. It was a cowboy haunt similar to the old honky-tonks of neighboring Texas.

Inside these dark, smoky places was a charade of motley characters intermixed in a kind of one-night, brewing still: regular patrons, interlopers, pretenders, bar hoppers, gold diggers, good-timers; and what came out of the spigot was sometimes rotgut. The interactions consisted of small talk, flirtations, game-playing, duplicity, pomposity, turn-ons, turn-offs, and put-downs. Cowboys, cowgirls, and cows are as common in Oklahoma as in Texas.

Country western music was popular for those who aspired to retreat into the sticks and find rural bliss. In Oklahoma or Texas, it is the same dream that will not die – cowboys wanting to remain on the open prairies and stressed-out urban folk yearning to retreat into an elusive rural haven.

The partying continued into the heat of the night. Sometimes passions flared, causing emotions to erupt. Throw in a few hillbillies, Indians, rednecks, Arkansas razorbacks, and wild women, and you have a strange and volatile concoction – a lot of incongruous vibes and a rowdy crowd. The parking lots were full of pickup trucks, many with guns hanging in the cabs' back windows. The spirit of the Wild West still thrives in rural Oklahoma. These were the descendants of frontier Celts and Indians – country folks living a fantasy in a rapidly changing world – their atavistic dreams appeased by drink, dance, and song.

Cowboys made these rounds and partied from sundown to almost sunup – boasting, joking, and just hanging out. But maybe, to cap it off, one might get lucky and score a romp in bed with a redneck woman or a honky-tonk queen. The ultimate goal for the cowboy was to get laid, but most, unfortunately, usually had to settle for a few drinks, dances, and laughs. When frustrations, jealousies, or petty annoyances surfaced and boiled over, there was often a quarrel or fight – maybe even a bar-room brawl.

The Wagon Wheel Dance Land was the favorite attraction along the strip. It sucked in large crowds from both sides of the state line – Okies and Arkies alike. It sported a huge ballroom dance floor and showcased popular country western singers and bands as live entertainment. Music legends Merle Haggard, Ray Price and the Cherokee Cowboys, Bob Wills and the Texas Playboys, and Hank Thompson and the Brazos Valley Boys, are reputed to have entertained at the Wagon Wheel.

During such extravaganzas, the house was filled to sardine-like capacity. The whiskey flowed, the music enthralled, and the dance floor hopped. The blue collar patrons needed to let loose and blow off a little steam after a boring and tiring forty hour week on the clock. Weekends were party time at the Dance Land.

The state line strip was reputed to have been an outlaw haven. The notorious Doc Callahan, the renegade doctor, was reported to have been an occasional patron at the Wagon Wheel – perhaps stopping off to visit the owner or drink a fast cold beer. He was not known to frequent the bar-line strip, but on the rare occasions he was spotted the ordinary folks, at least those who knew him, stepped aside to let a legend pass unhindered. People in McCurtain County and Sevier County, Arkansas were aware of his reputation, and both respected and feared him.

Doctor Leroy Callahan lived a double life as an upstanding medical doctor during the day and a "down-standing" heavy drinker, gambler, partier, brawler, and womanizer at night. Stories about his legendary exploits as a surgeon abound.

On one such instance during the 1950s, he was drinking beer at a tavern on the state line strip when a vicious brawl broke out. One man received a ghastly slash on the abdomen from a broken beer bottle and was bleeding profusely. He was laid atop the bar, which served as an operating table, and Dr. Callahan sewed him up on the spot. The man lived to drink another beer and swing another fist. Dr. Callahan did not even send him a bill. He was a true hero to the working class and bar patrons all over southeastern Oklahoma.

In another such incident, a married couple had a serious car wreck outside DeQueen, Arkansas, and both were brought to the local hospital where Dr. Callahan, stone drunk, was on standby in the emergency room. The husband was in critical condition. He, too, was drunk and had managed to bite his tongue almost off. It was hanging by a bare strip of skin.

Dr. Callahan sewed up the husband's tongue and patched his wounds to perfection. He performed first-class surgery while in an intoxicated state. Drunk or sober, he was one of the best surgeons in the land, and had sewn up many lumberjacks with their arms or legs dangling by threads. For Dr. Callahan, these two examples of "masterpiece surgeon feats" were the norm, rather than exception. Such stories go on and on, and are true, not fabricated or exaggerated.

Callahan had a family practice in DeQueen, Arkansas and despite losing his license in the '50s, was also a standby surgeon at the local Dickerson Hospital. He had also practiced medicine in nearby Texarkana, Arkansas, where he became a suspect in a string of serial sadist murders. It was believed that the "phantom killer," as popularized in the 1970s movie *The Town that Dreaded Sundown*, was a prominent member of the community. Doc Callahan certainly fit that bill, despite his flamboyant nightlife and outlaw reputation.

He was revered by the locals, considered by some a kind of Robin Hood, who often treated the poor for free. Also, it was reported by old timers that Doc Callahan had a populist streak. At least for awhile, he was known to have hung out on the bar row section of Broken Bow, located at Broadway and First Streets, and drank and mingled with the working people, including mill workers and tenant farmers. In the late '40s and '50s, the tavern strip in the city of Broken Bow boomed; but by the 1980s, all these taverns had closed for good.

Doc Callahan was tall, slim, mustached, and wore freshly-pressed western clothes, including stylish cowboy boots and hats. He was reputed to have carried a side arm while carousing. He was a throwback to the Old West – something like a reincarnation of the old Doc Holliday legend. He was notorious for drinking and "going out slumming," but more precisely, he was an avid gambler who liked to throw his money around in high places. He had ties to the wealthy in both recreational and business contexts and was believed to have been an associate of Lemuel Due, a prominent local moonshiner. Some believed he was a high-ranking associate of the Dixie Mafia.

Although he may have spent some time in working class taverns, his more frequent haunts were the exclusive deer lodges and hunting camps where he mingled with other high-rollers from among the top strata of society. Men of the upper-crust – fellow doctors, lawyers, businessmen, politicians, and judges – who had ample money for big-time drinking and gambling, partied in these exclusive havens on weekends and enjoyed their vices and leisure hours in comfort and style – with private security outside and high-class prostitutes inside.

Dr. Callahan, after losing his medical license, either fell on hard times or lost restraint of his restless spirit. In the late 1950s, he and a fellow outlaw, Tobo Rhoden, robbed a grocery store in Texarkana and killed a store clerk. Both were subsequently arrested and sent to prison. Rhoden, the actual killer of the clerk, later escaped from the Arkansas penitentiary and was killed in a car wreck on Bellah Mine Road near DeQueen while running from a police chase. Dr. Callahan was later released from prison and succeeded in regaining his medical license. He practiced medicine for only a short time at the Dickinson Clinic in DeQueen before his alcohol addiction and hard life in the fast lane had taken its toll on his health. He died within months after being released from prison.

Doc Callahan is an old local legend that has faded away. The course of time changes everything – old institutions and ways of life disintegrate into the mist of time. The state-line strip is now a ghost of its old self. Virtually all the taverns and dives are gone. The legendary Wagon Wheel ballroom burned down in the mid 1980s. A small replica of it was rebuilt and still exists – a mere shadow of its former glory. Highway 70 near the Oklahoma-Arkansas state line now looks almost empty. The notoriety of a once infamous nightlife along the strip will never return.

Dr. Callahan had been the Halls' family physician for years until he lost his license, then they began seeing Dr. Bill Dickinson, a Callahan associate in DeQueen. For a while, Joyce even worked as a receptionist at Dr. Dickinson's office. During this time, Cephis and Joyce's daughter Angie was treated by Dr. Dickinson for chronic allergies and bacterial infections and given repeated regimens of antibiotics over an extended time period.

Under the rules of the medical licensing board, Dr. Callahan, while on probation, was allowed to dispense medical services only under the supervision of another doctor, in this case Dr. Dickinson. Whenever Dr. Dickinson was absent, Dr. Callahan filled in. During one of those absences, six-year-old Angie came under the care of Dr. Callahan, who immediately questioned the excessive reliance on antibiotics. He suspected there was an underlying, unidentified culprit at work, believing that the allergies had plagued Angie too long.

After ordering blood work he found Angie anemic with her white blood cell count high and red blood count low, while running a low-grade fever. Alarmed, he admitted her to DeQueen General Hospital. She recovered to good health. Dr. Callahan found the cause of the allergies—chocolate—and Cephis and Joyce believe his actions saved Angie's life.

To reach the Halls' home from Eagletown one had to drive east on Highway 70 toward Arkansas for about six miles then turn left (north) immediately after passing the Wagon Wheel Dance Land. From there, one traveled east on the old Highway 70, which was nothing more than a gravel road roughly parallel to the new Highway 70. This was an area of pine trees, flat land, and swift-flowing creeks. Cephis' house was located about one mile down the narrow gravel road now known as the "Old Highway 70."

Cephis sat back down to finish his supper. The vegetables came out of his garden – some of it fresh, some canned the previous year. Cephis was a master gardener, Joyce, an adroit cook and home canner. Shortly, the visitor showed up at the front door. The stranger had easily found his way through the backwoods maze of narrow, gravel roads to the isolated and rustic bungalow perched on a hill – the humble abode of Cephis Hall and his family. The man had a good sense of direction, but what was he peddling?

Jeffrey Pittman lived somewhere near Shreveport. He was a rather large guy with dark, serious eyes, and in his late twenties. After introductions, Pittman asked to see a few pieces of the dinosaur. Cephis obliged, handing him a vertebrae and spine he kept in the house. After examining them, Pittman got down to business. His offer was simple and blunt. The university wanted to bring in a field team and finish the excavation. They wanted to take control and relieve him of any further burden.

Cephis asked Pittman if he had any experience himself in excavating dinosaurs. Pittman stated he had found a few pieces but had never participated in a major excavation. He further added that this was to be a student project under the supervision of university paleontologists. He was trying hard to sell Cephis on the need for professionals to enter the picture and complete the excavation. As Pittman explained it, Cephis and Sid were welcome to watch from the sidelines while their beloved dragon was scooped up by credentialed academicians fresh out of their air-conditioned classrooms.

What could Hall and Love gain by turning over the dig to university students supervised by professors? Other than the forfeiture of a little future sweat, the two diggers would gain nothing more than a fleeting "good feeling" at having briefly participated, certainly not a distinction for accomplishment. They would lose ownership and control of the skeleton as it departed into the outstretched hands of academia.

There was a subtle extrapolation of hubris in the air. Pittman's underlying attitude floated out in plain view … *only degreed professionals were capable and entitled to undertake such an important paleontological project.* Pittman inquired as to the location of the dig site and who owned the land, but Cephis was not about to give away that information. It was a secret. Pittman was treating Hall like a… well, dumb hillbilly.

The longer Pittman talked, the more Cephis was repulsed. He didn't trust Pittman and perceived him as rather snotty. Pittman appeared like one of those wise guys who thought he knew it all. His pushy approach was rather distasteful, but Cephis kept his composure.

In essence, Pittman's message was clear: Cephis and Sid were not qualified excavators and had no credentialed right to dig in the dinosaur pit. The "Pitt man" would absolve them of that onerous demand on their time and energy. All he needed was their consent and capitulation, and their burden would be lifted. *Sign on the dotted line.*

Cephis asked Pittman how he had found out about the dinosaur and if somebody from the university had sent him. Pittman didn't give a direct answer. He just spouted off some nonsense as if he had forgotten how he had actually learned about the dinosaur and was basically drumming up field prospects on his own.

Pittman may have been a scholar with impressive credentials, but he did not know how to talk to a genuine Arkansas hillbilly. The bayous and swamps of Louisiana might be rustic, but they were a world away from the hills of Arkansas. Cephis was a practical man, and he was not stupid. Pittman offered him no incentive, and besides, if Cephis turned over the dig to an out-of-state field team, he would be violating his agreement with Bueno. The decision was not his to make. It was not his land.

How would he and Sid feel watching what remained of their world-class specimen being carted off by student trainees? It was not an enticing proposition. Perhaps they could look back with heartfelt consolation knowing it was they who had found the dinosaur, and it was they who recovered more than 50 percent of its remains before succumbing to a superior intervention. To not finish the job would be like admitting defeat. Cephis said "no" about a dozen times. Pittman finally relented and left, but this would not be the last Cephis would see of the aspiring scientist-in-waiting. As Pittman walked out the door, he thanked Cephis for his time.

"I'll be in touch," Pittman said.

"Okie dokie," replied Cephis.

Pittman was persistent. He kept trying to convince the obstinate hillbilly that he and his university crew were the best qualified to delve into the mysteries locked inside the early-Cretaceous strata, no matter where that strata might be located.

Pittman was in repeated contact with Cephis over the coming months as he traveled back and forth on weekends from northwestern Louisiana to Austin and detoured out of the way to revisit Hall. With each visit he reiterated his sales pitch, but with a slightly different emphasis. He spun his spiel of scientific exclusivity, institutional preeminence, credentials, finances, entitlement, and state-of-the-art technology, while each time belittling amateurs like Hall and Love. Each offer was turned down by the hillbilly he had mistakenly taken for a fool.

CHAPTER TWENTY-SIX
The Bone Tally

Cephis and Sid needed to recuperate from their last ordeal at the pit. They rested while the open-pit mine dried out. How many bones had they lost? It was impossible to know. If a bone had disintegrated into dust, its secret aura would be disseminated into the forsaken earthen realm. While a large, hard appendage could weather the storm, a small, crumbly piece might not. Only four fossils were exposed at the time the storm blew and they were covered as quickly as possible.

The duo had worked frantically while struggling against the battering rain. Some water had seeped into the bone bed. How much damage had been inflicted?

The pieces nearest the surface needed to come out of the trench as quickly as possible and dry out. Water and pyrite contamination were a deadly combination. The Acro was encased beneath a wet substrate; fossils deteriorated when exposed to moisture.

The number of bones lost, if any, would remain a mystery. Another intriguing puzzle was the sudden appearance of Jeffrey Pittman, who, like the storm, had suddenly come out of the blue and left the duo bewildered. When Cephis told Sid about Pittman, he too was baffled. Who was Jeffrey Pittman? Was he really what he claimed to be, or was he a pretender? How had he found out about the dinosaur, and who had sent him?

Mysteries continued to cast a shadow over the Mountain Fork, the diggers, and the dinosaur. There was always some sinister and beguiling force lurking in the background. These dark forces continued to haunt the diggers. From grave to museum, there would always be something brewing in the background that ensnared the duo in some kind of snafu, conflagration, or conundrum. There was not just divine intervention, but human intrusion with which to contend.

After assessing the situation, they started where they had left off by liberating the most accessible fossils and evaluating each of them. As soon as a bone was freed from the crusty matrix, it would be treated, warehoused, and watched. A time of reckoning had arrived. It was not only imperative to save the water-logged bones, but to take an inventory. It was time for a bone tally.

The duo had recovered approximately 55 percent of the skeleton, but the most important piece, the skull, was still missing. Also still missing were the tail, a few vertebrae, parts of the spine, a femur, a tibia, the gastric ribs, and a hand and foot. Despite what remained unaccounted, the collectors had an impressive inventory.

On weekends, the duo continued to hack away at the sediments, while during the week they tended to the bones in the warehouse. It was an everyday affair for Sid, who owned both the warehouse and half the inventory of bones. Both men performed their routine inspections and therapeutic ministrations as spare time allowed. Since initiating the excavation, their lives had changed drastically. They dealt with a new work order—one that encompassed the routine occupational demands required to make a living and their after-hours devotion to caring for the bones.

Of course, there was always the random threat of some unforeseen disruption coming out of the stillness and wreaking havoc, not just on the bones, but on their lives and livelihood. Life is precarious for most people, and one sometimes faces a simultaneous assault on many fronts. This was even more the case for the two bone rescuers. Their lives were full of peaks and valleys, especially since having found the dinosaur. The scale of their achievement would be directly proportional to the sacrifices they made.

Sid and Cephis quickly recovered from the devastating storm and continued shoveling loose clay and sandstone amid the Cretaceous strata. They had undertaken an expedition back in time—a traversal through the unwritten pages of the era of *Acrocanthosaurus*. The story was in the strata and the bones. The secret was manifesting itself amid the excavated rubble on the edge of a worn and contaminated waste-holding pit owned by an ultra-powerful, mega-corporation. The dig continued for months in the wake of that dastardly storm, and more bones were evacuated to Sid's warehouse for safe keeping.

Each recovered bone was tainted with a golden patina of distinction—a blotch of glazed magnificence set against an austere exterior coating. Each precious, ossified piece was decorated by a golden inlay—a sparkle of radiant glitter overshadowing a stark silhouette. Each piece was black to the core and golden at the seam. The gleam was nothing more than pyrite, or fool's gold, but it cast a tantalizing and mesmerizing specter. The bright glow of gold contrasted sharply with the dark glare of coal-black coarseness.

A magnificent ensemble of captivating bones was now stored in a drab storefront warehouse. Bones were on shelves, on tabletops, inside bins and wooden crates, and lying atop pallets and sheets of plywood resting on the floor. Maintaining valuable fossils, whether in a crude warehouse or a lavish laboratory, can be as expensive and cumbersome as excavating them. The electric bill was mounting and supplies were diminishing. It was just a part of the cost of doing business in bones.

Giant appendages looking much like monstrous turkey bones were strategically placed inside the confines of the building with each bone accorded its own space, description, note pad, demographic, photo, and approximate contextual location in correspondence to the other bones. This was a strange conglomeration of earthly products housed inside an abandoned commercial building. The warehouse felt dreary—even haunted—more because of the nature of the products housed within its walls than the condition of the building itself.

The warehouse was an abandoned appliance store about two thousand square feet in size. Built in the late 1960s, it featured wood frame construction, a concrete slab foundation, tile floors, and suitable lighting, ventilation, and indoor plumbing.

The duo kept the interior clean and free of dust. The diligent warehousemen did their best to maintain a moisture-free environment inside the building. They soaked the fossils in trays, tubs, or sinks with acid baths to get rid of any residue. Working at a large workbench, they used a variety of small dental tools for scraping away dirt and mudstone, and applied glue as necessary to seal up cracks.

Whenever the two proprietors were not in the field digging bones, they were inside the warehouse tending them. They treated the diseased bones for a common affliction often encountered with paleontological products—pyrite contamination. Pyrite disease fosters a decomposition caused by the influx of sulfuric acid and moisture.

They knew they were operating on borrowed time. The fossils needed to be professionally treated in the finest paleontological lab in the nation. With their limited facilities and expertise, they were doing their best, but a primitive warehouse would not suffice for the long term.

This huge crop of bones raised questions about several issues: the value of the skeleton to science, the monetary value of the collection, how to proceed in locating a university lab competent enough to cure the diseased bones, and how to protect their financial interest in the specimen.

Who could best preserve and protect this bone treasure? What university might they contact? Who was this Jeff Pittman guy? Was he really from the University of Texas? How could he have known about their dinosaur excavation?

Finally, something clicked in Cephis's mind as he remembered a connection to the University of Texas. It was Dr. Dalquest who had contacted Dr. Langston at UT. Langston had confirmed Dr. Dalquest's identification of the Acro.

The two men had no communication with Langston and had simply forgotten about him. They had not given Dalquest any detailed information about their excavation—no mention was made of a bone bed, an articulated skeleton, or a productive quarry. But somehow, Langston had figured out that a considerable dig was going on somewhere in McCurtain County.

Despite this realization, Pittman's real motive was still hazy. Had he acted alone, or had he been sent by the university's chain of command? Was he merely trying to drum up excavation projects to facilitate student training in field techniques? Or perhaps Langston had sent him as a spy?

Pittman seemed to know about the ongoing excavation, but maybe he really didn't know. Possibly, he was merely feeling Cephis out and trying to read between the lines. Now that he thought about it, Cephis realized that he had not denied digging a dinosaur, but simply refused to give the location of the excavation. And of course, he had turned down the offer of university assistance. Pittman had never even asked what kind of dinosaur it was. Why?

From what Cephis had seen of Pittman, he did not want to be involved with UT. Pittman had visited him again since the initial meeting on the storm day. Pittman was unpleasant, but was he showing his true face? Was he employing devious psychology in an attempt to ferret out the location, or did he really think he could talk the duo into throwing in the towel and allowing the university to take over? UT had to know something. Why else would it keep sending Pittman?

Cephis was ready to let the matter rest. It was all a matter of speculation anyway. For certain, they needed to persuade university scientists to undertake the preservation-restoration phase of the project. Positively, they were not allowing any intruders near their secret cache of bones. The dig site was their secret, and as long as there was a chance of a single bone still left to be found, especially the all-important skull, it would remain their province alone. Besides, if they wanted to bring in a university field team, they needed to tell Bueno, and that would really complicate things.

Certainly, they needed to sort things out. They had much to learn, but wanted to remain in control of the dinosaur. It was a dream come true for both men, especially for Cephis. They needed clarity and a sense of direction. They knew that once the bones were removed from the pit and warehouse and were in the custody of another caretaker, control—even ownership—might slip away. It was a tiresome and treacherous path to circumvent, but their recourse was narrowing day-by-day.

These thoughts were perplexing. Cephis and Sid needed some rest and recreation. Tomorrow was a Saturday, and for once, they had a different plan. They had neglected their wives and families for many months as they dug and tended bones. They decided to take a day off to attend the annual Gem and Mineral Show in Oklahoma City with their wives, who always enjoyed the rock shows. There, the two families could showcase their finest mineralized treasure—and something else—their astounding dinosaur bones. Might their fossils be the star attraction of the exhibition? If so, perhaps the allure of the bones would rub a little celebrity status upon them. It would be fun, they thought.

CHAPTER TWENTY-SEVEN
The Strange Encounter at the Gem and Mineral Show

In the still darkness of the early morning while McCurtain County slept peacefully, the Loves and Halls loaded their separate trucks with their finest showpiece items and headed northwest toward the state capitol. They were off on a five hour, 300-mile journey to the State Fairgrounds of Oklahoma City (OKC) for their annual pilgrimage to the Oklahoma Gem & Mineral Show—an extravaganza for displaying exotic stones.

They were eager to showcase a sample of their most exquisite collections of quartz crystal and other minerals mined from the finest veins of McCurtain County's outback quarries. This was also an opportunity to connect with old friends within the rock and mineral community and see some dazzling gems.

Their collections, contained in specially-crafted wooden crates, included not just the finest gem and lapidary collections from McCurtain County, but also a sample of exquisite fossils from the skeleton of the most elusive dinosaur known to man.

By the time the local populace slipped out of bed, the Halls and Loves had traveled almost half their journey. Counting time out for a breakfast and a refueling stop, they expected to arrive in Oklahoma City about 11:00 AM, Friday morning—in time to set up their display cases and be ready for the weekend show.

Traveling on State Highway 3, they veered northward to Shawnee and entered onto Interstate 40 on the east side of Oklahoma City. Misty darkness concealed the most scenic part of their drive.

Closer to OKC they encountered a rather drab panorama as the pine trees, hills, and emerald pastures of the east were replaced by a more arid and flat landscape. At the height of summer in the OKC area, the vivid green turned dull or bleak brown as the surrounding terrain emblazoned a heat-tormented, scorched appearance—a vastly different geographical vista than their beloved McCurtain County. Pine forests gave way to the dullness of thirsty grasslands.

OKC is noted for more than just being the state capitol and the home of the fairgrounds. The University of Oklahoma (OU) and the Sam Noble Museum of Natural History are located in nearby Norman, a suburb on the southern fringe of the city. Like Tulsa, the other major metropolitan area of the state, OKC is a major enclave of the

Bible Belt. Conservative roots, both religious and political, run deep here. Amidst this bastion of religious fundamentalism and conservatism is a sprinkling of independent-minded folks and a tiny mixture of environmentalists and naturalists. Area rock hounds and greenies attend the Gem and Mineral Show. Some come from the local university.

Heading west on I-40, the two-truck caravan soon reached the outskirts of OKC and shortly entered the fairgrounds. The fairgrounds were located within an older business district on the west side of the city. They arrived at the ramp entrance of the Expo Building about noon that Friday and unloaded their wares. In a few hours their display cases would be set up and ready for the following day's show. They planned to have supper at a nearby restaurant and get to the motel early for bed.

Saturday would be exciting, but hectic. They knew what to expect; they had attended this annual event for more than a decade. But this time it would be different. They would have a chance encounter with two strangers that would perplex and perturb them.

As usual, Cephis would show his finest quartz crystals and Sid his unique lapidary collections, which included handmade jewelry made from the finest polished stones. Rockhounds from all over the nation attended the event. The most spectacular exhibits were usually the rare topaz gemstones and the exquisite quartz crystals brought from McCurtain County. Because of the reputed value of these unique collections, security was tight. Their showpieces were unpacked and arranged inside pre-designated display cases.

Mineral enthusiasts always admired the collections of Sid and Cephis. But this time the two McCurtain boys enhanced their displays with a sampling of their enthralling bones mined from the Mountain Fork riverfront—a few pieces of a mysterious lizard of remote antiquity.

The weekend show lasted from 9 AM to 5 PM on Saturday and Sunday. Rock and mineral collectors from all over the state were setting up their mineral displays. More than 2,000 visitors usually dropped in to examine these exhibits.

Typically there were 200-300 people on the floor at any single time, but on Saturday afternoons the crowd was larger and the showroom more congested. During the clamor of the afternoon, excitement punctuated the showcase arena as people marveled at the precious stones. The rules for the State Gem and Mineral Show prohibited club members from selling their collections to the audience. This was not a bazaar, but a large scale, show-and-tell festival for rockhounds. The audience was mostly curious browsers. Contacts were made, but sales or trades were not consummated on the showroom floor.

The display cases were custom made and furnished by local members of the various gem and mineral clubs throughout the state. They were about six feet long and housed the show items inside a wooden cabinet with a glass viewing cover and fluorescent light. There were ordinarily about 150 separate displays set up inside the Expo Building. Each collection was owned by individual members of various gem and mineral clubs. The cabinets were arranged in neat rows and took up most of the floor space in the center of the building.

As the show got underway that Saturday morning, it seemed like just another ordinary day at the fair, except for the special interest in the fossils. The Halls and Loves recognized many of the same people who attended year after year as the passing viewers paused for a closer look at the fossil exhibit. One case contained a femur and a set of claws; the other displayed a shoulder bone, a vertebra, and a rib. They had chosen not to label the pieces as being from an Acrocanthosaurus. Instead, they labeled the pieces as unidentified fossils from McCurtain County. Some people were perceptive enough to recognize them as dinosaur bones, but had not the faintest clue as to what kind. The onlookers asked questions that Cephis and Sid could not answer. The most versed in dinosaur anatomy asked if the bones were from a T.rex or some other Cretaceous theropod.

That afternoon as the crowd intensified, Sid and Cephis walked away from their case exhibits to visit with fellow rockhounds on the other side of the building, and Joyce and Floy stepped aside to chat with old friends clustered nearby. As they conversed, two strangers walked up to the glass cases containing the fossils and began pointing fingers and shouting like banshees in dripping repetition. "This is it! This is it! They have no business with these!" They made a scene and attracted attention. A small crowd gathered.

Joyce and Floy noticed the commotion and walked over to the two animated gentlemen. Somewhat annoyed, they asked what was wrong. The two men replied that these were some fossils a couple of amateurs had found and had no legitimate right to have them. Joyce responded, "Well, we're the half- owners of those bones. Would you like to meet the other half?" The two men just walked off without saying a word.

Sid and Cephis returned a few minutes later and learned about the incident. Wow! What was going on? They went looking for the two mysterious men and located them about eighty-feet away, admiring some exotic gems. Cephis and Sid introduced themselves and politely inquired as to who they were. One identified himself as Rich Cifelli, a paleontologist at the Sam Noble Museum; the other was Michael Mares, the director of the Museum.

The four men talked briefly, but the two strangers seemed rather cautious. Cephis asked them to walk with him to their fossil display and see if they could identify the pieces. The two men reluctantly followed. After coyly glancing inside the glass case, they offered no opinion whatsoever, not even a ventured guess. Their tone had changed. They now seemed to imply that the bones meant nothing. The conversation ended and the two men walked out of sight. It was a weird face-off, and a mystery to boot.

Cephis and Sid were dazed and confused. They wondered if the affair was over. What did these men know? What were they up to?

Sid became nervous. "Those guys are going to cause trouble," Sid quipped to Cephis. At that moment, Sid was ready to pack up and leave. Cephis, however, reminded Sid that if they left early, they would be violating the rules. Display owners could not remove their wares before the end of the show, and that was not until 5:00 PM on Sunday. Sid regained his composure and both men realized they needed to think about and understand the situation. How on earth could a couple of scientists from the local university know about an assortment of odd-looking dinosaur bones dug up in McCurtain County, more than three hundred miles away?

They had no answer, only rank speculation. Obviously, the two strangers now knew their names and from where the fossils had come. Their names were on the display cases along with a label identifying the origin of the fossils. Somehow, the university men recognized the fossils as belonging to a rare dinosaur. Perhaps they owned some Acro bones or had seen a similar set and made a connection. Maybe they were envious because their museum didn't own such a rare collection of theropod bones. Were they biased against amateurs possessing such valuable fossils? Were they blowing off a little steam to relieve pent-up resentment?

The disoriented showmen would never figure it out. Several years later, however, long after the last bone was retrieved from the pit, Cephis and Sid learned that the museum actually had a set of matching fossils from an Acro skeleton. These were the same pieces donated a half decade prior by Christi Silvey, the naturalist at Beavers Bend State Park. Perhaps the two scientists connected the showpiece bones to the fossils in their museum storage room. The two sets of bones came from the same species and were a size and color match. There was only one other possibility. Maybe Professor Langston at UT contacted Cifelli and Mares and advised them to be on the watch for some loose Acro bones rumored to be floating around somewhere in McCurtain County?

CHAPTER TWENTY-EIGHT
In the Clasp of Academia

The two exhausted families were glad to be home that Sunday night. Early Monday morning, Cephis would be in the timber patch and Sid, inside a commercial refrigeration hatch. When a blue-collar worker indulges in a weekend recreational binge, he often has to sacrifice a few hours sleep and returns to work on Monday feeling a little worn down.

The incident involving the two scientists at the rock show made an indelible impression. Time was creeping up on them; and the walls closing in. Their space to maneuver was narrowing. Their "command and control" over the dinosaur was weakening, day by day. A showdown with academia seemed inevitable.

It was not just the imperious intrusion of the "scientific mind" that concerned them; the bones needed professional attention. They needed a university accommodation that accorded an arrangement with a scientific lab to preserve the fossils, while also safeguarding their self-interest. A substantial amount of time and money was tied up in the dinosaur, and they needed to recoup at least part of their investment.

They sought to enlist professional support and mediate favorable terms. Negotiating a viable agreement might take months.

Due to the rare quality of their specimen and the high dollars at stake, they limited their contacts to major universities. Only the best universities with a high-caliber paleontological staff and advanced lab-preparation facilities could tackle the work order.

After their recent encounters with university staff, they were wary. Their contact with SMU's Dr. Slaughter was negative. Pitman was unpleasant. Dr. Dalquest's facilities at Midwestern were inadequate. To whom could they turn?

Cephis did not relish the onerous chore of soliciting university scientists. Both men's hearts and minds were still in the pit, not the lab. Having mastered excavation, lab preparation was entirely out of their league.

Since there were still loose bones awaiting recovery, they prepared to revisit the mine that Saturday. During the course of the week, they tried to slip in a few extra hours sleep to make up for the weekend deficit.

Only a few days after their return from the show, an unexpected call came in from the University of Texas (UT), and this time it wasn't Pittman. Dr. Wann Langston was on the line and wanted to talk business. The University knew about their discovery and wanted to make a deal. Instead of trying to edge in on the dig, Langston was offering lab services to professionally clean and preserve the fossils in return for a cast of the specimen. The caller commanded Cephis's complete attention.

Langston's proposition was enticing for several reasons. The two men felt pressured to act promptly to preserve the bones and get academia off their backs. Dr. Dalquest had told them that UT had the strongest paleontological endowment of any university in the country. Also, the Stovall-Langston partnership had recovered the first set of Acro bones on record.

Wann Langston, Jr., was one of the big names in American paleontology. Born July 21, 1921, in Oklahoma City, Oklahoma, he had a long, distinguished career spanning back to the late 1940s. Highly acclaimed in the field, he had been selected to fill the vacant position of curator of fossil vertebrates at the National Museum of Canada upon the retirement of the legendary Charles M. Sternberg.

While curator at the museum, Langston spent eight summers collecting in the western Canadian provinces and uncovered an impressive array of vertebrate fossils. In 1962, he and his family traded the cold, northern climate of Canada for the southern heat of central Texas after he accepted a faculty position in Geological Sciences at UT, Austin. During his long, distinguished tenure at UT, he held several prominent positions, including Director of the Vertebrate Paleontology Lab from 1969 to 1987.

Dr. Langston also served distinctively as President of the Society of Vertebrate Paleontology in 1975 and was editor of its *News Bulletin* from 1977 to 1979. He was the twentieth recipient of the Society of Vertebrate Paleontology's highest honor – the A.S. Romer-G.G. Simpton Medal. The medal was awarded annually in honor of the two twentieth century giants in paleontology and evolution.

Langston collected heavily in West Texas for 30 years, particularly in the Big Bend National Park area. He and his students uncovered a number of unique species, including the giant pterosaur, *Quetzalcoatus*, and *Deinosuchus*, an ancient crocodile relative.

His mentor was the late J. Willis Stovall of the University of Oklahoma (OU). In 1950, while Langston was still a graduate student, the two men uncovered a few fossils in Atoka County, Oklahoma, belonging to a previously unknown North American theropod. Stovall and Langston documented the new species and named it *Acrocanthosaurus atokensis*. Langston later became the world's most authoritative expert on this giant, apex predator.

It was no coincidence that Langston had a special interest in the Hall-Love specimen. Since his original Acro discovery, few new pieces had been found in the field. The American scientific community was thirsty for more detail on the elusive beast, and the only way to get it was through new findings. Unfortunately, new discoveries had not surfaced over the ensuing decades. Almost nothing had been added to the existing stock of knowledge.

The Acro story was a personal one for Wann Langston. His name and career were inextricably linked with the dinosaur. A new collection of approximately 20-30% of an Acro skeleton might be sufficient to fill in the missing pieces and solve the puzzle. With an adequate inventory of skeletal parts, Langston could construct a cast replica showing with accuracy what the animal looked like.

Hall and Langston conversed and gradually merged toward a meeting of the minds. Although additional negotiations might be needed to refine the details, a tentative understanding was ironed out over the phone. The oral agreement would be supplemented with a typewritten contract prepared by Hall and Love.

The basic tenets of the contract were as follows: UT agreed to clean and prepare the fossils in return for the right to make a molded cast of them within an eighteen-month time period. After securing a cast for UT, Langston agreed to return the original pieces and a cast of each bone to the two men. As a further stipulation, if the duo found additional Acro fossils, they were to present them to the lab.

Langston agreed to drive to Idabel to pick up the skeleton at Sid's warehouse. Upon taking possession, he would sign the contract and a packing list acknowledging the inventory of fossils received.

It seemed like a win-win situation for both parties. The two amateurs were to finish the field work, the University, the lab work. Both parties would end up with a marvelous cast of this extraordinary creature.

Cephis and Sid awaited the arrival of Langston with guarded optimism. If UT failed to perform, they had little recourse. They could not fathom the prospect of suing a major, out-of-state university. Still, with the bones at imminent risk of pyrite-induced deterioration, the two men had no choice but to place themselves and their precious bones at the mercy of academia.

CHAPTER TWENTY-NINE
A Clash of Cultures – Trickle-Down Fossil Manna

It was "morning in America" during the fall of 1986. Ronald Reagan, America's first and only Hollywood actor president had inspired a new consciousness in middle class Americans. The working class soon abandoned the Democratic Party in droves, much like the regional South had done in the 1970s after Lyndon Johnson signed the Civil Rights legislation into law. The American Dream was reawakened – even if it was a scaled-down version. "Conspicuous consumption" was back in vogue after years of "austerity and self-abnegation" under President Jimmy Carter. (Remember the oil embargo, gas shortages and long lines at the pump, economic malaise, stagflation, the Iranian hostage crisis, and the misery index?).

The American Dream as envisioned in the nineteenth century was broadly defined. As a young nation with a sparse population and abounding frontier, the dream was cast as an illimitable opportunity to seize new land in the West, or a chance to start a new business within a burgeoning national economy, or to simply strike it rich. Opportunity seemed boundless. The distant horizon always seemed within reach.

In the 1980s, with the frontier long vanished and the economy dominated by giant, multi-national corporations, Reagan redefined the American Dream in purely urban and consumptive terms. It was now merely a mortgaged home with two cars in the driveway and a lifestyle of suburban affluence in the new middle class. Business ownership was reconfigured in line with an evolving neo-service economy as typified by a plumber, hairdresser, or fast foods franchiser. The family-owned store, farm, or factory was a distant memory from a fading industrialism.

"Free market capitalism" was ballyhooed as a divine perpetual wealth machine that showered manna on America. Trickle-down corporate capitalism became the new plutocratic mantra. The high priests of conventional wisdom blessed the unwashed masses with a divinely sanctioned enculturation of true faith in the new economic order, and the masses clamored for more blessings. Only an obscure few had peeked behind the curtain to see the wizards of wealth disparity and realized that markets were not free and what some called crony capitalism (not to be confused with vulture capitalism) was the new economic reality (Frank, *What's The Matter With Kansas*).

The blessing of faith inspired a consumer spending splurge and the measure of personal success was redefined by conspicuous materialism. The new prosperity was driven and financed by massive debt – most of it made possible by the liberal use of credit cards and mortgage refinancing, which allowed consumers ample opportunity to tap into their growing home equities. Both spouses had to work outside the home to attain the equivalent standard of living earned by the male breadwinner in the 1950s-1970s. To maintain their affluent lifestyle, the middle class borrowed beyond their capacity to repay.

Lenient mortgage debt fueled real estate speculation, and a formula for a uniquely American housing boom was conceived and implemented. It was multifaceted and rose to its greatest prominence during the subprime mortgage fiasco of the George W. Bush presidency. Reagan once described America as a shining new city on a hill; more accurately it was a shining new suburb.

Savings and loan institutions provided the financing. The Federal Reserve furnished the easy money. Large corporations dominated the home construction industry and put small, independent builders out of business.

A porous border allowed the importation of millions of Mexicans who became a source of cheap labor. They were employed en masse as construction workers to build the sprawling new housing subdivisions and supply fresh occupants for the older stock of housing left vacant in the inner cities as "American Dream seekers" flocked to the shiny, outlying suburbs. Fertile farmlands on the fringe of metropolitan areas were transformed into large-scale housing developments and shopping malls. It was a recipe for urban sprawl and total dependency on the automobile and imported oil from the Middle East.

Government debt exploded. The annual budget deficits of the Reagan years exceeded all prior administrations combined. They were eventually surpassed by the George W. Bush and Barack Obama administrations. While Bush had inherited a surplus from Clinton, the Obama administration not only inherited the largest federal deficit in history, but two wars and a financial system on the verge of collapse that required tens of trillions in bailouts to "too big to fail" institutions to avert another Great Depression.

In the cases of Reagan and Bush, both administrations cut taxes to the wealthiest 3 percent of the population; became heavily involved in foreign entanglements, including wars; and ramped up defense spending to levels far beyond anything ever seen – the sole exception being World War II. While Reaganites and Bushites hypocritically extolled the virtues of free, unregulated markets, they simultaneously enjoyed lucrative government contracts and turned to the government for bailouts when banks "too big to fail" become insolvent due to bad loans and rank speculation. (In the case of Reagan, it was Savings and Loans, rather than banks, being bailed out.)

Reagonomics and its heirs – Clintonomics and Bushonomics – were essentially de-Rooseveltization schemes to eliminate government regulations, privatize every public function (even the military), and end social programs that served as safety nets for the middle class. Bushonomics, the most ambitious plan of all, failed in its overt attempt to privatize Social Security. The Bush II administration squandered the Clinton surplus on tax cuts to the wealthy and wars in Afghanistan and Iraq not financed with current revenues; the debt was passed on to future generations.

Beginning in the Reagan years, a new "American exceptionalism" was touted as if a fundamental paradigm shift had brought about an idyllic, utopian reality. A fiscal policy of "borrow and spend" created rising incomes and wealth at the top and a trickle-down benefit to the patriotic working classes.

America's preeminent defense contractors like Halliburton gloated with each new round of spending as their share of the federal budget soared to new heights. Empire and consumption-based prosperity became linked in the hearts and minds of the public. The nation had become addicted to cheap immigrant labor, cheap imported goods, and expensive imported oil, which required a worldwide projection of military power to maintain the status quo.

With Reagan at the pinnacle of popularity, it didn't matter that federal deficits were shooting through the roof, the environment was deteriorating at a rapid clip, and the nuclear clock had been set at two minutes before high noon. (This clock supposedly measured the intensity of the Cold War hostilities and the risk of an itchy finger on the nuclear arsenal.) Nuclear missiles were on hair-trigger readiness on both sides of the Atlantic throughout the 1980s.

What did matter was that the stock market was booming, profits were high, "greed was good," credit was easy, corporate CEO compensation was soaring, and America was sitting on the precipice of world domination. The Soviet Union was ebbing toward insolvency as a result of escalating expenditures required by the arms race and its own war in Afghanistan. As apparent winner in the Cold War, a nationwide revival was celebrated across America, especially along the Washington Beltway and within the lavish boardrooms of the largest corporations. Even the working class was encouraged to imbibe the "feel good Americanism."

During Reagan's reign, big government was blamed for everything, while big business and lobbyists were blamed for nothing. The white working class had taken Reagan's cue; right-wing anti-government militia groups proliferated during the Clinton years, and big media like Fox News began constructing an anti-Clinton, anti-democratic, anti-government regulation, pro-corporate spin zone. The Reagan ideology served as the zeitgeist for the ensuing decades. George W. Bush took up the Reagan mantle and expounded the ideology to new heights of extremism. (Reagan grew the budget by 189 percent and nearly tripled the national debt; George W. Bush added 4.9 trillion to the national debt (MSNBC, *The Rachel Maddow Show*).

For most of the local populace of McCurtain County, things did not feel so grand during the 1980s. McCurtain County, like most of rural America, had not found joyous prosperity under Reagan, nor had they in the two ensuing decades since his economic and social policies became firmly rooted. Beginning with the long-term policy of globalism and deregulation unleashed by the Reagan Revolution, a slow, steady decline of small town America began. Two trends were driving American demography during the 1980s and thereafter; the suburbanization and Southernization of America. Republicans had timed their Southern strategy perfectly.

The tinkle-down effect was scarcely palpable to the sons and grandsons of sharecroppers, tenant farmers, and lumberjacks in this largely blue-collar, once Democratic, but now Republican county. For a sizeable portion of the working class, wages seemed to have stagnated, and few new jobs were created locally since Reagan's tenure. The brightest employment prospects for working class people in McCurtain County were still found at the Weyerhaeuser-owned pulp mill at Valiant or the Tyson poultry processing plant near Broken Bow. Federal spending on rural projects for America fell from $10 billion to $1 billion during the Reagan years. As federal debt soared, the trickle-down effect trickled out to cheaper labor in Mexico and China. (McCarthy 160) The country was rhetorically-committed to small government, except when it came to the defense budget.

Compared to many of their blue collar peers, Sid and Cephis were doing relatively well. As conventionally defined by Reagan, the two men had already attained the American Dream, or certainly made a considerable down payment on it. Both men, disregarding the banker's lien, owned their own houses (modest as they were); both usually had two vehicles parked in their driveways; and both owned their own businesses – Sid, a commercial refrigeration repair business and tire shop, and Cephis, a rock shop and tour guide service. Although overworked and tired, they were relatively stable in their finances. They were not rich or conspicuously affluent, yet neither were they mired in poverty. Still, as hard as Cephis worked over the decades, he never became wealthy, not even notably affluent. He was Exhibit A in negating the old fashioned myth that hard work always equated wealth. He was no poster child for Horatio Alger.

Cephis Hall's American Dream was intertwined with nature. That fact would not have surprised anyone who knew him. His life's vocation, his recreation, his business, his self-esteem, his ideas about aesthetics and tranquility, were all swaying to the mooring of geological and biological manifestations. Of course like all Americans, he wanted his share of the pie and a secure abode to call his own, but even that part of the dream needed to be anchored in the midst of a rustic and secluded setting that harbored treasure of exotica within the physical realm.

The two country boys were not driven to impress anyone with the latest fad or fashion and did not own the finest three-piece suit or the most sophisticated formal attire. They rarely resorted to credit cards or consumption-driven debt. Lavishness, extravagance, an expensive swimming pool or swank patio was of no interest to them.

Hall and Love did not live in a shiny new suburb. Cephis lived in the sticks not far from honky-tonk row, and Sid lived in a small house in a small town where vast cotton fields once enveloped the surrounding landscape. In their unique life situation, materialism was subordinate to naturalism, and individualism overshadowed conformism. While the new American suburbs reflected the transience of American life, Hall and Love were rooted in the local community – a community of stability where neighbor knew neighbor and life-long friendships endured.

The two men favored the basics of life and avoided conspicuous luxury. They were not garish or ostentatious in their styles, tastes, manners, or displays. More than anything else, they wanted to be close to nature. They wanted to experience it firsthand – literally being able to see, feel, taste, smell, hear, and touch it. Also, they had a great desire to share nature with others. Nature was like a second religion for them. It was beautiful and offered a spiritual transcendence. Both were ardent nature explorers and coveted the raw products mined directly from God's good earth. They were greenies, pure and simple. The social and economic forces of the 1980s had not touched them.

On a Saturday morning during the fall of 1986, the two Boomer-Sooners had a scheduled meeting with Dr. Wann Langston, also known as "Mr. Dinosaur," and his graduate assistant, Jeffrey Pittman. The two paleontologists were traveling all the way from central Texas, and were to meet the Okies at Sid's commercial building in Idabel to examine their warehoused bones.

The Langston-Pittman association was much like the Stovall-Langston partnership of lore – a mentor-protégé relationship that yielded tangible results. Although different in temperament and personalities, the partnership blended the unique talents, specialties, and responsibilities of each man into a kind of division of labor that accomplished real goals.

The two scientists were expecting to see the remains of an articulated Acro skeleton housed in a private storage shed. Such a specimen was extremely rare – in fact, so rare that none was known to exist anywhere in the world. The two scientists had agreed that if the bones were confirmed to be those of an *Acrocanthosaurus,* the parties were to enter into an arrangement whereby the university would take possession of the skeleton, with Hall and Love retaining ownership.

Cephis and Sid knew that if Langston, a world-class paleontologist, was willing to drive more than a thousand miles to inspect an unattested set of fossils stored at an obscure warehouse in a small town of the Red River valley, Langston had insight into the merit of their specimen.

For the two university men, it must have seemed like a leap of faith. Other than to take Cephis, an amateur, at his word, the two professionals had little else to go on—they had not seen the fossils. Cephis and Sid had tried to keep the discovery a secret. Somehow, academia had penetrated their crusty veneer and sorted the basic facts. Perhaps the academics had literally sniffed out bones from afar. Possibly, they had sent spies to infiltrate the community and gather a dossier on the diggers and their elusive bones. The two scientists had to know more than they pretended.

Langston and Pittman were driving all the way from the campus at Austin, Texas, a distance of more than 500 miles, and were expected to roll into town about noon. Sid and Cephis agreed to meet them at the McDonald's in Idabel, a universal icon.

The two Okies arrived early at Idabel's popular burger and fries franchise and began filling up on caffeine. They were immersed in mixed feelings as they contemplated the transfer of their beloved dinosaur into UT's possession. It had been over two years since the first bone was pulled from the pit. The fruits of their labor were about to slip out of their hands, perhaps forever.

They did not know if they could trust these out-of-state scientists. Doubts and skepticism clouded their consciousness. Still, for the mere sake of "peace of mind," they had little choice but to put their trust and hope in Dr. Langston and UT.

Cephis had met the obnoxious Pittman. The conniving "Pitt man" had visited him at his home on several occasions in an apparent attempt to hone in on the location of the excavation and nudge in on the dig. Cephis refused to cooperate. The pushy and fast-talking Pittman had not impressed him.

Dr.Langston, however, had impressed Cephis. The Arkansas native knew about his remarkable career, his scientific reputation, and his first-hand knowledge of the *Acrocanthosaurus*. In their prior phone conversations, Dr. Langston had come across as rather suave and amiable. Unlike Pittman, Langston was soft-spoken and had a pleasant tone and manner of conversation. Langston was cultured and sociable, an excellent communicator, and could put an anxious person at ease. He did not talk over his listener's head and wasted few words.

Like Hall and Love, Langston had deep roots in Oklahoma. He was born in Oklahoma City and studied at the University of Oklahoma. The native son was highly respected by the citizens of that city and had earned the honor of having a public library named for him. Despite having been away for decades, he was still remembered as one of OKC's favorite sons.

A pair of Sooners on the north side of the Red River sat in the local McDonald's sipping coffee as they awaited the arrival of a couple of Longhorns from south of the river. At about 12:15 that afternoon, the two scientists arrived in Pittman's late-model, half-ton Ford pick-up. Cephis recognized the truck immediately. The two scientists had not kept the two amateurs waiting long.

The four men exchanged greetings as Langston and Pittman joined the two locals at their table. Langston, with a distinguished persona and dignified demeanor, immediately garnered the attention of the two Okies.

Langston was about six feet in height and average build. He had a fair complexion, a few freckles, and a rounded face. He had a receding hairline that was visible whenever he removed his elegant-looking hat. His hair was closely clipped and graying. He had a calm, masterly expression that resolutely inspired trust and respect. For an aged man of sixty years, he was spry and active.

As the two travelers consumed hamburgers and soft drinks, the four men became better acquainted. Langston and Pittman had come all the way from the southern portion of the Lone Star State. The dinosaur was the only thing on the agenda. After a little small talk to thaw the ice, the sole subject was the *Acrocanthosaurus*.

The two homespun Okies ostensibly clashed with the two academicians – culturally, regionally, educationally, occupationally, socially, and economically. There was an unmistakable divergence between their backgrounds. This became even more apparent the longer the two blue-collar workers sat across the table from the two white-collared scholars, and their interaction noted by curious burger-devouring patrons sitting nearby. There was an unbridgeable difference between their hardscrabble world, and Langston's refined, scholarly sphere.

Cephis and Sid were not leisurely gentlemen in the classic sense. One only had to look at their fingers to determine that – dirt under the nails and rough, calloused hands were telltale signs of recent manual culpability. Theirs was a world of hard, honest work with their hands – the use of tools, spades, machines, and chainsaws to make a daily living.

At the local McDonald's, an egalitarian, fast foods restaurant, different classes of folk commingled. Locals were distinguishable from non-locals in their manner of informal dress, demeanor, and language, and workers discerned from professionals via similar distinctions. The wealthy or highly-successful, on the rare occasions such persons patronized McDonald's, usually had some aura of self-importance, bearing, or condescension that could be detected by the local rank and file diners.

As the impromptu business meeting proceeded, the watchful diners sitting nearby recognized the incongruence between the two local rustics and the two out-of-state gentlemen. In this instance, McDonald's played host to an odd conference involving two provincial commoners and two erudite professionals. Langston had enough cosmopolitan panache to conspicuously stand out in a prosaic setting like McDonald's; Pittman, on the other hand, was less a stark contrast, seemingly more mundane.

Herein, with McDonald's serving as an open forum, the mechanically endowed mingled with the academically enshrined; two working stiffs interacted with the intelligentsia of high academia; and an older industrial order of machines, tools, and brawn contrasted with a newer order of books, intellect, computers, and air conditioned classrooms. The meeting represented a clash of cultures: remnants of a fading industrial order intersected with an emerging world of science and technocracy.

Dr. Langston had done his share of hard, physical labor in his earlier years while prospecting as a graduate student or untenured professor, but that was many decades prior. He now supervised the field projects, and the heavy work was done by students or field assistants.

While the four men sat together and chatted, Cephis took advantage of the opportunity to question Langston about how he had learned so much about their local fossil collection. Mr. Dinosaur's reply was terse and evasive. He stated he had looked over the photos sent by Dr. Dalquest, which led him to believe that a sizeable quantity of recovered fossils actually existed. This presumption enticed him to make the trip to Idabel to personally inspect their warehoused collection of fine bones. In the case of the *Acrocanthosaurus,* the number of fossils on record was so scarce that even a mere handful of new pieces might shed valuable light on the story of the species. Langston's answer provided no new insight into the university's motives or their behind-the-scenes machinations.

The restaurant meeting was short. The two travelers needed to proceed with business. They had come a long way with no time to waste, and had a long drive back to Austin. Shortly, they were back in their truck and following the two Okies to Sid's storage building only a few blocks from the eatery.

Within a few minutes, the two vehicles arrived at the warehouse. The plan was for the two paleontologists to examine the fossils, and if satisfied, load them up and take them to the university's lab in Austin, where they could be cleaned and molded into cast replicas. The two warehousemen had already packed the bones in crates lined with foam rubber. The bones were secure and ready for transport.

Cephis Hall and Sid Love, purveyors of fine and hard bones, readied themselves for the psychological distress of seeing their wondrous dragon depart from their control. It was somewhat painful – almost like losing a stepchild or family member. The enchanting bones had given them purpose and meaning beyond their routine life experience; their embarkation to a new home might engender a void or empty feeling.

The four men got out of their vehicles and promptly went inside. Langston and Pittman made a concerted effort to conceal their excitement as they entered the bone-holding morgue.

As the storage room lit up, their eyes opened to the curious wonder of what remained of a giant killer who had once elicited sheer terror across a great expanse of valleys and swamplands along the southern shores of North America. This was not just any ordinary dinosaur. This was *Acrocanthosaurus* – a regal theropod from the lower Cretaceous. **Behold the bones of *Acrocanthosaurus*!**

The two academics wasted no time in examining the treasure. The lids were removed from each crate, allowing the gentlemen to inspect the contents of each box. Langston and Pittman showed little emotion as they peered inside each crate and assessed the valuables.

The two fossil experts made a cursory examination of each bone, and found most to be in relatively good condition. Langston made positive comments about what a good job the two locals had done in recovering the fossils without inflicting collateral damage. He noted their distinctive black color and expressed concern regarding the pyrite contamination.

Langston was satisfied with what he had seen. Most of the crates weighed less than a hundred pounds and required two men to carry and load each box. The boxes filled up the entire bed of Pittman's truck. After the last crate was loaded, Langston handed

Cephis a signed copy of the contract and packing list that identified each individual bone included in the inventory.

Presumably, the skeleton was only being loaned; ownership was not passing to UT. Although the university was now responsible for the bones, what could the two amateurs actually do if they became damaged, stolen, or disintegrated into dust? Could the university be held accountable? Langston seemed like a credible scientist. They were willing to give him and UT the benefit of the doubt, but had a feeling of guarded optimism as the bones slipped out of their grasp, and the truck disappeared into the distant vista.

While it had taken Cephis and Sid almost three years to dig up this fine inventory of *Acrocanthosaurus*, it had taken only about thirty minutes to load the truck. Within minutes, Pittman and Dr. Langston would cross the Red River into Texas with a truck load of exotic Oklahoma fossils. This collection represented the most significant Acro inventory in paleontological history, indeed, one of the greatest theropod specimens of all time. Before their departure, Langston had given the two bone conveyors a business card and invited them to Austin for a guided tour of the lab. For Langston and Pittman, this was merely business; for Cephis and Sid, it was an emotional ordeal.

As the weighted-down truck left Idabel with its load of treasure, the minds of the two Okies were again filled with uncertainty. They hated losing control of the dinosaur. This reminded them of the emotional vacuum they experienced after their dig was halted while awaiting approval from Weyerhaeuser to resume. The loss of the dinosaur was deeply sobering.

At this point, all they could do was sit back and wait on the university to perform. Until then, there was more work to do at the dinosaur pit. They were hoping to recover the skull and the remaining bones. They still had a reasonable chance of fulfilling their version of the American Dream.

CHAPTER THIRTY
The Visit to Langston's Bone Lair

After surrendering their bones to the university, the two peevish Okies were engulfed in a vacuous state of mind. Their bones were gone and their warehouse emptied. They now had to contend with a gnawing feeling of emptiness and impotence. As with the tedious arrangement made with Bueno two years prior, they now had to wait it out. And again, they found themselves in a state of limbo and dependency.

These were men of action. They could not sit still for long. They had given UT a timetable of eighteen months to perform their part of the contractual agreement. If it actually took that long, their patience was sure to wear thin. The only remedy to their dilemma was to plunge ever more deeply into the underlying stratum and recover the remaining contents.

They wanted to retrieve every bone still entrapped in the crusted Cretaceous bed. Bone emancipation was back on the agenda and the principal target was now the skull. Their response was simple. Digging was better than sitting, action better than inaction. Through a resumption of intensive digging, they hoped to find more bones and convert their apprehension into something constructive.

The agreement with Langston was straightforward and represented a reciprocal deal. Langston was supposed to make a cast of each and every piece, and then assemble them into a mount for display. Cephis and Sid were to get the original fossils back, not assembled, but as a collection of loose pieces, cleaned and treated. Langston now had a rare opportunity to examine and study the remains of a genuine Acrocanthosaurus. Both parties had signed the written agreement, but it was not notarized.

The fossil collection was out of their hands and seemed rather tenuous, but the pit was still accessible. One thing remained constant – their perseverance. Freed from the burden of tending bones, they had a slight feeling of liberation and more time and energy to delve into the remaining secrets still sealed off from human purview. With renewed vigor, they picked and scooped deeper into the stratum in a new excavation phase.

Their newly-ordered dig soon turned into disappointment. The recovery of fresh bones was going slowly. After several weeks of excavation, they were now certain that there had been less than a 100% articulated skeleton buried at the site. They had successfully retrieved more than half of the original skeleton.

The expedition had largely been stanched. There was no longer an expedient flow of bones from the pit to the warehouse. It was more like a trickle. The bone bonanza had already been struck; diminishing returns had set in.

A few bones here and there were uncovered – mostly small, insignificant pieces. What about the skull? The most important piece of all was still missing. A few new pieces were now stashed at their warehouse, but other than that, the warehouse was empty. And the duo felt kind of empty.

Still, they had much to be proud of. Their excavation marked the first time in history that two amateurs, operating totally independently of a major university or commercial fossil company, had carried out such a massive undertaking with remarkable success. It was definitely the first time that self-educated amateurs had excavated their own discovery of a nearly complete dinosaur with no outside financing or intervention. Nobody could deny them that accomplishment, not even the highest order of academia.

After a couple of months of "bone pettiness," it was time for a break. They were now more concerned about their fossils in the lab than the remaining pieces in the pit. Dr. Langston had invited them to come to inspect the lab facility and see the progress being made on preserving their specimen. It was time to take him up on his offer. Cephis called the University to make an appointment. Langston reserved that following Monday afternoon for their personalized tour of the lab. The locals were going to the great university in Austin as personal guests of one of the greatest dinosaurologists of all time.

Their Acro bones were housed in the Balcones Research Lab at the University of Texas. This massive laboratory contained one of the largest assemblages of vertebrate fossils in the world. The facility principally warehoused unarticulated specimens of mammals, reptiles, and dinosaurs. This large research center was sealed off from the public by a chain-link fence with guards stationed at the gate entrance.

A visitor had to have a scheduled appointment to get inside. Langston's bone lair was not located on the campus and was essentially private in the way it operated. In contrast, there was a science museum on campus that housed impressive archaeological and finished paleontological exhibits and was open to the public. The format for the flow of specimens through the system was expediently simple: from field to lab to museum. However, the lab was already weighted down with decrepit fossils. Unfortunately, the more the bones accumulated, the more they became an albatross for the scientific staff.

The paleontological wing of the Balcones Laboratory was a giant repository and keeper of both prepared and unprepared fossils. Thousands of specimens had been collected during the 1930s when FDR's New Deal unleashed droves of workers from the Civilian Conservation Corps to perform construction projects across an impoverished nation. Many specimens dug up in 1938 by WPA labor were now collecting dust as they sat decrepitly on shelves. Despite being backed by a generous endowment and a world-class technology and knowledge base, the lab looked rather cluttered and disorganized with a huge backlog of unworked fossils.

Dr. Langston and his able assistant Jeff Pittman met his trans-Red River guests at the front entrance and guided the duo around the lab. The tour was superficially friendly, but a little unsettling for the two amateurs. They discovered that their extraordinary specimen was being treated in a rather ordinary manner—as if it was just another minuscule collection of neglected bones. This was rather humbling for the two out-of-state bone connoisseurs who thought their dinosaur was special.

Their observations did not instill confidence. Their rare and unique product was considered no different here than the typical heaps of bones lying about. All were aging with each passing day, and now their specimen appeared to be losing out in the race against time. Furthermore, they learned that their Acro had been catalogued as a student project and might not get the master's attention it deserved. And to their further dismay, they learned that Pittman had been put in charge.

Cephis and Sid subtly expressed their concerns. Langston responded to each question and reassured them that the lab would soon get started on their Acro project. Even the "obnoxious Pittman" put on a happy face. Being calm and dignified, he seemed like a different person now that he was no longer badgering Cephis about taking over the excavation. Still, reassurances left room for doubt. The conversation between the four men leached out new issues that were not transparent during their visual inspection of the lab.

Dr. Langston, normally engrossed in scientific detail, didn't have much time for a couple of "schmucks" from across the river. But on this occasion, he showed considerable patience and deference. However, the two "scraggly hayseeds" detected ambivalence in his choice of words and tone. Red flags were thrown.

Langston reiterated his concern about the pyrite contamination, but this time with a more somber tone as if he had just discovered that the pyrite affliction was a more serious problem than originally thought. The ball was now in the university's court. Instead of Pittman snooping around and trying to pry out any lead or information about the dinosaur site, now the two Acro owners were trying to ferret out information from Langston-Pittman. As the conversation continued, Hall-Love looked for clues to interpret what was really going on behind the bone facade.

The conversation involving the four men proceeded in an orderly and sequential manner. Each time Cephis or Sid pointed out a deficiency observed while touring the great repository, "Mr. Dinosaur" countered with an explanation or alibi. Whenever Cephis inquired about the inordinate quantity of fossils lying around and apparently unattended, Dr. Langston explained that this was typical for most university labs. There simply were not enough personnel and funds available to tend to all the fossils.

Langston's words rang true. Hall and Love could see the obvious — a baffling pastiche of miscellaneous bones that were either consolidated into small clusters or lying loosely as single, distinct pieces. Scads of jumbled bones were arrayed wall to wall – an unimaginable stockpile housed inside a single building.

Each precious compendium of related bones had to wait its turn, but given the significance of the Acro specimen, the lab planned on making it a priority project. Although the inquisitive bone owners did not know it at the time, Langston had given a true and accurate statement reflecting the reality of most paleontological labs and museums across the nation – typically they were understaffed, underfunded, and overworked.

Finally, the conversation stumbled upon the matter of the skull. Cephis informed the esteemed scientist that he and Sid were still hoping to find the skull. The highbrowed Langston sneered at the "oafish hillbilly" with condescending skepticism. In a knee-jerk response, Langston authoritatively informed the backwoods rube that it was very unlikely – dinosaur skulls are hard to find.

Apparently, it was highly unusual for an embedded skull to remain intact over the eons because the slightest movement of the earth breaks them apart. Normally, if they are found, they are already broken to pieces and unsalvageable. This claim made by Langston was also true.

Defiantly, Cephis informed Dr. Dinosaur that he did not think that the earth had shifted at the location where the dinosaur was discovered, and if the skull was there he was going to find it. Langston emitted a doubtful stare. "I don't think you will," he reiterated. Such disparaging remarks from one of the most respected paleontologists in the world would have stopped most amateurs in their tracks, but not Cephis Hall. "I plan on proving you wrong," countered Hall.

CHAPTER THIRTY-ONE
In Search of the Skull

The two resolute naturalists sought refuge from the complexities of the modern world by immersing themselves in the search for elusive bones hidden inside a waste-holding pit near the brim of a forlorn river. Although desiring closeness with nature, more than anything else they aspired to uncover the prized specimen that had for so long eluded professional paleontologists – an intact skull of an *Acrocanthosaurus*.

Until their articulated skeleton was recovered, only a few, scattered pieces of the rare theropod had ever been found. A discovery of an Acro skull was not even contemplated by mainstream scientists. Not until the scientific world got wind of their recent discovery had it even been conceivable that a fifty-percent articulated Acro could be found, let alone a nearly pristine skull.

As the day dawned, the two men were back inside the trench, peerlessly probing its outer fringe for any clues or signs. At times, whenever they penetrated hard clay or stone, they were forced to use a jackhammer. Rattled by the bone-jarring work, they had to be careful not to sink the bit too deeply or ream out too big of a chunk, lest they shatter a precious bone.

The fecund foliage and beautiful florescence adorning the riverbank awed the two nature lovers, even as they toiled in an artificial pit. The majesty of the towering oaks and pines inspired reverence. The brilliant blue of the sky and the light ambience of the misty morning overhang blended serenely with the diverse, riverine setting. But the luring beauty of the majestic landscape did not prevent their feelings of isolation and loneliness.

Despite the secluded, insular backdrop and the paucity of human intruders, the diggers were never truly alone. Insects, snakes, lizards, and small mammals sometimes invaded their workspace. The obsessed bone hunters frequently contended with menacing assaults by swarming mosquitoes, gnats, ticks, and ants. Hungry coyotes were sometimes heard howling along the river as dusk eclipsed into darkness, on the days they worked late. The hoots of owls and swoops of hawks were detected in the early hours of darkness. Armadillos, ever shy and peculiar creatures making odd grumbling and hissing noises when cornered, were sometimes seen scuttling about. The chirpings of crickets and birds punctuated the evening twilight as dusk settled over the Mountain Fork.

The wildlife captivated their senses as much as the sheer beauty of the scenery. Their most enjoyable diversion was watching hummingbirds dive for the fresh, succulent nectar of nearby blooming flowers. The most harrowing experiences came when the pit was encroached by pit vipers. The aggressive cottonmouths thrived in water. These fearsome and venomous black snakes, also known as water moccasins, will swim near a person without pause and bite without provocation. When in water, they are in their element.

On one occasion, Sid scooped up a large cottonmouth as it swam toward his unsuspecting partner, tossed it on the dry edge of the gully, and killed it with his shovel. Whenever the gully contained water — about 80 percent of the time, it seemed – the two diggers had to be wary of snakes. During their long tenure inside the pit – a course of several years – they smashed the heads of dozens of serpents. Mean, black snakes were the bane of the two men's riverine exposure.

On the good side of nature, they relished the opportunity of getting a glimpse of a passing deer as it darted through the high grass, fleeing from the sight and sound of humans. Rabbits, squirrels, raccoons, skunk, and opossums all came under their radar.

The forest's nocturnal pulse was vibrant and seethed with fecundity. At times, the two men left scraps of food for the coons and possums, or for whatever animal wandered up first. The food was always gone by the time they returned. Over time, the raccoons became friendly and scampered about as darkness approached – perhaps waiting for a handout. The spontaneous shenanigans of forest-dwelling animals provided some measure of escape from the drudgery of shoveling dirt along a lonely river.

There were never enough hours in a day. On weekends, they often worked after dark. As the light dwindled in the forest, they toiled by lantern, spotlight, or flashlight. Sunburned, sullied with mud, and annoyed by insects, the stubborn diggers continued laboring for hours after sunset. Their obsession was bordering on madness.

Cephis was most driven, but Sid, despite being almost twenty years his senior, stood up to every demand and fully accommodated his steadfast partner. They knew they had a marvelous discovery under their belt, but they wanted to cap it off with a few more fossils and the all-important skull. Their bone horizon had not yet been reached.

They avowed to hunker down, overcome the perennial forces of nature, and emerge from the pit with a trophy skull to present to a skeptical world, most importantly, to Dr. Langston.

But where was the skull? And where was the tail? The tail was important as a marker based on the dinosaur death pose and might give an indication of where the skull could be found. In the classic dinosaur death pose, after rigor mortis sets in, the head and tail both curve inward and face each other—much like a fetal position.

Unfortunately, their enthusiasm was not matched by reality. After weeks of continuous digging, their bone horizon looked clouded. They uncovered a few bones here and there, but no skull. Their optimism was starting to wane.

Had the storm taken a malevolent toll on their bone supply? The mine seemed almost depleted. Since the storm, the number of bones coming out of the pit had been reduced to a dribble. Had the bones washed away? Had they rotted in the ground? Had they seeped ever deeper into their underground lair? Or had the balance of the skeletal pieces simply leached out decades earlier and vanished in the mist of time? The fabric of their bone infatuation was beginning to unravel. Doubt was creeping in and starting to skew their bone-headed determinism.

Feeling a trifle down and a little devoid of luck, their only remedy was more digging. The hard-boned realists had transmuted into hard-headed dreamers—die-hards seining an empty net and refusing to admit failure. Although hovering at the margins of exhaustion, they would not quit—especially Cephis, and Sid was determined not to abandon him.

Their enduring sacrifice and shared experience had bonded the two men in a kind of brotherly affection. A sense of duty and obligation bade them ever forward in pursuit of their mission, regardless of the consequences.

In their continued search for the Acro skull, they uncovered the remains of another prehistoric animal. A 100-million-year-old turtle was recovered in the same Cretaceous level. There was nothing contained in the scientific record about this species of turtle. Its limestone-crusted shell was 18 inches across. A rare specimen in its own right, it accorded no consolation. They wanted the real prize—a skull worth a million words, perhaps a million dollars.

A few months had elapsed since their trip to Austin, but the words spoken by Dr. Dinosaur still rang clearly: "You will never find the skull." "You will never find the skull." Other PhDs had told them the same thing.

In a concerted effort to prove the experts wrong, they had concentrated their search at both ends of the trench. They knew the skull was probably embedded at one corner or the other of the skeletal bed—not distributed in the center, but on the margins.

Before the backhoe work was performed, they had breached a 14-foot tunnel into the north side of the gully. The backhoe operator had shaved off the top of the cave, converted it into an open trench, and then extended it by an additional 12 feet to make a total trench span of 26 feet. They then spearheaded the principal thrust of their spades on the north end of the trench—reasonably assuming that if the skull had been situated on the southern edge, they would have already stumbled across it.

Finally, a shred of luck came their way. At last, a piece of the tail cropped up near the southeast corner of the trench and seemed to be facing northward. In sorting the puzzle, locating the placement of the curved tip of the tail was all-important in providing a sense of bearing, because it often pointed in the direction of the skull. But they had not found the tip of the tail, only the mid-section. With limited directional perspective, they conjectured as to which direction the tip of the tail faced. Based on speculation, the skull might be located within the northeast zone of the trench.

It now looked like the trench needed to be extended outward, to the east. To find the skull, they might have to tunnel by hand into the northeast side of the trench. At the twilight of their exhausting ordeal, this seemed like more than they could handle. A backhoe was no longer feasible, but perhaps with luck they might not have to trench too far.

They redirected their excavation at the northern end of the east wall. After scooping dirt for several more days, there was still no sign of the skull. Having no accurate assessment of the actual height or length of the dinosaur, their only option was to span-out the dig.

They had found nothing resembling fragments of a crushed skull, and that was a good sign. They dug an adjoining five-foot wide trench six feet into the east wall of the trench, but still the skull eluded them. As they say, the skull is always the hardest part to find. The two weary amateurs knew it would not be easy.

Cephis had lain awake at night, brainstorming about where to look next, and was beginning to think that the PhDs might be right after all. He tried to shake off negative thoughts and reminded himself that perseverance was the key to success. He was determined not to be sidetracked by negativity and despair. Although he had no formal college training, the mutterings of PhDs did not intimidate him. He had shaken off the negative feedback from professionals to this point, but could he rise to the occasion and overcome the many obstacles still ahead?

Cephis knew the skull was somewhere within an eastward extension of the tunnel. He suspected that it had been washed outside the actual confines of the bone bed, and that was likely the reason it was proving difficult to find. With extreme concentration, his perceptive senses finally kicked in and accorded focus on a resolute mental picture of the cranial case as it lay within its hidden lair. While pondering the intricacies in detail, he mentally pinpointed the location of the skull.

The following morning he called Sid and told him that they should extend their dig about four feet further to the north. Two days later, on a bright Saturday morning, the two men initiated their dig at Cephis' projected location. They cut northward about two feet from the edge of their previous dredge and immediately hit pay dirt.

CHAPTER THIRTY-TWO
A Skull Worth A Million Dollars

Despite it being an overcast, misty day, the spirit of the duo was buoyed as they toiled inside the trench. Suddenly, they probed something solid and detected a vague outline of an ossified encrustation. They felt a sudden rush as their hearts raced.

The first protrusion distinguished was a tooth. In the predawn hours, they had tapped the edge of a jaw – indicating the possibly of an intact skull. Jubilantly, they combed the matrix in an attempt to determine the outline of the hard object they felt.

In the midst of willow leaves, tall grasses, creeping vines, and majestic pines, the two naturalists had sunk their shaft into the Antlers clay and touched the rim of one of the rarest, largest, most complete, and pristine dinosaur skulls ever probed. The prize was located to the west of a clutch of willows and at the base of a gnarled maple tree.

After probing more closely, they detected with amazement more of the teeth still intact inside the jaw. With a little more scraping, the contours of the skull became discernible. Like an apparition from the unrecorded past, the skull with its monstrous, protruding teeth glistening in the jaw seemed to have an expression and meaning of its own. "Bring me back to life and restore my magnificence," it suggested, "for I am the Terror of the South, and I once ruled these lands."

Eventually recognized as the third largest theropod skull ever found – four feet, seven inches long – only two adult T. Rexes, Stan and Sue, had larger skulls. Nineteen curved, serrated teeth lined each side of the upper jaw. Virtually all the teeth were in place inside the jaw—67 total.

Just as ennui was about to overtake them, they made the discovery of a lifetime. While not yet sure of the value and significance of their boney encrustment, they were in a joyous mood.

It was axiomatic among the scientific community that they would never find this marvelous piece, let alone successfully excavate and transport it. Now the challenge was staring them in the face.

Devoid of the imprimatur of the scientific establishment, they now had proof that they had been right and the academics wrong. The ordeal of finding the skull had tested their strength and resolve. Now they charted the course for the most important part of their entire excavation – the actual extraction of the Acro skull. Merely finding it was hard enough, now it would be equally hard to liberate, move, load, and transport it without inflicting undue damage. With wry caution, they began digging around the prize, leaving an earthen base beneath it.

The ordeal of freeing and preparing the skull for movement took about thirty days. The two McCurtainites, due to the importance of the specimen, spent more time at the pit during this intense period than any other timeframe since the dig commenced, often working into the still hours of darkness. At the end of each day, they covered the skull to protect it from the elements while they were away from the grave site.

After careful planning, their strategy to excavate and move this huge block of bone was mapped out. The project required a daunting feat of engineering. They needed winches, ramps, cables, come-alongs, chains, and an assortment of construction materials. A sturdy wooden bridge needed to be built over the abutment to move the 1000 pound skull across the gully. Also, they needed to construct a ramp into the bed of their pickup so they could man-handle the bulky prize up the incline.

Before tackling the task of separating the skull from the compacted stratum, they took measurements of the skull and readied rebar inserts that could be bent to extend the length of the measurements. The rebar could be folded to fit the perimeter of the skull and the ends cut with a bolt cutter.

After removing the clay concretement from around the top and sides of the skull, it was left sitting atop a solid clay pedestal. With the earthen debris cleared, they could begin their delicate removal of the pedestal base.

They chiseled out three small trenches through the pedestal beneath the skull and placed a piece of ¾ inch plywood about 3 ½ feet long and 12 inches wide inside each trench. To prevent sagging, 2x4 boards were placed underneath the plywood in the two outside trenches. Next, they inserted the unbent rebar underneath the plywood sheets. Finally, they began reaming out the clay pedestal still supporting the weight of the skull, but left two narrow mounds to keep the skull from collapsing downward. To protect the skull in transport, they built a protective case around it – or perhaps more fitting – a sealed coffin.

Through the cleared space underneath, they folded burlap strips around the skull. Whenever all the accessible area underneath the skull was covered with burlap, they cleared out the support mounds and began wrapping the remaining portion of the skull. The skull was plastered with burlap strips after plastic wrap and a 1/8" screen wire mesh had been wrapped around it. Over 200 pounds of plaster were used to encase the precious fossil.

Once the skull was completely coated with burlap, the rebar pieces were bent upward with a homemade pipe bender to encircle the entire skull, and then were tied together where they crossed. New pieces of rebar were then fashioned into four hooks and connected to the encircling rebar at the corners, which made it possible to connect a chain and cable and then hand crank the skull casket onto a large, wooden pallet. After anchoring the skull to the pallet with nylon strips, the pallet could be levered and wafted across the makeshift bridge.

Lifting the skull from the earth and loading it into the truck was a dawn-to-dusk affair. The skull could only be moved a fraction of an inch with each crank of the winch. The two men struggled for hours to move the casket across the gully, and still faced the daunting task of moving it up the ramp into the truck. However, luck was with them on this day. Harold James, the water quality tester, arrived and lent a hand.

With the skull secure atop a durable wooden pallet, using hand-operated winches and cables, they slowly skidded the giant block of bone over the gully and onto the grassy knoll and then slowly cranked it up the ramp into the back of their truck.

At each important phase of the move, Sid took photos to document one of the greatest extractions of a dinosaur skull on record. Mr. James, a Weyerhaeuser employee, was photographed making paleontological history. Without his assistance, the two men might not have been able to move the skull into the truck. Two men, with an extra set of hands for the most grueling phase of the ordeal, had accomplished what is normally done by a fully-financed scientific team with student assistants, perhaps as many as two dozen bodies.

The two amateurs had done the impossible – not just miraculously finding the skull, but successfully excavating, moving, and transporting this thousand-pound hunk without inflicting collateral damage.

Although a little flattened, the skull was not shattered or damaged and was actually in pristine condition. This ossified rarity offered considerable new insight into a species that had long been a mystery for the scientific community. It was time to send a herald to the outside world – an Acro skull had been found in McCurtain County, Oklahoma, USA.

CHAPTER THIRTY-THREE
The Dig Comes to an End – the Valuable Cargo is Transported to the Lab

Cephis and Sid were elated. They had accomplished the impossible and were eager to make their discovery known to the scientific world. They felt vindicated, especially Cephis, who had kept them focused and on track, even in their darkest hours. The two men had gone against the grain to prove that individual initiative combined with a willingness to think outside the box and challenge undisputed authority sometimes pays off. The two Okies had uncovered the greatest dinosaur specimen ever found east of the 100th meridian and they had done it Indiana Jones style. Their skeleton pre-dated the pre-Adamite Age by one-hundred million years.

Cephis wasted no time in contacting Dr. Langston. He wanted to uphold his part of the agreement, which required him to turn over the skull to the university in the event it was found. His ego inflated as he prepared to confront the preeminent dinosaurologist with the news of his finding. Still, he did not wish to embarrass the esteemed Dr. Langston; he didn't need to be told that he had been proven wrong.

The communication was cordial and businesslike. Now it was imperative that UT scientists come to Idabel to pick up the skull and the balance of the bones. The palletized prize was parked beneath a large oak tree in Sid's backyard and ready to be loaded and shipped to the highest university in the adjacent state.

When Cephis called Dr. Langston and told him he had found the skull he thought for a moment that Langston had hung up on him. The acclaimed paleontologist was stunned, but quickly recovered his composure. The extraordinary news of their discovery beckoned the professor and his able assistant, Jeff Pittman, to leave Austin that very evening to inspect the treasure.

Since the skull was too heavy to be housed inside Sid's warehouse, it was left outside where it could be loaded using the strength of the old oak tree for a lever and pulley attachment. Being exposed to the elements, the prize needed to be transported to the lab immediately. Because of its extraordinary value, the specimen required meticulous handling.

A revolutionary study of Cretaceous theropods was in order. This rare McCurtain collection provided a groundbreaking opportunity for paleontologists to examine and research the skull and skeletal anatomy of one of the largest predators known to science. The unique specimen might shake up conventional wisdom about North American theropods, even usher in a paradigm shift in evolutionary and dinosaurian theory.

Whoever possessed this specimen could cause a stir in paleontological circles. The skull, even more than the appendages, provided invaluable clues to the animal's origin and ancestry and served witness to its evolutionary connection to other dominant theropods of the Dinosaurian Age.

These bones told the life story of the dinosaur and signified the hard life it apparently had. This Acro was banged up by other large meat eaters (most likely Acros) in contests for meals and mates. Also, its prey offered considerable resistance and inflicted scores of injuries. The Mountain Fork specimen had suffered numerous broken bones during its struggle for survival, including a crushed scapula and a broken toe that never healed, and signs of arthritis and inflammation of the joints. Curiously, the skull showed similar signs of trauma; the animal had a crocodile tooth embedded in its jaw, a shark tooth lodged in its skull, and a cracked nose.

In his latest speculation concerning the demise of the dino, Cephis conjured up another scenario in which the Acro had died during a volcanic mud flow, in which lava covered the carcass before scavengers could scatter its remains. Previously, he had conjectured that the creature had become trapped in a bowl-shaped lagoon, died, then was subsequently buried in sediments.

On a spring Sunday morning in 1987, the two UT scientists arrived at Sid's house in Idabel to claim the balance of probably the rarest dinosaurian collection of the twentieth century. In addition to the skull, there were a few other assorted fossils, including a claw, a vertebrae, a shoulder blade, a few sections of the tail, and a few loose ends.

The skull was loaded quickly, but cautiously. With the use of come-alongs and cables supported by a large branch of a large oak tree, the skull was lifted up into the back of Pittman's truck. A few boxes of miscellaneous fossils were brought out of the warehouse and loaded up alongside the skull.

While Langston had shown little emotion when he and Pittman picked up the skeleton on their first trip, this time he was visibly excited when he saw the skull. This was a specimen that had continuously evaded him throughout his long and illustrious career. Finally, it had come into his hands. The very species that catapulted his reputation and alerted the world to his rising stardom was on its way to his lab. It was like rekindling an old association. If only Dr. Stovall were here to see it. This was the only one of its kind in the world.

Cephis and Sid watched with trepidation as the sagging truck with the precious cargo departed for the Lone Star State. The skull and bones were now in a new venue and out of their control.

This concluded the dig, but their struggle would continue against a new kind of foe. They had successfully navigated the realm of nature and won; now they would be maneuvering in the arena of man. Powerful human institutions would pry into their bone business, invade their space, and rattle their security and sensibilities. Controversy loomed, rumors emanated, jealousies abounded, and conflict was inevitable. This would become a war over bones.

CHAPTER THIRTY-FOUR
Haggling With the Professor

The dig was finished and the two naturalists now had spare time on their hands. After working eighty or more hours per week for over three years, the two toughened dirt scoopers needed to mellow out. But the more free time they had, the more anxious thoughts clouded their perceptions. They tried to stay occupied to defray their impatience by working around their houses, searching the outback for more treasures, or doing a little fishing and hunting. But while waiting, concerns about their skeleton remained a constant preoccupation.

They knew that their specimen had been made a student project, and Pittman had been put in charge. Were the students actually cleaning the bones? How much oversight would Langston, a top-notch researcher, devote to the project? Would he be actively involved in watching over the work in progress? Would he peer over Pittman's shoulder to make sure everything was done properly? Or would he put his trust in his loyal aide and involve himself in other matters? Cephis and Sid felt uneasy.

The question of what was going on in the lab weighed heavily on their minds. Soon, a spree of communications began flowing back and forth between Cephis, the down-home naturalist, and Langston, the up-town scientist. The humble country boy soon found himself at odds with one of the greatest scientific minds in the world and one of the most prominent educational institutions in the nation. A duel of wills and wits ensued.

As weeks passed by, the tone of the correspondence became ever more negative. One letter from Langston hinted that preservation would prove too costly and time-consuming. In another, Langston implied that the specimen was too unstable to be prepared into a viable cast. In still another letter, he stated he had been advised by the British Museum of Natural History that the specimen could not be saved and was on the verge of disintegration. Yet, despite these doomsday scenarios, Langston still wanted to keep the skeleton. The professor soon initiated a tedious campaign to persuade the two country boys to donate their bones to the university.

How could a pine-coned, rustic hillbilly dispute the scientific opinion of a world-class scientist with corroborating opinions from other scientific authorities?

For months, Langston kept averring that the fossils were worthless and could not be preserved and insisted that the best solution to the problem was a donation made in the interest of public education. Cephis balked at the suggestion.

What did a rough-shorn woodcutter and small town Indian from Oklahoma have to gain by donating their skeleton to a prominent, out-of-state university? Perhaps their names might be memorialized on some wooden plaque on the wall of the university lab. Or maybe a tax deduction; but if the bones were adjudged to be worthless, might their tax deduction be paltry, if not zero? If they were lucky, they might get their names mentioned in the local press as munificent benefactors of the university. But if the bones had negligible value, that would be a bit of a stretch.

Langston must have thought the two Okies were a couple of fools possessing big hearts, but gullible minds. After spending thousands of hours toiling and digging up bones, accompanied by constant mental anguish, the prospect of donating them to some ivory-towered institution in a rival state did not seem palatable to Cephis and Sid. Could they even deduct their labor and expenses on their tax returns?

Langston's university was not in Oklahoma, but across the Red River and in hostile football territory. If they had to donate the bones to a university, they wanted it to be to an Oklahoma institution. Texans might like the dinosaur, but they damned sure didn't care about two obscure Sooners from across the river.

For the two Oklahomans, having their names posted on some billboard marquee or wall placard meant nothing. Texas residents might look in awe at the dinosaur cast (if it ever got mounted), but could care less about the remote names posted at the bottom of the pedestal. The two Okies were generous at heart, but not that generous.

They were not a couple of money-toting do-gooders looking for a generous tax deduction or an esteemed title on the Board of Regents or the university alumni. The beleaguered naturalists needed to at least recoup their out-of-pocket expenses. Donation was not an option. They were not rich philanthropists hoping to spread good will far and wide, or buy prestige and elevate their egos to the next level.

Dr. Langston, with his incessant pleadings that the bones be donated to UT, was assuming that Cephis was either a very generous man or a fool. Cephis and Sid knew their specimen had monetary value, especially now that the skull had been recovered. Langston was expecting them to make a charitable contribution out of their monumental laborious effort. You couldn't get more generous than that. Most university donations accrue from wealthy individuals who make their money from the brain power or sweat of others, but in this case, Hall and Love were expected to donate their own sweat labor, not to mention their non-deductible, out-of-pocket expenses.

The haggling went on back and forth until Langston became convinced that the hillbilly could not be persuaded or cajoled into donating for a good cause. Shortly thereafter, Cephis received a letter from Langston offering to buy the specimen. Cephis responded that he would take $275,000 in cash and explained that most of the value reflected in the dollar figure was based on labor. The dollar figure reflected their labor at the minimum wage rate, as well as other associated costs.

Langston recoiled at the figure. The negotiations bogged down. Langston may have had a bigger vocabulary, but he couldn't get the vocal edge on the hillbilly, who argued back with his simple, hillbilly jargon. Langston's highfalutin' dialectics did not intimidate the backwoodsman.

Cephis was a fast talker and a fast walker, and one underestimated him at his own peril. In this duel of words, a professional was arrayed against an amateur; a bone analyzer against a bone digger; a man of sophisticated intellect against one of simple, down-home wit. This struggle became a face-off of nerves and verves. The final outcome would determine possession of the skeleton.

Langston countered back with an offer of $15,000. Cephis refused. Langston asked: "What will it take?" Cephis stated he would lower the price to $175,000. Langston responded back by letter and stated that the university did not have that kind of money. No funds were available due to a shortage of grants.

Cephis reiterated that the parties should stick to the original terms and inquired as to what progress had been made, if any, in cleaning the bones. He was willing to give the university more time, even though the eighteen-month deadline was fast approaching.

Despite the negativity, Langston seemed to imply that there was still a chance that the lab might be able to stabilize the bones. He conveyed just enough positive sentiment to keep the two yeomen hanging on, grasping for a tidbit of hope.

The eighteen months soon elapsed with little or no progress made. Cephis, with limited options, sat tight for a few more months. It now appeared obvious that Langston did not want to give the bones back. If he was dead set on keeping them, more beseeching would have about as much effect as a leaf falling in a pine forest. The apotheosis of Langston and the lab was tarnished by a lack of funds and a possible regency intervention. Langston's rigidity had narrowed the options.

A dramatic decision was staring Cephis in the face. He wanted guidance, but had nobody to turn to. What was really going on at the research lab in Austin? Was the budget busted? Was Langston telling the truth? Was it a question of an unsalvageable specimen or a shortage of money?

Whom could Cephis contact to get the inside scoop? Dr. Dalquest probably did not know. Nobody at the University of Oklahoma could be trusted. But there was one man who might know something. That man was Allan Graffham, the commercial paleontologist in Ardmore.

Graffham and Langston were friends and had professional contacts. They spoke with each other from time to time. Graffham had insight into what was going on at the Balcones Lab.

Cephis had recently forged a friendship with Graffham, who had once visited him at his home in Eagletown to buy quartz crystals. Not to mention the Acro, Hall and Graffham had several things in common. Both Graffham and Hall were prototypes of Edward Drinker Cope, the Gilded Age commercial paleontologist, and both operated without academic or governmental sponsorship. Graffham, a bourgeois capitalist, was cut more in the mold of the wealthy Cope than Hall, an entrepreneur of the proletarian rank. Othniel Marsh of the 1880s was symbolic of academic and institutional prerogative. Institutional money from government, academia, and corporate trusts flowed into his expeditionary budget. As for Hall and Graffham, they were subject to the limitations of finances and markets.

Through his contact with Graffham, Cephis found out that the Board of Regents were threatening to close the Balcones Research Lab because it was losing money. The paleontological wing had massive stockpiles of un-worked fossils just lying around, taking up valuable space without earning their keep. The Board had threatened to haul the many mastodons and mammoths to the city landfill, and dinosaurs were likewise threatened with disposal. Cephis began to fret that his own specimen was headed for the dump. Even if it were not, he still feared it would soon turn to dust.

Langston was telling the truth about the lab's deficit of funds, but Cephis and Sid doubted that their specimen was beyond redemption. It just needed to be in the right hands at the right lab. Due to the nagging problem of budget shortfalls, a university lab was not a good home for their specimen. If they could ever get it back, they wanted it in the possession of the most competent hands at the most reputable commercial lab.

Cephis, now apprised of the dire situation at Balcones Lab, promptly called Sid. They needed to forge ahead with a plan to recover their trophy. They couldn't bank on Langston's goodwill. Any venture to recover their property would require guile and deception. They would recover it legally, by stealth. Another dinosaur coup was on the drawing board. This conquest would not be from the grudges of nature, but from the stingy clasp of man. Preparations for a face-off with Mr. Dinosaur were being made.

CHAPTER THIRTY-FIVE
The Low Down Filthy Capitalist

While Cephis and Sid discussed plans for a dinosaur coup to recover their property from Langston and UT, Cephis re-encountered his old nemesis Jeff Pittman. Pittman made a surprise "Pitt stop" while in transit to his home in Louisiana. Although UT's dismal caretaking of the bones was on the verge of igniting conflict between the contractual parties, Pittman stepped into the vacuum to further compound the maelstrom already brewing.

Pittman sensed the "bone affair" between Langston and the two Okies was going sour and teetering on divorce, so he was making a final encore in an attempt to salvage something from the deal that might prop up his sagging career aspirations.

Cephis was getting ready for a "barbecue afternoon" when Pittman steered into his driveway. For Cephis, it was one of those rare days off from the normal grind, and he merely wanted to relax. Dinosaurs and academics were the least of his concerns. This was a day for barbecue, family, and Southern fried chicken. The charcoal had not even been lit, the steaks still cold and in wrap, the iced tea not even brewed.

The keeper of the "land-worn secret" reluctantly greeted the familiar but uninvited visitor, and the conversation got underway. Pittman had something on his mind. The opposites engaged in another whirlwind of wits as if for the sake of a last hurrah.

In a prior letter to Langston, in which he lowered the sales price for the dinosaur from $275,000 to $175,000, Hall had inadvertently piqued the interest of Pittman. For the ambitious graduate assistant, this was no bargain. He had an "academic bias" in regard to dinosaur sales. In his mind, the dino automatically belonged to the university since its initial discovery. Pittman, however, was intrigued by one aspect of the letter in which Hall implied that paleontological products likely still existed at the dig site, even remnants of their own "beast from the southeast," and was offering to guide UT to the site.

This was likely hyperbole. Hall knew the Acro bed was dry and empty. Although he felt certain that other dinosaurs were concealed nearby, Cephis knew Weyerhaeuser would have to give approval for a university-sponsored excavation. If Cephis could dispose of the dinosaur for a pocket of cash, he was out of there. Langston and crew could be left to their own devices. Of course, it was all a vain attempt. No sale was ever consummated.

Nevertheless, Pittman was inspired by the prospect of exploring the site further and maybe writing a thesis or research paper about the project. He needed first-hand field experience at a productive quarry in order to shore up his resume.

Hall and Pittman sat down under a large shade tree, and over iced tea, voiced their respective opinions regarding paleontology in general and a furtherance of the dig in particular. Although the relationship had its tense moments, sometimes the two men joked and conversed informally. Pittman got pushy at times, but Cephis treated the affair rather good-naturedly. The two men liked to argue with each other, but at times got under each other's skin. This was Pittman's fourth or fifth "Pitt stop" while traveling back and forth from Austin to Shreveport.

"I'm the person who should be doing this," Pittman stated as he tried again to convince Hall to show him the dinosaur site.

Pittman argued that the dig was not yet complete, maybe even blotched, because almost 30 percent of the skeleton had not been accounted for. In a monotone familiar to Cephis, Pittman further declared that only academic professionals were capable of determining the extent of completion of a project.

"The only value was scientific," he added.

The young aspirant to "dinosaur prominence" then emphasized his plan to strip a large area at the site of its overburden in a broad sweep to widen and deepen the quarry. He would perform this meritocratic project by using a backhoe or bulldozer instead of hand tools. This kind of talk always irritated Cephis.

In fact, Hall was rather stunned by this radical approach. He had indeed found a few other fossils in the closing days of the dig, including the vertebrae of a small raptor and the ankle bone of a sauropod, which he subsequently donated to a museum. Loose bones, even skeletons, were lingering amidst the clay rubble within the gully parameter but had to be approached in a conservative and meticulous manner. While sipping tea, he tritely informed Pittman that he could not transfer permission since he didn't own the property. Permission would have to come from Weyerhaeuser. He knew if he took Pittman to the pit, he would be violating his "low profile" agreement with Bueno, which presumably was still in effect.

On this note, Pittman became agitated. He was desperate, hoping a little of the Acro's grandeur might rub off on him. Apparently, he did not want to go through Weyerhaeuser to obtain official permission to research the site. Maybe he knew something Cephis and Sid did not.

The conversation grew more tense and gravitated toward the topic of UT's buying the Acro specimen. The whole idea was anathema to Pittman. He persisted in his hard talk, never stooping to a plea or begs; he was too proud for that. Had he been more humble, Cephis might have been sympathetic, but the logistics simply militated against his caving in to Pittman's demands.

Cephis, quickly losing patience with the badgering, finally asked Pittman why he did not just buy the specimen. Pittman did not answer, but gave the irate hillbilly an angry glare. There was a moment of silence as the conversation shifted to economics and labor issues, rather than bones and excavation.

"The university does not have $200,000 to pay for a bunch of diseased bones," Pittman said.

Hall countered with a question. "Why doesn't UT appeal to some white knight oil tycoon like T. Boone Pickens to get the money?"

Pittman did not answer.

Here was a situation where a man of hard labor, sweat, and danger, a true working class protégé, even an icon, talked down to a middle class scholar who had not yet paid his dues in the world of toil and grind.

As words grew tenser and Pittman more anxious, Cephis questioned Pittman's work ethic and history in a rather abrupt and brutal way. "There is a big difference between earning money and getting money. With all due respect, Dr. Langston started his career with funds provided by the WPA. Jeff, unless you finish your doctorate and get a job as a curator of a museum, you might have trouble supporting yourself. You are a classic 'armchair paleontologist'."

At that point, the seething Pittman lost his composure. "Well, you're nothing but a low down, filthy capitalist."

Cephis narrowed his eyes and gritted his teeth. "Before I was a low down, filthy capitalist, I was a low-down, filthy log cutter."

Pittman leaned back in his chair, clinched his fist, and gave Cephis a hard look.

The conversation had grown terminally stale. "I think we have nothing further to discuss. Please give Dr. Langston my regards," said Hall.

Pittman walked off, got into his truck, and drove away. This was to be the last personal conversation Hall and Pittman would have. Pittman had immodestly called Cephis a "low down filthy capitalist," but at least he did not call him a "vulture capitalist," the term Newt Gingrich used to describe Mitt Romney in the 2012 Republican presidential primary.

Shortly after his departure, Cephis got Sid on the phone. "Sid, I think we need to go ahead and carry out that bone sting as soon as possible. Let's refine the plans and prepare to activate it."

The two men began making plans for another trip to Austin.

CHAPTER THIRTY-SIX
The Bone Heist

Tension was mounting on both sides of the river. Langston could sense Hall's impatience and was a little edgy. He perceived Hall as a kind of loose cannon – a simple country boy at best, a rough-edged redneck at worst. The renowned scientist had leverage over the two Okies and would use it to extract a major concession.

Hall had detected Langston's intransigence and had lost all confidence in him. From Hall's point of view, Langston was an opportunist who had taken advantage of their trust and betrayed them. He now contrived a plan to recover the controvertible bones of the elusive creature and bring them back to the good soil of Oklahoma.

As for the erudite scientist, he had possession of the dinosaur and the ball was in his court. He had the two Sooners between a rock and a hard place. However, that would not resolve his twin problems of monetary and manpower shortages.

Fortunately for Cephis, a positive development was rolling in the background. Cephis was expecting his older brother, Bob, to visit him that week. Bob, a self-employed, long-haul, moving van operator who owned his own rig, was wheeling through town and had a few days to spare. Cephis' younger brother, Roger, worked for Bob and was with him; both brothers planned to stop and rest a few days before resuming their trip to the east coast.

Their plan to recover the bones revolved around Bob and his big rig. Bob called that Monday morning to say that he would arrive about 6:00 PM. As soon as he hung up the phone, Cephis called Langston to schedule an appointment. Langston obliged and set the appointment for Wednesday at 3:00 PM. It was necessary for the appointment to be made personally with Langston; the guards would not let a non-scheduled person through the gate. The names of Cephis Hall and Sid Love and their vehicle would be on the guards' appointment list.

That afternoon, Cephis' brother wove his way through the pine-laden trail in his shiny, new Peterbilt cab with a Mayfair moving van attached. The two brothers arrived in time for a fine, home-cooked meal specially prepared by Joyce.

As they sat and dined, Cephis asked Bob, "Have you ever been to Austin, Texas?"

"Yea, brother, I've been just about everywhere."

"Well," said Cephis, "I need for you to go with me there early Wednesday morning. I can buy your diesel; that's about all I can do. We'll leave about 3:00 AM. We'll have a whole day to rest until then. Are you with me?"

After enjoying such a delightful meal and his brother's down-home hospitality, how could he refuse? Both brothers were glad to help. The trip was set.

Cephis called Sid to discuss the plan. Both men would have to take off work. All the necessary arrangements were made. Cephis and Sid would ride together in Sid's pickup. Bob and Roger would follow behind in the Peterbilt. The trip would take at least six hours. They needed to arrive early, so they allowed extra time for breakfast, refueling stops, and the slow traffic in the Austin area. Everybody needed to hit the sack early Tuesday night.

As the night wore on in the small southern village, a blast sounded in the silence of the night and the moon sent glimmers off a shiny, blue Peterbilt with chrome stacks rising two feet into the air. While the moon shined against the serene cottage, the trucks set off from Eagletown on their way to Austin for a journey of recovery — recovery of a pile of loaned bones that were held in close surveillance inside a secure building ringed by a chain-link fence with guards manning the gate.

The eighteen-wheeler was following the wheels of a customized, baby blue 1967 Chevrolet pickup truck owned and driven by Sid. Cephis sat in the front seat. The truck was Sid's pride and joy. Everything had been rebuilt at his family's tire shop, including the motor, but it was still twenty years old.

They crossed the Red River north of Paris and entered Texas. There would be no turning back. It was Austin-UT or bust. The plan was a big gamble. If it failed, Langston might take legal action to ban them from ever entering the premises. If that happened, their only recourse was the courts, and that was never a viable option for the underdog. If it worked, the dinosaur would again be theirs.

Begging and pleading with Langston to return their property would probably not work; besides, it was below their dignity. This bold plan to snatch their bones from the iron grip of the great institution was their only hope of recapturing their fossil collection intact. If Langston returned it voluntarily, some bones might turn up missing, and there would be nothing they could do.

Lawsuits seldom solved anything, Cephis believed. The system allowed lawyers to enrich themselves, whether justice was served or not. Judges were arbitrary and juries fickle. The whole process was just too expensive for the ordinary man, and too slow. The legal system was designed for the big institutions and rich folks. Of course, the courts were reserved for the poor when they got caught up in the criminal-judicial system.

Better to simply outsmart the fox and avoid the courts. In the courts, they would be out-gunned by Dr. Dinosaur and UT. A civil suit against a great, educational institution and Dr. Langston, a pillar of society, was just not a viable option. While Langston had scheduled a meeting with the two men merely for the purpose of discussing the future of the skeleton, he had no idea that they were coming to pick up their property and haul it back home. A plan for a bone heist had been hatched, and Langston was an unwilling accessory. This was a case of two down-home boys squaring off against an icon of uptown cosmopolitanism.

When they arrived in Austin, Cephis called Dr. Langston and told him he was looking forward to meeting with him and would be there in about an hour. Dr. Langston invited them to meet him at Jim's Restaurant to discuss the issue over coffee. Cephis politely declined, stating that the office would be fine and he had given up coffee because of caffeine reactions.

Cephis wanted to remind Langston of their scheduled meeting and simultaneously put him at ease. Actually, they were only about twenty minutes away from the gate of the Balcones Lab and expected to arrive nearly an hour early. Part of their plan was to arrive early and pretend they were confused about the meeting time. They had not driven more than 500 miles to drink coffee and socialize with Dr. Langston. They had come to stage a coup and recover their prized possession.

As the two-truck caravan proceeded down the streets of Austin, the state capitol, the two instigators started to feel uneasy: they had butterflies in their pits, sweaty palms, dry lips, and edgy nerves. They were worried, but tried to blot out the possible embarrassment of failure. Could they outwit the scientific genius?

The guard would be expecting them and might even fall for the ruse. So what if they arrived early? Ordinarily, they would have to sit and wait for the boss, anyway. They were hoping that Langston was occupied somewhere in the back corridors of the giant lab complex and far away from the gate entrance. They knew that with a scheduled appointment, the guard would let them drive in, but could they slip the eighteen-wheeler past him? The Peterbilt would have to follow closely behind, hugging their bumper.

At approximately 2:00 PM, Sid's cream puff 1967 Chevrolet pickup arrived at the gate of the research laboratory. Cephis got out of the pickup and walked over to talk with the guard. The guard checked their IDs and cleared them. As the Chevrolet truck proceeded forward, Cephis turned to the guard and informed him that the moving van was with them and they were supposed to haul off some junk fossils. Before the guard could respond, the eighteen-wheeler glided past the gate entrance and followed Sid's pickup over to the loading dock.

Cephis thanked the guard and quickly walked over to the loading dock and helped his brother back the rig up to the dock. Sid and the two brothers went inside the warehouse to begin loading the truck. Cephis headed straight for Langston's office. The UT employees inside the facility, not knowing what was going on, were baffled. But because the two men had a scheduled appointment and the guard had cleared them, the employees were not overly suspicious.

Cephis, feeling tense and nervous, anxiously set out to confront Langston before he figured out what was going on. Beads of sweat poured off his eyebrows as he tried to maintain his composure. He spotted Langston sitting inside his office and immediately engaged him. While standing rigidly in the doorway, Cephis fired off several questions before Langston grasped what was happening. Shortly later, Sid also entered Langston's office while the two brothers, being professional movers with all their lifts and equipment, stayed behind to load the van.

With a steady and resonate voice, Cephis commenced. "Dr. Langston, I understand that no work can be done on the skeleton."

"Yes, that's right."

"And I also understand that you don't have the money available to buy the fossils."

Langston agreed again.

"Isn't it also true that another expert paleontologist has observed that the skeleton is deteriorating at a fast rate?"

Langston replied, "Yes, that is true."

Finally, Cephis stated, "I also understand that the Board of Regents is threatening to close down the lab and have this huge inventory of fossils hauled to the dump."

Langston was silent on that, but began to act edgy.

Cephis took advantage of the silence and unloaded his bombshell. "We have come to get the bones of the monster and take them across the Red River to give them a decent Oklahoma burial. We want to save you the trouble of having to take them to the dump. We are backed up at the dock and ready to load."

Dr. Langston was visibly shaken and before he could respond, Cephis concluded, "Would you kindly unlock the doors so we can get what is rightfully ours?"

Langston stormed out of the office and headed for the back door. He knew he had been outfoxed. He unlocked the cabinets that held the remainder of the pieces and quietly walked back to his office.

It took more than an hour to load the truck. The two brothers did all the work. The skull was sitting on a pallet atop a cart that could be rolled up to the loading dock. The moving van was equipped with lift devices to handle heavy objects. The heavy pallet was lifted off the cart and situated inside the van.

Langston appeared a little unraveled and belligerent, but otherwise remained cool. He was standing by the loading dock when the two brothers finished loading the last piece. Cephis told Langston he was disappointed that the university had not kept up its end of the bargain, and then added that he hoped there were no hard feelings. Langston did not respond.

As he readied to leave, Cephis turned and thanked Langston for his interest and effort. While Langston stood motionless and stunned, Cephis blurted out, "It's ours; we're taking it home." The pickup truck then drove past, with the eighteen-wheeler close behind. The Peterbilt exhaled a miasma of foul, noxious exhaust as it departed the gate. A perturbed Dr. Langston glowered at the vehicle tide as it passed out of sight.

The procession headed north across the state line and into the Red Man's State of Oklahoma. The bones had been brought to the University in the back of Pittman's

Ford pickup. The rescuers were bringing them back home in style – in a forty-foot, air-ride, moving van.

The convoy headed north with the cargo of precious bones that rightfully belonged to the native soil of Oklahoma. There was a great feeling of relief and glee. As darkness was about to overtake them after turning eastward through Texas, a fitting song blasted on the radio.

East bound and down, loaded up and truckin
a' we gonna do what they say can't be done
We've got a long way to go and a short time to get there
I'm east bound just watch ol' Bandit run...
Keep your foot hard on the pedal.... Son, never mind them brakes
Let it all hang out 'cause we've got a run to make
The boys are thirsty in Atlanta, and there's beer in Texarkana
And we'll bring it back no matter what it takes
East bound and down, loaded up and truckin'

The song was joyous; the occasion, euphoric. They had won again, and this time against a powerful institution of man. But as they celebrated their crossing of the Red River, they could not have known that dark forces would soon be coalescing and conspiring against them. Dr. Langston bristled at the gall and vulgar initiative of the two amateurs and silently seethed with resentment.

The tables had turned, feelings were stirred, jealousies aroused, egos inflamed, and cognizance of lost opportunities emerged. Bone envy became couched in the indented wrinkles of elite scientific minds. Cephis and Sid's escapade had unleashed a powerful and unsettling chorus which would reverberate across the state line and reach the ears of Oklahoma scientists, Weyerhaeuser officials, and other powerful institutions and persons.

Langston was later reputed to have told Allan Graffham that he had never met anyone quite like Cephis Hall in his entire career and at that point, he was retiring. But before he did, he would instigate powerful forces against the two Okies who had hijacked the marvelous *Acrocanthosaurus* right out of his own lab. The real troubles of the two bone emancipators were about to begin. They faced a **Byzantine** labyrinth of intrigue, conflict, and perplexity. The dream would soon turn into a nightmare.

CHAPTER THIRTY-SEVEN
Dark Conspiracies Forming

On a bright southern day, the quiet, brooding scientist left Austin, Texas and headed north to Ardmore, Oklahoma to visit Allan Graffham of Geological Enterprises. The two men had been associates for years. On this day, Langston had a bone to pick with Cephis and sought assistance from his long-time friend. He was going to pull a few strings in high places and needed all the support he could muster.

Langston had learned his lesson the hard way and would no longer underestimate the backwoodsman. The bone heist had jolted him. He was now going to use his influence within the Oklahoma scientific establishment to vent his fury and exact retribution on the audacious hillbilly and taciturn Indian for their brazen heist of university-controlled fossils right out from under his nose. In his mind, the bones properly belonged to the public, meaning the university. He hoped that his influence within high-level scientific circles would succeed in bringing the specimen back into the public realm. Little did he know that Graffham had other ideas.

Graffham and Hall had formed a kind of bone bond, motivated by a mutual desire for money. The two had been in contact over the past few months while the bones sat in the university storeroom and the Hall-Langston dispute unfolded. Graffham had told Hall that if he ever recovered the dinosaur, he wanted first crack at making a deal to become its new owner. Hall concurred and an informal, tentative business arrangement had been made. Money is often thicker than friendships.

Graffham listened curiously to Langston's malevolent diatribe against the wily woodcutter and his slick maneuver to wrest the bones from university control. Unaware of the communications that had transpired between Graffham and Hall, he told his friend more than he should have.

When Langston finished venting his rage, he got into his vehicle and headed north to the collegiate core of Oklahoma's elite, scientific establishment. He was intent on evening the score. As soon as he disappeared from sight, Graffham got on the phone with Hall, advising him of what was coming down.

The two partners had unloaded the precious cargo at Sid's warehouse and were hoping to get a few days' rest to recover from the strain of their latest conquest. The news from Graffham was stunning. Langston was on his way to the University of Oklahoma (OU) in Norman and had an angry bent. The university was certain to take an interest in his plea. OU scientists shared Langston's bias that the bones belonged in the hands of the public, not the private hands of two hicks from the sticks. They needed only to be instilled with Langston's passion and galvanized into action. Hall and Love would soon face the wrath of a small cartel of esteemed scientific elites.

Hall was aware that George Weyerhaeuser, Jr. was on the Board of Regents at the University of Oklahoma. This connection concerned him, as it portended the formation of a university-Weyerhaeuser alliance being arrayed against them. The two amateurs now faced retaliation from both the public and private sector. This could have political implications, and if Weyerhaeuser became devious, possibly even criminal. Maybe they needed to hide the bones. They began discussing the prospect of relocating the skeleton to a safer place. But where?

OU had friends in high places, including the Oklahoma State Legislature. Weyerhaeuser had political influence, not only at the local and state level, but across the entire nation. The two men felt totally overshadowed as their minds sank into despair—but not for long.

Cephis soon regained his composure and became determined to stand his ground against whatever powerful forces might be thrown against him. He could not rule out the possibility that Weyerhaeuser might trump up bogus charges against them. Whether facing a civil or criminal affront, their rights as free citizens might be threatened by a possible conspiratorial collusion between Oklahoma's highest educational institution and the state's most powerful corporation.

In the minds of the "lords of the forest," Hall and Love had revealed their true predilections. Originally thought to be lunkheads and clodhoppers, they were now considered as scheming and treacherous deceivers who had taken advantage of the company's good will. Accusing the two men of plunder, the Corporation and its friends in academia and government honed in on the two men and their elusive treasure.

A thin veneer of law protected Hall and Love from an arbitrary arrest if Weyerhaeuser chose to drum up charges and pursue the dispute as a criminal matter. A vestige of constitutional protections might prevent them being injudiciously arrested and thrown in jail and their property confiscated. The writ of habeas corpus and the fourth, sixth, and eighth amendments to the US Constitution, otherwise known as The Bill of Rights, provided elemental safeguards for individual freedom against arbitrary state action—against such things as unlawful detention, unreasonable searches and seizures, excessive bail and fines, and cruel and unusual punishment. These constitutional protections, which ultimately stemmed from the Magna Carta and English common law, might keep them barely hanging on by the threads against overarching corporate influence exercised at the local criminal-judicial level.

The Magna Carta was an English legal charter issued in 1215 in an attempt by barons to rein in the abusive and arbitrary rule of King John and protect their own powers. Article 39 of the Magna Carta ultimately protected yeomen like Hall by creating conditions that gave rise to the middle class in England, which, in turn, established the conditions needed for non-aristocrats to thrive under the protections of English common law. Although the Magna Carta was a deal strictly between barons and kings and intended only for the benefit of the nobility, it represented the novel idea that nobody, not even the king, was above the law. In that same token, nobody should be falsely imprisoned. Article 39 of the Magna Carta reads, in part: "No free men shall be arrested, or imprisoned, or deprived of his property or outlawed or jailed…unless by legal judgment of his peers."

Before the establishment of the Magna Carta, people were owned. Afterwards, they were still owned, but awareness had grown among the yeoman class, a sort of proto-middle class in England, that the civil protections accorded barons under the laws of the Magna Carta should extend to commoners as well. The yeoman class, in consonance with Enlightenment era philosophers, succeeded in bringing the ideas of liberty, equality, and justice to the modern world. The Magna Carta laid the blueprint for rule of constitutional law in the English-speaking world.

In extreme medieval society, the social hierarchy under feudalism resembled a pyramid with the king at the apex, the nobles as a tiny percentage (about 3%, or less, of the population) directly below the king, followed in descending order by the city burghers, merchants, and artisans in the burgeoning middling ranks, and the mass of serfs (over 90% of the people) at the base. After the Crusades, a tiny contingent of returning bowmen, the yeomen, formed a new hegemonic class beneath the aristocrats and middling order but above the serfs. This tiny yeoman class was the underpin that prodded the monarchs into extending concessions of the Magna Carta to yeomen, thereby paving the way for the gradual rise of the middle class.

Although feudalism had long vanished, traces of this medieval institution still lingered on in backwater, provincial areas where a single, giant corporation dominated the landscape and a kind of economic vassalage still existed. In the pre-World War II era, this local economic arrangement was referred to as the "company town." Despite the end of serfdom, McCurtain County's economy was still much like a plantation economy. Weyerhaeuser was the plantation owner, the pine forests were the plantation, the mills were the shops, the workers were the vassals, and the county citizens the de facto subjects — at least whenever they were on Weyerhaeuser's vast domain. The local populace was dependent on Weyerhaeuser to provide jobs, paychecks, and livelihoods. Usually, Weyerhaeuser got whatever it wanted in return.

Hall and Love had been forewarned that a lobbying effort in Oklahoma City was underway, and a conspiracy against them might be brewing in the halls of academia and the board suites of Weyerhaeuser. But what could they do? Langston was going for blood and hoped to ensnare the wayward bone snatchers with wicked fangs and claws stretched out from the slithery maneuvers of gargantuan institutions.

They decided to sit tight and see what happened next. They did not have to wait long before learning of the dark forces converging in the background. Becky Eustace, one of Sid's friends and a clerk at the court, soon notified him that Weyerhaeuser officials had been talking to the District Attorney and intended to file trespassing and grand theft charges against the two inauspicious bone diggers. The Corp was seeking access to all documents, photos, and bones. The two yeomen braced themselves for a deluge of problems.

In a vast and heavily forested province overseen by corporate barons and local sheriffs, Hall and Love had become outlaws of the forest. But the two yeomen had not been driven deeper into the darkness of the forest, but deeper into the morass of a neo-feudalistic system. They would soon find themselves involved in a tempestuous imbroglio with the corporation, academia, the legal system, the state legislature, and scores of other antagonists.

CHAPTER THIRTY-EIGHT
The Free Market in Bones

While darkness loomed in the background, Cephis and Sid continued to negotiate with Allan Graffham in an attempt to consummate a sale involving the transfer of bones from the world of amateur paleontology to the world of commercial paleontology. There were some thorny issues pricking the aura of the dinosaur and impeding a possible deal.

Graffham was well aware of the clouded title. Ownership was disputed by high academia and a powerful mega-corporation. Three conditions needed to be met before Graffham would fork over his cash: a marketable title; evidence that the specimen could be properly cured of the pyrite disease; and an awaiting buyer. After the specimen was prepared, he needed to put the finishing touches on the sale.

Graffham was not a buy-and-hold kind of guy. He was more dealer than collector. As a commercial trader in fossils, he was basically a middleman or wholesaler who flipped dinosaurs the way real estate entrepreneurs flipped houses – buying, fixing up, and reselling for a profit. World-class museums, fossil exchanges, international marketing networks, and even wealthy, eccentric individuals who just wanted to own their own dinosaur were all willing to pay top dollar for a rare and unique specimen. The Hall-Love *Acrocanthosaurus* certainly met the criteria for rare and unique.

Before Graffham would commit any hard cash, even just for a deposit or down payment, he had to do some networking and investigating. He made contact with Pete Larson at the Black Hills Institute (BHI) in Hill City, South Dakota, and began contacting potential buyers.

BHI featured a world-renowned commercial lab in which dinosaurs were repaired for a fee and then sold to a willing third-party, who relied on the integrity and quality of their workmanship. Graffham informed Larson that the pyrite contamination was acute and wanted his best estimation as to whether the specimen could be saved and made marketable, and how much it would cost. Graffham could then estimate the probable value of a rejuvenated *Acrocanthosaurus* on the open market and set his price. Larson was optimistic that his laboratory could salvage the skeleton, but needed to actually see it before making a commitment.

While arrangements were made for Larson to fly in from South Dakota, Graffham was in discussion with possible buyers from Japan. The Japanese were interested in the specimen only if it could be given a clean bill of health from BHI or some other reputable lab. They were not aware of all the swirling controversy and ownership quagmire.

The Japanese fossil dealers came to Ardmore to discuss a possible purchase with Allan Graffham. The bone financier spent over $800 hosting a black tie dinner party in an attempt to entertain his guests and convince them that everything was in order. The Japanese became nervous about the clouded title controversy and were afraid the US government would intervene. The bone dispute was too hot for them. They were conservative businessmen and naturally skeptical. They enjoyed Graffham's wining and dining, but had otherwise wasted a trip.

Cephis and Sid were unaware that Graffham was negotiating with foreign buyers, but they would soon read about it in the local press. Rumors of all sorts were circulating. One rumor numerically headlined in the newspapers claimed that the two men were in tender negotiations to sell the mysterious dinosaur to the Japanese for two million dollars. The local media had gotten wind of it and was hyping the story. With their names plastered on the front pages, the two locals would become household names in McCurtain County — heroes to some, villains to others. Weyerhaeuser, or somebody, had disseminated nebulous rumors that generated bad press.

How the local newspapers obtained the inside scoop on a confidential dinosaur deal would remain a mystery. Graffham certainly did not tell them. He did not share his private business with the world. Obviously, the stories about the behind-the-scenes dealings had been planted. The newspapers had been tipped off by Weyerhaeuser or OU. There was no other logical explanation. Weyerhaeuser had an extensive spy network and had uncovered Graffham's confidential wheeling and dealing. If Weyerhaeuser wanted a story printed, it likely would be printed.

A few days after the Japanese returned home, Pete Larson flew in from South Dakota and Graffham picked him up at the airport in Dallas. Larson had come to evaluate the specimen and offer a professional opinion regarding its viability. The following morning, the two men drove eastward out of Ardmore to a secretive storage building in rural Arkansas where the bones were stashed.

Cephis and Sid were animated about this moment. The future of their paleontological specimen and their reputation rested on this one man's opinion. If Larson gave a negative report, they were finished. They might as well just hand the bones over to Weyerhaeuser or take them back to Dr. Langston, if he would even accept them.

The two professionals met the two amateurs and initiated a friendship for the sake of fossils and dollars. Larson and Graffham were eager to inspect the skeleton, so the four men immediately went inside the makeshift dinosaur mortuary. The moment of truth had arrived.

The two amateurs took the lids off every box and eagerly awaited any positive signs or comments. Larson was part owner of one of the most reputable paleontological labs in the world; if anybody could save the bones or determine their merit for restoration, it would be Pete Larson and his innovative staff at BHI.

Larson began silently inspecting individual appendages, but soon got to the core of the bone matter.

"Where is the skull?" he asked.

Cephis moved over to his right and lifted the plastic tarp. The skull was resting on the same wooden pallet. Larson reacted quickly. "Wow!" He threw up his arms in excitement. It was like a light flashing. He was stunned. "This is remarkable!" He could see the teeth protruding from the mouth.

This was a complete skull of one of the rarest dinosaurs known, and he had never seen a skull this pristine, pyrite or not. The skull was huge, much bigger than he anticipated. After a careful examination, he stated: "This is one of the greatest dinosaur skulls in the world."

Allan then curiously asked Pete, "Well, what do you think?"

After a moment's hesitation, Larson replied, "Yes, we can do it. Because of the pyrite, it will be difficult and expensive, but I am confident that this specimen can be preserved."

Cephis and Sid were elated and certain that they were on the verge of making a sale. Maybe their years of struggle had not been in vain. But Graffham would make no commitment at that moment. There were other considerations. He informed Cephis and Sid that he would be back in contact with them. The two fossil dealers gingerly headed back to Ardmore.

Within a few days, Graffham called Cephis and set up a meeting to discuss possible terms. The dealer and his two potential suppliers would engage in a series of meetings and discussions over the ensuing weeks. After taking turns driving back and forth from Ardmore to Broken Bow and vice versa, the parties finally succeeded in hammering out a tentative oral agreement. The stipulations were clear and specific. The agreement was conditional. It depended on Hall and Love getting a clear title to the dinosaur.

In addition to the title dispute, the two amateurs had unwittingly become snagged in the middle of an enduring ideological feud between academic paleontologists and commercial paleontologists. The two sides were on opposite ends of the fossil ownership question, and the continuing rancor between the two camps went back decades. At the heart of the debate was whether or not commercial collectors should have access to fossils buried on public lands.

While amateur and commercial collectors contend that public lands should be open to all fossil seekers, many paleontologists affiliated with public universities oppose universal access and contend that fossils of scientific merit should be deposited only in public institutions with established research and educational programs. They voice a particular concern about commercial collectors removing valuable specimens from scientific inquiry, even selling them to foreign individuals or institutions.

One side of the argument holds that all fossils are the common property of the nation's people and should be held in public trust for the academic paleontologists of that nation to study. Private ownership and a free market in fossils should never be allowed because important fossil specimens and site information would be lost to science. Science is best served, they feel, by leaving fossils in the field as they lie until degreed paleontologists can study them in their natural context and choose whether or not to excavate and preserve them. If amateur or commercial fossil hunters are allowed unhindered access, important fossil specimens may be damaged or contextual locality facts lost. Unauthorized collecting causes harm to the science of paleontology.

The other side of the debate contends that science is best served by using every possible eye and hand to find, collect, and preserve fossils in order to provide the greatest number of specimens for study. Although some fossils may be damaged on site, information lost due to amateur collection can be minimized in the larger scheme by a more liberal policy of open access. By allowing all interested parties the right to collect fossils, the number of fossils discovered and collected in the field would increase substantially and thereby significantly expand the national stockpile of fossilized research material.

The number of specimens lost to science because of unauthorized and illegal collecting is a tiny percentage compared to the vast quantities of fossils lost to the forces of weathering every day. Nearly all exposed fossils are eventually destroyed by the same natural forces that originally exposed them.

Some of the more strident purists of academia contend that selling fossils for a profit should be made illegal and criminal sanctions imposed. While the debate raged, these ideological contestants would soon come to blows over these long-standing core beliefs in the arena of the Oklahoma State Legislature. The legislature would up the ante. The assembly would soon delve into the fossil prospecting and ownership question, not merely pertaining to public lands, but private lands.

CHAPTER THIRTY-NINE
Bones of Contention

Sid and Cephis had been tipped off that Weyerhaeuser was trying to stir up trouble at the local level. The company was maneuvering behind the scenes in an attempt to have their skeleton, documents, and photographs confiscated. Cephis anticipated that a whole vortex of unpleasant surprises was gathering steam just around the bend. A door knock, a phone call, or flashing red lights could invade their privacy at any moment—and that moment came soon.

The phone call came in from Weyerhaeuser's office in Hot Springs, Arkansas, and Joe Bueno was on the line. Cephis anxiously answered the phone. It was Bueno who knew the truth about their dig, and it was he who might set the record straight.

Was he going to be honest, or was he going to be duplicitous? Was he going to toe the company line, or act on the basis of personal integrity? Were the higher-ups at Weyerhaeuser pushing his button and persuading him to join them in an attempt to railroad the two diggers and shake out their property? Higher management had leverage over him, and he knew it. His job might be at stake, and with all the controversy whirling about, he might suffer a personal rebuke for his unwitting complicity.

Higher management now contended that Mr. Joe Bueno, the Weyerhaeuser regional timberlands manager, did not have authority to grant permission for a dinosaur dig, certainly not to give away valuable scientific property to amateur moonlighters. Within Weyerhaeuser's inner circle, Bueno's unilateral action was deemed a mistake, if not anathema, and it was thereby his personal responsibility to recover Weyerhaeuser's lost property or be downgraded in the managerial ranks.

Cephis answered the phone and immediately detected that same overbearing and haughty tone. Also, Bueno's speech was a little slurred, as if he had been sipping Jack Daniels or Jim Beam whiskey.

Bueno quickly made his matter of interest known. He was calling about the dinosaur and wanted to know where it was. The gist of his conversation was simple and blunt: Cephis needed to turn over the bones immediately or face arrest and imprisonment. He was using strong-arm tactics, and buttressed his intimidating remarks with implied threats. Whom did the hillbilly think he was talking to? You were supposed to show proper submission and deference to the Corporation.

Partially reconstructed dialogue of the phone conversation between Bueno and Hall:

Bueno: Man, you got me in a lot of trouble.

Cephis: How's that?

Bueno: Over this dinosaur thing. Where is the skeleton?

Cephis: It's stashed in a secret place.

Bueno: You know it's not going to do you guys any good to try to hide that thing. We have ways of finding out what we need to know, and there are consequences for not cooperating. You guys know that you shouldn't have taken that dinosaur off Weyerhaeuser land. You've committed theft, and you need to return what you've taken.

Cephis: Now Joe, you know you gave that skeleton to us fair and square.

Bueno: I never told you that you could remove a dinosaur from Weyerhaeuser land. Man, they're twisting my arm. I need to get that thing back.

Cephis: Well, Joe, you would have been in real good shape if you would have just told the truth all along.

Bueno: You know how it is with big corporate people. We have to lie a lot with our superiors.

Cephis: Yea, but in this case, lying is not gonna do you any good.

Bueno: We have the financial means and power to get the skeleton back, and we will exercise that power.

Cephis: Uh huh

Bueno: I'll tell you something else. We know you're working on a deal to sell it to some people from Japan, and you need to stop that transaction immediately. If you sell that dinosaur to foreigners, you'll end up serving time in prison – we're talking a felony offense here. I'm warning you, if you continue contact with those Asians, we're going to catch you and pull a sting operation.

- Pause

Cephis: Joe, I got this thing all figured out. I solved the whole problem. Now, let's go over this step by step. You know you and your company is accusing me of taking this thing without permission—of actually stealing it.

Bueno: Yes, you did.

Cephis: Well, I just want to make sure we understand this right. What would you do if you went to a neighbor's house and he gave you a rock and then later accused you of stealing it?

Bueno: I would take it back.

Cephis: Well Joe, that's exactly what I done. I took it back. I took this thing back that I was accused of stealing and dumped it back into the river.

- A long silence fell on the phone

Bueno: You didn't

Cephis: Hey, what do you think?

- Silence again

Cephis: I solved it. Man, I've got a big box of fossils over here with some of the remaining pieces in it. If you want it, you need to be over at Sid's house in the morning at 8:00 a.m. to pick it up. This is it. This concludes it.

Bueno: Tomorrow morning? That's awful early.

Cephis: Well, I'm sorry. We've both got things to do.

Bueno: Okay, I'll be there.

Cephis: Good. I'll be glad for you to take the rest of these things off my hands. I'm tired of hassling with bones. Maybe Weyerhaeuser can find good use for them. They've been nothing but a burden for me. If you don't come over tomorrow to pick this thing up, I'm gonna' throw it in the river too.

Bueno: See you in the morning.

The hillbilly was using a little duplicity of his own. He was disappointed in Bueno. The man had willingly agreed to let them dig on Weyerhaeuser land, and had never suggested they turn any fossils over to the company. The agreement made between the two parties (at least as it was understood by the two diggers) implied that any bones they dug up would be theirs. Weyerhaeuser was not interested in fossils and had no written policy regarding fossil excavation on company timberlands.

Had they merely been mundane mammal bones, or just plain cow bones as Bueno had suspected, there would be no ruckus over them. But the two amateurs had uncovered a world-class dinosaur specimen that might be worth millions if it could be saved. The buck had stopped with Bueno. Now he was about to be made the fall guy. George Weyerhaeuser, Jr. or the other big shots in Tacoma might be coming down hard on him, even though they may have actually sanctioned his local decision. Bueno might redeem himself by recovering the skeleton, or what remained of it.

Cephis and Sid had moved the bones from Sid's warehouse to a more secure storage shed in rural Arkansas. If a police raid was conducted on Sid's property they would find nothing. The local authorities might throw them in jail, but they couldn't get their hands on the treasure. Bueno was now aware that he too had been outfoxed. He too had underestimated the plain-spoken woodsman.

Cephis had no intentions of ever turning over the bones, no matter how much pressure might be brought to bear on him. He would rather let them rot in an abandoned building than fork them over to a scheming, dishonest cadre of corporate officials. He resented the scenario that appeared to be unfolding—a scenario in which super-powerful forces with bags of money and widespread influence were attempting to steam-roll the little guy and unjustly take his property simply because they had subsequently learned of its intrinsic, high-dollar scientific value.

Cephis knew he was the underdog. But just as his ancestors had stubbornly stood their ground with William Wallace against the English crown in the thirteenth century, he was determined to stand on his own feet and go down fighting.

Yet at the same time he was not overly worried about the prospect of trumped-up criminal charges. He had an ace up his sleeve. If the criminal judicial system had any semblance of fairness and honesty, the prosecution would never be able to convict them for trespassing or theft. For the time being, he and Sid waited to see what Bueno was really up to and if Weyerhaeuser had some master plan to ensnare them. The scorched reality of their dismal predicament would cut close to the bone.

Photo Album

Acro at Museum of Red River

Backhoe

The Cast of the Monster is assembled at a park near Black Hills Institute.
1996

Cephis and Sid at the Black Hills Museum of Natural History.
September 1996

Cephis Hall standing atop the remains of the concrete abutment inside the dinosaur pit.
Photo was taken by the author in 2007

Dinosaur pit with standing water and eroded out remains of concrete weir.

Cephis and Joyce Hall with daughters Angela and April.
1994

Wayne Edgar, Cephis Hall, Dr. Adrian Hunt, and Alan Graffham (seated)
Museum of the Red River

Moving the Skull

Neal Larson at Black Hills Museum on day of unveiling of the Arco.
Note claws of Arco in foreground to the left.

A Rich Quartz Crystal Quarry struck in McCurtain County
by the treasure hunter and his partner Steve Due.

Sir Alan Graffham and Lady Fran beside the Dinosaur Fran.

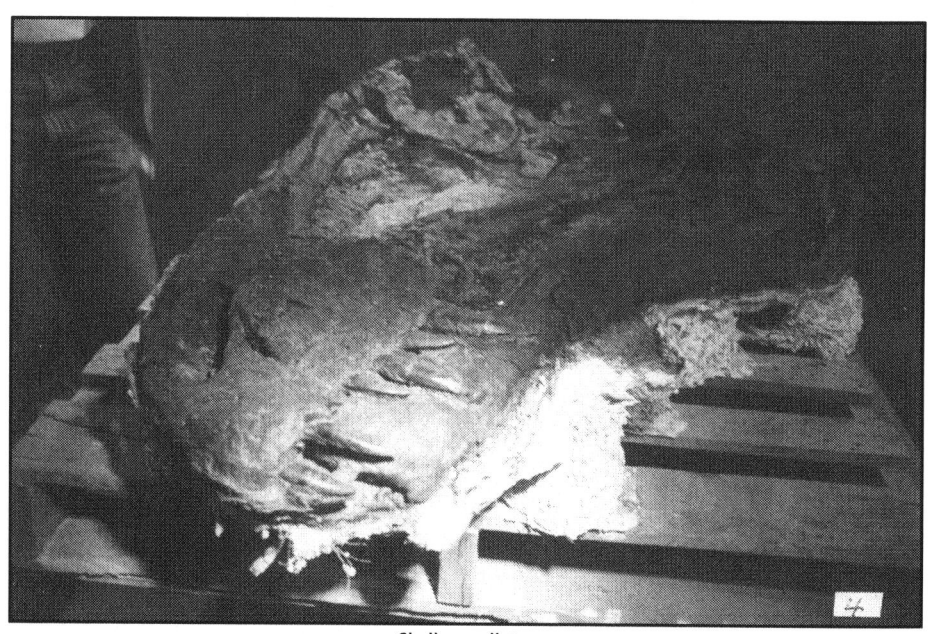
Skull on pallet.

Cephis and Joyce in Triumphal Celebration at Black Hills Museum.
1996

Treasure Cave in McCurtain County discovered by Cephis and Steve Due.

CHAPTER FORTY
The Box of Bones

The next morning, Joe Bueno arrived at Sid's house at 8:00 AM sharp. But he did not come alone. He also brought a young, unidentified attorney and something else — a formal document-receipt that he expected the two bone conveyors to sign. Sid invited the two men inside and asked them to sit down at the kitchen table while he went to get the box of valuables. The two visitors sat in anticipation of receiving not an entire skeleton, but a box of scientifically-scrutable bones they hoped might take the edge off the blade that higher management was using to slice into Bueno's flaccid flesh. For Bueno, this was all about mitigating losses and saving face with his bosses.

Within a couple of minutes, Sid nonchalantly walked into the kitchen with not a large or heavy box of miscellaneous bones, but a small Coke flat (about 24" X 20") full of fossilized wood and bone fragments. He very carefully placed the pseudo-treasure on the table as if it were worth its weight in gold. The two Weyerhaeuser men were aghast that such a puny-sized box allegedly contained the bones of the Mountain Fork monster.

"Is this it?" asked Bueno. "This can't be all?"

The two company men sullenly peered inside the box. They did not know the difference between a piece of fossilized wood or a dinosaur bone. They were unable to contest the contents of the box, and a law book was of no value in this situation. They were now in the realm of the bone diggers. It was simple, either one knew what a dinosaur bone looked like, or one didn't.

"Did you really throw those bones back in the river?" asked Bueno.

Cephis responded, "Now Joe, we've already gone over that. I've taken enough flack from you guys and don't want anymore. There are dinosaur fragments in this box. This is it. Take it or leave it."

Bueno drooped silently beside the box. He was trying to salvage whatever he could of the lost treasure. He knew this was not going to impress his bosses. But in his mind, a little box of pure dinosaur gold was better than nothing.

The slick lawyer then handed the two men the document and asked them to sign it. It was intended to convey to the bosses that Hall and Love had actually handed over a bit of the treasure trove, and their signatures were a testament to that fact. Although Bueno and his attorney were baffled, they figured that what they now owned must be bones, or at least fragments of bones. A few bones were better than none. If they could get the two men's signatures on the document, at least higher management would know they had run the gauntlet in an attempt to recover Weyerhaeuser's lost dinosaur. Besides, they could address the issue of the hidden fossils later. Weyerhaeuser had ways of shaking out all kinds of concealed commodities, even bones.

As Sid and Cephis looked over the masterful piece of legalese, Sid fidgeted.

Cephis then asked, "Gentlemen, would you excuse us for a couple of minutes while we discuss this thing in private?"

The legal expert acquiesced, and the lean, gangly hillbilly and the short, stocky Indian went in a back room to discuss the situation. The thing about the document that glared out at Cephis was the way the document was worded. In private, the two men were able to candidly discuss their options.

"Sid, this thing is not worth the paper it's written on," declared Cephis. "Look at the title and signature blanks. It says: 'Sid Love and Cephis Hall – the finders of fossils.' The thing we found has been identified as *Acrocanthosaurus,* not just fossils. We got a truck load of 'em out here. Let's sign this thing and be done. Here, sign it and then we'll get them out of here. Give 'em this box of junk."

The two men signed the document, then walked back into the kitchen and handed it to the cocky attorney, who must have thought he now had the two bone outlaws under the gun, at least in a legal sense. If the box did not contain true pieces of the dinosaur as the crime partners had attested, the two men had fraudulently misrepresented what they were conveying and their credibility would be tarnished.

Ownership of the box of "fossilized treasures" now changed hands. The two Weyerhaeuser henchmen walked out with a mysterious box of "Acrocanthosaur riches."

Cephis and Sid readied themselves for the next round of Weyerhaeuser intimidation. Although Weyerhaeuser had security guards, private police, spies, and investigators of their own, the two bone deceivers were not totally on their own in terms of intelligence gathering. McCurtain County had an informal communications network — an underground grapevine — where secrets, gossip, and inside information flowed clandestinely from one person to another.

That same evening, Cephis received a phone call from Bill Blankenship, a friend who worked at the Craig Plant as a maintenance supervisor. He had something interesting to report. Bueno had brought the box of treasure to the Craig Plant and locked it up hard and tight in a storage room. He then confiscated all the keys from the plant personnel who happened to have one, including Bill's own personal key to the room.

Bueno had bragged a little. "We got it. We confiscated a box of bones," he was heard to have said to the top Craig managers.

Bill described Bueno as having a rather guarded look of satisfaction and relief as he walked from the factory to his vehicle and drove off to Hot Springs. Perhaps he was suffering from self-delusion or wishful thinking, or maybe he was simply putting on an act to deceive whoever was gullible enough to believe him.

After this arbitrary management initiative, only Bueno had a key to the storage room. All the people who had personal possessions locked inside now had to wait until Bueno unlocked the door. Their own valuables were held hostage to management's whim. Blankenship was not happy. He had an extra set of clothes, shoes, and other miscellaneous personal items locked inside the room.

Blankenship, one of Cephis' close friends for years and the owner of the Hill Top Tavern located along the state line strip about a mile from Cephis' house, was curious. "Did you lose the bones? Did they get them back?" Cephis explained what had happened, and Blankenship burst out laughing. He did not particularly like Bueno anyway.

A couple days later, Bueno called Cephis again. "Did you really throw that thing back into the river?" he asked again.

Cephis didn't say yes or no. Instead he retorted, "I told you what I did. I throwed some bones in the river. Now you prove that I didn't." The conversation was short and tense, and was to be Bueno's last call to Hall.

Bueno was probably hoping that the meeting at Sid's house would be his last time to deal personally with Hall. Cephis, in turn, was now a little more confident and ready to lock horns with Weyerhaeuser management whenever and wherever they chose. He wondered what they would throw at him next. His combative passion to defend his rights and set things straight was about to open a Pandora's Box and instigate a bizarre chain of events.

He was later accused of being sly and shifty. "Yea, probably so," he agreed. "But that written form we signed did not define our dinosaur. It was too broad, too vague, and not specific."

The two bone-struggling veterans had battled the perennial forces of nature for nearly four years. Now they were set to struggle against dominant institutions at the local and state level, including educational, governmental, and bureaucratic strongholds. The two embattled discoverers did not know it at the time, but they had inadvertently been placed at the crossroads of science, religion, and politics.

While Bueno bragged about the confiscated box of bones, even more powerful and sinister forces were converging in the state capitol and manipulating the political sphere in an attempt to address the bone question from a legislative standpoint. Weyerhaeuser, a hive of duplicity and treachery, now reached amidst the corridors of power to rein in the treasure.

In a complementary stroke, Dr. Langston had pulled some strings at the University of Oklahoma and set in motion a series of events that would reverberate from the halls of the legislature out into the provincial hinterland. The two bone conquerors would be caught in the middle of it. Langston had worked his magic and achieved his last hoorah. He then retired from the scientific world.

CHAPTER FORTY-ONE
"Only Dead Fish Go With The Flow"

Cephis Hall realized he was in a serious legal quandary. Weyerhaeuser was privy to the high-dollar value of the dinosaur, and was ready to contest ownership. The dinosaur story that unfolded along the company's forlorn wasteland had incited intense rage, even envy, within the bosses' hierarchically-biased minds. Retribution against the rock hounds was being transacted behind the scenes. A couple of nativist, Southern bone pillagers and a transnational hardwood plunderer were locked in combat.

Weyerhaeuser's top regional officials resented the very idea that two local yokels had managed to pull off such a brazenly orchestrated feat without them even knowing about it. Local Weyerhaeuser officials had dropped the ball and allowed the two yeomen to give their corporation a black eye. The inflated egos of the corporate brass had been pricked, and hot air floated outward. Their aura of monolithic invincibility had been dealt a blunt blow. For the moment, they were a tainted officialdom—stained by the impudence of a couple of homespun naturalists who had inadvertently outwitted them.

The corporation had been thrown a "left curve," and it had sailed right past them. Their ineptitude was now a matter of public recognition. They were embarrassed and bent on evening the score. They had a standby repertoire of corporate and small-town lawyers ready to enter the fray at a moment's notice and work their legal magic within the criminal or civil courts.

Cephis sometimes viewed his institutional antagonists in a rather flippant way as big men with fancy titles but shriveled brains. Was Cephis naïve about the pitfalls of an ordinary individual battling a mighty corporation? Perhaps he had just enough naivete to cause him to struggle on against the impossible, rather than soberly assess the odds and step backward.

The two resolute naturalists had gone rogue as they played their hand of spades along the twists and turns of the riverine bend. Now it would be necessary to take a detour off the beaten path. As Sarah Palin would say, "Only dead fish go with the flow." Cephis and Sid realized that it would be futile to follow the normal course of legal fluidity. They were in a legal dilemma and needed a customized legal package free from the onerous, pay-by-the-hour terms. Normal recourse within the legal system would not work in their case. Having been continuously plagued by malodorous effluvium seeping out of the polluted pit and by an occasional miasma of putrefied fish floating near the river bank, they now feared the stench of decaying dinosaur bones.

Cephis was quite aware that the dispute with Weyerhaeuser was bound to wind its way into the courts. If it didn't become a criminal matter, it would surely become a civil one. If Weyerhaeuser did not soon file a civil suit in an attempt to recover the dinosaur through litigation, he and Sid might have to be the moving party (plaintiff). But they didn't have the money, or at least he didn't.

Weyerhaeuser had no issues with money; their resources for such a venture were almost limitless in this context. Such a legal initiative for a giant corporation required the expenditure of mere pocket change in terms of their overall budget and bottom line. In contrast, the attorney's fees for the two downtrodden sod busters would drive them to insolvency.

Sid, with more experience and resources, was wary of lawyers; he knew how they operated. It was clear to him that if they hired an attorney and paid him by the hour (about $150.00 hourly in a small town in the late 1980s), the counselor would have no incentive to settle the case, but an economic incentive to bill them voraciously for every conceivable minute of involvement and could quickly run up a staggering bill that would likely deplete their resources before they made it to court. If that happened, they would either have to borrow money or throw in the towel. It was not a rosy scenario. Sid knew the score. The courts were a sorry venue to obtain justice. Consequently, Sid was unwilling to expend his life savings in a "crap shoot" for justice.

Another issue with Sid's finances was his lack of liquidity. Although he descended from Choctaw aristocracy – the prominent Jones and Love families of southeastern Oklahoma – he had not inherited much wealth from those family fortunes. The assets had already been distributed amongst a large host of relatives before his time.

The old Robert M. Jones mansion near Hugo burned down sometime in the late 1860s. Rumors of buried treasure still remaining on the property persisted for a century later. Finally, sometime in the late 1960s, a local treasure hunter with a Geiger counter discovered a box of gold coins buried in the ground near the old home site. The value of the coins was estimated at about $100,000 based on the price of gold during that period, which was quite low. However, nothing was confirmed. The real value was likely much higher. What a pity for Sid; that box of coins was liquid and could have paid a lot of legal fees. His assets were tied up in real estate and small businesses.

Cephis had difficulty imagining a civil suit against a powerful corporation. The prospect of such a legal endeavor was sickening, but what other option did they have? One way or another, they would be dragged into the system whether they wanted it or not. The only place they could get a marketable title to the dinosaur was in the courts, and without a marketable title, they could never sell the dinosaur. With that sobering reality, Cephis began pondering the contingencies and intricacies of their legal dilemma. He knew they were out-gunned and out-financed. What kind of legal strategy could they conjure up from the "pit of desperation?" Like Sid, he hated the prospect of dealing with lawyers.

Cephis had little experience in working with legal counselors. He had dealt with a local, small-town attorney, Carl LeForce in Idabel, but only pertaining to minor business. A civil suit against Weyerhaeuser would take him, and his paltry legal experience, to a whole new level. Against Weyerhaeuser, he was a small fish in a big sea. Could Carl LeForce, or any local country lawyer, help span that great gulf merely through legal expertise?

As Cephis saw it, virtually all blue-collar people distrusted and despised lawyers. "Lawyer hating" is an enduring passion within the working class, and Cephis believed they had that sentiment mostly right. Other potential foes – gays, abortionists, gun regulators, atheists, liberals, etc. – are unlikely to do real harm, but a lawyer empties their pockets and takes advantage of their profound ignorance and impotence before the arcane tower of legalistic malfeasance. The court system intimidates working people and is perceived as an enormously expensive process with arbitrary judges, fickle juries, and capricious counselors.

Cephis knew that one could ask any blue-collar boor, except maybe some "divorce-driven hussy" who was "gold-digging" some poor schmuck for all he was worth, and he would set one's doubting mind straight – dealing with lawyers was pure hell, with one exception; when somebody banged you from behind in an automobile accident and did not really injure you – now that was pure "lawyer bliss." Ordinarily, lawyers chopped up the pocket greens of working folks and put them in their gourmet salads. (*Working class means wage earners without degrees. But even middle class professionals would fare little better against a formidable legal opponent with deep pockets.)

Republican or Democrat, rightist or leftist, easterner or westerner, cosmopolitan or small town, the lesson was the same: lawyers were leeches sucking the lifeblood out of the working class. There were "damned lawyers" and "no-good" lawyers, and none were friends to the "ordinary Joe" on the street. They could never be trusted, and neither could the bar associations that supposedly oversaw and regulated their ethics and business behavior, not to mention the lawyer-politicians who presided over the entire system. For Cephis, the prevailing sentiment was unmistakable: lawyers were a necessary evil when one had some money and no other recourse. Likewise, the courts were begrudgingly entered as a last resort when all other conceivable remedies had failed to materialize.

The working class might like trillion-dollar defense budgets, gas-guzzling SUVs, coal-fired electric generating plants, deep off-shore drilling, Sarah Palin (drill baby drill), deregulation (perhaps because Rush Limbaugh and Fox News tells them they should), guns, God, country, and apple pie, but they did not like lawyers – except maybe those lawyer-politicians they kept returning to Congress decade after decade as lobby-swayed, career politicians.

If one wanted to point fingers at who was responsible for the political, economic, social, and environmental mess the nation was in, and if one wanted to identify a particular occupational group who might be culpable, it would have to be lawyers. They run the legal, political, judicial, and corporate systems and make up the great majority of lobbyists, think tank pundits, and bureaucratic officials who pull the strings behind the scenes to influence and direct policies. Attorneys write the rules that govern society and stack the odds in favor of their preferred clientele.

While contemplating his legal quagmire, Cephis seized on a realization regarding legal representation for ordinary, rural folks. He concluded that dealing with a country lawyer who had a vested stake in their reputation within the community and wanted to treat his clients fairly was a lot better prospect than dealing with an unknown, transient lawyer in a mass society. In that regard, a small-town lawyer offered more hope than a big-city lawyer. But of course, it was all a matter of money; the deeper one's pockets, the more legal services one could purchase.

What about satisfaction and performance standards in the attorney-client relationship? When a consumer purchases a defective product from Walmart, he can take it back and get a refund, at least if he has a receipt. But with lawyers, a client usually has to take what he receives, even if the goods (services) are defective or mislabeled. There are no returns or refunds for legal services rendered.

If one had a complaint against an attorney, he might simply fire him and wait for the final bill. But what if you had a whole string of dysfunctional counselors and a sordid legal experience? What if unethical or immoral behavior were involved from one's own attorney or from the opposing side? It was usually just tough luck. Filing a complaint with the local or state bar against the conduct of an individual attorney rarely got one anywhere.

Lawyers controlled the state legislatures and judiciaries. They policed themselves and were a great deal more sympathetic to a fellow member of the club than John Q. Public. There is no independent, public interest body delegated to overseeing the conduct of individual attorneys or the legal system in general. Self-regulators were largely dismissive of abhorrent behavior of fellow insiders. The rules and codes of ethics supposedly enforced by the bar associations were rarely cited against one of their own members. Only in rare cases when an attorney stepped over the line into renegade territory by offending prominent and powerful persons inside the corridors of power did the self-regulators take a serious look at the offending behavior.

Although many attorneys will never rise to national prominence or conspicuous wealth, from the consumer's perspective it seems that the economic principles of free markets – of supply and demand –do not apply to attorneys. When the befuddled consumer begins a search for legal representation, he often discovers that the greater the supply of practitioners, the higher the fees.

Lawyers were seen as being part of that exclusively rich "green zone" (not botanical green, but dollar green) of the American landscape. This was a particularly vivid perception for disgruntled working stiffs who could not afford their services. Detached legal elitists perched on piles of cash and plush corporate nostrums have delusively presumed that everything was on par with John Q. Public; however, in reality, things were not as idyllic out in the hinterland as they imagined. There was a groundswell of disillusionment and outright contempt for the profession and system. To many people looking inward at the system from an outside vantage point, the system looked broken and hopelessly corrupt.

The criminal judicial system seemed just as capricious as the civil courts. Even there, people with money fared much better than those without. The laws were applied differently for wealthy and prominent people as opposed to the poor and downtrodden, where the brunt of the law was often weighted out in stringent doses. White-collar criminals who committed horrendous crimes against the entire society were coddled, while blue-collar criminals were thrown in the slammer for minor offenses like smoking pot.

Wealthy celebrities like O.J. Simpson got away with murder, while poor people charged with a similar offense went to death row. Almost one third of the black male population was reportedly in prison. People have been sentenced to life in prison, including a considerable number of homeless Vietnam veterans, for a mere four convictions of small marijuana possessions. To some people peering into the workings of the criminal judicial system, Americans are as fickle in the jury box as they are at the ballot box, and judges sometimes refuse to recuse themselves from cases in which they have a vested economic interest.

Records show that 130 people on death row were proven to be innocent and eventually exonerated. For every eight people who have been executed, one has been identified as being innocent. The very fact that the society tolerates these kinds of statistics reveals much about the society and the shortcomings of the criminal judicial system. (Bill Moyers' Journal, *PBS Television*, guest host Bryan Stevenson, 4-2-2010)

The civil courts were absolutely out of reach for the poor and working class unless an attorney was willing to litigate their case on a contingency, charity, or class-action basis. Even highly affluent middle class litigants had little prospect against an opponent with deep pockets, such as a corporation. The litigant with the most resources had only to drag out the case until the weaker opponent ran out of money and was forced to capitulate. It was in the best interest of the party with the most financial resources to delay the process and trial as long as possible; consequently, the process often crept at a snail's pace.

It was not usually the delay of one's day in court that sealed the fate of the financially weaker litigant; the routine legal tactics used in the discovery process were utilized to drive up attorney's fees and prevent him from ever making it to court. The party with shallow pockets was bombarded with all kinds of legal procedures and paper work, much of it redundant and unnecessary, but all intended to force him to empty his pockets – like a legal shakedown scheme where only lawyers who got paid by the hour benefitted. The financially stronger opponent had no incentive to hold down his costs, but did have an incentive to drive up the costs of his weaker opponent to ensure that his day in court never arrived.

The mere discovery process can drag on for months or years. A deluge of legal paperwork is generated at a cost of $100 to $500 per hour. In cases where the strategy of the stronger opponent is simply to outlast his adversary, there are endless streams of back and forth correspondence and various requests for information: requests for disclosure, requests for admissions, requests for production, requests for continuance, interrogatories, depositions, supplemental responses, designations of expert witnesses, amended petitions, motions, orders, letters of correspondence, attorney conferences, etc. The process generates a long paper trail, and much of it cannot, or will not, even be entered into trial. If somehow the weaker opponent survives the discovery ordeal, a sullen moment of truth is inevitable: it will still cost tens of thousands of dollars in court costs (including trial preparation) if the trial lasts several days.

Sid had set Cephis straight about the bleak prospect of fighting Weyerhaeuser in the courts. Even with both men sharing the fees, it would cost each about $75.00 for every hour of the attorney's time. If the case dragged out for several years and was finally placed on the court docket, the total cost, including trial, could literally be millions, and there was always the likelihood of an appeal, which might add tens of thousands more to the bill. Soberly, the legal reality was clear – paying legal services by the hour was not feasible. Alternatively, there was no possibility an attorney would take the case on consignment because the two were not likely to recover anything from Weyerhaeuser because they had not yet been damaged by Weyerhaeuser. At this point, it was a mere legal dispute over rightful title to a dinosaur.

Another tangible consideration was the roadblocks lawyer-politicians were endlessly erecting to protect their most favored clients (corporations) from the whims of suit-happy middle class Americans. Lawsuit reform had made it more difficult for ordinary people to sue a corporation, but not the other way around. It was easier for a corporation to sue an ordinary person because money was the decisive factor in any lawsuit, and corporations had plenty of it. Lobbyists like Citizens Against Lawsuit Abuse (CALF), supported by Phillip Morris and Anheuser Bush, have pushed for new laws to stop people from suing corporations.

On the other hand, ordinary plaintiffs who somehow managed to successfully bring suit against a powerful corporation or wealthy individual in a personal injury case had an uphill battle. When corporations and insurance companies became defendants in a lawsuit, they routinely concocted strategies to burn holes in the plaintiff's pockets by stringing the process out for decades. Plaintiffs in personal injury suits against powerful corporate polluters had little hope of recouping losses for damages to their health, environments, businesses, and livelihoods. The litigation could drag out for decades, with lawyers being the only apparent winners. Many of the Exxon Valdez oil spill lawsuits were not settled until 2010.

The prospect was depressing. There had to be a better way to resolve the issue, but how? Unfortunately, the legal system was their only recourse to gain title and justice. They had to find a way around the typical pay-by-the-hour, attorney-client relationship. Time was creeping up on them. If they were to take the case into the hallowed halls of American jurisprudence, they needed to figure out something fast.

CHAPTER FORTY-TWO
House Bill 2014

The two embattled underdogs tried to assess their situation in light of swirling controversies and sinister conspiracies. What could they do to affect the course of events that were rapidly unfolding? The situation seemed to be spiraling out of control as they found themselves at the mercy of scheming and foreboding forces. Troubles were brought down upon them from above, and they were forced to react. Some strategic thinking and planning were needed to balance the scales, but intervening events soon overtook them anew.

On a cool, breezy evening in March 1988, Sid and Floy Love sat down for supper at their modest three-bedroom, wood-frame house in Idabel and anticipated a relaxing evening. The two spouses were much alike – reserved, quiet, and private. Floy was not of American Indian heritage; she was typical European frontier stock.

As they discussed the latest gossip and other mundane matters over iced tea and sirloin steak, the phone suddenly rang. The unexpected call was from Mike Murphy, a long time friend of Sid's. Sid had known Mike since they were small boys growing up in Idabel. Mike had built a successful career as a politician in the state legislature and represented the Idabel district. He had risen in the ranks to become Speaker of the House.

Murphy called to tell Sid about a state bill that had just passed in the Oklahoma State House of Representatives by a vote margin of ninety-four to four. The bill addressed state fossils and was sure to be of interest to Sid. Mike believed the bill had a direct bearing on the *Acrocanthosaurus*. Although somewhat confused about the bill, he wanted to inform Sid of what he knew from the inside

House Bill 2014 initially had been portrayed as a bill to protect Indian cemeteries from grave robbers, but had a more serious, if not sinister, undertone. Indisputably, the heart of the bill dealt with fossils rather than Indian graves. Its passage into law would make criminals out of small-time amateurs collecting fossils on state lands without a permit issued by a newly proposed, quasi-governmental body called the Advisory Board for the Conservation of Paleontological Remains. And not just that – amidst the hype and confusion on the capitol floor, innuendos and accusations were being hurled against Sid and Cephis.

The bill was sponsored by Representatives Carolyn Thompson of Norman and Victor Wickersham of Mangum in the House, and State Senator Kelly Haney in the

Senate. It had earned the pseudonym "Grave Robbing Bill," perhaps because one proponent of the bill, Dr. Richard Cifelli, a paleontologist at the Oklahoma Museum of Natural History in Norman, had reportedly referred to Cephis as a "grave-robbing thief" in a prior conversation with Senator Haney.

The legislation, also referred to as the Oklahoma Fossil Preservation Act, was apparently directed at amateur and commercial fossil collectors and its underlying intent was to shut down all fossil sales and trafficking inside the state of Oklahoma. The newly proposed law had easily passed the House despite few members having read it. The scientists associated with the university-sponsored museum in Norman were apparently the lobbyists behind the bill and were believed to have actually written it.

Murphy asked Sid if he thought the scientists at OU had a vendetta against him. Sid responded that he was not sure, but believed the bill might just be a stepping stone in an attempt to ultimately recover the subject dinosaur for OU and single out amateur fossil collectors like him. In Sid's mind, such a bill could always be amended in the future to impose broader guidelines and more drastic penalties against amateur or commercial collectors, and if the current version applied only to state-owned lands, it might later be expanded to include private lands as well. The bill was likely the first step in a continuing process. It portended ultimate doom for free access to fossils on public or private lands in the state of Oklahoma.

House Speaker Murphy informed Sid that he had initially been in favor of the bill and voted for it, but now had second thoughts. At the time of the vote, he was not aware of the true nature of the bill because he had not read it. But since the vote, he had learned some new things which raised several questions. The bill had moved too fast and seemingly in a sly, secretive manner. He was now concerned about how the bill would play out in the home districts with local constituents who enjoyed collecting fossils and rocks.

Murphy added that the bill was currently tied up in the Senate Committee on Education and if he and Cephis wanted it killed, they needed to contact the Committee Chairperson, Senator Billie Floyd of Ada, or the Senate sponsor, Kelly Haney from Seminole. The bill might be coming out of committee any day and brought before the Senate for debate.

As soon as the conversation with Murphy ended, Sid got on the phone with Cephis. The news did not come as a surprise to him. The two men were already aware that something was stirring in the state capitol. They believed Murphy was right on target; after all, he was an insider. The two men also suspected that Michael Mares and Rich Cifelli of the Oklahoma Museum of Natural History, the very same scientists they had encountered at the Gem and Mineral Show in Oklahoma City, were the driving force behind the bill. They knew they had to act quickly if there was going to be any chance of stopping it. The two men hung up the phone and began making calls. Although they had not yet obtained complete details on the bill, they sensed the gravity of the matter. They had no time to waste; the specifics of the fine print could be learned later.

Allan Graffham was contacted first. They knew he would be personally interested because the bill was bound to impact commercial paleontologists and might even infringe on their planned business transaction. They hoped Graffham would, in turn, contact other commercial paleontologists across the state and nation.

Another person called was a friend of Graffham – Wayne Edgar, the director of the Goddard Youth Camp in Sulphur, Oklahoma. Edgar was a fellow naturalist whom Cephis had first met when he and Graffham once visited his Rock Shop to examine his quartz crystals. Hall and Edgar had struck up a friendship and stayed in close contact.

Edgar had ties to prominent families in the state, including the Goddard and Noble families. Graffham had once worked for Noble Affiliates, a major oil company, and still had personal ties to both the Noble family and the Noble Foundation. If they could get these powerful people on their side, they might be able to make some waves in the state capitol. Cephis was hoping that either Edgar or Graffham would be able to get the rundown on all the particulars of the bill and fill them in later.

Next, they began calling their friends and associates within the rockhound community in hopes that the local gem and mineral clubs throughout the state would take an active interest. They prayed that a grassroots furor would echo across the state and be heard by the state senators considering the bill.

Only a few days later, Wayne Edgar called Cephis to report what he had learned about the bill and what was going on at the state capitol. He had actually read the bill and had been talking to important people. He believed that Sid and Cephis were basically accurate in their initial assessment of the underlying intent of the bill, and that the two scientists at OU were the principal proponents. In addition, Weyerhaeuser might also be involved. Regardless, the dubious bill had been surreptitiously crafted and rammed through the House with little debate. The mere prestige of the University of Oklahoma, which ultimately stood behind the bill, had been enough to convince legislators that the bill was benign. He then summarized some of the highlights of the bill.

The bill was rather short and vague, but could be construed to have a broad application. The statute might easily accommodate future revisions and amendments. Fossils, particularly the Hall-Love *Acrocanthosaurus*, were the principal issue. Conceivably, with potential conspiracies abounding, title to the skeleton clouded, and pervading allegations of theft from private property, the language of the bill might later be expanded and made more specific. If that were the case, new language in the bill might target these controversies in a concerted effort to retroactively criminalize the acts of Hall and Love and seize the dinosaur for the public interest.

The *Acrocanthosaurus* was unquestionably a focal point of the bill. Section 10, to be codified in the Oklahoma statutes as Section 379 of Title 53 read as follows: "*Because of the extraordinarily rich paleontology of the State of Oklahoma, the Legislature hereby* declares <u>Acrocanthosaurus atokensis</u> to be the State Fossil of Oklahoma. This spectacular dinosaur, 'the 'high-spined dinosaur', occurred in Oklahoma 105 million years ago. It is known primarily from Oklahoma and rivaled <u>Tyrannosaurus rex</u>, the 'king of the dinosaurs' as the greatest predator of earth's history."

The logic behind this glorified acclamation appeared obvious. By making the "high-spined dinosaur" the State Fossil of Oklahoma, pressure would mount on Hall and Love to forego any sale and hand over the specimen to the public. The public interest as defined in the bill meant the Advisory Board for the Conservation of Paleontological Remains, a newly created state bureaucracy that was a front for the Oklahoma Museum of Natural History. Stiffer penalties for not turning over the Acro, or any other specimen in question, could be written into the law at a later date. Conceivably, Hall and Love could be made felons and imprisoned. In that event, their dinosaur would be confiscated without compensation and held for the benefit of the public interest at the Oklahoma Museum of Natural History.

The language of the bill seemed evasive, and key terms like "fossil" and "state lands" were not adequately defined. Section 2(1) defined "fossil" as follows: *"Fossil' shall mean the recognizable remains and traces of prehistoric nonhuman organisms that are incorporated into the earth's rocks."* Section 2(2) of the bill read: *"State lands' shall mean all lands owned by or under the jurisdiction of the state, or any agency thereof."* Of course, there was room to rewrite and extend the meaning of "state lands" to encompass private lands, but in reality, for some people, all lands were ultimately under the jurisdiction of the state, and thereby the original meaning could be construed to mean not just governmentally owned lands, but privately owned lands as well.

The bill would bureaucratize the hobby of collecting fossils by vesting all power to decide the facts on "who, when, where, what, and how" concerning fossil collecting on "state lands" in the new scientific-governmental Advisory Board for the Conservation of Paleontological Remains.

Section 4, 373 of Title 53 stated: *"Where fossils are found to exist on state land and the Advisory Board for the Conservation of Paleontological Remains determines that such fossils are worthy of special conservation effort, the Board may recommend the procedures best calculated to ensure conservation."*

Section 5C, 374 of Title 53: *"The Advisory Board for the Conservation of Paleontological Remains shall encourage persons having knowledge of the location of or any unlawful excavation project for fossils on state land, to communicate such information to the museum."*

Section 6A: *"Unless the proper permits have been issued by the Advisory Board for the Conservation of Paleontological Remains, collecting fossils for profit, and quarrying for fossils on all state lands are prohibited, as is the sale of fossils obtained from said lands."*

Section 6B read, in part: *"A permit may be granted by the Board upon application for the permit accompanied by an application fee not to exceed Twenty-Five Dollars ($25). Permits shall be issued when it is shown that investigations, excavations, gathering, and* *removals shall be undertaken for the benefit of science and education. Additional requirements may be established by the Board, including but not limited to the requirements that a portion of any fossil materials recovered may be deposited within the State of Oklahoma and shall forever remain the property of the state."*

Section 8A: *"The illegal collection of, or unlawful traffic in, fossils from state lands shall be considered a misdemeanor. Upon conviction of illegal collection of, or unlawful traffic in fossils, punishment shall be imprisonment for a period not to exceed three (3) months, or a fine not to exceed Two Thousand Five Hundred Dollars ($2,500.00) or both such fine and imprisonment. All objects and materials obtained in violation of this act shall be forfeited to the state, as will all photographs and records relating to such materials."*

Section 9: *"The State of Oklahoma may institute a civil action in district court for recovery of any unlawfully taken fossil. The fossil shall be forfeited to the state if the State of Oklahoma proves that the fossil has been taken illegally from state lands, and that the person, institution, or other entity that is found in possession of the fossil is not authorized by permit to possess such fossil."*

The underlying intent of the bill seemed clear. This was a stealthy means to bring the *Acrocanthosaurus* into the limelight and sully Love and Hall with aspersions in the media and public discourse, thereby creating a public clamor for confiscation of the State Fossil. Also, it was rather clear that the newly created Board would have neither the funds nor the capacity to administer or enforce such a law. There were only a handful of university paleontologists in the state, and the museum was already understaffed and underfunded.

Edgar informed the two men that the bill was currently bogged down in the Senate Education Committee, and there had been some tense verbal exchanges between the sponsors and Committee Chair Billie Floyd. It had been reported that Michael Mares, in an appearance before the Senate Education Committee, had pointed his finger at Senator Floyd and stated to this effect: We will get this dinosaur no matter what we have to do. Apparently, the Senate, under the guidance of Floyd, was taking a more serious look at the bill.

As a result of Cephis and Sid's contacts, many state senators were now getting calls or letters from their constituents back home who voiced strong opposition to the bill. The word had gotten out to the rock and mineral enthusiasts across the state, and they wanted no part of the bill. Consequently, with momentum stalled in committee, the proponents of the bill were starting to get a little frustrated.

Edgar concluded the conversation by informing Cephis of the plan. He and a few others were going to Oklahoma City to talk personally with Senators Haney and Floyd. They were representing the other side of the public interest. He advised Cephis and Sid to sit tight and wait. They would be informed of the results as soon as there was news to report. They were leaving for the state capitol that evening.

The following day, Wayne Edgar, Allan Graffham, Dixie and John Alf, representatives of the Oklahoma Mineralogical Society, and Neal Larson of the Black Hills

Institute, entered the office of Senator Kelly Haney to discuss the bill in person. Senator Haney was a powerful state senator who had been around long enough to know the system and how things worked inside and outside the legislature. He was a full-blooded Seminole Indian and had other things to his credit.

Kelly Haney was an internationally recognized Native American artist who specialized in paintings and sculpture. In 1972, he was named as one of the outstanding young men of America. Before serving in the legislature, he had served the Seminole Nation of Oklahoma as a tribal councilman, band chief, business consultant, and planner. In 1976, the Five Civilized Tribes Museum declared him a Master Artist. He would later go on to create "The Guardian", a twenty-two foot bronze sculpture which now adorns the Oklahoma State Capitol, and run as a Democratic candidate for Oklahoma governor, only to be defeated in the primary by Brad Henry.

Senator Floyd had now taken sides against the bill in conference and was rocking the boat inside the committee. She had actually read the bill and was now speaking out against it. If Senator Haney could be persuaded to drop his support of the bill, the bill would likely die in committee.

Edgar was personally acquainted with Haney, and his contact had likely gotten the party access. The two men greeted each other as if they were old friends.

Haney asked, "Who are these other people?"

Edgar allowed each person to introduce him or herself.

Haney then pointed at Graffham and Larson and exclaimed, "Get them out of here. They're nothing but lobbyists." Graffham and Larson immediately left the room, leaving only Edgar, John, and Dixie to sit down with the Senator.

As the meeting continued, Senator Haney pulled a small fossil out of his coat pocket and informed Edgar that his grandson had found it. "What is it?" he asked.

Edgar responded that it was a brachiopod, and then, while pointing at the object, declared, "Senator Haney, if this bill passes, your grandson could be arrested."

Haney, looking stunned, quickly read the six-page bill sitting atop his desk.

With the Senate Chamber still in conference right outside his office, Senator Haney looked up and stated in a rather solemn tone, "I have been lied to again."

Seeming a bit irritated, he told Edgar to wait inside his office and then stormed into the Senate Chamber where committee members were waiting and whispered to Senator Floyd, "There is no longer a sponsor in the Senate." At that point, the bill was doomed. It never came out of committee.

On his return to his office, Senator Haney informed Edgar and the Alfs that he wanted them to write a fossil bill that was more suitable for the people of Oklahoma. He asked if they could bring him a typewritten version the following day. They stated they would do their best.

The bill-writing consortium, an alternative proponent of the public interest, also included Graffham and Larson, who had specialized knowledge and insight into the commercial aspect of fossils. The contingent worked frantically overnight in their hotel to cobble up a new fossil bill based more persuasively on the perceived sentiment of the general public.

Edgar, John, and Dixie returned the following morning with the new bill in hand and presented it to Senator Haney. Haney, somewhat impressed, thanked them and handed the manuscript to his legislative aide and instructed him to get it properly prepared in the capitol print shop. He then asked his bill writers to hang around and see what happened next. They complied.

By the time the aide returned with a printed version of the alternative bill, the political atmosphere in the chamber had changed. A crowd of state senators was clamoring outside Haney's office with a clear message to convey. Their constituents back home had spoken and wanted no part of any fossil bill. The newly crafted bill was not even introduced into committee. The committee was in no mood to entertain any kind of fossil bill. Not just plain folks had contacted their offices; wealthy and powerful people like the Goddards and Nobles had also lent their voices. The whole matter was dead.

Despite the failure of the alternative bill, Edgar had good news to report to Hall and Love, who were eagerly awaiting the outcome. Upon getting the news, the two men were ecstatic. Their side had won another round.

The Acro had suddenly generated a lot of interest at the state level as it was temporarily placed in the spotlight, but for ulterior reasons. After the bill failed, the Acro was forgotten and expunged from the public record. The Sam Noble Museum of Natural Science and the State of Oklahoma looked elsewhere for a suitable icon to be dubbed the title of State Fossil of Oklahoma.

The honor of State Fossil would eventually be awarded to that great predator of the late Jurassic Era, *Saurophaganax Maximus*, under Title 25, Chapter 3, State Emblems and Honorary Positions, Section 98.6. State Fossil, April 14, 2000.

CHAPTER FORTY-THREE
The Enforcer

Within a week after the aborted attempt by university lobbyists to rush the dubious Fossil Preservation Act through the state legislature, Weyerhaeuser sent down one of their hot-shot security agents to conduct a private investigation and shake out some bones. Eugene Marrs was a private investigator modeled after the old Pinkerton private detectives who routinely sprayed bullets and cracked skulls during the episodes of labor unrest in the late nineteenth century.

His mission was to find and confiscate the bones. Intimidation was his principal method. Through the use of Gestapo-like tactics, he hoped to scare the hell out of the bone outlaws and persuade them to hand over their stash. A corporate bully was about to be unleashed on Cephis Hall.

Eugene Marrs looked like a hulky Irishman: red-headed, burly, about 6'7" and 300 pounds. The man towered over most of his contacts and instilled fear in the hearts of the physically weak or meek. He was not just an investigator; he was also an enforcer. He executed the corporate will on uncooperative subjects and persuaded them to toe the company line. He specialized in knocking on doors and securing the desired information by strong-arm tactics. It was not just his physical appearance that unraveled the nerves of targeted suspects; his tone of voice and overbearing demeanor could melt the subversive resistance of virtually any corporate foe. He was pure muscle.

This corporate policeman from Tacoma called Hall on a late evening in the middle of the week. Upon answering the phone, Cephis detected the same overbearing tone he had experienced with Joe Bueno, but this was somebody different.

Marrs identified himself as a security official from Tacoma who had been sent down to resolve the dinosaur dispute and wanted to meet with him in a private, neutral place to discuss a possible settlement. Cephis wavered on giving an answer, but decided he would rather let this guy show his face in the open; at least then he could flesh him out and uncover his real motive. He would need to have his own secret witnesses staked out nearby to observe what transpired.

Weyerhaeuser's private security police had no authority to arrest him. If the sheriff wanted him arrested, he would already have done so. Cephis reluctantly agreed, but with the stipulation that both he and Marrs be alone. Marrs concurred. They would meet face-to-face at the Dairy Queen in Idabel.

That following evening, the two men exchanged greetings inside the restaurant and sat down across from each other at a dining booth. The corporate agent introduced himself as Gene Marrs, investigator for the Weyerhaeuser Timber Company. The meeting started off on a rather sour note, and the discourse quickly became testy and nasty. Fortunately, the Dairy Queen was almost empty and Marrs and Hall were sitting in an isolated corner.

Marrs was not friendly; rather, he was confrontational and uncompromising. Marrs bluntly informed Hall that he had been commissioned to take possession of the dinosaur, and rudely added that he had been sent down from Tacoma to "bury his (Cephis') ass."

Cephis responded, "It will take a pretty big hole. I will dig my way out."

Marrs, with a sour look on his face, retorted, "I used to play football with the Nebraska Cornhuskers and I'm mean as hell."

Hall stood up and quickly countered, "I've weighed about 150 pounds most of my adult life and have carried a 26 pound chainsaw up and down the mountains all day long for years. You have to be pretty tough to do that. You're either tough or you die. I can and will kick your ass all over McCurtain County."

Diners inside the restaurant started looking around at the commotion. Hall knew it was time to leave. Before turning around, he concluded, "This meeting is not productive. I see no reason to continue. If you want to talk again, I will do so only in the presence of my lawyer." The lean and mean lumberjack then walked out of the Dairy Queen leaving the stunned giant speechless.

The bulky enforcer, somewhat embarrassed and bewildered, walked out afterwards and drove off the premises. Pure intimidation was apparently not going to work. He had failed to scare the lumbering hillbilly into submission.

Cephis had quickly figured out the towering hulk's tactic. He knew Marrs was trying to shake him up by throwing his weight around and acting tough. In response, Cephis utilized the same intense mental concentration he had long-practiced in the crystal field to allay any signs of fear. The man who had lived through numerous chainsaw accidents and had stood up and walked away after having giant trees crash down on him was not intimidated by pure muscle.

But a realization had dawned on him. Hall knew it was now time to start consulting an attorney; there was no other option. He could not outsmart or outmaneuver Weyerhaeuser much longer. The corporation had more muscle, brains and money and was not going to quit. They had to be stopped.

Cephis believed that if he and Sid could file a civil lawsuit and bring the dispute into the legal system, this might quiet Weyerhaeuser's attempt at pressing criminal charges against them. He figured that if the district attorney knew there was a civil suit pending, the prosecutor might defer to the civil courts. It might seem rather incongruous for the state to bring an indictment against two men who had filed a civil suit against the party alleging the crime.

Cephis had recently come up with a plan and it was now time to implement it. There was one possible way that he and Sid might be able to afford legal representation. He would visit the law office of Carl LeForce, knowing that it would require some hard convincing. He and Sid needed to step up to the plate and initiate further negotiations with Graffham. Cephis would call both Graffham and LeForce tomorrow to set up meetings.

Weyerhaeuser obviously meant business. The two bone benchers needed to step out in front of the curve and slug back at the hard-hurling corporation. It was time to play hard ball, but Cephis wanted his team to be the hard-balling pitcher. Cephis was tired of Weyerhaeuser always being the mover and shaker, and with them being forced to respond off the cuff. They were hoping to strike a deal with both LeForce and Graffham and move the ball into Weyerhaeuser's court. Their plan was another big gamble and one with long odds, but their options were limited. It was David against Goliath. They would need to strike out the opponent and hit a grand slam home run. They could not slay the giant corporation, only detract or deter it. It would be impossible to cut off the titular head of a far-flung corporate empire; about all they could do was send a message and hope the colossus would back off.

CHAPTER FORTY-FOUR
Legal Recourse

On a weekday afternoon, Cephis Hall walked into the law office of Carl LeForce at 117 North Central Avenue in Idabel, Oklahoma. He wanted LeForce to represent him and Sid in a lawsuit against Weyerhaeuser. Hall and Love had worked out a sales agreement with Allan Graffham and this time it was in writing – signed and notarized. Cephis had a proposal for LeForce and thought there was a chance he might be interested, even though he knew lawyers did not usually take cases that might not pay off. Good attorneys were shrewd businessmen and were picky about the cases they accepted.

LeForce was a family lawyer for the Halls and Cephis had used him on a few occasions for minor things. Cephis had known LeForce since his earliest days of practicing law in Idabel. At the time Hall and LeForce initiated their legal relationship, both were young, LeForce being a few years older.

On their very first meeting, Cephis entered LeForce's law office with a ticket issued to him by a state trooper for uttering profane language in a public place. Cephis had blurted out the profanity after receiving a traffic citation for some petty mechanical defect like a blown license tag bulb. The trooper then nailed him for that indiscretion. Cephis wanted to contest the profanity charge and handed the citation over to the young LeForce, who rendered his service for a small fee and was successful in getting the ticket dismissed. From that day forward, he was the Hall family's personal attorney.

On this particular visit, Hall's need for legal representation was crucial. This was not some petty issue. He was now treading in the big leagues and embroiled in a legal dispute with one of the most powerful corporations in the world.

Normally, the attorney sets the terms for legal representation and is inflexible in granting concessions to a potential client. A client either accepted the attorney's proposal or looked elsewhere. Regarding this legal matter, Hall was offering the terms and the attorney listened. LeForce had to look beyond the typical attorney-client arrangement and see the potential in the deal. Only LeForce knew what was potentially feasible within the world of legal maneuvering and finessing inside McCurtain County. Like all attorneys, he was practical. If the proposal offered no potential lucrative payoff, it would be rejected. A cordial relationship with a client was preferable, but LeForce was no bleeding heart dispensing discounts on legal services.

As he walked in the door, Cephis was greeted by a young attorney named Walter Hamilton who was fresh out of law school and had just joined LeForce's legal team. Hamilton escorted Hall to a small conference room where they were soon joined by LeForce. The two attorneys then listened attentively to Hall's pitch.

Hall explained that he was in a legal dispute with Weyerhaeuser over ownership of a dinosaur skeleton he had dug up on Weyerhaeuser's land. He needed to get the issue settled in order to sell it. He already had a buyer who was offering a good price.

Cephis showed them a copy of the contract for sale to Allan Graffham of Geological Enterprises. The purchase price was $225,000, plus a $50,000 allowance for a cast of the bones, making a grand total of $275,000 that was to be paid in installments. As soon as the case was settled, Graffham agreed to make a down payment of $25,000. Hall offered the law firm a consignment on a portion of the sale proceeds in return for legal services. Hall stated that he had no money and his partner Sid was unwilling to pay an attorney by the hourly rate.

Hall proposed certain stipulations, which included the following: The payment installments were to be transacted and cleared through the law office, and then the firm could take its portion out of the proceeds and distribute the remaining balance to the two clients. Hall-Love, as plaintiffs, wanted the case settled out of court, preferably within six months, and needed the firm to specify a percentage portion to be taken out of each installment for legal fees and a maximum dollar figure to be exacted from the total proceeds; and, if the case did not settle before trial, the parties could agree to renegotiate the terms, or drop the case. Cephis suggested $25,000 as a reasonable fee and wanted to know if that figure would be acceptable to LeForce. LeForce could not address a dollar figure at that point, but of course he would have the last word on that.

The legal arrangement proposed by Hall was similar to the typical consignment deals attorneys routinely make with injured parties in automobile accidents. The attorney takes a percentage – typically 1/3 (33%) of what is recovered from the insurance company. The injured party pays all their medical bills and expenses out of their own pockets, or out of the settlement sum dispersed from the insurance company. The insurance company pays the monetary settlement to the lawyer, who then takes his cut and distributes the balance to his client. It is a neat little package that relies on the deep pockets of the insurance company and its willingness to cough up the funds, which it usually does. If the attorney recovers nothing from the insurance company, the client owes nothing in legal fees.

However, this contingency deal was a little different from the normal settlement terms in cases involving injured parties in automobile accidents. In this case, the attorneys would receive their funds not from a liable party (usually the insurance company), but from a neutral third party (the buyer of the dinosaur), who awaited the outcome of the case. The attorney had to secure a settlement that quieted the title in order for the sellers to transfer a clear title to the purchaser.

The deal envisioned by Hall was based on the hopeful contingency that LeForce could settle the case prior to trial. If he could settle the case quickly without expending much time or money, the firm would make a hefty return on their speculative investment. But if they could not settle the suit or recover any monies, the firm might have to mark it off as a loss. Settling the case meant convincing Weyerhaeuser, or at least its attorneys, to acquiesce and accord Hall and Love a clear title to the dinosaur. As a sound business proposition, LeForce would set the total dollar figure for his legal fees on the high end to justify the potential risk. Perhaps he figured, as is quite common, that if the case did not settle prior to trial, his two clients might locate the funds to cover the legal fees and court costs. But based on the situational facts of the proposed deal, LeForce had every incentive to settle quickly while cutting litigation costs to the bare minimum.

Hall brought in some documents and facts that were highly favorable to his case. He stated that he had two personal meetings with timberlands manager Joe Bueno, and at the second meeting, Bueno agreed to let he and Sid dig on Weyerhaeuser land. Furthermore, Bueno had also stated that the company had no interest in anything they dug up. Cephis then showed the two attorneys a notarized affidavit signed by Gregory Perino, the director of the Museum of the Red River in Idabel, as proof of what he just said.

The affidavit attested to the fact that Perino witnessed Bueno give Hall and Love oral permission on behalf of Weyerhaeuser to proceed as they deemed fit in their excavation, asking only that they maintain a low profile. Also, Perino's statement attested that Bueno indicated that Weyerhaeuser had no interest in the paleontological products recovered by Hall and Love.

Next, Cephis provided photographs of a Weyerhaeuser employee, Harold James, assisting them in loading the thousand-pound skull into their pickup bed. The evidence was compelling. Bueno could lie all day long on the witness stand, but would that refute an admissible document signed by a prominent member of the community (or his personal testimony) along with photographs showing evidence of Weyerhaeuser's complicity in the dig?

LeForce was an insider within the legal community. Lawyers talked to each other all the time. They bargained and traded behind the scenes while settling cases. Sometimes favors were bestowed, which often left obligations to accrue in the future. When an attorney helped an opposing attorney settle a case, a favor was owed that represented a debt to be collected in the future. This was how lawyers worked – a quid pro quo arrangement.

Weyerhaeuser retained local attorneys in Idabel. LeForce could wheel and deal with those familiar bargainers. If it was in his best interests to settle a case promptly, he knew whom to talk to and what to say. All cases settled before trial were settled not just in the best interests of the clients, but in the best interests of the attorneys involved. "Best interests" for the attorneys might pertain to the benefit of the moment or a benefit to accrue in the future when new negotiations were underway and new settlements at stake.

It was clear to LeForce that they needed to file some kind of quiet title action. A quiet title action involves a lawsuit brought because one fears another party may assert a counterclaim, a right, or an interest against one's title to property which could infringe on rightful enjoyment of that property. The action was an equitable remedy for real property, but could the principle be applied to personal property? Was the dinosaur real or personal property? LeForce needed to do a little research before making a commitment. On that note, the meeting ended.

Cephis had done his best to convince LeForce to take the case on a customized contingency arrangement. But lawyers are cautious and deliberate when it comes to accepting new cases.

"We will get back with you soon on this," stated LeForce as Cephis walked out the door.

LeForce then instructed Hamilton to investigate the merits of the case and determine if it might pay off. The legal action necessary to save the dinosaur hung in the balance, and Weyerhaeuser was still making noise. The two dinosaur proponents were in legal limbo.

CHAPTER FORTY-FIVE
In the Shadow of Perdition

Cephis was waiting eagerly for any word from LeForce. He desperately needed to get a lawsuit initiated and on the record. A lawsuit might take some of the steam out of Weyerhaeuser's attempt to logjam them. The suit needed to be settled promptly to allow them to get a clear title, sell the dinosaur, pay the attorneys, and pocket the remainder. After all their troubles, they deserved to get a decent return on their time and investment. This was what any reasonable businessman expected, or at least hoped for. They were businessmen in bones. Why should they be treated as outlaws? The answer was simple. Powerful institutions and persons wanted the bones and were willing to run rough-shod over them to get them. They were lucky they were not already in jail on trumped-up charges. Perhaps if they obtained legal representation, the rules of engagement might change.

The bones were aging by the day and needed professional treatment for the pyrite affliction. Unless properly treated, the disease could spread across the entire girth of each and every bone, portending certain disintegration. Stopgap measures would not suffice over the long term. Langston-Pittman had done little treatment on the specimen while it was in their custody. It was amazing the skeleton was still relatively resilient considering the bane of the bone disease.

The skeleton was stored in a shed in rural Arkansas about six miles east of DeQueen. The shed was owned by Cephis' brother, James. Cephis had given him instructions on how to control the pyrite. James and his family were doing their best to care for the bones. He was like his brother's keeper, but tending bones instead of flesh.

Cephis did not want to spend much time at his brother's shed. Being concerned that somebody might follow him, he was afraid to drive out to the place. Cephis had recently observed strange cars parked in front of his house and alongside the gravel road. The roadway on which he lived was not a pike for joy riders or sightseers. People did not normally travel this back road unless they either lived on it or were lost. There was absolutely no explanation for strange cars being staked out along their road or in the vicinity at odd hours of the day or night. And what was even more suspicious, when a family member spotted one of these mysterious vehicles and the occupants knew they had been seen, they quickly moved out of sight.

Obviously, Cephis was being watched, but by whom? It was an eerie feeling, and caused him to be concerned about the safety of his family. But what could he do, call the sheriff? He knew that Weyerhaeuser had been talking to the sheriff about him. Cephis had contacts and ways of finding out certain things. Many friends and members of the community now knew his plight and were sympathetic.

As the Acro had once lurked in the primal swamps of primordial conifer forests, fearsome and gigantic institutions now stalked the bone stashers, especially Cephis. While the Acro wanted fresh meat, the institutions now sought a treasure trove of bones and were ready to expend blood and cash to get it.

Although Cephis was a man of action, he found himself feeling like a passive bystander waiting helplessly for the next incident to happen. He did all he could to wrest control of the situation, but he knew he was just plain folk and unable to take destiny into his own hands. He was at the mercy of powerful people with money and influence. There was no way he could convince Weyerhaeuser to back off, or LeForce to take the case. They each had their own agenda and were motivated by personal gain.

LeForce would take the case only if he deemed it was in his best interest. That was a reasonable business practice, and lawyers were certainly good businessmen. Understandably, looking out for one's self-interest was how one survived in the business world. But how could Cephis survive in this dire situation of powerlessness? Why were a couple of well-meaning bone merchants being so maligned? He thought businessmen were supposed to understand each other. Although he was part scientist, he was an entrepreneur at heart. He now felt more like a pariah than a businessman.

It was an agonizing thought to look back and realize that their struggle might have been in vain – thousands of hours of work, worry, and strain for nothing. There was much at stake, and he could not quit. He would struggle on with the same degree of determination and fortitude he had expended in the dig, but the situation looked bleak. Only hope and determination could keep him moving forward, but was that enough? Not likely, but he had little other choice.

He continued to be proactive and stayed in touch with key people. He contacted Graffham about fine details and continued to state his concern about the dinosaur being sold to international buyers. He wanted the specimen to remain in Oklahoma, or at least in the United States. For that very reason, he had stipulated in the sales agreement that he and Sid receive a cast of the monster. If nothing else, he and Sid would provide a mounted replica to an Oklahoma museum.

He also stayed in contact with the Black Hills Institute – seeking reassurance that they actually could preserve the specimen and make them a cast. The staff at the Institute remained confident that they could accomplish the task.

If only he could get the specimen to Black Hills, he would not have to worry about the bones dissolving into powder. Of course, that was out of the question; he and Sid didn't have the funds to pay for such a massive and expensive project, even if they managed to get a clear title.

Their best hope was to consummate the sale as quickly as possible. Graffham was reputedly wealthy. His rich financial resources could make it all happen. But that prospect was stymied over a legal dispute – a course of action that would be very expensive in its own right. They had to win in the legal contest before they could win in the scientific test. At this point, everything hinged on them getting affordable legal representation.

A miracle soon arrived in the way of a phone call from Carl LeForce. LeForce was bearing surprisingly good news. He had decided to accept the case under the terms proposed by Cephis.

"We can handle this case for you. We will need $50,000 out-of-sales proceeds," stated LeForce. "Walter doesn't have a single case right now, so he has ample time to devote to it. This will be his first case," explained LeForce. "Come on in and talk to Walter as soon as you can."

Cephis was overjoyed, but tried to contain his excitement. *There must be some catch*, he thought. He was wary of all lawyers, even LeForce. He heard the dollar figure. Fifty thousand dollars was a substantial sum of money, but he didn't care. If Leforce was shooting straight and stuck to the deal, he would not have to pay anything unless the case settled and Graffham forked over the money. After the lawyers got their cut and he and Sid divvied up the rest, they would each get about $87,500. That seemed a fairly reasonable amount for all their sacrifices. It seemed almost too good to be true. Settling the case seemed quite remote.

"I'll be in tomorrow morning," Cephis cheerfully replied.

The following morning, Cephis met his new lawyer, Walter Hamilton, at the front desk and the two men initiated their legal relationship. This was the rookie lawyer's first case since becoming licensed, and what an intriguing one it was – all the plots and sub-plots of a theatrical thriller. But lawyering in a small town did not usually accommodate melodrama or idealism; it was strictly hard-line business with straight-forward negotiation and deal making. Theatrics and histrionics were for a television audience addicted to drama – mere fantasy to titillate and entertain the mindless viewers.

Cephis expected to be presented with a lengthy contract with all the trimmings – pure legalese that he did not want to read, even if he could understand it. He merely wanted to sign on the dotted line and be done. He was a mere pawn in a legal scheme—a means to an end in the pursuit of a cash payout—and he knew it. He could only pray that the system would treat him fairly and that the lawyers wouldn't take all his money. His and Sid's overriding concerns about typical attorney-client arrangements had galvanized him to secure legal representation in a customized package. He had delineated the terms and expected his legal counsel to comply. Now he learned that the terms were not going to be specified in writing—it was to be an oral agreement. It was a customized deal for the attorneys, not him. There was nothing to sign. It reminded him of the Bueno affair.

He was turning over the destiny of the bones to the lawyers and the legal system. For a man of engagement, the situation was perplexing. Here again, things were being taken out of his control. He would have to sit and wait for the legal experts to work their magic. But could he trust the system? The answer was no.

He was filled with hope, rather than trust. The bones were again to be held hostage. Instead of their destiny being in the hands of a great educational institution, they were now in the hands of the legal system. What would Sid say? He had obtained legal representation without a written contract specifying the terms. He said yes to everything and walked out in a daze.

Promisingly, there was one ray of hope; the young attorney might be anxious to make a name for himself, and if he had plenty of time on his hands, he might actually do something. He wanted to trust this attorney, but knew he was not the man behind the deal. LeForce was telling him how to conduct business. The underling attorney was merely following orders from his boss. Did the boss have Cephis Hall's best interest in mind?

Hamilton had asked some questions and opened a case file. If he did not plan on doing anything, why would he go to even that little bit of trouble? Hamilton had given every indication that he was going to file some kind of legal action in an attempt to quiet the title. Some legal document was going to be drafted – at least that was the understanding Cephis had as he walked out of the law office. He at least felt some consolation; if a legal question came up, perhaps now he had somebody he could turn to. If Hamilton had no other cases on his plate, he could at least answer a question over the phone. That question would come soon.

CHAPTER FORTY-SIX
A Dream Turns Into A Nightmare

It was on a Sunday evening that Cephis received a phone call from a friend who had connections inside the sheriff's department. Rumors were teeming about Cephis and the dinosaur, and the most portentous rumor of all was that a warrant for his arrest was about to be issued. The sheriff was ready to nab the two bone outlaws and place them in custody – a polite term for jail. There was no way to confirm the veracity of the rumor.

Perhaps Weyerhaeuser figured that if it could scare the two bone thieves into panic, possibly they might unload their treasure. Maybe they might gather their bones and attempt a getaway with the police following and apprehending them. If the police took possession of the fossils, what would happen then?

Cephis and Sid contemplated the rumors, but avowed to maintain their composure. They were not stupid enough to run with the treasure, even if arrest was imminent. The police had not even attempted to interrogate them, let alone arrest them. They were not overly worried. If they ended up in a criminal court, perhaps the truth would come out. If Weyerhaeuser pressed bogus charges and its accusations proved spurious, the company's credibility might be tarnished.

Although the prospect of a false arrest was abhorrent, if it happened and they were later vindicated, pressure might mount for Weyerhaeuser to settle the civil suit or relinquish its claim. Settling the ownership dispute in a criminal court would be less expensive than in a civil court, but more immediate concerns came to mind.

If they were arrested for theft, might they be pressured by the police into revealing the location of the bones, or ordered by a judge to turn them over to the custody of the court? Another question kept worrying them: If they were arrested, could a judge issue a search warrant to probe into their premises, or even the premises of friends or relatives suspected of harboring the fugitive bones? They had the skeleton hidden in a secure place, but good detectives had ways of uncovering almost any hidden valuables. An investigation of their backgrounds might reveal the names and addresses of their friends and relatives. With that knowledge, multiple search warrants could be issued and multiple places searched. But that prospect was unlikely. Nobody, except maybe Weyerhaeuser or OU, wanted the bones badly enough to do that.

If the corporate nabobs discovered where the skeleton was hidden, could they persuade the sheriff to issue a search warrant and execute a raid? Could the court order its seizure? Cephis and Sid delusively reassured one another that everything was all right, but still another question registered. Should they ask their legal counselors these kinds of unsettling questions? Their whole panorama of fearful concerns might send the wrong message. They wanted the attorneys to be comfortable with their case. Were their fears bordering on paranoia?

But a new, troubling issue put all these other concerns on the back burner. Another call came in from Gene Marrs. In a more moderate and measured tone, Marrs asked if he and Cephis could have another meeting. Cephis reminded him of the outcome of their previous one, and to ensure that the discussion was civil, he stated that he would bring an attorney. Marrs agreed and inquired as to where they might meet.

"I know a quiet, public place in Idabel. The address is 117 North Central Avenue. I can meet you there," answered Cephis. Marrs, probably assuming it was a restaurant, obliviously wrote down the address and agreed to meet Cephis at 1:00 PM that Monday afternoon. Cephis then advised Marrs that if he was unable to keep the appointment, he would notify him. "Good," replied the enforcer, giving a phone number where he could be reached in Hot Springs. "I will see you tomorrow afternoon."

An appointment with Marrs was set, but it was tentative. Cephis was prepared to cancel the meeting on a moment's notice if Hamilton was unavailable to sit in as his legal representative. If Hamilton had no casework pending, what excuse would he have for not being referee at a hardball meeting with Marrs?

Cephis refused to deal with Marrs again without an attorney present. He would be at LeForce's law office early the following morning to explain everything to Hamilton and enlist his presence at the impromptu conference. This would also put Hamilton to the test. If he was serious about litigating the dinosaur case and representing his clients' true interests, he should not object, even if it was a slight inconvenience. With $50,000 in potential attorney fees at stake, how could he object to sitting in on a short meeting as representative for his first (and only) clients? If he was not receptive, there were only two options left for Hall and Love: cancelling and rescheduling the Marrs face-off; or, finding a new attorney.

Cephis arrived at the law office early the following morning and explained the situation to Hamilton, who agreed to sit in. He had no other appointments or pressing business. As the two men waited for Weyerhaeuser's private policeman to show up, Cephis briefed Hamilton about his prior encounter with Marrs. Hamilton was amazed at his client's predicament and curious about Marrs' motives. Did Marrs want to interrogate his client? If so, what exactly was he hoping to uncover? His job as attorney was to safeguard his client's legal rights and prevent verbal or physical abuse. What a way to start a law career!

Marrs was not privy to the fact that he was dropping in on a law office. He was met at the door by Hamilton and directed to the conference room. Marrs hesitated. After introducing himself, he explained that he didn't know the meeting was being held at a law office and asked to be excused for a few minutes until he could return with a company attorney. Hamilton agreed to wait.

Marrs had only to walk across the street to the law offices of John Shipp, a prominent corporate spokesman for southeastern Oklahoma. Shipp was a silk-stocking attorney who was born of wealth, and now was wealthy in his own right. On his maternal side, his mother was a Dierks; on his father's side there was also great wealth. Money always married money. It was anathema for wealth to marry poverty. That just did not happen in southeastern Oklahoma, or anywhere.

Shipp had a brisk law practice. He represented large corporations and wealthy individuals and was the principal legal proponent for the financial interests of Weyerhaeuser, the new timber empire of southeastern Oklahoma since Dierks sold out and faded from the scene. He was on a year-round retainer. If any problem came up at the local level, he would be assigned to quash it. A patrician, he had served as president of the State Bar Association of Oklahoma. His family members were prominent lawyers, bankers, businessmen and judges.

Although Shipp resented being interrupted on a moment's notice, he grudgingly walked across the street and entered the more modest law suite of Carl LeForce. Shipp and Marrs were led into the conference room, and after short introductions, the meeting got underway.

This was the young Hamilton's first conference as a practicing attorney and sitting across the table was the highest ranking member of the State Bar of Oklahoma and, in Marrs, one of the most imposing physical figures he had ever seen.

The meeting was not intended to settle any dispute. It was, as Cephis suspected, an interrogation – perhaps it could aptly be called an inquisition, witch hunt, or fishing expedition. Cephis, the commoner, was being questioned by two stern representatives of the sovereign timber realm.

As the underdog, Cephis had one thing in his favor – Shipp knew virtually nothing about the case and was not prepared. Marrs, the corporate strong man, had to pinpoint many of the questions. Everything was geared toward intimidation. Cephis was cross examined by both Marrs and Shipp in an apparent attempt to blow a hole in his testimony and cause him to unravel. Both asked the same probing questions, but each in a slightly different way, hoping to cause the hillbilly to slip up and divulge where the bones were hidden. Hamilton had to intervene on several occasions, and cautioned the two inquisitors about their tactics and language.

The principal thrust of the questioning was to determine whether or not Cephis had really thrown the dinosaur into the river as he had told Joe Bueno. And if he had not discarded it, where was it? They really did not believe he had actually dumped the bones, but they had no proof one way or the other.

"I can't believe you actually tossed that valuable dinosaur in the river," growled Shipp.

Cephis responded, "Well, think what you want. I will not clarify whether I did or didn't because you will not shoot straight with me. If I have the last word, I will say that I did dispose of it."

Shipp was stunned, probably thinking to himself: "Was this poor, backwoods hick really stupid enough to do such a thing?"

Shipp was obviously impatient and irritated; he rapped his knuckles on the table in an apparent act of contempt or boredom. "You mean you actually threw a two-million dollar skeleton in the river? If that's the case, what are we doing here?"

Cephis retorted, "I did not ask for this meeting. You should direct that question to Mr. Marrs. By agreeing to come to this miserable session, I have accommodated Mr. Marrs' request."

That blunt retort almost ended the meeting. Shipp gave Marrs a spiteful glance and then resumed the questioning. "We have been told that you sold the dinosaur to Japanese businessmen, is that not true?"

"No, it is not. I have received no monies for any sale of a dinosaur," answered Hall.

Shipp then followed up, "Did you enter into negotiations to sell the dinosaur to anybody, including Mr. Graffham over in Ardmore?"

Cephis responded, "How could I enter into negotiations to sell a dinosaur that I have already thrown away, and who would buy missing or damaged goods? I have no intentions of trying to salvage it out of the river."

The longer Shipp queried the hillbilly, the more irritated Shipp became. He was not happy about being there in the first place. He had more important business to attend to than questioning some obstinate chump about a trashed dinosaur. He had to keep reminding himself that it was Weyerhaeuser that wanted him there; it was not his choosing. If his corporate paymaster wanted it done, somehow he had to manage it, no matter how distasteful it might be.

Uncertainty and confusion clouded the conference. The two interrogators were getting frustrated and on the verge of lashing out at each other. Although they had attained some respect for this plain-spoken woodsman who stood his ground, they had gained disdain for each other. Shipp suddenly got up and walked out. The meeting was over. Marrs sullenly walked off like a hang dog covered with fleas. After the two corporate henchmen left, Hamilton and Hall burst out laughing. Hamilton lightheartedly asked aloud, "Is this what lawyering is like?"

Eugene Marrs, a giant Pacific westerner, was undergoing a learning curve on Southern culture. Backwoods Southerners were a different social animal than he was accustomed to dealing with. These pine-dwelling Okies and all their Southern kindred – crackers, rednecks, and good old boys – were pugnacious and obnoxious, and even worse, they were resistant to authority.

Marrs was starting to unravel under the strain of confronting Little Dixie's recalcitrant ruffians. Would he learn the ropes and get his act together in time to salvage the remains of Weyerhaeuser's lost dinosaur?

CHAPTER FORTY-SEVEN
The Gestapo Knocks on the Door

Allan Graffham, a scientist with money in his pockets – a pillar of the community and a fixture within the Ardmore commercial establishment – was a man with business and dinosaur savvy. He salvaged and sold dinosaur parts for a living and had plenty of spare parts lying around – stores of resplendent, stockpiled pieces – some mundane, others exotic. He pieced them together into something saleable. Every once in a while, he came across something world-class, and he knew a deal when he saw one. Hall and Love's *Acrocanthosaurus* offered one of those rare moments in paleontology when a deal became a steal.

He had a small (at least by major university standards) but innovative laboratory and a sizeable warehouse as part of a perfectly-synchronized, dinosaur-finessed operation. He preserved, stored, assembled, and cast bones. When he gained possession of a valuable articulated specimen needing specialized attention, he shipped it out to the best fossil preparation facilities in the world – like the Black Hills Institute located in the shadows of Mount Rushmore at Hill City, South Dakota.

Graffham had worked as a geologist in the oil fields and for years had rubbed elbows with the wealthiest oil barons in the state. Oil was the matrix of economic prosperity. In Oklahoma, reservoirs of black gold percolated beneath the surface and could be tapped by those possessing the specialized resources and equipment to capture it. In Oklahoma during the 1980s, it was easier to find an oil gusher than an articulated dinosaur skeleton.

Oil flowed out of the ground through pipelines, and money flowed into the deep pockets of wealthy oil men, who subsequently pipelined cash into the wellsprings of politicians and the coffers of charitable institutions. Oil money changed the minds of many state legislators who contemplated bills inside the state capitol. Oil was the lifeblood of the Oklahoma economy. Fossils were merely a hobby for eccentrics or the scientifically minded. Graffham had a bit of it all – money, science, flair, conspicuous consumption, respectability, eccentricity, and social and political connections. His economics combined fossil fluidity with fossil tangibility.

Graffham had ridden the boom until the oil crest peaked. He had since cashed out and abandoned the oil rigs for a more relaxed, entrepreneurial style – mining for tangible fossils, rather than fossil fuels. But despite his diversion into hard tangibles, he still traveled in the elite circles of regional oilmen and Ardmore businessmen. He didn't mind lavishly entertaining when there was a lucrative business deal hinging on the tilt of a glass of bourbon or a bite of a crab tendril.

As a businessman, Graffham was one of the most influential persons of Carter County. He was on the boards of directors of several foundations, including the Goddard Foundation and, according to some, the Noble Foundation. The wealth of the Nobles and Goddards stemmed from oil. The families had set up charitable foundations to distribute some of that surplus wealth and enjoy the tax breaks that go with munificence.

The Noble family was known to be very generous. Both the Noble and Goddard families provided grants for many worthwhile causes. Allan Graffham had a voice in how these charitable institutions handed out small portions of their great fortunes for noble causes.

Allan and his wife Fran lived on the north side of Ardmore in an upscale home within a prestigious subdivision. They were private persons – a security fence ringed their exclusive premises. Their place of business, Geological Enterprises, was located on Stoffa Street in the southeast part of the city next to a large cemetery. Bones lay about under the cemetery grounds as well as in their building. Other than that, the premises were quite impressive.

The business was housed inside a two-level building – above and below ground. The business office, showroom, and storage-warehouse were on the top floor; the workroom-lab was on the bottom floor. The facility was rather spacious.

The business model was efficient and well-organized – the display showroom, quite notable. The showroom contained samples of specimens that could be bought for the asking price. Some mounted replicas of smaller mammals and dinosaurs were modeled on display stands. A rich inventory of fossils was held in stock and if a potential buyer liked a particular product, very likely that item was available for purchase.

The storage-warehouse contained one of the largest commercial fossil inventories in the world. If Graffham did not have what a customer wanted on hand, he could likely find it elsewhere and have it shipped anywhere in the world for the right price. Even dinosaurs were on the list, except, of course, an articulated *Acrocanthosaurus*. Such a rare specimen was extremely hard to come by; only two such specimens were known to exist in the world, and they were just partial collections (less than 25%) without the all-important skull. Of course, there was the Acro skeleton housed in a secret shed in rural southwest Arkansas that was 70% articulated and had the most complete and best preserved theropod skull in the world. But who would want to buy such an exquisite specimen? Who could afford it?

Graffham showcased numerous exotic specimens – saber toothed cats, archaic reptiles and lizards, and small dinosaurs – his most precious being a full cast replica of an *archaeopteryx*, a transitional species between a reptile and a bird. He specialized in small prehistoric organisms like trilobites and brachiopods. In fact, he owned his own trilobite quarry – hundreds of acres located in Amish territory near Clarita, Oklahoma, which was just north of Wapanucka and southwest of Atoka, the site where the first Acro bones were found by Stovall and Langston.

Graffham mined trilobites, prepared them into beautiful collector items, and sold them on his showroom floor or through mail order. A raw, ordinary trilobite was not worth much – typically $25 to $100 – but a rare, exquisite piece might fetch $5,000 on the open market. Graffham's trilobites and brachiopods, dug right from his own quarry, were sold and shipped worldwide. They were known as the Rolls Royces of trilobites – impeccably crafted and valuable on demand. Graffham had refined and advanced the esoteric techniques in the preservation and beautification of small fossils. A top-notch preparer, he performed his work in his own laboratory, which was furnished with the finest tools, instruments, and equipment in the world.

Graffham's clients were not from the local area; they were principally affluent purchasers from around the world. One did not merely walk into Graffham's showroom for a casual browse-around to see what was on display and what one might afford. Visitation was by appointment only. Drop-in shoppers were promptly asked to leave. Graffham did not keep normal business hours, anyway. If he was at the facility, he was usually either working in the lab or catering to pre-arranged customers.

There was a peculiar mystique attached to Allan Graffham. People did not get to know him easily. His private life was rather cryptic. He shunned strangers or solicitors. Certainly to strangers he seemed aloof and all business. Social affairs, for him, were usually wrapped inside an orderly, compartmentalized business deal. Only upscale naturalist-collectors knew the nature of his business; the general public knew nothing of his abstruse operations conducted on the edge of Cemetery Hill within the city limits of Ardmore. His wizardry with bones was veiled. Only his best customers knew his uncanny ability to impart dinosaurian magic in the lab. He routinely converted crude and ordinary fossils into aesthetic marvels of beauty and art which brought hefty prices on the open market.

On one cool Monday morning in 1988, when he heard a loud knock on the entrance door, he was rather surprised and annoyed. Waiting at the door were two intrusive policemen – not public, but private, lawmen. Marrs and a man named Reagan (his title and first name unknown) were conducting a private investigation of his premises. The two men had come to seize the *Acrocanthosaurus,* if they could. Apparently they thought, or at least hoped, that they could flash their badges, throw their muscle around, and intimidate Graffham into turning over the dinosaur or revealing its hiding place. If they could not get the dinosaur, maybe they could get some useful information.

Graffham was outraged, but sensing these men were official in some capacity, he contained his temper. They flashed their ID badges, brandished their three-pieces, identified themselves as private investigators, and stated the purpose of their visit, which was to examine the fossilized remains of the *Acrocanthosaurus.* Their demeanor, physical stature, and presence were imposing. Graffham reluctantly opened the door and let them in.

As the two men followed Graffham into his storage room, Graffham calmly asked, "So, you are looking for the 'High-Spined Lizard'?"

Graffham then proceeded to show them shelf after shelf of assorted fossils. "I suppose you fellas would recognize one if you saw it?" The two investigators did not respond.

"Here, is this it?" Graffham asked, as he pointed to a duckbill fossil.

The two private cops could not tell the difference between an Acro or any other kind of dinosaur. Although impatient with Graffham's belligerent and uncooperative attitude, there was not much they could say. Graffham, too, was agitated and about to blow his top.

These goons had no appointment, had violated his privacy and business protocol, and were acting pompously and disrespectfully. "Did they really think they could just barge into his facility and search his property without a warrant or court order?" he wondered. Within minutes, he had already taken enough of their crap. Their attitude, behavior, and language were quite offensive.

"Do you know a Cephis Hall?" Marrs inquired.

Graffham did not answer.

"Did you purchase an *Acrocanthosaur* from him?" Marrs further inquired.

Graffham still did not respond.

Marrs, a little irritated, fired off another question: "Are you in negotiations to sell the dinosaur to Japanese investors?"

Graffham snarled back, "Look, I do not share my personal business with strangers." He then exploded into a tirade. "Hear this, you tin horn cops. Nobody comes out to my place of business without a scheduled appointment. Visits are by appointment only, and you guys didn't bother to make one. Another thing — what makes you think you can enter my premises and search it? Do you guys have a search warrant or legal document that gives you that right?" After a moment of silence and no response from the two agents, Graffham screamed out his final line. "You're trespassing! Now get off my land, or I'll call the real cops on you!"

The two private detectives, a little dejected, did not press the issue. They knew their limits and were getting nowhere with this "insolent bastard". Silently, they walked out, got into their company van, and drove off. This was the last time Marrs was seen in southeastern Oklahoma.

Immediately after they left, Graffham called Cephis and informed him about the incident. "The Gestapo was just here looking for the elusive dinosaur," he exclaimed.

CHAPTER FORTY-EIGHT
The Fog of Legalities

The two rock hounds-turned-amateur paleontologists were about to steer their helm into the arcane realm of legal jurisprudence. Could they trust lawyers and courts? They didn't have much choice. They needed a lawsuit filed in an attempt to both quiet the title and Weyerhaeuser.

Their best hope was to initiate a civil suit that both addressed and clarified the issues and forced Weyerhaeuser to confront the facts head-on. They needed legal recourse that forced the corporate leviathan to face the fallacies and incongruities of its legal argument. If Weyerhaeuser was forced to digest the truth, it might balk and walk away. The truth might put the company in a kind of "social limbo" and conceivably tarnish its standing within the community. Weyerhaeuser needed truth on its side to maintain local trust, but could their brand of truth be purchased?

Truths aside, might Weyerhaeuser beat them to the punch and bring its own suit? Perhaps, but the two naturalists were more nimble on their feet than the giant hierarchical octopus with many tentacles. Important corporate decisions had to filter up and down layers of managerial niches encased within bureaucratic molds. Or did they?

Could not the local attorneys representing the interests of the corporate behemoth settle disputes on their own, or at least prod the minds of higher officials on what should be done at the local level? In whose minds did the answer to the dinosaur question reside? Obviously, the decision was Weyerhaeuser's. The company could either settle or bury the two out-gunned litigants, along with their dinosaur, in a pit of legal morass.

The future of one of the greatest dinosaur specimens in the history of paleontology hung in the balance and was at the mercy and prerogative of the stubborn mind of a giant timber oligopoly. The two hard-nosed entrepreneurs could envision only two possible outcomes: settle the title dispute (win) or pull the plug on life support for the dinosaur. As a matter of principle, they were not going to turn over the bones to Weyerhaeuser unless court ordered, and they had no other option.

If Weyerhaeuser became the plaintiff, this might put the legal onus on Hall and Love and give the corporation leverage and legal momentum. Going to court, whether the decision was made by a judge or jury, was not a reassuring prospect. Or, if Weyerhaeuser's suit was proven to be without merit, perhaps the two bone-worn combatants might accrue damages against Weyerhaeuser that would enable them to recover their legal fees.

Whether the two small-time litigants ended up as plaintiffs or defendants, a legitimate legal concern germinated. Would the timber barons bring out their heavy legal armor and ram full scale over Hall-Love? Would Weyerhaeuser blow Hall-Love's underfinanced case off the docket with their massive arsenal of legal weapons? The forces of LeForce and Associates looked puny compared to Weyerhaeuser's army of attorneys. The LeForce contingent had no heavy cannon or armor and had assigned their case to Hamilton, a rookie lawyer.

What about Weyerhaeuser's ties and influence within the community – its connections to local officials, police, media, judges, and politicians? Potential jurors who worked for Weyerhaeuser, or had relatives or close friends employed by the company, might not be sympathetic in the jury box. What if the judge received campaign financing from Weyerhaeuser? The corporation held the reins to local power economically, judicially, socially, and politically. People inside the corporate domain who were dependent on timber for jobs and income might not be favorably disposed toward two wretched outsiders battling their employer. A jury was a whimsical prospect. The men had to settle outside of court, and quickly, but how? They couldn't force anybody's hand; everything was at the lawyers' (and court's) whim.

With Weyerhaeuser being the moving force or driver of costs, would the two be forced to settle and relinquish their bones to the corporate titan? With all the adverse publicity that was sure to emerge, they could never make a quick sell to any reputable museum or scientific institution. Maybe they could give the bones away if it looked like they were going to lose — anything to void the prospect of relinquishing possession to Weyerhaeuser while receiving no compensation in return.

It just wasn't fair for the two well-intentioned miners to have borne all the burdens and bruises of digging the dinosaur and then stand idle as a corporate gargantuan moved in to legally take ownership without having made any sacrifice. The two men provided all the sweat and sowed all the seeds, while the corporation would come in to reap all the rewards and garner the crops. This outcome was tantamount to a landed baron reaping the harvest of a peasant's tilled field, and then leaving the tiller to starve. The arrangement was neither just nor compassionate. A modern-day peasant could expect to fare little better in a contemporary "corporatized court" than he might in the medieval lord's court. But still, he had to try.

It was all a haze. Their legal dilemma was not clearly defined. They were ensnared in the fog of a "bone war" and would have to learn the legal ropes as the noose tightened and the controversy heightened. Also, the case might be tried on the pages of the newspapers as headline stories about an enigmatic legal dispute between two local "outbackers" and a corporate colossus. Their story implied a tussle over elusive bones, and the narrative might become a partisan line.

How would their case fare judicially in a society where faith was sold as science, spin treated as fact, and propaganda indistinguishable from truth? In the South, and that meant Little Dixie, thinking and decisions often emanated from within the gut, rather than the cognitive mind. Whoever had the best public relations gimmickry, or the best flare for showmanship, might have the edge. The decision might be made on emotion, rather than judiciable fact or reason. Which argument, theirs' or Weyerhaeuser's, might resonate within the gut and persuade the jury? With slick PR puffery, Weyerhaeuser could pull the wool over the eyes of any citizen panel.

Would their side of the dispute receive fair coverage in a local press highly influenced by Weyerhaeuser and other corporate insiders? It was a very one-sided dimension. Bias in the local press might adversely affect their trial. Like all Southern cities, Idabel and Broken Bow were conservative and run by business leaders more sympathetic to Weyerhaeuser than a couple of rogue bone merchants.

Finally, what would happen if they did settle and got a clear title, but Graffham didn't come through with the funds? What if he backed out of the deal and refused to pay? What if LeForce was unwilling to invest any additional time in the case and refused to follow up, even with $50,000 in legal fees balanced on the scales? In that case, they would still be stuck, but at least they could search for another buyer, or could they? They would be saddled with a pending contract in which the attorneys had a vested stake.

But disregarding that legal concern, could they find a new buyer in time? Could they make a sale before the bones disintegrated? Who else might buy the specimen? If the University of Texas was any indication, a public university could afford little more than paltry cash. They were caught in a legal time drag, but time was of the essence. Scores of questions enumerated, and few, if any, answers emanated.

Cephis and Sid began to worry. It seemed as if the two discoverers had been "engulped" in the crunching jaws of a giant mystifying lizard that was thrashing them about and ready to consume them. They wished Hamilton would hurry up and do something. Please file the damn thing! File something! Hamilton had only one case – theirs. What was he waiting for?

CHAPTER FORTY-NINE
Legal Action

After a hard day cutting timber on the rough side of a mountain, the tired, thirsty and hungry lumberjack arrived home and discovered good news. In his mailbox was an envelope from the attorneys' office and it was thick enough to contain a legal document rather than a one-page letter. Maybe, at last, something legal was cooking. Cephis had already paid $350.00 out of his own pocket to cover the cost of the filing fees. Unless LeForce was in a habit of skimming his clients, it was reasonable to expect a legal instrument to be instituted within a short span. It was about time. Anxiously, Cephis opened the envelope.

Inside was a copy of a legal action, a COMPLAINT ASKING FOR DECLARATORY JUDGMENT, filed September 14, 1988 on their behalf naming CEPHIS HALL and SID LOVE as PLAINTIFFS and WEYERHAEUSER CORPORATION, A WASHINGTON STATE CORPORATION as DEFENDANT, NO: 88-544-C filed in THE UNITED STATES DISTRICT COURT, EASTERN DISTRICT OF OKLAHOMA, Tulsa, Oklahoma.

The most salient arguments put forth in the Complaint were:

(2) That the Plaintiffs began their work with the consent of one Joe Bueno, who was at the time, Woodlands Manager for Weyerhaeuser in the aforementioned region.

(3) That the Plaintiffs relied to their detriment on this consent, and began excavation on the site. (4) That upon excavation of the aforementioned paleontological site, the Plaintiffs made an extremely rare find, that being the fossilized remains of an Acrocanthosaurus, or "high spined dinosaur".

(5) That said excavation took approximately five years to complete, and until completion and discovery of the value of said fossil, Weyerhaeuser Corporation made no claims to said remains.

(6) That as the developers and preservers of said fossil, the Plaintiffs are entitled to have a jury of their peers determine them to be the absolute owners of said fossil, free of all claims and/or liens whatsoever by any third party.

(7) That Weyerhaeuser Corporation has claimed that it now owns the fossil.

(8) That this claim is without merit, as Weyerhaeuser is estopped from denying the Plaintiffs' ownership.

(13) That the ownership of said dinosaur find constitutes a justiciable issue that could be and should be determined by the court.

There were some 13 paragraphs, each setting forth a statement of fact from the Plaintiffs' standpoint. One such paragraph (12) *stated that the Plaintiffs have been damaged in the amount of $500,000.00 as Weyerhaeuser's claims of ownership have prevented the Plaintiffs from taking advantage of several sales and exhibition opportunities.*

The Affidavit signed by Greg Perino was attached and incorporated by reference with the Complaint. A jury trial was demanded. The complaint was signed by L. Walter Hamilton, OBA #012687, as attorney for the Plaintiffs.

The attached affidavit attested to the fact that Gregory Perino, Director of the Museum of the Red River, was present at a meeting held on museum premises between Sid Love and Cephis Hall on one part, and Joe Bueno, Oklahoma Land Management Supervisor for Weyerhaeuser, in which Perino witnessed Bueno give oral permission to the two men to dig on Weyerhaeuser land as they deemed fit, asking only that they maintain a low profile. The statement also affirmed that Bueno indicated that Weyerhaeuser had no interest in the paleontological finds of Mr. Hall and Mr. Love. The affidavit was signed June 27, 1988.

The document gave Hall a glimmer of hope. The ball was now rolling, and Weyerhaeuser would have to confront both the facts and the truth. This legal action was intended to signify to the corporation that the two bone hoarders were not going to just lie down and take Weyerhaeuser's crap without a struggle. A legal fight was about to get underway, and the two men intended to stay, if not for the course, at least for the first round. They knew that truth was on their side, whether Weyerhaeuser wanted to admit it or not. Truth was always a strong point, even in a severely flawed legal system where money counted more than truth.

What seemed most promising about the legal action was paragraph 12, which set forth a claim for damages if Weyerhaeuser continued to contest ownership, thereby causing a delay of proper treatment for the pyrite disease. The statement was true. Weyerhaeuser was preventing them from selling the bones and recouping their enormous investment in labor, time, sweat, money, and worry. The bones could not be saved unless they were sold.

The longer Weyerhaeuser stalled, the more likely destabilization, even disintegration, threatened the specimen as a result of pyrite contamination. The specimen needed to be turned over to the Black Hills Institute for immediate remedial treatment, but that could not be accomplished without Weyerhaeuser's acquiescence.

To Cephis and Sid, this seemed like a strong argument. The Black Hills Institute had certified that they were capable of restoring the specimen, whereas the University of Oklahoma might have the same peculiar problem exhibited by the University of Texas – a shortage of money and manpower – and might also lack the necessary technique and craft. A middle man with deep pockets like Allan Graffham was sorely needed as a white knight. He had the wherewithal and resources to intercede and save the distressed dinosaur. He could afford the expensive upfront costs required to initiate remediation of the bones at a world-class fossil preparation facility, or at least that was what everyone believed. Weyerhaeuser stood in the way of progress. Consequently, Weyerhaeuser was now inflicting damages on Hall and Love's property (the dinosaur) and investment (time, labor, money, etc.).

If Weyerhaeuser got possession of the specimen, they would likely either sell it themselves for a hefty profit or turn it over to the University of Oklahoma for a charitable donation and tax deduction, but would that save the dinosaur? Hall and Love were convinced that the Graffham-Black Hills nexus was the only path to dinosaur salvation. That pathway was contingent on their settling or winning the lawsuit. Weyerhaeuser continued to block the path.

CHAPTER FIFTY
The Bone War

Weyerhaeuser soon learned it was in a legal battle, but for the giant, transnational corporation, it was a small affair. True, the property being disputed might be worth millions, but in the larger scheme, the value of the dino was of little consequence and the cost to Weyerhaeuser of defending against Hall-Love's pitiful lawsuit represented paltry cash. The dinosaur affair was more an issue of prestige, honor, and discretion. The corporation's aura of invincibility had been tarnished and it needed to save face. Retaliation was a natural response.

A couple of raw-boned hayseeds had gotten one over on the corporation, and the behemoth wanted to exact retribution. If the corporation could not shake loose a decrepit pile of bones, at least it could show the local yokels who was boss – who was really in charge. It was the brashness, boldness, and impudence on the part of the two rogue miners that needed to be addressed. They had to be put in their place, or at least reminded that it was necessary to show proper deference to the sovereign.

The two treasure hunters had violated the sacred rules of dynastic protocol and decorum that commoners were expected to heed at all times. To dig up a world-class dinosaur on company land without apprising the organization of its inherent value and merit was unforgiveable; in fact, it was downright disrespectful. A commoner was not supposed to circumvent the rules of convention when interacting with the Majesty of the Timber Realm. In their brazen and cavalier dismissal of corporate propriety, the bone diggers had offended the mighty corporation, and that was the crux of the problem – not to mention that OU had registered its annoyance and vented its steam at the two bone rustlers.

What would Weyerhaeuser do about it? The verdict was still out. At the moment, the company had to answer the complaint. It was customary for a powerful defendant – whether guilty or complicit or not – to deny all the charges set forth in a legal action and to force the underdog to start grasping for straws and worrying about legal costs. Weyerhaeuser had plenty of time and money, but the dinosaur was reeking in pyrite deterioration and its viability was threatened. In this case, the winner would take all or nothing – depending on what was left of the dinosaur by the time the case was adjudicated. There was no happy medium or room for compromise. The winner would get the title and what was left of the dinosaur; the loser, nothing.

Weyerhaeuser had a chip on its shoulder. It was perfectly all right for a pair of loose cannons to dig up a heap of bone trash on company land, but a genuine dinosaur classic – that was beyond the pale of corporate correctness. The company now felt cheated. "Imagine the gall and temerity of those irksome bone hustlers. They could at least have shown proper respect by notifying us of what they had found," Weyerhaeuser officials likely said among themselves. But if the two diggers had complied with that sort of corporate expectation, the brass would have simply thanked the two men for their candor and submission and sent them packing with a "ya'll don't come back down here" farewell.

The problem was simple: the two men did not know they had uncovered a specimen of significant monetary value until almost three years into their dig. At that point, if they had shared their knowledge with the corporation and submitted the bones, it would have been like giving a charitable contribution to a for-profit corporation without receiving a tax deduction. Beyond that, the two men were too deeply wrapped up in their own dreams and ambitions to entertain the idea of a donation to the corporation. Besides, Bueno had set the tone and terms of their excavation by clearly stating that Weyerhaeuser did not want to be involved in the project and was not interested in their paleontological products. Now, after the fact, and after the product was exhumed and presumed to be of significant value, Weyerhaeuser was singing a different tune and wanted to change the rules of the game. Neither party was altruistic; each side was looking out for its own self interests.

Weyerhaeuser filed an answer to the plaintiffs' Complaint-Petition on October 11, 1988. The company admitted what was expedient and refuted all allegations of managerial complicity in the dig. Nothing in the lawyers' response was a surprise. The corporation denied everything.

The defendant "denies that the plaintiffs had any authority whatsoever to dig on Weyerhaeuser lands, and specifically denies that Joe Bueno gave any authority, and further specifically alleges that if, in fact, Joe Bueno did give permission (which defendant specifically denies) that he was acting outside the scope of his authority."

The defendant "specifically denies that the plaintiffs relied to their detriment on the consent of Joe Bueno, and began excavation on the site."

The defendant "specifically alleges that the defendant was not informed and had no knowledge of any excavation until after a discovery of the fossil, and defendant further specifically alleges that it has at all times claimed and does claim that any find upon the property of this defendant belongs to the defendant."

The defendant "specifically denies that the plaintiff is entitled to a jury trial and specifically denies that the plaintiffs are the owners of the find upon the properties of this defendant."

The defendant "denies that the plaintiffs have been damaged in the amount of $500,000 because they have been prevented from taking advantage of several sales and exhibition opportunities."

The defendant "denies that the plaintiff has set forth facts to raise justiciable issue and specifically alleges that this defendant is the owner of the properties in controversy."

The answer was routine and typical for a powerful defendant facing such charges. A blanket denial was pretty much standard operating procedure, but the lines had been drawn, the controversies spelled out, the issues framed, and the dispute highlighted. The dispute had entered the formalized legal system and would result in adjudication with a conclusion in some form or another.

As usual in such a case, the basic facts were being disputed and it was the province of the system to ferret out the truth and provide remedy based on that truth and the rule of law. The system now had jurisdiction over the fate of the dinosaur. The case had been inputted and a justiciable output was awaited.

The two men knew clearly that enormous economic power translated into pervasive political and judicial power, and this power gave Weyerhaeuser a decisive edge within the system. As a matter of routine, corporate lawyers profile state and federal judges and have the rundown on courts and judges far in advance. They know their friends and enemies, and have tactics to bring non-friends into the fold, or to have them replaced by friends.

If a corporation has influence over the court clerk, it can leverage that relationship to influence what cases are assigned to specific judges and when the cases will be heard. These large corporations use their insider connections to stack dockets so their case has a good chance of being heard by a favorable judge. If the corporation doesn't like a particular judge on the docket, it may ask for a continuance and have the case redocketed, thereby increasing the prospect of a friendly judge hearing their case. A series of continuances increases their prospect. There was no doubt in the minds of the two legal lightweights— the system favored the corporation. The two men had an eerie feeling of gloom whenever they contemplated the harrowing prospect of doing legal battle with the dominant institution of McCurtain County.

Weyerhaeuser, with all its economic and political clout, did not exist in a vacuum; rather, it was the titular head and foundational prop for the entire local infrastructure. The community revolved around the giant timber firm, and in reciprocity, the omnipotent corporation cast out its tentacles and garnered what it needed from the community.

Cephis was a firm believer in the concept of fully understanding and knowing the face of the enemy. As with dinosaurs, the key to understanding the present pivoted on understanding the past. Weyerhaeuser had to be understood both in the present "community context" as well as the "historical context." What had shaped the community in the past would likely have a bearing and influence over the present and future. The past was often prologue.

Weyerhaeuser likely had a corporate profile – a corporate personality, image, or record that defined its character. As Mit Romney said in 2012, "Corporations are people my friend."

Cephis also strongly believed that one should never underestimate the opponent, and in order to avoid that trap, one had to fully understand the opposition. Weyerhaeuser was the adversary and needed to be understood in relation to the community and its past behavior.

What kind of corporation was Weyerhaeuser, and how did it relate to the community? How had it acted in the past, and how was it expected to act in the future? How did it treat its subjects whenever they interacted in an adversarial situation? What about the disposition of the corporation in regard to truth and a semblance of justice? What chance did a couple of unfinanced, local rustics have against such a monstrosity of economic and political power?

CHAPTER FIFTY-ONE
The Lamb and the Beast

Cephis and Sid had gone rogue and now faced the prospect of being judged as apostates within their own conservative religious community. The dinosaur ordeal had turned into a roller coaster ride that threatened to derail their lives. They had climbed a mountain of worry to reach the summit only to learn that more worries lay ahead.

The men worried about their status in the community. What if the local newspapers jumped on the story and started sensationalizing? What would the editors say about a mud-encrusted dinosaur skeleton dug out of a toxic waste pit on land owned by the most powerful corporation in the state? Would the media choose to emphasize the more divisive aspects and stir up anti-evolutionary sentiment?

Dinosaur fossils have for decades portended a hotbed of controversy over their meaning, importance, and value to modern society. Darwin was a reclusive invalid who shrank from the commotion aroused by his new theory and shied away from trying to defend it. Would these two "iconoclastic diggers" be cast in the role of trying to defend their involvement in a sacrilegious exhumation of a controversial dinosaur?

Cephis worried about what the local anti-Darwinians would say about his dinosaur with a hundred-million-year vintage. The thought of the discord it might stir left him with uneasiness in the pit of his stomach. He was bold and determined, but did not like to incite dispute among his peers. Would the local creationists look askance upon his dinosaur digging and accuse him of blasphemy? They were strident absolutists with sharp tongues and were quick to judge. Hall and Love were simple, authentic men swept up in a spiraling tide of acrimony and reproach.

One should not forget that the South won the Monkey Trial and John Scopes was convicted of teaching evolution to students. Only ten percent of Americans believe in Darwinian evolution, while forty-four percent believe God created the world in only seven days about 6,000 years ago (Graham 126). But these lopsided figures in favor of creationism did not mediate the issue of Biblical timelines, always a thorny obstacle in bridging the great divide between evolution and creationism. Cephis did not believe that dinosaurs and humans lived contemporaneously in time and space. This stance might bring him into conflict with the local fringe of religious fundamentalists. Mainstream Protestants were more open-minded on the dinosaur question.

Non-fundamentalist churches were largely reticent, if not indifferent, concerning dinosaurs. Many just ignored the subject or had no official position. Others mediated the Genesis creation story with the tenets of science in multifarious ways. Dinosaurs were not a popular topic among many religious congregations. Cephis, a man of strong religious conviction, integrated religion and science and dinosaurs and Genesis in a balanced and complementary guise by simply being open-minded to new discoveries while maintaining his foundational belief. He strove to balance faith with reason, and scripture with science.

Like his inspiration E.D. Cope, Cephis believed that the divine hand of the Creator had shaped evolutionary design and created the earth and heavens and all the living creatures, including dinosaurs. But he also understood the inflexibility of the scientific imperative and was aware that scientific mandarins like Marsh and Langston had little tolerance for his kind of Biblical beliefs. Othniel Marsh had succinctly stated the sentiment of the evolutionists with these words: "To doubt evolution today is to doubt science and science is only another name for truth."

Such remarks today, one hundred years later in modern America, ring with as much divisiveness, if not more, than they did in the Gilded Age of Marsh and Cope. America is the only advanced, post-industrial nation where the majority of the populace still believes in literal Genesis-based creation.

In a social quandary, Cephis realized that despite his religious beliefs, he might become a divisive symbol within the community. How would he, a religious man who delved into science and nature, be viewed locally by the two polarized camps of Biblical fundamentalists and scientific secularists? Would he be considered as proto-scientist or pseudo-religionist? It seemed like an empty void – a pit of vacuity he wanted to avoid. Divisions ran deep in fundamentalist Oklahoma, and he risked alienating both camps.

For Cephis, the passages of the Bible were not literally etched in stone, but meant to be instructive – using allegory and parable to teach lessons about life and morality – often subject to one's own interpretation. Thus, to him, the windy-spirited, wealthy tele-evangelists spouted their interpretations that were not necessarily his own.

In his experience of navigating the dualistic religious and scientific worlds of southeastern Oklahoma, it was often pure faith set against pure reason. He strived to occupy the middle ground – preferring flexibility to unwavering dogmatic interpretations. In his view, the issue of belief was not an immutable repertoire of partisan sentiments, but a living and constantly changing symposium that encompassed new discoveries, new evidence, new theories, and revised beliefs and suppositions.

Cephis, in the late 1980s with a dinosaur under his belt, was a moderately devout and pious man about to be swept up in that great swirling tide of evangelism and fundamentalism unfurling across the nation, especially in the remotest hamlets of the American South. As the region was undergoing a transformation in religiosity, secularism, liberalism, humanism, and scientific empiricism was being supplanted in favor of more passionate sentiments. Fundamentalist expressions such as snake handling, faith healing, End Times theology, and reactionary political ideology were back in style. Republican Social Darwinism coupled with crony corporatism set the social tone and economic mantra of the times. The South was undergoing another paradigm shift as it repudiated political pragmatism and religious rationalism.

There were social and economic forces at work that lay behind this transition in religious tone. To understand it, one had to look back a decade or two at the most recent trends in economics and religious expression. William Faulkner once remarked that "the South is a placed where the past is never dead, it isn't even past."

The Southern economy had not followed the same trajectory as the Northern and Midwestern economies. As Northern and Midwestern rustbelt cities declined due to the outflow of large corporations to the Sunbelt in the 1970s, Southern cities began to thrive, at least until cheaper labor and lower manufacturing costs enticed these same manufacturers to relocate elsewhere. From 1970 to 1977, over one million jobs disappeared in the North and Northeast – most of them reallocated to the anti-unionist South (Wray and Newitz, *White Trash*, 202).

A new mantra of boosterism and urban prosperity was transplanted to major cities like Atlanta, Charlotte, and Nashville (Hemphill 13). The Good Old Boys were out in the shining new suburbs, mortgaged to the hilt, shopping at Walmart, and acting like the Babbitts. A new, but short-lived, prosperity tempered Southern religious expression.

The Southern economic miracle emerged during the early 1970s when cheap, non-unionized labor and enormous subsidies and tax concessions lured large corporations to relocate from the northern and midwestern states to the South. The prosperity of the New South did not reach out to its remotest fringes such as McCurtain County, but was mostly confined to the large cities and suburbs.

With the end of the one-horse farmer and the emergence of the new Southern economy in the 1970s, the new affluence also brought a transformation of the religious landscape as the newly-emergent middle class Southerner sought a more moderate sermonizer to go with his new respectability and prosperity. Instead of the hell fire and brimstone revivalist, he wanted the respectable mega-church preacher in fine tailored business suits.

While faith healing and snake handling still existed out in the boondocks, the big city churches became ornate, sedate, and sophisticated. The new prosperity-based religiosity of the New South thrived in places like the giant, high-tech First Baptist Church of Dallas.

As the new urban South thrived, McCurtain County remained a provincial backwater devoid of skyscrapers, high-technology, traffic congestion, sprawl, fashion design, sleek housing subdivisions, and modern shopping malls. The McCurtain landscape was a picturesque piece of rustic Americana more attuned to an earlier beat and the thralls of nature. But by the 1990s, the Southern economy was teetering and in decline as multi-national corporations began leaving for even cheaper labor in Mexico, China, and other developing countries.

These same fickle corporations that had enjoyed their economic inducements – payoffs, subsidies, tax moratoriums and abatements, taxpayer-funded infrastructure development, etc. – showed no loyalty to these generous municipalities and taxpayers that had showered them with public beneficence. After reaping short-term benefits, they abandoned these communities wholesale and relocated their factories and jobs to foreign jurisdictions also playing the Southern game. Forty years after Reagonomics promised prosperity to the nation, 25 percent of existing manufacturing jobs in the South were shipped overseas (McCarthy 160).

As goes the economy and prosperity, so erodes the more moderate and less-impassioned practices of worship, even tolerance itself. A fundamentalist, emotional appeal in religious services was now needed more than ever as the economy offered fewer prospects and less hope. Marx once stated that "religion is the opiate of the people." Perhaps now it is sports. But the need for emotionalism in religious services always rises during hard times. It was probably Cephis' science forte that kept him from going full hilt to the fundamentalist-emotionalist bent, as he was heavily impacted and unsettled by the economic and technological transformation occurring all around him during the late 1980s.

The transformation of global economic structures is destabilizing and oppressive to millions. The spiritual capital of the displaced compensated in some measure for their lack of money. They resisted globalization by identifying trilateralism, Illuminate, and the loss of the gold standard as signs of the advent of an evil one-world government. Such sentiments of apocalyptic religious belief flourished, not in the center, but along the margins of mainstream Christianity (Wray, *White Trash*, 195, 204).

The danger of the crisis was displaced from the material, economic realm to the spiritual realm. The impending apocalyptic crisis mirrored the global economic crisis of a world capitalist system in transition (Wray 202). Charismatic Christianity brings a sense of power and righteousness to those suffering from a fundamental lack of social and economic power – and for people with deep antipathies towards modern life (Wray 207). Only very strong people like Cephis Hall could avoid the sway of this anti-modernist revanchism, as impersonal and externally-imposed transformative forces swept away the last vestiges of their southern insularity.

It is this feeling of displacement among rural southerners that has so often been reflected in the lyrics of country western music about personal tragedies – the perpetual struggles with temptations, guilt, and redemption – including the burdens of choice between sin and salvation; hard living and drinking as opposed to religious conformity; and, depravity versus holiness. Such conflicts are seen in the erratic lives of rambling southern entertainers like Hank Williams, Jimmy Rodgers, and Johnny Cash, who mixed music, love, religion, alcohol, and hell-raising into a whirling maelstrom of personal dissonance.

Now, as the 1980s were drawing to a close and Cephis delved more deeply into the mysteries of the High-Spined Lizard, there was a gradual shift back to the more primitive as the new Southern prosperity waned and anti-modernist sentiments burgeoned. In a kind of Second Great Awakening, religious fundamentalism reasserted itself across the South, including the southeastern corner of Okieland known as Little Dixie.

The South was moving full circle back to its pristine roots of old fashioned evangelism and revivalism in the expression of religious fervor. This anti-secular retrenchment foreshadowed antipathy for dinosaur hunters and science. Dinosaurs might again become controversial subjects. Less reason and more fundamentalist purity meant less tolerance for dinosaurs and the people who exhumed their remains. Enlightenment rationality and secular humanism in any form, including science, was scorned by rural Pentecostals and charismatic religionists.

By the late 1980s, the big, fancy Protestant churches of downtown central and suburbia had become too bland, too stolid, and too boring as Southern congregations needed more intensity and emotion in their services. For the relatively affluent who didn't want to go all the way back to the "holy roller" phase, the new gospel of prosperity theology bridged the divide. As the Southern economy waned, charismatic Christianity waxed.

This revived Southern evangelism abandoned the rational stoicism of mega churches, but left the basic organizational infrastructure in place. Faith-based emotionalism merged with mega dollars and big business. Tele-evangelism supplanted tent revivalism. Formalism and congregational restraint gave way to charismatic, emotional services. Fundamentalism and Pentecostalism were back in vogue across the Deep South. As with their politicians, the South again wanted its preachers to be showmen and the audience wanted to be part of the act.

By the 1980s, Oklahoma, especially southeastern Oklahoma, had become the most fundamentalist and pious state in the Union. It was now more fundamentalist than the ex-faith healer Oral Roberts of Tulsa, who had become something of a modernist in recent decades. Hall and Love were pitted not just against corporate over reach, but religious zealotry.

The politically-conservative, Southern humorist Michael Graham, in his book *Red Neck Nation,* has described Southern religiosity as "a circus of nonsensical superstitions, overbearing zealots, and borderline lunacy." According to Graham, there are three fundamentals of Southern spirituality: "rejection of reason, embrace of passion, and prohibitions and regulation of individual behavior." (Graham 121) In the aftermath of the Scopes Trial, H.L. Mencken once ridiculed Southern fundamentalists as "full of degraded nonsense which country preachers are ramming and hammering into yokel skulls." (Grantham112)

French historian Alexis de Tocqueville prophetically observed, "There is no country in the whole world in which the Christian religion retains a greater influence over the souls of men than in America (de Tocqueville 214). The central role of religion in Southern urban life reflects the rural heritage of the people. The Baptists, Methodists, and Presbyterians came South to the forest clearings in the early nineteenth century. When the people moved to the cities, so did the churches (Escott & Goldfield 69).

Since then, there has been a blurred line between business and politics and the religious and secular in Southern life. Since the emergence of post-Civil War textile industries and mill towns, a small group of conservative businessmen have run Southern cities – translated as the chamber of commerce in recent times. These are merchant-dominated governments with an interlocking directorate of business and governmental leaders (Escott & Goldfield 74, 75). Cephis and Sid figured that because of their ongoing conflict with Weyerhaeuser, few, if any, local business or political leaders would be warmly receptive to the announcement of their discovery.

The South is replete with ironies and contradictions. One example is an emphasis on individualism, yet a disdain for individual dissent. Since the days of slavery and Antebellum cotton plantations, Southern leaders have been suspicious of democracy (Escott & Goldfield 70, 82). Stifling dissent is as Southern as corn pone, grits, and turnip greens (Graham 28). The South is more willing to use the coercive force of government to regulate thought and behavior. In some quarters at least, Hall and Love's discovery certainly bordered on dissent.

In other examples of Dixieland contradiction, Southern leaders railed against the tyranny of big government and government spending, yet the South is the largest recipient of federal tax dollars (Graham 28). The federal government built the Southern infrastructure, much of it constructed by Franklin Roosevelt's government make-work projects during the Great Depression. Federal assistance has pump-primed the Southern economy and stimulated new industries, especially under war time assistance (Escott & Goldfield 84). Indeed, all southern states, with the exceptions of Texas and Arkansas, get back more from the federal government than what they send in taxes. Alabama gets $2.03 back for every $1.00 it sends to the federal government. South Carolina receives $1.93 from the federal government for every $1.00 it pays in federal taxes (Cenk Ugur, The Young Turks, *Current TV*, 11-13-12).

The South is the largest regional beneficiary of government defense contracts. Dixie, more than any other region, has enshrined defense spending and war-making as sacrosanct, despite the hemorrhaging red of federal budget deficits. Military bases and defense industries dot the Southern landscape. During WWII, the federal government sent some seven billion dollars to the South in the form of defense contracts; the trend continues, even during peacetime. Southerners are passionate about God, guns, the military, and defense contracts. Dinosaurs had no particular appeal.

It is not strictly fact that the white Southerner favors bloated military budgets solely because of the economic benefits accrued from employment in defense industries; the Scots-Irish have a warrior ethos that is passed from generation to generation, which ideologically orients them favorably toward the manufacture of armaments. The pugnacious Scots-Irish gave America some of its greatest military commanders: Andrew Jackson, Stonewall Jackson, Ulysses S. Grant, George S. Patton, and the list goes on and on. In the South, the military tradition is strong and stems from the Scots-Irish frontier tradition, which presumably made these people more suitable for soldiering. There are two pillars of Scots-Irish culture: fighting and religion.

All in all, the rural South or "Little Dixie" as it were, was not an ideal social and religious environment in which to introduce the mysterious High-Spined Lizard to a world-in-waiting. The rural South, for the most part, was not interested in dinosaurs with their troubling evolutionary implications. For Cephis and Sid, it might be necessary to keep their dinosaur secretly under wraps in a safe place somewhere outside the confines of Little Dixie until the controversy died down, and the idea of the dinosaur could be gently implanted in the collective mind of the local community. Then, they hoped to bring it back to town and present it – in all its mystique and majesty – to the locals for their consideration.

CHAPTER FIFTY-TWO
Official Inquiry – An Inside View

The legacy of the Dierks began in the early 1900s when the family purchased surplus lands from the Choctaws at dirt-cheap prices. The Dierks brothers, Hans and Herman, ended up with some 1.8 million acres of timberlands in southeastern Oklahoma and southwestern Arkansas, and began building the massive timber infrastructure of saw mills, mill towns, logging camps, paper mills, and a shipyard, all tied together with the DeQueen & Eastern Railroad, which they also owned.

The Dierks family had operated lumber mills in Broken Bow, Nebraska, and knew the value and demand for national timber. They had witnessed the first great Gilded Age of the 1880s when timber barons pushed the national timber supplies to the brink of virtual depletion. Loggers treated the western timberlands as if they were an inexhaustible resource—often stripping the landscape bare with no attempt at reclamation.

President Theodore Roosevelt, a naturalist-conservationist, saw the danger and created the National Forest Service, which sought to balance a reverence for nature with responsible exploitation. It was Roosevelt who laid the foundation for modern scientific management of the national timberlands. The Dierks family, while setting out to emulate the Rooseveltian model of scientific management, laid the foundation for the emergence of a Southern-based timber empire on lands once controlled by the Choctaws. The Dierks aptly named their new company the Choctaw Lumber Company. The company, whose name was later changed to Dierks Lumber and Coal Company, thrived in the land of Little Dixie for some seventy years before being bought out by Weyerhaeuser in 1969.

Dierks was a rather progressive company for its time and recognized the value of reforestation and sustained yield forests. The paternalistic company maintained harmonious relations with its employees and dealt with them on a personalized basis. If an employee was injured on the job, he was paid half his regular salary while recovering, an industrial policy virtually unheard of for that time. Normally, in Gilded Age America and prior to FDR's reforms, if a worker were maimed or killed on the job neither he nor his family were compensated.

McCurtain County was an idyllic setting for the traditionally minded who enjoyed the geographical amenities that made rural life attractive: hunting, fishing, scenic vistas, a perceived clean environment, and a slow paced lifestyle. The rural people of McCurtain County cherished a frontier mentality that had its own unwritten rules and social codes for regulating individual and collective behavior. These rules were based on custom, rather than formal law. Through custom, the cement that held the rural society together, social control mechanisms for individual behavior were implanted into individual consciousness. But with the coming of Weyerhaeuser in 1969, the old way of life was threatened. Weyerhaeuser, insensitive to local traditions and values, unilaterally challenged these codes as it attempted to impose its will.

With a rule of custom, social control is internalized through a shared consensus among community members. The law, as practiced in McCurtain County prior to the arrival of Weyerhaeuser, was oriented as much to the customs of the community as the legal-rational codes of corporations. Unwritten rules and social codes had always regulated behavior. These traditional regulatory mechanisms within the community were worked out between neighbors through trial and error over decades. Suddenly, Weyerhaeuser came in with its corporate imperatives of efficiency, rationality, formality, impersonality, and profit above all other considerations, and upset the social order.

Weyerhaeuser wanted to impose a formalized rule of law with sanctions imposed by courts and judges, which the company largely controlled, whereas local citizens wanted informal moral sanctions exacted by the family, kindred, or local community based more on a rule of community custom, rather than a rule of corporatized law.

There were hundreds, if not thousands, of small landowners living astride and amidst Weyerhaeuser's massive new land holdings. An impersonalized, bureaucratized, and rationalized approach to managing the land and people was bound to incite resistance from the locals. Weyerhaeuser, as a large-scale, impersonal organization operating alongside a rural and traditional community built on face-to-face communications and unwritten codes of personal conduct had a major impact on community relations.

Weyerhaeuser's philosophy, technology, and methodology for managing its timberlands had a far greater impact on the community than Dierks. The shock and trauma caused by these new land-use practices had to be absorbed by the community, and adjustments would take years, if not decades.

Whereas Dierks represented a form of organization reflecting a small-company and small-town mentality, Weyerhaeuser, with its profit-oriented organization dictating economies of scale, vertical integration, and the constant drive for efficiency of operation, posed a callous affront to the sensibilities of many local residents. The new emphasis on private property rights and legal rights clashed with community social codes worked out over many decades based on custom and tradition.

Weyerhaeuser's commitment to large-scale clear cutting practices in the mid 1970s, the assertion of private property rights on open range, and tree farming with the latest machinery and chemical applications were a radical departure from the more sustained and flexible practices of Dierks. High-tech feasibility was the new expedient rather than ecological flexibility. While Dierks had utilized selective cutting, Weyerhaeuser radically implemented large-scale clear cutting.

A large, profit-oriented company like Weyerhaeuser has a fiduciary responsibility to its shareholders to cut out extraneous costs and increase the profit margin by simplifying and streamlining production in a rationalized formula for maximum efficiency. Weyerhaeuser used a system of high-yield, monoculture timber farming—raising timber like corn—which required heavy use of herbicides and chemicals. The implementation of this model required massive clear cutting, clear burning, aerial spraying of herbicides and fertilizers, and closing off of the open range—all of which offended many rural residents. The formula did not adequately take into account the impact it would have on the local community. Weyerhaeuser had created a public relations nightmare. Whereas locals had worked closely with Dierks in protecting the forests and putting out fires, disgruntled citizens were torching Weyerhaeuser's pine farms by the early 1980s.

Once the clear cutting, aerial spraying, burning of clear cuts, stressing of wildlife, fencing off of lands, regulating cattle herds, restricting the open range, blocking off roads, and other adverse land-management practices began, the traditional, rural community reacted with strong opposition. This conflict heated to a fever pitch in the early 1980s.

Following citizen unrest over aerial spraying of the 2,4,5-T herbicide, a concoction which allegedly contained the deadly defoliant dioxin (or Agent Orange as it was known in Vietnam), a series of twenty-three deliberately set fires occurred on Weyerhaeuser plantations. During this same period, labor unrest led to a strike at the Craig Plant, which was now owned by Weyerhaeuser, and a security officer was beaten severely. A letter to the editor of the McCurtain Gazette dated April 16, 1980 protested biased reporting in regard to its coverage of Weyerhaeuser-related issues. At the same time, race riots erupted in Idabel following the shooting of a young black man, and more than 100 fires in the city were reported with estimated damages of nearly two million dollars.

The extensive disturbances caused Weyerhaeuser to look inward at its practices and assess what was motivating the community to engage in such commotion. Commensurate with this introspection, the company funded an independent study made by the sociology department at Oklahoma State University, which provided a very objective and unbiased analysis. The study was completed in 1983, and the results compiled into a report entitled *Land Use Change in South McCurtain County, Oklahoma*. The study allowed the airing of grievances by local residents against the giant timber corp. Many complaints registered, giving clear evidence of the issues needing addressment.

The cutting and spraying of trees along the streams caused the most ire. The practice expelled sediments and poisons into creeks and allegedly killed fish and wildlife. A sizeable percentage of the local population was opposed to clear cutting and aerial spraying in principle. Weyerhaeuser used helicopters piloted by Vietnam vets in space suits for both aerial spraying and clear burning. A torch from a helicopter was used to spray and burn out hardwoods to clear space for monoculture pines.

Scattered across more than 800,000 acres of Weyerhaeuser timberland in southeastern Oklahoma are many private plots. Nationwide there is a constant problem with large landowners being insensitive to the owners of small acreages adjoining them. The arrogance is not peculiar to Weyerhaeuser; small property owners often confront this insensitivity when dealing with any large corporation or wealthy individual.

The diversity of complaints by locals against their gargantuan neighbor was extensive and included the following: a total disregard for streams and wildlife; large fish kills caused by toxins from aerial spraying released into the streams; planting pine stands along adjoining fence lines causing a fence problem; blocking roads and sealing off private access to property owned by small landowners; claiming public roads as their own private roads; the hiring of illegal aliens through subcontractors; a general disregard and disrespectful attitude toward adjoining small landowners; control and manipulation of the police and judicial system so that laws were enforced to Weyerhaeuser's advantage; and the closing off of the open range.

In 1971, Weyerhaeuser announced the closing of grazing on its lands; but after an angry uproar from cattle owners and threats of arson, the company backed down and continued issuing grazing permits. When Weyerhaeuser later reneged on cattle leases a lawsuit was filed by cattlemen, but a federal judge ruled in favor of Weyerhaeuser. Weyerhaeuser then followed up with a suit to compel cattlemen to remove their cattle. The open range was phased out; permit grazing was totally ended by 2007.

Besides its range and clear cutting policies, there was a great deal of controversy in the county concerning Weyerhaeuser's use of the roads. Some locals complained that Weyerhaeuser re-graded old existing roads, added some shale, and then received government reimbursement. Some of those roads, they claimed, were built by pioneers, maintained by the community, and improved by the WPA and public funds. Although Weyerhaeuser had built many new roads throughout their lands, it now claimed control, if not ownership, of virtually all roads traversing its property, and were even gating them to limit public access.

Pollution of the water shed was an ongoing concern, especially concerning the Craig Fiber Board facility, which discharged some 2.7 million gallons of wastewater into the Mountain Fork River per day during 1980 and, based on a hazardous waste inspection report, six to seven million gallons in 1981. Virtually all that wastewater flowed through the dinosaur pit on its course to the Mountain Fork.

"According to EPA hazardous waste site inspection reports, solid wastes produced from the Craig Plant were separated from the wastewater sludge in a settling basin. The liquids were dumped into a raw storage pond, which then flowed into one of four aerated ponds and discharged into one of two natural oxidation ponds. Effluent from oxidation ponds flowed into an unnamed creek or ditch which discharges a half mile to the east into the Mountain Fork. The record shows that waste flowing into this chain of ponds at a minimum consisted of 75,000 gallons per year of paint, pigments, solvents and inorganic cleaners, 6,000 gallons per year of used oil-crank case and hydraulic lubricating oils, unknown amounts of halogenated solvents, and unknown chemicals only described as "Acids." The report contained in the letter stated that the ponds had no membrane liners and that the groundwater table is 3.5-15 feet below the pond floors. (Letter, dated Oct. 6, 2005, written by Attorney Christopher Jones of the Texas Committee on Natural Resources to Don Maisch, Water Quality Division, Oklahoma Dept. of Environmental Quality)

One local employee at the plant, Kenny Joiner, a bulldozer operator, described his observations quite succinctly with these words: "I was in charge of dumping all that crap into a landfill and I saw what spilled over into those waste lagoons. You could see all kinds of paint cans and fifty-five gallon drums of toxics floating in those lagoons. Sometimes, they would explode like sticks of dynamite." (Jackson, "How Safe is the Mountain Fork?" *Daily Oklahoman*) There were accounts of bizarre sightings in and around those ponds: frogs with three heads and massive lesions; fish with large heads and small bodies, or small heads and large bodies, etc.

Cephis and Sid knew that the majority of complaints against Weyerhaeuser were related to how the company interacted with the local environment, which, in turn, impinged on the health, safety, and well being of the community. The company's land management practices had alienated a considerable portion of the local population. The fact that Weyerhaeuser had sought and funded an impartial university study concerning its impact on community relations denoted that it was interested in rectifying some of those grievances, but the damage had already been done and could not be papered over with public relations gimmicks. It would take years, or decades, to earn the public's trust.

In the meantime, after careful contemplation, Cephis and Sid saw a ray of sunshine amidst a cloud of legal turbidity. The legal system was expensive and treacherous, there was no denying that; but while weighing the ramifications of a suit against Weyerhaeuser, they recognized an "Achilles' Heel" – Weyerhaeuser's relations with the local community. Weyerhaeuser did not have a good corporate image in the eyes of a considerable portion of the local population. As they looked closer at the "timbered giant," cracks in the imperial edifice began to appear.

Weyerhaeuser might be monolithic within the county, but in the hearts and minds of the people, it confronted a human face that grimaced at its conduct and impact on the community. The controversies had radiated out across the state, even as far away as Tulsa or Muskogee. Objectively, Sid and Cephis realized that although the Corporation had its supporters, at least 50 percent of the county's population was alienated. It was as if polarization over Weyerhaeuser's management practices had divided the community in half.

The strategy of Weyerhaeuser was always to get a case transferred to a federal court, where it held a decisive edge. But even there, a jury trial might offer an advantage for the legal underdog. It was better to have the case decided by a jury, rather than a judge, because it was easier for the company to control a judge than a jury. As for community relations, that was best turned over to its experts in public relations who could impart a dazzling spin and a happy face on any dour, sourdough mug.

If the case ended up in court and Weyerhaeuser could not stack a jury in its favor, the company might be in trouble. Within McCurtain County, where at least 50 percent of a potential jury felt estrangement from Weyerhaeuser, all the two men needed was at least a few others on the panel who placed more importance on truth than loyalty to a corporation. It was a mixed bag.

But the case might be heard in Muskogee or Tulsa, where Cephis and Sid had less to fear from partisans with economic or family links to the giant corporation. Although this realization gave room for hope, the optimism quickly subsided when the hard issue of legal costs reasserted itself. Getting their case into court might prove more difficult than winning. Their best chance was to settle out of court, but that prospect rested solely on Weyerhaeuser's shoulders. The two men could not budge or compromise. Weyerhaeuser was in the driver's seat.

While the two litigants waited in legal limbo, an unexpected call came in from a high-ranking Weyerhaeuser official (name unrecounted), who had been sent down to the local area from North Carolina. This man was no Joe Bueno; he was a company turn-around specialist charged with assessing the viability of Weyerhaeuser's Craig operations and reviving the struggling plant, if possible. Apparently, the local managers of the plant had failed to maintain profitability despite the hard work and dedication of the rank and file employees.

Unexpectedly, this key management troubleshooter called Cephis at home and wanted to hear his side of the story. Despite the man's conciliatory tone, Cephis was skeptical. The man was proposing a personal meeting to discuss the case and see if there was any possible way to settle out of court.

In a last ditch effort to salvage the Craig Plant, the manager stated he was concerned about human relations – both inside the plant and in the community – and that this lawsuit over the dinosaur was a community relations issue. He proposed that Cephis come out to the Craig Plant and talk to him in person. Cephis responded that he would need to have his attorney present. The manager concurred, and an appointment was made.

Cephis was stunned. This man did not talk like any Weyerhaeuser official he had previously met.

A few days later, Hall and Hamilton walked inside the Craig office. People seemed to be rustling and shuffling about as if in a panic mode – not over them, but in response to the presence of a high-level manager who held their employment destiny in his hands.

The gentleman appeared from out of the maze and greeted them with a friendly gesture. He quietly stated that it would be better to talk in complete privacy and suggested that they step outside to discuss the matter. The parley was held in an outside pavilion and lasted about thirty minutes.

It did not take Cephis long to realize that this man was made of different mettle than the typical Weyerhaeuser officials with whom he had dealt. This forum provided an opportunity Cephis could not have previously imagined as he poured out his heartfelt feelings. The man seemed sincere and repulsed by what he heard.

"The company needs to get along with the local community," the official stated. Then he asked, "What would it take to resolve this issue?"

"Management keeping their word and living up to the truth," responded Hall.

After hearing Hall's side of the story, the executive acknowledged that Cephis had been dealt with in a heavy-handed manner and agreed that management should keep their word. He then concluded by saying, "I am serving merely as a mediator and do not have authority to settle the case right here and now. I will relay what I have learned to the officials who will have the final say on this matter. Good luck to you, and I hope everything works out."

This was the first and last time Cephis and Hamilton would see this high-ranking, atypical Weyerhaeuser manager. They could only hope that he, unlike Bueno, would keep his word and place truth above managerial self-interest.

The elusive company revivalist would not be in McCurtain County long. Within a mere few months, the Craig Plant would be closed – locked down permanently. The abandoned facility became a desolate apparition – the premises sealed off with a high-fenced barrier, the gate padlocked, and the property patrolled by security guards. Other than a few watchmen, there was no sign of life inside the complex. Since its closure, it has remained an unfriendly blight on the landscape.

Today, as one drives along the isolated Craig Road that contains remnants of the once-bustling fiberboard factory and views the abandoned complex, an eerie feeling sets in. The plant conjures up tainted images of toxic waste as if a ghost from the remote past had brewed up malodorous concoctions upon the premises and cast out all shadows of life. The plant was permanently closed sometime in the late 1980s because it had become unprofitable; but it also had other issues. The facility now looks sinister as it sits idle without a trace of the vibrant manufacturing activity that once thrived on the premises. It had a self-contained history and lore that played out over the course of decades. Local people earned a living there, while the plant supplied materials needed for America's housing boom.

One building on the site was torn down and the machinery, equipment, and structural support beams sold and transported to the premises of Pan Pacific, a smaller fiber board manufacturing plant located west of Broken Bow, which has since suspended operations. Two hundred acres of the original 1,000-acre site comprising the manufacturing complex, the three landfills, and seven waste-holding ponds were deeded over to the City of Broken Bow. The two hundred acres, believed to have been an EPA super fund site, is now under the city's control, but monitored by the EPA and the Oklahoma Department of Environmental Quality (ODEQ).

Locals believed the facility had been taken over by the city in a sweetheart deal designed to spare Weyerhaeuser the horrendous costs of cleaning up the site. Some believed that Weyerhaeuser had spent as much as $60 million to clean up a similar mothballed plant in nearby DeQueen, and did not want to incur that kind of cost burden again.

CHAPTER FIFTY-THREE
The Legal Showdown

After the meeting with the official at the Craig Plant, the two men had a feeling of optimism. Something must be stirring within some corporate boardroom. They expected positive news, but after waiting weeks and months, the bone hoarders became fretful. Had they and the dinosaur been forgotten? Who was pulling the strings behind the scenes? The corporation simply would not cooperate; a different set of prerogatives was driving its agenda.

They knew the decision to settle rested with Weyerhaeuser, but the company was a corporate being, not a human being. Some swank, high-caliber executive inside a lavish suite likely held the fate of their case and the dinosaur in his polished, non-calloused hands. Egos were at stake. Arbitrary managerial discretion was obstructing both justice and science. Everything centered on a decision that, in turn, was swayed by corporate intrigue and the interplay of personalities, biases, influences, and power politics.

The two men became preoccupied with the question of who might be holding up the bag and stifling a settlement. Who within the far-flung corporate empire had a vested interest in not settling the case, and why? By dragging the case out for months or years, everyone could lose, even science, because the bones might deteriorate to an unsalvageable status. At what point would Graffham grow wary, throw in the towel, and cast his eyes and fortunes elsewhere? The two men did not relish the idea of searching for another buyer. They were not bone marketers with extensive business connections. If Graffham backed out, they would be in a world of hurt.

Most certainly, Weyerhaeuser was mad at them, and that did not help matters. In Weyerhaeuser's mind, the two bone rustlers had not yet atoned for their sins, but could they be forgiven? Could bygones be bygones?

Weyerhaeuser was not mad solely at them; the megalithic organization was also angry at Greg Perino, who had signed an affidavit and agreed to testify in court. Through the grapevine, Cephis and Sid learned that the company was now alleging that Perino was expecting to be paid out of the proceeds of the dinosaur sale. The two men knew the real facts; the truth was nothing of the sort.

After some contemplation, they did not think local managerial personalities were the roadblock. If the upper crust of management in Tacoma or North Carolina were indifferent, that meant the obstinacy rested at some level of the hierarchy higher up than Joe Bueno – somewhere in the middle of the chain.

They figured Bueno could care less about the dinosaur, even after he learned it might be worth millions, because none of it was going into his pockets. He had been made the fall guy. He was caught in a vise that squeezed the life force out of him. The man had sold his soul to the corporation and was now paying the price. He had long ago been relegated to a "company man" and forced to kowtow to his immediate superiors. He was insecure about his job. Somebody directly above him in the chain of command had applied pressure and he capitulated, thus sacrificing independence and personal integrity to the dictates of the organization. The corporate machine had denigrated him to the level of a groveling sycophant who buckled at the knees in the face of executive whim. But who could blame him? His job and future hung in the balance.

Obviously, Bueno was not involved in the decision. Very likely it was a corporate official with a particular agenda and bias, or at least a connection to such a person or organization. That organization very likely was the University of Oklahoma (OU). But who, other than George Weyerhaeuser, Jr., had such a connection?

The minds of Hall and Love were filled with intrigue, and their imaginations worked overtime until they finally realized that speculation and finger pointing were getting them nowhere. They needed to start applying pressure on their legal representatives. Why weren't they making any progress? What had they accomplished toward bridging the great divide? Why couldn't they cajole or persuade the corporate mind to see the big picture? Just a little good will, a little independence of mind and foresight might go a long way. They decided to bypass the rookie and made an appointment to talk to the head man, Mr. Carl LeForce, himself. They were ready to air their concerns.

After setting an appointment with LeForce, the specter of lawyers and the system once again came to the fore, and their blame concerning inactivity was redirected at the counselors who seemed to be dragging their feet. That is the way lawyers usually worked. Attorneys never settled cases too quickly – they might be able to squeeze a few additional thousands out of a case by dawdling around the margins and extending it to the max.

What was in the case for the lawyers? Maybe the issue needed to be reframed. Instead of a win or loss for Weyerhaeuser, perhaps the case could be chalked up to the self-interest of the attorneys. Maybe when they were ready, something would finally happen.

The lawyer on the other end, they soon learned, was the aristocratic John Shipp. He had plenty of money. Why would he feel compelled to drain Weyerhaeuser's treasury over a small affair? Surely he had more important cases on his plate and did not need to squabble over the bones of a long-deceased dinosaur.

The two men did not know it at the time, but things were brewing in the background. John Shipp and Carl LeForce had been talking directly to each other – like lawyers always do – a tit for a tat. Weyerhaeuser's position had remained firm. The company held that it had never given the two men permission to go onto the premises, and consequently, they were interlopers; thus, in accordance with law, the fruit of their trespass belonged to Weyerhaeuser.

LeForce, in a meeting at Shipp's office, laid out the evidence. There was an affidavit signed by a leading citizen attesting to the fact that he had witnessed regional timberlands manager Joe Bueno give oral consent for Hall and Love to excavate on the company's land, and that Weyerhaeuser had no interest in the fruits of their dig. In addition, LeForce presented pictures of a Weyerhaeuser employee, Harold James, a supervisor at the Craig Plant, helping the two men load the skull into their pickup.

By this stage, Shipp was well aware of these facts. They had not swayed him earlier, but something or somebody had finally changed his mind. If not Carl LeForce, perhaps Weyerhaeuser's upper management had pushed his button and lit the fire. Maybe somebody had made a cost-benefit analysis and determined that the case wasn't worth the company's time. Whether it was company pragmatics or politics, a legal debt owed to LeForce, or because he had milked the case dry, Shipp now accepted old evidence that had been staring him in the face for months as if it had suddenly elicited compelling new facts. He now admitted that Weyerhaeuser's defense was weak, and the logistics of the case not in the corporation's favor. The Corporation had decided to settle. The settlement agreements would be drawn up for the parties to sign. Legal title to the dinosaur was to be vested in Cephis Hall and Sid Love.

Hall and Love soon received the news. Instead of a face down meeting with LeForce over legal minutia, they would be going to LeForce's office to sign settlement agreements. Nothing could be sweeter. The two men were overcome with ecstasy. But their problems were far from over.

CHAPTER FIFTY-FOUR
Full Pockets – Time for A Spending Spree?

Hall and Love entered the law offices of Carl LeForce, signed the settlement agreements, and walked out in a joyous fog. At this moment it was presumed that the ownership issue was settled, the Weyerhaeuser dispute ended, and the burden of the bones lifted. They felt liberated. Would their euphoria last? Everything now pivoted on Allan Graffham and the Black Hills Institute.

Hats off to Weyerhaeuser! If Weyerhaeuser's decision to settle did not show it had a heart, it at least showed it was a rational being. The corporate Goliath had to be given credit. Many giant corporations or wealthy individuals endowed with monetary clout would have dragged the case out until financially ruining their legal opponent. They might do it merely out of spite, or simply because they could. It was all about the expression of power; but in this case, Weyerhaeuser rose to the occasion and did the right thing, thus according a reasonable prospect that the marvelous specimen could be saved for the benefit of science, the nation, and humanity.

The two modest bone proponents immediately contacted their upscale peer, the ultimate deal maker and fossil progenitor, Mr. Allan Graffham of Geological Enterprises Inc. Arrangements were made for a meeting to convey the large store of bones for a small down payment of cash. A deal was a deal. The problem was that the deal had been structured in such a way that Graffham had great latitude, while the two sellers had little leeway. The demure dino damsel needed to be rescued by a valiant knight like Graffham. The two yeomen had prepared the ground and made the sacrifice. It was now up to the lord to complete the bargain.

In a need to entice LeForce with a solid-looking, enforceable contract offering a potentially lucrative payout, Graffham had largely set his own terms, which meant deferred payment and a long wait for the two men who had made the real sacrifice and investment in the dino through their own toil and sweat.

The basic terms of the agreement specified a down payment of $25,000, with the balance of $200,000 to be paid within two years. At the far end of the deal, the true finders of the high-dollar "product of nature" were to get a cast, and an allowance of $50,000 was to be paid by Graffham to BHI to cover the cost. The deal was struck in such a way to accord Graffham maximum flexibility in making the capital expenditures required to preserve and prepare the specimen – a project that would take years to complete and cost over a million dollars.

It was simply not sound business practice to invest all the money up front in one lump sum. The payoff (the sale of the dinosaur) was too far into the elusive future, and payments to BHI for preparation would be strung out in increments over years as work progressed inside the lab.

Graffham was a shrewd businessman; he had set up a customized financial arrangement that limited his risk and capital outlay while delegating Hall and Love to subsidiary lenders with no collateral or security received for their loan. It was not just that the lenders in this case were gullible; Graffham held the upper hand at the time the contract was negotiated. He made sure all the fine details were in his favor.

The terms of the sale were specified to deal specifically with Graffham's unique situation as a dinosaur preparer and trader. Time, money, a marketable finished product, and a credible buyer were the crucial ingredients that made up the gourmet transaction. It would take years for a finished product to emanate from the lab, and because of the enormous costs involved in preparation, the final product, considering its rarity and uniqueness would be worth millions on the showroom floor.

A suitable buyer could not easily be found, and that was the crux of the issue. A sale of such a specimen was touch and go; potential buyers were sparse and scattered across great distances. A public auction such as Sotheby's might have to be tapped. The investment was highly speculative but offered a dramatic return on capital. A high mark-up meant a high profit. Allan Graffham was a real capitalist, not some petty, small town, pretentious entrepreneur like Hall or Love. Years of restoration and infusions of cash were needed to rejuvenate the specimen into a marketable product.

These were the facts and inescapable reality of "big business in fossils." Hall and Love were aware of this and had liberally accommodated Graffham. Besides, the arrangement had a favorable inducement for them: by stringing the sale out over a couple of years, the bone conveyors theoretically would not incur an onerous tax on a lump sum distribution. They envisioned Graffham making payments in installments as the work progressed and the term of the loan lapsed.

However, Graffham had every incentive to defer payment until the very end of the two-year term. This placed the two bone stragglers in another extended waiting period. Although Graffham could choose to make periodic installments, he could also conserve his capital for the duration and not make any payment until the final bill came due, or even past due. A rainbow of $200,000 (plus their own Acro cast) was waiting over the clouded horizon for the two "bone toilers" now turned dinosaur financiers. But, of course, the lawyers would have to get their cut.

The two lenders derived their capital (bones) through ordeal and sweat, and loaned it out under precarious terms with a receipt of a minimal $25,000 down payment. They never envisioned themselves becoming bankers in bones. This was a wholesale arrangement in which blue-collar amateurs transferred wealth to white-collared professionals. Two men who had been debtors most of their lives had suddenly become creditors. A wealthy icon of Oklahoma's sublime bourgeois strata was now in hock to them.

This was an owner-financed deal favoring the buyer, rather than the seller. The lesson to be learned from such an arcane financial arrangement was to be patient and not count one's chickens before they hatched. Instead of prudence, Cephis Hall would make a leap of faith and incur large debts that relied on Graffham's upholding his contractual obligation and divvying up by the end of the contract period. If Graffham failed to perform, Cephis would be in the debtor's hot seat. In the meantime, they still had two years to wait and hope.

A few days after all the settlement papers were signed and the deed officially transferred, Hall and Love met the commercial fossil maestro at the clandestine bone shed and conveyed the Acro skeleton for a measly $25,000. A check in that amount was written out to Sid Love as a down payment on the "bone loan." It was not (in an old Southern expression) that Cephis and Sid were going to "live high-on-the-hog." That was beside the point. They were making a statement to the world, as well as being compensated.

Graffham and an associate, Leon Theison of the Black Hills Institute, loaded the bones into a one-ton U-Haul truck and immediately headed north for the drier and colder climate of South Dakota, leaving the two micro-merchants high and dry—devoid of their magnificent treasure and in a long waiting mode. A massive assemblage of tangibles had been exchanged for a token paper check worth only a tiny fraction of the value of the exchanged product. They felt rather hollow as they watched the truck drive off with their wondrous theropod collection.

They had a check to cash and an obligation to the lawyers. The two honest bankers promptly drove to LeForce's office to have the proceeds distributed. Approximately 25 percent of their reparation was earmarked for the legal representatives as a down payment on the balance due of $50,000 for attorneys' services. The two bone-harried veterans pocketed about $8,500 each, the balance went into the coffers of LeForce and company. It was July 1989, and they had a long wait in from of them.

CHAPTER FIFTY-FIVE
Cephis Stretches for the American Dream

The months and years ebbed by with no payments received from Graffham. The two- year contractual term was nearing its end. Would Graffham perform his fiduciary duty in the last minutes of the duration?

Cephis and Sid had put nearly $8,500 in their pockets at the time the dinosaur was transferred into the hands of Graffham and the Black Hills Institute. A bill of sale had been transacted and the balance still due enumerated. Hall and Love had a lien on the bones, but could they enforce it? Could they repossess the skeleton if Graffham defaulted on the loan? Big bankers certainly have no problem in foreclosing on defaulted mortgages, but could small bankers extending "credit for bones" do the same? Forking over the cash before the deadline arrived was the right thing for Graffham to do, and that much was expected of him.

This was a period of transition for the two champions of "Acrocanthosaurus Eminence." Their lives were about to be drastically changed. By this time, Sid had become seriously ill, and his health rapidly declining. The "bone war" had taken a toll on him. Cephis, on the other hand, had gone on a consumer splurge and incurred considerable debt obligations.

Hall, never one to sit idle, now set out to engage his repressed fancies. His earlier simple tastes and moderate means were giving way to sumptuous savor and materialist dreams. A man of "inconspicuous consumption" had transitioned to an ostentatious "consumptive syndrome." At last he had joined the ranks of the American mainstream as a consumer conformist. Rugged individualism and austere self-abnegation went out the door—and why not? The man had worked hard all his life, sacrificed, and deferred self-gratification. These were the old virtues, more akin to the frontier and a basic, simpler era. Why not be modern and indulge in the good life? All it took was heavy reliance on credit and debt. That was the American way: buy now, and pay later. If one couldn't pay the bill when it came due, he borrowed more and extended the loan.

Cephis' unconventional dream to recover a world-class dinosaur mint and make his mark on the scientific helm was too esoteric and non-conformist. Such a dream would never be sanctioned or condoned by the hierarchical order. Thus, it was fully acceptable for him to try to strike it rich and fail; but to excavate a rare dinosaur and succeed, that was beyond the pale. Such a wistful and maudlin venture would not garner the blessings of the entrenched elites within corporate America, the government, academia, and the bureaucracy, public or private. But now that he sought a more mainstream consumptive objective, he was blissfully encouraged to reap the reward or fail in the effort. Materialist ambition underpinned the American economic paradigm.

For many years, Hall and his family had lived in a modest, rustic, backwoods bungalow. It was now time to enjoy the good life and look prosperous – even if the "new prosperity" was based on a collapsing house of cards. The American Dream had been laid at his front door and he reached out and grasped it. Debt was the means to make the dream become reality. He now had surplus cash and possessed a promissory note from one of the wealthiest and most prominent businessmen in the state.

Cephis was now a creditor himself, and the note security would serve as collateral to accord him an opportunity to placate his untapped desires and revel in splendor for the first time in his life. Like Jedd Clampitt of *The Beverly Hillbillies*, he had struck a "gusher in black bones," and the money scheduled to flow from that "paleontological well" would allow him and his family to "go away from there." Now his family could move to an upscale section of the city, a swank suburb, or perhaps even a quaint village. It was time to leave forever the wild, dim backwoods setting on the fringes of honky-tonk row. It was also time, at last, for Cephis and family to reap the pleasure of worldly goods.

Shortly after racking in the dough, Cephis went out and bought a brand new, shining red Chevrolet pickup on the easy payment plan. He expected his wages to cover the payments. It seemed a reasonably prudent move.

Soon afterwards, he found a deal on an impressive piece of real estate for only $75,000, which suited his neo-tastes and needs. The seller offered owner-financing terms that could be customized to meet Hall's unique financial situation. Cephis presented his collateralized debt instrument as assurance for payment of the loan. It was certainly an indication that he had the capacity to pay on a future day; all a potential creditor had to do was look at the name and verify the guarantor, Allan Graffham, and the sale was a done deal.

The financing for Hall's dream home was simple: a down payment of $8,000 to be paid at closing with the balance due in a balloon payment within thirty days of the close of the two-year contract with Graffham. When Graffham timely forked over the funds, Cephis was scheduled to turn around and pay off the note on his new house and be free and clear. It all seemed so simple.

Cephis and Joyce purchased a two-story, four-bedroom, 2 ½-bath, 3,500 square foot house on 4 ½ acres near Hochatown, just a few miles north of Broken Bow and in the heart of the crystal zone. A price of $75,000 for such a luxurious piece of real estate might sound dirt cheap these days, even in the aftermath of the George W. Bush sub-prime-derivatives fiasco, but in the early 1990s, real estate in Oklahoma was in a cyclical depression, and deals galore were prevalent for qualified buyers. Bargain basement prices for prime real estate were the rule, not the exception.

All Hall had to do was wait for Graffham to deliver the funds so he could then pay off the loan and be free of all liens and encumbrances. There was no doubt that Graffham had the resources to make it all come true. The "bones tycoon" could easily pay off Black Hills and the two cash-strapped bone lenders, but it was still a waiting game.

CHAPTER FIFTY-SIX
Empty Pockets – Cephis Feels the Pain

The bones were at Black Hills and finally getting the care and attention they deserved. But what about Cephis and Sid? Were they being taken care of? Certain obligations to them had accrued as their waiting period ensued. The two-year loan contract with Graffham had expired, and the payment was past due.

Could the creditors charge a late fee? Where was the money? It was time for Graffham to step up to the plate and perform his duty. Like the bones, the two "back roads" financiers needed attention. If they were Wall Street or even Main Street, payment would come forth or heads would roll (financially speaking), yet their pockets were empty. What about Graffham's? It was assumed that his pockets were still deep and full, but he was now derelict in his financial responsibility. What did that say about the upper crust of Oklahoma society?

Cephis was anxious. Time was ticking away, and he was in a financial squeeze. If Graffham did not come through with the funds, he risked losing his new home. The balloon payment of approximately $65,000 was due within thirty days following the end of the two-year contractual timeframe, and that time had long passed. Unless Graffham paid his debt for his dinosaur purchase, Cephis could not honor his obligation on his newly-purchased real estate.

Suddenly, luxury had become a despicable burden. The noose tightened around his neck and threatened to stifle his new lifestyle. Debt had suddenly changed his whole outlook and became an albatross weighting him down as he sank into despair. Was this the face of consumerism and ostentatious display? It did not seem liberating. The whole specter of overextended debt was looming larger and larger and had already soured his short-lived infatuation with the so called "good life." If this was the American Dream, he wanted no part of it.

He called Graffham to remind him of his obligation; the response was not reassuring. He called LeForce to relay his concern, but LeForce likewise seemed unresponsive. He was simply told to sit tight and wait, but he had already been doing that. He next contacted his creditor who had owner-financed his new house. He told his mortgage holder that there was going to be a delay, but he expected to be able to make the payment shortly. On this contact, he finally got a positive response; the seller-financier stated he would try to work with him and, if necessary, they could set up a temporary payment plan until the money flowed in. Cephis decided he could wait six more months, but after that time period, he would have to act.

As Cephis sat and worried about the money, Sid's health continued to deteriorate. He had recently been diagnosed with throat cancer and would have to undergo expensive treatment. Sid now would have to delegate full authority to Cephis to handle the financial affair. He gave Cephis his moral support, while Cephis tried to reassure him. Cephis now began to worry about his best friend. As usual, he had too much on his plate. He was over-extended, but what could he do? The entire "bones experience" had tested his endurance. It had been both a blessing and a curse. Exciting and thrilling at times, the adventure also had a down side. Stress and intermittent worry were a major part of it. He now began to worry about his own health as his blood pressure gradually escalated.

The bones were receiving treatment, and Black Hills was making slow, steady progress. Graffham was making payments on the remediation bill as it accrued, yet why was payment on the bones loan being deferred? Why did the lawyers seem disinterested? What was driving Allan Graffham? Was it solely money or something else?

The mystique of Allan Graffham began to wear thin. He was no longer seen as a white knight that had come to the rescue. The man whom the Association of Applied Paleontological Sciences (a trade organization of fossil sellers) had honored on numerous occasions; the man who had more than a dozen fossils bearing his name (*Graffhamicrinus matheri,* for example); the man who sold dinosaur eggs from China; amber-encased insects from South America; and camasain teeth from Canada was now beginning to look like a shyster in the eyes of the two small-time fossil merchants.

As the months passed, the nature of the finance had changed. There was no art in this deal, as Donald Trump might say. It was not enthralling for Hall and Love; maybe it was "creative finance" for Graffham. The financial arrangement was no longer just a loan on bones; it was now a loan on $200,000, and the lenders were not earning interest. There was nothing in the contract that allowed for penalties, late fees, legal fees, interest, or repossession charges. The big-time "fossil capitalist" had outwitted the two naïve, home-grown and hard-boned aspiring capitalists. Again, their only recourse was the legal system.

Allan Graffham showed no inclination to pay anything on the loan. They were now in a monetary dispute with a wealthy tycoon who demonstrated no good will or inkling of compassion. Cephis needed the money to save his home; Sid needed the money to pay his medical bills.

Cephis was not stupid; but at times, he was a little too trusting. He was from the old school where a real man kept his word and never lied to or cheated a friend. A friendship was a bond that cemented trust, affection, and fidelity. He thought Graffham was his friend. They had talked dinosaur language, laughed, shared amusing stories and naturalist tales, exchanged crystals for dollars, drank coffee and a few cold ones together, and even formed a bones partnership. Now it all seemed to be unraveling as Graffham appeared to be taking advantage of their trust. A ruthless, "calculating capitalist" could indeed place money over friendship, but was Allan Graffham such a person? Cephis began to fear the worst.

More than five months had elapsed since the note had matured and the deadline for payment had expired. Cephis was growing weary. Telephone conversations with Graffham just irritated him more: Graffham said nothing definitive or decisive; he was just putting him off and dismissing his concerns. Cephis visited LeForce again and explained his situation, but the attorney was not moved. His answer was more of the same – sit and wait on the edge of the couch until the seat wore a hole – Cephis was more concerned about the hole in his wallet.

LeForce continued to be indecisive and uncertain about what should be done. He implied that it was best not to antagonize Graffham, lest he refuse to pay out of sheer spite. LeForce knew Graffham had money; he also knew that Graffham owed his clients and was therefore indirectly in debt to his law firm to the tune of some $44,000. Did Graffham's social and political prominence intimidate LeForce? Had he been taken in by the "Graffham mystique" and his leftover reputation from the oil patch or maybe even by his awesome stature as one of the most successful independent businessmen in the state?

There was no doubt: Graffham was a fixture within high circles of south-central Oklahoma society. He belonged to the exclusive country clubs, was invited to the most extravagant social parties, and attended the toniest black-tie affairs. Even high-level politicians and executives listened when he talked. He held the purse strings on numerous charities and was influential in how wealthy foundations funded such causes.

As a highly-successful attorney, LeForce was a notch below Graffham on the social-economic-political scale. Was this a case where men of high social ranking shared empathy and identified with each other to the exclusion of those outside their club? Men of money often colluded with their kind while discounting penury, but Cephis did not believe that to be the case, and even if so, all he wanted was his money so he could pay some bills. Money talks, but it certainly wasn't speaking to Hall or Love.

Cephis was feeling the pain. More weeks had passed and he was in desperate straits. His contractor-employer had also been snagged in a "debt hook and sinker" and was forced to cut back work hours for his crews. A reduction in work hours put a crimp in Hall's cash flow and made it more difficult for him to make payments on his new truck.

Cephis, out of desperation, made another appointment to see LeForce. He had been dickering with LeForce and Company for months to no avail. Would this meeting be different?

The debt-ridden entrepreneur entered the conference room and immediately got to the core of the issue.

"Carl, something needs to be done. I can't pay you until Graffham pays me."

Leforce stared blankly at the pleading hillbilly and offered few words. He still seemed hesitant to pursue the matter. Did LeForce know something that Hall didn't? Was Graffham about to file bankruptcy or perhaps leave the country? Without a quick monetary fix, the bones were doomed, and so were their finances, or at least Hall's.

Cephis emphasized that the contract needed to be enforced, and he was flexible as to what approach the attorneys might take to enforce it.

"It's up to you to decide what to do, but you must do something," said Hall.

LeForce did not reverberate with passion and zeal; instead, he slumped in his chair with a rather sullen glare. The seriousness of Hall's plea did not faze him.

The facts of the matter were clear. Graffham had signed a notarized contract and was obligated to buy the bones if and when a marketable title was obtained. That stipulation had been met, and Graffham had taken possession of the fossils after making a petty down payment. He was obligated to pay the balance due. Why was that so hard to understand? Did not modern-day Oklahomans take their debt obligations seriously? A simple Letter of Demand would be a good starting point in an attempt to compel Graffham to comply.

What was holding back LeForce and Hamilton? The LeForce law firm had $44,000 hinging on a collection of the debt. Was that not enough to propel them toward one last push to garnish the funds? This mystery was more perplexing than the cloud over the dinosaur – a case where lawyers neglected to pursue action for their own monetary interest. Was filing one more document and perhaps staging one more conference in pursuit of hard cash just not worth the expenditure in legal time and energy? The lawyers had a counterclaim against Graffham, and, as a result of his non-performance, compensation for their legal services was being impeded. Yet still they did nothing. The mere drafting of a Letter of Demand or petition might get Graffham's attention. A judgment against Graffham should easily be worth the dollar amount of the contract. After all, he had hordes of hard assets that were visible and conspicuous. If the two men couldn't get hard cash, maybe they could at least get hard bones.

The two men from "down under" had saved the dinosaur, but it looked like they could not salvage their own finances. Cephis Hall walked out of the law office in bewilderment and disgust. He had no skeleton, no money, and no representation. His situation was bleak. He had struck rock bottom, and there were no bones on the horizon.

CHAPTER FIFTY-SEVEN
Southern Comfort

The mounting debt pinched Cephis' rough integument. Like the Acro's prey, the wicked claws had snagged and penetrated deep into his interior, thrashing his flesh and expelling the lifeblood from his mainstream, materialist ambitions. His so-called American Dream was fading, even threatening to turn into a nightmare. A pang of anguish now gripped his consciousness. He sought relief, but how could he obtain it? Cephis braced himself to confront the only personage who could make a difference and change the situation – Allan Graffham.

The two yeomen from the "Manor of McCurtain" now contested the bone baron from the "Fiefdom of Carter." The dispute was not just over bones, but also about a financial vassalage that had gone awry and needed to be adjusted. It was up to Cephis Hall to set things straight.

He strapped his bow and sheathed his arrows in his quiver, but soon realized it was all a futile, feckless endeavor. He knew he was at the mercy of a feudal, pecuniary-minded, lordly order. Commoners apparently did not count for much in the royal "Province of Carter." Despite the feudal futility, the barter-strapped backwoodsman set out on a trip to "Graffham Castle" to see the "Lord of Bones." Hall would first try to negotiate before calling his opponent onto the field of honor. It would be a face-off between an archer and a knight.

Hall's debt situation had taken a turn for the worse. He was behind on his truck payments and the banker was threatening to repossess his $20,000 truck. He, as a creditor to the tune of $200,000, was being hounded by a lienholder over the measly sum of $20,000. It just didn't seem fair; a high-caste lender could enforce a low contract, while a low-caste lender could not enforce a high contract. It was difficult being only one notch above a peasant in a medieval-styled economic scenario, even if he was a creditor to a member of the high nobility.

Cephis was a man who tried to think and plan ahead – even envision the outcome – and sometimes he thought outside the box. Maybe it was part of his overall strategy, or perhaps it was merely out of a daunting sense of intimidation over the prospect of facing Allan Graffham alone under the shadowy pall of a lender versus debtor relationship. Whatever it was, he decided to take a companion – a documenter-reporter who could peer into the mystique of Allan Graffham and render an interpretation. Jim Honeywell, the man of the hour, would be his traveling companion.

Honeywell was a writer-reporter for a local, small-town newspaper, but he had once been in a journalistic hot seat. He had shined as a star reporter and columnist for the mega-media newspaper, the *Dallas Morning News*, and had won numerous journalist awards during his better days. He had returned home to McCurtain County to finish out his last days as a local reporter before retirement. He had seen the big time and was now bored with small-town gossip, trivia, obituaries, and mundane crime stories. The dinosaur story was the biggest thing happening around McCurtain County, and now he wanted a piece of the dinosaur action, even if his glory days had already faded. Besides, he was a personal friend of Hall's; they'd known each other for decades. To steady Hall's nerves, he even agreed to chauffeur the downtrodden bone creditor to the scene.

Graffham agreed to meet them and planned to entertain his two obscure guests in lavish style. It was his way of doing business – wine and dine the associate to impart a relaxing atmosphere and good feeling. They could mix business and pleasure, although in the case of Graffham, he hoped it was mostly pleasure. Regardless, business details always flowed better under conditions where the tone was right and the environs amicable. If contentment was attained, dissension would melt away. In the case of Hall and Honeywell, Graffham was most likely hoping to feed them, butter them up – even inebriate them, if he could – and then send the two schmucks on their merry way. His lordship would have the last say, or so he hoped.

Around high noon on a weekday of 1990, Hall and Honeywell followed Graffham as they drove from his business premises on Stoffa Street to an upscale dining and bar facility outside the city limits of Ardmore – Dakota's. It was a fancy restaurant, frequented mostly by the business elite of Carter County. Dakota's was the most exclusive and lavish eatery in the area. The prices were not even listed on the menu. Graffham would set them up and pay for everything. They were to be given the red carpet treatment. He was hoping a little plenitude, fine eats, and exotic drinks would melt all opposition, at least for the moment.

Allan Graffham knew the clientele – at least all the upscale diners. This was not just a fancy dining experience, it was also expensive. Informal, working-class people in t-shirts and blue jeans just did not walk in and dine comfortably. This was a formal setting, and a customer was expected to be appropriately dressed – if not in a three-piece suit or black-tie attire, at least in professional wear. It was easy to distinguish a white-collar businessman or professional from "white trash." The people who frequented this establishment did not buy their clothes at Walmart.

The problem with this social dining arrangement was that Hall and Honeywell were dressed informally. But that infraction would be overlooked. They were the personal guests of Allan Graffham and were to be bestowed with the VIP works – a full course of whatever their dining fancies might desire. Everyone who frequented the restaurant knew Graffham, and if diners were in his company and happened to be dressed in casual blue jeans, like Hall, or khaki pants, like Honeywell, it would be accepted, maybe even ignored. Graffham would pick up the tab, and he entertained his guests in the most stylish means the ornate eatery could provide. While the opulent ambience and decorum overshadowed the drab attire, dollars flowed into the pockets of the restaurant owners – compliments of the free-spending Graffham.

Hall and Honeywell sat down in their luxurious seats at a specially reserved table and prepared to indulge their palates. Cephis and Honeywell, despite the VIP treatment, felt out of place, but their gnawing appetite needed to be satiated. They savored the delicate smells, and, for the moment, were distracted from their real purpose.

The eatery clients sitting near their exclusive table were all formally dressed in fine-tailored business suits. Ardmore, Oklahoma, at one time, was reputed to have had the most millionaires per capita of any city in America, largely as a result of the oil boom. Graffham was likely counted in that statistic. Perhaps it was still so; regardless, Graffham was still on the list.

As the two outsiders tasted the preliminaries, they noticed that "uppity people" sitting nearby were glaring at them and their common, casual dress as if they were misfits – Graffham's friends in low places. The two informal diners were taken aback, but brushed off the cold, aloof stares and refocused on the tender delicacies that had just been served. The waiter reminded Cephis of old Southern-style butlers serving masters and guests on television dramas. An expensive meal, steak and ale, or any fancy trimming that they desired was on the menu. They could have whatever they wanted. There was no need to be bashful or concerned about the impact on Graffham's pocketbook. They could dig right in to their heart's content.

As the dining experience progressed toward the main course, the issue of the bones and the loan was finally thrust into the serene ambience of the plush setting. Cephis, while sipping on vintage wine originating from the finest vineyards and perfectly mellowed in the exquisite distilleries of Bordeaux, France, had finally conjured up the nerve to delve into the financial controversy.

Cephis stated his case: "We have been waiting long enough for you to deliver payment. I am at risk of losing my house, pickup, and all that expensive furniture I bought for Joyce. Poor Sid is undergoing radiation and chemotherapy for cancer and needs the money for medical expenses. Can we count on you to come through with the funds? We delivered the bones; it is now time for you to deliver the cash. Your payment is seven months past due."

The question was rather stale and entirely unfitting for the setting, but Cephis had to speak what was on his mind. Hall had interjected hard reality into an otherwise lighthearted dining experience. The tone changed, but Graffham tried to detract the serious edge of the blunt question. He responded with a joke and a little more casual small-talk about his trilobite mine being flooded out as a result of the deluge of recent rains.

Graffham's ordeal with the flood did distract Hall for the moment. It reminded him of how fortunate he and Sid were to have recovered the dinosaur before the hundred-year flood inundated Oklahoma in 1990. Such a flood would have destroyed the dinosaur if it had still been embedded in the gully. As the thought quickly passed, Cephis reminded Graffham that he was more concerned about hard cash than hard, water-logged fossils. But Graffham had water on his mind – namely, a particular river. He stated he was trying to come up with the cash, but he would not be available for the next thirty days. He planned a trip to sail down the Amazon. He would address the issue of his fiduciary duty after he returned from vacation.

Cephis sank in his seat and Honeywell was stunned. This old man Graffham had a lot of nerve. Where were his priorities? Did he not have a conscience or moral compass? He had displayed astonishing insensitivity toward a man who had just pleaded his cause. It was apparent that his obligation to Hall and Love was at the bottom of his priorities, if it even qualified at all. It was as if he had entered into a midlife crisis and sought adventure to quell the misery or indulge his fantasy. Obviously, pleasure came before business, at least in regard to his debt obligation owed to Hall and Love.

Cephis was aghast. He wagered that Graffham did not give his high-profile, celebrity associates or big-time bankers the same kind of consideration. He could afford to take an expensive trip down the Amazon, but not pay him and Sid. At that point, the luxurious dining experience had turned into a fiasco, if not a travesty. Cephis gulped a whole glass of rich red wine and quickly finished his steak. Graffham asked if he wanted more.

"No, I'm getting out of here," said Cephis as he got up and silently walked out the door. Honeywell, equally disgusted, followed closely behind.

The two men got into their vehicle and left the scene. Although Honeywell was fairly quiet at the restaurant, he had plenty to say on the way home.

"I don't think he will ever come through. He'll always put you off for another day. You're going to have to compel him to pay. He's more interested in sailing down the Amazon than paying you and Sid. My son-in-law is an attorney in Oklahoma City. Here is his card. Wait a few days until I have had a chance to talk to him, and then give him a call."

Cephis stuffed the card in the pocket of his jeans. To him, it was just another lawyer and he was unable to spring any enthusiasm. Could this referral solve his legal problems? Or would it lead to just more legal quagmires?

CHAPTER FIFTY-EIGHT
Legal Pleading

Cephis did not sleep well that night after the restaurant folly in Carter County. The situation got worse the following morning when he woke up with a hangover and heard a loud commotion outside. He opened the door and watched as his brand-new pickup was being towed away. *That was what happened when poor people or over-extended debtors did not pay their bills*, he thought. Everything was not bleak, however; he still had his old clunker, and Joyce had a low-mileage, eight year old minivan to drive. Besides, he had already learned that driving in style was not all it was cracked up to be.

He would make do with his dilapidated vehicle with its worn tires, torn seats, dings and pings, faded paint, sagging liner and slipping transmission. At least he didn't have to worry about making the payments anymore. What bothered him more was his employment situation.

He had been cut down to a three day work week as a result of the real estate collapse and declining timber demand. The savings and loan scandals and restrictive monetary policy (high interest rates) experienced under the Reagan Administration had finally taken their toll. The economy, at least the real estate and housing industries, was in recession.

Hall was a man who lived a hard life closely intertwined with nature. Yet he now sat idle – one of the lowest points of his life. Oddly, he did not even feel like going out into "the rough" to dig crystals. He now felt passive, inactive, even powerless. His debt pinch was about to turn into financial plight. He sank into a pit of despair, but not for long. He got a grip on his situation and bounced back from his forlorn state of adversity. After all, he still had battles to fight. He would grind it out in the same old tried-and-true way. The sheer force of his determination would propel him onward.

He got into his worn-out but debt-free truck and drove down to LeForce's office – an appointment be damned. He needed to talk to the man. LeForce would have to listen and if he would not act, Cephis would write him off and move on. This was LeForce's last chance to redeem himself. If he would not get off his haunches for the sake of his clients, perhaps he could be enticed by the pot of cash at the end of the rainbow that was earmarked for legal fees. Forty-four thousand dollars was a lot of money. *I've waited long enough, why was LeForce still waiting?* Cephis asked himself.

After arriving at the law office, he had to wait still more. It seemed like several hours before LeForce freed up about five minutes to talk to his disparate and desperate client. The meeting was short. LeForce was not charging by the hour.

As Cephis and Sid had noticed earlier, there seemed to be a shortcoming in the language and remedy of their legal petition: There was nothing mentioned about legal fees. The provisions did not allow for any recovery from their legal opponent (Weyerhaeuser) or their own attorneys. That was understandable of course; attorneys are not going to refund their fees under any circumstances.

The two men held up their end of the deal by forking over approximately 25% of the proceeds from the down payment made by Graffham. Now, with the big money at stake, their attorneys sat immobilized and there were no refunds for legal non-performance.

Although they had not yet paid any legal fees out of their own pockets, technically speaking, they assumed they had an obligation to pay the attorneys $44 thousand even if they had to enforce the contract themselves – through any means. It was not unreasonable to demand that their lawyers show some initiative in taking action to further their own and their clients' monetary interests.

The rockhound pleaded his case – almost begging LeForce to do something in a legal vein – but it was to no avail.

LeForce's response was short and crude. "It looks like you're going to lose your ass."

That was all Cephis needed to hear. He scratched LeForce off his list and walked out the door. He was left to his own devices, but was not finished, for he had other rocks to turn over.

CHAPTER FIFTY-NINE
The Hard Sell

Within days after his last meeting with Mr. Carl LeForce, Cephis was already pulling out of his slump and maneuvering behind the scenes. A true man of action, he devised a plan and then carried it out. He started by addressing his many problems on a broad front. The dinosaur had cost him more than he could ever have imagined – tarnished relationships, neglect of personal responsibilities, perpetual stress, lost opportunities and business possibilities – but he was in a process of sorting it all out and putting the pieces back together. Momentum was building for a revival of old revenue streams. Calls and inquiries about his tour guide services were starting to roll back in. He was hoping to get his economic house back in order.

Hall was now trying to resurrect his popular nature tours. People from all over the nation came to McCurtain County to be a special guest of Cephis Hall and partake of his uncanny ability to impart nature in a simplistic and hands-on form. Hall would show the way, locate the treasure, demonstrate the technique and assist in ferreting out the treasure from its hidden enclave, and finally, heap praise on his students as astute, quick studies in true grit rockhounding. Since his ordeal with the dinosaur, he had put his crystal digging expeditions on hold. Like the T.rex bone cruncher, his nature worship had become one-dimensional. He had traded tangible rocks and crystals for the mystical bones of an elusive dinosaur, and the obsession had cost him dearly and almost killed him.

For over five years, his tour guide service had basically been shut down. It was as if he had gone out of business. The dinosaur demanded too much of his time and energy and proved costly beyond his wildest imagination. Far from getting rich, he was likely going to take an enormous economic hit that he could not write off his taxes. The loss was multi-dimensional, impacting many areas of his life. He was a tired man, having worked seven days a week for most of the prior seven years.

Although the dinosaur dig and ensuing legal battle had taken up virtually all his spare time, he still managed to conduct occasional field trips for local schools, and he did those for free. Elementary school kids from all over the state loved Cephis Hall – not because of the dinosaur, but because he taught them how to find and dig rare minerals and small fossils and to look for Indian arrowheads and artifacts. He took them on field trips to interesting places. Hall's colorful persona represented a kind of quaint yokelicity – a melding of the picturesque Appalachians, Ozarks, and Ouachitas into one idyllic, contemporaneous personhood. His Arcadian foibles and quirky eccentricities endeared him to the young.

His tours were not just popular with students, but with educators. Teachers and parents seemed to enjoy the trips as much as the kids. Now that the dinosaur dig was completed, he had spare time to conduct school field trips and was soon bombarded with requests.

Although his school tours did not bring income to a cash-strapped family budget, they were an intrinsic reward in their own right. For Cephis, it was sheer delight to see the sparkle and awe in the animated eyes of youngsters who had just found their first nature product. The children, teachers, and parents knew they were in the company of the foremost nature guide of southeastern Oklahoma. Cephis still proudly displays scrapbooks full of letters from individual students, whole classes, teachers, parents, and principals thanking him for their nature experience and exclaiming about how wonderful it was to find quartz crystal or other exotic rocks or relics.

Now, as his finances sagged and his logging employment faltered, he was hoping to supplant lost wages with extra revenue earned from an expanded tour guide business. He began advertising and contacting old clients and customers who had written him off years prior. As business picked up, instead of cutting trees, Cephis guided tours on the weekdays that he was not otherwise in the timberlands.

Naturalists and rock hounds began to flock back to the crystal zone. A short-term sedentary and depressed phase for Hall had given way to the normal seven-day work week. In the meantime, he still had unfinished business concerning the dinosaur transaction, but in the intermediate span, he would be back in search of new buried treasures – not just small-time quartz pockets, but true bonanzas in crystal mines and other riches, even on a commercial scale. He would become the Cephis Hall of old – the great multi-dimensional explorer of the outback and backwoods.

There was another bright spot added to the picture: Sid was doing better and becoming more active. Before long, he even started going with Cephis on some of his group tours, and the two men began exploring for new veins of mineralized quarries, but with less zeal and vigor than they had enjoyed in the past. Both men had aged, and their pace had slowed considerably.

As a commercial tour guide on an exceptionally good day, Cephis could earn $800 minus out-of-pocket expenses. With revenue from his tourist business, Cephis inched his way back up from the abyss of financial doom. Both Hall and Love, after hitting rock bottom, were resurging. Sid's cancer was in remission, and Cephis was smitten with new ambitions. That great thirst for finding a truly viable commercial crystal mine was unquenched and old dreams rekindled—although the dinosaur and ensuing debt was still very much on their minds.

After weeks of neglect, the two men sat down to devise a plan. They had largely written off Graffham; it seemed he either could not or would not pay his bill. They suspected the latter. Since Graffham had failed or refused to pay, perhaps they could strike a deal that would allow them to recoup part of their horrendous expenses and refund Graffham's investment. However, they knew if they had to bite the bullet and sacrifice their dinosaur equity (most of it in the form of sweat), they could not afford to pay LeForce $44,000 out of their downsized sales proceeds. LeForce had already collected a tidy percentage of their sweat equity. They had spent years toiling and wrestling the elements, while LeForce and company had expended only a few hours in an air-conditioned law office doing legal paperwork and had garnered 25% of the income from the fruits of their labor. It certainly was not fair for the lawyers to garnish the remaining 25% of what the two diggers could salvage out of a discounted sale to an alternative buyer, who, as the customized deal would dictate, would have to buy out Graffham's equity and pay them a token amount for their sacrifice. The two men were now willing to substantially discount their equity and sell the dinosaur at a cut-rate, dirt-cheap price. Any kind of deal was better than none. They were tired of hassling with lawyers and commercial fossil dealers. They just wanted to be freed from the fracture of the fissured bone deal. They hoped the dinosaur could find a good home, preferably somewhere in the hospitality of a museum in the state of Oklahoma.

Not long after confronting the reality of their predicament and scaling down their expectations, Cephis and Sid jumped back into the dinosaur dispute. Cephis called Graffham and gave him a piece of his mind – he extrapolated the essence of a new perceived "dinosaurian corporeality."

Cephis proposed the terms and Graffham listened: "Mr. Graffham, since you don't have a buyer and we don't have any money, how about us all just baling out of this situation? Why can't we just make a deal where we can all recover our out-of-pocket expenses? If we can refund all your expenditures and recoup some of ours, that would just tickle me and Sid and maybe even relieve a big burden on you. What do you think?"

Graffham hesitantly replied, "Go ahead and contact your buyer and see what you can work out."

But was Graffham sincere? Only he knew how much money he had already invested. Black Hills also knew, but that knowledge was confidential client information. And only Graffham knew the time and expense of saving and preserving the dinosaur – years of technical treatment and quarters of millions of dollars – that lay ahead. Graffham knew the score, but pretended ignorance. He knew such big-time buyers were few and far between. He and his entourage were now dealing in the esoteric world of high-profile fossil mercantilism. Universities did not have that kind of money unless they had access to a big corporate sponsor that was willing to bestow the largess.

"Sure, go right ahead and find you a buyer and have him contact me and Black Hills so we can fill in the details," said Graffham.

Cephis proceeded to do just that. He had been talking to OU and several other institutions, and they sounded interested, at least enough to set up a meeting for discussion. He was not as naïve as Graffham had imagined. He knew university science departments were strapped for cash, but they also had wealthy benefactors. In the case of the University of Oklahoma, the Noble Foundation could ride in on a white horse and save the dinosaur and greatly enhance the science museum with a new shrine to "carnivorous magnificence."

In a prior conversation with Dr. Cifelli of OU, Cephis asked "Dr. Cifelli, would you be interested in buying an articulated skeleton of Acrocanthosaurus?"

"Of course," said Cifelli.

Cephis explained, "Well, we will need to figure out our costs and try to recover some of our investment."

"Certainly," agreed Cifelli. "Don't under price yourself." Cifelli must have been thinking small, as in low dollars. "As soon as you're ready, call back and we'll set up an appointment."

"I shore will," concluded Cephis.

Next, Cephis called LeForce to get his take on the situation. Cephis and Sid had already decided that if LeForce would not consent to relinquish his claim on the sales proceeds, they would act on their own and leave LeForce and Associates out of the loop. Since the two men had to find a new buyer as a result of LeForce's refusal to enforce the existing contract with Graffham, they would leave LeForce to his own legal means. He could then enforce the existing contract for himself. In that case, they would see LeForce in court in a defendant-plaintiff relationship, rather than a client-attorney relationship.

Fortunately, LeForce consented. He told Cephis, "Go ahead and try to get your money. If you sell to a different buyer, that will negate your obligation to us under the prior arrangements specified in the Graffham transaction."

Freed from the shackles of onerous legal terms, Hall and Love began searching for a new buyer. Although they knew that Graffham and Black Hills still had possession of the dino and nobody could touch it without reimbursing them (and maybe even throwing in a tip or bonus for their troubles), there was a slight glimmer of hope.

Cephis and Sid set about to iron out the details for an upcoming meeting with Dr. Rich Cifelli, the head paleontologist at OU. This was the same gentleman the two men had earlier encountered at the Gem and Mineral Show and the same lobbyist-scientist who had allegedly called Cephis a "grave-robbing thief." Nevertheless, all that had been forgotten. Although no price was mentioned, the meeting was set for the following week at Cifelli's office at the Sam Noble Museum of Natural History on the grounds of the university campus. Cephis and Sid would be traveling to Norman, Oklahoma. In addition, they would take along Jim Honeywell as a witness to what transpired. Honeywell had relatives in Oklahoma City – his daughter and son-in-law, Eric Gray, a high-powered corporate attorney whose business card was still packed away in Cephis' wallet. Honeywell planned on driving ahead and visiting with his daughter and would later show up at Cifelli's office at the scheduled time.

THE HARD SELL

On a cloudy day in late 1991, Cephis and Sid entered the well-stocked and tended office of Dr. Rich Cifelli. The three men sat down and initiated the preliminaries regarding a potential "dinosaur deal." The conversation had barely gotten underway, when Jim Honeywell, a little disheveled and wet from the outside rain, arrived. Honeywell, the man chasing the "tale of the dinosaur", joined the association.

"Dr Cifelli, this is Jim Honeywell. He brought in some documentation to share with us," said Cephis. Actually that statement was a ruse to deter Cifelli's questioning about Honeywell's presence.

Honeywell had a role in the affair; he was to document what was discussed, like any good journalist would do. Honeywell sat down and the discussion resumed. The journalist had his notepad and pen to take notes. He was an accessory to the bargain. The deal was then laid out on the table and Cifelli took a look. The stats were compiled on a professional itemized print out, compliments of the accounting acumen of Sid Love. One quick glimpse and a dismayed Cifelli fell back in his seat.

The list of expenses included such things as hours worked, costs for supplies and materials, and a sundry tally of miscellaneous out-of-pocket expenditures – all for the sake of saving the dinosaur. The dollar figure for labor was based on the minimum wage — less than $5.00 an hour during this period of American labor munificence. The total costs were well in excess of $200,000.

"Don't worry," said Cephis. "We are not asking that bottom line price you see down there in bold. We are writing off most of our costs and selling at a big loss. Here is the deal: Sid and I want $85,000 total ($42,500 each) for our troubles, about one third of our total expenses. There is no profit in this deal for us. As for Graffham, we estimate he has about a $50,000 to $75,000 investment tied up in the beast, but you'll have to confirm that figure with him. Please remember that the specimen has already undergone considerable treatment for its pyrite affliction. Unless you want to finish off the specimen yourself, you can continue footing the bill for the remainder of the preservation, molding, and casting. As you might very well know, Black Hills Institute is a first-class preparation facility. When finished, you will have a classic dinosaur. You can take ownership of the magnificent creature for probably less than $150,000. It will cost more to complete the work at Black Hills, but when it is finished you will have the only one like it in the world, and it is a native of Oklahoma. We want to keep the dinosaur within the state, so we are willing to sell cheap."

Cephis had succinctly stated their cause. He sounded polished – not like some stereotypical backwoods hillbilly. The presentation was to the point, although lacking florid embellishment. Cephis was a straight talker and tried his best to conceal his accented, Southern woodlands origin. Perhaps he rehearsed, or maybe the fluency just came out naturally. Despite his rough aura, he was actually well read. Even Honeywell, who crafted words for a living, was impressed. Cifelli, however, was not. He was from New Jersey or somewhere on the East Coast, where simple, down-home dialect did not resonate. The paleontologist could see no potential in the deal. He was taken aback by the high-dollar figure that had initially been thrust in front of him and was unable to recover from that initial shock.

What Cifelli did not appreciate was that these two modest outdoorsmen had used old, tried-and-true, but safer, paleontological methods that were more labor intensive. Thus, the majority of the costs of the excavation were in labor. Although they had taken longer to complete the dig, they had saved virtually every piece accessible since thrusting their spades. Rather than using a "Pittman-style excavation method" that might have crunched and scoured a large percentage of the bone crop, the two raw naturalists had done the job the hard way in a slow, meticulous, and deliberate manner – thus driving up labor costs. But at the minimum wage or less, who could argue about that? They had worked cheaper than wetbacks. They were discounting about 70% of their costs, including labor, selling their work at $2.00 an hour or less. Still, Cifelli did not see the merits. He was a hard sell. Cheap labor did not entice him.

Perhaps Cifelli just didn't believe the figures. Maybe the figures were padded or the men's excavation methods so unorthodox that they had escalated the costs beyond any realistic model. Maybe inefficiency sealed off the deal. Cifelli was a pure skeptic and apparently unable to envision the ultimate value of a finished-out model of a complete *Acrocanthosaurus* cast on the exhibition floor. He would later need to go to the North Carolina Museum of Natural Sciences to see the real thing.

Cifelli had an inability to appreciate the fact that the specimen was unearthed by two men working alone without help from dozens of student volunteers. The only charity embedded in the deal was the excavators' own discounted labor. This was a case where amateurs labored in pursuit of a life-long dream (at least in Hall's view). It was not done for student credit, recreation, or learning, although there were similar underlying motives. Despite the constant pang of strenuous labor, the two explorers had set out to assuage their curiosity, satiate their ambitions, and divert their life-stressors; they also hoped to learn and receive credit for their accomplishment. They had learned plenty, but the recognition and compensation were lagging. The two men had saved the dinosaur, but nobody wanted to recognize or appreciate that simple fact, least of all Cifelli.

"Well, thanks for sharing that with me. Could I please make a copy of that?" asked Cifelli.

"Sure," said Sid.

Cifelli concluded by saying, "To be honest with you guys, we were thinking in terms of about $15,000. We don't have that kind of in-house money. I need to talk to some of our funding sources to see what we might be able to come up with. We will get back to you later."

"Thanks, Dr. Cifelli, we will be waiting to hear from you. We don't expect an answer in the next two days, but would appreciate one within the next two weeks," responded Cephis.

"I'll talk to my resource people and do my best," stated Cifelli as he walked his guests to the door.

That final note sounded reassuring for Cephis and Sid because they knew to which source Cifelli was referring – the Noble Foundation. It easily had the funds to reimburse them for their watered-down, paltry labors and lavish Graffham and Black Hills with a big bonus. If Graffham was still on the Board of the Noble Foundation, he might even be able to pad his own bill. It was all in service to science and public beneficence. If the Noble Foundation would cough up the dough, the *Acrocanthosaurus*, the rarest apex predator in the world, could adorn the showroom of the Sam Noble Museum to enchant and enthrall Oklahomans from near and far for decades to come.

The meeting ended on a cordial and positive note. As usual, the two spirited naturalists would have to sit and wait for some backroom decision to filter out into the stale Oklahoma air. They felt certain that if the decision were totally up to Cifelli, they might as well scratch off the sale. But if he turned the proposition over to the Nobles, perhaps they, with their nobility, gentility, and generosity, might see it differently. In the meantime, all the bone salesmen could do was wait and hope.

CHAPTER SIXTY
Legal Intercession

In the final minutes of the meeting with Cifelli, Cephis requested that the museum contact them within two weeks with an answer. When the two weeks elapsed and the salesmen received no reply from the university, they got edgy. The respectful thing for the institution to do was to give the two men a courtesy call and brief them on the status of the proposal. Was the proposition even being considered?

Cephis decided to sit tight for another week. He realized it would take time for the museum staff to discuss the full ramifications of such a purchase. Besides, Graffham needed to be contacted and arrangements worked out; and still more time was needed to relay the proposal to the potential donors – namely, the Noble Foundation – and even additional time for discussion on their end.

At least Cephis managed to work out new arrangements with his mortgage lender. Additional time was accorded, but refinance charges and late fees were incurred. Interest was now accruing at 10% per annum on $65,000. The longer Graffham deferred his debt obligation, the more Cephis became saddled with debt. Also, Sid's cancer, which was thought to be in remission, was back with a vengeance, and he was growing weaker by the day. Again, it would be necessary for Cephis to carry the weight of the obtruding overhang of bones.

Cephis knew the decision was not up to Dr. Cifelli but the Noble Foundation, the museum benefactors who held the purse strings. He waited still longer for a courtesy call, but none came. Obviously, he needed to contact the curator and inquire about the status. Things did not look promising. Were the Nobles not interested in enhancing the highly regarded science museum which bore their name?

Rather than call the university personally, Cephis decided to have a neutral third party make the contact. He chose Steve Due, a long-time associate and family friend, to make the inquiry.

Steve Due was the nephew of Lemuel Due, one of the big-time moonshiners of the county during the era when moonshine was the prime cash commodity. Lemuel was a top-of-the-line moonshine crafter, and his clandestine product was nationally famous. He was practically a legend in his own right. In the more colorful era of Lemuel's moonshine empire, timber and liquor dominated the local economy. Now, alcohol had been supplanted by marijuana, while timber was fading and poultry flourished.

Connoisseurs and dabblers in his drink, as well as outright alcoholics and white lightning freaks, were on Due's waiting list. People from all over Oklahoma, Arkansas, Louisiana, and Texas drove hundreds of miles to buy a few cases, or, if short on cash, merely a few bottles. Many prominent people partook of Lemuel's craft. Orval Faubus, the notorious governor of Arkansas and arch-segregationist of the 1950s, was a prime customer. Specially custom-blended and aged whiskey was set aside for his indulgence.

Many other prominent people were on the list. Governors and judges in surrounding states made personal calls to Mr. Due. Perhaps it was these widespread political and judicial connections that kept Lemuel out of the purview of the courts for decades, but eventually the law caught up with him and he served time in Leavenworth, Kansas.

As for Lemuel's nephew Steve, he was considered a local eccentric genius, a sober thinker, and philosopher of sorts – homegrown, yes; cracker barrel, no. He had once made good money as an engineer, consultant, and technocrat within the vast corporate-military-industrial complex, but had since fallen on hard times. Some locals now considered him a recluse. Nevertheless, Steve was an ardent rock hound and amateur geologist, and had accompanied Cephis on many treasure hunts.

Steve Due, a man of brilliant intellect even though his star was waning, made the call. He did not talk to Cifelli. Instead, he talked to a manager of finance who dispersed funds for natural treasures. The response Steve received was stark: "We're not in the habit of buying stolen property."

Upon hearing this, Due knew the cause was hopeless. He hated to relay that kind of message to Cephis and Sid, but knew the two men banked on the truth. It would be useless to sugarcoat or tweak the response.

Due pondered the nature of the answer and questioned whether this was really the attitude of the Noble Foundation or simply an insider sentiment?" He suspected the latter. Steve knew that the Nobles practiced an old-style southern chivalry—nobles oblige, but they had been factored out of the equation.

When Cephis was informed of the retort, he too doubted that the Noble Foundation had even been contacted. Apparently somebody at OU didn't appreciate the two amateur traders or their paleontological product, and their inherent bias coated the coarseness of the response. Was it Cifelli, Mares, or somebody else? It didn't matter; the two men had to move on.

What would they do now? Would they continue looking for a new buyer or jump back into the legal morass? Cephis and Sid still distrusted the legal system and did not want to go there. But what other choice did they have? LeForce and Company had jilted them, so they needed to find new representation. But where? And how could they afford it? Another bleak, perplexing pall hung over the amateurs. But that was nothing new – just the same old predicaments and blowbacks they had perennially experienced in their decade-long journey to wrest the dinosaur and recoup their investment.

Sid, who possessed more resources than Cephis, still maintained the same morbid skepticism about legal experts – perhaps even more so – but now he had major medical expenses and needed his resources to pay medical bills.

Cephis stoically called Honeywell to inform him of OU's answer. Honeywell was not surprised, but had something to say. "Dammit, you've got to do it. I know you don't like dealing with lawyers, but you've got to give Eric (Honeywell's son-in-law attorney) a call. I talked to him, and he has been waiting on your call. He will shoot straight with you and help you."

Cephis concurred. "Jim, I don't have any place else to turn. I will call him tomorrow."

A contention over the bones had transformed into a contention over money – via the contest regarding payment of the outstanding loan owed by Graffham. There was no question that Graffham owed the money, but how could the two men enforce the contract without getting tied up in expensive litigation? They needed a new legal voice strong enough to compel Graffham to perform his fiduciary duty.

Eric Gray practiced law in Oklahoma City and normally represented big corporations. But sometimes he handled cases at a deep discount for small-time clients like Hall and Love against powerful corporate interests, or even pro bono for financially destitute clients. Given Hall and Love's unraveling financial situation, perhaps they qualified. Honeywell had put in the good word. What in the way of legal services might that good word bring?

Gray was no small-town lawyer who relied on backslapping and backroom deal making to settle a case. He was a sophisticated metropolitan attorney who had been tested in the big leagues and relied on par excellence legal finesse to win cases. The momentum of his legal prowess carried him and his cases forward. He had an excellent track record and a distinguished career.

Cephis called Mr. Gray the following morning and liked what he heard. Gray was offering to intercede on his behalf not for a sharply discounted rate, but pro bono. This was a kindly act of legal charity. Of course, Cephis was no moocher. He was willing to accept a short-term fix in the way of a minor or quick legal intervention over a gnawing, long-term contract violation, but if more extensive legal involvement was necessary, arrangements needed to be made so his legal representative could be compensated.

Gray's response went right to the heart of the matter: "Either Graffham's going to pay you, or you're going to get your skeleton back. If you don't get your skeleton back, you're going to own a part of Geological Enterprises. I will prepare a brief, a so-called Letter of Demand concerning the eminent commencement of suit, for you to present to Mr. Graffham. I suggest that you hand deliver it to him and tell him if he has any questions to call me. If he doesn't come back with a credible response, we will move to the next step. In case we have to proceed further, I will enclose a proposed fee engagement letter for your review and mail the package in a few days. If you have any questions feel free to call me."

In addition to that, Gray provided legal advice and instructions pertaining to various related topics such as a power of attorney, trusts, and incorporation as possible avenues of recourse to protect their interests in the dinosaur.

The letter, provided on behalf of Hall and Love, was addressed to Allan Graffham and his attorney, Kenneth Delashaw, and was blunt and to the point. The letter stated in part.... "Based on a review of the contract and the correspondence between the parties, it appears there has been a failure of consideration and/or breach of the contract by Mr. Graffham and Geological Enterprises Incorporated." In the final paragraph, the letter further proclaimed, "In light of the above, demand is hereby made upon Mr. Graffham and Geological Enterprises Incorporated for rescission of the contract. Alternatively, demand is hereby made for immediate payment to Mr. Love and Mr. Hall of the balance of the purchase price, plus damages for non-delivery of a cast of the dinosaur in the total sum of $500,000. Unless rescission or payment is made within (10) days from the date of this letter, suit will be commenced accordingly. If you have any questions please do not hesitate to contact the undersigned." Very Truly Yours, Eric S. Gray."

Sid, upon receiving news about the letter, insisted that he personally deliver it to the slacker. He now felt strong enough to make the drive to Ardmore and as soon as he could make an appointment he would be on his way. This was his way of lifting some of the burden off Cephis. Cephis consented, but he was concerned about the strain on Sid.

When Sid hand delivered the demand letter Graffham was taken aback and looked at Sid with a tinge of trepidation.

After reading it he asked Sid, "Would Cephis really do this to me?"

Sid responded, "Yes, he has no choice. Cephis and I are in need of the money and we are ready to enforce the contract to get it. Frankly, I feel you have taken advantage of Cephis' good nature. If you do not comply, we will see you in court. You have ten days."

Sid then quietly walked off, leaving Graffham alone with his thoughts.

Graffham was concerned because he recognized the name of the attorney – Eric S. Gray – and knew that Gray did not play games. The man took his legal responsibilities seriously. This was the same Eric Gray who had ignited a fire under Arkla Gas, a Jerry Jones company. Jones was the Arkansas oilman and big-time sports franchiser who utilized the largesse of taxpayers to construct high-dollar sports domes for his favorite team – the Dallas Cowboys.

Gray had won a few high-profile cases for small-time litigants, like Hall, against powerful corporations. Corporate tycoons across the state paid attention when Gray's name was mentioned. They were afraid of court-ordered restitution. Graffham now took heed. He had only ten days to act.

First he called Cephis, and this time the roles were reversed. Instead of Cephis begging for remuneration, Graffham was pleading for time and clemency. Cephis now established the tone and terms while Graffham listened submissively. Cephis' words were short and brutal. "You have ten days to pay us the balance due, or we will turn this affair over to you-know-who (Mr. Gray)."

"Can we work out some kind of payment plan? I will get some money on the table very shortly," squawked Graffham.

"Well, you may present your proposal to us, but if we don't like it, we will insist on payment in full," explained Cephis.

Graffham had other commitments at the time and did not wish to hand over $200,000 in one lump sum. He wanted to drag the payment plan out for another two years.

"I will see what I can do and get back with you soon. Please don't do anything rash," concluded Graffham.

Graffham wanted no part of dealing with Mr. Gray. He contacted his own attorney, Ken Delashaw, and the two men discussed the predicament. They needed thirty days instead of ten to come up with a new payment plan. Although the fire was lit by Gray, they now turned to a more palatable firm, where deal making and more flexible terms could be attained. Delashaw immediately contacted LeForce by letter and phone in an attempt to reestablish an old legal precedent and more friendly tone.

Theoretically, at least the way Graffham and Delashaw saw it (or wanted to see it), LeForce and Associates was still the legal representative of Hall and Love. It was through LeForce that the original contract and terms had been drafted, the lawsuit crafted, the case settled, and the proceeds of the down payment distributed. LeForce still had a vested interest in the disbursement of the payments. It would be to Graffham's advantage to utilize the intercession of LeForce in an effort to keep Gray at bay. In an attempt to get him off their backs, they would sway and court LeForce.

Delashaw, in an effort to placate Gray and the contractual parties, sent a written plea to LeForce, apologizing for his client. There was an uneasy tone as denoted by the posturing and phrasing used to explain his client's unique pinch and difficulty in marketing the dino. In a letter dated March 20, 1991, Ken Delashaw (the future District Judge of Love County) obtained a reprieve for his client by ironing out the details with LeForce, who had reinstituted his services in lieu of Gray. Gray was waiting on the sidelines to see what happened. Cephis held his breath.

In a conciliatory tone, Delashaw's plea on behalf of his client pointed out the delicate difficulties of marketing the specimen and the limited market for un-prepared dinosaur skeletons. He further remonstrated, by citing an article in the *Daily Ardmoreite* and naming Professor Cifelli, the unkindly distractions of newspaper articles about foreign buyers, which set a discordant tone for intricate negotiations with potential American buyers.

Delashaw further added, "We respectfully ask your clients to forego any further communication with anyone save and except through you, as their attorney concerning this matter, for a period of at least thirty days in order that my client may secure a contract for the purchase of the fossil."

LeForce was amenable to a thirty-day delay in implementing new financial terms suitable to all parties. He had already waited more than two years for his fees, so why not wait two more? With the amiable consent of LeForce, Graffham was given a little breathing room. When the news finally reached Cephis, he relented. What else could he do? Lawyers have a way of working things out behind closed doors to their clients' satisfaction, and sometimes, their detriment.

And so it was. Graffham got his thirty days, and he and his attorney came up with a suitable payment plan. They wanted to make semi-annual payments of $50,000 each over a two-year period. Of course, LeForce and Hamilton would get their share of the proceeds as attorneys' fees. To seal the deal, Graffham had $50,000 ready to lay down on the table. A meeting of the minds occurred. Graffham was now serious about paying off the loan as the revised financing arrangement stipulated.

As Graffham had promised, in less than two weeks he delivered a check for $50,000 to the law office of Carl LeForce. LeForce called his two estranged clients in and distributed the proceeds according to the original terms. Naturally, LeForce took his cut (about $15,000) and paid the remainder to the two debt-strapped and legal-weary combatants. Graffham was on his way toward redemption. Now he could rest easily; Gray wouldn't be coming after him, at least not anytime soon.

Cephis was relieved that he and Sid did not have to find another buyer, and was glad that the sale to Cifelli had fallen through. Even without paying LeForce the oppressive legal fees, they would have realized a significantly smaller return on their gritty-soiled investment. They had learned the basics of dinosaur finance the hard way.

Still, he wondered, what happened to the Nobles? Why were they not interested in funding the purchase of the Acro for their own magnificent museum? Were the Nobles even contacted? Cephis knew how to find out. He actually had a contact with the Noble Foundation, and it wasn't through Graffham.

Joe Lobell was the communications director of the Noble Foundation and a personal friend who knew about the business matters that sifted through the foundation's communications network.

Lobell was also the communications director of Ouachita Tours, Hall's own fledgling charitable institution. Joe was a producer of low-budget documentaries and videotaped Hall's nature tours conducted along the winding course of the scenic Glover River.

Cephis finally asked Lobell if the Noble Foundation had been contacted about purchasing the Acro for what was believed a bargain basement price. "No," he declared, "the foundation had not been contacted and no proposal had been submitted."

Lobell was stunned and disappointed to learn that the museum actually had a chance to buy the specimen. The Noble Foundation might have actually funded the dino purchase had it been asked. The answer did not surprise Cephis, who was glad the deal had fallen through. He had underpriced the Acro. Cifelli, or somebody, had done him a favor.

CHAPTER SIXTY-ONE
To the Core of the Bones

The bones of the Acro had been shuffled from place to place – from private storage buildings to the lab of a great academic institution, and were now housed at one of the most respected commercial fossil preparation facilities in the world. The fate of the bones had been transacted through the hands of two obscure amateurs, an omnipotent corporate timber baronage, academia, the Oklahoma legislature, the legal system, a prominent fossil merchant, and had finally come under the care of the scientists and lab technicians at the Black Hills Institute (BHI).

The various caretakers of the bones had blazed a suspenseful paleontological trail with wailing episodes of travail confronting them all along the way. The story had incorporated a whole confounding comportment of protagonists and antagonist – heroes and villains – depending on the partisan minds of the viewer. Diverse and obverse contestants and role players had stepped into vacuums and open pits, seeking clarity and deliverance. The struggle for control and ownership of the skeleton had engendered an assortment of losers, as the winners progressed toward the final stage of the drama. The winners, while trying to consolidate gains, mitigate losses, and move on to the next level of the contest, suffered duress as powerful extraneous forces complicated matters and obstructed progress. In the long path across the discovery, recovery and preparatory phases, losers in the contest fell by the wayside, while the survivors grasped for straws in monetary, legal, technical and marketing forums.

The endeavor to save the bones had started out as a laborious chore by two rustic backwoodsmen, traveling through several distinct junctures before finally ending up at Black Hills. It was here where labor again became the prime factor in the story of the dinosaur as it underwent massive treatment to eliminate the perfidious pyrite affliction. The destiny of the bones now rested in the hands of lab technicians whose efforts were being funded by Sir Allan Graffham of Geological Enterprises. It was the business of BHI to collect, conserve, curate and display extraordinary geological and natural history specimens. The expert Terry Wentz would play a major role in the preservation of the specimen, particularly the skull.

Pyrite, an inherently unstable material found in the form of iron sulfide can decompose quickly under the right conditions. When iron sulfide combines with water from the air, sulfuric acid is created, which slowly dissolves bone. As the bone and pyrite dissolve, calcium sulfate is created. As calcium sulfate (a gypsum) disperses, bones can split apart. In conjunction with pyrite, moisture and temperature variations in the environment can accelerate the process and cause the fossils to expand and contract, eventually causing breakage or disintegration.

White-robed men and women of BHI now delved into the core of the dark bones: grinding, drilling, sanding, scraping, chipping, brushing, polishing and finishing the raw product via the use of small tools and instruments much like those used by a dentist. The bones had turned jet black by minerals migrating in ground water through the sediment in which they had lain for millennia. Such a tone imparted a mysterious aura to an already intriguing paleontological enticement.

The profuse pyrite (iron disulfide) grew out of and around the bones like moss on a rock. When the pyrite was pulverized and removed, acids were subsequently released into the air. Technicians wore respirators and tried to seal off the bones in vacuum boxes. Baking soda was used to remove debris from around the fossils.

A team of expert caretakers were given the task of saving the prized specimen and invested thousands of hours in the painstaking process of cleaning the fossils, restoring the skeleton, and creating a museum-quality mount. The Acro was on its way to becoming a showpiece specimen as a quality cast replica. Molds were made of the bones —and missing pieces—to provide a complete cast skeleton for exhibition.

To make a mold, a clay base is built around each bone, then silicon rubber is poured around the clay base so that the liquid enters every crack and crevice. When it is completely set, a perfect replica is created. In this way, hard plastic casts are made ready for mount. BHI had taken on a job that most paleontologists said could not be done: they defied the scientific establishment by endeavoring to preserve the Acro. The project turned out to be one of the most difficult the institute ever undertook.

As Sid and Cephis awaited full recovery of their investment and Graffham nervously anticipated a finished product, dark clouds descended on the horizon. The road toward final recovery and preservation would not go easy.

CHAPTER SIXTY-TWO
Dark Forces Converge

At Black Hills Institute, while the specimen was being treated and prepared, the scientific world learned about the discovery: the most complete Acro skull and skeleton ever found. The bones were inventoried and made available for examination. Scientists inquired and peered into the bone assemblage while studies of the giant carnivore were undertaken. The story of the Acrocanthosaurus gradually reached the outer periphery of the scientific establishment.

The so-called "Terror of the South" was classified within the following beastly genre: Order: Saurischia; Suborder: Theropodia; Family: Allosauridae; Genus: Acrocanthosaurus; Species: Atokensis. It was found in the Paluxy Sandstone (approximate to the Antlers formation) of the early Cretaceous and was related to the Jurassic *Allosaurus* and the mid-Cretaceous African dinosaur *Carcharondontosaurus saharicus*. The specimen had nearly complete arms and shoulder girdles. It also showed evidence of a near-fatal hunting accident in a punctured shoulder blade and several broken ribs that had healed.

The specimen was believed to be a female. Female dinosaurs were usually bigger and better fighters than males, probably a result of having gained more experience fighting to protect their young. Males had more color and adornment: more plumage like male birds.

BHI was world famous for its specialized work with theropods, particularly the T.rex. The facility has been involved with the excavations of at least nine T.rex skeletons since 1990, including Sue, Stan, Bucky, Duffy and Wyrex. These five are among the top ten most complete T. rexes in the world.

Certainly T.rex was more famous, but the Acro was more rare and mysterious. For a while, during the early 1990s, the Acro was the center of attention at the BHI complex. Although it was not owned by the institute, it was a world class specimen that deserved first-class treatment, especially with a high-profile client like Graffham footing the bill. But while the Acro, named "Fran" after Mr. Graffham's wife, was entering the last stages of its remediation regimen, a new theropod was brought in and became the star attraction in competition for expert intervention.

The new trophy, "Sue," was a T.rex and had been named for Pete Larson's girlfriend, Sue Hendrickson. It was she who had first stumbled across its remains while on a hiking expedition in the nearby plains and was credited with the discovery. Although

T.rex was not a novelty, this specimen was unique: the biggest and baddest T.rex ever found and 90% complete, also a record. The Black Hills team had dug up the remains of the creature from a nearby cliff and brought it to the institute's workroom. The giant carnivore now occupied a large space in the central core of the first floor. The Acro would now take a back seat to this marvelous creature from the late Cretaceous. BHI had taken on the burden of simultaneously preserving and preparing two of the greatest theropod specimens in history, all under one roof.

Sue was owned by BHI, while Fran was owned by an outside private investor who was distracted by a lien on the treasure. The fossil preservation center was now pressed to bless both specimens with its utmost devotion. The staff was spread thin, but the work had to be done. Big hopes and dreams now rested on the backs of these two great monsters from the prehistoric past. The institute was in a unique situation.

A specimen like Fran or Sue came once in a century, but suddenly BHI had two of them housed in its facility at the same time. The staff now had to put in more hours as the work continued on both specimens. Thousands of hours would be expended in the preparation of these two foremost dinosaurian predators.

To gain possession of Sue, Pete Larson had paid the owner of the land, Maurice Williams, a Sioux Indian of mixed blood, for the paleontological rights to dig and recover the trophy, but the transaction concealed a hidden problem. Williams had previously placed the land in trust to the federal government; as a result, the land became part of tribal lands within the exterior boundaries of the Cheyenne River Sioux Reservation. The trust arrangement prohibited the sale of the land to a non-Indian without the permission of the Bureau of Land Management. Williams did not secure permission to sell the dino to Larson.

The dinosaur, it could be argued, was fixed to the land or was incidental or appurtenant to it and therefore could be construed as real property. The Federal Antiquities Act of 1906 – at least in the minds of some legal experts – supposedly prohibited the removal of fossils from any lands owned or controlled by the federal government, including trust land.

Federal authorities became privy to the transaction between Larson and Williams. The transaction had, with this revelation, sown seeds of destruction for Larson and his business. In May of 1992, two agents approached Larson and handed him a search warrant, alleging he committed felonies by stealing from government and tribal lands and had violated the Antiquities Act. The warrant demanded that the fossil remains of the T.rex commonly referred to as Sue and other fossil specimens taken from the excavation site on the property of Maurice Williams be handed over to federal agents. A raid on the Institute ensued.

Twenty-five gun-wielding FBI agents descended on the premises. The facility was cordoned off with yellow evidence tape. Sue was loaded into boxes, hoisted onto flatbed trailers, and hauled away by the National Guard while 200 men, women, and children protested outside the building.

The magnificent Sue was gone. The remains of Fran still lay unmolested on the workbenches inside the preparation room, but the feds had eyed it and were now questioning its legitimacy as well. The feds were not finished. The Acro treasure was still threatened by federal confiscation. The nightmare had not yet ended. Larson and Black Hills were under investigation.

CHAPTER SIXTY-THREE
The Dinosaur Tempest – The Feds Move In

Like obsessed storm troopers, the feds poured into Hill City, South Dakota and demanded reams of documents and records in a quest for criminal evidence. They had taken a look around, seized Sue, and were now inquiring into the origins and circumstances regarding the other dinosaurs housed at BHI. Even the Acro came under scrutiny and it too was threatened with seizure when the feds struck a second time on June 8, 1992. During this second whirlwind, thirty FBI agents unceremoniously revisited the scene with another search warrant and began invasively scouring the premises.

The agents spent seven hours collecting fossils and documents, loading them into more than 50 boxes, then carried them out to trucks to be transported away. Again, a portion of the institute was cordoned off with yellow tape and Hill City residents protested vociferously. The agents were referred to as the "Keystone Cops" by one prominent local attorney, but the feds had the upper hand. (Fiffer 135)

When the coterie of FBI agents, sheriff's deputies and national guardsmen started to take possession of the Acro, attendants rushed to protect the treasure with their bodies while scurrying to present documentation showing that the Acro specimen was not actually owned by the institute. With much imploring, BHI finally persuaded the feds that the Acro had not been dug, bought or traded by BHI, but that the institute was merely a contractor providing preparation services for the specimen's real owner, Allan Graffham (and lien holders Sid Love and Cephis Hall). The agents first balked, but eventually backed off.

When it was all said and done, the halls of BHI seemed devoid of treasure. The greatest T.rex in history had been carted off and would never return. The staff was startled and bewildered, and the townsfolk bereaved and perturbed.

The staff mulled over several questions and concerns. What would happen to Sue, and would the federal bone snatchers return to seize Fran? Would the feds go the full course? Would they come back and confiscate everything merely to demonstrate their power? The scientists knew that it was not the agents who were to blame; after all, they were merely following orders. Federal judicial authorities were pulling the strings. This sordid, nightmarish affair was about to become a legal fiasco. The Larson brothers and staff at BHI braced themselves and awaited their fate.

A forthcoming 33-page, 39-count indictment would name Pete Larson, Neal Larson, Bob Farrar, Terry Wentz and BHI in 154 separate offenses alleging improper transactions involving the sale or purchase of fossils. Larson counter-sued for custody of Sue and garnered his legal defense. (Fiffer 146)

The fossils listed in the indictment included Triceratops, duck-bills, mosasaurs, whales, turtles, ammonites, crinoids and catfish allegedly collected illegally from public and private lands in South Dakota, Wyoming, Montana and Nebraska. Some of the fossils had been sold to the Smithsonian Institution and Field Museum. But the feds had no clear evidence in a single instance that the institute had intentionally or knowingly collected, purchased or sold illegally obtained fossils. The alleged crimes for theft could potentially earn Pete Larson 353 years in prison and $13 million in fines. Larson would need big-time legal representation to stave off federal prosecution on what he and many others believed were bogus charges.

The bones of Sue were stored in a desolate warehouse at the School of Mines in Rapid City. As lawyers wrangled and the ownership controversy played out over several years, Sue lay in a degenerative state as a crop of pyrite-coated, untended bones.

The longest and costliest criminal trial in South Dakota history got underway. The decision was left to a jury supposedly comprised of Pete Larson's peers. After millions of dollars were spent prosecuting and attempting to convict Larson and BHI, only two minor misdemeanor convictions were obtained. After hundreds of thousands were spent on the defense, the jury dismissed. Pete Larson and BHI were exonerated on all federal charges of stealing bones on government land.

Neither the Larsons nor BHI was ever compensated in any form for their excavation and preservation work to rescue and preserve Sue – some 5,630 hours in total. A suit for a mechanics lien to cover the institute's expenses was thrown out of court. The ownership issue was finally settled in favor of Maurice Williams, who garnered all the proceeds (minus commissions) from the sale of Sue to the highest bidder at a Sotheby's auction. The Field Museum paid $8.36 million for the monstrous T.rex named Sue – the highest price ever paid for a dinosaur specimen.

CHAPTER SIXTY-FOUR
A Buyer Steps Forward

Allan Graffham was a shrewd and astute businessman. He knew all the tricks of the trade – in the field, in the lab, in the market, and in the world of dinosaur high-finance. A couple of prodding and hungry rock hounds were nothing more than a petty annoyance. Cash flow was everything. He would pay Black Hills on an expedient timeframe suitable to his needs; as for the rock hounds, he would throw them a few scraps when he got good and ready. Graffham would pay the lien holders in full only when he collected all his monies from the sale of the dinosaur, and even then he wouldn't be in a hurry.

The sale of Sue had whetted scientific and curatorial appetites. There was only one successful bidder – the Field Museum. And they had gone over the top – to the tune of 8.6 million dollars – to purchase the magnificent beast. Every buyer has a limit on how much can be spent to obtain a rare, world-class paleontological mint. Some of the losers in the bid for Sue still sought a comparable prize they thought might dazzle and enchant their audience.

Naturally, it was always better if a dinosaur could be credited as being a former native of a particular state, region, or community. Such recognition bestows a feeling of identification and imparts community pride. Why else would states brandish and extol such symbols as state dinosaurs, state fossils, state birds, state flowers, etc.? It was all about state heritage and state prestige. "Look at this monstrous local denizen from the ancient past; it trampled across this very landscape where we now stand." "It's unique! It's magnificent! It's ours!"

North Carolinian museum curators had certainly picked up on the cue. Although they had lost out in the bidding frenzy for Sue, they still wanted a marvelous manifestation of beastly preeminence to showcase in their new natural science museum slated to open in 1999.

The benefactors for the $55 million N.C. Museum of Natural Science were in the market for the right kind of dinosaur for the right price. They didn't want to get caught up in another frenetic bidding war against wealthy individuals and institutions with more financial muscle. They began searching the lofts, nooks, and crannies of paleontological labs and storage rooms for something that would suit their needs.

When the North Carolinian contingent located the Acro at BHI, they knew they had found their dinosaur. It was a perfect match for their situation. The specimen fit the bill as a star attraction in every conceivable way. The Friends of the Museum, a non-profit support group of anonymous donors, were ready to put their money where their patriotic fervor lied by supporting a project denoting state pride.

They propitiously made their purchase offer while the specimen was still in the planning-preparation phase, rather than after it hit the auction floor as a full cast mount. A bidding war always escalated the price. The specimen might be purchased as an unfinished product in the lab for less than half of what it might bring at a high-class auction like Sotheby's.

While turmoil and confusion still buzzed all around the Black Hills facility, the North Carolinians investigated the prospect and made their move. As long as the feds did not return to seize the Acro, Black Hills was set to accommodate the proposed purchase arrangement.

The offering price was $3 million as the Acro lay dressed-out on the workbenches, but BHI would be required to complete the process and provide a quality finished product. Graffham relented, although he might've been able to get considerably more for the finished specimen on the auction block. A solid contract now was better than an "uncertainty" being dragged into the dismal future. Besides, two strapping rock hounds nipped at his heels. If everything worked according to plan, the "Beast of the Southeast" was headed for a new state-of-the-art museum at Raleigh, N.C., in the southeastern United States. Cephis had always said that if the beast could not stay in Oklahoma, he at least wanted it to go to a reputable institution like the University of North Carolina. The price of $3 million was reported to be the second highest price ever paid for a preserved dinosaur and the highest price ever paid for an unfinished and uncast specimen still in the preparation stage.

Restoration expenses were projected to be about one million dollars, which meant Graffham could pay off the two hungry hounds and pocket at least $1.5 million. After socking in almost two million, what was a measly $200,000 to be paid to the lien holders? It was nothing more than a drip, or short-term blip, in an otherwise free-flowing cash faucet.

But the deal could not be finalized until BHI put on the finishing touches and certified the Acro as fit, clean, and clear of all tarnish and pyrite. It was one of those contingency deals where the bargain was made but the deal not sealed until all the conditions were met. Although the agreement was made in late 1992, it would still be several years before a finished product was attained and the funds transacted. Graffham could rest on his own laurels; he had plenty of money to tide him over.

The museum's financial backers were excited over the prospect. "If we had the first pick in the dinosaur draft there is no doubt that we would have selected this one," said John McMillan, president of the Friends of the Museum. "It's equally as large and ferocious as T.rex, but unlike that dino (a native of the western U.S.), Acrocanthosaurus likely lived in North Carolina. Plus, there is no other mountable Acrocanthosaurus in the world at this time. Its rarity makes it extremely valuable to science." (Press Release, North Carolina Museum of Natural Sciences)

"The Museum's specimen is the most complete early Cretaceous large carnivore ever found in North America," said Dr. Dale Russell, the Museum's senior curator of paleontology. "The skeleton can be used for comparative anatomical studies. The ancient coastal plains where the "Acro" hunted are now submerged, making discovery of their bones nearly impossible."

Russell continued: "A delta containing sediments the same age as those where Acro was found lies buried under the waters of Pamlico and Albemarle Sound. It's the right age, contains evidence of similar environments, and probably also Acro bones, but they are hidden from us." (Press Release, N.C. Museum of N. S.)

The new $55 million Museum of Natural Sciences in Raleigh was to be four times larger than the existing facility. The state legislature had earmarked construction funds of $31 million. The Museum was purchasing the original inventory of treated bones and a cast replica of the fossil for traveling exhibitions at a bargain of $3 million dollars. If the deal was sealed, Fran would find a new home as a patriotic symbol of the southeastern United States, part of her regional homeland.

CHAPTER SIXTY-FIVE
Acrocanthosaurus Versus T-Rex

Tyrannosaurus Rex and *Acrocanthosaurus*, two of the greatest terrestrial theropod predators of all natural history, arouse great curiosity and controversy. Both were the dominant terrestrial apex predators of their day. *Acrocanthosaurus* was the king of the early Cretaceous, whereas T.rex sat on the throne in the late Cretaceous. When the paleontologists weigh in, there are differences of opinion which elicit considerable debate and dissension. How would these two great monsters stack up in a contest for the heavyweight championship of beastly pugilistic combat?

T.rex gets all the press and glory. Is it just a matter of habit of mind, attention deficit disorder, closed-mindedness, or a form of xenophobia or nationalistic fervor? T.rex was pure North American and went down in the dino holocaust 65 mya at the close of the late Cretaceous, but *Allosaurus* and *Acrocanthosaurus* were also North American, just of an earlier age. Why do patriots always exclude them? Is T.rex overrated? Is it unpatriotic to worship another beastly icon?

Carcharodontosaurus "shark-toothed lizard" and *Giganotosaurus* were equally fearsome and equivalent in stature, if not larger, than T.rex. Why are they never mentioned? The answer is rather obvious: *Carcharodontosaurus* is African, while *Giganotosaurus* is South American. Students can understand this; it is question of national pride, if not racism. Despite its size, another African, *Spinosaurus*, does not measure up as a deadly land killer. More swamp and water niched, it ate more fish than red hot flesh. It was more like a giant crocodile that occasionally walked upright.

When the Jurassic is mentioned, *Allosaurus* gets listed, but what about the early Cretaceous? Conjure up the early Cretaceous, and Acro doesn't register. Why not? The reason may lie in the fact that it is a relatively new discovery and has not yet caught on in the public's fancy or limited imagination. Or is there so much obsession and fascination with T.rex that patriots can't shake the mystique loose or be distracted long enough to recognize the merits of the magnificent "beast from the Southeast?" North Carolinians certainly know about *Acrocanthosaurus*. She (Fran) is the prized exhibit of the North Carolina Museum of Natural Sciences in Raleigh.

Acrocanthosaurus, Allosaurus, Giganotosaurus, and Carcharodontosaurus are all proven predators with the great attributes and tools of terror and fleshly indulgence. What about Oklahoma's state fossil, *Saurophaganax?* Perhaps it is just an overgrown specimen of *Allosaurus*. All these fearsome predators have one thing in common: they are all related; not through direct descent, but as side branches from the same family tree. All were evolutionary dead ends, whereas T.rex did not merely die out; it was extinguished in a hellish inferno 65 mya. The tyrannical Rex lived only three to five million years before succumbing to a godly intervention. It did not live long enough for the workings of evolution and environmental change to take it down gradually. T.rex went out in a blaze of glory when the asteroid hit the earth.

While all these multi-national, unincorporated beasts were closely related and equally ferocious, they all stemmed from the same family of theropods. The allosauroids – Allo, Acro, Giga, and Carchar – were of the common carnosauria line of descent, whereas T.rex was an entirely different beast of a different race (coelurosaurian) and origin.

Although T.rex is a beloved national treasure – purely American and deemed worthy of worship as a patriotic icon, its tools of the trade are questioned, even impugned, by some noted paleontologists – namely the highly respected Jack Horner, who, like Robert T. Bakker, is on the cutting edge of new theories, new heresies, and new ideologies regarding dinosaurian hegemony. In paleontology, the debate lingers regarding the true nature of this beast. Was it a predator or scavenger?

The issue of predation was never in doubt for the *Allosaurus, Giganotosaurus, Acrocanthosaurus,* or the shark-toothed *Carcharodontosaurus.* The evidence is manifested in the serrations and cutting edges of their teeth. But T.rex is a different matter. Instead of knife-like slicers or thrashers, its giant conical teeth are shaped like railroad spikes or bananas – indisputably designed for bone crunching rather than meat dicing. Based on the "tale of the teeth," it is more hyena or vulture than lion.

Jack Horner, while committing outright heresy, continues to expound the theory that T.rex was an overrated, bone-crunching scavenger. If he is correct, the tale of two dinosaurs would suggest that the Acro is the greater and more ferocious predator, and would have an odds-on chance of dispatching T.rex and seizing its worn crown as the king of all earthly beasts.

Despite Horner's obstinacy, the experts continue to assert that T.rex was larger and fiercer than Acro, but does this reflect a true reading of the fossil record or some kind of patriotic bias? More than two dozen articulated skeletons of T.rex have been found. (In a century of searching, scientists have discovered over thirty T.rex specimens, with four exceeding sixty percent articulations.) T.rex is pervasive on the landscape in a relative paleontological sense, while the Acro is scarce. The measurements weigh in on T.rex and science knows the range. But with the Acro, only one articulated specimen over sixty percent complete has been discovered, and that one specimen alone was nearly the size of the largest T.rex (Sue) ever found. So without more sampling and comparisons, how can it be said incontrovertibly that the T.rex was indisputably larger than Acro? If objectivity prevails, the verdict on that question is still out.

Originally, the Acro was assigned to the allosauridae by Stovall and Langston, but later reassigned to the carcharodontosauridae by Sereno. But a new consensus seems to imply that the creature had characteristics of both divisions, but had more allosauridae characteristics than carcharodontosauridae – more North American than African. The Acro looked like a large *Allosaurus* with fins (or a ridge) on its back. It had a typical allosauroid skeleton, but its forelimbs were shorter and more robust than that of *Allosaurus*.

The Acro's brain was similar to the allosauroids and it had large and bulbous olfactory lobes, indicating it had a good sense of smell. The brain did not have much expansion of the cerebral hemisphere, more like a crocodile than a bird brain. That made sense; the Acro was a non-coelurosarian theropod. Its brain resembled the *Carcharondontosaurus* and the *Giganotosaurus* more than the *Allosaurus*. The Acro, as part of the carnosaurian branch of theropods, had no line of descent. Whereas the coelurosaurian branch, which included T.rex, gave rise to the avian dinosaurs that eventually became birds.

The Acro's close relative, the *Allosaurus* of the Jurassic, did not have good binocular (forward) vision; instead, it used lateral vision and probably had to wait until its prey came within sight to spring an ambush. Lateral vision means the eyes are on the sides of the head, rather than facing forward. The Acro's eyes were set more to the front than the Allo's; thus it was in evolutionary transition and on its way to obtaining true binocular vision. T.rex had binocular vision and likely had better eyesight and depth perception than the Acro.

The Acro's femur was longer than its tibia, suggesting it was not a very fast runner. But the monster did chase down prey; the fossil record confirms this. Fossilized footprints reveal that it ran alongside its prey, and then lunged laterally using its strong forelimbs to grip its victim. It attacked much like a modern lion attacks an antelope, only slower. It was a three-ton meat eater that left three-toed tracks. Its prey included 30- to 50 ton sauropods.

The Acro was about 13-14 feet tall from the ground to the top of the pelvis and about 40 feet long – slightly shorter on both measurements than the T.rex – at least based on current limited recordings of the fossil record. Its hind limbs were shorter than T.rex, but its forearms were longer, more muscular, and more powerful. The Acro had three wickedly curved claws on the ends of its forearms, whereas T.rex had only two-fingered forelimbs with less impressive claws.

The Acro was an active hunter. Paleontologists of the North Carolina Museum of Natural Sciences have identified four phases of the Acro's attack, which are elaborated in conjunction with the quite impressive Acro display at the museum. First, the Acro relentlessly stalked its prey and used precision strikes – not elegant or graceful, like a lion, but effective nonetheless. Once it sensed its prey from behind, it moved to the left and adjusted its position, then launched its vicious strike in planned precision – no mere wrestling match unless thwarted by a massive sauropod. Its teeth sank deeply into its victim's body while ripping the flesh apart at the same time its deadly claws clasped and thrust deeply into the unfortunate prey's flesh. While the prey was caught in the claws, the searing bite delivered the *coup d'etat* (*Acrocanthosaurus* exhibit, North Carolina Museum of Natural Sciences).

One bite ultimately proved fatal. As with T.rex, the efficient killer housed bacteria inside crevices of its teeth serrations which would later cause a deadly infection if the animal survived the initial attack. The Acro had only to defer its dinner and follow, but likely encountered other Acros or raptors in competition for the feast.

Big meat eaters must go after big animals to avoid expending too many calories while chasing smaller prey. T.rex, as a big, heavy, and bulky carnivore, would naturally use more energy in predation than a more streamlined animal like the Acro. A T.rex had to be on a more restrictive energy budget. T.rex, however, had one advantage: its bite force, which was a maximum of 4,000 pounds per square inch of force – the most powerful bite force of any known terrestrial animal. One bite from T.rex and it was all over. This may have been the reason why its forelimbs were so small – it didn't need them, natural selection had weeded them out. Although the bite force had rendered its forelimbs obsolete, this posed new challenges and questions. If T.rex ever fell down, it could not get up. In a chase, it had to get close enough for the bite because its forearms were of little value. In order to have been a true predator, T.rex had to be fast. But the speed of T.rex is in question. If it was as slow as the famed paleontologist Jack Horner suggests, it must have been a pure scavenger. However, there is an intermediary hypothesis that, if accurate, solves this puzzle to some degree.

The noted paleontologist Phil Curry has done extensive research on theropod hunting strategies and has posited some intriguing considerations. Curry believes T.rex hunted in packs. The juveniles were the stalkers and chasers; the adults, the ambushers. The juveniles and adults used teamwork in a highly efficient way to herd the game into a trap, garner the meat, and share the spoils. T.rex pre-adults were relatively fast and herded the game, while the adults, much heavier and slower, lay in ambush. It was a brilliant strategy demonstrating that T.rex was a social family animal with enough intelligence to strategize and organize its hunting technique. According to Curry, the T.rex was an opportunist – both predator and scavenger – depending on which stage of life the animal was in.

The teeth of the T.rex are consistent with this model. Its teeth changed as it progressed from a juvenile to adult – from seventeen meat-slicing teeth in each jaw as a juvenile to twelve bone-crunching teeth as a full grown adult. A hunter is more active than a scavenger and relies on fresh meat, rather than leftover bones.

The Acro, on the other hand, was more predator than scavenger, hunting in family pairs, or solitary, rather than in packs. The adult Acros must have been more active and better hunters than T.rex adults. As attackers of giant sauropods, they must have been more muscular and conditioned killers. Their arms were certainly stronger and their claws more deadly. While T.rex had the stronger bite, Acro had the stronger arms and was more agile and balanced – a true grappler of sauropods.

While the Acro ate sauropods, T.rex ate triceratopses – its teeth may have evolved to bite into the tough armor of the horned low grazer. Whereas T.rex was a chomping machine, the Acro was a slicing machine. The 60-ton *Sauroposeidon* was on the Acro menu. The Acro evolved to kill high browsers; the T.rex, low grazers.

According to Jack Horner, the T.rex did not fit the bill of a true predator; instead, it was pure scavenger. Horner maintains a rather irreverent and blasphemous attitude toward the "regal beast of theropodia." His heresy posits that the tiny arms of T.rex are inconsistent with predation and contends that most successful predators have large, powerful arms relative to body size. T.rex teeth, in the words of Horner, are designed for crunching bones, not tearing flesh from bones. Bones are what are left after the work of true predators. The typical teeth of predators are sharp with serrated edges, like steak knives. Bone crushers are scavengers, like hyenas and jackals. Even the T.rex's olfactory lobe is more consistent with that of a scavenger.

In any ecosystem, predators are extremely rare compared to plant eaters, but scavengers are common. T.rex olfactory bulbs were designed to smell carcasses at great distances, like a turkey vulture. This may explain why more T.rexes have been found than any other theropod; as scavengers, they were simply more plentiful.

It is not just olfactory lobes that tell the story, but optic lobes as well. In another disparaging snipe at the great icon of beastly dino-hood, Horner avers that the T.rex had very small optic lobes, suggesting poor eyesight. Other scientists disagree.

In the view of Horner, scavengers like buzzards or hyenas are scary, ugly, nasty-looking creatures that evolved to scare off predators that had already made the kill. T.rex was designed to seize or steal prey, not capture it. It was a matter of intimidation, in which a large and repulsive intruder startled and invaded the meal space of a carnivorous competitor. T.rex was built for long walking, not fast chasing. It was not very agile or swift and had small claws. Horner stated his case succinctly with these words: "The predators got the meat; and T.rex, the bones."

Dr. Rich Cifelli of the University of Oklahoma and Neal Larson of the Black Hills Institute disagree with Horner, and they are in the majority. But sometimes the majority is wrong. In a personal interview, Dr. Cifelli, highly dismissive of Horner's T.rex scavenger theory, scoffed "What has he been smoking?"

Dr. Kyle Davies, also of the University of Oklahoma, stated in a personal interview that T.rex was a better hunter and would likely prevail in an out-and-out fight with an Acro. Davies stated that T.rex was a later age predator and could have inherited or evolved more tricks of the trade in predation over time. That certainly seems true in regard to eyesight and pack hunting strategy, but may seem simplistic in other ways. Predators evolve and adapt to a specific ecosystem. The fine-tuning and improvement of its predatory skills are contingent on the features of the environment and the type of prey available. The Acro lived in a subtropical environment; the T.rex, in a drier climate. A wet climate has more flora and fauna and presents more opportunities for active predation, which allows a predator to hone its skills through extensive, hands-on experience.

Both the Acro and T.rex may have been slow, but T.rex was likely more lethargic and made fewer kills. The Acro would likely have the edge in aggressiveness, endurance, and fighting skills, but T.rex had an advantage in bite and weight. The outcome might boil down to speed and agility, but unless T.rex could score a knockout bite, the advantage would likely go to the more balanced, conditioned, and skilled Acro with its varied arsenal of weapons. While the T.rex was one dimensional, the Acro had all the ingredients for a successful hunter, and the better hunter would likely be the better fighter – like that of the lion and hyena. If Horner is right, the Acro would certainly prevail; if Cifelli, Larson, Davies, and most other paleontologists are right, the T.rex would win.

Despite its great hunting prowess, the Acro eventually lost out in the survival of the fittest, becoming extinct about 100 mya. Its origins and ancestors are still not clearly delineated. It likely inherited and revamped the best features of *Allosaurus* in order to rise to the top of the chain as heir to the throne following the downfall of *Allosaurus*. After its extinction, no other giant carnivorous theropod was known to have stepped into the vacuum as undisputed apex ruler of North America during this interregnum gap between Acro and T.rex.

The Acro was a more successful sauropod killer than *Allosaurus*, which accounts for its resilience and domination of the North American landscape for perhaps as long as 30 million years. T.rex had a reign of less than 4 million years, but might have ruled longer if the asteroid had not struck.

Although catastrophes play major roles in extinctions, the Acro's demise was more gradual than that of T.rex. Several factors simultaneously worked in conjunction to seal its fate. The migration or decline of the sauropods diminished its food supply. Climate change altered the flora and fauna, thus bringing it into direct competition with raptors. Large predators require large space and tend to be spread out over an extensive territorial range in a low-density population demographic. Any sudden adverse change in the environment makes these apex predators highly susceptible to population crashes because of their relatively slower reproduction rates.

Although the magnificence of *Acrocanthosaurus* reached an evolutionary dead end, it may have been the most successful and longest reigning apex predator in the history of the North American continent, perhaps even the entire planet. It was a step up in majesty and adaptive vigor over its smaller relative and predecessor, the *Allosaurus*. The creature deserves to be ranked at the top of "beastly preeminence" for the North American continent. It was a more compelling predator than T.rex. The successive dynasties of *Allosaurus* (Jurassic), *Acrocanthosaurus* (early Cretaceous), and T.rex (late Cretaceous) ruled supreme over the continent during their respective eras and represent a series of tyrannical kingships that took up the mantle when their predecessors faltered. This sequential threesome dominated the North American landscape for much of the dinosaurian age. Despite their longer reigns, the *Allosaurus* and *Acrocanthosaurus* are rarely mentioned in modern media. T.rex garners all the honor and recognition, despite its questionable credentials.

The tyrannosaurs are not related to the large predators of the Jurassic. They are derivatives of specialized, bird-like dinos – the raptors – that became smaller, lighter, and faster over millions of years before evolving feathers and taking to the air. The Jurassic dinosaurs like *Allosaurus*, a relative of *Acrocanthosaurs*, may have become too specialized to tweak their predatory techniques and evolve a new body plan in consonance with a changing hunting strategy and environment. Consequently, they underwent extinction.

Tyrannosaurs are a central Asian export. Scientists have traced their origin to the *Tarbosaurus*, who lived some 74 mya in Mongolia. The *Tarbosaurus* was the Rex of Asia and resembled the T.rex bone for bone, but was bulkier. The *Tarbosaurus Rex* made the journey across a temporary land bridge to North America and evolved to become the *Tyrannosaurus Rex* – the exalted iconic beast of the American empire. While the T.rex was an Asian transplant, the Acro's roots were likely in Africa.

The T.rex inspires the true spirit of the great American West and is equated with the American cowboy – a cowboy of lizards. The slightly smaller, but ready to rumble Acro is symbolic of the rebellious "Southern redneck." State geo-eccentrics partially lay behind the motivation for the North Carolina Museum of Science to purchase the Acro for 3 million dollars. The Acro was an ancient North Carolinian native and represented a manifestation of state pride. Hall and Love's Acro ended up as the showpiece specimen of North Carolina's greatest museum. It is the most complete early Cretaceous carnivore skeleton ever found. While the dearth of articulated regional skeletons from that era made it a state treasure, the creature remained largely unknown to the rest of America.

CHAPTER SIXTY-SIX
The Jewel of the Ouachitas

Once the dinosaur had been dug and spare time made available, Cephis and Sid were back in the hollows, hills, gullies, and cliffs looking for more treasure. Whereas they had traded a pursuit of mineralized treasure for that of fossilized investiture, they now reversed course and sought "jewels in the rough" – just like old times. It was far less stressful and demanding, and each excursion was an adventure in its own right. Something new was always hidden under the earth or around the bend and lured them into new places and new endeavors.

Although fossils were always an intriguing and enticing proposition, they now felt a touch of trepidation, as if some omen was attached to each relic. Cephis got somewhat nervous whenever he picked one up. Old memories of dinosaurian misery seemed to haunt him. Would he do it all again? Probably not.

He now knew what awaited a fossil-hunting adventurer who was bold enough to undertake an excavation of a bone quarry within the sovereign timber realm. Metals and minerals were back in vogue for the two backwoodsmen. New and old, abandoned mines dotted the landscape of southeastern Oklahoma, and the two men began to peer inside the shafts.

Mining for metals had once been a more practical economic endeavor in McCurtain County. Mines were economically feasible in the decades prior to the Great Depression. Lead, copper, and zinc were actively sought and commercially mined during those simpler times. During the Civil War, mining for lead was common because of the great demand for bullets. The vertical shafts are typically about 300 feet deep. Most of these old, abandoned mines are now full of water, and it is not feasible to pump them out. It is cheaper to import minerals from Mexico.

Potential mines abound in McCurtain County, but Weyerhaeuser is not interested in developing them. The mining of important minerals could mean good-paying jobs (certainly better than timber and chickens); however, there are numerous considerations and roadblocks. Although oil and gas might be more enticing and easier to extract, the area is environmentally sensitive because of its many streams and waterways. Locals have questioned whether or not mining of any kind can be done in a sound, ecological way. Cephis believed that it could, but it would be a real challenge. There are considerable environmental restrictions related to running water. Aerial herbicide spraying into the streams was one thing, releasing heavy metals into them, another.

Permit fees and start-up costs are burdensome, and heavy expenditures for equipment is necessary. Such investments require massive loan and debt exposure. Consequently, commercial mining is not seriously contemplated. For Cephis, it was a kind of economic bereavement as the local economy remained in bondage.

Cephis knew the potential. Even gold and silver were reachable. Hall had found gold veins in the back lanes of remote places and had gone to the trouble of having the rock material assayed in Elko, Nevada. The assayer said the gold content was mineable, even though it was of low grade, like most other mining veins. A reporter from the *Daily Oklahoman* once asked the treasure hunter what else he had found besides dinosaurs and quartz crystals.

Hall responded: "Gold and silver."

The reporter dismissed Hall's answer as a kind of wisecrack, but little did the newspaperman know that this rock hound was telling the truth.

Quartz crystals are still mined in McCurtain County, principally for recreation and hobby. The local quarries, about which Cephis was well versed, were not known to be commercially viable. Quartz crystal veins are known to extend across a belt 30 to 40 miles wide over a distance of 170 miles from Little Rock to Broken Bow.

Most of the commercial production of quartz crystal still occurs in western Arkansas, where the veins are more prolific. These commercial operators extract quartz for manufacturing use. The output is sold principally to large industrialists who utilize the commodity in manufacturing processes. The quartz crystal veins in McCurtain County are more accessible to amateurs and hobbyist collectors, at least to those who know their locations.

The lucrative, commercial veins in Arkansas are largely under the control of mining consortiums, which has stifled amateur collector involvement. Cephis was primarily a crystal recreationist, but sold quality crystals for extra income. He extracted crystals with various hand tools: small shovels and picks, hammers and chisels, crowbars, and small screwdrivers. He immersed the crystals in water and then soaked them in oxalic acid for a week before rinsing and drying. He had mastered the technique as both an art and science.

Quartz is formed when minerals deep inside the interior of the earth are dissolved by extreme heat and pressure. The hot solution seeks an escape route to the surface as it flows through crevices in the rock. While moving, the minerals are deposited in the formations along the way. When cooled, they form crystals and other mineral deposits.

Cephis, the crown prince of quartz crystal glitz, had been active in searching for new veins of metals for decades. He found pockets of mineable minerals throughout the county on both private and public lands. Feasibility was always an issue, so a friendly relationship had to be struck with the landowner, particularly on private lands. Still, despite his continuously intense exploration, a truly commercially viable lode had always eluded him. But soon after the dinosaur was secured in the early 1990s, Hall resumed his search for a rare, quantifiable, and potentially profitable mine. As Sid's health deteriorated, Cephis began taking along a new partner, Steve Due.

Hall and Due soon located a significant quartz deposit on U.S. Forestry Service land in the northern part of the county. They dug a small open-pit mine about eighteen feet deep and struck a unique quartz vein with titanium and green chlorite. Even the tailings contained traces of high-quality quartz. All evidence at the pit indicated the probability of commercial grade ore. The quartz was conspicuously visible inside the hole once they removed almost a ton of high-quality crystal. After realizing the prospects, they decided to request a permit from the Forestry Service. Also, they paid the administrative entrance fee and began the process of applying for a hard rock mining permit with the Bureau of Land Management Office in Santa Fe, New Mexico.

Contemplating a lease on the land, Hall and Due submitted an application to the Forestry Service to commercially mine quartz crystal on public lands. They learned, after applying for a lease on twenty acres, that the lease fees were not high. As part of the application process, John Nichols, the head geologist for the Ouachita National Forest in Hot Springs, Arkansas, and Ron Bush from the EPA, inspected the site and confirmed the presence of a potentially productive quarry that could yield commercial quantities of high-grade quartz crystal.

Getting the lease and permit to mine was not the major roadblock; other factors were more obtrusive and soberly forced them to seal off the mine and scrap the whole idea. Reality had shattered a dream; practicality had sublimated a vision. The capital investment and start-up costs were beyond their reach. Both men's health was failing. Sadly, Hall and Due filled in the hole, leaving the pit in its original condition. They then walked away, never to return.

It was not just Hall's declining health and the prohibitively high capital requirements that stifled his dream of a commercial mining venture. The county was changing rapidly and open lands were gradually being blocked off and public entrance denied. Private lands became more difficult to access as large landowners like Weyerhaeuser were less tolerant of public encroachment. The Commons were becoming privatized and corporatized.

CHAPTER SIXTY-SEVEN
The Crystal Lode – Cephis Strikes Again

The saga of Cephis Hall did not end with the resurrection and exhibition of the dinosaur, the recovery of a debt owed by Graffham, a ceremony and a little recognition, or even the discovery of the first-known commercially feasible quartz mine in the county. Field exploration was in his blood; Cephis' veins flowed with the rich, oxygenated fluid of a true naturalist-rockhound who was forever engaged in pursuit of raw, earthly treasures. He was always looking for something more spectacular and enthralling, and needed the thrill and rush that accompanied a discovery of only the most rare and ornate of natural relics ferreted from the entrails of Mother Earth. Dinosaurs now had less appeal. He had been there and done that and succeeded in fulfilling his life-long dream. He had nothing more to prove and sought recreational stimulation in a search for the most exquisite treasures created by natural geological processes.

The long career of naturalist Hall progressed basically in three stages as he transitioned from a purely recreational rockhound, to a tour guide and amateur paleontologist, and finally, to an adventurer-explorer oriented toward finding large mineral deposits. After briefly working mines and extracting bits of treasure, he established their commercial potential and then, finally, due to impracticalities and contingencies, simply covered them up and moved on. The secrets remained buried in his mind as he carried with him the knowledge of the locations of countless caches of untold, hidden booty scattered throughout the county.

He and Steve Due were back on the move in search of something new. They had found a prolific vein on Weyerhaeuser terrain and did a little amateur mining. The low-level managers posted at the entrance to the outback lands were given beautiful and exotic minerals, and were so satisfied with their gifts that they did not question the clandestine motives of the two miners.

Cephis and Due spent a few days assessing the prominence of the backwoods mine while keeping a few of the most precious pieces they found to add to their collections. They had discovered another potentially commercial vein, but would again have to cover it up and walk away in vain. Only Weyerhaeuser could establish a commercial mining operation at the site, but the company was not enticed. If the two men wanted to continue plucking the finer pieces, they needed to continue bribing Weyerhaeuser fiefs and that was going to get old. They paid their last bribe and moved on, taking their secret with them.

That same summer of 1990, the two men began exploring the Hochatown line near Broken Bow Lake, knowing that if they could penetrate its interior structure, they were apt to find top-quality quartz crystal – the kind Cephis sold to German buyers.

They tunneled into the side of a mountain along a bluff for twenty-one days and hit an interesting vein. They dug deeper into the cavity, and at a depth of about twenty feet, found something most exciting and unique. They had hit the core of a vein that was not only commercially feasible, but also exotically beautiful. The prize was what Hall and Due called jeweler points, which are smaller, well-defined crystals that are of such uniform length that they are used in jewelry. These high-grade crystals are in high demand by the jewelry industry.

"Some of the quartz was sheared off thousands, perhaps millions of years ago," Hall told the local news media after they got wind of the story. "We can pick these crystals off the tunnel floor by the handfuls, or we can scoop them up by the shovelfuls. In most cases, you have to pry them out from the adjacent rock formation, but not here," Hall explained (*McCurtain Gazette*, November 7, 1990).

Cephis and Steve worked the mine with low-tech tools, using a variety of steel bars to loosen and pry the rocks apart and five-gallon buckets to carry out the dirt and debris from inside the tunnel. Although they tried using jackhammers inside the mine, this proved too unwieldy and forced them to abandon power tools in favor of primitive hand digging. The mine itself was barely large enough for one man to work inside while another on the outside sifted through the rocks and picked out the unbroken, high- quality pieces that were passed back to him (*McCurtain Gazette*, November 7, 1990).

They had found one of the finest quartz crystal jewelry-point mines in the country. This crystal strike was not industrial grade, but jewelry grade. The pile of jewelry-point crystals reminded Cephis of huge, fine-point diamonds lying loose on the floor of a prolific diamond mine.

The two men had struck a bonanza in crystals, but it was doubtful that they could mine it. Did Weyerhaeuser own the land? The men didn't know what to do. How could they walk away from something like this? They figured they had little other choice.

Before the mine was covered up, Steve Due decided a little publicity was due him. He transformed himself from a rock hound to a publicity hound and contacted the local newspaper. He told them the story of the mine and even provided photos. The story came out in the *Gazette* with photos showing Due with handfuls of jeweler-point crystals, while a pile of crystallized treasure lay at his feet.

Weyerhaeuser found out about the story and started inquiring as to whether or not the mine was on company land. A raucous protest followed, but the noise soon died out.

Cephis later had the mine filled in with a backhoe to avoid a safety and liability issue. A road had to be built to get the heavy equipment up to the mine. The operator was paid well for his work. The mine's location remains a secret to this day – now covered and forgotten. Only Cephis and Steve know its location and what is hidden inside.

CHAPTER SIXTY-EIGHT
OU Scientists Probe the Bone Site

The dinosaur story had taken on a new twist as things were looking up for Fran. The female dinosaur had been christened "Fran" after the noted lady from Ardmore who knew the nuts and bolts of the dinosaur business. She stood at Allan Graffham's side during the entire ordeal to convert raw bones into a prized showpiece collection and secure a credible buyer. If everything worked out according to plan, Fran was on her way to a new home in Raleigh, North Carolina.

She had started out in an impounded bone bed on the edge of a toxic waste pit, then through the outstretched hands of amateurs and professionals, next from crude, rural sheds, and finally to esteemed scientific labs. She was soon to be embellished and featured at one of the greatest science museums in the nation. With $3 million at stake, all the technical work had to be perfect. Black Hills had its work cut out for it, but the staff remained optimistic. Allan Graffham felt cautiously hopeful, whereas Cephis and Sid were somber and prayerful.

Even though the dinosaur was on the pedestal, intriguing contemplations lingered about the prospect of other dinosaur skeletons still buried at the Acro site. Despite the enchantment in the minds of dinosaur enthusiasts and the public at large, the window of opportunity was rapidly closing. Weyerhaeuser didn't want Cephis traversing its lands to dig up anything, let alone dinosaurs. Public encroachment on the mighty corporation's lands was being curtailed.

At least Weyerhaeuser now had a company policy regarding fossil finds on its vast timber holdings. The policy mandated that any such findings automatically became the property of the Sam Noble Museum of Natural History at OU; therefore, it would be theft if anybody removed a fossil without permission from Weyerhaeuser or OU.

Only OU scientists would be allowed on Weyerhaeuser lands. As for Cephis Hall being granted access to lead another expedition, Weyerhaeuser's official answer was trite and impolite: "We aren't in the habit of working with thieves." Weyerhaeuser even denied entrance to the vaunted Dr. Dale Russell of the University of North Carolina. The Black Hills Institute had expressed interest in exploring the site, but was also thwarted. All paleontological rights had been reserved for OU, and Weyerhaeuser refused to budge on the issue. Either OU made the dig or none did.

About late 1993, before the dinosaur story began to recede from the recesses of the public mind, paleontologists from OU decided to make one last attempt to penetrate the strata at the dinosaur river front. Cephis had earlier called for more investigations to be conducted at the site; he believed dinosaurs were still embedded in the clay embankment.

"A storehouse of treasure still exists near the Mountain Fork just east of Broken Bow," Hall declared in an interview conducted with the local press.

Was OU responding out of intense interest, or was it just putting on a public front to feign enthusiasm and deflect lingering public curiosity and desire for more discoveries?

Did more dinosaurs reside at the Mountain Fork site? That question still remained after the lands bordered by the Mountain Fork to the east, the Little River to the south, and the Red and Glover Rivers to the west, was brought to the attention of the paleontological establishment. Cephis had told local rock hounds that he found parts of another dino skeleton on the Mountain Fork just a quarter mile south of the Acro site. He claimed to have found a pelvic bone and other pieces belonging to an ornithopod near the river's edge. He had noticed some peculiar, petrified wood where logs were distended from the river bank in a distorted jam. The fossilized wood he recovered was identified by Allan Graffham as an ancient chordate (a conifer or cone-bearing tree) of the early Cretaceous. Armed with this new knowledge, Hall proposed that more searches be done in the immediate area where the Acro was found.

Spurred on by curious public sentiment and hype, OU finally sent two scientists to investigate the site and tap into the strata heights. Weyerhaeuser provided the backhoe and operator; the university, the scientific brain power. Cephis Hall, given a short reprieve and temporary access, guided the two scientists. This was the last use the Corporation had for Hall; he would quickly be discarded like a bag of rotten potatoes.

The two scientists were Dr. Rich Cifelli and a friend and fellow paleontologist named W. Desmond Maxwell, a research associate at the Sam Noble Museum and also a professor at the University of the Pacific. Cephis did not stay long at the site; his presence was not appreciated by Weyerhaeuser, maybe not even by Cifelli and Maxwell. Cephis offered some suggestions regarding where they might focus their excavation, but the two scientists dismissed him. Their inherent scorn and bias against amateurs like Hall and commercial paleontologists like Larson and Graffham were never hidden far below the surface. Cephis thought the two scientists to be both arrogant and derisive. While he felt uncomfortable with them, they acted, at least in his view, as if they didn't want to be seen in public with him. They refused to listen to any of his recommendation despite his familiarity with the location. They would dig wherever they wanted, and that would likely be anywhere but the place Hall suggested. While Cephis had broken ground on the north side, Cifelli and Maxwell penetrated an area west of the location of the bone bed.

Dr. Cifelli was a world-class paleontologist, not yet on the level or stature of a Dr. Langston, Dr. Bakker, or Dr. Dale Russell; but he was young and his star rising. This was the same Dr. Cifelli who had proposed a credible scenario explaining the demise of the Acro and how the skeleton found its resting place amidst the clay rubble of what became a modern-day waste-holding pit. According to Cifelli, the Acro did not wade its way to its place of interment or become bogged down in a lagoon or tar pit. It did not die at the site, but was washed in from upstream – transported there not by lava, but fast-flowing water. The dinosaur had either died or drowned on the floodplain and the carcass became lodged against a barrier island where it was entombed in sediments.

This was a storm scenario, maybe a hurricane blowing near the shoreline just east of the present-day Mountain Fork, some 110 mya. The animal was washed in with the rest of the debris along a fifteen-mile span north of the shoreline. The storm knocked down trees and deposited logs, debris, and organic material in low, obstructed places. The debris washed in with the flood covered the Acro. This flowing avalanche of wood, mud, and mixed sediments covered the Acro and preserved it unmolested until Hall and Love arrived on the scene some 110 million years later. The large quantities of carbonized wood and fossilized plant material found atop the bone bed are believed to have been a part of that great deposition.

After guiding the two scientists and half-heartedly thrusting his spade within an entirely new substrate, Cephis, quickly overcome by a feeling of dejection, left the scene after only thirty minutes. He would never return (except when he guided this author). The backhoe operator, Bobby Trusty, was later asked what had happened after he left. Trusty stated that the two scientists did a little digging with shovels and picks for about an hour and then had him scoop and move some dirt. They concentrated in a 20x20 foot area to a depth of about six feet. The excavation by shovel and pick was minimal; almost all the dirt was moved by the bucket of the backhoe.

The OU excavation project spanned a few hours over a two-day period. Trusty moved the dirt and the scientists inspected for traces of fossils. The venture failed to turn up anything.

This was a two-man crew from the same university believed to have sent a previous team to the site in the early 1980s after Beaver's Bend naturalist Christi Silvey contacted OU and donated those original bones recovered by the Jones family. The first OU team reportedly also came up empty handed. OU still has that small inventory of Acro bones on its museum shelves.

Cephis offered an opinion as to why OU never found anything at the site. He contended that the institution didn't want to invest sufficient manpower and resources. "No teams of college students were brought to the site apparently because of the expense of transportation and lodging," he claimed. Consequently, as the glamour of the dinosaur faded, the site was abandoned. Open-pit mining was prohibited for everybody except OU scientists, who apparently, or at least it seemed, lacked motivation to stir up a sufficient amount of dust.

The century-long era of free public access to the great forested estate was coming to an end; Weyerhaeuser and community relations would be altered forever. The Corporation's gradually implemented policy of gating and leasing to hunting clubs virtually ended fossil hunting, crystal digging, and educational tours. The Oklahoma Department of Wildlife Conservation would be given oversight over some 450,000 acres of Weyerhaeuser land, with the balance of about 400,000 acres gated off and reserved exclusively for high-class hunting clubs who pay high fees to Weyerhaeuser for private access. Meanwhile, Weyerhaeuser continued to enjoy the advantage of its land being classified on the tax rolls as wasteland.

CHAPTER SIXTY-NINE
A New Order is Imposed on the Forests

The time when the macho stars of rock and bone-hounding like Sid Love and Cephis Hall could roam the lonely lowlands and isolated uplands of great feudal estates in search of earthly riches was coming to an end. The great dinosaurian expedition conducted right under Weyerhaeuser's nose in the heart of the corporation's vast estate had caused a swirl of controversy. The triumph of Hall and Love in their struggles on the manorial lands, within the community, in the legislature, the halls of academia, and the courts had embarrassed and alienated the landed barony. Consequently, company officials, reacting with a feeling of rage and rancor, were bent on revenge. Thus, the old order of liberal public access to the vast, corporate domain was overthrown. The timber barons were intent on sanitizing the forests from the detritus-littered encroachments of poachers, loiterers, collectors, and recreationists.

As outback explorers, Hall and Love were particularly targeted by the corporation. They were treated as outlaws, much like Robin Hood. Bone poaching or rock pilfering would be strictly forbidden and suppressed, just as hunting and trespassing had been in the medieval forests of England by the sheriff during the time of Robin Hood, who, like Hall, was also a yeoman and an archer to boot. The Weyerhaeuser kingpins saw Hall and Love as scofflaws with no respect for the Company's forest decorum and wanted to keep them, more than any other class of intruders, out of the sovereign forests forever.

Weyerhaeuser used its clout to win friends and placate enemies. The company pulled strings behind the scenes and lobbied the political sphere to get its way – as usual. A new lobbyist-inspired land policy was being implemented. After the deal was struck, people were banned from walking on Weyerhaeuser's vast terrain to peer and probe around. Such uninvited activity was now considered trespassing, and tickets and fines would be incurred. The lords of the forest would again have total sway and final say over the people and the land.

A new, customized land-use package was inspired with the connivance (or deference) of the Oklahoma Wildlife Commission, regional political officials, and the state legislature. Weyerhaeuser's lipid holdings of some 850,000 acres were to be reclassified, so to speak. Some 400,000 acres were gradually gated off and reserved for affluent, hunting-club clientele. For a high-dollar annual fee per acre, gun clubs had the run of the land. The general public, on the other hand, was particularly appeased with a special deal for them.

Approximately 450,000 acres of Weyerhaeuser lands on the western confines of the county was reserved for "legalized public trespass and egress," meaning a vehicle could drive through on Weyerhaeuser roads without obtaining a permit so long as it did not stop or any passenger get out of the car. If a family wanted to step out of the vehicle to have a picnic, inhale fresh air, or take in the scene, they had to obtain a permit. If the permit was not visible, the driver could be ticketed for illegal trespass, or even arrested. Under no circumstances would a passerby be allowed to pick up anything.

The cost of a recreational outing was now rather expensive. A $16 permit fee for anyone over the age of 18 was required. Park rangers supervised the new corporate-spirited, land-use program with the revenue from fees presumably divvied up in some peculiar way between the State of Oklahoma and the corporation. Such a non-neutral, revenue-partisan arrangement put a crimp in Hall's guided tour business, including the non-profit school programs. This was a case of government and corporate regulation stifling business activity and charity.

When the new rules were eventually implemented, such a restrictive policy imposed burdensome costs. For Hall's educational tours, adults accompanying the children paid the state a $16 permit fee to enter Weyerhaeuser's managed lands. No educational waivers were allowed from the State Wildlife Department, at least not for tours conducted by Cephis Hall. Although neither Cephis nor the state-Weyerhaeuser consortia charged fees for students, the adults were hit with the new revenue-enhancing scheme. For instance, a school party including fifteen parent chaperones would incur a cost of $240, provided the tour guests were from the state of Oklahoma. If visitors came from out of state, as many of Hall's clients and students did, the imposed charges were almost double the in-state fees.

Even before his wheels rolled across Weyerhaeuser's back roads, Cephis was already in the red after paying the state for his own $16 entrance fee, plus gasoline and other out-of-pocket expenses, because he did not charge for school nature tours. But it was not just revenue enhancement that hindered education; the new land policy was also about control and restrictions on public access. The restrictive policy harkened back to medieval times when the forests and resources within were exclusively reserved for the king and nobility, and represented another instance in which corporation and government had merged. Little Dixie was still a microcosm of the Old South – a rural landscape dominated by big landowners overseeing not cotton plantations, but pine plantations.

Before the new policy was fully implemented, Hall, Love, and other noted rock hounds were already on the company's (and state's) radar and got a foretaste of what was to come. There was certainly no shortage of rocks – only money. But permission would not be given to the once-venerable Hall, who had already been rebuffed by OU in a stinging rebuke, which accused him of bone thievery. The sentiment was the same for Weyerhaeuser, if not stronger.

The rules were drastically changed. Even with a permit, a person would not be allowed to remove anything – not even a rock, a sack of poke salad, or a jug containing pure water freshly scooped up from Blue Springs. In May of 2004, the woodsman-turned-educator was taking a group of second graders from Dierks Elementary on a field trip to examine rocks and nature when the reality of the new order hit him like a hard bone thrown out of the pit.

On that blue day in May, Hall's field trip group of students, teachers, and parents was accosted by a gun-toting state wildlife official who informed them that he did not approve of their presence and that Weyerhaeuser no longer allowed tours in its Three Rivers Wildlife Management Area. A few days later, a gate was erected to seal off the area.

The hyped publicity surrounding the now controversial nature tours conducted by Hall finally made its way onto the front pages of the newspapers. Even though the new policies had not been fully orchestrated, Weyerhaeuser now alleged that Hall and Love, based on a written agreement previously made with the corporation, had assented to not enter company lands without expressed written consent from company officials.

The company was likely referring to a legal document called a *Motion To Dismiss*, which was never signed by the two Acro avatars, only the attorneys. The original *Settlement Agreement*, which was signed by the two litigants and their attorneys, did not contain such a stipulation. Cephis contended he had not signed any such document as worded by John Shipp in the *Motion To Dismiss*. On the other hand, the *Order Of Dismissal*, which was signed by the district court judge and the two attorneys Hamilton and Shipp, did not contain such language. Regardless of legality, Hall's fate as a tour guide was sealed. Weyerhaeuser had the final say.

In an attempt to rectify the situation, Hall made a visit to local Weyerhaeuser officials at the Beaver's Bend office and discussed the matter with Jim Sovenson, who blatantly told him he could not take students onto Weyerhaeuser lands for recreational activities. Such services, as Cephis was told, could only be performed by OU. He was told point-blank that he would receive no written permission for school children to participate in any future nature tours or rock gatherings. The gates were closed. Educational tours, at least those conducted by the county's foremost nature guide, were effectively ended.

CHAPTER SEVENTY
The White Knight

At long last, the two dinosaur lien holders could breathe a sigh of relief. Graffham had been making his semi-annual payments and was scheduled to make his final $50,000 installment in just a few days. The ensuing hours slipped by – and bingo – the man with the "dinosaurian touch" (and the cash) came through with the restitution. The balance was paid in full except for the remittance of the two men's cast, which was part of the deal (and reward) that Graffham had been obligated to bestow upon the actual founders, who were hence out of the limelight.

As the finished product and sale came to fruition, Graffham was the man in transition who would garner the celebrity spotlight and recognition. The Acro cast was supposedly being constructed by the staff at Black Hills and would soon be presented to the two original agents of Acro acclamation who stood in the luminous glitz of the Acro blitz.

In the interim, Allan Graffham may have appeared not exactly as a shining emblem of high nobility riding on a white horse, but instead, as a dark, coarse figure who cast a shadowy glare. Now, the dark cavalier had saved the dino damsel (Fran) in distress with his rich infusions of cash.

Graffham, once truly considered a white knight come to rescue the bones and the two bone warriors, had become tainted by the stench of non-performance (of the contract). But virtually nobody noticed that unchivalrous ignominy, except, of course, the two bone lenders on the other end of the deal. Now, after legal performance, Graffham's nobility was no longer questioned and he smelled like a rose, at least to the two reimbursed debt holders. The "fief of Carter County" now stood upright as a gallant knight in disposition, if not in form. In the end, he had saved the day, and quite literally the bones and the two bone prospectors. The errant knight had become chivalrous again.

As the two "outbackers" gathered to claim the last installment of their reward, Graffham was now a hero, maybe a saint (in a dinosaurian sense), at least in regard to "*Acrocanthosaurus* salvation", and was garnering recognition from the entire community of commercial paleontologists, if not from the armchair academics.

Much the same could be said of the Larsons and BHI, who played a monumental role in the preservation of the dino. As the mystique of the Acro was reiterated, commercial paleontology was reinvigorated. The profession now had an icon (Fran) and a symbol (Graffham) of eminence to parade as scientific protuberance.

Once the funds were transferred into the hands of the two men of rock-hard diligence, the once-blotched deal would be exonerated in paleontological grandiloquence. As the final phase of restoration and transaction moved forward, wordy salvos of praise emanated from the helms of both commercial and academic paleontology.

When the lien was released, no longer would there be an encumbrance on the bones. Graffham could then pursue the final ministrations of his multi-million dollar sale without a trace of red tape. After the last check was delivered to LeForce's office, the two bone lenders would revel in Graffham's nobility and credibility, as his knighthood (at least in their eyes) was fully restored. They now stood in awe of both the almost-complete dinosaur replica and the knightly stature of Graffham, the man who had made it all happen.

The original two-year loan with Baron Graffham had been extended to a four-year term. But the two amateur lenders had not complained too loudly. If they had collected the entire amount in one lump sum, Uncle Sam would have come in and skimmed the cream off the top. In one big stroke of legal income confiscation, their miniscule return on their hard labors would have been reduced even more drastically. To avoid that reality, the two men, in a routine manner of tax abeyance, strung out the receipt of the proceeds over a four-year period. Although the arrangement had reduced his tax bill, it had also cost Cephis extra interest, fees, and charges on his home loan, which had to be refinanced. When the money flowed in from Graffham, Cephis paid on his mortgage. Now as the last payment came in, he would pay the balance.

The final meeting to distribute the funds would not be held at LeForce's office. Instead, it would be finalized at a more neutral site – the McCurtain County National Bank in Idabel. Instead of LeForce tallying the funds and divvying the spoils, the vice president of the bank, Mary Tidwell, was vested with that chore. She was the wife of the same Royce Tidwell who was among the first to find and retrieve bones from the pit – the man who still, to this day, has vertebra and other pieces in his possession as keepsakes. Mary Tidwell knew full well the significance of the bones, and she also knew about the importance of funds – especially those in her custody and about to be parceled out. This was a transaction for a bank, not a law office; the funds had to be accounted and signed for. It was altogether fitting, and besides, Carl LeForce was on the bank's board of directors. This was the final payoff, and the debt and lien on the bones would be expunged after the transaction. On this final note, the two bone creditors ended their short-term career as banker-financiers and rejoiced in their receipt – they could pay some bills.

When it was all over, LeForce remarked that the Hall-Love suit for quiet title ended up being the most expensive quiet title suit he had seen in his entire forty-seven-year law career. How expensive was it?

The record (or at least what is left of it) shows that virtually no discovery work was conducted by either party. Of course, many such records obtained during discovery do not end up in the permanent file jacket maintained in the court records and later transferred to the archives. The archives contained not one single discovery document. In a personal interview with Walter Hamilton, he stated that little or no discovery was done. There were no depositions, no interrogatories, no letters of correspondence between the opposing attorneys (save one), etc.

When we lay what is known about the case on the table, we can come up with an arbitrary figure for an estimated hourly charge for legal services performed. After a review of the case file from the National Archives and an interview with both Hamilton and LeForce, the author has estimated the number of hours of legal services rendered at somewhere between six and seventeen hours. At the higher projection of seventeen hours of service, the hourly fee would have been about $3,000 based on a total charge of $50,000. However, only Carl LeForce knows for sure what was actually charged per hour. Regardless of any ballpark figure, LeForce was right on the money with his comment about the Hall-Love quiet title suit being the most expensive.

But who can blame LeForce? After all, a deal is a deal, and Hall consented. Perhaps it was the best deal Cephis could find under the circumstances, and LeForce did bear risk of not being able to recover anything. The charges may have been approximate to the risk. However, lawyers are seldom accused of not taking advantage of an enriching business opportunity, and why not? No accusation of legal exploitation should be leveled at the LeForce law firm. In the end, everybody got their money.

CHAPTER SEVENTY-ONE
Fran is Unveiled at Black Hills

With a sense that the eyes of the world were upon them, the staff at BHI worked diligently on the Acro specimen for seven years, spending thousands of hours in a painstaking process of cleaning the bones, restoring the skeleton, and monitoring a quality cast. While the discovery created ripples in the field of paleontology, showing the world that other meat-eating dinos as intimidating as T.rex existed in North America 45 million years earlier, the preservation and assembly of the Acro was also a milestone in reconstructive paleontology with scientists accomplishing new feats through innovations within the lab – cleaning, treating, restoring, molding, casting, and mounting.

The Acro was a member of the *Allosauroids* – a group of three-fingered, two-legged meat eaters with bony head ridges – that had taken up the torch from *Allosaurus* and re-emerged fiercer than ever during the early and mid-Cretaceous. A close examination of the skeleton revealed that Fran had lived a hard life and was plagued with numerous injuries and disabilities, including broken ribs and infection of the right scapula. The left maxilla tooth bearing element of the upper jaw had been bitten by a crocodile (a tooth of a crocodile was found imbedded in the jaw), and poor Fran had a broken toe on the left foot. The Acro had apparently walked around on a broken foot and toe. Its right shoulder blade was infected and never fully healed; thus, it was partially disabled and its hunting prowess impaired.

The cast of each bone was made of polyurethane and first assembled for display in a park at Hill City, South Dakota. The assembling of the mount in the summer of 1996 was an awe-inspiring but tiring and intricate task. In typical laboratory protocol, the original skeleton is never mounted for display purposes, but is instead held for scientific study. In the case of Fran, the original skeleton was assembled (without the skull) at BHI in a modular style, with the bones strapped or cradled so that they could be left accessible for future study. The original skeleton and mounted cast for display would soon be on their way to the new N.C. Museum of Natural Sciences.

"Even those of us involved in the preparation of this skeleton are awed by the sense of power we feel in the presence of the mounted skeleton," explained Terry Wentz, chief preparatory for the project.

After seven years and over one million dollars, the mounted cast of the Acro was ready for display. In September of 1996, the reconstructed skeleton replica was unveiled at the Black Hills Museum of Natural History in Hill City, South Dakota. In one day, over 700 people lined up to see the dinosaur inside a museum that normally holds only 100 people.

The ceremony went on for two days. On the first day, the skeleton was assembled in a Hill City park near the Institute; on the second day, it was displayed inside the museum showroom. Although it was a frantic pace for Neal Larson and the staff, he found time to visit and interact with each of the major players in the Acro story. Cephis and Sid strolled through the facility, taking in the sights and talking to important people. It was during these informal proceedings that the issue of the cast came up in a conversation between Cephis and Neal Larson.

Earlier, Sid had visited the laboratory area where the cast was being prepared and did not like what he saw. He noticed that the cast pieces being prepared did not contain the steel rods, the major components that provided structural support and allowed the pieces to attach. Sid immediately reported what he saw to Cephis, who in turn, confronted Neal.

Cephis informed Larson that the contract made with Graffham stipulated that he and Sid were to receive a complete, mountable cast. As Larson starred at him with a stunned glare, Cephis explained that the cast being constructed inside the lab did not contain the steel rods and pins.

Larson explained that what was being constructed was based on Allan Graffham's order and what he had agreed to pay for the cast. The conversation got tense, as Cephis became disappointed, and Larson confused. Cephis reiterated his position, but Larson remained firm.

Larson was very busy with the unfolding extravaganza and could not delve into the matter at that time. He did mention, however, that for an additional $25,000 he would put the rods in for them. Cephis retorted that he felt he and Sid had already paid for their part of the bargain. Since Cephis did not want to create a ruckus and spoil the gaiety, he dropped the issue. Cephis walked away and settled in for the balance of the festivities.

The ceremony included several dignitaries, as well as all the important people involved in the Acro story: Allan Graffham and his wife Fran, Cephis Hall and his wife Joyce, Sid Love (although in poor health), Neal Larson, Terry Wentz, and Bob Farrar.

The monster cut a striking image – 13 feet tall at the hips and 40 feet long – and every bit as fearsome as T.rex. In fact, it looked even larger as the two giants (Stan and Fran) stood on display side by side.

Other than the Acro, Graffham was the "célèbre-de-status" who garnered most of the attention and publicity. Although the two rockhounds had dug it up and saved it, Allan Graffham's cash provided the means to preserve it. The celebration emphasized the preservation phase of the Acro story more than the excavation phase. Cash talked louder than toil and sweat. While heaps of praise were piled on Graffham, the suppliers were doled only a few tidbits.

Nothing was mentioned regarding the simple truth that without Hall and Love's dogged determination, one of the greatest dinosaur finds of the century would have never been retrieved from a toxic waste pit, let alone modeled as a finished cast. Indeed, without them, there would be nothing at all to celebrate.

But the two earnest rockhounds were given an honorable mention, identified as Allan Graffham's suppliers – the men in the field who had brought the crops to the table. Professional paleontologists and geologists preferred to praise one of their own rather than amateurs outside the club. Still, it was a special moment for all parties concerned. The Acro was a symbol of beastly preeminence that all could view with a feeling of pride, no matter what roles they played or conventions by which they might abide.

Everyone who contributed toward the making of the towering exhibit now had a feeling of being "one with the beast" and with each other. The dinosaurian accomplishment changed paleontology for the better and the lives of the participants forever. As this paleontological moment reverberated across America, the media was on hand with crew and camera; however, the newsmen were more interested in the majesty of the iconic beast than the men who had accomplished the splendid feats it took to get it there.

A unity in beastly exuberance now radiated forthrightly, at least for the short duration of the formality. While a feeling of earnest pride proliferated amongst the motley crowd, an external audience was notified and mystified as the television film crew beamed the story to the outside. The accomplishment would be recognized and celebrated beyond the confines of Hill City and the festivities that were held that day in September. In 2004, The Association of Applied Paleontological Sciences, a trade organization of fossil sellers, awarded Allan Graffham the Sternberg Medal (its highest award) for his steadfast devotion and fidelity to the principles of commercial paleontology.

CHAPTER SEVENTY-TWO
The Raid

In late summer of 1997 Joyce Hall was undergoing chemotherapy for cancer, which was not considered unusual for McCurtain County residents. Sid's wife Floy, a non-smoker, had died of lung cancer less than two years prior. Sid was now a widower and he too was undergoing treatment for both colon and throat cancer. Many locals contended that McCurtain County comprises one of the highest measured rates of cancer for any local population in America. But how can such assumptions and claims be verified? Perhaps they are exaggerated. Statistics are hard to come by.

Such arcane medical and demographic data is not readily accessible to the general public. Government (and corporations) at all levels cloak such unnerving statistics in a veil of secrecy — perhaps because the free and open reporting of such data raises too many troubling implications in a number of demographical areas. The public makes outrageous speculations based on emotional observations and piecemeal facts and opinions reported in the mass media, and therefore cannot be trusted with such hard data. Nobody sees the real, true statistics.

This was a period when Cephis and Sid were fading into obscurity, at least in the realm of amateur paleontology. Both were fraught by pressing concerns: Sid by health problems, Cephis by family issues.

Cephis and Joyce's twenty-three-year-old daughter April had just gone through a bitter divorce and had a two-year old baby. April had temporarily moved back into her parents' house while she picked up the pieces and tried to get her life back together. Their eighteen-year old son Alan had just graduated from high school and was needed at home to take his mother back and forth for cancer treatment in Texarkana. Cephis was working his usual seven days a week — on weekdays as a logger and on weekends as a tour guide. Notwithstanding Cephis being tired and over-worked, a flurry of personal, medical, and family problems palled over the Halls' rural residence in northern McCurtain County.

It was during this time that Cephis received word from BHI that his cast was ready for him to pick up — the same defective cast that did not contain the steel rod inserts needed to assemble the segmented pieces into a complete mounted cast. Still, even with that shortfall, the cast was supposedly worth $50,000.

Cephis cursed Graffham for cutting costs and skimping on production. He assumed that since Graffham was footing the bill for the cast, he was responsible for the deficiency. In his mind, BHI had geared its production based on the specifications in the work order and the amount of funds earmarked by Graffham (probably $25,000); but the two men were never sure how much Graffham actually paid BHI for the cast.

Apparently, the two men did not do their homework, or at least not very well. They had bargained, or at least thought they bargained, for a mountable cast, because that was what was specified in the contract. Graffham had told them that it would cost $50,000, and he would throw that amount into the financial pot to be poured over the two amateurs as their liquid return on assets.

They had been short-changed. Apparently Graffham (or somebody) had skimmed the cream off the top of the pot in order to cut costs and save dollars. The two men would have to make up the deficit through some other means. They did not have an extra $25,000 to hand over to BHI. Twenty-five thousand dollars was the amount Neal Larson had quoted Cephis to have the steel rods inserted and the cast complete.

Had they been flimmed and flamed by Graffham? The issue of the deficient cast involved a consumer complaint. But the two men could not simply take the defective parts back to the store for a refund or factory replacement. Cephis had to take whatever he could get and lump it. What recourse did he have — the courts, possibly? It all boiled down to a technicality over what was considered mountable. Apparently, Graffham had made that determination for them. Regardless of the technical glitch, somebody else had to supply the cash needed to make the defective product a finished, mountable cast. Graffham had customized the deal to his advantage, causing infeasibility.

Whatever product Cephis might end up with was probably worth the trouble of driving all the way to Black Hills. Perhaps he could further discuss the issue with Larson, and some concession made. Cephis felt shorted by a measly $25,000; perhaps it was a windfall for Graffham. If he could just get his hands on the cast, maybe he could sort it all out. A dream was still in place. He would find some way to make it come true. After the ordeal they had been through, a deficit of $25,000 seemed a minor detail.

To make a trip from Oklahoma to Black Hills, South Dakota, and back would take several days. Cephis made the arrangements. He contacted his boss, a prime timber contractor for his old nemesis Weyerhaeuser. Because of a critical timber harvest already underway, Cephis had to talk a blue streak to get his boss to relent. The lumberjack had to fill in detail, particularly about his expected date of return.

The logger left on a Saturday morning in mid-November. His son Alan and Alan's friend, Mark Hanna, accompanied him. They had traveled into southern Nebraska when a blizzard blew in and South Dakota became blanketed with snow and ice. The party became stranded at a motel. And even worse, the inclement weather was expected to last several days and a second front was on its way. The cast of travelers was molded into a frigid frieze and were also in a tight squeeze.

They had little choice but to turn around and head south as soon as the icy roads thawed. If they continued north it would be tough sledding and they faced another blizzard. The expense of a motel and lost time from work was unpalatable, Mark was attending classes at Southeastern State University in Durant, and only short-term arrangements had been made to transport Joyce for chemotherapy treatment. They would have to return home empty-handed. Cephis could always figure out another way to get the cast, even if it meant another trip. It was frustrating, but that was the way "Old Man Winter" behaved – he was capricious and cantankerous. The elements had dealt Cephis a bad hand on numerous occasions.

Cephis and party returned to McCurtain County and settled back into routine. But following the aborted trip, still more problems intervened. Soon, another extraneous incident warped reality and added more stress. At approximately 6:30 A.M. — about an hour after Cephis had left for work — there was a loud, unexpected knock on the front door. The loud clamor woke everybody. Who could be banging on the door this early in the morning? Given the unusual time, maybe it was somebody important. Joyce, April, Alan, and the baby grand-daughter were startled and shaken from a deep, early-morning snooze.

As Joyce opened the door, four rifle-toting police officers in fatigues barged in, flashed their badges and search warrant, and began barking orders. Joyce squawked that she needed to call "Carl" (LeForce). The intruders growled back that she was not calling anybody. Joyce, April, and the grandbaby were confined to the living area and denied access to a phone. A dazed and barely-dressed Alan was taken outside at gunpoint and put inside a police vehicle and interrogated for almost four hours while some thirty camouflaged officers brandishing assault rifles scoured the outside premises, including the garage, shed, and rock shop. The two women were not even allowed to go to the restroom without a guard being present. This was more than a mere raid — it was an assault, except no weapons were fired.

This was a terrifying situation. Indeed, it was an act of state terror — the kind of police sting people hear about but presume will never happen to them. The Hall household was put under house arrest, but no rights were read or explanations given. A swoop of federal and state agents had descended on a hapless family already overwhelmed with problems of their own. Six known police agencies were believed to be involved, including the Oklahoma State Bureau of Investigation (OSBI), the FBI, the Drug Enforcement Agency (DEA), the U.S. Forestry Service, the Oklahoma Department of Wildlife, and the county sheriff. The real motive for the raid was a matter of pure speculation. The whole sordid affair lasted approximately six hours, and Alan may have been coerced into saying things that raised more questions in the minds of the authorities.

The police struck only a few days after Cephis had returned from the trip and on his second day back to work. They conveniently waited until after he left for work. Was the timing coincidental? Would the raiders have confiscated the casted bones if found on the property? Were the lawmen looking for cast bones, joints of marijuana, or something else? It was hard to say because there was no real basis for any suspicion of marijuana smoking or dealing upon the premises. Nobody in the family had a criminal record, and there was no portent of criminal activity on the grounds or behind the walls.

The raid hosted a fleet of police vehicles parked along the road and in the driveway with their lights flashing the whole time. The two-story house was located along Highway 259, a major state highway, and invited curiosity and questioning from area residents who noticed the commotion. The whole thing was a conspicuous invasion of the family's privacy, a sore-rubbing embarrassment, and a taint on their standing within the community. It would take days, if not weeks, to get their house back in order.

The court-empowered officers ransacked the premises as they tore through closets, suitcases, bedrooms, and furniture drawers. No corner or storage space was spared. Any organization or order that previously existed was thrown into utter disarray. Chaos ensued and perplexing bewilderment followed. When Cephis arrived home from work and learned what had happened he was devastated. A whole assortment of disquieting emotions intruded his disoriented consciousness: fear, worry, horror, anger, disgust, distrust, even revenge. But what could he do? The answer was nothing.

He asked himself, "Whatever happened to the Fourth Amendment to the U.S. Constitution, which supposedly protected the rights of people to be secure in their persons, houses, papers, and effects against unreasonable searches and seizures? And what about safeguards against arbitrary warrants issued without probable cause supported by oath or affirmation that described the place to be searched and the persons or things to be seized?" He answered his own question within his own mind – a patriot had to enforce the right himself after the fact in cases where the government was unwilling to follow the letter of the law. But how?

Who had asked for the warrant and who had issued it? He knew that nobody in his household was an illicit drug user or seller. Neither he nor Alan had a police record or any outstanding tickets or warrants. Cephis had experienced only one brush with the law in his entire life, and that was the incident when he cursed a state trooper, and Carl LeForce was supposed to have taken care of that. However, he did have a long-standing feud with Weyerhaeuser.

What basis did the authorities have to invade his premises and terrorize his family? They had flashed their badges and the warrant so fast that neither Joyce nor any other family member could see or read anything. As bizarre and troubling as the implications were, Cephis wanted to get to the bottom of the matter. With suspicions flashing in his mind, there was one consolation; he now felt fortunate that he was unable to bring the cast home. The blizzard had ended up being a blessing in disguise. If the cast had been stored on his property at the time of the raid, the agents might have seized it. Were they looking for a mere cast of a dinosaur? Or were they looking for the real bones?

Were the police incited to such drastic action on a mere chance of seizing a $50,000 plastic cast of a skeleton?

Cephis rethought the situation and remembered that he had told a few friends about his planned trip to get the cast, but he knew he could trust them. He also remembered that he had not chosen his words wisely when he talked to two parties — his timber boss and his inquisitive neighbor — about his trip to South Dakota to pick up his dinosaur cast. He used the word "dinosaur" instead of "cast". This implied he was picking up a real skeleton, rather than a plastic one.

His suspicions now centered on his mysterious neighbors who had recently moved-in next door. He and Joyce had observed repeated incidents of suspicious behavior, which now, as he looked back, seemed more dubious than ever and raised alarming questions. Were the neighbors planted as spies? Were the police expecting to seize real bones, rather than artificial ones? Within thirty-six hours following the raid, the neighbors had packed up and moved. They inexplicably fled in the middle of the night without saying a word to anybody.

CHAPTER SEVENTY-THREE
After Shocks

In the aftermath of the raid, Cephis Hall's life spiraled into utter chaos. Life had thrown him a few wicked curves now and then which had either "beaned him" or sailed right past him, and each time he had quickly recovered. But this time, he, like the rest of his household, was shaken and disoriented. The raid had to be based on flimsy or trumped-up suspicion. Whatever the cops were looking for was not found.

Joyce's health deteriorated more and Alan sank into a state of despair. It seemed likely that he was the suspect, or at least he (or his behavior) offered some pretext for a raid that may have been motivated by some hidden agenda. Apparently, Alan had done something that attracted the attention of the authorities. Perhaps they had been looking for anything that might raise a question about illegality. Conceivably, some dubious activity might be stretched into a suspicion that formed the basis for a raid in search of something, maybe even an extra bonus – the bones. But what might that suspect behavior have been? What could have prompted the authorities to become suspicious, or who could have persuaded them to be suspicious?

Alan now cowered inside his own house. Fearing that the authorities might return to arrest him on some bogus charge, he lived in darkness and fear for months after the incident, trembling at any strange knock, noise, or sound of a vehicle pulling into the driveway at odd hours.

Maybe the suspicion had something to do with his friend Mark Hanna, a college student at Southeastern State University in Durant majoring in criminal justice. Within a few years, Mark would get his degree and become a police officer himself, but at the present, he was constantly battling police suspicion and harassment because of his family connections.

Mark came from a family of known professional criminals. Many of his close relatives, including parents, uncles, and cousins had run-ins with the law. A couple of his uncles were notorious criminals serving time in prison. Other family members were caught up in the criminal judicial system at some level and under constant police surveillance.

Raw statistics from sociological research suggest that criminal behavior is often learned and can be traced to associations within the family or community. Major theories in criminology link a subculture of criminality to a process of socialization rooted in peer groups, gangs, or family ties. Criminal behavior is reinforced when the young adopt the prevailing values and lifestyles of this subculture through emulation of role models. Once branded as a criminal by the police or society, youngsters tend to fulfill role expectations.

In the case of Mark Hanna, police investigations were tapping into orthodox social theory that generally holds true. However, there are many exceptions to the rule. Sometimes sons or daughters rebel and adopt different role models. That was likely the case for Mark Hanna, but theories and biases put into action had made him a potential suspect merely because of his family background, a sort of guilt by association. Some members of Mark's family were involved in drug dealing, but there was no indication that he was. He lived with his grandparents and tried to maintain some distance from much of his kin, at least from their criminal dealings. He did not, however, disavow his family and continued to interact with them.

Mark was on the police radar, not for anything he had likely done, but because of his family background and connections. As one of Mark's close friends, Alan might also be caught in the same dragnet. If the authorities were watching Mark with suspicion, they might also be watching Alan. One thing was certain: something was brewing in the background.

Shortly after the raid, Cephis called Sid to explain what had happened. Sid was very ill, but his mind was still clear. He believed two possible motives were behind the raid: Weyerhaeuser security had gotten wind that Cephis was bringing back the bones (real or cast) and used the company's influence to instigate a conspiracy with state or federal authorities to raid Hall's home, possibly under some other pretext such as possession of marijuana. In the process of searching for pot, they could confiscate the bones (or cast), which the police could then hold, pending completion of an ongoing investigation. In Sid's mind, although it was just conjecture, a second motive may have been revenge. But if that were truly the case, why hadn't the authorities just planted marijuana somewhere on the property to seize as evidence?

Cephis tended to agree with Sid, but he was somewhat distracted. Sid's voice sounded weak and shaky; his health had obviously taken a turn for the worse. He asked Sid if he needed anything.

Sid responded: "I want you to finish the last leg of our dream. Get the cast of the dinosaur home and get it put on display at a local museum so we can get the recognition we deserve for all our hard work."

Cephis assured his friend that he would do his best. "Rest assured. I will make it happen. Take care of yourself. I will call you back tomorrow."

After the phone conversation, Cephis tried to collect his composure. He was concerned about Sid, but somehow he had to restore his household to normalcy. He went to bed early that night.

The following evening, Cephis received some very disheartening news. Sid had passed away that morning, November 21, 1997.

It was a great loss for Cephis, but it was also a loss for the worlds of amateur paleontology and rock hounding. Sid Love was one of the greatest amateur naturalists in history.

Cephis, already stressed, now became depressed. It was as if he no longer had a companion in the struggle. He felt isolated and alone with seemingly dark forces conspiring all around. For almost two weeks, he retreated into a shell. He was a pall bearer at the funeral, and shortly afterwards, he took time off from work. A few days of rest was helpful, but he needed to become active again to avoid sinking into a perennial pit of depression. A shroud of darkness haunted him for weeks, but gradually the light became brighter. While he would dearly miss his friend Sid, it was time to get back to work.

Once his mental state improved, he resumed the struggle and again contemplated the events and facts surrounding the raid. He asked himself, "Who could have tipped off the police? Were they looking for bones or drugs?"

He knew that Alan, Mark, and Mark's cousin were under suspicion and being watched by the police. He had already advised both Alan and Mark to stay away from that cousin who was believed to be involved in drugs.

Cephis and Joyce discussed the possible motive for the raid. They each had noted strange and suspicious behavior on the part of their next-door neighbors. The neighbors were nosy and seemed always to be prying into their personal business, and marijuana was a frequent topic. The wife was either a pot head or pretended to be. She repeatedly offered joints to Joyce, trying to entice her to use it to alleviate pain. Cephis and Joyce noticed the couple walking in their yard or along the fringes of their property on different occasions, as if they were stalking or casing it. Joyce became afraid the woman might be attempting to plant marijuana on their land. They started keeping a closer watch on them, refusing to let the mistrusted neighbors inside their house.

In the aftershock of the raid, the Hall family braced themselves for what was coming next, and their concerns naturally focused on Alan. Cephis and Joyce believed the state was trying to cook up evidence against Alan and Mark on marijuana possession or some related charge, but what could they do? Nothing, unfortunately, except wait on the authorities to make their move.

Alan, Mark, and Mark's cousin were having their movements on rural county lands monitored by state game and federal forestry wardens. The three boys had been observed working cattle on what had become (or was about to become) U.S. Forestry Service lands after Weyerhaeuser traded lands in the northern part of the county to the federal government for more desirable timber lands in the southern part of the county. The land swap required cattle grazers to remove their cattle from the northern lands. The three teenagers were hired to assist in the endeavor, and their movements somehow became intertwined with suspicions about marijuana growing.

In another incident denoting suspicious activity, a game warden had taken a photo of Alan and Mark with shovels in their hands while digging crystals on a crystal tour.

Apparently, the shovel was a potentially incriminating tool implicating the two boys in marijuana cultivation. Armed with the photo, the state now decried illegal activity.

The game warden showed the photo to an Eagletown convenience store owner named Chadwick and asked if he could identify the other boy in the picture. (The "other boy" was Alan Hall. The warden already knew Mark Hanna.).

Chadwick informed him that it was the "Hall boy." The game warden later turned the photo over to either the Oklahoma State Bureau of Investigation (OSBI) or the Drug Enforcement Agency (DEA) as possible evidence of marijuana cultivation. The photo and innuendo formed the basis of a short-sighted investigation.

A few weeks later in December 1997, Alan, Mark, and Mark's cousin all received letters ordering them to appear in federal court in Muskogee to face trumped-up criminal insinuations. Because of circumstantial suspicion and contact (or association) with potential drug users/dealers, Alan and Mark were also believed to be one. There were no charges, no arrests, and the evidence spurious; in fact, there was no evidence at all – only mere speculation.

This was a period of considerable stress for Cephis and Joyce. Their house had been ransacked, Joyce was undergoing chemotherapy for cancer, Cephis had just lost his best friend, their daughter April was in transition following a life crisis, and now their son was facing counterfeit charges of criminal activity.

Cephis feared the boys were about to be railroaded and something needed to be done to protect them. He visited his prior counsel Walter Hamilton, who had long since left LeForce's law firm and was currently the county district attorney. Hamilton had made his mark on his own as a highly respected prosecutor.

Hamilton knew nothing about the raid or the accusations against Alan; he was a county official, not state or federal. He was sympathetic, but there was nothing he could do. He would later be elected to a second term, but declined to continue in office. He left the legal profession to become a teacher and cattle rancher and never returned. It was presumed by many that he left due to his dissatisfaction with the ethics of the profession and disenchantment with the political pressures brought to bear on the office of county prosecutor to serve powerful special interests at the expense of the general public.

Cephis still needed to find a legal representative for the three teenagers, but who? In his mind, he would rather deal with the familiar than the unfamiliar, and besides, there were not many to choose from within the known slate of local attorneys. None were very palatable as far as he was concerned. He decided to turn to the attorney he knew best – Carl LeForce. He hired LeForce to show up at the court hearing as the legal counselor for the three boys. The charge would be $5,000.

LeForce was hired to project a legal presence at the court hearing, a kind of insurance policy. At least with a legal spokesman on their behalf, the boys stood a better chance of avoiding bogus charges. LeForce could at least force the court to present incriminating evidence (and in this case there was none) before bringing a charge. But he was an expensive insurance policy.

LeForce merely had to appear in court as spokesman for the three teenagers. A few hours of travel time, a court appearance, and he was done. In addition, he did a background check on the three boys and found they all had clean juvenile records, including the seventeen-year-old cousin who was still in high school but believed to have a checkered past. In the case of Alan, LeForce learned that he had been a good student, made good grades, and was well liked by his teachers and principals.

The judge heard what LeForce and the three boys had to say and weighed the spurious evidence. There were no witnesses, perhaps only a photo showing two boys with a shovel and maybe an accusatory report based on circumstance rather than hard evidence. The whole case was a fishing expedition, if not an outright farce. The judge was not impressed with what the state had presented as allegations, and the investigation of the three boys ended. Cephis wondered if Weyerhaeuser had manufactured the whole charade as some kind of retaliation over the dinosaur affair.

The court hearing was the last Alan and Mark would make as potential suspects on any kind of criminal charge. However, the stress and worry had caused the family considerable harm. It had cost Cephis $5,000, but much worse, he suffered a stroke a week later on January 17, 1998.

CHAPTER SEVENTY-FOUR
The Dreamer

Cephis was down and out and still did not have his cast. Although he was lucky the cast was not on his property when the raid happened, he still dreaded having to drive all the way back to South Dakota, especially during the winter. He sat for a few weeks waiting for an opportune moment. However, he was getting restless and feared BHI might start charging storage fees, or something might happen to the cast. He had no guarantee or warranty. If something came up missing, BHI had an alibi – the lab had told him he needed to pick up the product. As he began making plans for another trip to Hill City, a window of opportunity appeared.

A close friend, local veterinarian Dr. Lewis Stiles, notified Cephis that he was traveling to Rapid City to visit his daughter and could bring back the cast on his return home. Cephis took him up on the offer. He knew Dr. Stiles was reliable and trustworthy. Stiles would bring the cast back in his pickup.

Stiles and Hall went way back. They had shared interests and had collaborated for years. Dr. Stiles was also an avid outdoorsman and rockhound. He operated the Gardner Family Mansion, a local museum located near the Mountain Fork Bridge east of Broken Bow, only a few miles from the dinosaur site. The museum was the former home of Jefferson Gardner, a former chief of the Choctaw Nation. Dr. Stiles had lived in the house while growing up, and now as a museum, it contains many relics from the local area, including some of the finest quartz crystals in the southwest, compliments of Cephis Hall. The museum also contains a few of the original bones from Hall's Acro that were given to him by the iconic Louis Jones. Retired, Stiles lives in a newer house adjacent to the mansion.

Although he had to have sideboards fitted on his pickup bed, Stiles successfully hauled the cast pieces and delivered them to Cephis. Thanks to the kindness of Stiles, Cephis had a $50,000 cast of *Acrocanthosaurus* housed inside his rock shop. The cast represented a joint-ownership venture between him and Sid. Now that Sid was deceased, Cephis was the full owner. Although Graffham had presumably paid only $25,000 for the cast as part of the deal, the cast was figured to be worth $50,000 on the open market. However, Cephis wondered if that appraised amount reflected the dollar value of a complete cast containing the steel attachment rods. His pieces did not contain the rods and pins, thanks to the order request submitted by Graffham. The cast needed some refinement to make it a viable standing mount. This cast of the original skeleton was the basis for a new museum Cephis and Sid had hoped to build in McCurtain County. Now Sid was dead and money in even shorter supply.

Sid and Cephis had also considered the possibility of working with the Herrons, a local patrician timber family and founders of the Museum of the Red River, in expanding their existing facility. The museum, consisting principally of Indian artifacts, might be fitted with a new geological wing. Their initial contact with the Herron elders did not bear fruit. The timber patricians did not seem interested and preferred to keep their museum as a repository for Indian heritage only.

Cephis had been looking around for a suitable location and had his eyes on a 6.5-acre tract of land near Hochatown. Cephis and Sid's original dream was to build a museum near Beavers Bend which would contain gems, minerals, and ancient artifacts from the local area, and, of course, the dinosaur. Hall had a mediocre talent for clairvoyance and could visualize an outcome much like what later became the new Museum of the Red River in Idabel.

To realize this dream, they needed a loan or grant. Sid had planned to front the money from his own savings until his severe illness struck. Now Cephis was all alone with his hopes and dreams. He talked to a banker, but was turned down. A wealthy widow had offered to donate land near the chicken plant for Hall's dream, but that deal also fell through.

With all the obstacles and difficulties he faced, Cephis again entertained the possibility of striking a deal with the Herrons. Somehow, he needed to convince them to expand. Could the awesome mystique of the dinosaur do the talking for him? It would be no mundane consideration. The undertaking would encompass a major capital expenditure. Hall's cast could be upgraded to become a first-rate, quality-mount replica of the county's most famous and fearsome prehistoric monster. Cephis needed to convince the Herrons to buy his cast.

CHAPTER SEVENTY-FIVE
The Cast

As the months passed by, Cephis saw little hope of fulfilling his dream of a new independent museum. Even the watered-down dream of an enlarged Museum of the Red River looked bleak. Although his fate was intertwined with his dream, his personal life was in shambles.

Joyce was still dealing with cancer, and he was recovering from a stroke. Medical bills were mounting, while the family's income was tanking. Neither Joyce nor Cephis was able to work.

This was no time for luxury or ostentation. They sold the fancy two-story house along with 2 ½ acres from the original 4 ½ acre tract, keeping the remaining two acres on which to build a rather modest log home. As their health was changing, so were their tastes. They no longer felt the need for the space and luxury the big house offered; a logger's tastes were more modest. They made a sizeable profit from the sale and had sufficient funds to build their new home while using the balance for medical and living expenses.

But soon they learned that modesty has its limits. Until their new home was finished, they temporarily moved into a 28-foot travel trailer, and the cramped quarters nearly drove them crazy.

When their log house was finally constructed, it had the sort of rustic look that Cephis wanted and was spacious enough with three bedrooms and about 1,800 square feet of living space. The customized builder's package, however, did not include all the interior finish work, such as wall tile, floor coverings and paint. The Halls would incur extra expenses to finish the interior. Meanwhile, their finances were hemorrhaging profusely.

Joyce and Cephis had plenty of space for themselves inside, but Cephis' rock shop was crowded and cluttered. The pieces of the dinosaur cast were taking up too much space. He needed to sell the cast to raise money, but his dream was standing in the way. He wanted the cast to become part of a local museum display, but his options were limited.

In Cephis' mind, the Acro cast had to be exhibited at the Museum of the Red River or nowhere. He attempted to renegotiate with Mary and Quintus Herron. If he could somehow convince them to buy the cast, perhaps a new and expanded museum would follow in its path.

Sir Graffham had told Cephis that the true value of the cast was $50,000 if it could be sold to the right buyer, but because he had paid only $25,000 for its manufacture, that was all it was actually worth to him.

"The materials used to make the cast were not expensive, but the work involved was very laborious," explained Graffham, without alluding to the missing steel rods and pins. Graffham admitted that he didn't need the cast, although he would appraise it at $50,000 if he were selling it.

Could Cephis sell it for $50,000? If he could, it would certainly be beneficial. What if he could kill two birds with one stone by selling to the Herrons? If they would buy it for $50,000, he could put some needed cash to work and pay off some medical bills, while also enticing the Herrons with an incentive to move forward on an expansion of their museum.

Cephis soon revisited with Quintus and Mary Herron, the respective patriarch and matriarch of the clan, to discuss the possibility of their buying the cast. The Herrons, however, were not receptive. They likely had an inherent bias against Cephis.

The Herrons were a long-standing McCurtain timber family going back to the mid-19th century who utilized the select-cut method of timber management. Cephis suspected the Herrons looked down on him as being merely a filthy log cutter. He believed the family's loyalty was still with big timber and had sided with Weyerhaeuser in the feud he and Sid had with the giant timber company

When he conversed with the Herrons, he pointed out that the occasion was probably the first time they had ever seen him when he was not either dressed as a logger or actually out on the job. Cephis had worked on the Herron's timber lands — some 30,000 acres — and had interacted with family members a time or two. The Herrons knew him only as a logger, not as a highly-versed naturalist, tour guide, amateur geologist, or educator. Their opinions were tainted by mere impression, not fact.

Cephis believed the Herrons tended to see all loggers in the same vane: from the perspective of a boss versus worker scenario. The Herrons, he believed, had an inherent bias; to them, the log was a more important component of production that the logger.

Cephis informed the Herrons that his asking price for the cast of the only true theropod predator ever dug from the soil of McCurtain County was $50,000 (but he would have taken less). The Herrons were totally unreceptive and refused to entertain a purchase at any price at that particular time.

Cephis, somewhat desperate and dejected, next contacted Sid's son, Mike, a local businessman who owned the tire and automobile repair shop in Idabel that he recently inherited after his father's death. Cephis and Mike were not close like he and Sid. In fact, Cephis had stated that Mike and his father were not cut out of the same cloth. But as Sid's son, Mike was the closest blood connection to his partner, whose half of the cast Cephis had inherited.

Since Cephis badly needed the cash and extra space in his rock shop, he ended up selling the cast to Mike Love for only $12,500. That wouldn't pay many medical bills, but it was enough to make some badly needed improvements on his new house.

In a way, the cast was still in the family — at least in Sid's family — and it was still in McCurtain County. Cephis hoped that Mike would see that it remained there.

Within a week or two after his purchase, Mike had succeeded in selling the Acro cast to the Herrons for $50,000.

Cephis' dream was still alive.

CHAPTER SEVENTY-SIX
Fundraising –
Making the Dream Come True

Cephis Hall's dream inched closer to reality day-by-day. His original dream was to discover and recover a world-class dinosaurian specimen. He had accomplished that grandiose task and was still alive, although there had been some close calls. He now contemplated the second phase of his dream vision: finding a local home for his wondrous theropod dragon, a fearsome monster of McCurtain County's Cretaceous flood plain.

The controversial cast configured an awesome skeletal replica of the fiercest predator to ever stalk the southern homelands. Although it did not spit fire, it did tear apart huge chunks of flesh and devoured whole carcasses, leaving only a nominal pile of bones for the despicable scavengers.

The defective cast that Cephis sold to Mike Love for $12,500 was now in the hands the folks at the Museum of the Red River in Idabel. Through the astute salesmanship of Mike Love and the generosity of the Herrons, a full-cast replica of the former local denizen was on its way to becoming a spectacular showpiece exhibit in its own designated hall. The museum's existing building needed to be expanded with a new paleontological wing in order to accommodate the beastly celebrity.

The cost of the new wing was pegged at some $750,000, but cost-overrun contingencies could drive the price still higher. In addition to the costs of new construction, the faulty Acro cast would have to be reconstructed at a cost of roughly $25,000. Inflation, however, and ensuing mark-ups might have driven the costs even higher since September 1996, when Neal Larson originally quoted the figure to Cephis.

Sure enough, the museum soon learned that rising material and labor costs had escalated the charge to over $50,000 (double the original price quoted to Hall) for a revamping of the cast pieces with new steel rod attachments, a process called articulation and mounting of the cast. The plastic molds of the Acro's bones would also have to be shipped back to Black Hills for additional reconfiguration and reconstruction.

When budgetary considerations were tallied and projected, final costs for the cast would exceed $100,000 ($50,000 paid to Mike Love and at least another $50,000 to be paid to Black Hills), plus ancillary service costs. In addition to the actual cost of the new mountable cast, there were other expensive services connected with the task of preparing the mounted cast on the showroom floor: exhibition preparation (1,200 square feet at $37.50 per foot) amounting to $45,000. In all, the total charges for the expanded museum project could reach as high as one million dollars if projected budgetary expenditures proved too conservative.

Nevertheless, it was too late to rationalize or cost-analyze the surcharges; the mystique of the beast had captivated the hearts and minds of local residents. Fund drives were under way with appeals made to corporate sponsors and charitable foundations. Roughly one million dollars would have to be raised to fulfill not just Hall's dream, but now the dream of a considerable portion of the county population. The Museum of the Red River was the peoples' museum, and the Acro had become the peoples' dinosaur. A true spirit of populism and community activism was now at work. A groundswell of public sentiment and support animated the previously skeptical and indifferent populace. Voices of dissent were drowned out. The people were determined to have their dinosaur, and have it in a big way. Pledges emanated forth, and fund-raising schemes proliferated. Generous people and institutions stepped in to fill the void.

The museum was founded by the patrician Herron family in 1973 and principally contained Indian artifacts. Now, if the planned capital expansion panned out, the facility would almost double in size and also showcase geological and paleontological specimens. The new Acro specimen was to be placed in a reserved exhibit hall within the new natural science wing.

Sallie Webb and Paulette La Gasse, two community-spirited patrons, headed the McCurtain Acrocanthosaurus Project and organized fund raising drives. They appealed to the haves and have-nots, mostly the haves who had the discretionary funds to serve as benefactors of the public interest. La Gasse and Webb raised $154,000 through their own initiatives. In addition, other independent-minded groups organized their own creative funding and solicitation drives.

Although the big money in the form of grants or matching funds came from big donors and charities such as Weyerhaeuser and the Herron Foundation, small-time contributors, including classes of school children, pitched in pennies, dimes and quarters. There were actually contests among local schools to raise the most money and garner recognition. This was a public-spirited involvement in the greatest grass roots fashion. The bottom line goal was to raise a minimum of $50,000 from small contributors, then go to corporate foundations for grants or loans.

The fund raising ideas were creative, if not ingenious, and included such activities as: pie walks (a "dimes for dinosaur" pie walk); trick or treat for dimes and nickels, instead of candy on Halloween night; auctions; cook-offs; car washes; jars placed inside business establishments for small donations; and various civic clubs and service organizations – especially the Gem and Mineral Club – staging special events to raise money.

Community fund raising was centered at the schools because it was the school children who loved Cephis Hall and the dinosaur the most. Pennies, quarters and dollars flowed in, and over time added up to a sizeable chunk. In one local elementary school, 200,000 pennies were raised in a few weeks.

But of course a large collective of small contributors can never match the largess of resource-rich corporations and charitable foundations. Weyerhaeuser, the Herrons, and other corporations and independent businessmen provided most of the funds and footed most of the bill. In the end, it was the people who hated Cephis Hall the most who were the most generous in making both his dream and the community's dream come true.

Despite the environmental affronts which often go hand-in-hand with manufacturing and intensive agri-business, Weyerhaeuser has given a lot in return to the community – not just jobs, but hard cash through grants, charity, and generous donations for a wide variety of worthy causes.

The museum staff and community held their breath in anticipation of success. The dinosaur offered hope as a landmark tourist attraction and a source of community pride.

CHAPTER SEVENTY-SEVEN
The Monster is Showcased – The Celebration at the Museum

Years of fund raising, planning, and construction were about to pay off and community pride instilled. New galleries of exotic exhibitions were in the making – most prominently, the Acro exhibit. In a celebration to be staged, new celebrities were about to be introduced to a soon-to-be dazzled crowd. Cephis Hall was a living, breathing exhibition. The dinosaur mount was an assembly of plastic bones, but it imparted an awesome sense of beastly magnitude as an artificial replica of the skeleton of the most fearsome creature that once stalked the ancient floodplains right outside the walls of the museum building.

It was left to the imagination of the beholders to visualize real flesh on the bones as they walked through the new gallery and got their first glimpse of the beastly reality that had generated so much controversy. The name of the creature had frequently been seen in the headlines of local newspapers along with the names of the founders, Sid Love and Cephis Hall. Sid was now deceased and unavailable to participate, but his dream too had been realized – won through a long, hard, bitter struggle and capped off by the finishing touches of his most dear friend who would share the limelight and garner the recognition on behalf of both of them.

Tribute was paid to a motley cast of characters and institutions, presumably in a ranking order equivalent to their contribution in making the beast a showpiece citizen. First and foremost on the list was the dinosaur, which elicited stunning sighs, grimaces, and awes from the beguiled spectators as the beast was showcased for the first time in McCurtain County. Throngs of curious examiners filed by the exhibit and caught "monster mania." This was the face of the same beast that had adorned flyers, billboards, and the front pages of the local newspapers. The image of the fearsome carnivore became more real and indelible as its mounted cast was unveiled at 10:00 AM on Saturday, February 25, 2005. After years of waiting in the wings, the original finders cast stored in McCurtain County had found a new home in the new wing of the Museum of the Red River and became the centerpiece exhibit.

Guest speakers narrated the story of how the dinosaur had come to occupy a place in the museum's gallery. Dignitaries and important persons introduced the celebrities and extolled the virtues each had demonstrated in their respective drives to make the dinosaur a kindred citizen. Sid Love was memorialized and Cephis Hall, glorified. In Hall, the crowd found another common figure, for his name had also been plastered on tabloid papers. Hall made his debut, and his name and face was forever linked to the beast despite his common and modest appearance falling far short of the striking pose of the dinosaur. Hall was ordinary, but his accomplishment, extraordinary.

Given enough time, and before his passing, the world would learn some inkling of the struggles and sacrifices Hall had made to save the dinosaur. As a plastic cast, the Acro would survive for near-eternity, while Hall's accomplishment and deeds might only decorate a memorial plaque or be cited as a footnote in some paleontological treatise, scientific report, or news article.

The story of the "Mountain Fork Specimen" and the struggles of Cephis Hall and Sid Love were coming to an end. The celebration of the grand opening on that bright Saturday morning in Idabel marked a milestone for both Hall and the dinosaur. The new gallery in the new wing brought forth tangible glimpses at underlying mysteries that heretofore had remained dormant and insipid, as the real-case exhibit enchanted the viewers.

Hall signed autographs and gloated in the celebrity limelight. Weyerhaeuser, the Herron Foundation, and other corporate sponsors received recognition and praise from the guest speakers, which included important people like then Lt. Governor Mary Fallen, State Senator Jeff Rabon from Hugo, the State Representative Terry Matlock of Valiant, and Dr. Lewis Jacobs, paleontologist at SMU.

But the story was not quite over. After years of dicing the dinosaur, State Senator Jeff Rabon introduced a bill that would make the *Acrocanthosaurus* the state dinosaur, and on June 6, 2006, Governor Brad Henry signed the bill into law. The title became official in July 2006. Another dino celebration was in order.

CHAPTER SEVENTY-EIGHT
The Last Controversy

Cephis, Sid, and the dinosaur, nicknamed Fran, were acknowledged in southeastern Oklahoma. The small, regional Museum of the Red River now had one of the most spectacular theropod displays in the nation. Only a handful of science museums throughout the world had a mounted cast of the Acro – perhaps the supreme sauropod killer of all time and certainly a top contender for the greatest terrestrial predator that ever walked the face of the earth. Still, there seemed to be an enigma regarding the status of the great theropodic carnivore.

While regional pride concerning the Mountain Fork monster was instilled in southeastern Oklahomans, why was the iconic beast not a celebrity showpiece elsewhere across the Red Man's State? The larger museums had no interest in the specimen. Why?

The Acro, a native of Oklahoma, could be seen on display at only two small museums in the entire state – the Museum of the Red River and Graffham Hall at the Goddard Museum Youth Camp in Sulphur, Oklahoma. The fact that the Acro is noticeably missing at the Sam Noble Museum of Natural History on the University of Oklahoma campus and at other large museums within the state remained a mystery.

Were there bad vibes in the air over the Weyerhaeuser affair? Did OU have an attitude or hidden agenda? The Acro phenomenon pitted a small cartel of important persons in amateur and commercial paleontology against pure academia. Were the establishment scientists offended? Dissension ran rampant among the ranks of academia. Was the Acro a symbol of that disunion?

The Acro affair had sown seeds of bitterness. Sour grapes had fermented. The "High-Spined Lizard" became a symbol of controversy and discord, but regional pride prevailed. The residents of southeastern Oklahoma felt kinship with Fran and wanted her bones distinguished as an "insignia beast." Oklahoma had a state fossil, so why not make way to celebrate the "Beast of the Southeast" with an honorary state title? This was not a new proposition. After all, the *Allosaurus* and *Saurophaganax* were from the Jurassic, while the Acro was from the early Cretaceous. Why not invoke a sovereign from the Cretaceous realm?

In 1988 the state legislature, under the sway of scientific lobbyists with a possible hidden agenda, had passed House Bill 2014 in the House which named the *Acrocanthosaurus* as the state fossil. The bill later died in the Senate Educational Committee, and along with it died the prospect of official state recognition of the *Acrocanthosaurus*. Since that aborted legislative attempt, the Acro was abandoned and forgotten within the highest political and educational institutions of the state. An inherent bias persisted against the Acro and its two parochial discoverers.

Due to the pervasive influence of Weyerhaeuser, an erroneous aspersion had unfairly tainted the Acro and its two excavators. The skeleton of Fran was generally perceived by much of academia – certainly, OU – as having been stolen from a pit on the corporation's river-front fringe. This deleterious stigma could not be shaken and seemed to disparage the allure and legitimacy of the specimen. Consequently, the controversy failed to abate. Subsequent to the failure of House Bill 2014, the *Saurophaganax* was named Oklahoma's state fossil on April 14, 2000.

Apparently, Hall and Love, within the parameters of their epic bone quest, had managed to alienate the corporate gentry, the academic scientocracy, and prominent politicians – namely Republicans, who always sided with the corporate legation. Consequently, only Democrats were in a position to take up the cause of *Acrocanthosaurus* jubilation. Political partisanship had descended to the level of a squabble over old bones – a sentimental reflection of the earlier era bone war of Marsh and Cope.

Reflexively, E. D. Cope had named one of his specimens "cophater" as a testament to his baleful acknowledgement of the scores of Cope haters that surrounded him. Cephis and the dinosaur also suffered from a host of detractors and haters who could barely tolerate the idea of the *Acrocanthosaurus* getting its due.

The situation was kind of like the following words Wallace Stegner, a Marsh partisan of the 1880s, had said about Cope during the Gilded Age I war: "The very bones of tertiary mammals, as he cleaned and arranged them in his Philadelphia home, cried out to him 'revenge'." In a similar vent, it seemed rather obvious that Weyerhaeuser, Langston, Cifelli, OU, and a whole coterie of revenge seekers had conspired against the Acro. A little lobbyist flim-flam had been brought to bear within the political arena to tarnish the Acro brand. Weyerhaeuser had called out for revenge.

The rancor against Hall and the Acro were not just seen inside the corridors of power, but in more prosaic places like the Forest Heritage Museum within Beaver's Bend State Park. Evidence of this can be seen when one goes through the artistic exhibits and comes to the Harry Rossoll diorama depicting the ancient McCurtain Cretaceous landscape and the dinosaurian predator that haunted that landscape. The audio narration erroneously identifies the creature as T.rex; but informed locals know that the Rossoll painting was made with advisory support from Cephis Hall and was intended to portray the Acro, rather than T.rex. There is no evidence that T.rex ever lived in the area; in fact, all its remains have been found in the West. This misnomer is a tiny hint of the inherent bias that still tarnishes the Acro image and is another slap at Hall and the Acro.

For nearly twenty years, the Acro was largely anonymous outside the southeast corner of the state. But Acro partisans wanted to change that. The citizens of southeastern Oklahoma demanded statewide recognition for their beloved Mountain Fork specimen. A fitting moniker needed to be officially imparted. The regional political base was galvanized.

Two public-spirited legislators, State Senator Jeff Rabon (D, Hugo) and State Representative Paul Roan (D, Tishomingo), backed Senate Concurrent Resolution 3 designating *Acrocanthosaurus atokensis* as the state dinosaur of Oklahoma. However, once the resolution was on the docket, it was not easy sledding. Within the state legislature, the last controversy over the Acro was played out. Apparently, there were partisan forces arrayed against granting the Acro its deserved official distinction. A concerted plan of political obstruction was orchestrated by the opposition.

The bill had been assigned to the House Rules Committee and seemed to be stifled in committee. Curiously, Representative Sue Tibbs (R, Tulsa), the Chairperson of the House Rules Committee, was impeding a committee hearing on the bill. In order to be placed on the agenda, the bill had to receive a hearing by the deadline of April 21, 2005.

"I really don't understand why Representative Tibbs is choosing not to hear this legislation. In my nine years of service, I have never encountered such an unusual stance as one that is going on in the House right now. The resolution should have gone straight to the House floor for a vote, and it should not have been assigned to a committee at all. This truly is an inexplicable, unprecedented display by the House Rules Chairwoman," stated Senator Rabon, author of SCR 3.

"I can't believe that the House Rules Committee is holding a 120-million-year-old dinosaur hostage," declared Representative Roan.

"We do not ask for a lot in southeastern Oklahoma, and I believe this is deserved recognition to the region. This unique dinosaur species is very important to our museum and the people in southeastern Oklahoma," concluded Rabon.

Despite the opposition, the bill gradually meandered its way through the legislative maze and was adopted on June 6, 2006. The Acro was finally bestowed with an aura of official regalia. The highest lawmaking body in the state had bequeathed the honor. This called for another celebration to be held at the Museum of The Red River on August 15, 2006.

Once again, local residents and dignitaries from across the state turned out for the festivities. The Acro was no longer just a regional symbol, but now a state icon. Cephis Hall again basked in the glow of public acclaim. But on this occasion, he shared the spotlight with the politicians who had pulled the strings and made the final hurrah possible. The politicians were extolled and celebrated as much as Cephis and the dinosaur, and deservedly so.

State Senator Jeff Rabon and State Representative Jerry Ellis, both instrumental in getting the Acro named as state dinosaur, were honored. Scientific celebrants included Dr. Adrian Hunt of the New Mexico Museum of Natural History as guest speaker, and Oklahoma's own top-ranked paleontologist, Rick Cifelli.

And so this final celebration marked the triumphal end of the dinosaur story – a posthumous award long overdue. No higher official award could possibly be given to a dinosaur. As for Cephis Hall, he made his last debut in the public eye as an amateur paleontologist. His dream had come true, and he knew that Sid could rest easy. He felt exonerated; he had kept his word and held up his part of the bargain. The long ordeal was finished. Cephis Hall, too, could rest easy.

CHAPTER SEVENTY-NINE
Creationists Hound Cephis

Cephis had become a sort of celebrity, or at least a curiosity, not just in McCurtain County, but across the nation. The dinosaur had been saved, the cast made, and Cephis cast into amateur acclaim. Scientists and laymen alike were making contact. He was bombarded with telephone calls, even from famous people. The celebrity of the dinosaur had rubbed off on him.

As his name and fame spread, he began to receive numerous calls from people who wanted to converse about dinosaurology, or some aspect of science or religion. Some callers were credible, while others were outright weird, even deplorable.

Two highly esteemed Ph.D.s, Dr. Louis Jacobs of Southern Methodist University and Adrian Hunt of the New Mexico Museum of Natural History, visited him to chat about the Acro and to inspect his collection of exotic minerals. It was a pleasant visit.

Dr. Jacobs had discovered another Acro skeleton in 1990 in Texas, which has since been excavated and formed the basis for another Acro exhibit at the Fort Worth Museum of Natural History. Dr. Hunt had been a guest speaker at the Museum of the Red River on the day that the Acro was unveiled.

The famed painter Harry Rossoll wanted to meet Cephis after the artist was commissioned by the Forest Heritage Center Museum at Beaver's Bend State Park to paint a diorama of the natural setting of McCurtain County during the early Cretaceous. Naturally, the piece would include an image of the dinosaur set amidst the landscape. Cephis was the technical advisor regarding the description of the beast. The painting is still on display at the museum and is perhaps the star attraction.

Since Cephis and Sid had dug up the dino and had the mounted cast made, they were on the radar of fundamentalist-literalist religionists. Science and religion have been in conflict with each other for centuries, and dinosaurs represent a dicey issue for hard-core Biblical literalists because of the dating controversy. A one hundred million year time frame did not equate with Biblical timelines, thus literalists were always looking for a way to explain away the contradiction. They were forced to go against the grain of prevailing scientific evidence and public fascination with dinosaurs. In order to make the Genesis timeline fit, they had to prove that humans and dinosaurs lived side by side during the same time period: about 2500 – 1600 BC.

Because of the inherent conflict with science over evolution and the scientific dating of rocks and fossils, a considerable segment of religious fundamentalists (particularly within the Christian and Muslim faiths) scorned dinosaur diggers and investigators. In rural Oklahoma and particularly the American South, the sentiment was strong within fringe fundamentalist congregations. Some extremists believed what Cephis and Sid had done was sacrilegious, if not a sinful act in its own right.

There are basically two fundamental ways of thinking about dinosaurs among strict creationists and "literal-interpretationists." One view held that dinosaurs got off Noah's Ark about 4,000 years ago and eventually died out due to depletion of their basic food stocks (coniferous trees, ferns, etc.) or were eventually exterminated by human hunters. In this view, dinos lived simultaneously with humans. This immutable time period went no farther back than 4,500 years ago, and that timeframe was etched in stone. Thus, any new dinosaur finds on the land merely confirmed existing precepts.

In another body of creationist opinion, dinosaur talk was basically taboo. Since the dinosaurs could not be rationally explained or credibly reconciled to fit with Genesis scripture, the subject was ignored. In this dino perspective, people should not talk about them and certainly not dig them – period. Any scientific field project that dug up dinosaurs was blasphemous by its very nature.

From this element of strict literalist constructionists, Cephis had met criticism and skepticism. He was called an atheist by one irate lady for merely having dug up the bones and believing in scientifically constructed theories.

"Ain't it sad that we have so many atheists around here?" she said, as she walked off.

These types of scientific skeptics simply could not accept modern scientific dating as being reasonably accurate because it did not conform to their belief systems. When they asked the dinosaur's age, and Cephis informed them it was about 100 million years, he was met with disbelief, even ridicule. "The world ain't even that old" was a typical response. They believed the dino was less than 4,000 years old, and nothing could convince them otherwise.

One faction of so-called creationists had a rather jejune explanation for the extinction of the dinos. Rather than having been wiped out by an asteroid impact 65 mya, they believed those descendents of the dinosaur pairs boarded on Noah's Ark met a tragic end about 3,000 years ago. Malnourished and emasculated by a depletion of their traditional food staples of conifers and ferns, the last of the hungry beasts were mercilessly cut down in the grain fields by valorous, dragon-slaying spearmen of the Bronze Age. As the hapless behemoths gasped their last breath upon crumpled grain stalks, anthropocentric butchers wielding bronze swords unceremoniously hacked them to pieces where they lay.

Like most people in Oklahoma, Cephis himself had a religious fundamentalist background. He grew up with a Bible in one hand, and a rock in the other. However, he was not a literalist and did not allow interpretative dogma to overwhelm his reason. He understood that the Bible was written by many different men over centuries, and some authors might have misinterpreted the divine translations given to them by God.

Cephis was actually tolerant of diverse shades of religiosity and did not allow a strict interpretation of the Good Book to subvert an objective pursuit of scientific truth.

As word of the discovery and the magnificence of the mounted cast reached the fringes of science and religion, creationists of all stripes came out of the woodwork. They wanted a piece of the dinosaur action and "salvation" too.

Cephis received a number of mysterious calls from the creationist fringe. Among the most baffling was a call from Carl Baugh, often known as "Dr. Baugh," despite having no known credentials of PhD or MD. Baugh was reputed to be the founder of the Creationist Museum in Glen Rose, Texas, and offered an alternative viewpoint for the rise and fall of the dinos rather than the more scientific explanations provided at the nearby Dinosaur Valley State Park, where fossils and dinosaur footprints were on display.

Baugh was pushing his own agenda and now pushed Hall's hot button. "Dr. Baugh" wanted to buy the Acro cast from Cephis. He also wanted something else, and for some mysterious reason, believed Cephis had it.

Baugh had somehow learned that Cephis had dug the dinosaur bones out of a "damned Oklahoma waste pit" and had also retrieved chunks and bits of rock nearby that contained footprints cast in stone – not dinosaur footprints, but human footprints. Baugh believed these fossilized human footprints came out of the same strata and bed as the Mountain Fork monster, making them approximate in age – perhaps within a few years or decades in geologic time from an earth less than 5,000 years old.

At first, Cephis thought this idea preposterous, maybe even a joke. But soon he realized the man was serious. Perhaps he had obtained erroneous information, but from whom?

Although the man persisted in his pitch, things got a little dicey when the cost of the cast came up. Actually, Cephis had already sold the cast to Mike Love for $12,500 and did not know how the caller had gotten the idea he had also discovered fossilized human footprints that were the same age as the dinosaur.

Perhaps just playing along, Cephis quoted him a price nonetheless.

"It will be $50,000 for the cast," he said.

The caller sighed in disbelief. "And what is your price for the barefoot human tracks?" asked the "doctor of creation science."

"I'm afraid it will cost you $100,000 for those pieces. You know they are very rare," Cephis said.

Although Cephis had neither the cast of the dinosaur nor the earthen slab with the human footprints, he let the man speak what was on his mind. "Dr. Baugh" finally admitted he really did not need the human foot prints as he already had some of those. He needed a genuine Acro cast because he knew the dino as a local Texas denizen, and he wanted to put it on display alongside his "rock embedded slabs of localized human footprints." Upon learning the high cost of the cast, he had a simple solution to his shortfall in blessed godly remuneration. He asked Cephis to donate the cast in benevolent service to his own divinely-inspired Creationist Museum in Glen Rose.

Here was a literal, creationist Christian talking to a more moderate or secularist Christian. Baugh must have assumed Hall talked the same language, walked the same walk, knelt at the same altar, and espoused the same literalist-fundamentalist viewpoint.

"Dr. Baugh" was likely the same kind of yokefellow who patronized and extolled science with patriotic zeal when it came to cell phones, the Internet, nuclear-tipped warheads, Star Wars defense systems, intercontinental ballistic missiles, nuclear-powered generating plants, deep offshore drilling, genetic engineering, robotization, automated-push button warfare, open heart surgery, agrochemicals, etc. But when it came to scientific dating and interpreting of rocks, fossils, or geological strata, he and his minions contended that science was still stuck in the Dark Ages, if not the Stone Age.

"You know you could make a contribution to the Lord by donating that cast to the church," stated the righteous diviner of fossils and rocks.

Cephis answered, "I will give it some consideration."

Once the conversation turned to money and no oral commitment to the Lord made, the Lord's servant in "creationist inspiration" decided to continue his search elsewhere.

Other calls from so-called creationists continued to come in, which kept Cephis on his toes. Another call from a creationist church or museum (or both) somewhere around Syracuse, New York, bobbled Cephis. The caller stated he already had the dinosaur (he did not say which one) and needed only the barefoot human tracks. Somebody had ostensibly told him that Cephis was a fellow creationist and had exactly what he needed.

Again, Cephis was baffled. Somehow these people had been told and apparently believed that he was eager to sell or donate his stone casts of fossilized human foot prints allegedly discovered amidst the same claystone with the carnivorous beast. How did all these callers get the idea he was a creationist cut in their same mold?

Now becoming annoyed, Cephis simply told the inquirer that he did not know about any such barefoot human tracks, but if he did find some, he would contact him and gladly donate them for the cause. However, the man was still persistent. He did not believe Cephis was shooting straight with him. It took a while for Cephis to convince the man he had received erroneous information.

"Well, please do contact us when you find them or wish to make a donation," the caller retorted as he abruptly hung up the phone.

After a while later, the calls from creationists stopped coming. Perhaps the seekers had found what they were looking for elsewhere, or had just given up on Cephis.

CHAPTER EIGHTY
The Tail of the Tale

The story of Cephis Hall, Sid Love, and their fight to save the dinosaur ended in triumph. Hall and Love surmounted multiple hardships and obstacles and rose to the summit of amateur success in a battle across many venues — the field of discovery, the field of excavation, the field of recovery, and the field of dreams. The narration of Hall and Love's struggle against overwhelming odds is an account of a Herculean achievement of the human spirit.

Hall and Love took up the banner of the underdog in a world where the underdog is often programmed to fail. The elites have gone to great lengths to make sure of that. The lofty and the privileged stacked the deck in their favor, but Cephis and Sid climbed the ladder — broken rungs and all — to raise their banner. In a bizarre way, Cephis won revenge against the very social system that had "caste" him as a kind of social pariah and oddity since his earliest days. Against bullies old and new, Hall parlayed his struggle into an extraordinary account of the lowly surpassing the lordly.

The pages of this book have celebrated that struggle — a struggle drenched in romanticism and contrarianism as it revels in the mystery and majesty of untamed nature and the lonely heroism of the individual. Foreboding naturalism was transformed into perturbing factionalism as the conflict assumed many forms and progressed through many stages. The bone war of McCurtain County hearkens back to an older crop of dino explorers and a bone war of an earlier era — the bone war of the two eccentric scientists O.C. Marsh and E.D. Cope during the late nineteenth century.

But Hall and Love's war was different. Their war was fought against many adversaries, particularly the intervening forces of bureaucratic institutions, rather than the inflamed egos of rival aristocratic scientists. Instead of battling eccentric personalities and polemics, Cephis and Sid defeated an intact political-economic system that wanted to confiscate their property. Their story is a tale of the triumph of the common man against entrenched elites.

The tables were reversed in their Gilded Age II bone war. While Marsh, the man of paramount institutional power, won the earlier bone war of Gilded Age I, the paragons of institutional power lost in the modern provincial Bone War of McCurtain County.

Hall and Love had timed their conquest well. In the bare nick of time, they finished the excavation phase of their mission. Not long after their dig was complete, a Hundred Year's Flood cascaded through Oklahoma. Shortly thereafter, entrance into

Weyerhaeuser lands was gated, thus denying access to the former grave of the beast and company lands elsewhere across southeastern Oklahoma. The mysteries and secrets still hidden amidst the clay bedding of the Acro quarry and adjacent lands were sealed off to the outside world.

Although the Great Flood of 1990 came too late to wash the bones away from where they lay, these precious relics defeated their most daunting adversary (pyrite) to ultimately become a showpiece in a world-class museum. Surpassing the moniker "bones of contention," they became the "bones of distinction" when the North Carolina Museum of Science ordained the skeleton as its star spectacular and Oklahoma officials proclaimed it their state dinosaur.

Despite the Acrocanthosaurus genus succumbing to extinction, the bones of Fran received their just distinction. In the course of her story becoming reality, the principal characters in the plot revealed their true intentions and predilections. In due course, new celebrities emerged to bask in the limelight and brandish the mystique of the dinosaur, at least for a time.

As the dinosaur story unfolded, it was given a new twist. The cast of characters was replete with egos, passions, conspirators, winners and losers, and heroes and villains. The multifarious cast included the following individuals, who were cast in conspicuous molds as they played out their roles and left indelible marks: Graffham might have been mysterious; Dr. Langston, duplicitous; Pittman, invidious; Weyerhaeuser, treacherous; the police raiders, nefarious; the dinosaur, astounding; the bones, confounding; and, the pyrite affliction, alarming. But Cephis Hall and Sid Love topped them all — being genuinely "bone-a-fied," mystified, anthologized, and sanctified in the unpublished annals portraying the manifest conquest of the downscale, miniscule amateur over the upscale, grandiose professional. All this while being red-necked, sun-bleached, and sweat-drenched in the mists of the hollows, hills, peaks and troughs of pine forests, pot fields, toxic pits, submerged mines, bone beds, crystal glitz, and dinosaur bliss. The high and mighty had met their match in Hall and Love, and succumbed to more determined and luckier foes. But the press did not see it quite that way.

The official world did not celebrate their victories over their foes, but instead celebrated their contribution in saving the dinosaur from certain destruction. But credit was not always given where it was due. Allan Graffham, the man with the cash, got most of the glory for saving the dinosaur, while the two men from "down under" were mentioned only in short lines and passing phrases — a kind of honorable mention in small print tucked beneath heaps of praise for the wisdom and techniques of Graffham, BHI, and the wealthy benefactors behind the scenes who received their tax benefits for their donations and munificence.

But there were several phases of the rest of the dinosaur story: the conquest of nature; the defeat of numerous foes in the struggle over rightful ownership and possession of the creature; the cash infusions to rejuvenate the dilapidated bones; the splendid expertise, technique, hands-on labor, and intensive care to bring the bones back from the brink; and, the tides of generous monetary donations for the skeleton's ultimate purchase.

In the end, the two obscure excavators did get their monetary reward—duly compensated at less than the minimum wage—for all their sacrifice. But they were not complaining; instead, they were pleased they had saved the dinosaur and made their own contribution to science and community. But most of all, their names would be forever etched on an elusive and tenuous monument to amateur paleontology.

Hall and Love received no royalties from any future sales of casts made of their fossilized tangibles. Unlike fossilized plant material (oil, natural gas, or coal), animal fossils do not bestow monetary riches, at least it didn't for Hall and Love. While oil or coal earns royalties, dinosaur fossils return none, unless one happens to be an Alan Graffham (who owned his own quarries) or a Maurice Williams (whose royalties were paid compliments of the hard work of Pete Larson and BHI and in virtue of his tribal affiliation). Fossilized bones might earn enough of a cash payout to cover the costs and labor of excavation.

Cephis Hall and Sid Love are two of the hardest-working stiffs in the history of American labor — each holding down several jobs and working seven days a week, almost continuously, for over a decade. The mounted cast of the *Acrocanthosaurus* now adorning the halls and galleries of some of the best museums in America is a testament to the hard, enduring labor that was expended in pursuit of their dream. As their story radiated out from the backwoods of southeastern Oklahoma, a tiny snippet of the heroic age of American vertebrate paleontology was recaptured.

Old-fashioned naturalists such as Hall and Love are a vanishing breed in a land drastically transformed by ever-expanding urban development and renewal. With the great frontier ended and open lands sealed off by corporations, government, and large, private landowners, there is little free and open space for the indulgent passions of adventurous men like Hall and Love. Modern populations have become estranged from the land and the land-bearing wonderments, not to mention a growing irreverence toward nature itself. One can see this in the declining memberships of gem and mineral clubs – at least in America – where the average age looks to be about 65 years old, and few young faces are seen at monthly meetings. The Cephis Halls of the world may become rarer than the treasures they once hunted.

Cephis and Sid are champions of the underdog in a society apparently more sympathetic to the super rich (the so-called 1%) than the working class. They are an inspiration to anyone who has ever directly confronted the raw, naked power of towering institutions.

In the end, it was likely their credibility and reputation within the community that kept the full weight of the law from crashing down on them with the same blunt force that had crushed medieval peasants and yeomen who were bold enough to trespass on the lord's vast estates. The record suggests that Cephis and Sid had stature within the community. In a scenario in which the diggers were unknowns, quite certainly the county sheriff, like the sheriffs of the medieval forests, would have conceded to the demands of the modern-day lords of the forest and nabbed the men and their fossils.

The transition of McCurtain society during the late twentieth and early twenty-first century mirrored the nation as it evolved from a backwater, provincial, semi-open frontier to an integrated, corporate-dominated, closed-frontier. The struggles of Hall and Love against entrenched corporate power parallel the experience of the American industrial worker.

As the gates close on open access to great landed estates, factory doors are also being locked and keyed. Workers are shut out, and their jobs taken by robots or exported to cheaper labor havens overseas. Both blue-collar naturalists and blue-collar, industrial workers are being disenfranchised from open access to nature and factory, respectively, while land ownership patterns gradually return to a proto-medieval style. The medieval world was nothing if not a series of private fiefdoms organized into regional jurisdictions under the ownership and control of a local lord, who owed allegiance to no one but the Church and King.

As larger and larger conglomerations of land are consolidated into fewer and fewer hands, great private lordships in the form of corporations, oligarchs, and plutocratic-landed barons will reemerge. Under the emerging neo-feudalistic society, the corporations and super-wealthy will be the lords, while everybody else a vassal or peasant. In such a scenario, the ideal of individual freedom and the spirit of the open frontier will become an archaic relic from the long-vanished Jacksonian democracy.

The story of Cephis Hall and Sid Love represents a rare instance in history when two little guys defeated giants. Their story is unique, mainly because they themselves are unique. Cephis and Sid are men of uncommon fortitude and rectitude, who stood their ground against overwhelming odds and won—a David and Goliath story if ever there was one. With the nation spiraling into crisis, American society needs more men like Cephis and Sid—men who obey the laws and are patriotic, but capable of questioning the status quo; men of uncommon honesty, simplicity, and integrity who are willing to sacrifice and stand strong against overwhelming adversity; men of fierce, independent minds and spirits; men with strong internal values and moral convictions; men who respect nature and the environment and stand in striking contrast to those who don't. Such men are a dying breed at a time when they are needed most.

Science and posterity owe tribute to these two men. Without their unbridled perseverance and undaunted courage, the most complete skeleton of one of the greatest predators in all earth's history and the corresponding scientific knowledge that ultimately accrues from the study of those rare, tangible remains would have been lost forever.

Lest the world forget, these were two men who endured hardships they did not have to bear. Their mark lives on through the memories they shared, the tales of their conquests laid bare, and the magnificent exhibits for the world to compare.

Notes-Sources

Chapter 2
Blevins, Brooks, *Arkansas/Arkansaw: How Bear Hunters, Hillbillies, and Good Ol' Boys Defined A State*, Univ. of Arkansas Press, Fayetteville, AR, 2009

McCurtain Daily Gazette, June 1, 1990

Hemphill, Paul, *The Good Old Boys*, Simon &Schuster, New York, 1974

Hogeland, William, *The Whiskey Rebellion*, A Lisa Drew Book/Scribner, New York, NY, 2006

Ste. Clare, Dana, *Cracker*, Univ. Press of Florida, Gainesville, FL., 1998

Chapter 5
Charig, Alan, *A New Look At The Dinosaurs*, British Museum of Natural History, New York, 1979

Bakker, Robert T., *The Dinosaur Heresies*, William Morrow and Company, New York, 1986

Dingus, Lowell, *Hell Creek Montana*, St. Martin's Press, New York, 2004

Fiffer, Steve, *Tyrannosaurus Sue*, W. H. Freeman, New York, NY 2000

Haines, Tim, *Walking With Dinosaurs*, BBC Worldwide LTD, London, UK, 2000

Horner, Jack, *Digging Dinosaurs*, Harper & Row Publishers, New York, 1988

Horner, Jack, *How to Build a Dinosaur*, Dutton, of the Penguin Group, New York, 2009

Jacobs, Louis, *Lone Star Dinosaurs*, Texas A&M University Press, College Station, Texas, 1995

Larson, Peter and Donnan, Kristin, *Rex Appeal*, Invisible Cities Press, Montpelier, VT, 2002

Jaffe, Mark, *The Gilded Dinosaur*, Crown Publishing, New York, NY, 2000

Lessem, Don, *Kings of Creation*, Simon & Schuster, New York, 1992

Norell, Mark, Dingus, Lowell, and Gaffney, Eugene, *Discovering Dinosaurs*, U. of California Press, Berkeley, CA, 1995

Parker, Steve and Mertz, Leslie, *Extreme Dinosaurs*, Harper Collins, New York, NY, 2008

Wallace, Joseph, *The Rise and Fall of the Dinosaur*, Gallery Books, New York, 1987

West, David, *Encyclopedia of Dinosaurs*, Parragon Publishing, Bath, UK, 2002

The Dinosaur Monsters Emerge: The Elite Killers, wHYY, Turner Broadcasting System, PBS Home Video, Turner Home Entertainment, Atlanta, GA, 1992

Dinosaur Enclyclopedia, Igloo Books Ltd., Oxfordshire, UK, 2006

The Planet, Charon Film, Sveriges TV, AB Dokumentia with AS Videomaker, A film by Michael Stenberg, John Soderberg, Linus Torrell, Produced by John Kellagher and Michael Stenberg

Chapter 6
Agin, Dan, PH.D., *Junk Science: How Politicians, Corporations and Other Hucksters Betray Us*, St. Martin's Press, New York, 2006

Colbert, Edwin H., *The Great Dinosaur Hunters and their Discoveries*, General Publishing Co., LTD., Toronto, Ontario, 1968, 1984

Dingus, Lowel, *Hell Creek Montana*, St. Martin's Press, New York, 2004

Jaffe, Mark, *The Gilded Dinosaur*, Crown Publishers, New York, 2000

Fiffer, Steve, *Tyrannosaurus Sue*, W. H.Freeman and Company, New York, NY, 2000

Laham, Url, *The Bone Hunters, The Heroic Age of Paleontology in the American West*, Columbia Univ. Press, New York, 1973

Travels With The Fossil Hunters, Edited by Peter Whybrow, Cambridge University Press, UK, 2000

Miller, Kenneth R., *Only a Theory – Evolution and the Battle for America's Soul*, Penguin Group, New York, 2008

Mooney, Chris, *The Republican War on Science*, Basic Books – A Member of the Perseus Books Group, New York, 2005

Pierce, Charles, *Idiot America*, Doubleday, New York, NY, 2009

Wallace, David Rains, *Bonehunter's Revenge*, Houghton Mifflin, New York, 1999

Creation Museum, from Wikipedia, The Free Enclyclopedia,

Wapshott, Nicholas, *Third World Traveler*, The Darwin Exhibition Frightening Off Corporate Sponsors, www.telegraphco.uk, November 20, 2005

En.wikipedia.org?wiki/creationist_museum

Scienceblogs.com./Pharyngula

Crooksandliars.com/2007/05/28/the-creation museum

Chapter 7

Applebome, Peter, *Dixie Rising*, Harcourt Brace & Co., New York, 1996

Ayers, Edward L., *What Caused the Civil War? Reflections on the South and Southern History*, W.W. Norton & Company, Inc., New York, 2005

Bageant, Joe, *Deer Hunting With Jesus*, Crown Publishing of Random House, New York, 2007

Biggers, Jeff, *The United States of Appalachia*, Shoemaker & Hoard, New York, 2006

Bledsoe, Jerry, *Just Folks*, East Woods Press, Charlotte, NC 1980

Blevins, Brooks, *Arkansas/Arkansaw, How Bear Hunters, Hillbillies & Good Ol' Boys Defined a State*, The Univ. of Arkansas Press, Fayetteville, AR., 2009

Bultman, Bethany, *Redneck Heaven*, Bantam Books, New York, NY 1996

Burkhard, Bilger, *Noodling for Flatheads*, Touchstone, New York, 2000

Cash, W. J., *The Mind of the South*, Vintage Books, Alfred A. Knopf, Inc. and Random House Inc., New York, 1941

Dugan, Myles, *How the Irish Won the West,* Skyhorse Publishing, New York, 2011

Dunbar-Ortiz, Roxanne, *Red Dirt – Growing Up Okie,* Verso, New York, 1997

Egan, Timothy, *The Worst Hard Time,* Houghton Mifflin, New York, 2006

Escott, Paul. D. and Goldfield, David R., *The South For New Southerners*, Univ. of N. Carolina Press, Chapel Hill, NC., 1991

Fry, Michael, *How the Scots Made America,* Thomas Dunn Books, New York, 2003

Goad, Jim, *The Redneck Manifesto*, Simon & Schuster, New York, 1997

Graham, Michael, *Redneck Nation*, Warner Books, New York, 2002

Hemphill, Paul, *The Good Old Boys*, Simon & Schuster, New York, 1974

Lavin, Patrick, *The Celtic World*, Hippocrene Books, Inc., New York, 1999

Ignatiev, Noel, *How the Irish Became White*, Rutledge, New York, 1995

Magee, David, *The South is Round*, Jefferson Press, Lookout Mountain, TN., 2007

McCarthy, Karen, *The Other Irish*, Sterling Publishing, New York, NY 2011

Mead, Walter J., The Jacksonian Tradition, *National Interest*, Winter, 1888-2000, pp. 11-12

McCurtain County – A Pictorial History, McCurtain County Historical Society, P.O. Box 922, Idabel, Oklahoma, 1982

McWhiney, Grady, *Confederate Crackers and Cavaliers*, McWhiney Foundation Press, Abilene, Texas, 2002

McWhiney, Grady, *Cracker Culture: Celtic Ways in the Old South*, The University of Alabama Press, Tuscaloosa, Alabama, 1988

McWhiney, Grady, *Southerners and Other Americans*, Basic Books Inc., New York, 1973

Pierce, Charles, *Idiot America*, Doubleday, New York, NY., 2009

Ste.Claire, Dana, *Cracker*, Univ. Press of Florida, Gainesville, Fl., 1998

Thompson, John, *Closing the Frontier – Radical Response in Oklahoma, 1889-1923*, the University of Oklahoma Press, Norman Ok, 1986

Webb, James, *Born Fighting – How the Scots-Irish Shaped Americ*a, Broadway Books, a division of Random House, Inc., New York, 2004

Wray, Matt, *Not Quite White: White Trash and the Boundaries of Whiteness*, Duke University Press, Durham, NC, 2006

Wray, Matt, and Newitz, Annalee, *White Trash: Race and Class in America*, Routledge, New York, NY, 1997

Oklahoma Territory – Wikipedia, the free encyclopedia; en.wikipedia.org/wiki/Oklahoma Territory

Land Run of 1889 – Wikipedia, the free encyclopedia; en.wikipedia.org/wiki/Land_Run_1889

The Oklahoma Land Rush of 1893, www.eyewitnesstohistory.com/landrush.htm

Boomer Movement, digitallibrary.okstateedu/encyclopedia/entries

Sooners – Wikipedia, the free encyclopedia; en.wikipedia.org

The Land Run – Boomers versus Sooners; cityoftulsa.org/our city/budget/documents/Sec03a – Departmental Budget Highlights/Public Safety And

Trail of Tears, Wikipedia, the free encyclopedia; en.wikipedia.org/wiki/Trail_of_Tears

The States, The Oklahoma Territory, Nicholas Stern, Producer, Robert Hughes, Co-Producer, Steve Mellom, Editor, Green Scripts Graphics, Crazy Ridge Studios; for the History Channel

www.oklahomacasinocitytimes.com

en.wikipedia.org/wiki/Choctaw_casino_and_resort

Chapter 12

Malam, John and Parker, Steve, *Encyclopedia of Dinosaurs*, Parragon Publishing, Bath, UK, 2006

Dinosaur Encyclopedia, Igloo Books LTD., Oxfordshire, UK, 2006

Haines, Tim, *Walking with Dinosaurs*, Metro Books, New York, 2008

En.wikipedia.org/wiki/spinosaurus

En.wikipedia.org/wiki/suchomimus

www.projectexploration.org/suchomimus

Chapter 13

Farlow, James, "Acrocanthosaurus and the maker of Comanchean large theropod footprints," Tanke, Darren and Carpenter, Ken, *Mesozoic Vertebrate Life*, Indiana University Press, pp 408-427

Forest Heritage Museum, the Harry Rossol Diorama, Beavers Bend State Park, Broken Bow, Oklahoma

McCurtain Daily Gazette, June 28, 1990, Volume 85, Number 15

Rockhounding and Earth Science Activities in Oklahoma, 1995 Workshop, Oklahoma Geological Survey Special Publication, 96-5, 1996, Kenneth S. Johnson and Neal H. Suneson, Editors

www.ogs.ou.edu/pubsscanned/guidebooks/GB-29pdf

en.wikipedia.org/wiki/geology_of_Oklahoma

en.wikipedia.org/wiki/Geography_of_Oklahoma

geology.about.com/od/geology_ok/Oklahomageology.htm

Chapter 19

Bakker, Robert T., *Raptor Red*, Bantam Books, New York, 1995

Jacobs, Louis, *Lone Star Dinosaurs*, Texas A & M University Press, College Station, TX, 1995

Larson, Neal, *Dinosaurs Illustrated*, Winter Edition, 1996

Lessem, Don, *Kings of Creation*, Simon & Schuster, New York, 1992

Wilford, John Noble, *The Riddle of the Dinosaur*, Alfred A Knopf, New York, 1985

Chapter 20

Gillette, David, *Seismosaurus The Earth Shaker*, Columbia University Press, 1994

Bakker, Robert T., *Raptor Red*, Bantam Books, New York, 1995

Chapter 23

Bacevich, Andrew J. *The Limits of Power*, Henry Holt & Co., New York, 2008

Bageant, Joe, *Deer Hunting With Jesus*, Crown Publishing, of Random House, New York, 2007

Frank, Thomas, *One Market Under God*, Anchor Books, of Random House, New York, 2000

Frank, Thomas, *What's the Matter With America?* Secker & Warburg, London, England, 2004

Frank, Thomas, *What's the Matter With Kansas?*, Metropolitan Books – Henry Holt and Co., New York, 2004

Frank, Thomas, *Pity the Billionaire*, Henry Holt & Co., New York, NY, 2012

Galbraith, James K., *The Predator State*, page 116, Free Press, of Simon & Schuster, New York, 2008

Geenwald, Glenn, *With Liberty and Justice For Some*, Metropolitan Books, New York, NY., 2011

Hamel, Gary and Prahalad, C.K. *Competing for the Future*, Harvard Business School Press, Boston, MA, 1994

Hedges, Chris, *Empire of Illusion – The End of Literacy and the Triumph of Spectacle*, Nation Books, a member of the Perseus Books Group, New York, 2009

Hightower, Jim, *Thieves in High Places*, Penguin Group, New York, 2003

Horner, Jack, *How to Build a Dinosaur*, Penguin Group, New York, 2009

Huffington, Arianna, *Pigs at the Trough*, Crown Publishers, New York, 2003

Jaffe, Mark, *The Gilded Dinosaur*, Crown Publishers, New York, 2000

Johnson, David Cay, *Free Lunch*, Penguin Group, New York, 2007

Judis, John B., *The Folly of Empire*, Oxford Univ. Press, New York, 2004

Kennedy, Robert F. Jr., *Crimes Against Nature*, Harper Collins Publishers, New York, 2004

Korten, David C., *When Corporations Rule the World*, Kumarian Press, Bloomfield, CT, 2001

Larson, Peter and Donnan, Kristin, *Rex Appeal*, Invisible Cities Press, Montpelier, VT, 2002

Lifton, Robert J., *Super Power Syndrome*, Thunder's Mouth Press/Nation Books, New York, 2003

Mooney, Chris, *The Republican War On Science*, Basic Books, a member of the Perseus Books Group, New York, 2005

Stiglitz, Joseph E., *The Three Trillion Dollar War*, W.W. Norton & Co., New York, 2008

Thompson, John, *Closing the Frontier*, University of Oklahoma Press, Norman, OK, 1986

White, Curtis, *The Middle Mind – Why Americans Don't Think For Themselves*, Harper Collins Publishers, New York, 2003

Zinn, Howard, *A Peoples' History of the United States*, Harper Collins Publishers, New York, NY

Chapter 29

Applebome, Peter, *Dixie Rising*, Harcourt Brace & Co., New York, 1996

Bacevich, Andrew J., *The Limits of Power – The End of American Exceptionalism*, Henry Holt and Company, New York, 2008

Briody, Dan, *The Halliburton Agenda – The Politics of Oil and Money*, John Wiley & Sons, Hoboken, NJ, 2004

Greider, William, "The Contractor Scofflaws," *The Nation*, pages 4-6, March 22, 2010

Juhasz, Antonia, *The Bush Agenda*, Harper Collins Publishers, New York, 2006

Kleinknech, William, *The Man Who Sold the World – Ronald Reagan and the Betrayal of Main Street America*, Nation Books, New York, 2009

McCarthy, Karen, *The Other Irish – The Scots-Irish Rascals that Made America*, Sterling Publishing, New York, 2011

The Rachel Maddow Show, MSNBC

Thompson, John, *Closing the Frontier – Radical Response in Oklahoma, 1889-1923*, The U of OK Press, Norman, OK, 1986

www.paleo.org/meeting/2007/romersimpsonmedalwinner.cfm

www.utexas.edu

en.wikipedia.org/wiki/Wann_Langston_Jr.

Chapter 41

Greenwald, Glenn, *With Liberty and Justice For Some*, Metropolitan Books, New York, 2011

Chapter 49

U.S. Archives, Cephis Hall and Sid Love Versus Weyerhaeuser Corporation, A Washington State Corporation, No. 88-544-C, State District Court, Eastern District of Oklahoma, Tulsa, OK

Chapter 51

Applebome, Peter, *Dixie Rising*, Harcourt Brace & Co., New York, NY 1996

Bageant, Joe, *Deer Hunting With Jesus*, Crown Publishing, New York, NY 2007

Bultman, Bethany, *Redneck Heaven,* Bantam Books, New York, NY 1996

De Tocqueville, Alexis, *Democracy in America,* Dearborn and Co., New York, NY 1838

Escot, Paul D. and Goldfield, David R., *The South For New Southerners,* Univ. of N. Carolina Press, Chapel Hill, NC 1991

Graham, Michael, *Redneck Nation,* Warner Books, New York, NY 2002

Grantham, Dewey W., *The South in Modern America: A Religion at Odds,* University of Arkansas Press, Fayetteville, AR 2001

Hemphill, Paul, *The Good Old Boys,* Simon & Schuster, New York, NY 1974

Hedges, Chris, *American Fascists,* Free Press, Simon & Schuster, New York, NY 2006

Magee, David, *The South is Round,* Jefferson Press, Lookout Mountain, TN 2007

McCarthy, Karen, *The Other Irish,* Sterling Publishing, New York, NY 2011

Pierce, Charles, *Idiot America,* Doubleday, New York, NY 2009

Scheer, Robert, *The Pornography of Power,* Hachette Book Group, New York, NY 2008

Wray, Matt, *Not Quite White: White Trash and the Boundaries of Whiteness,* Duke University Press, Durham, NC 2006

Wray, Matt and Newitz, Annalee, *White Trash: Race and Class in America,* Routledge, New York, NY 1997

Chapter 52

Forest Heritage Museum, Beavers Bend State Park, Broken Bow, OK

McCurtain County A Pictorial History, Volume 1, McCurtain County Historical Society, Idabel, OK

Jackson, Ron," How Clean is the Mountain Fork?" *The Daily Oklahoman,* Redorbit.com, Feb. 17, 2006

Letter dated October 6, 2005 from Christopher Jones, Texas Committee on Natural Resources to Don Maisch, Water Quality Division, Oklahoma Department of Environmental Quality (ODEQ)

Report of the National Wildlife Federation Blue-Ribbon Panel on Wildlife and Forestry, Assessment of the Weyerhaeuser Company's Forestry Operations in Southwestern Arkansas and Southeastern Oklahoma, funded under a grant from the Winthrop Rockefeller Foundation, Little Rock, AR, October, 1982

River and Environmental Issues, Southwest Paddler.com/docs/MtnFork1.html

Turner, John C. and Perkins, Larry M., Department of Sociology, Oklahoma State University, Final Report: Land Use Change in South McCurtain County, Oklahoma, in cooperation with Weyerhaeuser Company, Wright City, Oklahoma, 1983, Idabel Public Library, Idabel, Oklahoma

Chapter 62

Fiffer, Steve, *Tyrannosaurus Sue,* W.H. Freeman and Company, New York, 2000

Chapter 64

Acro Exhibit, N.C. Museum of Science, Raleigh, N.C.

Franzosa, Jonathy and Rowe, Timothy, (2005) "Cranial endocast of the Cretaceous theropod dinosaur Acrocanthosaurus atokensis" Journal of Vertebrate Paleontology 25 (4)

Horner, Jack, *Digging Dinosaurs,* Harper & Rowe Publishers, New York, 1988

Larson, Peter and Donnan, Kristin, *Rex Appeal,* Invisible Cities Press, Nation Books, Montpelier VT, 2002

Museum of the Rockies, T.rex displays, 600 W. Kagy Blvd., Bozeman, MT

Utah Museum of Natural History, dinosaur display, 1390 Presidents Circle, Salt Lake City, Utah

When Dinosaurs Ruled China, David TIdballs, Director and Producer, Jonathan Hews, Simon Lloyd, Executive Producers, BBC Worldwide America, Discovery Channel Images, American Museum of Natural History, Home Planet Productions

Wolfe, Ron, Digging up Dinosaurs, *Arkansas Democrat Gazette,* June 2, 2012

Chapter 66
McCurtain Gazette, November 7, 1990

Chapter 75
The Hochatown Tourist, May 2001

West, Bob, *McCurtain Gazette*, September 29, 2000, Volume 95, No. 64

DeQueen *Daily Gazette,* March 3, 2005, Volume 71, No. 214

Index

A

Advisory Board for the Conservation of Paleontological Remains, 322
Age of Dinosaurs 43, 44, 170
Agrarian South, 66
Alf, Dixie, 264, 266
Alf, John, 264, 266, 267
Alger, Horatio, 18, 198
Allosaurus, 58,106, 114, 136, 137, 355, 356,357, 360, 361, 401
American cowboy, 361
American Dream, 18, 19, 20, 195, 196, 198, 319, 203
American Museum of Natural History, 139
American South, 13, 60, 69, 74, 75, 298
American West, 53, 54, 56, 58, 62, 76, 77, 89, 139, 162, 169, 174
Ancient Celts, 69
Anglo Saxon culture, 68
Antlers Sand Formation, 37, 106, 110, 148
Appalachia/Appalachians, 4, 7, 9, 10, 11, 66, 67, 331
Appalachian-cloned hillbillies, 9
Appalachian frontiersmen, 29
Ardmore, OK, 230, 282, 284, 326, 327, 341
Arkansas hillbilly, 5, 6, 7, 182
Arkansas razorback, 9, 70, 178
Arkies, 1, 5, 7, 9, 10, 66, 72
Association of Applied Paleontological Science, 322
Asteroid impact, 46
Austin, TX, 226, 227, 230

B

Badlands, 60, 61
Baer, Max, 100
Bakersfield, CA, 5
Balcones Research Lab, 205, 221
Bakker, Robert T, 137, 138, 139, 167, 168, 370
Barbecue, craze of, 70
Battle of the Boyne, 7
Battle of Sterling Bridge, 8
Beast of the Southeast, 353, 401
Beaver's Bend State Park, 12, 191, 402
Bible Belt,189
Bible thumpers, 69

Big Foot, 18, 129
Bird, Roland T., 139
Black Hills Institute (BHI), 23, 174,234, 235, 264, 265, 276, 285, 291,315, 316, 317, 318, 322, 333, 334, 335, 346, 347, 348, 349, 350, 351, 353, 359, 360
Boar cult, 70
Broken Bow, OK, 9, 10, 11, 12, 74,148, 180, 198, 289, 310, 370
Broken Bow Lake, 24, 366
Bronson, Charles, 100
Brown, Barnum, 59, 62, 63, 64, 139, 163

C

Caesar, Julius, 69
California dreaming, 1, 7
Callahan, Leroy, Dr, 179, 180, 181
Campbell Soup Company, 2
Carnegie, Andrew, 50, 58, 59, 163
Carnegie Museum, 58
Carcharodontosaurus, 355, 356, 357
Carter County, 119, 327, 329, 375
Catholic Irish, 68
Catfish noodling, 72
Celts, 68, 69, 70, 71, 72, 74
Celtic ancestors, 74
Celtic folkways, 72
Celtic homelands, 74
Celtic cotton culture, 68
Celtic mountain culture, 68, 69
Celtic Nation, 69
Chief Red Cloud, 55
Choctaw/s, 9, 10, 11, 12, 28, 71, 74, 90, 93, 167, 168, 169, 304
Choctaw aristocracy, 9, 30, 255
Choctaw Lumber Company, 9, 10, 12, 304
Choctaw Nation, 9, 10, 29, 99, 391
Cifelli, Rich PhD, 190, 191, 262, 333, 334, 335, 336, 337, 338, 339, 342, 343, 359, 360, 369, 370, 371, 402, 403
Citizens Against Lawsuit Abuse, 359
Civilian Conservation Camps, (CCC), 12, 13, 101, 205
Clear cutting, 16, 307
Cody, William "Buffalo Bill", 55
Cold War, 8, 168, 196
Cockfighting, 73, 74

Confederacy, 68, 69, 75, 93
Confederate gold, 18
Confederate Nationalism, 70
Confederate South, 11, 93
Cope, Edward D, 53, 54, 55, 56, 57, 62, 63, 76, 77, 133, 155, 162, 164, 167, 220, 298, 402, 409
Coprolite, 160
Coon hunting, 72, 73
Cotton South, 11
Cowboy/s, 178
Cowboy of lizards, 361
Cracker/s, 8
Cracker culture, 8, 68, 69
Craig Fiberboard Plant, 102, 124, 152, 304, 306, 307, 308, 309, 310, 312, 314
Cretaceous Period, 22, 31, 37, 43, 45, 46, 109, 113, 136, 148, 150, 355, 369
Crystal zone, 12, 319
Curry, Phil PhD, 358

D

Daily Ardmorite, 342
Dalquest, Walter PhD, 132, 133, 136, 137, 140, 186, 193, 220
Davies, Kyle PhD, 359, 360
Deep South, 68, 69
Deinonychus, 111, 115, 116
Delashaw, Kenneth, 341, 342, 343, 359, 360
De Tocqueville, Alexis, 301
DeQueen, AR, 9, 10, 179, 180, 275, 311
Dierks/Dierks brothers, 10, 15, 16, 84, 102, 304, 305, 306
Dinosaurian Age, 215
Dinosaur National Monument, 57, 58
Dinosaur Valley State Park, 139
Dixie/Dixieland, 9, 11, 302
Dixie Mafia, 180
Douglas, Earl, 58, 62, 63, 163
Due, Lemuel, 180, 338, 339
Due, Steve, 338, 339, 363, 364, 365, 366, 367
Durant, Ok, 74, 93
Dust Bowl, 7

E

Eagletown, OK, 9, 10, 12, 23, 24, 76, 113, 172, 178, 225
Edward 1, King, 8
Ellis, Jerry, 403
Elkhart, IN, 1
Enlightenment/Enlightenment Age, 128
ESP, 17, 34

Evolutionists, 54

F

Fallen, Mary, 400
Faulkner, William, 299
Faubus, Orval, 339
Farrar, Bob, 351, 378, 379
Fender, Freddie, 2
Federal Antiquities Act, 348
Feudalism, 232, 412
Field Museum, 351, 352
Field of dreams, 5, 409
Five Civilized Tribes Museum, 266
Floyd, Billie, 262, 265, 266
Forest Heritage Museum, 97, 402, 405
Fort Worth Museum of Natural History, 405
Fort Smith, AR, 100
Fort Towson, Ok, 11
Fran, the dinosaur, 347, 348, 349, 375, 402, 409, 410

G

Gardner Family Museum, 39, 391
Gardner, Jefferson, 391
Gardner Mansion & Museum, 98
Gastroliths, 161
Gates, Bill, 165
Geological Enterprises, 230, 272, 284, 315, 341, 345,
Giganotosaurus, 106, 355, 356, 357
Gilded Age America, 52, 67, 162, 163, 164, 165, 166, 167, 298, 304, 402, 409
Gillette, David, 142, 148
Gingrich, Newt, 10, 224
Goddard Youth Camp, 263, 401
Golden State, 5
Grapes of Wrath, The, 5, 7
Gray, Eric S, 334, 340, 341, 342
Great Depression, The, 1, 4, 12, 13, 67, 72, 73, 100, 101, 168, 196, 302,
Great Lakes region, 1
Great Philadelphia Wagon Road, 67
Green Corn Rebellion, 67
Guardian, The, 266
Guthrie, Woody, 76

H

Hadrosaur, 41
Haggard, Merle, 6, 178
Hamilton, Alexander, 14
Hamilton, Walter, 272, 274, 276, 278, 280, 281, 288, 289, 309, 324, 343, 377, 389,

Haney, Kelly, 261, 262, 266, 267
Hard Times, (the movie), 100
Hatfields & McCoys, 7
Hatton-Tuff volcanic layer, 112
Heartland, American, 5
Heart of Dixie, 68
Henry, Brad, 266, 400
Henry VIII, King, 73
Herron Foundation, 397, 400
Herron, Mary and Quintas, 393, 394
Hickok, "Wild Bill", 53
High-spined Lizard, 401
Highway 70, 11, 25, 76, 180, 181
Hobos, 100
Hochatown, OK, 12, 13, 15, 17, 319, 366, 392
Honeywell, Jim, 325, 326, 327, 328, 335, 340
Hoover camps, 6
Horner, Jack, PhD, 357, 358, 359
Hot Springs, AR, 238
House Bill 2014, 261, 401, 402
Hugo, OK, 93
Hunt, Adrian, PhD, 246, 403, 405

I

Idabel, OK, 11, 12, 23, 203, 260, 273, 289, 306
Indian-Celts, 71
Indian Removal Act of 1830, 74
Indian Territory, 93, 100
Indiana Jones, 23, 117, 118, 168, 169
Isles of Britannia, 68

J

Jackson, Andrew, 73, 74, 169, 303
Jacksonian Democracy, 68, 142, 412
Jacobs, Lewis, PhD, 400, 405
James III, King, 7
Jefferson, Thomas, 54
Jensen, Dinosaur Jim, 173
Joiner, Kenny, 308
Jones, Christopher, 306
Jones, Jeff, 96, 97, 98
Jones, Levi, 97, 98
Jones, Louis, 97, 99, 100, 101, 391
Jones, Robert M, 9, 29, 93, 255
Jurassic Gold Rush 55
Jurassic Park III (the movie), 107, 137, 164
Jurassic Period, 43, 106, 114, 136, 138, 139, 357, 360, 401

K

King Cotton, 11, 74
King of the Dinosaurs, 43

K-T Boundary, 46, 47

L

Lake Michigan, 1
Langston, Wann Jr. PhD, 136, 140, 186, 191, 193, 194, 199, 200, 201, 202, 203, 205, 206, 207, 215, 216, 218, 219, 220, 221, 222, 223, 224, 225, 226, 227, 228, 229, 230, 231, 235, 298, 232, 239, 402
Larson, Neal, 247, 265, 266, 351, 359, 378, 396
Larson, Pete, 23, 119, 234, 235, 236, 348, 350, 351, 378, 379, 411
LeFlore County, 7
LeForce, Carl, 256, 270, 271, 272, 273, 274, 275, 276, 281, 288, 289, 290, 313, 314, 315, 321, 323, 324, 329, 330, 331, 333, 334, 343, 376, 377, 383, 389, 390
Leidy, Joseph Dr, 53, 54, 166
Lewis and Clark, 54
Little Dixie, 11, 30, 66, 77, 169, 282, 289, 301, 303, 304, 373
Little River, 24, 25, 370
Little Rock, AR, 9
Lincoln, Abraham, 73
Lobell, Joe, 343, 344
Logging/contract logger, 17, 19, 33
Lone Star State, 201
Long, Huey, 167
Lumberjacks, 70

M

Magna Carta, 231, 232
Mares, Michael, 265, 339
Marsh, Othneil C, 54, 55, 56, 57, 58, 62, 63, 76, 77, 155, 162, 164, 166, 167, 221, 298, 402, 409
Matlock, Terry, 400
Mason Dixon Line, 76
Maxwell, Desmond W PhD, 370
McCurtain County, 39, 62, 63, 64, 71, 84, 85, 87, 97, 101, 104, 105, 108, 109, 110, 112, 119, 121, 129, 134, 151, 154, 160, 162, 169, 170, 174, 179, 189, 190, 191, 198, 232, 235, 299, 303, 381, 394, 395, 405,
McCurtain County Gem and Mineral Club, 29, 30
McCurtain County Genealogical Society, 29
Mccurtain County National Bank, 376
Medieval Europe, 54, 87
Mena, AR, 11

Midwestern State University, 132, 133
Moonshine, 6, 9, 13, 14, 15, 16, 71, 102
Monoculture plantation system, 16
Monoculture timber farming, 306
Morgan, J.P, 58, 163
Mountain Fork River, 12, 13, 22, 25, 27, 76, 90, 91, 92, 96, 113, 154, 172, 174, 307, 308, 369, 401
Mountain Fork valley, 76
Mountain Fork specimen, 400
Museum of the Red River, 144, 291, 273, 392, 393, 396, 397, 399, 401, 403, 405
Murphy, Mike, 262

N

National Geographic, 3
Native Americans, 71, 74, 75
New Deal, 4, 101, 106, 205
New South, 10
Noble Foundation, 263, 337, 338, 339, 343, 344
Nobles oblige, 67
North Carolina Museum of Natural Science, 335, 351, 352, 354, 357, 360, 378, 410
Northern Ireland, 7

O

Okies, 4, 5, 66
Okie Noodling Tournament, 72
Oklahoma City, 328, 334
Oklahoma Dept. of Environmental Quality, 311
Oklahoma Dept. of Wildlife Conservation, 371, 372
Oklahoma Fossil Preservation Act, 262
Oklahoma Gem & Mineral Show, 187, 188, 189
Oklahoma Mineralogical Society, 264
Oklahoma Museum of Natural History, 262, 264
Oklahoma State Bureau of Investigation, 384, 489
Old South, 9, 11, 69, 75, 373
Old West, 178, 180, 75
Old Virginia, 33
Open range, 307
Ouachitas/Mountains, 1, 4, 9, 12, 19, 24, 25, 66, 331
Ouachita National Forest, 364
Owen, Sir Richard, 166
Ozarks, 4, 9, 331

P

Palin, Sarah, 224, 254, 256
Paris, TX 89, 226
Parker, Judge Isaac C, 99, 100
Pastoral legacy, 75
Peabody, George, 166
Perino, Greg. 145. 146, 147, 291, 312
Pickens, T. Boone, 224
Pine Knot Crossing, 18
Pittman, Jeff, 181, 182, 183, 184, 187, 199, 200, 202, 203, 206, 218, 222, 223, 224, 228
Prohibition, 13, 15
Pterosaur/s, 41, 42

Q

Quartz crystal/s, 3, 12, 17, 19, 20, 21, 30, 189, 363, 364, 366

R

Rabon, Jeff, 400, 403
Reagan, Ronald, 195, 196, 197
Raptor/Utah Raptor, 41, 42, 137, 138, 139, 166
Rebels of Ole Dixie, 66
Red River, 93, 110, 200, 203, 206, 219, 225, 226, 228, 229, 370
Red River valley, 11
Redneck/s, 13, 32, 33, 69, 70, 76, 178
Redneckery, 33
Redneck mystique, 70
Redneck pastimes, 76
Red Slough Wetlands Management Area, 79
Roan, Paul, 402
Robbers Cave State Park, 100
Robin Hood, 86, 372
Rockefeller, John D, 163
Rogers, Will, 76
Romer, Alfred, 173
Romney, Mitt, 224, 296
Roosevelt, Franklin, 4, 12, 106, 302
Roosevelt, Theodore, 30, 304
Rossoll Harry, 402, 405
Route 66, 5, 6
Russell, Dale PhD, 354, 368, 370

S

Sam Noble Museum of Natural History, 188, 190, 266, 337, 401
Sacrison, Stan, 173
Saurophaganax Maximus, 106, 266, 355, 401, 402

Scientific Age, 135
Scopes Monkey Trial, 297, 301
Scots-Irish, 6, 7, 10, 29, 30, 32, 67, 68, 70
Scots-Irish frontiersmen, 11
Scots-Irish pioneers, 66
Scottish highlands, 68
Seismosaurus, 142
Senate Bill 1185, 106
Serf/serfdom, 67, 231, 232, 412
Sevier County, Arkansas, 179
Sharecroppers/sharecropping, 67, 73
Shenandoah Valley, 67
Shipp, John, 281, 282, 313, 314
Simpson, O.J, 258
Sitting Bull, 53
Slaughter, Bob, PhD, 122, 132, 133, 192
Smithsonian Institute, 163, 351
Southeastern State University, 383, 386
Southern Celts, 74, 75
Southern gentility, 67
Southern obesity epidemic, 32
Southernized/southernization, 8, 69
Southern redneck/culture, 69, 361
Southwestern Arkansas, 4
Spinosaurus, 106, 107, 115, 116, 137, 139,, 140, 355
Steinbeck, John,, 5
Stiles, Dr. Lewis, 97, 391
Stovall, J. Willis PhD, 106, 140, 193, 216, 356
Sue, the dinosaur, 347, 348, 349, 350, 356
Sunneson, Neal H, 18, 112

T

Tarbosaurus, 361
Tenant farmers, 67
Tenontosaurus, 111, 115, 116
Terror of the South, 114, 170, 171, 212, 346, 347
Tertiary Period, 11, 47
Tertiary strata, 47
Theison, Leon, 315
Thompson, Carolyn, 261
Thorpe, Jim, 75
Three-piece suitification, 168
Tibbs, Sue, 403
Tidewater aristocrats, 33
Tidwell, Mary, 376
Tidwell, Royce, 98, 99, 376
Tyrannosaurus Rex/T.rex, 23, 41, 43, 52, 82, 83, 106, 107, 114, 122, 136, 137, 138, 140, 141, 166, 174, 212, 331, 347, 348, 350, 355, 356, 357, 358, 359, 360, 361, 362, 378, 402
Trail of Tears, 74
Triassic Period, 43, 44, 45, 104
Triceratops, 41, 351
Trump, Donald, 322
Tyson Foods, 12

U

Ulster Irish, 7, 29, 68
Ulster Plantation, 7
University of Arkansas, 70
University of Oklahoma (OU), 188, 230, 231, 235, 293, 313, 333, 334, 339, 340, 359, 368, 370, 373, 374, 402
University of South Carolina, 74
University of Texas (UT), 177, 192, 193, 194, 203, 204, 215, 216, 219, 222, 223,224,226,227, 289
U.S. Forestry Service, 364, 383

W

Wagon Wheel Dance Land, 178, 180, 181
Wallace, George, 8
Wallace, William (Brave Heart), 7, 241
Washington, George, 14, 73
Wentz, Terry 351, 378, 379
Where the Red Fern Grows, (movie), 73
Whiskey Rebellion, 14
White Lightning, 6
White trash, 69
Wickersham, Victor, 261
Wilburton, OK, 100
Wild West, 76, 100, 178
William, Prince of Orange, 7
Williams, Maurice, 348, 351
Winstar Institute, 58
Works Progress Administration (WPA), 307

Y

Yeomen, 231, 232, 233